# Accounting 1 Second Edition

# Accounting 1

## Second Edition

**G. E. Syme** B. Com., C.A.

Eastview Secondary School
Barrie, Ontario

Prentice-Hall of Canada, Ltd. Scarborough, Ontario

Canadian Shared Cataloguing in Publication Data

Syme, G. E.
    Accounting 1 Second Edition

Includes index.
ISBN 0-13-001370-6

1. Accounting.   I. Title.

HF5635.S98 1976          657

Prentice-Hall, Inc., Englewood Cliffs, New Jersey
Prentice-Hall of Australia, Pty., Ltd., Sydney
Prentice-Hall of India Pvt., Ltd., New Delhi
Prentice-Hall International, Inc., London
Prentice-Hall of Japan, Inc., Tokyo
Prentice-Hall of Southeast Asia (PTE.) Ltd., Singapore

Design / Maher & Garbutt Ltd.

ISBN 0-13-001370-6

    4  5  BP  80  79  78

Printed and bound in Canada.

# Contents

# Acknowledgments

The author wishes to express his appreciation to those who assisted him in the preparation of this book. The contribution of three people in particular is gratefully acknowledged:

K. Douglas Dixon, Commercial Director, Hammarskjold High School, Thunder Bay, Ontario, who taught from this text while it was still in manuscript form and was thus able to offer many helpful suggestions and to confirm many of the ideas incorporated therein. He was also responsible for the preparation of Workbooks A and B, and Teacher's Manuals A and B.

John Litt, Commercial Director, Sir Winston Churchill C. & V.I., Thunder Bay, Ontario, who experimented with a new course in applied bookkeeping and accounting which required the writing of a great deal of exercise material. He also wrote the chapter on payroll for this text.

W. F. (Bill) Riggs, Commercial Director, Sutton District High School, an innovator in the teaching of accounting, who authored and class-tested the case studies in the second edition.

G.E.S.

# Preface to the First Edition

The teaching of introductory accounting is taking a different direction than in the past. It is concerned with the development of a more positive understanding of accounting principles and concepts, as well as with a broader appreciation of the office environment. It aims to prepare the student of accounting for the technologically dynamic society in which he will one day be employed.

## Objectives

For the first six chapters **Accounting 1** follows fairly traditional lines in developing a firm understanding of basic concepts. Then, it breaks away – proceeding along new and original lines in an attempt to satisfy the following objectives:

1. To provide for the student the means of acquiring a thorough understanding of basic accounting principles, concepts, and procedures.
2. To provide a solid foundation for possible further study.
3. To develop in the student the qualities of versatility, flexibility, and initiative that will be of certain benefit to him in a world of persistent change.
4. To achieve the above three objectives through the application of genuinely functional practice material which of itself will benefit the student.

## Organization

The broad coverage of the text, together with the availability of independent optional chapters, provides the teacher with a flexible tool that he can adapt to suit the needs of all students in regular courses.

The text consists of fifteen chapters. The first nine chapters are considered to be the minimum coverage for a satisfactory one-year course. However, it is expected that most students will proceed beyond this point.

The first ten chapters are developed on a continuous basis. After completing Chapter 10, the student may proceed to any of four additional independent units of study. These are:

Ch. 11 – Cash Registers, Banking, Bank Reconciliations.

Ch. 12 – Basic Accounting Systems and Procedures.

Ch. 13 – Payroll.

Ch. 14 and Ch. 15 – Adjustments, Closing Entries, Classified Financial Statements, Reversing Entries.

Where it is desirable to offer a two-year course, **Accounting 1** may be combined with one semester of an additional subject such as Applied Accounting or Data Processing.

## Individualized Instruction

**Accounting 1** explains the subject matter thoroughly, an approach that benefits both the student and the teacher.

It enables the student to work more independently. This is a habit that he should develop, in many instances wants to develop, and often is forced to practice. For the superior student, complete independent study is possible.

Because the student can rely on the text, the

teacher is provided with a less demanding class-room situation, a very important consideration in view of the increasing workload of teachers.

## Problems and Exercises
A wealth of exercise material of varying degrees of difficulty is included. It is not expected that all students will work all of the exercises, but rather that by careful selection the needs of all students will be satisfied.

## Scope of Business Transactions
This text attempts to include every routine business transaction that falls within the domain of the accounting clerk. Sales Tax, Petty Cash, Cash Registers, Returns and Allowances, Credit Notes, Cash Refunds, Cash Discounts, Payroll, N.S.F. Cheques, Bank Debit and Credit Notes, and Bank Reconciliations are among the many topics discussed.

## Office Systems and Procedures
The last ten to twenty years have witnessed tremendous changes in accounting techniques. During that time, the traditional role of the book-keeper has disappeared and the role of the accounting clerk has emerged in a new accounting environment of systems, procedures, and automation.

Accounting 1 reflects the new state of accounting and relates accounting theory to current practices.

## Total Business Concept
The text is organized so that it is not necessary to devote a separate chapter to each of the Purchases Journal, the Sales Journal, the Cash Receipts Journal, and the Cash Payments Journal. The organization of Accounting 1 makes it possible to introduce these four special journals all in one chapter. This method has the advantage of showing all transactions in their proper perspective; that is, in relationship to total business activity.

## Subsidiary Ledgers and Control Accounts
Subsidiary ledger accounting is an important phase of every business and is the type of accounting work most likely to fall to a new or junior employee. Therefore, the study of subsidiary ledgers and control accounts is given an early and prominent place in Accounting 1.

## Flowcharts
This text teaches basic flowcharting techniques and utilizes them to describe graphically the basic accounting systems and procedures. With the advent of greater use of mechanical and electronic accounting techniques, flowcharts have become a most effective method of describing business systems.

## Business Source Documents
The entire accounting process is dependent on a variety of business documents. Accounting systems and procedures are geared to the flow of business papers. These business papers represent a means of communication from business to business and from person to person. They represent the supporting evidence of most business transactions and the source of most accounting entries. As such, they deserve a place of importance in a text on introductory accounting and receive it in Accounting 1.

## Adjusting and Closing Entries
The text includes two different treatments of adjusting entries. Either or both methods may be studied according to the individual's preference. The first is the traditional method, using adjusting entries. The second is the professional's method, by means of which the adjustments are effected through the closing entries.

## Mechanical and Electronic Accounting
This text is designed to provide a thorough introduction to fundamental accounting principles and practices. Where appropriate, mechanical and electronic devices are acknowledged and discussed. However, it is not a purpose of this text to overlap into the field of data processing.

# Preface to the Second Edition

The second edition of **Accounting 1** has been written expressly with a view to improving the text by acting upon suggestions from teachers in the field. The book has been expanded by the addition of two new chapters, thereby making it fully sufficient for a two-year program. The end-of-chapter material has been strengthened by the inclusion of a number of graduated exercises designed to be steppingstones in the student's progress. Case studies have also been included in every chapter, and the entire text has been updated and had the benefit of classroom experience brought to bear upon it.

It has been a persistently expressed view that the text should be expanded to make it suitable for a full two-year accounting program. This has been achieved by the addition of Chapter 16 on partnerships and Chapter 17 on corporations. These two topics were selected as being the most suitable for rounding out an accounting program. Students should be familiar with the work sheets and financial statements covered in Chapters 14 and 15 before proceeding to these two new chapters.

An often expressed suggestion has been that case studies be included. Case studies are popular because they are interesting, motivating, and thought-provoking. They demand a kind of response different from that of traditional exercises, thus adding variety to the classroom experience. Teachers who are partial to case studies will find a plentiful supply in the new **Accounting 1**.

In today's schools, students of widely differing abilities are often placed together, presenting the teacher with a demanding classroom situation. A number of simpler exercises designed to allow students to progress in graduated steps have been added to **Accounting 1** to make it a more effective resource in such class groupings.

The Council of Ministers of Education, Canada, has published the *Metric Style Guide*, which defines the metric terminology and symbolism to be used in Canada.

The notation used for money amounts in **Accounting 1** now conforms to this style guide. This is the only aspect of accounting that is significantly affected by metrication.

**Accounting 1** was never put forward as a fully comprehensive accounting text. The chief claim made for it has been that it is pedagogically excellent for introducing the subject. Because teachers have responded to the text enthusiastically, its structure has not been changed. Its essential features are:

1. The order of presentation of the topics has been carefully selected to combine two objectives. The first is to emphasize understanding over and above rote learning. The second is to give early placement to topics that may benefit the student who is destined for early employment. The introduction of subsidiary ledger accounting in Chapter 7 is an example of this second objective.
2. The exercise material is of sufficient variety and abundance to meet the needs of all students. Some students may need to work through a number of the simpler assignments before attempting those of greater difficulty. Others will gain mastery by doing only a few of the more difficult assignments in each chapter. It is not intended that all students do all of the exercises, but that under the

guidance of their teacher, they select those appropriate to their own particular needs.

3. The text is written to read easily. A book that reads easily can be used to promote reading and thinking on the part of students. This is an important feature in this time of concern about reading. Equally important, it can be used to facilitate individual progress and, for some students, even completely independent study.

It is doubtful if an accounting text can be written to suit the wishes of all teachers. There are differing points of view and individual preferences in the subject that cannot be accommodated in any single book. A teacher having a strong preference for an alternate approach to a particular topic or point should seize upon that opportunity to augment the text with his own materials, thus enriching the course for the benefit of his students.

# Introduction

## Accounting and your Future

Accounting and related functions play an important role in the structure of our economy. You will find that in numerous ways a knowledge of accounting can be of considerable value to you in your career.

Those of you who decide to go into the working world of business, commerce, trade, and industry, will find employment in one of the countless numbers of business establishments that make up our economic system. Within these business establishments, however, so many of the individual jobs are either directly or indirectly involved in the accounting and recording processes that there is every chance of your job being one of them. It is not difficult to see that an understanding of accounting may help you perform your duties and increase your value as an employee.

As an employee improves his position in the business world he finds that his responsibilities grow accordingly. The higher positions in business require a more able and knowledgeable employee. If you hope to improve your position in business, either by moving up the ranks or by changing employers, an understanding of accounting will be helpful. It will round out your appreciation of the aims and objectives of the whole business organization, the interdependence of the various departments and the relationship of your own job to the whole enterprise. Also, it will direct your attention to matters that concern management, such as profit, systems and procedures, and efficiency.

It is the ambition of many a person to become one day the owner of a business. Anyone who achieves this goal will soon find himself concerned with matters related to accounting. There is the banking, the customers' accounts, the paying of bills, the sales tax, the income tax, the payroll, and so on. For the owner of a business, a knowledge of accounting is of obvious benefit.

Some of you may choose a career as a professional accountant. By completing the requirements of one of the professional bodies of accountants, you can become a Chartered Accountant (C.A.), a Certified General Accountant (C.G.A.), or a Registered Industrial Accountant (R.I.A.). The work performed by a qualified accountant depends to some extent on which particular group he is associated with. In general, qualified and experienced accountants are eligible for senior management positions and have the right to practise as public accountants; that is, to offer their services to the general public for a fee in the same manner as a doctor or a lawyer. Professional accountants earn good incomes and enjoy a respected place in the community.

An appreciation of accounting will influence your personal and social life. By understanding the financial aspects of the family and of various community organizations, you will be better able to take your place in the community.

# 1 The Balance Sheet

## Purpose of Accounting

Although the science of accounting is useful to business people in a variety of ways, it is fundamentally a system designed to accomplish two things. These are –
1. To maintain an accurate and up-to-date record of the **financial position** of a business or individual.
2. To keep a detailed record of the changes which occur in the **financial position**.

## Financial Position

The concept of financial position is simple and logical. Ask yourself, 'How can I determine someone's (an ordinary homeowner's or my parents') financial position?' Then, using pure common sense, find the answer.

You will likely decide that the following three steps are necessary:
1. List and total the things he owns that have some monetary value; these are called his **assets**.
2. List and total his debts; these are called his **liabilities**.
3. Calculate the difference between his total **assets** and his total **liabilities**; this difference is called his **capital**, or **equity**.

*Example*

To determine the financial position of A. R. Proctor on June 30, 19—.

*Step 1*

List and total the things of value that he owns. These **assets** might be as follows:

| | |
|---|---:|
| Cash on hand | $      35.60 |
| Bank balance | 647.40 |
| Government bonds | 1 200.00 |
| Amount loaned to Jack Burns | 300.00 |
| Automobile | 2 700.00 |
| House and lot | 46 500.00 |
| Furniture and equipment | 1 956.00 |
| **Total assets** | **$53 339.00** |

*Step 2*

List and total his debts. These **liabilities** might be as follows:

| | |
|---|---:|
| Acme Finance Co. (automobile) | $      962.00 |
| Western Furniture Company | 264.00 |
| Mortgage on home | 11 363.50 |
| **Total liabilities** | **$12 589.50** |

*Step 3*

Calculate the difference between total assets and total liabilities. The calculation is as follows:

| | |
|---|---:|
| Total assets | $53 339.00 |
| Less total liabilities | 12 589.50 |
| Difference | $40 749.50 |

The difference of $40 749.50 is the amount that A. R. Proctor is worth. It is generally referred to as his **capital**, or **equity**.

**Note:** Other less common terms for capital are **proprietorship** and **net worth**.

# The Balance Sheet

A. R. Proctor's financial position may be presented formally by means of a financial statement or financial report called a **balance sheet**.

A simple form of balance sheet is illustrated below.

A. R. Proctor's balance sheet is that for a person. It is just as easy to prepare a balance sheet for a business, club, church, or any organization.

| A. R. Proctor<br>Balance Sheet<br>June 30, 19— | | | | | |
|---|---|---|---|---|---|
| **Assets** | | | **Liabilities** | | |
| Cash on Hand | 35 | 60 | Acme Finance Co. | 962 | 00 |
| Bank Balance | 647 | 40 | Western Furniture Company | 264 | 00 |
| Government Bonds | 1 200 | 00 | Mortgage Payable | 11 363 | 50 |
| Jack Burns | 300 | 00 | | 12 589 | 50 |
| Automobile | 2 700 | 00 | **Capital** | | |
| House and Lot | 46 500 | 00 | A. R. Proctor, Capital | 40 749 | 50 |
| Furniture and Equipment | 1 956 | 00 | | | |
| | 53 339 | 00 | | 53 339 | 00 |

*Balance sheet for an individual.*

Some additional sample balance sheets are shown below:

| Wesley Saxton, Lawyer<br>Balance Sheet<br>December 31, 19— | | | | | |
|---|---|---|---|---|---|
| **Assets** | | | **Liabilities** | | |
| Cash | 1 407 | 10 | Bank Loan | 2 000 | 00 |
| R. Mason | 350 | 00 | Mercury Finance Co. | 1 475 | 00 |
| H. Moran | 1 056 | 75 | | 3 475 | 00 |
| Office Supplies | 264 | 00 | **Owner's Equity** | | |
| Furniture and Equipment | 2 600 | 00 | Wesley Saxton, Capital | 5 467 | 85 |
| Automobile | 3 265 | 00 | | | |
| | 8 942 | 85 | | 8 942 | 85 |

*Balance sheet for a small business.*

| Center High School Student Council<br>Balance Sheet<br>March 31, 19— | | | | | |
|---|---|---|---|---|---|
| **Assets** | | | **Liabilities** | | |
| Cash | 156 | 50 | Glendale Company | 52 | 03 |
| D. Fraser | 37 | 24 | | | |
| Art Supplies | 17 | 00 | **Net Worth** | | |
| Decorating Materials | 56 | 00 | Student Council Net Worth | 214 | 71 |
| | 266 | 74 | | 266 | 74 |

*Balance sheet for a small organization.*

## Important Features of the Balance Sheet

1. A three-line heading is used. The heading tells three things –
   a. the name of the business, organization, or individual;
   b. the name of the financial statement: Balance Sheet;
   c. the date on which the financial position was determined.

2. The assets are listed on the left side of the balance sheet and the liabilities and the capital are listed on the right side.

3. The details of any item are fully disclosed on a balance sheet. For example, on the balance sheet of A. R. Proctor, shown above, his automobile is shown in the Assets section at its value of $2 700 and the amount that he owes on the automobile, $962 to Acme Finance Co., is shown in the Liabilities section. This is a more informative presentation than to show the car at a value of $1 738, the amount that Mr. Proctor has paid on it.

4. Abbreviations are not used on financial statements except when listing a company name which includes an abbreviation; for example, International Trading Co.

5. The two final totals, one for each side of the balance sheet, are recorded on the same line.

## Use of Columnar Paper

It is important for a student of accounting to learn to use columnar paper. When columnar paper is used, notice how the figures are placed carefully in the columns; this is to help the accountant total the columns correctly. Observe also the omission of dollar signs, periods, and commas when recording amounts of money in the columns.

It is permissible when using columnar paper to indicate even dollar amounts by inserting a dash in the cents column, as shown below.

|  | 506 | 21 |
| 1 | 000 | – |
|  | 51 | 20 |
|  | 12 | – |

## Debtor and Creditor

When a sum of money is owed to our business or organization it is listed on our balance sheet as an asset. Conversely, when a sum of money is owed by our business or organization it is listed on our balance sheet as a liability.

Considering this from a different viewpoint, whenever the name of a business or an individual appears on our balance sheet in the assets section, that business or individual owes us a sum of money. Such a business or individual is one of our **debtors**.

Similarly, whenever the name of a business or an individual appears on our balance sheet in the liabilities section, we owe a sum of money to that business or individual. Such a business or individual is one of our **creditors**.

**Note:** It is customary when discussing the business for which we work to use words such as 'we', 'us', 'our'. On the other hand, when talking about another business it is customary to use words such as 'they' and 'their'.

## Use of Ruled Lines

If a column of figures is to be totaled (added or subtracted), a single line is drawn beneath the column and the total is placed beneath this single line as shown below.

| 131 | 10 |
| 14 | 11 |
| 31 | 05 |
| 176 | 26 |

If a total happens to be a final total, such as the last amounts on the balance sheet, a double ruled line is drawn immediately beneath the total as shown below.

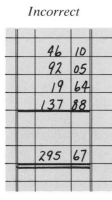

On most balance sheets, when placing the two final totals on the same line, it is necessary to leave one or more blank lines between the figures in a column and the total. When this is done, place the single ruled line immediately above the total and not immediately beneath the figures in the column. Examine the following examples:

*Incorrect*        *Correct*

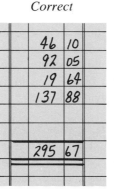

## Neatness

It is most important that an accountant's work be neat and perfectly legible. He must see to it that no one misinterprets his writing or figuring. Although his work should never be unsightly, at the same time it is not necessary that it be beautiful – only neat and legible.

From the very beginning you should make it a habit to strive for neatness and clarity in all of your exercises. Be sure to use your ruler to underline headings.

# The Fundamental Accounting Equation

It is a fundamental truth in accounting that a balance sheet always balances. It is not possible to prepare a correct balance sheet that is not balanced.

The relationship between the assets, liabilities, and capital as shown on the simple balance sheet indicates the 'fundamental accounting equation' (also known as the 'fundamental bookkeeping equation'). This equation is shown by the illustration below.

The fundamental accounting equation is:
$$A = L + C$$
By simple mathematical rearrangement:
$$A - L = C$$

This relationship is an extremely important concept in the study of accounting. As you will soon see, the whole science of accounting is based on it.

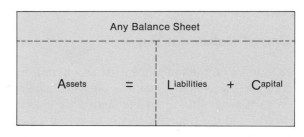

# Bookkeeping and Accounting Terms

**Balance Sheet** A statement showing the financial position (the assets, liabilities, and capital) of an individual, company, or other organization on a certain date.

**Capital** The difference between the total assets and the total liabilities. Also known as **equity, proprietorship,** or **net worth**.

**Asset** Something owned that has a monetary value.

**Liability** A debt, owed to another individual, company, or organization.

**Creditor** An individual, business, or other organization to which our business owes a sum of money.

**Debtor** An individual, business, or other organization that owes a sum of money to our business.

## Review Questions

1. Name the two basic purposes of accounting.
2. Describe how a person's financial position is arrived at.
3. Define 'asset'. Name five different assets.
4. Define 'liability'. Name three different liabilities.
5. Define 'capital' (or 'equity').
6. Name two other less commonly used terms that mean the same as capital.
7. What is a balance sheet?
8. What three things must the heading of a balance sheet show?
9. When may the name of the owner of a business be used in the heading?
10. On which side of the balance sheet are the assets listed? On which side are the liabilities listed?
11. Describe the way in which an automobile that is only partially paid for is shown on a balance sheet.
12. When listing figures on columnar paper, what items may be omitted?
13. Define 'creditor'.
14. Define 'debtor'.
15. Describe where debtors and creditors are listed on a balance sheet.
16. What is meant by a single ruled line drawn beneath a column of figures?
17. What is meant by drawing a double ruled line beneath a total?
18. What is the exception to the rule 'never use short forms or abbreviations on financial statements'?
19. Give two forms of the fundamental accounting equation.

## Exercises

Study the balance sheets illustrated on page 2. Then complete the following exercises using the illustrated balance sheets as a guide.

**Note:** You will never be a successful accountant if, as you work through the exercises in this text, you merely memorize the solutions. Therefore, as you proceed through the text, always do your best to understand each topic completely.

1a. List eight assets that a small business might own.
  b. List three liabilities that a small business might owe.
  c. If the total assets of a business are $37 486.49, and the total liabilities are $11 749.71, calculate the owner's equity.

2. Classify each of the following as an asset, liability, or capital item: office furniture; an amount owed to H. Smith; land; buildings; cash on hand; the owner's investment in the business; an amount owed by R. Jones; an unpaid heating bill; trucks; supplies; bank loan.

3. S. Stevens's assets and liabilities are listed below in alphabetical order:

Bank loan, $4 000; Building, $40 000; Cash, $1 435; City Service (a debtor), $960; Emerson Electric Ltd. (a creditor), $1 200; Equipment, $13 750; Francis and Company (a debtor), $350; Frank's Service Station (a creditor), $375; Mortgage on building, $25 000; Supplies, $370.

List the assets in one column and total them. List the liabilities in another column and total them. Calculate S. Stevens's equity.

4. Jack Plummer, a factory worker, asks you to help him find out how much he is worth. From a discussion with him you find out the following facts:

1. His bank balance is $754.
2. He owns a home valued at $42 500 which has a mortgage on it of $12 500.
3. He owns furniture and household equipment valued at $6 000.
4. He owns a summer property valued at $15 000 which he bought with money borrowed from the bank. Since the time of purchase he has paid back $1 000 of the loan.
5. He has unpaid bills amounting to $1 560.
6. He owes his father, M. Plummer, the sum of $10 000 which he borrowed interest free several years ago at the time he bought his home.

List Jack Plummer's assets in one column, his liabilities in another, and calculate his net worth.

5. From the following information prepare a balance sheet for M. H. Clark, a public accountant, on December 31, 19—.

| | |
|---|---|
| Cash | $ 356.75 |
| R. Swift (a debtor) | 100.00 |
| G. K. Falls (a debtor) | 500.00 |
| Y. S. Banton (a debtor) | 275.00 |
| Office Supplies | 135.50 |
| Office Equipment | 462.00 |
| Automobile | 2 850.00 |
| Colewell Office Supply (a creditor) | 225.00 |

6. The Western News Company, owned by C. D. Proctor, had the following assets and liabilities on March 31, 19—. Prepare a balance sheet for the company on that date.

| | |
|---|---|
| Cash | $ 896.52 |
| S. Miller (a debtor) | 750.60 |
| P. Hayes (a debtor) | 400.00 |
| Supplies | 351.00 |
| Automobile | 1 850.00 |
| Furniture and fixtures | 965.00 |
| Bank Loan | 2 500.00 |
| Ace Finance Company (a creditor) | 920.00 |
| General Trading Co. (a creditor) | 642.98 |

**7.** From the following list of assets and liabilities prepare the personal balance sheet of T. G. Russell as of June 30, 19—.

| | |
|---|---:|
| Cash on hand | $ 402.16 |
| Bank balance | 1 002.34 |
| Stocks and bonds | 3 560.00 |
| House and lot | 48 005.00 |
| Household furniture | 4 095.00 |
| Automobile | 2 400.00 |
| Mortgage payable | 12 569.00 |
| Sabot Finance Co. (creditor) | 853.50 |
| Click Finance Co. (creditor) | 1 235.40 |

**8.** From the following information as of June 30, 19—, prepare a balance sheet for Morgan & Associates, which is owned by A. Morgan.

| | |
|---|---:|
| Bank balance | $ 1 449.55 |
| J. Arthur (a debtor) | 75.00 |
| N. Jackson (a debtor) | 100.00 |
| Land | 15 000.00 |
| Buildings | 42 000.00 |
| Equipment | 1 975.00 |
| Trucks | 4 925.00 |
| Hardware Supply Company (creditor) | 461.20 |
| General Merchants Co. (creditor) | 1 105.63 |
| Marvel Finance Co. (creditor) | 163.00 |
| Mortgage payable | 23 251.00 |

**9.** B. M. Kramer is the owner and operator of The Kramer Company. On September 30, 19—, The Kramer Company had the following assets and liabilities. Prepare the September 30 balance sheet for The Kramer Company.

*Assets*

| | |
|---|---:|
| Cash on hand | $ 106.70 |
| Bank balance | 530.00 |
| J. Crothers | 100.00 |
| R. Smart | 370.00 |
| Supplies | 200.00 |
| Furniture and equipment | 1 700.50 |
| Delivery equipment | 2 100.00 |

*Liabilities*

| | |
|---|---:|
| Anglo Supply Co. | 740.46 |
| C. P. Gregg | 1 000.00 |
| Bank loan | 2 000.00 |

**10.** C. B. Travis, the proprietor of Travis and Company, gave the following list of assets and liabilities to a public accountant and asked him to prepare a balance sheet as of March 31, 19—. Prepare the balance sheet as if you were the public accountant.

Amounts owed to Travis and
Company:
| | | |
|---|---|---:|
| –G. Fordham | $ | 42.16 |
| –W. Gaines | | 743.86 |
| –D. Samuelson | | 346.95 |

Amounts owed by Travis and
Company:
| | |
|---|---:|
| –Raymond and Company | 125.00 |
| –Bank of Montreal | 2 500.00 |
| –Gem Finance Co. | 1 236.45 |
| –Dacana Insurance Co. | 50.00 |
| –Radelect Company | 1 567.25 |
| –Realmont Mortgage Co. | 15 540.00 |

| | |
|---|---:|
| Office supplies | 326.40 |
| Building | 35 000.00 |
| Bank balance | 946.03 |
| Land | 16 000.00 |
| Office equipment | 1 960.00 |
| Shop equipment | 535.00 |
| Delivery equipment | 4 240.00 |

# Cases

## Case 1

G. Armstrong is the new owner of Armstrong Hardware Store. He believes that he knows enough about accounting to prepare his first balance sheet before starting business, May 1, 19—.

G. ARMSTRONG
BALANCE SHEET
AS OF MAY 1, 19—

| Assets | | | Liabilities | |
|---|---|---|---|---|
| Supplies | | $ 500.00 | Mortgage on House | $ 6 000.00 |
| Cash | | 4 500.00 | Bank Loan | 3 000.00 |
| Building | 30 000 | | | $ 9 000.00 |
| Less Mortgage | 12 000 | 18 000.00 | | |
| Office Equipment | | 10 000.00 | Capital | |
| Delivery Equipment | | 5 000.00 | Armstrong Hardware, | |
| Household Furniture | | 3 000.00 | Capital | $32 000.00 |
| | | $41 000.00 | | $41 000.00 |

Do you agree with Armstrong that he knows accounting practice? Give specific reasons for your answer.

## Case 2
Shown below is the balance sheet of J. Prosser.

J. PROSSER
BALANCE SHEET
JANUARY 31, 19—

| Assets | | Liabilities | |
|---|---|---|---|
| Cash | $ 6 000.00 | T. Johnston Co. | $ 7 000.00 |
| A. Galloway & Son | 4 000.00 | P. Hamilton | 5 000.00 |
| Land | 10 000.00 | K. Lawson | 4 000.00 |
| Building | 30 000.00 | | $16 000.00 |
| | | Capital | |
| | | J. Prosser, Capital | $34 000.00 |
| | $50 000.00 | | $50 000.00 |

1. Based on the limited information at your disposal, would you say that Mr. Prosser is in financial trouble? Give reasons.
2. Describe the various ways Mr. Prosser may obtain additional cash.

## Case 3
J. Mundy's capital balance as of December 31, 19–1, was $62 000.00. At the end of December 19–2 his capital balance was $43 000.00. What could have caused Mundy's capital to decrease from one year to the next?

## Case 4
R. Allen, owner of Allen Enterprises, states that he is one of the creditors of his business. Is he correct? Explain.

## Case 5
On December 31, 19—, you have presented your balance sheet, shown below, to the manager of the local bank with the hope of obtaining a bank loan. During your conversation with the manager, certain facts are brought out.
1. About $8 000.00 owing from debtors is considerably overdue.
2. A yearly mortgage payment of $4 000.00 is due next March 1.
3. All creditors' accounts are due within 30 days.

BALANCE SHEET
DECEMBER 31, 19—

| Assets | | Liabilities | |
|---|---|---|---|
| Cash | $ 5 000.00 | Creditors | $17 000.00 |
| Debtors | 25 000.00 | Mortgage Payable | 35 000.00 |
| Land | 10 000.00 | | $52 000.00 |
| Equipment | 20 000.00 | | |
| Building | 30 000.00 | Capital | $38 000.00 |
| | $90 000.00 | | $90 000.00 |

Would the bank manager grant the loan? Give your reasons.

### Case 6

S. Beck is the owner of a local coin laundromat. He has an automatic washer in the basement which is no longer in use. The machine is still in good running condition, but he has now purchased better machines. Although it could be sold for scrap for $30, it would cost that much to move it away. Is this machine an asset? Explain.

### Case 7

If the proprietor's equity is $4 000, should that amount of cash be on hand? Explain.

### Case 8

Rogers Real Estate has listed among its assets a coffee dispensing machine placed in the office by a vending company. Would you classify it as an asset in the books of Rogers Real Estate? Explain.

# 2 Changing the Financial Position

You now know how the financial position of a business (or individual) is found and how it is presented by means of a balance sheet. But the financial position does not remain constant. In an active business it is forever undergoing change. Whenever a payment is made, an article is bought, money is received, goods are sold – whenever any **transaction** takes place, the financial position of the business changes.

It is your next step in the study of accounting to learn how the various business transactions affect and change the financial position. To begin, consider the balance sheet of Metropolitan Cartage on a certain date.

| Metropolitan Cartage Balance Sheet – – – DATE – – – | | | | | |
|---|---|---|---|---|---|
| **Assets** | | | **Liabilities** | | |
| Cash | 1 500 00 | | Bank Loan | 2 000 00 | |
| K. Lincoln | 500 00 | | Garrott Supply Co. | 1 574 00 | |
| Supplies | 321 46 | | Central Hardware | 656 74 | |
| Trucks | 7 261 30 | | Mercury Finance Co. | 600 00 | |
| Equipment | 1 426 75 | | | 4 830 74 | |
| | | | **Capital** | | |
| | | | H. Harrison, Capital | 6 178 77 | |
| | 11 009 51 | | | 11 009 51 | |

## Transaction 1

**A regular monthly payment of $100 cash is made to the Mercury Finance Company.**

After this payment is completed, the financial position as shown by the balance sheet above will no longer be correct. Can you make the changes that are necessary to bring the balance sheet up to date? Try to do this before looking at the adjusted balance sheet shown below.

| Metropolitan Cartage Balance Sheet – – – DATE – – – | | | | | |
|---|---|---|---|---|---|
| **Assets** | | | **Liabilities** | | |
| Cash | 1 400 00 | | Bank Loan | 2 000 00 | |
| K. Lincoln | 500 00 | | Garrott Supply Co. | 1 574 00 | |
| Supplies | 321 46 | | Central Hardware | 656 74 | |
| Trucks | 7 261 30 | | Mercury Finance Co. | 500 00 | |
| Equipment | 1 426 75 | | | 4 730 74 | |
| | | | **Capital** | | |
| | | | H. Harrison, Capital | 6 178 77 | |
| | 10 909 51 | | | 10 909 51 | |

*Balance sheet showing results of transaction 1.*

Transaction 1 has had the following effect on the financial position of Metropolitan Cartage and is reflected in the new balance sheet:

(i) Cash has decreased by $100.
(ii) The amount owed to Mercury Finance Company has decreased by $100.

## Transaction 2

**K. Lincoln, who owes us $500, pays us $300 cash in part payment of his debt.**

Can you make the changes necessary to bring the balance sheet up to date?

The corrected balance sheet is as shown below.

In analysing transaction 2, note the following:
(i) Cash has increased by $300.
(ii) The amount owed to us by K. Lincoln has decreased by $300.

You will see these changes by comparing this balance sheet with the preceding one.

| Metropolitan Cartage Balance Sheet ---DATE--- | | | | | | |
|---|---|---|---|---|---|---|
| Assets | | | | Liabilities | | |
| Cash | 1 700 00 | | | Bank Loan | 2 000 00 | |
| K. Lincoln | 200 00 | | | Garrott Supply Co. | 1 574 00 | |
| Supplies | 321 46 | | | Central Hardware | 656 74 | |
| Trucks | 7 261 30 | | | Mercury Finance Co. | 500 00 | |
| Equipment | 1 426 75 | | | | 4 730 74 | |
| | | | | Capital | | |
| | | | | H. Harrison, Capital | 6 178 77 | |
| | 10 909 51 | | | | 10 909 51 | |

*Balance sheet showing results of transaction 2.*

## Transaction 3

**A cash purchase of $50 of additional supplies is made.**

Make the changes necessary to bring the balance sheet up to date.

The corrected balance sheet is as shown below. In analysing transaction 3, note that:
(i) Cash has decreased by $50.
(ii) Supplies has increased by $50.

| Metropolitan Cartage Balance Sheet ---DATE--- | | | | | | |
|---|---|---|---|---|---|---|
| Assets | | | | Liabilities | | |
| Cash | 1 650 00 | | | Bank Loan | 2 000 00 | |
| K. Lincoln | 200 00 | | | Garrott Supply Co. | 1 574 00 | |
| Supplies | 371 46 | | | Central Hardware | 656 74 | |
| Trucks | 7 261 30 | | | Mercury Finance Co. | 500 00 | |
| Equipment | 1 426 75 | | | | 4 730 74 | |
| | | | | Capital | | |
| | | | | H. Harrison, Capital | 6 178 77 | |
| | 10 909 51 | | | | 10 909 51 | |

## Transaction 4

**Mr. Harrison purchases for his store a piece of equipment costing $500 from Garrott Supply Co. Not wishing to pay the full price at the time of purchase, Mr. Harrison makes a cash down payment of $125 and owes the balance of $375.**

Make the changes necessary to bring the balance sheet up to date. The corrected balance sheet is as shown below.

In analysing transaction 4, note the following:
- (i) Cash has decreased by $125.
- (ii) Equipment has increased by $500.
- (iii) The liability to Garrott Supply Co. has increased by $375.

| Metropolitan Cartage Balance Sheet | | |
|---|---|---|
| - - - DATE - - - | | |

| Assets | | Liabilities | |
|---|---|---|---|
| Cash | 1 525 00 | Bank Loan | 2 000 00 |
| K. Lincoln | 200 00 | Garrott Supply Co. | 1 949 00 |
| Supplies | 371 46 | Central Hardware | 656 74 |
| Trucks | 7 261 30 | Mercury Finance Co. | 500 00 |
| Equipment | 1 926 75 | | 5 105 74 |
| | | Capital | |
| | | H. Harrison, Capital | 6 178 77 |
| | 11 284 51 | | 11 284 51 |

## Transaction 5

**Metropolitan Cartage completes a storage service for G. Taylor at a price of $50. Mr. Taylor pays cash at the time the service is completed. (Remember that Metropolitan Cartage is in the business of providing a service to make a profit.)**

Make the changes necessary to bring the balance sheet up to date.

The corrected balance sheet is as shown at the top of the next page.

It is a little more difficult to understand transaction 5 than it was the previous four. But to understand the transaction is of the utmost importance. You must make a determined effort to master completely the reasoning in each transaction before proceeding to the next.

Transaction 5 may be explained as follows:
- (i) Cash has increased by $50, the amount received from the customer, Mr. Taylor.
- (ii) No other assets or liabilities have changed.
- (iii) H. Harrison's capital has increased by $50.

Remember that the fundamental accounting equation tells us to calculate capital by subtracting total liabilities from total assets. In each of the first five balance sheets shown in this chapter you will find that the total assets minus the total liabilities is the same – $6 178.77. The total assets figure does not remain the same, nor does the total liabilities figure, but the difference between them – capital – does remain the same.

The situation as a result of transaction 5 is different. After making the changes to the assets or liabilities affected by the transaction you will find that the difference between the total assets and the total liabilities is now $6 228.77 – which is $50 more than it was before. The new figure of $6 228.77 is the up-to-date capital figure and the one that must be shown on the new balance sheet.

| Metropolitan Cartage Balance Sheet --- DATE --- | | | | | | |
|---|---|---|---|---|---|---|
| **Assets** | | | **Liabilities** | | | |
| Cash | 1 575 00 | | Bank Loan | | 2 000 00 | |
| K. Lincoln | 200 00 | | Garrott Supply Co. | | 1 949 00 | |
| Supplies | 371 46 | | Central Hardware | | 656 74 | |
| Trucks | 7 261 30 | | Mercury Finance Co. | | 500 00 | |
| Equipment | 1 926 75 | | | | 5 105 74 | |
| | | | *Capital* | | | |
| | | | H. Harrison, Capital | | 6 228 77 | |
| | 11 334 51 | | | | 11 334 51 | |

## Transaction 6

**A piece of equipment which cost $120 and which is included in the equipment figure on the balance sheet at that amount is found to be no longer necessary and is sold to Morrison Brothers for $95 cash.**

Make the changes necessary to bring the balance sheet up to date.

The corrected balance sheet is as shown below.

The explanation for transaction 6 follows:

(i) Cash has increased by the amount of cash received, $95.

(ii) Equipment has decreased by $120. The item that was sold was included in the Equipment figure at $120. Since it is no longer on hand, the Equipment figure must be $120 less than it was before in order to be correct.

(iii) Capital has decreased by $25. After changing the necessary assets and liabilities, the difference between total assets and total liabilities is $6 203.77, a decrease of $25.

| Metropolitan Cartage Balance Sheet --- DATE --- | | | | | | |
|---|---|---|---|---|---|---|
| **Assets** | | | **Liabilities** | | | |
| Cash | 1 670 00 | | Bank Loan | | 2 000 00 | |
| K. Lincoln | 200 00 | | Garrott Supply Co. | | 1 949 00 | |
| Supplies | 371 46 | | Central Hardware | | 656 74 | |
| Trucks | 7 261 30 | | Mercury Finance Co | | 500 00 | |
| Equipment | 1 806 75 | | | | 5 105 74 | |
| | | | *Capital* | | | |
| | | | H. Harrison, Capital | | 6 203 77 | |
| | 11 309 51 | | | | 11 309 51 | |

# Change in Financial Position—Any Transaction

You have studied the effect of six transactions on a financial position. You should now be ready to consider the concept of financial change in general.

The first step in the accounting process is the analysing, or breaking down of a transaction to determine the financial changes that result from it. It is imperative that you recognize the importance of performing this step correctly. Accounting must be accurate. For this reason you must be very careful in executing all steps in the accounting process.

You must realize, too, that the possible number of different transactions is very large. To illustrate them all so that you might commit them to memory is not practicable. In the first place, it is unlikely that you could remember them all. But secondly, and more important, if you were to rely on the technique of committing transactions to memory, you could never become a truly accomplished accountant. A good accountant relies not on memory but on common sense, ingenuity, and clear thinking. He is able to handle any transaction, not just certain ones. In your work, you must endeavor to follow his good example.

The following suggestions will assist you in analysing transactions:

1. In general, try to make your decision logically and to understand the results.
2. For each of the given transactions, analyse the information carefully to decide what changes have occurred in any of the assets, liabilities, or both.
3. Recalculate the assets total and the liabilities total. Then calculate A–L to see if C has changed.
4. Make sure that at least two of the individual items on the balance sheet (any of the assets, liabilities, or capital) have changed. It is possible that several items may have changed but never only one.

# Exercises

1. Explain how a transaction is analysed.

2. In each of the following transactions name the accounts affected and indicate which accounts increase and which decrease.

*Transactions*
1. A cash payment is made to Ace Supplies, a creditor.
2. A new desk for the office is purchased for cash from Equipment Supply.
3. D. Murray, who owes us a sum of money, makes a cash payment on his debt.
4. We perform a service for a customer, J. Cooke, who pays us cash.
5. We purchase a new truck from Pine Motors but pay only one third of the cost in cash.
6. We buy stationery and supplies from Doug's Stationers but do not pay for them at the time of purchase.
7. The owner, J. Pitt, takes a sum of money out of the business for his personal use.

3. Indicate the accounts which increase and the accounts which decrease, and by how much in each case, for each of the following transactions:

*Transactions*
1. $400 of supplies are purchased from Paper Servicenter but are not paid for.
2. A new truck is purchased from Modern Motors at a cost of $7 500 with a $2 500 down payment.
3. $880 cash is received from H. Vernon in part payment of the amount owed by him.
4. Paid $750 to Vacation Inns in payment of the amount owed to them.
5. The owner of the business withdraws $500 cash from the business funds for his personal use.

4. After recording a particular transaction, the equity figure for P. Watson, a lawyer, increased by $250. Explain how this could happen.

5.  P. Givens's balance sheet is as follows:

GIVENS CARTAGE
BALANCE SHEET
JANUARY 31, 19—

| Assets | | Liabilities | |
|---|---|---|---|
| Cash | $ 126.31 | Francis Manley | $ 57.40 |
| E. Foster | 24.75 | Burton Bros. | 267.50 |
| I. Noonan | 10.50 | Chartered Finance Co. | 2 095.65 |
| Truck | 4 946.00 | | $2 420.55 |
| Supplies | 115.00 | *Capital* | |
| Equipment | 1 150.00 | P. Givens, Capital | 3 952.01 |
| | $6 372.56 | | $6 372.56 |

Givens is unable to make the payment on the truck to Chartered Finance
Co. He is therefore forced to sell the truck, which he does for $4 500
cash, and to pay off the liability of $2 095.65 to Chartered Finance Co.
The balance of the funds is kept in the business.

**Prepare the balance sheet for P. Givens as it will appear after completion of
the above transaction.**

6.  **The balance sheet of Triangle Real Estate, at the close of business on
September 30, 19—, is as follows:**

TRIANGLE REAL ESTATE
BALANCE SHEET
SEPTEMBER 30, 19—

| Assets | | Liabilities | |
|---|---|---|---|
| Cash | $ 216.00 | Acme Supply | $ 562.00 |
| P. Adams | 375.00 | | |
| N. Serle | 200.00 | | |
| J. Walker | 150.00 | | |
| Office Supplies | 175.40 | *Capital* | |
| Equipment | 967.00 | J. Morse, Capital | 1 521.40 |
| | $2 083.40 | | $2 083.40 |

**Analyse the transactions of October 1 listed below and record the necessary
changes.**

*Transactions*
1.  Received $100 cash from N. Serle in part
    payment of the amount owed by him.
2.  Paid $200 cash to Acme Supply in part
    payment of the debt owed to them.
3.  Purchased supplies costing $29.50 from the
    Standish Company and paid cash for them.
4.  Triangle Real Estate sells a home for Mr.
    A. J. Baxter. For this service Triangle Real
    Estate is paid a commission of $2 700 cash.
5.  A new office desk is purchased from Ideal
    Office Outfitters for $195 cash.

**Prepare the balance sheet at the close of business on October 1, 19—.**

7. Merrymen Window Washers is a business owned and operated by C. Clyde. On November 30, 19—, at the end of the day, the financial position of Merrymen Window Washers is as shown by the following balance sheet:

MERRYMEN WINDOW WASHERS
BALANCE SHEET
NOVEMBER 30, 19—

| Assets | | Liabilities | |
|---|---|---|---|
| Cash | $ 750.00 | Simplex Finance | $1 560.00 |
| D. Washer | 75.00 | Cleanall Supply | 124.00 |
| T. Bird | 120.00 | Piper's Garage | 175.00 |
| Supplies | 80.00 | | $1 859.00 |
| Truck | 3 050.00 | | |
| Equipment | 947.00 | Capital | |
| | | C. Clyde, Capital | 3 163.00 |
| | $5 022.00 | | $5 022.00 |

Analyse the transactions of December 1 listed below and record the necessary changes.

*Transactions*
1. Paid the regular monthly instalment payment to Simplex Finance, $125 cash.
2. Purchased $56 worth of supplies from Arthur Soaps but did not pay for them.
3. $100 cash is received from T. Bird in part payment of his debt to the business.
4. A new cash register is purchased from International Register Company. A cash down payment of $100 is made; the balance of the $325 purchase price is to be paid at a later date.
5. The old cash register, included in the Equipment figure at $150, is sold to B. Lasby for $40 cash.

**Prepare the balance sheet of Merrymen Window Washers at the close of business on December 1, 19—.**

8. P. Severs is a lawyer in business for himself. On the morning of May 6, 19—, the business has the following assets and liabilities:

| Assets | | Liabilities | |
|---|---|---|---|
| Cash | $ 761.25 | Jack Wilson's Co. | $ 56.86 |
| V. Brabson | 100.00 | Starter Finance Co. | 1 320.00 |
| T. Carlisle | 50.00 | | |
| Office Supplies | 42.00 | | |
| Office Equipment | 330.00 | | |
| Automobile | 2 500.00 | | |

On May 6, Mr. Severs transacts the following business. Analyse the transactions and record the necessary changes.

*Transactions*
1. $750 cash is paid for an air conditioner for the office.
2. Because the cash position of the business is very low, Mr. Severs transfers $500 cash

from his personal bank account into the business.

3. A cash payment of $115 is paid to Starter Finance Co.

4. A. Bates, a client, is given legal advice by Mr. Severs. For the service performed for his client, Mr. Severs charges $75. Mr. Bates pays in cash.

5. Mr. Severs has his automobile washed and pays $2 cash.

**Prepare the balance sheet of P. Severs at the close of business on May 6, 19—.**

---

9. **Alliance Appliance Service, owned by W. Wills, has the following assets and liabilities at the close of business on October 20, 19—:**

| *Assets* | | *Liabilities* | |
|---|---|---|---|
| Cash | $ 516.20 | Bank Loan | $1 000.00 |
| N. Brock | 100.00 | Mortgage Payable | 2 700.00 |
| P. Jones | 27.50 | | |
| Supplies | 92.00 | | |
| Equipment | 316.00 | | |
| Delivery Truck | 2 750.00 | | |
| Building | 10 000.00 | | |

**On October 21, the following transactions occur. Analyse them and record the necessary changes.**

### Transactions

1. The owner, in need of money for his personal use, draws $200 cash out of the business.

2. P. Jones comes to the store and pays his debt of $27.50.

3. A service is rendered for a customer. The customer pays the full amount of the bill in cash, $45.

4. A new electrical tester is purchased and paid for in cash, $110.

5. The regular monthly mortgage payment is made, $150 cash.

**Prepare the balance sheet of the business at the close of business on October 21, 19—.**

# Cases

### Case 1
P. Lang owned property that had originally cost his business $15 000. He sold this property for $25 000. Lang recorded this as follows: he increased the Cash by $25 000 and decreased the Property by $25 000. Even though the accounting equation will remain in balance as a result of the above entry, explain to Lang that his analysis is incorrect.

### Case 2
Jay Potter purchased a typewriter for $500 and typewriter ribbons for $10 from Ace

Supply Company. He paid $100 cash down and promised to pay the balance in 30 days. In his records he showed the Equipment increased by $510 and Ace Supply Company increased by $510. Explain why this is not correct.

## Case 3
Do the following events represent business transactions? Explain your answer in each case.
1. Supplies are ordered for delivery next month.
2. A truck is purchased.
3. A prospective employee is interviewed.
4. The owner of the business withdraws cash from the business for his personal use.
5. A service is performed for a customer.

## Case 4
Don Austin has been recording all debts owed by his business as one item called Accounts Payable. Included are amounts owing to suppliers, a bank loan, and a mortgage on the building. As the accountant, how would you explain to Austin that this procedure is not the best? What method should be used?

## Case 5
Bill Phillips, the owner of Phillips Hardware Store, has followed the practice of increasing the item Automobile for purchases of gasoline and oil for the car and for any minor repairs and tune-ups. During the current year the motor in his car was completely overhauled, which caused the item Automobile to be increased by $400.

As the accountant for Phillips, do you agree with this procedure? Explain.

## Case 6
On January 2, 19—, J. Morse purchased land and an office building at a total price of $36 000. The terms of purchase required a cash payment of $16 000 and a promise to pay $20 000 at a later date. The records of the tax assessor indicated that the value of the building was one half that of the land. Mr. Morse recorded the above transaction on his balance sheet as "Land and Building" $36 000.

How should the land and building be shown on the balance sheet?

## Case 7
D. Parker decides to go into business for himself. He has $10 000 of his personal funds and borrows an additional $10 000 from the bank. His monthly payment on the bank loan is $325. On March 1, he opens a bank account in the name of his business, Riveredge Motel. With these funds he purchases a motel for $80 000 with a cash down payment of $10 000 and a mortgage for the balance. The monthly payment on the mortgage is $900. In addition he buys a truck from Howes Motors for use in the business at a cost of $5 000, paying $1 000 cash and the balance to be financed over 2 years with a monthly payment of $250. He also purchases 7 color television sets from the T.V. Shop at a cost of $525 each. He pays half down and will pay the balance in twelve equal instalments. He takes one of these television sets for his personal use.
1. Based on the information in the above paragraph prepare a balance sheet as of March 1, 19—.
2. Calculate the total monthly payment for the bank loan, motel, truck, and T.V. sets.

3. If additional expenditures for supplies and repairs amounted to $300 per month, how much money would the motel have to take in each month in order to break even?
4. If Parker is a carpenter with a monthly salary of $950, do you think it wise for him to open up his own business? Explain.

## Case 8

At December 31, 19–1, Dowse Corporation had assets totaling $85 000. At December 31, 19–2, the assets totaled $115 000. During the same period, liabilities increased by $35 000. If the equity at the end of the first year amounted to $60 000, what was the amount of the owner's equity December 31 of the second year? Show how you arrive at your answer.

# 3 The Simple Ledger

## Financial Position Presented by Means of Ledger Accounts

The exercises in Chapter 2 have given you practice in keeping certain financial positions up to date. But the method employed – as you may already suspect – is not the one used by practising accountants. The method of Chapter 2 is much too cumbersome and untidy to be used in business. But if you fully understand the effect that transactions have on financial position, Chapter 2 has served a very worthwhile purpose.

In current accounting practice a most efficient and orderly system is used. But because of its design it cannot be explained in a few words, or even in a few chapters. Several chapters are necessary to unfold the full accounting story.

The accounting function with which you are immediately concerned is the maintaining of an up-to-date financial position. The universal method of performing this function is the **double-entry system of accounting**. As you are about to see, it is a marvellously effective system.

Let us begin the study of this new method by looking at the balance sheet of City Moving and Storage, shown below. It presents financial position in the form with which you are familiar.

| City Moving and Storage Balance Sheet - - - DATE - - - | | | | | |
|---|---|---|---|---|---|
| **Assets** | | | **Liabilities** | | |
| Cash | 765 | 35 | Bank Loan | 3 000 | 00 |
| R. Caswell | 400 | 00 | Packham Supply Co | 946 | 24 |
| B. Atwell | 220 | 00 | Jenkins and Sons | 1 000 | 00 |
| W. Randall | 150 | 00 | Proctors Limited | 516 | 28 |
| Supplies | 465 | 20 | | 5 462 | 52 |
| Trucks | 5 075 | 00 | **Capital** | | |
| Equipment | 4 674 | 00 | B. J. Wilson, Capital | 6 287 | 03 |
| | 11 749 | 55 | | 11 749 | 55 |

You have already learned that the balance sheet itself is not a suitable means of dealing with a financial position that is undergoing change. Accountants long ago recognized this problem and overcame it by developing a unique system of 'ledger' accounts. This system gives to each balance sheet item a separate and specially designed page on which the changes are recorded in a special way. Before explaining the system in detail let us examine the financial position of City Moving and Storage as presented by means of ledger accounts, shown on the next page.

| Cash | | R. Caswell | | B. Atwell | | Equipment | | Bank Loan | | Packham Supply Co. | |
|---|---|---|---|---|---|---|---|---|---|---|---|
| 765.35 | | 400.00 | | 220.00 | | 4 674.00 | | | 3 000.00 | | 946.24 |

| W. Randall | | Supplies | | Trucks | | Jenkins & Sons | | Proctors Limited | | B. J. Wilson, Capital | |
|---|---|---|---|---|---|---|---|---|---|---|---|
| 150.00 | | 465.20 | | 5 075.00 | | | 1 000.00 | | 516.28 | | 6 287.03 |

*The simple ledger accounts of City Moving and Storage.*

There are a number of important features of this new presentation that must be carefully examined.

1. Each individual balance sheet item is given its own specially divided page with the name of the item at the top. Each of these pages is called an **account**. In the illustration there are twelve accounts altogether. You must learn to refer to them as the Cash account, the R. Caswell account, the Packham Supply account, the Bank Loan account, the B. J. Wilson, Capital account, and so on.

2. The dollar value of each item, as taken from City Moving and Storage's balance sheet, is recorded in the account on the first line. It is especially important to record the dollar value on the correct side of the account. For any item, the correct side is the side on which the item would appear on a simple balance sheet. Observe that for each of the **assets** the dollar amount is placed on the left side of the account page and that for each of the **liabilities** and for the **capital** the dollar amount is placed on the right side of the account page.

3. All of the accounts together are called a **ledger**. A ledger may be prepared in different forms. For instance, the accounts may be printed on cards, thus forming a card ledger; the accounts may be printed on loose-leaf pages, thus forming a loose-leaf ledger; or the accounts may be recorded on magnetic tape that can be read by a computer.

4. The ledger and the balance sheet both show financial position, although in different ways. It follows, therefore, that given a ledger, a balance sheet can be prepared from it, and conversely, given a balance sheet, a ledger can be prepared from it.

*Card ledger (courtesy of Luckett Loose Leaf, Ltd.)*

*Loose-leaf ledger (courtesy of Luckett Loose Leaf, Ltd.).*

*Magnetic tape (courtesy of IBM Canada Ltd.).*

## Debit and Credit

In your work so far you have come to know that the matter of the left-hand side or the right-hand side is of considerable importance in accounting. When dealing with accounts, this is especially true. The theory of accounting by means of ledger accounts is based entirely on the understanding that there are two distinct sides to every account page.

In referring to the two sides of an account, modern accountants use terms that have their origin in the Latin language. The left-hand side of an account is given the name **debit** (he owes) and the right-hand side is given the name **credit** (he trusts).

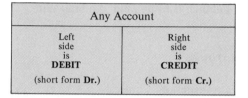

| Any Account | |
|---|---|
| Left side is **DEBIT** (short form **Dr.**) | Right side is **CREDIT** (short form **Cr.**) |

These two words have become what are probably the two most important words in the accountant's vocabulary. As the accounting system is developed you will see that they are used constantly.

Let us begin to use these two new terms right away. In looking back at the simple ledger on page 22 you will notice that the values of the assets were set up individually on the left-hand or debit side of their accounts, and that the values of the liabilities and of the capital were set up individually on the right-hand or credit side of their accounts. You may correctly conclude from this that the assets are considered to be debit accounts and that the liabilities and capital are considered to be credit accounts.

## Changing the Financial Position When a Ledger is Used

Now that you have been introduced to the simple ledger and to the terms 'debit' and 'credit', you can learn how they are used in performing the

task at hand, namely, the recording of changes caused by transactions.

In order to record correctly the changes caused by transactions, follow the rules set out below:

**Increases in Accounts**
1. To increase an asset, the amount of the increase is recorded on the debit side of the appropriate account.
2. To increase a liability or capital, the amount of the increase is recorded on the credit side of the appropriate account.

**Decreases in Accounts**
1. To decrease an asset, the amount of the decrease is recorded on the credit side of the appropriate account.
2. To decrease a liability or capital, the amount of the decrease is recorded on the debit side of the appropriate account.

These rules are summarized in the chart below. It will be wise for you to impress them indelibly on your mind.

**DEBIT AND CREDIT SUMMARY**

| | TO INCREASE | TO DECREASE |
|---|---|---|
| ASSET | DEBIT THE ACCOUNT | CREDIT THE ACCOUNT |
| LIABILITY | CREDIT THE ACCOUNT | DEBIT THE ACCOUNT |
| CAPITAL (EQUITY) | CREDIT THE ACCOUNT | DEBIT THE ACCOUNT |

The importance of understanding the theory being introduced here cannot be overemphasized, for if you do not master the technique of analysing and recording transactions correctly, all of your subsequent work is apt to be rendered useless by inaccuracies.

To provide you with the opportunity of developing a facility with the new rules as quickly as possible, let us discuss a series of transactions pertaining to City Moving and Storage. In applying these new rules to the transactions, it is preferable that you perform the analysis mentally before reading the explanations that follow. You will remember, of course, that the beginning financial position of City Moving and Storage is represented by the ledger on page 22. It will be necessary for you to refer to this ledger in performing your analyses.

## Transaction 1

**$200 cash is received from R. Caswell in part payment of his debt.**

### Analysis

This transaction requires –
(i) That the Cash account be increased by $200. You will recall, of course, that Cash is an asset. As such, in accordance with the new rules, a debit entry (an amount recorded on the debit side of the account) is required to increase it. Or, as the book-keepers say, 'Debit Cash, $200'.
(ii) That the R. Caswell account be decreased by $200. A look at the ledger tells you that the R. Caswell account is also an asset account and as such, in compliance with the rules, requires a credit entry to decrease it. In the language of the bookkeeper, 'Credit R. Caswell, $200'.

After recording the changes, the two accounts involved in the transaction appear as follows.

| Cash | | R. Caswell | |
|---|---|---|---|
| 765.35 | | 400.00 | 200.00 |
| 200.00 | | | |
| | | | |
| | | | |
| | | | |

## Transaction 2

**A storage service has been provided for a customer at a price of $100. As the storage contract has just been completed the customer pays cash for the service.**

### Analysis

This transaction requires –
(i) That the Cash account be increased by $100. Since Cash is an asset, the rules require that it be debited for an increase; the amount, $100.
(ii) That the B. J. Wilson, Capital account be increased by $100. To increase Capital the rules state 'credit'. Therefore, credit B. J. Wilson, Capital, $100.

After recording the changes, the accounts involved in the transaction appear as follows.

| Cash | | B.J. Wilson, Capital | |
|---|---|---|---|
| 765.35 | | | 6 287.03 |
| 200.00 | | | 100.00 |
| 100.00 | | | |
| | | | |
| | | | |

## Transaction 3

**A used moving truck costing $1 000 is purchased from Packham Supply Co. A cash down payment of $250 is made at the time of the purchase and the balance is to be paid at a later date.**

### Analysis

This transaction requires –
(i) That the Cash account be decreased by $250. According to the rules, since Cash is an asset, $250 must be entered on the credit side of the Cash account. Or, expressed in the new terminology, Cash must be credited $250.
(ii) That the Trucks account be increased by $1 000. According to the rules, since Trucks is an asset account, $1 000 must be entered on the debit side. Or, expressed in the new terminology, Trucks must be debited $1 000.
(iii) That the Packham Supply Co. account be increased by $750. According to the rules, since the Packham Supply Co. account is a liability account, $750 must be entered on the credit side of the account. Or, expressed in the new terminology, Packham Supply Co. is to be credited $750.

After these changes are recorded, the accounts involved appear as follows.

| Cash | | Trucks | | Packham Supply Co. | |
|---|---|---|---|---|---|
| 765.35 | 250.00 | 5 075.00 | | | 946.24 |
| 200.00 | | 1 000.00 | | | 750.00 |
| 100.00 | | | | | |
| | | | | | |
| | | | | | |

## Transaction 4

**$540 is paid to Jenkins & Sons.**

### Analysis

This transaction requires –
(i) That the Cash account be decreased by $540. According to the rules, since Cash is an asset, $540 must be entered on the credit side. Expressed in the new terminology, Cash must be credited $540.
(ii) That the Jenkins & Sons account be decreased by $540. According to the rules, since Jenkins & Sons represents a liability, $540 must be entered on the debit side. Expressed in the new terminology, Jenkins & Sons must be debited $540.

After these changes are recorded, the accounts involved appear as follows.

| Cash | | Jenkins & Sons | |
|---|---|---|---|
| 765.35 | 250.00 | 540.00 | 1 000.00 |
| 200.00 | 540.00 | | |
| 100.00 | | | |
| | | | |
| | | | |

See page 27 for some additional transactions.

### Finding the Balance of a T Account

The accounts used in this chapter are very simple accounts called T accounts. The T account obtained its name from the fact that its main rulings resemble the letter T. T accounts are used only for the purpose of explaining accounting theory. The formal account – the one used in actual practice – is introduced in Chapter 4.

In a ledger there are several accounts. Each account stores information about one specific item. The question to be answered now is this: what information does an account hold?

In addition to its name, which is written at the top, an account tells two things:
1. The dollar value of the account.
2. The type of value it is – debit or credit.

These two things together are called the **account balance** or **the balance of the account**. To determine the balance of a T account two steps must be performed. These two steps are illustrated below using two accounts of City Moving and Storage.

Step 1. Add separately each of the two sides of the account. Write down the totals beneath the last item on each side in tiny pencil figures, as illustrated below. These tiny figures are called **pencil footings** or **pin totals**.

Step 2. Subtract the smaller total from the larger total and write the difference beside the larger of the two totals. Circle the amount just written (as illustrated).

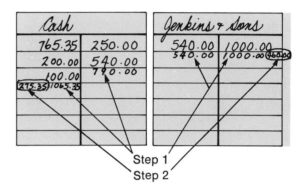

It now remains to interpret the information produced in these two accounts. Looking at the two accounts above, you should be able to see easily that the Cash account has a debit balance of $275.35, and that the Jenkins & Sons account has a credit balance of $460.00. But it is not enough just to determine the balances; they must have some meaning for you. At this stage (as far as your knowledge has progressed), the fact that an account has a debit balance should mean to you that it is an asset account. Similarly, the fact that an account has a credit balance, and is not the Capital account, should mean to you that it is a liability account. The Jenkins & Sons account, for example, having a credit balance, is a liability account which means that City Moving and Storage owes a sum of money to Jenkins & Sons. But if by chance a debit balance had been produced in this account it would have been an asset account and would have meant that Jenkins & Sons owes a sum of money to City Moving and Storage.

On page 28 you will see the ledger of City Moving and Storage with all of the accounts showing the balances after transaction 9.

## Accounting Entry

In addition to its use in its dictionary sense, 'a writing of something in a book', the word 'entry' is used in a special way. Whenever a transaction occurs and the resultant changes in accounts are decided upon, all of the account changes together are referred to as the accounting entry for the transaction.

In this chapter, so far, there have been four transactions and consequently four accounting entries. These four accounting entries are shown below.

| Trans- action No. | Account | Debit | Account | Credit |
|---|---|---|---|---|
| 1 | Cash | $200 | R. Caswell | $200 |
| 2 | Cash | $100 | B. J. Wilson, Capital | $100 |
| 3 | Trucks | $1 000 | Cash Packham Supply Co. | $250 $750 |
| 4 | Jenkins & Sons | $540 | Cash | $540 |

If you have been observant, you will have noticed something about these four transactions that is very special, something that is basic to the whole accounting process. Each of these four transactions balances within itself; that is, the total of the debit amounts is equal to the total of the credit amounts. This is a condition that will hold true for every possible transaction. If, in your work, you ever arrive at an accounting entry that does not balance within itself, you can be absolutely certain that the entry is not correct. On the other hand, just because you have worked out a balanced entry is no guarantee that the entry is correct. It merely means that it might be correct. If it doesn't balance, there is no such possibility.

## Balancing the Ledger

A ledger is an alternate method of presenting the information on a balance sheet. Since a balance sheet must balance, so too then must a ledger.

When setting up a ledger, such as was done on page 22, it is the usual practice to obtain the information for the accounts from a balance sheet. This ensures that the ledger begins in a balanced position; that is, the money total of the accounts with debit balances is equal to the money total of the accounts with credit balances. Thereafter, the ledger is used to record the changes caused by business transactions. These changes are in the form of accounting entries. And, as was just explained, each individual accounting entry itself balances. As a result, after each full accounting entry is recorded, provided of course that it is done correctly, the ledger will still be balanced.

## The Trial Balance

The procedure to ascertain whether or not a ledger is in balance is quite simple. It is merely necessary to see if the total value of all the accounts with debit balances is equal to the total value of all the accounts with credit balances. If the two totals are the same the ledger is said to be **in balance**. If they are not the same the ledger is said to be **out of balance** or **not in balance**. The whole process is called **taking off a trial balance**.

In carrying out the balancing procedure your work may be done with pen and paper as illustrated on page 28, or it may be done by means of an adding machine. Other illustrations and a further discussion of trial balances will be found in Chapter 5.

## Importance of the Trial Balance

It is important to an accountant to have his ledger in balance. He knows that if his ledger is not in balance his work cannot be accurate. To him a ledger out of balance is a sign that one or more errors have been made in the accounts and that he cannot rest until he finds and corrects them. He knows, too, that he must test the ledger fairly frequently. It is standard practice to take off a trial balance at least every month.

A ledger that is in balance proves only that it is mechanically or mathematically correct. It may be in balance and still have inaccuracies in it. These could be caused by the fact that the accountant made incorrect entries even though they were balanced ones.

When a ledger is not in balance it has mechanical errors in it. The errors may be in addition, or in entering an item on the wrong side, and so on. Sometimes, the error or errors can be found easily; at other times, they are quite obscure and difficult to detect. The technique for finding errors when a trial balance is out of balance is fully discussed in Chapter 5.

## Some Additional Transactions

Some additional transactions of City Moving and Storage are now given. Review the work of this chapter and see if you can work out the entries for yourself before looking at the analyses that follow.

5 **The owner, B. J. Wilson, brings into the business $1 000 from his personal funds.**
6 **$1 000 is paid to Packham Supply Company in part payment of the debt owed to that company.**
7 **$85 of supplies is purchased and paid for in cash.**
8 **A $123 item of equipment is purchased from Majestic Machinery Co., a new business supplier for City Moving and Storage. The item is not to be paid for until two months have passed, giving the store an opportunity to try out the new item.**
9 **One of the lifting machines (part of Equipment) breaks down. $112 cash is spent on repairing the machine. (A common mistake made by beginners in respect to this type of transaction is to increase Equipment. To assist you over this hurdle, here is a clue: the owner is worse off financially because he has to repair the machine.)**

## Analyses of Transactions 5 to 9

5 This transaction requires that —

(i) Cash be increased by $1 000. (Increase an asset.)
(ii) Capital be increased by $1 000. (Increase capital.)
The required accounting entry is:
Debit Cash, $1 000; credit B. J. Wilson, Capital, $1 000.
6 This transaction requires that —
(i) Cash be decreased by $1 000. (Decrease an asset.)
(ii) Packham Supply Co. be decreased by $1 000. (Decrease a liability.)
The required accounting entry is:
Debit Packham Supply Co., $1 000; credit Cash, $1 000.
7 This transaction requires that —
(i) Supplies be increased by $85. (Increase an asset.)
(ii) Cash be decreased by $85. (Decrease an asset.)
The required accounting entry is:
Debit Supplies, $85; credit Cash, $85.
8 This transaction requires that —
(i) Store Equipment be increased by $123. (Increase an asset.)
(ii) Majestic Machinery Co. be set up as a liability of $123. (Increase a liability.) Since there is no account in the ledger at present for this company it will be necessary to prepare one.
The required accounting entry is:
Debit Store Equipment, $123; credit Majestic Machinery Co., $123.
9 This transaction requires that —
(i) Capital be decreased by $112. (Decrease capital.)
(ii) Cash be decreased by $112. (Decrease an asset.)
The required accounting entry is:
Debit B. J. Wilson, Capital, $112; credit Cash, $112.
The ledger of City Moving and Storage, after the nine transactions have been recorded and the balances brought up to date, is shown on the next page. Notice in particular, in the Cash account, how as new balances are determined old balances are crossed out.

*The simple ledger of City Moving and Storage after transaction 9.*

| Cash | | R. Caswell | | B. Atwell | |
|---|---|---|---|---|---|
| 765.35 | 250.00 | (200.00) 400.00 | 200.00 | (220.00) 220.00 | |
| 200.00 | 540.00 | 400.00 | 200.00 | 220.00 | |
| | 790.00 | | | | |
| 100.00 | 1000.00 | | | | |
| (275.35) 1065.35 | | | | | |
| 1000.00 | 85.00 | | | | |
| (78.35) 2065.35 | | | | | |
| | 112.00 | | | | |
| | 1987.00 | | | | |

| W. Randall | | Supplies | | Trucks | |
|---|---|---|---|---|---|
| 150.00 | | 465.20 | | 5 075.00 | |
| (150.00) 150.00 | | | | | |
| | | 85.00 | | (6075.00) 1 000.00 | |
| | | (550.20) 550.20 | | 6 075.00 | |

| Equipment | | Bank Loan | | Packham Supply Co. | |
|---|---|---|---|---|---|
| 4 674.00 | | | 3 000.00 | 1000.00 | 946.24 |
| | | | 3 000.00 (3 000.00) | 1 000.00 | |
| 123.00 | | | | | 750.00 |
| (4797.00) 4 797.00 | | | | | 1 696.24 (696.24) |

| Jenkins + Sons | | Proctors Limited | | Majestic Machinery | |
|---|---|---|---|---|---|
| 540.00 | 1 000.00 | | 516.28 | | 123.00 |
| 540.00 | 1 000.00 (460.00) | | 516.28 (516.28) | | 123.00 (123.00) |

| B.J. Wilson, Capital | | Trial Balance | |
|---|---|---|---|
| 112.00 | 6,287.03 | --- DATE --- | |
| 112.00 | | | |
| | 100.00 | Dr's | Cr's |
| | | 78.35 | 3 000.00 |
| | 1 000.00 | 200.00 | 696.24 |
| | 7 387.03 (7275.03) | 220.00 | 460.00 |
| | | 150.00 | 516.28 |
| | | 550.20 | 123.00 |
| | | 6 075.00 | 7 275.03 |
| | | 4 797.00 | |
| | | 12 070.55 | 12 070.55 |

*Balancing the ledger.*

# Bookkeeping and Accounting Terms

**Account**   A specially ruled page used to record financial changes. There is one account for each different item affecting the financial position.

**Ledger**   A group or file of accounts that can be stored in the form of pages in a book, cards in a tray, or tape on a reel.

**Debit**   To record an amount on the left side of an account.

**Credit**   To record an amount on the right side of an account.

**Account Balance**   The value of an account showing the dollar amount and an indication as to whether it is a debit or a credit value.

**Accounting Entry**   All of the account changes caused by one transaction, expressed in terms of debits and credits. For each accounting entry the total of the debit amounts will equal the total of the credit amounts.

**Trial Balance**   A special listing of all the account balances in a ledger, the purpose of which is to see if the dollar value of the accounts with debit balances is equal to the dollar value of the accounts with credit balances. The process of obtaining this special listing is called 'balancing the ledger' or 'taking off a trial balance'.

**Pencil Footings**   Column totals or other totals written with tiny pencil figures. Also known as **pin totals**.

# Review Questions

1. What is an account?
2. What is a ledger?
3. Each side of an account is given a special designation. Name them.
4. Describe the rule for recording an increase in an asset account; in a liability account; in the capital account.
5. Describe the rule for recording a decrease in an asset account; in a liability account; in the capital account.
6. Using a chart, summarize the rules of debit and credit.
7. Explain the procedure for finding the balance of a T account.
8. Three important pieces of information are stored in an account. What are they?
9. What are pin totals? What is another name for pin totals?
10. If the R. Jones account has a debit balance, what does it mean?
11. The Hunt Brothers account has a credit balance. Explain.
12. What kind of balance does an asset account have? a liability account? the capital account?
13. Define 'accounting entry'.
14. Describe a special characteristic of all accounting entries.
15. Describe a special characteristic of the ledger.
16. What is a trial balance?
17. Explain the importance of a trial balance.
18. How does one know if a trial balance does not balance?
19. What is meant by a trial balance that does not balance?
20. Describe the procedure for taking off a trial balance.

# Exercises

1. The balance sheet for Woods Woodworking is shown below.

WOODS WOODWORKING

BALANCE SHEET

— DATE —

| Assets | | Liabilities | |
|--------|--------|-------------|--------|
| Cash | $ 2 000 | Bank Loan | $ 1 000 |
| C. Prentice | 1 150 | Gem Lumber Company | 2 500 |
| A. Marks | 375 | Mortgage Payable | 20 000 |
| Land | 10 000 | | $23 500 |
| Building | 25 000 | | |
| Equipment | 7 800 | Owner's Equity | |
| Truck | 4 500 | T. Woods, Capital | 27 325 |
| | $50 825 | | $50 825 |

Name the accounts that would appear in the ledger of Woods Woodworking.
Indicate the dollar value of each account, and tell whether it has a debit or credit
value.

2. Calculate the balance of each of the following T accounts.

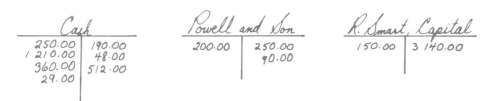

What does the debit balance in the Cash account indicate?

What does the credit balance in the Powell and Son account indicate?

What do you think the debit entry in the Capital account indicates?

3. In each of the following transactions indicate which account is debited and
which account is credited.

*Transactions*

1. F. Baker invests cash to begin a business.
2. A supply of envelopes is purchased from Ace Stationers and paid for in cash.
3. A debt to Little Brothers is paid for in cash.
4. Cash is received from S. Mann, a debtor, in payment of his debt.

5. The owner withdraws cash from the business for his personal use.
6. A typewriter is purchased and received from Olympic Supply but is not paid for.
7. A service is performed for P. Glass. He agrees to pay for the service at the end of the month.

---

**4. For each of the following transactions indicate the account to be debited, the account to be credited, and the amount.**

*Transactions*
1. Our liability of $500 to the International Union is paid by cash.
2. A new car costing $3 500 is purchased for cash.
3. $2 000 in cash is borrowed from W. Irwin.
4. Purchased equipment costing $700 from Dorsey Bros., but did not pay for it.
5. Supplies worth $125 are spoiled by a water leak and are thrown out.

---

**5. From the following information prepare a trial balance for the R. K. Smith Company. Date the trial balance September 30, 19—.**

*Account balances:*
Cash, $7 000 Dr; W. Philips, $300 Dr; Equipment, $1 400 Dr; Land, $15 000 Dr; Buildings, $25 000 Dr; Willwest Company, $1 700 Cr; Mortgage on Building, $15 400 Cr; R. K. Smith, Capital, $31 600 Cr.

---

**6. Reliable Janitorial Service, owned and operated by M. Finley, begins business with the following assets. There are no liabilities.**

| Assets | |
| --- | --- |
| Cash | $ 750.00 |
| Supplies | 56.00 |
| Equipment | 175.00 |
| Truck | 2 500.00 |

**Set up the beginning financial position in T accounts.**

**In the T accounts record the accounting entries for each of the transactions listed below.**

*Transactions*
1. Purchased $150 of cleaning supplies from Special Chemicals Limited but did not pay for them.
2. Purchased a large vacuum cleaner from Proust Bros. and paid $300 cash.
3. Performed a cleaning service for S. Pearson at a price of $115. Mr. Pearson paid cash.
4. Performed a service for M. King at a price of $70. Mr. King agreed to pay in thirty days.
5. Paid $50 cash to Special Chemicals Limited.

**After all of the transactions have been completed, calculate and record the balances in the accounts.**

**Take off a trial balance to see if the ledger is in balance.**

7. T. Barkley, an accountant, is in business with the following assets and liabilities.

| Assets | | Liabilities | |
|---|---|---|---|
| Cash | $ 500.75 | Proctors' Limited | $ 112.15 |
| R. Burke | 25.00 | A. Rose and Son | 64.25 |
| P. Chapple | 150.00 | Familiar Finance | 1 621.42 |
| O. Patterson | 78.00 | | |
| Supplies | 85.00 | | |
| Equipment | 1 956.25 | | |
| Automobile | 3 050.00 | | |

Set up the financial position of T. Barkley in T accounts.

In the T accounts record the accounting entries for the transactions listed below.

*Transactions*
1. Received $78 cash from O. Patterson in payment of his debt to the business.
2. Paid $64.25 cash to A. Rose and Son.
3. The owner withdrew $250 cash from the business for his personal use.
4. An accounting service was performed for R. Burke at a price of $170. Mr. Burke agreed to pay for the service at a later date.
5. The office air conditioner (included in the Equipment figure) broke down and had to be repaired at a cost of $47. Cash was paid for the repair.
6. An accounting service was performed for E. Green for $75 cash.

Calculate and record the balances in the accounts.

Take off a trial balance to see if the ledger is in balance.

8. For each of the following transactions of East End Electric Repairs, owned by V. Marsh, record the accounting entry. Show the accounts that are debited and those that are credited as well as the corresponding amounts.

*Transactions*
1. Purchased $50 of supplies and paid cash for them.
2. Received $25 cash from C. Fells, a debtor.
3. Repaired a motor for a customer and received $35 cash.
4. Paid $100 cash to R. Tweed, a creditor.
5. The owner withdrew $110 cash from the business for his personal use.
6. $150 cash was paid for repairs to the delivery truck which was damaged in a collision.
7. Performed a repair service for J. Wiley at a price of $82 but Mr. Wiley did not pay for it immediately.
8. A new typewriter was purchased for the office from Standard Typewriter Company at a cost of $350. $100 cash was paid at the time of the purchase and the balance was to be paid at a later date.
9. $200 cash was given to the bank for the purpose of reducing the bank loan.

9.  A. Frost is a sign painter and truck letterer. His business has the following assets and liabilities:

| Assets | | | Liabilities | | |
|---|---|---|---|---|---|
| Cash | $ | 216.00 | Bank Loan | $ | 500.00 |
| G. Anderson | | 57.00 | Consumers' Supply | | 375.20 |
| N. Paul | | 102.00 | Nu-Style Furniture | | 951.65 |
| Office Supplies | | 80.00 | Economy Finance | | 1 980.00 |
| Painting Supplies | | 120.00 | Mortgage Payable | | 5 092.25 |
| Office Furniture | | 1 090.00 | | | |
| Building | | 20 000.00 | | | |
| Automobile | | 3 000.00 | | | |

Set up A. Frost's financial position in T accounts.

For the transactions listed below record the accounting entries in the T accounts.

*Transactions*

1.  Received $25 cash from a customer for painting a sign.
2.  Paid $100 to Consumers' Supply.
3.  Received $102 cash from N. Paul.
4.  An extra office desk (which is included in the Office Furniture figure at $150) is sold to G. Brand at a price of $60. Mr. Brand paid $10 cash and owed the balance.
5.  An additional $500 was borrowed from the bank.
6.  Paid the regular monthly mortgage payment of $175 cash.
7.  Paid the regular monthly finance payment to Economy Finance, $125.
8.  Paid the balance owing to Consumers' Supply in cash.

Calculate the account balances and balance the ledger.

10.  Rainbow Real Estate is a business owned by C. Rogers. The assets and liabilities of the business are as follows:

| Assets | | Liabilities | |
|---|---|---|---|
| Cash | $1 056.25 | Bank Loan | 9 000.00 |
| A. Carlisle | 516.00 | Capitol Corporation | 520.00 |
| D. Murray | 351.00 | | |
| Office Supplies | 115.00 | | |
| Furniture and Equipment | 916.00 | | |
| Properties Owned | 8 042.00 | | |
| Automobile | 2 965.00 | | |

In T accounts set up the financial position of Rainbow Real Estate.

For the transactions which follow record the accounting entries in the T accounts.

*Transactions*
1. Received $516 cash from A. Carlisle.
2. Sold a home for V. Morris. For this service Mr. Morris owed $750 to Rainbow Real Estate.
3. Paid $35 cash for office supplies.
4. One of the properties owned by Rainbow Real Estate (included in the Properties Owned figure at $2 000) is sold for $3 000 cash.
5. $4 000 cash is paid to the bank to reduce the amount of the bank loan.
6. $100 cash is paid to Capitol Corporation.
7. $16 cash is paid for a new headlight for the automobile.
8. $351 cash is received from D. Murray.
9. The owner withdrew $200 cash for his personal use.
10. Received $250 cash from V. Morris.
11. Paid the balance of the debt to Capitol Corporation in cash.
12. Purchased a new office desk at a cost of $195 from Pioneer Furniture but did not pay cash for it.
13. Sold a home for A. McIntosh. Mr. McIntosh paid Rainbow Real Estate $2 100 cash for the service.

Calculate and record the balances in the accounts and take off a trial balance.

# Cases

### Case 1
Mr. J. Drysdale is the owner of a hardware store. At the end of the year, in the absence of his accountant, he attempted to prepare a trial balance of the accounts in the general ledger as shown below. The balances themselves are correct, but since Mr. Drysdale has no knowledge of double entry bookkeeping, he has made many errors in listing the balances. He asks you to find the errors and prepare a corrected trial balance.

J. DRYSDALE
TRIAL BALANCE
DECEMBER 31, 19—

|  | Debit | Credit |
|---|---|---|
| Cash | $ 3 000.00 | |
| Land | 4 680.00 | |
| Accounts Receivable | | $10 940.00 |
| Supplies | 690.00 | |
| Office Equipment | 7 150.00 | |
| Automobile | | 5 200.00 |
| Building | 40 000.00 | |
| Accounts Payable | 5 160.00 | |
| Bank Loan | | 12 000.00 |
| J. Drysdale, Capital | | 46 000.00 |
| Mortgage Payable | | 8 500.00 |
| | $60 680.00 | $82 640.00 |

## Case 2

G. Kerford, owner of Kerford's Moving and Storage, purchased a truck at a cost of $5 800. He traded in his old truck which originally cost $4 000, and was given an allowance of $2 000. He promised to pay the balance in 60 days. When Kerford entered the transaction in the ledger, he debited $1 800 to the Truck account.

Do you agree with the debit entry of $1 800 to the Truck account? Explain.

## Case 3

Your accounting clerk has prepared his trial balance as of June 30, 19—, and determines that total debits equal total credits. He breathes a sigh of relief and informs you that his ledger is in balance and that therefore the accounts are correct. Do you agree with his statement? Explain.

## Case 4

The trial balance prepared by your company at the end of the month did not balance. In reviewing the entries for the month, the accountant noticed that one of the transactions was recorded as a debit to Furniture & Fixtures, $500, and a debit to Cash, $500.

Answer the following questions and explain your answer for each:
1. Was the Furniture & Fixtures account overstated, understated, or correctly stated on the trial balance?
2. Was the total of the debit column of the trial balance overstated, understated, or correctly stated?
3. Was the total of the credit column of the trial balance overstated, understated, or correctly stated?

## Case 5

The accountant for M. Finney, owner of a janitorial service business, prepared a trial balance at the end of December. When Mr. Finney examined the trial balance, he noticed that the S. Pearson Co. had a debit balance of $375. Mr. Finney remembered depositing a cheque received from Pearson for that amount. He wants to know why a debit balance still exists on the records. Explain to Mr. Finney how this could happen.

## Case 6

State whether the following errors would cause a trial balance to be out of balance. Explain why or why not.
1. The entry to record the purchase of delivery equipment was omitted from the Delivery Equipment account.
2. A new desk was purchased for cash. Cash was credited but the Office Supplies was debited instead of Office Equipment.
3. Cash of $100 was received from a client for services performed. Cash was debited for $100 and Capital was credited for $10.
4. Cash of $500 was borrowed from the bank. Cash was credited for $500 and Bank Loan was debited $500.

## Case 7

The owner of K. Rose and Co. has never studied accounting and employs you to keep books for him. He does not understand why you debit Cash, debit Capital, and credit Office Equipment when an old typewriter used in the business is sold for less cash than it is worth. What explanations can you give him?

## Case 8

An employee beginning his first trial balance discovers that the Furniture and Equipment account has a credit balance of $5 000 and a customer's account has a credit balance of $200. Has the accountant made a mistake in his records or is this situation possible? Explain.

# 4 Formal Journalizing and Posting

Although the simple system described in Chapter 3 is theoretically sound and accurate, it is still not in the form used by today's businessmen. Businessmen and professional accountants have found that by modifying and expanding the simple system a far greater effectiveness is possible.

## The Journal

The theory described so far suggests that only one device – the ledger – is used in the accounting process and that as accounting entries arise the only thing that happens to them is that they are recorded promptly in the accounts.

Unfortunately, this simple system contains a serious weakness. Since each accounting entry affects at least two, and sometimes several accounts, its various parts become scattered throughout the ledger. After a period of time, these scattered parts become buried in the accounts in a great mass of accounting entries, the result of continually occurring transactions. Eventually, for all practical purposes, it becomes impossible to reverse the accounting process; that is, to reconstruct any particular accounting entry from the bits and pieces that are spread throughout the ledger. But this reverse procedure is an essential function in the accounting process. For it seems always to be necessary to investigate some transaction which, for one of a variety of reasons, suddenly becomes troublesome.

To overcome this difficulty, another book is introduced into the system. This new book, called a **journal**, is used expressly for the purpose of listing the accounting entries individually in the order in which they occur (chronologically). Each entry is first, or originally, recorded in the journal before being recorded in the ledger. The accounting entries as they appear in the journal are referred to as **journal entries** and the process of recording them in the journal is called **journalizing**. And, because the journal entries are the first or original recording, the journal is known as a **book of original entry**.

### The Two-Column General Journal

There are several types of journals in actual use today, each one designed for a special purpose. The simplest journal and the one to be studied first in this text is the **two-column general journal**. It is illustrated on page 38.

Familiarize yourself thoroughly with the two-column general journal. Examine the illustration on page 38 carefully, noting the general appearance and the column headings. Then, more specifically, observe the following:

1.  Each accounting entry is listed in a special way, balances within itself, and is separated from other accounting entries by a blank line. The debit accounts are listed first and are placed at the extreme left-hand side of the Particulars column. The debit amounts are placed in the Debit column. The credit accounts are listed in the Particulars column beneath the debit accounts but are indented approximately one inch. The credit amounts are placed in the Credit column.

2.  Immediately beneath the accounting entry, and in the Particulars column only, a simple explanation is written. Each line of the ex-

planation begins at the extreme left-hand side of the column. The explanations are simple, brief, and meaningful. They are to be thought out – not memorized.

3. In respect to the date it is necessary to consider the year, the month, and the day separately.

a. On each page, the year is entered in small figures in the top half of the first line of the Date column. The year is not repeated for each journal entry; the figure at the top of the page is meant to serve all of the entries on the page. Occasionally, however, it may happen that the year changes

| Date | | Particulars | P.R. | Debit | | Credit | |
|---|---|---|---|---|---|---|---|
| | | General Journal | | | | Page 16 | |
| 19-8 Dec | 17 | Cash | 1 | 17 | 42 | | |
| | | J. Hill | 2 | | | 17 | 42 |
| | | Paid the balance of his account | | | | | |
| | 23 | Supplies | 6 | 50 | 00 | | |
| | | Cash | 1 | | | 50 | 00 |
| | | Letterhead and envelopes from Dover Stationery | | | | | |
| 19-9 Jan | 7 | Store Equipment | 7 | 165 | 00 | | |
| | | Cash | 1 | | | 50 | 00 |
| | | Raynor Bros | 22 | | | 115 | 00 |
| | | New Display cases | | | | | |
| | 18 | King Finance Co | 21 | 126 | 74 | | |
| | | Cash | 1 | | | 126 | 74 |
| | | Monthly payment on auto | | | | | |
| | 18 | Cash | 1 | 25 | 00 | | |
| | | W. Foster | 4 | 75 | 00 | | |
| | | R. Jennings, Capital | 31 | | | 100 | 00 |
| | | Sale to W. Foster | | | | | |
| | 28 | R. Jennings, Capital | 31 | 200 | 00 | | |
| | | Cash | 1 | | | 200 | 00 |
| | | Owner's withdrawal | | | | | |
| Feb. | 2 | Raynor Bros | 22 | 115 | 00 | | |
| | | Cash | 1 | | | 115 | 00 |
| | | Payment of balance of account | | | | | |

*A page from a two-column general journal.*

before the page is completed. Then the new year is entered in small figures at the point on the page where the year changes (see illustration).

b. On each page, the month is entered in the month section of the Date column on the first line. It is not repeated for each journal entry, the intention being that the notation on the first line will serve all of the entries on the page. However, if the month changes before the page is completed, the new month is entered at the point of change.

c. For each journal entry, the day is entered once in the day section of the Date column on the line which corresponds with the beginning line of the journal entry. It is important to note that the day is recorded on the first line of each journal entry no matter how many journal entries may occur on any given day.

4. The Posting Reference (P.R.) column, often called the Folio (Fo.) column, is used to cross-reference the journal and the ledger. Cross-referencing is explained fully in a later section on posting.

5. It is permissible to use abbreviations in the journal (or in the ledger). The only place where abbreviations are not permitted is on financial statements, and the only financial statement with which you are acquainted up to this point is the simple balance sheet.

6. The pages of the general journal are numbered.

# The Three-Column Account

In Chapter 3 the theory of entry-making (the determining of accounting entries from the transactions) was demonstrated through the use of a simple two-sided account called the T account. It was explained at that time that the simple two-sided account, although ideal for theoretical explanations and discussion, is of little value in actual practice. Today's accounting requires an account that provides more detailed information in a more formal way.

The style of account that is most widely used today is the three-column account. Two illustrations of this type of account appear at the top of page 40.

Your first reaction is probably that the formal account is radically different from the one used in Chapter 3. But you will find, upon closer examination, that the differences are simple, logical, and easily understood.

You will see in the formal account a Debit column and a Credit column. These two columns form the core of the account and they correspond to the simple T account that you have already used. In addition, the formal account has the following columns:

**Date**  This column is used to record the date on which the entry is recorded in the journal.* With the introduction of a Date column, it becomes necessary that each amount recorded in the account be entered on a separate line. The rules in respect to the year, month, and day are precisely the same as for the journal.

**Particulars**  This column is not used for every posting. You will not be required to use it until Chapter 7, at which point it will be used to record invoice numbers. This column is often called **Items**.

**Posting Reference**  This column is used to cross-reference the journal and the ledger and is fully explained in a later section on posting. This column often goes under the name **Folio**.

**Dr/Cr**  This column is used to indicate the type of balance that the account has. It must be used in conjunction with the Balance column.

**Balance**  The Balance column is the most important addition to the account. With this column the balance in the account is now always readily at hand since, after each new amount is entered, the new balance is usually calculated and recorded. Note carefully that the most recently determined balance is entered on the same line as the most recently entered amount and represents the balance up to and including that entry; it must not be entered on any other line. It is most essential that you become proficient in the handling of this important column.

*The word 'entry' has different meanings in accounting. It may mean the full accounting entry with which you are already familiar. Or, as is intended in this instance, it may mean just one part of the full accounting entry.

| Account | Cash | | | | | | | No. | 1 | |
|---|---|---|---|---|---|---|---|---|---|---|
| Date | | Particulars | P.R. | Debit | | Credit | | DR. CR. | Balance | |
| 19— June | 3 | | J 1 | 1 750 | 00 | | | DR. | 1 750 | 00 |
| | 10 | | J 2 | | | 106 | 00 | DR. | 1 644 | 00 |
| | 12 | | J 2 | 174 | 70 | | | DR. | 1 818 | 70 |
| | 18 | | J 3 | 64 | 26 | | | DR | 1 882 | 96 |
| | 30 | | J 4 | | | 250 | 00 | DR | 1 632 | 96 |
| July | 2 | | J 5 | 25 | 00 | | | DR. | 1 657 | 96 |
| | 4 | | J 5 | | | 135 | 46 | DR | 1 522 | 50 |

| Account | Acme Finance Company | | | | | | | No. 23 | | |
|---|---|---|---|---|---|---|---|---|---|---|
| Date | | Particulars | P.R. | Debit | | Credit | | DR. CR. | Balance | |
| 19—1 Nov. | 15 | | J 9 | | | 1 500 | 00 | CR | 1 500 | 00 |
| 19—2 Feb. | 15 | | J 11 | 150 | 00 | | | CR | 1 350 | 00 |
| May | 15 | | J 14 | 150 | 00 | | | CR | 1 200 | 00 |
| Aug | 15 | | J 16 | 150 | 00 | | | CR | 1 050 | 00 |
| Nov. | 15 | | J 19 | 150 | 00 | | | CR | 900 | 00 |

## Numbering the Accounts

Although it is not absolutely necessary, it is customary to number the accounts in the ledger in order to improve the efficiency of the system. The technique of numbering the accounts varies depending on the size and complexity of the business, and on the views of the accountant. In this text the numbering system begins with the very simple scheme shown below.

Assets        No. 1 to No. 20 inclusive
Liabilities   No. 21 to No. 30 inclusive
Capital       No. 31

In larger businesses having automated accounting systems, coding of the accounts by means of numbers is essential.

## Opening an Account

As transactions occur in business, it often happens that an accounting entry affects an item for which there is no account in the ledger. When this happens, it is necessary to prepare an account for the new item and place it in the proper place in the ledger. This is called **opening an account**. To open an account it is necessary to:

1. Obtain an unused page of account paper.
2. Write the name of the new item at the top of the page in the space designated. This is called the **account title**.
3. Write the number given to the new account in the space designated.
4. Place the new account in its proper place in the ledger.

## The Basic Accounting Procedure

You now know that there are two important books in the accounting process. These two books – the journal and the ledger – are commonly referred to as the **books of account**, or the **books**.

You have also learned that each accounting entry is recorded in the journal before it is entered in the ledger. This is a cardinal rule in accounting except in advanced systems using complex equipment. As far as you are concerned, do not record entries in the ledger without first journalizing them.

For every transaction the basic procedure is:
1. Determine ⸻ ing entry and record it ⸻ thod of doing this – ⸻ ly been discussed.
⸻ shown in the jour- ⸻ unts in the ledger. ⸻ called posting, is

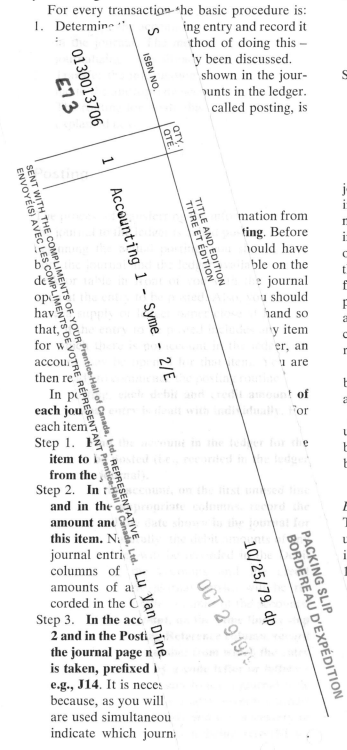

⸻ mation from ⸻ **ting**. Before ⸻ ould have ⸻ ble on the ⸻ journal ⸻ u should ⸻ hand so that, ⸻ y item for w⸻ er, an accou⸻ u are then re⸻

In p⸻ each debit and credit amount **of each jou**⸻ **or** each item

Step 1. I⸻ the account in the ledger for the **item to** ⸻ **from the** ⸻

Step 2. **In** ⸻ account, on the first unused line **and in the** ⸻ record the **amount and** ⸻ date shown in the journal for **this item.** N⸻ the debit amounts ⸻ journal entri⸻ ⸻ columns of ⸻ amounts of a⸻ corded in the C⸻

Step 3. **In the ac**⸻ **2 and in the Posti**⸻ **the journal page n**⸻ **is taken, prefixed** ⸻ **e.g., J14.** It is nece⸻ because, as you will ⸻ are used simultaneou⸻ indicate which journ⸻

The code for the general journal may be any one of the following three: J, G, or G.J. But once one of these is selected, it is used consistently throughout the ledger.

Step 4. **Calculate and enter the new balance of the account in the Balance column and indicate whether it is a debit or a credit balance in the small column to the left of the Balance column.**

Step 5. **In the journal, in the Posting Reference column and on the same line as the amount being posted, record the number of the account to which the posting was just made.** Steps 3 and 5 constitute 'cross-referencing', to which reference has been made previously.

The recording of the account number in the journal is the final step in the posting of any one individual item. The presence of the account number in the journal is evidence that the posting of an item is completed. And the absence of the account number in the journal is evidence that the posting of an item is not completed. If for any reason, perhaps for a telephone call, your posting of the journal is interrupted, you will be able to tell by a glance at the Posting Reference column where to recommence posting upon your return.

There are some accountants who do not number the accounts in the ledger. Where this occurs, a check mark ($\sqrt{}$) or some other symbol (e.g., $\int$) must be placed in the Posting Reference column of the journal instead of the account numbers to indicate that the posting of the item has been completed.

*Example*

The two illustrations on the next page will be used to demonstrate the posting process. These illustrations are –
1. A page of a general journal on which the latest recorded journal entry is not yet posted (as indicated by the absence of any account numbers beside that entry in the Posting Reference column).

The ledger accounts that will be affected by his entry, as they appear before the posting the entry under discussion. (You will see the Office Suppliers Company account a d method of indicating that an account no balance; i.e., that the balance is nil.)

## General Journal　　　　　　　　　　　　　　　Page 3

| Date | Particulars | PR. | Debit | Credit |
|------|-------------|-----|-------|--------|
| 19—<br>June 17 | Supplies | 7 | 37 50 | |
| |     Anderson Bros. | 25 | | 37 50 |
| | Ledger and typing paper | | | |
| 18 | Cash | 1 | 100 00 | |
| |     C. Winston | 4 | | 100 00 |
| | Partial payment of account bal. | | | |
| 18 | Office Furniture | | 125 00 | |
| |     Cash | | | 50 00 |
| |     Office Supplies Company | | | 75 00 |
| | New desk from Office Suppliers | | | |

*A partially posted journal page. The PR. column indicates that the first two entries have been posted, but that the third one has not been posted.*

---

**Account** Cash　　　　　　　　　　　　　　　　　**No.** 1

| Date | Particulars | P.R. | Debit | Credit | DR.CR. | Balance |
|------|-------------|------|-------|--------|--------|---------|
| 19—<br>May 31 | | J1 | 2 000 00 | | Dr. | 2 000 00 |
| June 6 | | J2 | | 1 475 00 | Dr. | 525 00 |
| 12 | | J2 | 746 47 | | Dr. | 1 271 47 |
| 18 | | J3 | 100 00 | | Dr. | 1 371 47 |

**Account** Office Furniture　　　　　　　　　　　**No.** 11

| Date | Particulars | P.R. | Debit | Credit | DR.CR. | Balance |
|------|-------------|------|-------|--------|--------|---------|
| 19—<br>May 31 | | J1 | 1 250 00 | | Dr. | 1 250 00 |
| June 15 | | J2 | 310 00 | | Dr. | 1 560 00 |

**Account** Office Supplies Company　　　　　　　**No.** 24

| Date | Particulars | P.R. | Debit | Credit | DR.CR. | Balance |
|------|-------------|------|-------|--------|--------|---------|
| 19—<br>June 2 | | J1 | | 500 00 | Cr | 500 00 |
| 7 | | J2 | 500 00 | | | -0- |

*The ledger accounts in which the last entry in the journal shown above will be posted.*

To begin the posting of a journal entry, each amount in the entry is usually considered in turn. In this example, the first item to be considered is the debit of $125 to the Office Furniture account. Step 1 in the posting process, assuming that the journal is opened at the correct page, is to open the ledger at the Office Furniture account. Steps 2, 3, 4, and 5 (as stated on page 41) are then performed mechanically in turn as shown by the top two illustrations on the next page.

The second item to be considered (in posting the sample entry) is the credit of $50 to the Cash account. Step 1 in the posting process is to turn to the Cash account in the ledger. Then, steps 2,

## Office Furniture Ledger

| Account Office Furniture | | | | | | | No. 11 | | |
|---|---|---|---|---|---|---|---|---|---|
| Date | Particulars | P.R. | Debit | | Credit | DR. CR. | Balance | | |
| 19— May 31 | | J1 | 1 250 00 | | | Dr | 1 250 00 | | |
| June 15 | | J2 | 310 00 | | | Dr | 1 560 00 | | |
| 18 | | J3 | 125 00 | | | Dr | 1 685 00 | | |

Step 1: Open the ledger at this account

Step 3: Record the journal page number

Step 2: Record the date and the debit amount as shown in the journal entry

Step 4: Enter the new balance

## General Journal — Page 3

| Date | Particulars | P.R. | Debit | | Credit | |
|---|---|---|---|---|---|---|
| 19— June 17 | Supplies | 7 | 37 50 | | | |
| | Anderson Bros. | 25 | | | 37 50 | |
| | Ledger and typing paper | | | | | |
| 18 | Cash | 1 | 100 — | | | |
| | C. Winston | 4 | | | 100 — | |
| | Partial payment of account bal. | | | | | |
| 18 | Office Furniture | 11 | 125 — | | | |
| | Cash | | | | 50 — | |
| | Office Suppliers Company | | | | 75 — | |
| | New desk from Office Suppliers | | | | | |

Step 5: Enter the account number

## Cash Ledger

| Account Cash | | | | | | | No. 1 | | |
|---|---|---|---|---|---|---|---|---|---|
| Date | Particulars | P.R. | Debit | | Credit | DR. CR. | Balance | | |
| 19— May 31 | | J1 | 2 000 00 | | | Dr. | 2 000 00 | | |
| June 6 | | J2 | | | 1 475 00 | Dr. | 525 00 | | |
| 12 | | J2 | 746 47 | | | Dr. | 1 271 47 | | |
| 18 | | J3 | 100 00 | | | Dr. | 1 371 47 | | |
| 18 | | J3 | | | 50 00 | Dr. | 1 321 47 | | |

Step 1: Open the ledger at this account

Step 2: Record the date and the credit amount as shown in the journal entry

Step 3: Record the journal page number

Step 4: Enter the new balance

| | 18 | Office Furniture | 11 | 125 — | | |
|---|---|---|---|---|---|---|
| | | Cash | 1 | | 50 — | |
| | | Office Suppliers Company | | | 75 — | |
| | | New desk from Office Suppliers | | | | |

Step 5: Enter the account number

3, 4, and 5 follow mechanically, as shown in the bottom two illustrations on page 43.

Notice in the journal how the Posting Reference column serves to indicate the point at which the posting has been completed. If you were called away from your work at this point, you would be able to tell by a glance at this column upon your return that you should recommence your posting with the $75 credit to the Office Suppliers Company account.

The final item to be considered (in posting this sample entry) is the credit of $75 to the Office Suppliers Company account. It is necessary to repeat the posting process for this item in a manner identical to that already executed for the first two items.

After completion of the posting of this third item, the journal and the three accounts involved appear as illustrated in the four figures shown below.

**General Journal**      Page 3

| Date | Particulars | PR. | Debit | Credit |
|---|---|---|---|---|
| 19—<br>June 17 | Supplies | 7 | 37 50 | |
| |    Anderson Bros. | 25 | | 37 50 |
| | Ledger and typing paper | | | |
| 18 | Cash | 1 | 100 00 | |
| |    C. Winston | 4 | | 100 00 |
| | Partial payment of account bal. | | | |
| 18 | Office Furniture | 11 | 125 00 | |
| |    Cash | 1 | | 50 00 |
| |    Office Suppliers Company | 24 | | 75 00 |
| | New desk from Office Suppliers | | | |

**Account** Cash      No. 1

| Date | Particulars | P.R. | Debit | Credit | DR.<br>CR. | Balance |
|---|---|---|---|---|---|---|
| 19—<br>May 31 | | J1 | 2 000 00 | | Dr | 2 000 00 |
| June 6 | | J2 | | 1 475 00 | Dr | 525 00 |
| 12 | | J2 | 746 47 | | Dr | 1 271 47 |
| 18 | | J3 | 100 00 | | Dr | 1 371 47 |
| 18 | | J3 | | 50 00 | Dr. | 1 321 47 |

**Account** Office Furniture      No. 11

| Date | Particulars | P.R. | Debit | Credit | DR.<br>CR. | Balance |
|---|---|---|---|---|---|---|
| 19—<br>May 31 | | J1 | 1 250 00 | | Dr | 1 250 00 |
| June 15 | | J2 | 310 00 | | Dr | 1 560 00 |
| 18 | | J3 | 125 00 | | Dr | 1 685 00 |

**Account** Office Suppliers Company      No. 24

| Date | Particulars | P.R. | Debit | Credit | DR.<br>CR. | Balance |
|---|---|---|---|---|---|---|
| 19—<br>June 2 | | J1 | | 500 00 | Cr | 500 00 |
| 7 | | J2 | 500 00 | | | — |
| 18 | | J3 | | 75 00 | Cr | 75 00 |

## The Opening Entry

You have already learned that, before any accounting entry is recorded in the ledger, it must first be listed in the journal. You must be sure to do this at all times, even for the very first entry – the one that begins a set of books.

To begin or 'open' a set of books, the beginning financial position must be set up in the accounts. But, in compliance with the rule above, before the amounts are placed in the accounts, they must be recorded in the journal as a journal entry. This **opening entry**, the one which starts the books off, is then posted to the ledger accounts in the usual way.

For example, Tom Wilson begins business on April 30, 19—, with the financial position shown by the balance sheet below.

To open the books of Tom Wilson, it is necessary to record the beginning financial position in the form of a journal entry as shown below. This journal entry, the opening entry, will then be posted to the ledger accounts in the usual way.

| Tom Wilson Balance Sheet April 30, 19— | | | | |
|---|---|---|---|---|
| **Assets** | | | **Liabilities** | |
| Cash | 1 564 67 | Courier Mfg. Co. | | 3 649 16 |
| C. Ferris | 126 50 | London Wholesale | | 1 472 90 |
| F. Bancroft | 300 00 | | | 5 122 06 |
| Merchandise | 7 641 32 | | | |
| Office Supplies | 125 00 | **Capital** | | |
| Equipment | 4 765 00 | Tom Wilson, Capital | | 9 400 43 |
| | 14 522 49 | | | 14 522 49 |

| General Journal | | | | Page 1 |
|---|---|---|---|---|
| Date | Particulars | P.R. | Debit | Credit |
| Apr. 30 | Cash | | 1 564 67 | |
| | C. Ferris | | 126 50 | |
| | F. Bancroft | | 300 00 | |
| | Merchandise | | 7 641 32 | |
| | Office Supplies | | 125 00 | |
| | Equipment | | 4 765 00 | |
| | Courier Mfg. Co. | | | 3 649 16 |
| | London Wholesale | | | 1 472 90 |
| | Tom Wilson, Capital | | | 9 400 43 |
| | To open the books of Tom Wilson | | | |
| | – financial position of Apr. 30 | | | |

*The opening entry for Tom Wilson.*

## The Trial Balance

Periodically it is necessary to test the mechanical accuracy of the ledger by means of a trial balance. This is usually done at the end of each month. The reasons for a trial balance being necessary are discussed on page 26.

Three different types of trial balances may be used by the accountant. The method chosen will depend on his particular point of view.

One method of preparing a trial balance is to list separately on a piece of paper the debit balances and the credit balances from the ledger. When these two lists are totaled, the two totals should agree. The piece of paper on which the trial balance is written is headed with the name of the business or individual, the words 'Trial Balance', and the date of the balances.

A second method of preparing a trial balance is to list the balances from the ledger on a paper tape using an adding machine. With this method the debit balances are entered into the machine as plus amounts and the credit balances are entered into the machine as minus amounts. The total of all the balances should be nil since the plus amounts entered into the machine should equal the minus amounts entered into the machine. As in the first method, the tape should be headed with the name of the business or individual, the words 'Trial Balance', and the date of the balances.

Although prepared in an informal manner, the first two methods are perfectly sound. Some accountants, however, use a third method, insisting that the trial balance be prepared in a formal way. With this method each account is listed in order and the account balance is placed in a Debit column or a Credit column depending on the type of balance. After all the accounts have been listed the two columns are totaled and agreed. The formal trial balance is headed in the same way as the informal ones. It is illustrated below.

Regardless of the method used, a trial balance should be kept on file for a short time, at least until a subsequent one is prepared at the end of the following month, but more commonly until after the visit of the official auditors.

*Trial balance (method 1).*

*Trial balance (method 2).*

| | | | DEBIT | | CREDIT | |
|---|---|---|---|---|---|---|
| Cash | | | 962 | 01 | | |
| J. Wraltham | | | 715 | — | | |
| S. Spears | | | 200 | — | | |
| J. Gardner | | | 76 | 41 | | |
| Merchandise | | | 2 798 | 95 | | |
| Supplies | | | 315 | 50 | | |
| Furniture and Equipment | | | 3 900 | — | | |
| Delivery Equipment | | | 5 641 | 75 | | |
| Erie Hardware Supply Co | | | | | 1 317 | 42 |
| Handley Tool Company | | | | | 417 | 73 |
| A. M. Finance Company | | | | | 2 641 | 36 |
| J. Hunter, Capital | | | | | 10 233 | 11 |
| | | | 14 609 | 62 | 14 609 | 62 |

*Trial balance (method 3 – the formal method).*

## Correcting Errors in the Books

Over the years, it has become an established rule in the accounting profession that the making of erasures is never permitted. Since erasures may arouse the suspicions of the auditors (the official examiners of the books and records), it has become standard practice not to make erasures under any circumstances. Consequently, it is necessary to make the corrections in some other way.

An error which is detected very soon after it is made usually presents no problem in making the correction. It is simply a matter of stroking neatly through the incorrect words or amount and inserting the correct words or amount immediately above. Examples of this type of correction are shown below.

It should be evident from the examples that a person who has a large style of handwriting will encounter difficulty in making corrections. In his regular work, an accounting clerk should make his letters and figures small enough to facilitate the subsequent correction of possible errors.

Any single error may necessitate the making of several corrections to completely rectify the books of account. For instance, a journal entry with a wrong amount could be posted to the accounts and new account balances determined before the error is detected. To rectify this error it would be necessary to change the amount in the journal, to change the posting in the account, and to recalculate and enter the correct account balance.

On many occasions the accountant may not notice an error until after quite some time has elapsed. By the time it comes to his attention many subsequent entries, postings, balances, and even trial balances, all incorporating the effect of the error, may have been made. Making the correction in the manner just described usually requires a number of changes.

Some errors can be corrected by means of a correcting journal entry. By this method, the incorrect entry is left untouched and a new (correcting) entry is worked out and journalized. The correcting entry must cause the accounts to reflect correctly the original transaction.

For example, suppose that a clerk incorrectly recorded a cash purchase of supplies as a credit purchase of supplies. The incorrect journal entry made by the clerk might be as follows:

| Supplies | 105.00 | |
| Weaver Brothers | | 105.00 |

On discovering the error, it will be necessary for the accountant to make the following correcting entry:

| Weaver Brothers | 105.00 | |
| Cash | | 105.00 |

The two entries considered together reflect the correct position.

*Correcting a name in the journal.*

| Account | *Supplies* | | | | | No. | 5 | |
| Date | Particulars | P.R. | Debit | Credit | DR. CR. | Balance |
| Feb 5 | | J3 | 64 10 | | Dr | 64 10 |
| 8 | | J6 | ~~151 75~~<br>151 85 | | Dr | ~~215 85~~<br>215 95 |

*Correcting amounts in the account.*

## On Account

The term 'on account' is used extensively in modern business. For that reason, it is an absolutely essential part of business vocabulary.

The term is used in four specific ways.

1. When something is purchased but not paid for at the time the purchase is made, i.e., a credit purchase, it is commonly referred to as a purchase on account.
2. When something is sold but no money is received for it at the time of the sale, i.e., a credit sale, it is commonly referred to as a sale on account.
3. When money is paid out to a creditor for the purpose of decreasing the balance owed to him, it is said to be paid on account.
4. When money is received from a debtor for the purpose of reducing the balance owed by him, it is said to be received on account.

## Forwarding Procedure

After a time, if an account page becomes filled, it is necessary to continue the account on a new page. It is customary to start the new page in a special way from the information on the last line of the finished page. This process is called **forwarding**, and the steps involved are:

1. Prepare a new account page by entering the account title and the account number which will be the same as on the finished account page.
2. On the last line of the finished account page, and in the Particulars column, write the words 'Carried Forward' or more simply, just 'Forwarded'.
3. On the first line of the new account page write the following information (obtained from the last line of the completed page):
   a. The date of the last entry.
   b. In the Particulars column, the words 'Brought Forward', or more simply, just 'Forwarded'.
   c. In the P.R. column, a dash.
   d. In the Balance column, the last balance including the balance indicator.

   Notice that nothing is written at this time in the Debit or Credit columns of the new page.

After completing the process, the completed account page and the new account page might appear as follows:

| Account J. G. Barker | | | No. 4 | | | | |
|---|---|---|---|---|---|---|---|
| Date | Particulars | P.R. | Debit | Credit | DR./CR. | Balance | |
| Feb 7 | | J 1 | 150 62 | | DR | 150 62 | |
| 9 | | J 3 | 374 50 | | DR | 525 12 | |
| 11 | | J 5 | | 150 62 | DR | 374 50 | |
| 12 | | J 5 | 216 51 | | DR | 591 01 | |
| 16 | | J 8 | 75 62 | | DR | 666 63 | |
| 18 | | J 9 | | 374 50 | DR | 292 13 | |
| 19 | | J 9 | 583 62 | | DR | 875 75 | |
| 21 | Forwarded | J 10 | | 292 13 | DR | 583 62 | |

*The finished account page after being forwarded.*

| Account J. G. Barker | | | No. 4 | | | | |
|---|---|---|---|---|---|---|---|
| Date | Particulars | P.R. | Debit | Credit | DR./CR. | Balance | |
| Feb 21 | Forwarded | — | | | DR. | 583 62 | |

*The new account page with the balance brought forward.*

# Bookkeeping and Accounting Terms

**Journal**  A specially ruled book in which accounting entries are recorded in the order in which they occur.

**Journalizing**  The process of recording accounting entries in a journal.

**Book of Original Entry**  Any journal, that is, the book in which the entries are originally recorded.

**Two-Column General Journal**  The simplest type of journal, in which there are two money columns, one for the debit amounts and one for the credit amounts.

**Three-Column Account**  The most commonly used type of account, in which there are three money columns, one for the debit amounts, one for the credit amounts, and one for the amount of the balance.

**Opening an Account**  The process of setting up a new account in the ledger.

**Account Title**  The name written at the top of an account.

**Books of Account**  The journal and the ledger.

**Posting**  The process of transferring the accounting entries from the journal to the ledger.

**Opening Entry**  The first entry in the general journal, the one that records the beginning financial position and starts the books of account.

**On Account**  Refer to page 48 for the explanation of the four uses of this expression.

**Forwarding**  The process of transferring certain information from the bottom of a completed page to the top of a new page.

**Opening the Books**  The whole process of beginning a set of books of account for a business, individual, or organization.

# Review Questions

1. Define 'journal'.
2. In what order are accounting entries recorded in the journal?
3. What are journal entries?
4. Define 'journalizing'.
5. Define 'book of original entry'.
6. Briefly name and describe the simplest type of journal.
7. When journalizing, which accounts are listed first?
8. When journalizing, which accounts are indented?
9. On a journal page where does the accounting clerk enter the year? the month? the day?
10. What is another name for posting reference?
11. Is it permissible to use abbreviations in a journal? a ledger?
12. Briefly describe the three-column account.
13. Why do most accountants number the ledger accounts?
14. Explain the meaning of 'opening an account'.
15. What are the books of account?
16. Briefly define 'posting'.
17. Give the five steps involved in posting.
18. How many of these steps are performed in the account? in the journal?
19. How is an accountant able to tell if a journal entry has been posted?
20. Briefly describe 'opening entry'.
21. Briefly describe three ways of preparing a trial balance.
22. Why are erasures not permitted in the books?
23. Describe two ways of correcting errors in the books.
24. Give four ways in which the term 'on account' is used.
25. Briefly describe the forwarding procedure.

# Exercises

1. R. Bell begins business with the following assets and liabilities: Cash, $1 200; Office Equipment, $900; Land, $12 500; Building, $35 900; amount owed to Diamond Equipment, $350; Mortgage on Building, $12 000.

Record the opening entry for R. Bell in a two-column general journal.

2. Using the accounts named below, journalize the transactions for February 1 to 5 on page 18 of the general journal of Mark Lambe, who operates a taped music service for dances.

The accounts in use by Mark Lambe are: Cash; T. Hall (debtor); Citizens' Hall (debtor); E. McGregor (debtor); Sound Equipment; Tape Recordings; Automobile; Perry's Tape Store (creditor); Mark Lambe, Capital.

*Transactions*
19—
Feb. 1 Purchased $120 of new tape recordings for cash.
  1 Provided taped music for a dance at Citizens' Hall for $150 on account.
  2 Received $75 from T. Hall on account.
  3 Paid $85 cash for repairs to the sound equipment.
  4 Paid $500 on account to Perry's Tape Store.
  5 Provided taped music for a dance at Municipal Arena and received $150 cash in full payment.

3. Syd Miller is a house painter who is in business for himself. In his ledger he uses the following accounts: Cash; various debtors; Materials and Supplies; Equipment; Truck; various creditors; Bank Loan; S. Miller, Capital.

On page 70 of his general journal journalize the transactions shown below for Syd Miller.

*Transactions*
19—
June 20 Received $75 on account from G. Ralph.
  21 Purchased a number of paintbrushes for $57 cash.
  21 Painted a verandah for Mr. V. Laing at a price of $135. Mr. Laing promised to pay in 30 days.
  22 Paid $150 to Performance Paints on account.
  23 Paid $28.50 cash to Jim's Garage to replace the old battery in the truck.
  23 Paid the bank $100 cash to reduce the bank loan.
  24 Completed a painting job for H. May and received $275 cash in full payment.

4. Note: This exercise should be done in the workbook that accompanies this text, or as directed by your teacher.

5. Note: This exercise should be done in the workbook that accompanies this text, or as directed by your teacher.

6. Note: This exercise should be done in the workbook that accompanies this text, or as directed by your teacher.

7.  Topflight Tool Rentals is a business owned and operated by Wm. R. Doyle. On October 1, 19—, the assets and liabilities of the business were as follows:

| Assets | | Liabilities | |
|---|---|---|---|
| Cash | $ 1 950.62 | Apoca Equipment | $4 750.00 |
| J. Hardie | 110.00 | Eastern Equipment | 2 500.00 |
| S. Seward | 25.00 | John's Garage | 65.00 |
| M. Singer | 175.00 | | $7 315.00 |
| Rental Tools | 12 050.00 | | |
| Shop Equipment | 2 470.00 | | |
| Delivery Truck | 2 950.00 | | |
| | | Owner's Capital | ? |
| | $19 730.62 | | |

**Journalize and post the opening entry.**
**(2 workbook accounts are required for Cash.)**

**Journalize and post the following transactions:**

## Transactions
October

2 Received $50 cash from J. Hardie on account.

3 Purchased $120 of rental tools from Apoca Equipment on account.

3 Rented a tool to a customer who paid $15 cash for the use of it.

4 Rented a tool to a customer who paid $25 cash for the use of it.

5 $500 was paid to Eastern Equipment on account.

8 M. Singer paid his account balance in full.

10 S. Seward who had rented a large piece of equipment for three weeks was issued a bill for $400.

11 $750 was paid to Apoca Equipment on account.

12 S. Seward paid $300 on account.

15 John's Garage account was paid in full.

15 A tool valued in the accounts at $75 was broken beyond repair and was thrown out.

15 S. Seward paid the balance of his account in full.

**Balance the ledger.**

8.  **Journalize the following transactions of John Miller on page 14 of his general journal. In preparing these journal entries use the account names that seem most appropriate to you.**

## Transactions
May

3 Received $180 from J. Jenson on account.

5 Paid $100 to Acme Supply Company on account.

6 A payment on account of $75 was made to City Finance Company.

7 Performed a service for P. Workman and received $40 cash.

10 Purchased $102 of supplies for cash from Anchor Supplies.

13 Performed a $100 service on account for O. R. Thomas.

13 A new delivery truck was purchased from Elite Motors. The cost price of the truck was $4 800. A cash down payment of $1 000 was made at the time of the purchase, the balance to be paid later.

14 $150 of store machinery was purchased from The Standard Company on account.

15 The owner withdrew $27 for his personal use.

15 Borrowed $1 500 from the bank.
15 Paid $25 for repairs to the delivery truck.

---

9. **The Crown Repair Shop, owned by W. T. Hall, is a business that has been in operation for several years. The trial balance of the business on March 31, 19—, is as follows:**

THE CROWN REPAIR SHOP
TRIAL BALANCE
MARCH 31, 19—

|  | Debit | Credit |
|---|---|---|
| Cash | $ 2 273.60 | |
| J. Watson | 47.20 | |
| Amber Bros. | 16.80 | |
| Supplies | 2 000.00 | |
| Machinery | 3 500.00 | |
| Truck | 2 068.00 | |
| Office Furniture and Equipment | 900.00 | |
| Parker's Service Station | | $ 27.60 |
| Harold's Hardware | | 563.65 |
| Regal Supply | | 729.56 |
| W. T. Hall, Capital | | 9 484.79 |
| | $10 805.60 | $10 805.60 |

**Set up the ledger of The Crown Repair Shop as of March 31, 19—. (2 workbook accounts are required for Cash.)**

**Note:** In this particular exercise, it is not correct for you to record and post an opening entry. An opening entry is proper only when a business is being started. In this exercise, the business has been in operation for some time.

To begin this exercise, set up each of the ledger accounts by merely entering the account balance and the date as shown on the trial balance.

**Journalize and post the following transactions, beginning on page 32 of the journal. (Remember that the business has been in operation for several years and as a result some portion of the journal will already have been used.)**

*Transactions*
April
1 Received $500 cash from the owner to increase the cash position of the business.
2 Received cash from J. Watson in full payment of his account.
3 Paid cash to Parker's Service Station in full payment of the account.

4 Received $25 from Amber Bros. on account.
4 Paid Amber Bros. an amount sufficient to adjust their account which they had overpaid.

5 Purchased $800 of supplies from Regal Supply on account.

8 Purchased new machinery, $246, from Peerless Machinery on account.

9 Paid $400 on account to Harold's Hardware.

9 Sold a piece of office equipment, which was no longer required, for $35 cash. The item had originally cost $50 and was included in the Office Furniture and Equipment account at $50.

10 Paid Regal Supply account in full.

10 Purchased a filing cabinet for $70 cash.

11 Paid $100 on account to Harold's Hardware.

15 The owner withdrew $200 cash for his personal use.

15 Paid the balance of Harold's Hardware account.

Balance the ledger.

---

10. The Northtown Gardening Service, owned by T. C. Harlow, begins business on February 1, 19—, with the following financial position:

NORTHTOWN GARDENING SERVICE
BALANCE SHEET
FEBRUARY 1, 19—

| Assets | | Liabilities | |
|---|---|---|---|
| Cash | $2 650.20 | Holland Bulb Growers | $1 150.00 |
| F. Greig | 165.00 | Baxter Chemical Co. | 164.91 |
| C. Charles | 174.00 | | $1 314.91 |
| M. Rogers | 316.00 | | |
| Supplies | 116.50 | Owner's Equity | |
| Equipment | 967.20 | T. C. Harlow, Capital | 3 073.99 |
| | $4 388.90 | | $4 388.90 |

Journalize and post the opening entry. Number the accounts in the usual way.

Journalize and post the transactions which appear below.

Take off a trial balance as of February 15.

*Transactions*

February

1 Received $200 from M. Rogers on account.

2 Paid $700 on account to Holland Bulb Growers.

4 The proprietor withdrew $75 for his personal use.

5 Performed a gardening service for G. Easter and charged him $32, which he paid right away.

7 Performed a gardening service for F. Greig on account, $56.

9 Purchased $300 of fertilizer on account from Baxter Chemical Co.

12 The Baxter Chemical Co. account was paid in full.

15 M. Rogers paid the balance of his account.

# Cases

## Case 1
Mr. Schulze arranges all his ledger accounts in alphabetical order in a bound book. Describe some of the problems that will be created by his using this system.

## Case 2
As the accountant for the J. R. Hudson Co. you have been assisting the junior clerk in recording all transactions to the general journal and posting the amounts to the general ledger. After a month's work, the junior clerk expresses the opinion that a great deal of time could be saved if a business would record transactions directly in ledger accounts rather than entering transactions first in a journal and then posting the debit and credit amounts from the journal to the ledger.

   Discuss the disadvantages of this proposal.

## Case 3
D. Holland, the accounting clerk for H. R. Jackson Co., is constantly being called away from his job of posting from the journal to the ledger. With these constant interruptions how does Holland know where he left off in his postings?

## Case 4
P. Cooper prepares a trial balance at the end of each month. In recording the balances onto the trial balance, he finds three creditors' accounts with debit balances. He thought this highly unusual because the trial balance did balance.

   What could be the reason for these debit balances?

## Case 5
An employee of Elite Motors made an error in posting from the journal to the ledger. The same entry was debited twice to the same Office Equipment account. Would this error be disclosed by taking a trial balance? Explain.

## Case 6
In recording transactions in a general journal, T. Stremos, a junior accountant, indicates the accounts to be debited and the accounts to be credited, but he never writes any explanation of the entries he records. Why would this be considered poor procedure?

## Case 7
Suppose that you as proprietor bought showcases for $75.00 cash, and that you entered this transaction directly into the ledger accounts without first setting up the complete transaction in the journal. In making the entries you debited Office Equipment $75.00, and credited Cash account $7.50. When you prepared a trial balance, your accounts would be out of balance.
1. Why would it be difficult for you to locate the error?
2. If you had used a general journal, how could you have located your error more easily?

## Case 8

You have been employed by Wilson Building Supplies as an accountant clerk. Your main duty is to record journal entries daily and post to the general ledger. Your procedure in posting is to post the entries by account order. For example, you first go through all your journal entries and post all Cash entries. You then proceed to the second account, and so on.

Are there advantages to this system of posting to the ledger? Explain.

## Case 9

Ray Campbell-Rogers has been posting to the general ledger only monthly. State the disadvantage of this method.

## Case 10

Dean Perry posts from the journal to the ledger at the end of each week. Because he prepares a balance sheet once a year, he believes it is necessary to prepare a trial balance only once a year. What are the disadvantages of taking a trial balance only once a year?

# 5 Income, Expense and Drawings

The theory of double-entry accounting is being developed in a gradual way. In the first four chapters you have been introduced to a great deal of basic accounting theory. The work in Chapter 5 is the next logical step in the accounting process.

This is an extremely important chapter as it finalizes the rules for the making of accounting entries. That is, the rules of debit and credit, except for advanced transactions, will be completed.

## Expanding the System

The rules of debit and credit, as developed so far, are summarized in the chart below.

**DEBIT AND CREDIT SUMMARY**

| | TO INCREASE | TO DECREASE |
|---|---|---|
| ASSET | DEBIT THE ACCOUNT | CREDIT THE ACCOUNT |
| LIABILITY | CREDIT THE ACCOUNT | DEBIT THE ACCOUNT |
| CAPITAL (EQUITY) | CREDIT THE ACCOUNT | DEBIT THE ACCOUNT |

These rules, with which you are familiar, will not be changed. But the chart itself is to be expanded – to make the whole accounting system more useful.

In particular, it is the capital or equity section of the chart that is to be expanded. The rules for assets and liabilities remain unchanged.

To date you have been accustomed to having a single account for capital. Any change in the equity of a business has been recorded in this single account. Now you must become familiar with a system in which the ledger, instead of having a single account for capital, has a number of accounts in the equity section.

## Purpose of Expanding the System

It is the principal purpose of the new accounts in the equity section of the ledger to gather the information that is necessary for the preparation of another financial statement. This statement, the income statement, is illustrated below.

**HARRIS REAL ESTATE**
**INCOME STATEMENT**
**MONTH ENDED JANUARY 31, 19–4**

| *Income* | | |
|---|---|---|
| Commissions | | $3 572.60 |
| | | |
| *Expenses* | | |
| Advertising | $142.65 | |
| Car Expenses | 197.60 | |
| Entertainment | 204.73 | |
| Miscellaneous | 74.82 | |
| Rent | 350.00 | |
| Wages | 915.75 | 1 885.55 |
| Net Income | | $1 687.05 |

You can readily see from the illustration that the income statement tells a great deal about the progress of the business for which it is written. You may rightfully ask why this statement is necessary in a business. The answer is twofold. First, it is vitally important that the owners and managers know if the business is being run profitably. Remember that their livelihood depends on its successful operation. To them, the income statement is an extremely useful tool. From an analysis of it, these people are able to derive a great deal of useful information that guides them in their decision-making and assists them in formulating company policies. Second, the income statement is needed to satisfy legal requirements. It must be prepared to comply with various government and income tax regulations.

It is absolutely essential in any business that the income statement be prepared, and it is the principal purpose of the new equity section of the ledger to gather the information necessary for its preparation. This statement will be discussed more fully in the next chapter along with a new form of the balance sheet.

# Equity Section of the Ledger

In the expanded accounting system the ledger has an equity section that includes several accounts rather than a single capital account. In this new section there are the following accounts:
1. A **capital** account that is reserved for the beginning capital balance.
2. An **income** or **revenue** account. (In some cases there will be more than one of these.)
3. Several **expense** accounts.
4. A **drawings** account.

These new accounts, income, expense, and drawings, are now discussed in detail.

### Income or Revenue

The first of the new accounts to be introduced is the **income** or **revenue** account. Income may be defined as:

**An increase in equity as a direct consequence of usual business activity.**

Whenever a transaction occurs that involves an increase in equity as a result of usual business activity, you must be prepared to treat it differently.

An example of a business transaction that produces income is the following:

> D. Peters, a lawyer, draws up a legal agreement for a client and for his services is paid a fee of $75 cash.

This transaction has the effect of increasing both cash and equity by the amount of $75. (If you need a review of the reasoning underlying changes in equity refer back to page 13.) Previously, you would have debited Cash and credited D. Peters, Capital with the $75. But now, under the new and expanded system, you will debit Cash, as before, and credit an income account which we shall call Fees Income. In general journal form the entry is:

| | | |
|---|---|---|
| Cash | $75.00 | |
| Fees Income | | $75.00 |

Remember that Fees Income represents an increase in equity. Since it has been established earlier that an increase in equity requires a credit entry, it should come as no surprise to you that the Fees Income account normally receives credit entries. All Fees Income will be accumulated in this account and it will have a credit balance.

Usually, a business has only one income account and it is given an appropriate name. A 'loan' company, for example, which earns its income by charging 'interest' on money loaned, will probably have an income account called Interest Income or Interest Earned. Similarly, a 'real estate' company, which earns its income in the form of 'commissions' will very likely have an income account called Commissions Earned, Commissions Income, or just plain Commissions. Other suitable names for the income account of other businesses might be: Rental Income, Fees Earned, Revenue, Royalties, and so on.

### Expense

The second new type of account to be introduced is the **expense** account. Expense may be defined as:

**A decrease in equity as a direct consequence of usual business activity.**

Whenever a transaction occurs that involves a decrease in equity as a result of usual business operations, you must be prepared to deal with it in a special way.

An example of a transaction that involves expense is:

D. Peters pays to his secretary her regular weekly wage of $125 cash.

This transaction requires that both cash and equity be decreased by $125. The decrease to Cash is handled in the usual way, as a credit to that account. But the decrease to equity is now to be debited to a new account called Wages Expense. In general journal form the entry is:

| Wages Expense | $125.00 | |
| Cash | | $125.00 |

Keep in mind that Wages Expense represents a decrease in equity and as such requires a debit entry. It follows logically, therefore, that the Wages Expense account, or any expense account for that matter, will normally receive debit entries. All Wages Expense will be accumulated in the one account and it will have a debit balance.

A second example of a transaction that involves an expense is the following:

D. Peters receives the monthly furnace oil bill for $65.65 from Municipal Oil but does not pay the bill immediately.

As a result of this transaction it is necessary to decrease equity and to set up a liability to Municipal Oil. According to the rule just established, the accounting entry is:

| Heat Expense | $65.65 | |
| Municipal Oil | | $65.65 |

In any business, there are usually several expense accounts, each one representing a reduction in equity from a specific cause. The name given to each one of these accounts will tell the nature of the reduction. In addition to those already mentioned, other typical expense accounts are: Rent Expense, Delivery Expense, Insurance Expense, Bank Charges, Postage, Property Taxes. Notice that the word 'expense' is not al-

ways included as part of the account title but is sometimes implied. With experience you will come to know the names customarily given to the expense accounts.

## Drawings

The third of the new types of accounts introduced in this chapter is the **drawings** account. Drawings may be defined as:

**A decrease in equity that is not an expense.**

The drawings account may be thought of as the owner's personal withdrawal account. In it are accumulated any decreases in equity that are not *bona fide* expenses of the business and as such are considered to be the personal responsibility of the owner. Such decreases are charged* or debited to the owner through his drawings account.

An example of the most common type of transaction that involves drawings is the following:

D. Peters, the owner of the business, withdraws $125 cash for his personal use.

This transaction requires that both cash and equity be decreased by $125. The decrease to Cash is handled in the usual way, as a credit to that account. But the decrease to equity, not falling within the classification of an expense, must be charged to the owner's drawings account. The correct accounting entry to record the transaction is:

| D. Peters, Drawings | $125.00 | |
| Cash | | $125.00 |

This and all entries affecting drawings conform to the rules of debit and credit with which you are familiar. Since drawings represents a decrease in equity and since decreases in equity require debit entries, it follows that the drawings account normally receives debit entries. All drawings will be accumulated in this one account and it will have a debit balance.

Another common type of transaction that affects the drawings account occurs when the

---

*Professional accountants often use the word 'charge' instead of 'debit'.

owner buys something for his personal use but has the business pay for it. He may do this in order to take advantage of a special price that is offered to businesses but is denied to individuals. Or, he may do it just for the sake of convenience. In any event, the recording of the transaction requires that the debit be to Drawings and that the credit be either to Cash or to a creditor's account depending on whether the item is paid for or not.

A third type of transaction that affects drawings occurs when the owner takes assets other than cash permanently out of the business for his personal use. As an example, he may take home a spare office typewriter so that his family may have the use of it. If the typewriter is to be permanently left in the home, propriety requires that the value of it, as recorded in the books, be charged to him. The correct accounting entry will be one that debits Drawings and credits Office Equipment.

In your textbook exercises you will meet additional transactions that affect the drawings account.

## Relationship of Income, Expenses and Drawings

A definite relationship exists among income, expenses, and drawings. This relationship, reduced to a very simple form, is discussed below.

The income account together with the expense accounts (but not the drawings account) reflect what is known as the **net income** or **net loss** of a business. Net income occurs when the balance of the income account is greater than the total of all the expense accounts. Net loss occurs when the total of all the expense accounts is greater than the balance of the income account.

Usually, a man who is in business for himself depends on the business for his source of livelihood. It is his hope and intention that the business will earn a substantial profit and that he will be able to withdraw this profit for his own purposes. Normally, he will withdraw as much of the profit as he can without squeezing the business; that is, leaving the business so short of funds that it cannot operate comfortably. If the business happens to suffer a loss, the owner may

find himself hard pressed financially. Certainly no one will continue to carry on a business that loses money persistently.

To summarize, the income and expense accounts all together show the amount of the net income or net loss. The drawings account shows the extent of the owner's withdrawals.

## Expanded General Ledger

There appears below an illustration of a ledger with the expanded equity section. The accounts included in this ledger are much the same as those that you might find in a ledger in the business world today.

Examine the new ledger carefully and note the following:

1. The ledger has three sections: assets, liabilities, and equity. These three sections still conform to the fundamental accounting equation. If you were to evaluate the three sections you would find that the total value of the asset accounts is equal to the combined total value of the liability and equity accounts.
2. In the equity section are several accounts. The capital account is intended to show the capital balance at the beginning of the accounting period and the other accounts are intended to show the various changes in capital since that time. The expense and drawings accounts have debit balances because they represent decreases in equity. The income account has a credit balance because it represents an increase in equity.
   **Note:** There is one exception to the statement that the Capital account shows only the beginning capital balance. At times in business, usually to tide the business over a difficult period, it is necessary for the owner to bring new capital into the business in the form of cash. In such circumstances, the Capital account is credited with the amount of the new investment.
3. The numbering system has been expanded to include the new accounts in the system. The complete numbering system used in this text is summarized below.

Assets    Nos. 1 to 20 inclusive
Liabilities Nos. 21 to 30 inclusive
Capital   No. 31
Drawings  No. 32
Income    No. 41
Expenses  No. 51 and on.

4. The expense accounts are often arranged alphabetically. This is not obligatory but is a practice employed by many accountants.

Debit and Credit Summary — Final Form

|  | TO INCREASE | TO DECREASE |
|---|---|---|
| Assets | Debit | Credit |
| Liabilities | Credit | Debit |
| Equity Capital | Credit | Debit |
| Income | Credit | Debit |
| Expense | Debit | Credit |
| Drawings | Debit | Credit |

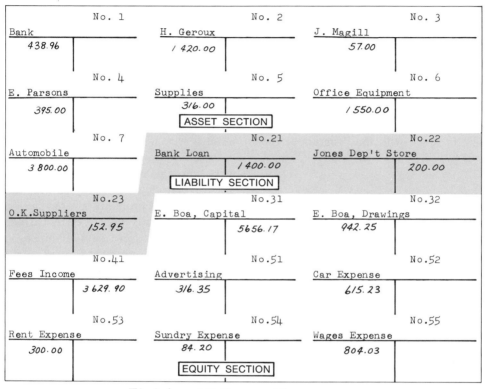

*The ledger of E. Boa, a public accountant.*

## The Fiscal Period

Now that we are introducing the income and expense accounts, it is proper to introduce another new concept in accounting. This new concept has to do with the measurement of earnings in relation to a certain period of time.

In order to have any meaning, the earnings figure of a business must be calculated in respect to a certain length of time. If not, the information is meaningless. If you were told the net income of a business was $1 000, you would not be very

well informed unless you also knew the length of time taken to earn it. For instance, if it took a period of one year, you would not be very favourably impressed, especially if you were the owner of the business and it was your only source of income. But if it took only one week to earn the $1 000 you would probably be very impressed indeed.

It is hoped that the foregoing paragraph has shown you that in respect to earnings it is necessary to know 'for how long?' as well as 'how much?' Bookkeepers and accountants accept this fact without hesitation and they refer to the period of time over which earnings are measured as the **fiscal period**, or as the **accounting period**, and sometimes as the **bookkeeping period**.

In business today, the usual length of time chosen for the fiscal period is one year. The choice of a year is a natural one. There are powerful forces at work in the world which have selected this period as the cycle of nature. It influences us in innumerable ways, from birthdays to income taxes. Its use as the most common accounting period should not surprise you, nor should the fact that it is the maximum length of fiscal period permitted by government regulations.

A period shorter than one year may be chosen as a fiscal period. Half-yearly, quarterly, or monthly fiscal periods are not uncommon. Short fiscal periods allow owners and managers to keep more closely in touch with the progress of the business.

## Chart of Accounts

A **chart of accounts** is simply a list of the ledger accounts and their numbers all arranged in ledger order. Most businesses, except very small ones, have copies of their chart of accounts available for the use of their own office staff, particularly new employees, and for their auditors. The chart of accounts of E. Boa, from the ledger on page 61, is shown here:

E. BOA

CHART OF ACCOUNTS

| *Assets* | | *Equity* | |
|---|---|---|---|
| Bank | No. 1 | E. Boa, Capital No. | 31 |
| H. Geroux | 2 | E. Boa, Drawings | 32 |
| J. Magill | 3 | Fees Income | 41 |
| E. Parsons | 4 | Advertising | 51 |
| Supplies | 5 | Car Expense | 52 |
| Office Equipment | 6 | Rent Expense | 53 |
| Automobile | 7 | Sundry Expense | 54 |
| | | Wages Expense | 55 |
| *Liabilities* | | | |
| Bank Loan | 21 | | |
| Jones Dep't Store | 22 | | |
| O.K. Suppliers | 23 | | |

## Debit and Credit Balances

It is very important that you be able to interpret readily the account balances in a ledger. At this stage it is not very difficult to tell whether an account is an asset or an expense, a liability or income. But there will come a time when it is not so simple. Be prepared for that day. As new accounting concepts are introduced, strive to understand them thoroughly.

At this point in the text, the accounts that have debit balances are either assets, expenses, or drawings, and the accounts that have credit balances are either liabilities, capital, or income.

## Other Forms of Ownership

The early chapters of this textbook deal exclusively with a form of business organization known as a single proprietorship. This is a business that is owned by one person whose investment is reflected by his capital account.

As you are probably aware, there are other forms of business ownership. A partnership, for example, is a form of ownership by means of which two or more persons may carry on business together. A partnership is a type of business organization that is suitable for small to medium-sized businesses having more than one owner. The accounts of a partnership are almost identical to those for a single proprietorship. The only difference is in the equity section where each partner must have his own Capital and Drawings accounts. It is in this way that the investment of each partner is accounted for separately.

Another major form of business organization is the corporation or limited company. Corporations are usually large enterprises requiring such large amounts of capital that it must be obtained from a number of people. Individuals invest their money in a corporation by purchasing share certificates which entitle them to a share in the ownership of the business. These investors are known as shareholders.

The accounts of a corporation are similar to those of the single proprietorship and the partnership, except for the way in which the capital is recorded. In the equity section of the corporation's ledger, there is an account called

Capital Stock or Shareholders' Equity, which shows the total capital contributions of all the shareholders. The individual contributions of the shareholders are kept track of in a separate record. The shareholders do not have drawings accounts.

## Buying and Selling on Credit

It is an accepted feature of our modern economy that businesses with good reputations are able to buy the things that they need on short-term credit, usually from 10 days to one month. By being able to delay payment for a short period of time, the buyer gains for himself the oppor-tunity of thoroughly inspecting or testing the goods. If they are found to be unsatisfactory, the buyer is in a commanding position; he can simply refuse to pay for the goods until they are made right.

A great deal of buying and selling on credit goes on in the business world of today. Each time a sale is made on account, it is necessary for the seller to prepare a business document called a **sales invoice**. The sales invoice form, such as the one illustrated below, shows all the pertinent in-formation in respect to the sale. One or more copies of the sales invoice are sent to the buyer for his records and also as a request for payment. (See also Chapter 12.)

## STAR ✳ SUPPLY

### 419 Mill's Gate, Oak City

SOLD TO W. Hay,
16 Mark's Road,
Oak City. P8F 4R2

INVOICE NUMBER 971

DATE March 15, 19—

TERMS 3/10,N/30

| Quantity | Description | Unit Price | Amount |
|----------|-------------|-----------|--------|
| 6 Pkg. | Typewriting paper | $7.50 | $45.00 |
| | 5% Sales Tax | | 2.25 |
| | | | $47.25 |

*An invoice.*

## Bank Account

Businessmen rely heavily on the banking system as the safest, cheapest, and most convenient way to make payments. It should be clear to you that the handling of large quantities of cash is unsafe. This is one important reason why a businessman chooses to keep his money in a bank account. Another and perhaps even more important rea-son is the convenience of being able to make payments by cheque. It is much easier to send a cheque to someone than it is to deliver cash to him in person. This is especially evident if the buyer and the seller are dealing with each other over a long distance. Except in the case of retail stores and their dealings with the general public, it is usual for all except very small payments to be made by cheque.

In the books of account, therefore, you can expect to see an account called Bank rather than one called Cash. You can also expect to see the paying of bills being effected through the issuing of cheques by the ones who owe the money and the receiving of cheques by the ones to whom the money is owed.

### Income Tax Regulations

The various governments of the country impose strict requirements on businesses for taxation and regulatory purposes. One requirement that is very important to a business is that it must keep the documents or business papers (called 'vouchers') as evidence of the authenticity of the business records. A government auditor may come at any time to verify the records by examining the supporting vouchers for the transactions.

### Trial Balance Procedure Unchanged

With the introduction of the new types of accounts you might expect that the trial balancing procedure would need to be amended. But fortunately there is no change in principle. It is still only necessary to total the accounts with debit balances, total the accounts with credit balances, and see that the two totals agree.

# Trial Balance Out of Balance

Now that you are able to journalize transactions, post them to the ledger, and take off a trial balance, you will be confronted with the problem of what to do when the trial balance does not balance. A trial balance out of balance indicates that one or more errors have been made in the journal, ledger, or trial balance. It is your responsibility as accountant to find and correct these errors.

Do not underestimate the importance of acquiring a real competence in this respect. For two reasons a real skill in locating errors can be extremely advantageous to the aspiring account-

ant. In the first place, it is not infrequent that a ledger is out of balance. In fact, in the more complex businesses it is a rare event when the trial balance is found to be in balance after the first attempt. Even in your relatively simple classroom exercises, you will find that on numerous occasions the trial balance does not balance.

Secondly, some errors are very elusive and can be detected only by a persistent and expertly conducted search. A person who does not possess the skill to conduct this search successfully is not a competent accountant. It is likely that this person will be constantly frustrated in his efforts to achieve success in business.

When a trial balance does not balance, it is a certainty that one or more errors have been made in the accounting process. To discuss all the ramifications of locating these errors is not practicable in a text of this nature. Instead, there is set out in brief form the general procedure to be followed when you are confronted with a trial balance out of balance. It will be wise for you to decide now to carry out this procedure to many successful conclusions. Only through persistent application will the necessary confidence and expertise be acquired.

Briefly, the steps to be taken and the order in which they should normally be followed are –
1. Re-add the trial balance columns.
2. Check the accuracy of transferring the account balances from the ledger to the trial balance.
3. Re-add the account balances beginning at the point at which the ledger was previously balanced. Ensure that the Dr. or Cr. prefix to the balance is correct.
4. Check the accuracy of the postings from the journal to the ledger, beginning at the point at which the ledger was previously balanced. In particular, watch for incorrect amounts, amounts not posted, amounts posted twice, and amounts posted to the wrong column. In performing step 4, it is generally necessary to make a distinguishing mark beside each of the amounts as they are checked.
5. Check to see that each individual journal entry is in balance.

Since on many occasions the error or errors will be detected at some intermediate stage, it is often not necessary to complete all of the five steps. On the other hand, if it so happens that after completing the five steps there still remain some undetected errors, it is not possible that the five steps were carried out properly. In this unhappy situation, it will be necessary for you to go through the sequence again, remembering to work with greater care. It is a positive fact that if the steps are carried out correctly, the errors will be revealed.

## Shortcuts in Detecting a Single Error

It can be a tedious and time-consuming task to carry out the full routine just described, and experienced accountants try to avoid it where they can. There is a strong possibility, provided that only one error has occurred, that the error can be located quickly by the application of a few short tests. These tests are set out below.

First, it is necessary to determine the difference between the two totals of the trial balance. Then any of the following tests may be applied.

1. If the trial balance difference is 1¢, 10¢, $1, etc., it is very likely that an error in addition has been made, in which case steps 1 and 3 of the previously discussed sequence should be performed first.

2. If the trial balance difference is an even amount, divide it by 2. Then scrutinize (i) the trial balance, and (ii) the ledger accounts for this amount. If found, check to see if a debit amount has been placed in a credit column by mistake, or vice versa. An error of this type always produces a trial balance difference equal to twice the amount of the error.

3. Scrutinize the account balances to see if one of them is equal to the amount of the trial balance difference. It may be that one account has been overlooked in the preparation of the trial balance.

4. Divide the trial balance difference by 9. If it divides evenly, it is likely that a transposition error has occurred. A transposition occurs when, for example, $35.60 is posted as $36.50, or when $1 200 is transferred as $120. Such errors always produce a trial balance difference that is exactly divisible by 9. When this happens, steps 2 and 4 of the checking sequence should be performed first.

# Bookkeeping and Accounting Terms

**Income** An increase in equity as a direct consequence of business activity. Also known as **revenue**.

**Expense** A decrease in equity as a direct consequence of business activity.

**Drawings** A decrease in equity that does not fit the definition of expense.

**Charge** A word often used instead of debit.

**Net Income** The difference between total income and total expenses if the income is greater than the expenses.

**Net Loss** The difference between total income and total expenses if the expenses are greater than the income.

**Fiscal Period** The period of time over which earnings are measured. Also known as **book-**

**keeping period** or **accounting period**.

**Chart of Accounts** A list of the ledger accounts and their numbers all arranged in ledger order.

**Cash Sales Slip** A business form prepared by the seller of goods or services at the time of a cash sale showing a description of the goods, the price, and other information.

**Sales Invoice** A business form prepared by the seller of goods or services, usually in respect to a credit sale, showing a description of the goods, the price, and other pertinent information.

**Voucher** A business document establishing the validity of accounting records.

**Transposition** An interchanging of the digits of a number when transferring the number from one place to another.

# Review Questions

1. What is the purpose of expanding the ledger?
2. Give two important reasons for preparing the income statement.
3. Name the four types of accounts that are to be found in the equity section of a ledger.
4. Define 'income'.
5. Give an example of an increase in equity that does not result from normal business activity.
6. Define 'expense'.
7. Define 'drawings'.
8. Give three examples of transactions that affect drawings.
9. What is meant by 'charge'?
10. How is the net income of a business determined?
11. What is the fiscal period?
12. Give two other names for fiscal period.
13. In today's business world what is the most common length of the fiscal period?
14. What type of balance is usually found in an income account? an expense account? the drawings account?
15. Draw a chart summarizing debit and credit theory in its final form.
16. What is a chart of accounts? Who uses a chart of accounts?
17. Why will a business that is buying something endeavor to arrange short-term credit with the seller?
18. Why do businesses rely heavily on the banking system?
19. What are vouchers? Explain the need for them.
20. Why is a real skill in locating errors an advantage to a junior accountant?
21. List the five steps to be taken in locating errors in the books.
22. Is it always necessary to carry out the five steps? Explain.
23. Describe the four shortcuts in locating errors.
24. What is a transposition?

# Exercises

**Note on the Handling of Supplies:** It is a fairly common practice in accounting to allow certain accounts to remain incorrect during the accounting period and to make them correct at the end of the accounting period. This is a technique used by accountants for convenience. The Supplies account is one account to which this shortcut technique is applied.

During the accounting period, make your accounting entries for supplies as follows:

1. Whenever supplies are purchased:
   Dr. Supplies
      Cr. Bank or the creditor
   } with the cost price of the supplies.
2. Whenever supplies are used in the business: Make no accounting entry.

The effect of step 2 above is to permit the Supplies account to become incorrect. The technique for updating this account at the end of the accounting period is explained in Chapter 14.

---

**1. From the following information for the month ended November 30, 19—, prepare an income statement for Atlas Associates.**

Fees Earned, $8 000; Salaries Expense, $600; Rent Expense, $750; General Expense, $185; Advertising Expense, $120; Car Expense, $158; Light and Heat Expense, $40.

2. For each of the accounts listed, indicate whether it would normally have a debit or credit balance.

Supplies; Advertising Expense; A. Bryce, Drawings; G. Wright, a creditor; Rent Expense; Fees Earned; Bank Loan; W. Magill, a debtor; A. Bryce, Capital; Mortgage Payable.

3. If a credit item for $265 in the general journal is posted in error as a debit, by how much will this cause the trial balance to be out of balance? How might you detect such an error?

4. If the trial balance difference is $63, what type of error would you suspect? What steps would you take to locate the error?

5. If the trial balance is out of balance by $10, what type of error would you suspect? What steps would you take to locate the error?

6. Journalize the following selected transactions of Alfred Murphy, a self-employed photographer. Use the accounts listed below.

1. Bank
2. M. Jackson
3. W. Potter
6. Office Supplies
7. Photographic Supplies
8. Equipment
9. Automobile
21. Master Chemical Co.

22. Saddler Photo Service
31. A. Murphy, Capital
32. A. Murphy, Drawings
41. Revenue
51. Car Expense
52. Miscellaneous Expense
53. Rent Expense
54. Wages Expense

*Transactions*
19—
June 5 Received $25 cash from M. Tyler who came to the studio for passport photos. (**Note:** It is normal procedure in business to deposit cash received each day.)
 9 Issued cheque No. 165 to Prince Motors for repairs to the car; $75.
 12 Issued cheque No. 166 to Milrig Investing for the rent for the month; $200.

 17 Issued invoice No. 97 to Ross Parkes for wedding photographs prepared for him on account; $150.
 20 Received an invoice from Master Chemical Co. for chemicals purchased on account; $64.50.
 25 Issued cheque No. 175 to the local telephone company in payment of the monthly phone bill; $24.75.
 25 The owner withdrew $100 for his personal use; cheque No. 176.

7. E. J. Steele is in business for himself as a groundskeeper and gardener. For a number of customers on a regular basis he cuts grass, weeds gardens, and trims trees and shrubs. Some of his customers pay him cash, making the payment immediately after receiving the service. Others pay him after they receive his invoice for services performed.
In E. J. Steele's ledger there are the following accounts:

1. Bank
2. G. Noble

3. F. Sawyer
4. W. Scott

| | | | |
|---|---|---|---|
| 7. | Equipment | 32. | E. J. Steele, Drawings |
| 8. | Chemical Supplies | 41. | Revenue |
| 9. | Truck | 51. | Advertising Expense |
| 21. | Bank Loan | 52. | Miscellaneous Expense |
| 22. | General Pesticide Products Ltd. | 53. | Telephone Expense |
| 31. | E. J. Steele, Capital | 54. | Truck Expense |

**Journalize the following selected transactions for E. J. Steele:**

19—

July 2 Received an invoice for $57.90 from General Pesticide Products Ltd. for a supply of insecticide.

5 Received an invoice from Tech Hardware for one new ladder; $64.25.

6 Issued cheque No. 70 to W. Silver in payment for part-time office assistance; $29.

10 Received $50 from a cash customer for services performed.

13 Issued invoice No. 103 to G. Noble for services performed; $100.

13 Received an invoice from *Local News* for an advertisement placed in the newspaper; $8.50.

16 Received $70 from a cash customer for services performed. The money was not put in the bank as usual. Mr. Steele paid $15 of it for gasoline for the truck and kept the rest for his personal use.

19 Received a notification from the bank stating that $10.25 had been taken from the business's bank account to pay for interest charges on the bank loan.

8. **T. J. Boyle, the owner of an engineering consultant business, has the following chart of accounts:**

| *Assets* | | *Proprietorship* | |
|---|---|---|---|
| Bank | No. 1 | T. J. Boyle, Capital | No. 31 |
| M. Black | 2 | T. J. Boyle, Drawings | 32 |
| F. Rose | 3 | Fees Earned | 41 |
| Office Supplies | 4 | Bank Charges | 51 |
| Office Equipment | 5 | Car Expenses | 52 |
| Automobile | 6 | Miscellaneous Expense | 53 |
| | | Rent Expense | 54 |
| *Liabilities* | | Telephone Expense | 55 |
| Bank Loan | 21 | Wages Expense | 56 |
| Mason Brothers | 22 | | |
| Regal Oil Co. | 23 | | |

**In the two-column general journal of T. J. Boyle, on page 162, journalize the following transactions; use the accounts shown above.**

*Transactions*

March

1 Issued cheque No. 615 for $165 to Royalty Trust Co. in payment of the monthly rent.

2 Issued cheque No. 616 for $200 to the owner, T. J. Boyle, for his personal use.

2 Received an invoice in the amount of $42.73 from Mason Brothers for office supplies that had been purchased.

3 Issued cheque No. 617 in the amount of

$355 to West End Garage, as directed by the owner. The payment was for repairs to Mrs. Boyle's personal car.

5 Issued invoice No. 214 to F. Rose for services rendered; $125.

5 Issued cheque No. 618 for $250 in payment of the wages of the office secretary for a two-week period.

9 Received an invoice from Regal Oil Company for gasoline and oil used in the business automobile; $56.46.

12 Received a cheque for $100 from M. Black on account.

15 Received a memorandum from the bank stating that $26.50 had been deducted by the bank from the business's bank account to pay for interest on the bank loan and other bank charges.

16 Issued cheque No. 619 for $15 to the post office to pay for the purchase of postage stamps.

19 Issued cheque No. 620 for $35 to the City Telephone Company in payment of the monthly telephone bill.

19 Issued cheque No. 621 for $250 to the office secretary in payment of her wages for two weeks.

22 Issued invoice No. 215 to M. Black for services rendered; amount, $500.

23 Received $25 from C. Sloan as a cash payment for services rendered. Cash sales slip No. 65.

25 Purchased several trade magazines for the office and paid for them by cheque No. 622 in the amount of $18.

---

9. The accounts required for this exercise are as follows:
(2 workbook accounts are required for Bank.)

No. 1 Bank
2 Jenkins and Co.
3 Office Supplies
4 Office Equipment
5 Automobile
21 Office Supply Company
31 N. A. James, Capital
32 N. A. James, Drawings
41 Fees Income
51 Advertising Expense

52 Car Expenses
53 Donations Expense
54 Miscellaneous Expense
55 Rent Expense

N. A. James, a public accountant, decided to begin a business of his own on October 1, 19—. At that time he invested in the business a bank balance of $2 497 and an automobile worth $2 000.

Journalize and post the opening entry.

Journalize and post the following subsequent transactions:

*Transactions*
October

2 Sundry office supplies were purchased from Martin Bros. at a cost of $165.55. Cheque No. 1 was issued in payment.

2 Issued cheque No. 2 to Premier Realty Co. for one month's advance rent; amount, $175.

5 An advertisement costing $15 was placed in a local newspaper; cheque No. 3 was issued in payment.

5 A desk, chair, and filing cabinet were purchased on account from Office Supply Company; cost, $305.

8 Mr. James was engaged by a client, Jenkins & Co. At the conclusion of three days' work an invoice amounting to $170 was sent to Jenkins & Co.

9 A bookkeeping service was performed for B. Masters and $35 cash was collected from him. A tax return was prepared for W. Shields and $20 cash was collected from him. The total of $55 was deposited in the bank.

12 A $25 donation was given to the United

Appeal. Cheque No. 4 was issued.

12 Received a cheque for $100 from Jenkins & Co. on account. The cheque was deposited.

13 Paid the Office Supply Company account in full. Cheque No. 5 was issued.

14 Issued cheque No. 6 to Louis' Service Station for gasoline and oil used in the business car; amount $16.50.

16 Performed a service for R. Andrews and received $100 cash in payment. The proprietor, N. A. James, did not deposit this money in the bank but kept it himself for his own use.

19 Purchased a quantity of office supplies from Daniel's and issued cheque No. 7 for $36.75 in payment.

22 Placed an advertisement in the local newspaper at a cost of $18. Cheque No. 8 was issued in payment.

23 Issued an invoice to Jenkins & Co. for several days' work; amount, $300.

26 Issued cheque No. 9 to the post office in payment for $20 worth of postage stamps.

27 Issued cheque No. 10 to N. A. James for his personal use; amount, $150.

**Balance the ledger by means of a trial balance.**

**Determine the amount of net income or net loss.**

---

**10. S. P. Proctor began a business called the General Repair Shop for the purpose of providing cleaning, repairing, and general handyman services to the public. His beginning balance sheet was as follows:**

GENERAL REPAIR SHOP
BALANCE SHEET
AUGUST 31, 19—

| *Assets* | | *Liabilities* | |
|---|---|---|---|
| Cash | $1 000.00 | Bank Loan | $1 500.00 |
| Supplies | 150.00 | | |
| Office Equipment | 732.50 | *Capital* | |
| Truck | 3 957.00 | S. P. Proctor, Capital | 4 339.50 |
| | $5 839.50 | | $5 839.50 |

**Record the opening entry in the journal and post it to the accounts. The complete chart of accounts for this exercise is as follows: (3 workbook accounts are required for Bank.)**

| | | | |
|---|---|---|---|
| Bank | No. 1 | Loss on Sale of Equipment | 51 |
| W. J. Thomson | 2 | Miscellaneous Expense | 52 |
| G. D. Fraser | 3 | Rent Expense | 53 |
| Supplies | 4 | Truck Expense | 54 |
| Office Equipment | 5 | Wages Expense | 55 |
| Truck | 6 | | |
| Bank Loan | 21 | | |
| Jones Hardware | 22 | A very important routine in business is to deposit in the bank daily all cash and cheques received. In this and all future exercises you are to assume that this function is performed as a matter of course – unless you are specifically told otherwise. | |
| Imperial Garage | 23 | | |
| S. P. Proctor, Capital | 31 | | |
| S. P. Proctor, Drawings | 32 | | |
| Service Income | 41 | | |

Journalize and post the following transactions:

## Transactions
September

1 Issued cheque No. 1 to P. Jarvis for the rent for the month of September; amount, $220.

3 Received an invoice from Jones Hardware regarding a purchase of supplies on account; amount, $135.

5 Issued invoices to W. J. Thomson, $180, and G. D. Fraser, $150, in respect to services performed during the week.

9 Sold an office desk for $50 cash. The desk had originally cost $175 and was included in the Office Equipment account at that figure. (Although a sale has been made, this transaction does not affect the income account which is reserved for the normal income of the business.)

10 Received $90 cash from a customer for services performed.

11 Issued cheque No. 2 to the owner for his personal use; amount, $150.

12 Issued cheque No. 3 to Jones Hardware on account; amount, $75.

15 Received an invoice from Imperial Garage for gasoline and oil used in the truck; amount, $42.

16 Issued cheque No. 4 to Cochrane Bros. for a cash purchase of supplies; amount, $65.45.

18 Received a cheque from W. J. Thomson in full payment of his account balance.

19 Received a memorandum from the bank to the effect that $16.50 had been deducted from the bank account to pay for bank charges.

19 Issued cheques for wages as follows:
No. 5 to R. Barnes – $190.
No. 6 to G. Bolton – $185.

19 Received $300 cash from a customer for services performed over a period of one week.

22 The owner, S. P. Proctor, requested the bank to reduce the bank loan by $500.

24 Issued cheque No. 7 to the telephone company; $12.

25 Received a cheque on account from G. D. Fraser; $75.

26 Received $200 cash from a customer for services rendered.

26 The owner withdrew $150 cash for his personal use; cheque No. 8.

29 Issued cheque No. 9 to Jones Hardware in payment of the balance of the account.

29 While on a job, S. P. Proctor needed some additional supplies immediately and purchased them at a local store paying cash from his personal funds; $19.

30 Received $375 cash from a customer for services rendered.

**Take off a trial balance.**

**Determine the amount of net income or net loss.**

---

**11.   P. Simpson began business as an engineering consultant on October 1, 19—.**
**He began business with the following assets and liabilities:**

| Assets | | Liabilities | |
|---|---|---|---|
| Cash in Bank | $2 651.20 | Ace Finance Company | $850.00 |
| Office Equipment | 465.00 | Grand's Stationers | 200.00 |
| Automobile | 2 460.00 | | |

Journalize and post the opening entry. The accounts used in this exercise are
shown in the following chart of accounts:
(3 workbook accounts required for Bank.)

Bank                     No. 1          P. Arthur                    2

| | | | | |
|---|---|---|---|---|
| J. Morrison | No. 3 | Star Oil Co. | 24 |
| N. Martin | 4 | P. Simpson, Capital | 31 |
| Supplies | 5 | P. Simpson, Drawings | 32 |
| Office Equipment | 6 | Income from Fees | 41 |
| Automobile | 7 | Car Expenses | 51 |
| Ace Finance Company | 21 | Office Expenses | 52 |
| Grand's Stationers | 22 | Rent | 53 |
| Industrial Suppliers | 23 | Wages | 54 |

**Journalize and post the transactions listed below.**

### Transactions
October

1. Performed a service for S. Stewart and received $20 cash in payment.
2. Received an invoice from Grand's Stationers for supplies purchased on account; amount, $103.78.
4. Issued invoice No. 1 to P. Arthur for services rendered; amount, $200.
5. Issued cheques for the weekly wages as follows:
   No. 1 – O. Mack – $175.
   No. 2 – W. Moss – $187.50.
8. Received an invoice from Star Oil Co. for gasoline and oil used in business car; amount, $31.24.
9. Paid the regular monthly payment to Ace Finance Company; cheque No. 3 for $120.
10. Issued invoice No. 2 to J. Morrison for services rendered; amount, $420.
11. P. Simpson withdrew $200 for his personal use; cheque No. 4.
12. Issued cheques for the weekly wages as follows:
    No. 5 – O. Mack – $175.
    No. 6 – W. Moss – $193.50.
15. Issued cheque No. 7 to J. Mahoney for the rent for the month of October; amount, $175.
16. Received a cheque on account from P. Arthur; $200.
17. Issued invoice No. 3 to J. Morrison for services rendered; $300.
19. Issued cheques for the weekly wages as follows:
    No. 8 – O. Mack – $175.
    No. 9 – W. Moss – $177.75.
19. Issued cheque No. 10 to Grand's Stationers on account; amount, $200.
23. Received an invoice from Star Oil Co. for gasoline and oil used in the business automobile; amount, $55.80.
25. Received an invoice from Industrial Suppliers for the purchase of supplies on account; $76.40.
25. Received a cheque from J. Morrison on account; $300.
26. Issued cheque No. 11 to the owner to repay him for out-of-pocket expenses as follows:
    Postage         $15.
    Car Repair      $40.
    Parking         $ 5.
26. Paid the weekly wages with the following cheques:
    No. 12 – O. Mack – $175.
    No. 13 – W. Moss – $190.
26. Issued invoice No. 4 to N. Martin for services rendered; $1 425.
29. Issued cheque No. 14 to Endover's Garage for repairs and servicing to the business automobile, $68.92.
30. Issued cheque No. 15 to Star Oil Co. in full payment of the account balance.
31. Issued cheques as follows:
    No. 16 – Telephone Company – $22.50.
    No. 17 – Hydro-Electric Co. – $6.45.

**Take off a trial balance at October 31.**

**Calculate the amount of net income or net loss for the period.**

# Cases

## Case 1

Mrs. E. Foreman owns and operates a small florist shop. She deposits all cash receipts in the bank and makes all payments by cheque. The Cash account at the end of the current year had a credit balance of $350 after all balances were found to be correct.

1. Assuming no errors, what might be the explanation for the credit balance? At the end of the fiscal year, how should this item be shown on the financial statements?
2. For May, Mrs. Foreman showed a net income of $2 000. During that period she withdrew $2 600 in cash for her personal use. Does this represent a net loss of $600 for May? Explain.

## Case 2

During the year Mr. Garvin received $50 000 for services rendered, borrowed $5 000 from the bank, and sold old equipment for $3 000 cash. On his net income statement for the year ended December 31, he showed total income to be $58 000.

As the auditor examining Garvin's books, would you verify this figure to be correct? State reasons for your answer.

## Case 3

Walter Crowe is a very stingy, yet diversified individual. He has a thriving business that operates from the basement of his home, and he also acts as his own accountant. He always boasts about his ability to handle accounting. Walter has various ways of cutting down on many of his costs. For example, he does not use a journal, but enters all his transactions directly into the ledger accounts.

Whenever Walter needs to visit a client, he charges the price of gas purchased to his Automobile account.

When preparing the balance sheet for the business, Walter includes his home and furnishings as an asset.

Do you think that Walter is really as good an accountant as he boasts to be? Explain.

## Case 4

Suppose that you were hired as an accountant for a small gas station. When looking over the records, you find that the proprietor, who kept the records previously, had recorded all his cash payments into one account headed 'Expenses'. Briefly outline what you would say to the proprietor in an effort to explain why this is not a good system.

## Case 5

The income statement for McGuire & Son prepared for the year ended December 31, 19—, showed the net income to be $36 500. During the year the junior accountant recorded some transactions incorrectly. Examining the general journal, the accountant discovered the following errors in transactions:

1. Revenue was debited, $4 000, and customers' accounts credited, $4 000.
2. Sold old equipment on the books at $4 000 for $2 000 cash. The junior accountant debited Cash and credited Revenue $2 000.
3. Recorded the withdrawal of $1 600 by the owner by debiting Wages expenses and crediting Cash.

Required:
a. Using the above figures, determine McGuire's correct net income as of December 31, 19—. Show all calculations.
b. Would the error in (3) have any effect on the final capital figure appearing on the balance sheet as of December 31, 19—? Explain.

## Case 6

The balance in the Capital account of the O.K. Suppliers on January 1, 19—, was $26 000. The balance in this account was $27 500 at the end of the year. Net income for the year was $5 000. Explain why the balance in Capital was not $31 000.

# 6 The Simple Work Sheet and Financial Statements

You have been told throughout this text that a vital purpose of accounting is to make possible the preparation of financial reports. Now that you have mastered the simple basic principles of accounting, it seems appropriate to follow these principles through to their ultimate and logical conclusion – the preparation of the financial statements. Therefore, you will now be shown how to apply the information shown in the books and records of a business, to produce an income statement and a balance sheet.

The purpose of introducing this topic at this time is to give you a broader view of the ultimate purpose of the system of accounting as a whole.

At the conclusion of every accounting period, and at any other time required by management, financial reports are prepared from the information accumulated in the ledger. The preparation of financial statements may appear to be a simple matter to you in view of the knowledge you have gained so far, but in reality it is work of an advanced and important nature, as you will see later. This work is usually done not by a clerk but by an accountant, a person possessing expert knowledge in such matters.

## The Simple Work Sheet

To assist him in organizing and planning for the financial statements, an accountant uses a working paper called a work sheet. This, as its name suggests, is an informal business paper. It is ordinarily prepared in pencil so that any necessary changes can be made easily. The work is done on columnar bookkeeping paper; the number of money columns used depends on the complexity of the business and the technique of the accountant. For our simple exercises, six money columns are used.

The steps in the preparation of a work sheet are detailed below. The information used in the examples is obtained from problem 11 of the previous chapter.

Step 1. The first step in the preparation of a work sheet is to **write the headings on the columnar paper**. Examine the headings in the illustration below very carefully. Observe, in particular, the precise way in which the accounting period is described.

Step 2. The second step in the preparation of a

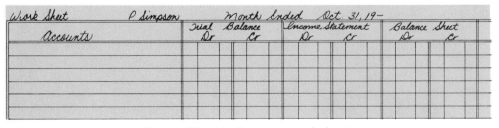

*Step 1. The headings of a work sheet.*

work sheet is to **record the trial balance in the manner shown below**. It is absolutely imperative that the trial balance columns be balanced and correct before any additional work is done on the work sheet.

Step 3. The third step in the process is to **extend each of the amounts from the trial balance columns into one of the four columns to the right**. The process is simple and logical. The Income Statement columns of the work sheet receive the income and the expenses — the items that make up the net income or the net loss. The Balance Sheet columns receive everything else — the assets, the liabilities, the capital, and the drawings. Remember that the drawings is definitely not an element of net income and therefore cannot be included in that section. Be careful to transfer the amounts accurately and to record debit amounts into Debit columns and credit amounts into Credit columns. Be sure, too, that no single amount is transferred to two places and that no item is missed.

Step 4. The fourth step in the process is to **balance the work sheet**. The objective in balancing the work sheet is —

| Work Sheet | P. Simpson | | Month Ended Oct 31, 19 — | | | |
|---|---|---|---|---|---|---|
| Accounts | Trial Dr | Balance Cr | Income Statement Dr | Cr | Balance Sheet Dr | Cr |
| Bank | 582 54 | | | | | |
| J. Morrison | 420 — | | | | | |
| N. Martin | 425 — | | | | | |
| Supplies | 87 68 | | | | | |
| Office Equipment | 465 — | | | | | |
| Automobile | 2 460 — | | | | | |
| Ace Finance Company | | 730 — | | | | |
| Grand's Stationers | | 103 78 | | | | |
| Industrial Suppliers | | 76 40 | | | | |
| P. Simpson, Capital | | 3 526 20 | | | | |
| P. Simpson, Drawings | 292 50 | | | | | |
| Income from Fees | | 1 365 — | | | | |
| Car Expenses | 200 96 | | | | | |
| Office Expense | 43 95 | | | | | |
| Rent | 175 — | | | | | |
| Wages | 648 75 | | | | | |
| | 5 801 38 | 5 801 38 | | | | |

*Step 2. Recording the trial balance on a work sheet.*

| Work Sheet | P. Simpson | | Month Ended Oct 31, 19— | | | |
|---|---|---|---|---|---|---|
| Accounts | Trial Dr | Balance Cr | Income Statement Dr | Cr | Balance Sheet Dr | Cr |
| Bank | 582 54 | | | | 582 54 | |
| J. Morrison | 420 — | | | | 420 — | |
| N. Martin | 425 — | | | | 425 — | |
| Supplies | 87 68 | | | | 87 68 | |
| Office Equipment | 465 — | | | | 465 — | |
| Automobile | 2 460 — | | | | 2 460 — | |
| Ace Finance Company | | 730 — | | | | 730 — |
| Grand's Stationers | | 103 78 | | | | 103 78 |
| Industrial Suppliers | | 76 40 | | | | 76 40 |
| P. Simpson, Capital | | 3 526 20 | | | | 3 526 20 |
| P. Simpson, Drawings | 292 50 | | | | 292 50 | |
| Income from Fees | | 1 365 — | | 1 365 — | | |
| Car Expenses | 200 96 | | 200 96 | | | |
| Office Expense | 43 95 | | 43 95 | | | |
| Rent | 175 — | | 175 — | | | |
| Wages | 648 75 | | 648 75 | | | |
| | 5 801 38 | 5 801 38 | | | | |

*Step 3. Extending the amounts on a work sheet.*

1. To total the four right-hand money columns.
2. To see that the difference between the two Income Statement columns is equal to the difference between the two Balance Sheet columns. This difference is known as the balancing figure.
3. To record the above information in a neat and orderly manner on the work sheet as shown below.

It is very important that the work sheet balance and so the balancing work must be done very carefully. If the two differences mentioned in 2 above do not agree, then the work sheet does not balance. This means that one or more errors have been made in preparing it and that you may not proceed to the preparation of the financial statements until the errors have been found and corrected. It is mathematically impossible for the work sheet to be out of balance and be correct.

The balancing figure on the work sheet will always tell you the amount of the net income or net loss for the accounting period. An intelligent look at the column totals of the Net Income section of the work sheet will tell you which it is. When the credits (income) are greater than the debits (expense), net income has been earned; when the debits are greater than the credits, a net loss has been suffered. The two illustrations below show the balancing work in a different color for purposes of emphasis. Balancing does not involve a great deal of work but it needs to be done carefully. Follow the upper example for a profit situation and the lower example for a loss situation. Observe carefully the slight but important variations in the finalizing of the work sheet for a loss situation.

| Work Sheet | P. Simpson | Month Ended Oct. 31, 19— | | | | | | |
|---|---|---|---|---|---|---|---|---|
| Accounts | Trial Balance Dr | Cr | Income Statement Dr | Cr | Balance Sheet Dr | Cr | | |
| Bank | 582 54 | | | | 582 54 | | | |
| J. Morrison | 420 — | | | | 420 — | | | |
| N. Martin | 425 — | | | | 425 — | | | |
| Supplies | 87 68 | | | | 87 68 | | | |
| Office Equipment | 465 — | | | | 465 — | | | |
| Automobile | 2 460 — | | | | 2 460 — | | | |
| Ace Finance Company | | 730 — | | | | 730 — | | |
| Grand's Stationers | | 103 78 | | | | 103 78 | | |
| Industrial Suppliers | | 76 40 | | | | 76 40 | | |
| P. Simpson, Capital | | 3 526 20 | | | | 3 526 20 | | |
| P. Simpson, Drawings | 292 50 | | | | 292 50 | | | |
| Income from Fees | | 1 365 — | | 1 365 — | | | | |
| Car Expenses | 200 96 | | 200 96 | | | | | |
| Office Expense | 43 95 | | 43 95 | | | | | |
| Rent | 175 — | | 175 — | | | | | |
| Wages | 648 75 | | 648 75 | | | | | |
| | 5 801 38 | 5 801 38 | 1 068 66 | 1 365 — | 4 732 72 | 4 436 38 | | |
| Net Income | | | 296 34 | | | 296 34 | | |
| | | | 1 365 — | 1 365 — | 4 732 72 | 4 732 72 | | |

*Step 4. Balancing the work sheet (net income situation).*

| Work Sheet | R. Graham | Month Ended June 30, 19— | | | | | | |
|---|---|---|---|---|---|---|---|---|
| Accounts | Trial Balance Dr | Cr | Income Statement Dr | Cr | Balance Sheet Dr | Cr | | |
| Bank | 601 17 | | | | 601 17 | | | |
| C. Foster | 125 — | | | | 125 — | | | |
| Wages Expense | 316 — | | 316 — | | | | | |
| | 4 701 17 | 4 701 17 | 2 172 47 | 1 816 40 | 5 167 21 | 5 523 28 | | |
| Net Loss | | | | 356 07 | 356 07 | | | |
| | | | 2 172 47 | 2 172 47 | 5 523 28 | 5 523 28 | | |

*Step 4. Balancing the work sheet (net loss situation).*

# Financial Reporting

The completed work sheet possesses, in an organized and readily accessible form, all of the information that is needed for the preparation of the financial statements. Develop the habit of looking only to the work sheet for this information. Later, with more advanced work, it will not be available in any other place.

The financial statements represent the accountant's report to the owners or managers on the financial affairs of the business. Owners and managers rarely need to look at the actual accounting records since they rely on the skill of the accountant to maintain them accurately. All that the owners want to see are the finished financial reports of the accountant. It would be a foolish accountant indeed who did not take the trouble to prepare his statements flawlessly.

In today's business world financial reports are most often prepared in typewritten form by skilled secretaries who copy from the accountants' handwritten work. But for you, as a student, it will be easier to prepare your statements in handwritten form.

## The Income Statement

It is important that you understand where to obtain the information necessary for the preparation of the income statement. Establish firmly in your mind that it is found in the Income Statement columns of the work sheet. At an advanced level of study these columns will be the only source of the correct information.

The income statement of P. Simpson appears below. It has been prepared from the work sheet on page 77. The style shown is not the only one possible.

Examine P. Simpson's income statement carefully. Observe in particular the following points:
1. The heading shows three things:
   a. The name of the business or individual.
   b. The description of the financial statement.
   c. The exact fiscal period.
2. The income or revenue and the expenses are each set out in separate sections.
3. The Net Income (or Net Loss – see below) is shown as the final item on the statement.

| MORRIS REAL ESTATE INCOME STATEMENT MONTH ENDED JUNE 30, 19— | | |
|---|---|---|
| *Income* | | |
| Commissions | | $3 874.60 |
| | | |
| *Expenses* | | |
| Advertising | $1 256.70 | |
| Business Tax | 57.50 | |
| Car Expenses | 746.51 | |
| Miscellaneous Expense | 92.46 | |
| Rent | 600.00 | |
| Telephone Expense | 96.24 | |
| Wages | 1 174.25 | 4 023.66 |
| Net Loss | | $ 149.06 |

*Example of income statement (net loss situation).*

*Example of income statement (net income situation).*

4. When a money column is totaled and the total is to be used in further calculations on the statement (e.g., the expenses column in the Morris Real Estate income statement) one standard way of showing the total is –
   a. Rule a single line beneath the column.
   b. Place the total in the next column to the right and beside the last figure in the column that was totaled.

## The Balance Sheet

All of the figures that are needed for the preparation of a balance sheet are found in the Balance Sheet columns of the work sheet. Select them as you need them for the preparation of the statement.

The balance sheets illustrated in this chapter differ from those you have used heretofore in two major respects: **appearance** and **content**. These two aspects are considered in turn.

1. **Appearance.** The balance sheets you are familiar with have had a horizontal or side-by-side arrangement as shown in the illustration below. This arrangement is known as the **account form** of the balance sheet.

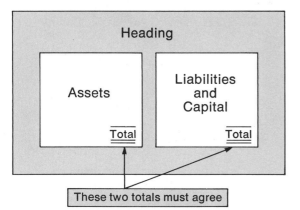

*Account form of balance sheet.*

The new style of balance sheet, introduced in this chapter, has a vertical or one-above-the-other arrangement as shown in the illustration at the top of the next column. This new style is known as the **report form** of the balance sheet. The report form, owing to the fact that it is more suitable for use with standard equipment and stationery, is commonly used.

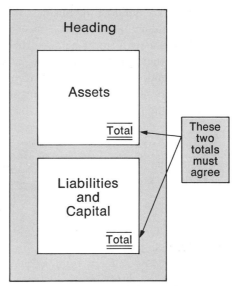

*Report form of balance sheet.*

Three sample balance sheets in the new report form are shown on pages 80, 81, and 82.

2. **Content.** The balance sheet discussed in Chapter 1 is very simple. The report form balance sheets shown in this chapter are of a moderately more advanced nature. As well as including additional information, this new form of balance sheet presents the usual information in more detail. You will find that much of the information is broken down into smaller classes or categories in order to make the statement more informative. It is at this stage that the balance sheet is considered to be a 'classified' financial statement.

Examine carefully the balance sheet samples that follow, observing in particular the points listed below.

1. **Current Assets** There is a separate section in the balance sheet for Current Assets. These consist of cash and assets that will be converted into cash within one year in the ordinary course of business. Current assets are listed in the order of their 'liquidity'; that is, their ability to be converted into cash.
2. **Fixed Assets** There is a separate section in the balance sheet for Fixed Assets. These are assets that normally last for more than one year; e.g., buildings, automotive equipment, and office equipment.
3. **Current Liabilities** There is a separate section in the balance sheet for Current Liabil-

ities. These are debts of the business that are due to be paid within one year.

4. **Capital** The new form of balance sheet has a section rather than a single figure for Capital. This section shows in broad terms the changes to capital that have occurred during the accounting period. Specifically, the major elements of capital – (a) the balance at the beginning of the period, (b) the net income or net loss for the period, and (c) the drawings for the period – are arranged on the statement in a way that permits the calculation of the new capital balance at the end of the accounting period. Remember that

| | | | | |
|---|---|---|---|---|
| | Western Company | | | |
| | Balance Sheet | | | |
| | September 30, 19— | | | |
| | **Assets** | | | |
| Current Assets | | | | |
| Cash | | 1 246 02 | | |
| J. C. Duncan | | 75 — | | |
| R. M. Prior | | 81 50 | | |
| P. G. Oliver | | 621 40 | | |
| Supplies | | 272 75 | 2 296 67 | |
| Fixed Assets | | | | |
| Furniture and Fixtures | | 863 20 | | |
| Delivery Equipment | | 3 500 — | 4 363 20 | |
| | | | 6 659 87 | |
| | **Liabilities and Capital** | | | |
| Current Liabilities | | | | |
| York Canning Company | | 951 — | | |
| Maple Leaf Manufacturers | | 652 75 | 1 603 75 | |
| A. M. Kendall, Capital | | | | |
| Balance September 1 | | 4 381 60 | | |
| Add: Net Income | 1 051 41 | | | |
| Less Drawings | 376 89 | 674 52 | | |
| Balance September 30 | | | 5 056 12 | |
| | | | 6 659 87 | |

*Report form balance sheet (net income greater than drawings). A fiscal period of one month is indicated by Capital section.*

capital is also referred to as **owner's equity**.

It is important to note that variations in presentation occur in the Capital section depending on (a) whether the business has earned a profit or suffered a loss, and (b) whether the profit is greater or less than the drawings. It will be necessary for you to follow the samples in the textbook carefully when you are working on the exercises.

**Notes:**

1. When financial statements are typewritten, as they are in most cases, dollar signs are used in a limited way. For typewritten statements the rule for the use of dollar signs is: use a dollar sign with the first figure in every money column and with the first figure beneath every ruled line in every money column.

2. On typewritten statements the 'cents' part of an even dollar amount is always shown by two ciphers and never by a dash.

3. In the Capital section the final capital figure is dropped one line to permit a description to be written in the same line as the figure it describes. This is a common technique.

EASTERN COMPANY
BALANCE SHEET
MARCH 31, 19—

ASSETS

| Current Assets | | |
|---|---|---|
| Cash | $1 040.80 | |
| B. Carson | 225.40 | |
| E. F. Fournier | 443.27 | |
| R. Nolan | 72.00 | |
| Supplies | 132.60 | $1 914.07 |
| | | |
| Fixed Assets | | |
| Furniture and Fixtures | $  931.00 | |
| Delivery Equipment | 3 950.00 | 4 881.00 |
| | | $6 795.07 |

LIABILITIES AND CAPITAL

| Current Liabilities | | | |
|---|---|---|---|
| Bank Loan | | $1 000.00 | |
| Standard Company | | 1 247.61 | $2 247.61 |
| | | | |
| R. C. Jensen, Capital | | | |
| Balance January 1 | | $4 696.86 | |
| Deduct: Drawings | $1 400.00 | | |
| Less Net Income | 1 250.60 | 149.40 | |
| Balance March 31 | | | 4 547.46 |
| | | | $6 795.07 |

*Report form balance sheet (drawings greater than net income). A fiscal period of three months is indicated by Capital section.*

## Northern Company
## Balance Sheet
## August 31, 19-6

### Assets

| | | | | |
|---|---|---|---:|---:|
| **Current Assets** | | | | |
| Cash | | | 951 06 | |
| Stewart and Martin | | | 43 — | |
| Sevigny Bros. | | | 777 46 | |
| O. F. Talbot | | | 731 32 | |
| Office Supplies | | | 185 21 | 2 688 05 |
| **Fixed Assets** | | | | |
| Land | | | 5 000 — | |
| Office Equipment | | | 230 — | |
| Furniture and Fixtures | | | 375 50 | |
| Delivery Equipment | | | 2 925 — | 8 530 50 |
| | | | | 11 218 55 |

### Liabilities and Capital

| | | | | |
|---|---|---|---:|---:|
| **Current Liabilities** | | | | |
| Central Supply Co. | | | 1 316 05 | |
| Silvanite Company | | | 871 63 | 2 187 68 |
| **H. H. Phillips, Capital** | | | | |
| Balance September 1, 19-5 | | | 9 893 47 | |
| Deduct: Net Loss | 512 60 | | | |
| Drawings | 350 — | | 862 60 | |
| Balance August 31, 19-6 | | | | 9 030 87 |
| | | | | 11 218 55 |

*Report form balance sheet (net loss situation). A fiscal period of one year is indicated by Capital section.*

## The Accounting or Bookkeeping Cycle

During a fiscal period a certain number of procedures are required to be carried out in a precise and orderly manner. The first three of these procedures, journalizing, posting, and balancing of the ledger, are the responsibility of junior employees. The remaining procedures have to do with the preparation of financial statements and advanced accounting matters. They are the responsibility of the accountant and are discussed in Chapters 14 and 15. All of the steps together constitute the **accounting or bookkeeping cycle**, the regular pattern of accounting functions that have to be carried out during each accounting period.

## The Ledger and Automation

In relatively recent times, automation and the computer have had a tremendous impact in the field of accounting. And it appears that the computer's influence is not diminishing.

Although it has not changed the theory of accounting, the computer has had an effect on the form and appearance of accounting records, in particular the ledger.

An example of a computer-produced ledger is shown below. It differs from the traditional ledger in two ways:

1. The traditional ledger consists of a file of account cards or a book of account pages. There is a separate page or card for each account in the ledger.

     The computer-produced ledger consists of a particular kind of listing of the accounts. There is not a separate page for each account; one or more accounts may be listed on each page of the listing.

2. The traditional ledger consists of a number of individual accounts each of which is cumulative in nature. That is, the same account page or card is used until it is completely filled, at which time the balance is carried forward to a new page or card and the process continued.

     The computer-produced ledger is not a continuous record. Each month a new monthly listing of the accounts is produced which shows: (a) the balances at the end of the previous month, (b) the debit and credit entries for the current month, and (c) the new balances at the end of the current month. Each individual listing shows the account information for a period of one month only. To examine a particular account for the entire year it is necessary to look at twelve listings.

| | | | | | | | |
|---|---|---|---|---|---|---|---|
| SYSTEMATIC SERVICES | | | | | | | |
| LEDGER | | | | | | | |
| SEPTEMBER 30, 19-- | | | | | | | PAGE 1 |
| DATE | ACCOUNT TITLE | ACCT CODE | REFERENCE | BEGINNING BALANCE | CURRENT MONTH | | CLOSING BALANCE |
| | | | | | DEBIT | CREDIT | |
| AUG 31 | BANK | 01 | BALANCE FORWARD | $5 016.25 DR | | | |
| SEPT 30 | | 01 | RECEIPTS | | $9 321.16 | | |
| SEPT 30 | | 01 | DISBURSEMENTS | | | $10 402.16 | |
| SEPT 30 | | 01 | JOURNAL ENTRY 65 | | 15.00 | | |
| SEPT 30 | | 01 | BALANCE | | | | $3 950.25 DR |
| | | | | | | | |
| AUG 31 | ACCOUNTS RECEIVABLE | 02 | BALANCE FORWARD | $10 416.95 DR | | | |
| SEPT 30 | | 02 | SALES ON ACCOUNT | | $16 402.19 | | |
| SEPT 30 | | 02 | RECEIPTS | | | $14 911.91 | |
| SEPT 30 | | 02 | BALANCE | | | | $11 907.23 DR |
| | | | | | | | |
| AUG 31 | MERCHANDISE INVENTORY | 03 | BALANCE FORWARD | $24 117.03 DR | | | |
| SEPT 30 | | 03 | BALANCE | | | | $24 117.03 DR |
| | | | | | | | |
| AUG 31 | SUPPLIES | 04 | BALANCE FORWARD | $315.20 DR | | | |
| SEPT 30 | | 04 | DISBURSEMENTS | | $74.20 | | |
| SEPT 30 | | 04 | PURCHASES ON ACCT | | $49.15 | | |
| SEPT 30 | | 04 | BALANCE | | | | $438.55 DR |

*Part of a computer-produced ledger.*

## Bookkeeping and Accounting Terms

**Income Statement** A financial report showing, in an orderly manner, the income, the expenses, and the net income or the net loss of a business, that is, the operating results of the business, for a specified fiscal period. Also known as a **profit and loss statement**.

**Work Sheet** An informal columnar business paper on which is organized, in convenient form, all of the information that is required for the preparation of both the income statement and the balance sheet.

**Account Form of Balance Sheet** A horizontal or side-by-side arrangement of the balance sheet.

**Report Form of Balance Sheet** A vertical or one-above-the-other arrangement of the balance sheet.

**Current Assets** Cash, and assets that will be converted into cash within a period of one year in the ordinary course of business.

**Fixed Assets** Assets that normally last for a number of years.

**Current Liabilities** Debts of the business that are due to be paid within a period of one year.

**Accounting Cycle** The total set of procedures that is required to be performed during each fiscal period.

## Review Questions

1. What is the ultimate purpose of keeping a set of books?
2. Why is a work sheet used?
3. What are the headings of a work sheet?
4. What is very important about the trial balance columns of the work sheet?
5. Briefly describe the third step in the preparation of a work sheet.
6. How is the work sheet balanced?
7. If the work sheet does not balance, what must be done?
8. Is the balancing procedure the same for a 'profit' situation as it is for a 'loss' situation? Explain.
9. When preparing financial statements where does one look for the information?
10. Why should an accountant take the trouble to prepare the financial statements very carefully?
11. In what ways is the heading of the income statement different from the heading of the balance sheet?
12. Explain the rules for the use of dollar signs in typewritten statements.
13. Explain the difference between the 'report' form and the 'account' form of the balance sheet.
14. What is meant by a 'classified' financial statement?
15. Define 'current asset'.
16. Define 'fixed asset'.
17. Define 'current liability'.
18. Explain the accounting cycle.

## Exercises

1. As the accountant for Simpler Devices you are just about to commence the preparation of the work sheet for the year ended December 31, 19—. Begin the work sheet for Simpler Devices by writing in the heading and the column headings.

2. Shown below are the accounts of G. Sloan. In your workbook, in two separate columns, list the accounts that are to be extended to the Income Statement columns of the work sheet and those that are to be extended to the Balance Sheet columns of the work sheet.

*Accounts*

Bank; M. Hamilton (debtor); Supplies; Equipment; Automobile; Bank Loan; Acco Finance Co. (creditor); General Hardware (creditor); G. Sloan, Capital; G. Sloan, Drawings; Revenue; Automobile Expense; Miscellaneous Expense; Rent Expense; Wages Expense.

---

**3.** The trial balance of A. R. Lewis at his fiscal year-end of June 30, 19—, is shown below:

A. R. LEWIS
TRIAL BALANCE
JUNE 30, 19—

| | | |
|---|---:|---:|
| Bank | $ 1 200 | |
| P. Anderson | 350 | |
| G. McEwan | 1 500 | |
| Office Supplies | 750 | |
| Office Equipment | 2 700 | |
| Automobile | 4 850 | |
| Bank Loan | | $ 3 000 |
| A. R. Lewis, Capital | | 7 622 |
| A. R. Lewis, Drawings | 10 000 | |
| Revenue | | 22 702 |
| Advertising | 961 | |
| Car Expense | 3 716 | |
| Miscellaneous Expense | 597 | |
| Rent Expense | 4 000 | |
| Salaries Expense | 2 700 | |
| | $33 324 | $33 324 |

Write in the headings on the work sheet.

Write in the trial balance on the work sheet.

Extend the trial balance items to the Income Statement and Balance Sheet columns.

---

**4.** The extended work sheet for R. Braun is to be found in your workbooks. In your workbooks, or as directed by your teacher, total and balance the work sheet.

---

**5.** In your workbook you will find the column totals of a work sheet. In your workbook, or as directed by your teacher, complete the balancing of the work sheet.

---

**6.** In your workbook you will find the column totals of a work sheet. In your workbook, or as directed by your teacher, complete the balancing of the work sheet.

**7.** The trial balance of The Arthur Company on October 31, 19—, after a fiscal period of one month, is as follows:

| | | |
|---|---:|---:|
| Cash | $1 722.16 | |
| Jack Young | 323.00 | |
| M. H. Watson | 72.00 | |
| G. H. Clarkson | 116.00 | |
| Office Equipment | 1 255.00 | |
| Automobile | 3 200.00 | |
| Office Supply Company | | $ 21.72 |
| Local Hydro | | 16.42 |
| Slick Oil Limited | | 31.19 |
| M. O. Arthur | | 6 000.00 |
| P. J. Arthur, Capital | | 1 277.50 |
| P. J. Arthur, Drawings | 1 000.00 | |
| Revenue | | 903.19 |
| Automobile Expenses | 65.12 | |
| Rent Expense | 170.00 | |
| Telephone Expense | 25.00 | |
| Salaries Expense | 280.00 | |
| Miscellaneous Expense | 13.74 | |
| Advertising Expense | 8.00 | |
| | $8 250.02 | $8 250.02 |

Prepare the six-column work sheet.

**8.** The trial balance of Morton Enterprises on February 28, 19—, after a fiscal period of three months, is as follows:

| | | |
|---|---:|---:|
| Cash | $ 462.12 | |
| Arthur Ball | 117.00 | |
| K. L. Rimmer | 92.55 | |
| Supplies | 150.00 | |
| Office Equipment | 741.00 | |
| Delivery Equipment | 2 840.00 | |
| Building | 17 340.00 | |
| General Supply Co. | | $ 94.80 |
| E. S. Thomas | | 52.00 |
| M. P. Morton, Capital | | 21 167.48 |
| M. P. Morton, Drawings | 200.00 | |
| Revenue | | 3 033.22 |
| Rent Expense | 360.00 | |
| Labor Expense | 1 530.00 | |
| Delivery Expense | 243.00 | |
| Power Expense | 162.63 | |
| General Expense | 109.20 | |
| | $24 347.50 | $24 347.50 |

Complete the six-column work sheet.

9. The completed work sheet for J. H. Devitt shows that he had a $20 300 credit balance in his capital account, that during the fiscal period he had drawings of $9 500, and that during the fiscal period the business had earned a net income of $12 800.

Using the above information, prepare the equity section of J. H. Devitt's balance sheet.

10. The completed work sheet for Mik's Delivery Service shows the following information:

1. The balance in the owner's (M. Hardy's) capital account was $5 040.50 credit.
2. The balance in the owner's drawings account was $15 000.
3. During the fiscal period Mik's Delivery Service had recorded a net income of $13 575.

Using the above information, prepare the equity section of the balance sheet for Mik's Delivery Service.

11. The finished work sheet of L. Nugent shows that:

1. The balance in his capital account was $14 000 credit.
2. His drawings during the year amounted to $8 500.
3. The business recorded a net loss of $2 000 for the year.

Complete the equity section of the balance sheet for L. Nugent.

12. The trial balance of Sturdy Insurance Agency on September 30, 19—, after a fiscal period of three months, is as follows:

| | | |
|---|---|---|
| Cash | $1 432.60 | |
| P. Norman | 76.00 | |
| V. Parker | 121.50 | |
| Supplies | 111.30 | |
| Office Equipment | 750.00 | |
| Automobile | 1 900.00 | |
| Winston Motors | | $ 441.00 |
| Harper Bros. | | 75.00 |
| D. K. Sandwell, Capital | | 3 995.80 |
| D. K. Sandwell, Drawings | 800.00 | |
| Commissions | | 2 240.80 |
| Rent Expense | 330.00 | |
| Car Expense | 277.50 | |
| Wages Expense | 540.00 | |
| Office Expense | 285.00 | |
| Miscellaneous Expense | 128.70 | |
| | $6 752.60 | $6 752.60 |

Complete the six-column work sheet and the financial statements.

**13.** The trial balance of P. C. Taylor, a lawyer, on June 30, 19—, after a fiscal period of six months, is as follows:

| | | |
|---|---:|---:|
| Cash | $ 516.20 | |
| C. Carlisle | 131.00 | |
| G. McGregor | 650.00 | |
| Office Supplies | 789.80 | |
| Automobile | 3 000.00 | |
| Office Equipment | 1 550.00 | |
| Professional Library | 1 270.00 | |
| Bank Loan | | $ 1 000.00 |
| T. D. Goodman | | 1 000.00 |
| A. E. Farrow | | 25.40 |
| P. C. Taylor, Capital | | 8 804.60 |
| P. C. Taylor, Drawings | 12 000.00 | |
| Fees Earned | | 14 721.61 |
| Rent Expense | 1 800.00 | |
| Salaries Expense | 2 645.51 | |
| Car Expense | 1 074.20 | |
| Miscellaneous Expense | 124.90 | |
| | $25 551.61 | $25 551.61 |

Complete the six-column work sheet and the financial statements.

**14.** The trial balance of Star Delivery Company on December 31, 19—, after a fiscal period of one year, is as follows:

| | | |
|---|---:|---:|
| Cash | $ 212.00 | |
| Chas. Green | 170.00 | |
| J. James | 351.00 | |
| V. Patterson | 12.60 | |
| Supplies | 651.00 | |
| Furniture and Fixtures | 900.00 | |
| Trucks | 7 050.00 | |
| Bank Loan | | $ 3 000.00 |
| Civic Trading Co. | | 746.00 |
| R. Rankin, Capital | | 11 925.60 |
| R. Rankin, Drawings | 5 000.00 | |
| Revenue | | 18 500.00 |
| Rent | 2 000.00 | |
| Gasoline and Oil | 1 800.00 | |
| Truck Repairs | 1 000.00 | |
| Insurance | 1 000.00 | |
| Miscellaneous Expense | 25.00 | |
| Wages | 14 000.00 | |
| | $34 171.60 | $34 171.60 |

Complete the six-column work sheet and the financial statements.

**15.** The ledger of General Laundry is prepared by the owner, S. J. Travis, who is not a skilled accountant. He arranges the accounts alphabetically. On November 30, 19—, the trial balance of General Laundry, after a fiscal period of one month, is as follows:

| | | |
|---|---:|---:|
| Ace Supply Co. | | $    43.20 |
| Bank Loan | | 1 000.00 |
| Cash | $1 610.01 | |
| Delivery Expense | 84.00 | |
| Delivery Truck | 1 800.00 | |
| Equipment | 4 750.00 | |
| R. Kirk | 15.00 | |
| J. Martin | 92.00 | |
| G. Leonard | 12.00 | |
| M. & S. Paint Co. | | 116.41 |
| H. Phillips | 157.51 | |
| Rent Expense | 100.00 | |
| Revenue | | 1 941.65 |
| Supplies | 220.90 | |
| S. J. Travis, Capital | | 6 290.16 |
| S. J. Travis, Drawings | 300.00 | |
| Wages Expense | 250.00 | |
| | $9 391.42 | $9 391.42 |

Complete the six-column work sheet.

**16.** You are to commence duties on November 1, 19—, at a salary of $265 per week, as accountant for J. Allen Lawson, a lawyer who has been in business for some years. In your new position you will be required to perform all the necessary accounting procedures to the point of preparing the financial statements at the end of each month.

The chart of accounts for this exercise appears below.

| Assets | No. | Liabilities | |
|---|---|---|---|
| Bank | 1 | C. H. C. Canadian Ltd. | 21 |
| Superior Cut Stone | 2 | Grande Oil Co. | 22 |
| Briggs Pharmacy | 3 | Toronado Furniture Co. | 23 |
| Arnold's Paving | 4 | Typewriters Limited | 24 |
| Warren Real Estate | 5 | | |
| Leyton and Leyton | 6 | | |
| Barter's Service Station | 7 | *Capital and Drawings* | |
| Weston Printing Co. | 8 | J. Allen Lawson, Capital | 31 |
| J. C. Carmen | 9 | J. Allen Lawson, Drawings | 32 |
| Office Supplies | 10 | | |
| Professional Library | 11 | | |
| Office Equipment | 12 | *Income* | |
| Automobile | 13 | Fees Earned | 41 |

| *Expenses* | | Miscellaneous Expense | 54 |
| Electricity Expense | 51 | Rent | 55 |
| Insurance Expense | 52 | Salaries Expense | 56 |
| Loss on Sale of Equipment | 53 | Travelling and Car Expense | 57 |

On October 31, 19—, the trial balance of the business is as shown below.

J. ALLEN LAWSON
TRIAL BALANCE
OCTOBER 31, 19—

|  | *Debits* | *Credits* |
|---|---|---|
| Bank | $2 062.54 | |
| Superior Cut Stone | 450.00 | |
| Briggs Pharmacy | 120.00 | |
| Arnold's Paving | 75.00 | |
| Office Supplies | 49.00 | |
| Professional Library | 330.75 | |
| Office Equipment | 501.60 | |
| Automobile | 2 475.00 | |
| C. H. C. Canadian Ltd. | | $ 75.00 |
| Grande Oil Co. | | 26.82 |
| Toronado Furniture Co. | | 125.00 |
| J. Allen Lawson, Capital | | 5 837.07 |
| | $6 063.89 | $6 063.89 |

Set up the ledger and the account balances as of October 31, 19—. If you are using the account paper that accompanies the text, it will be necessary to leave four accounts for Bank. Since this exercise involves a 'going concern', one that is continuing in business rather than just beginning, no opening entry is necessary. The technique for starting an exercise of this type is discussed in a special note on page 52.

The business transactions for the month of November are listed below. These transactions are to be journalized on journal page number 62. In recording the transactions, you are to assume that all money received is deposited daily in the bank account.

*Transactions*
November
3 Received $200 on account from Superior Cut Stone.
3 Issued invoice No. 76 to Warren Real Estate for services rendered; amount, $100.
5 Purchased $5 of postage stamps; cheque No. 71 was issued.

6 Paid the Grande Oil Co. account in full; cheque No. 72 was issued.
7 Mr. Lawson withdrew $100 for his personal use; cheque No. 73 was issued.
7 Paid the accountant's salary; cheque No. 74 was issued.
7 Paid $45 for professional books purchased for the office library; cheque No. 75 was

issued to the Provincial Law Association.

10 Purchased $36 of office supplies from Wilkins Brothers and issued cheque No. 76 in payment.

10 Issued invoice No. 77 to Leyton and Leyton for services rendered; amount, $375.

12 Received $120 on account from Briggs Pharmacy.

12 Purchased a new typewriter from Typewriters Limited on account. The price of the new typewriter was $315. As a down payment on the new machine, Typewriters Limited agreed to accept an old typewriter as a trade-in and gave an allowance of $75 on it. The old machine had originally cost $225 and was included in the Office Equipment account at that figure.

**Note:** At first glance, the above transaction appears to be a difficult one. But it and all other transactions can be worked out if you follow the rules that have been developed. Do not give up easily.

13 Paid $37.25 to the Local Garage for car repairs; cheque No. 77 was issued.

13 Received $10 cash from G. Frankland for services rendered.

14 Mr. Lawson withdrew $90 for his personal use; cheque No. 78 was issued.

14 Paid the accountant's salary; cheque No. 79 was issued.

17 Paid C.H.C. Canadian Ltd. account in full; cheque No. 80 was issued.

18 Received a phone call from Toronado Furniture Co. requesting payment of their account claimed to be $225. This phone call brought to light an error of $100 made by the previous accountant in recording the purchase of an office desk. After correcting the error, the Toronado Furniture Co. account was paid in full. Cheque No. 81 was issued.

**Note:** Think carefully about the above transaction; all the information that you need is

available.

19 Issued invoice No. 78 in the amount of $125 to Arnold's Paving for services rendered.

20 Received $20 cash from P. Morgan for services rendered.

20 Purchased $55 worth of office supplies from Dean's Stationery; cheque No. 82 was issued.

21 Mr. Lawson withdrew $100 for his personal use; cheque No. 83 was issued.

21 Paid the accountant's salary; cheque No. 84 was issued.

24 Paid the monthly insurance premium of $7.20. Cheque No. 85 was issued to Consumer's Insurance Company.

25 Issued invoice No. 79 for $100 to Barter's Service Station for services rendered.

25 Issued invoice No. 80 for $150 to Weston Printing Co. for services rendered.

26 Purchased $5 of postage stamps; cheque No. 86 was issued.

26 Received a cheque from Superior Cut Stone for the balance of their account.

26 Received $75 on account from Arnold's Paving.

27 Issued invoice No. 81 for $1 275 to J. C. Carmen for services rendered.

27 Paid the monthly telephone bill; cheque No. 87 in the amount of $16.50 was issued to the local telephone company.

27 Paid the electricity bill for the month; cheque No. 88 in the amount of $8.27 was issued to the local hydroelectric company.

28 Received an invoice from Grande Oil Co. for the gasoline and oil used in the automobile during the month; amount, $18.60.

28 Paid the rent for the month; cheque No. 89 in the amount of $125 was issued to E. French.

28 The proprietor withdrew $110 for his personal use; cheque No. 90 was issued.

28 Paid the accountant's salary for the week; cheque No. 91 was issued.

**Remember that you are to perform all the accounting functions required to the point of completing the financial statements.**

# Cases

## Case 1

On January 1, 19—, the capital of the Star Supply Company was $65 000. A local freight company had been hired in the past to make their deliveries. Once a month their statement was paid and Truck Expense account was debited. During the year the company decided to purchase its own truck, which cost $4 000. Since the truck would replace the local delivery service, the accountant debited the $4 000 to Truck Expense.

1. Do you agree that the cost of the truck should have been debited to Truck Expense? Explain.
2. If new tires are purchased for the truck, would they be debited to Truck Expense?

## Case 2

J. Orr sets up his general ledger in such a way that all his accounts with debit balances are listed first, followed by all his accounts with credit balances. He finds this method faster and easier when he takes a trial balance on an adding machine tape.

Do you agree with Orr's method? Explain.

## Case 3

John Roberts, the proprietor of a hardware store, withdrew $1 275.00 cash on December 31. His father, an automobile dealer, gave John a new delivery truck valued at $6 000.00 as a Christmas present. In auditing the books, you find that the transactions were combined and entered thus:

|  | Dr. | Cr. |
|---|---|---|
| Delivery Truck | $4 725.00 | |
| John Roberts, Capital | | $4 725.00 |
| To record additional investment in the business | | |

1. Did the accountant record the transactions correctly?
2. Will the trial balance balance?
3. Make any adjusting entry or entries necessary.

## Case 4

As the company accountant, you have just presented the financial statements to the owner showing a net profit of $45 000. 'That is impossible,' exclaims the owner. 'The company has fifteen thousand dollars less cash than it had last year.' What explanations can you give to the owner?

## Case 5

The accountant for the Mac Delivery Company incorrectly transfers the balance of the Truck Repairs account to the Balance Sheet Debit column of the work sheet.

1. Will this error be discovered when the net income is calculated on the work sheet?
2. What is the effect of this error on the net income as calculated on the work sheet?
3. When is an error of this type likely to be discovered?

## Case 6

William Kosmik, manager of Lawson Enterprises, prepares his income statement for May.

INCOME STATEMENT

MAY 31, 19—

WILLIAM KOSMIK, MANAGER

*Receipts:*

| | | |
|---|---|---|
| Cash Sales | | $ 8 950.00 |
| Bank Loan | | 1 000.00 |
| Total Revenue | | $ 9 950.00 |

*Payments:*

| | | |
|---|---|---|
| Office Salaries | $1 000.00 | |
| William Kosmik's Salary | 600.00 | |
| Salesmen's Salaries | 2 400.00 | |
| Payment for Truck | 4 500.00 | |
| Utilities | 500.00 | |
| Rent | 300.00 | |
| Furniture Purchased | 952.00 | |
| Total Expenses | | $10 252.00 |
| Net Loss | | $ 302.00 |

Prepare a list of all the errors which you can find in Kosmik's income statement, and indicate why each is an error.

## Case 7

R. Prince is in the process of preparing his first work sheet at the end of the year. In the process he has transferred a liability account from the trial balance to the debit column of the balance sheet section of the work sheet. Explain to Prince why the work sheet will not balance. What incorrect figures would result from this error?

## Case 8

A. R. Smith began a business on January 1 by investing $12 000 cash in the business. During the year the business had sales of $40 000 and incurred expenses of $34 500. He withdrew cash of $4 000 during the year for his personal use. He turned over to the business for use by the business his personal automobile valued at $3 000.
1. What was the amount of net income of the business for the year?
2. What was the amount of net assets at the beginning of the year? At the end of the year? What caused the increase or decrease in net assets during the year?

# 7 Subsidiary Ledger Accounting

## Growth of a Business

Businessmen are of a special breed. Because their personal prosperity, and to a considerable extent their social status, depend on their businesses, they work hard to make their businesses succeed. Most do achieve success and growth; they would not be in business for long otherwise.

As a business grows, a point is quickly reached at which one person no longer can handle all of the required accounting and office duties. At this point, the owner is forced to hire additional office staff. In so doing, keeping one eye on the profit of the business, he will normally try to hire as 'low-priced' help as he can; that is, persons whose skills and training are just enough to do the jobs that he has in mind for them.

## Division of Labor

The pressure to keep costs down has been responsible for the development of a technique that permits the bulk of the office duties to be handled by a number of junior employees under the direction of a few senior persons.

**Subsidiary ledgers** and **control accounts**, the subject of this chapter, is one such universally used accounting technique that permits an efficient and economical division of duties in a business office.

## Growth of a Ledger

As a business grows, its ledger grows too, but in a special way. In a ledger, most of the growth takes place in respect to the accounts of customers and creditors – as new customers and suppliers are sought out by an aggressive management. The other ledger accounts remain fairly stationary in number; they seem to change only in respect to the size of their balances.

The way in which a ledger grows may be illustrated by the following diagram. It shows most of the expansion taking place in the accounts of customers and creditors, the other accounts remaining fairly stationary in number.

Illustration of the Growth of a Ledger

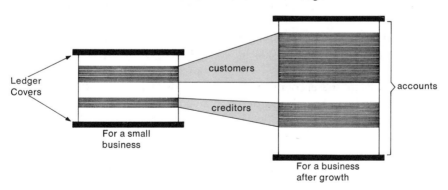

Ledger Covers

customers

creditors

For a small business

accounts

For a business after growth

Observe that once a business gets beyond the small stage, its ledger may be dominated by the accounts of customers and creditors. In many large companies the number of customers' accounts is phenomenal; for example, consider the accounts of The Bell Telephone Company.

## Subsidiary Ledgers and Control Accounts

It has already been pointed out that in a mature business the office work is divided so that the bulk of it can be performed by less highly trained junior personnel under the guidance of a few senior persons. This is an economical way to run an office.

The recording of customers' and creditors' accounts is ideally suited to a division of duties. You have already seen that a large part of the ledger consists of customers' and creditors' accounts. Too, you may have guessed that these accounts involve a great deal of accounting activity.

To begin the study of subsidiary ledgers, examine the ledger shown in Illustration A at right. This ledger (shown in T accounts for simplicity) is typical except for the fact that the number of customers' and creditors' accounts is small.

**Note:** The theory of subsidiary ledgers holds true regardless of the number of customers' and creditors' accounts. It is easier, but equally correct, for the author to explain the system using only a few such accounts. Remember, though, that the practical advantage of the system is in situations where the number of such accounts is large.

From this ledger extract all of the accounts of customers and creditors and set them aside in two separate groups.

In each new group, delete the account numbers, arrange the accounts in alphabetical order, and place the customers' and creditors' addresses on their account pages.

By definition, a group of accounts constitutes a ledger. Each of the two new groups of accounts

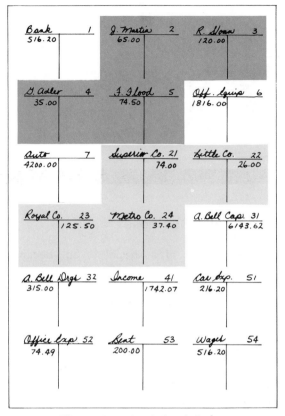

*Illustration A. A simple ledger.*

conforms to this definition and is, therefore, itself a ledger. The two new ledgers, arranged alphabetically for greater convenience in handling, are shown in Illustration B on page 97. They are known as subsidiary ledgers.

The ledger of customers' accounts, representing amounts receivable from customers, is known as the **accounts receivable ledger** or sometimes as the customers' ledger. The accounts in it usually have debit balances. Occasionally, a credit balance may occur; for example, when a customer overpays his account. The ledger of creditors' accounts, representing amounts payable to creditors, is known as the **accounts payable ledger**. These accounts usually have credit balances. Both of the new ledgers are called subsidiary ledgers, a term that will be specifically defined later in this chapter.

Now that there are three ledgers in the system it is necessary to be able to identify each one individually in order to avoid any possible confusion. For this reason, the main ledger, the one

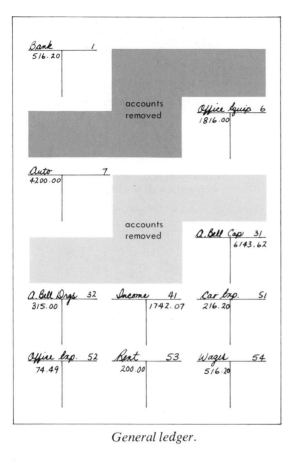

*General ledger.*

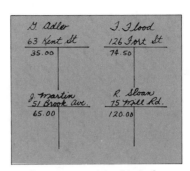

*Accounts receivable ledger (a subsidiary ledger).*

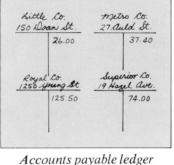

*Accounts payable ledger (a subsidiary ledger).*

you are accustomed to using, is given the name **general ledger**.

The changeover to the three-ledger system is not yet completed. Since certain accounts were removed from it, the general ledger in Illustration B is no longer in balance; that is, it no longer balances within itself. For two reasons it cannot be left in this state. First, the concept of the ledger 'balancing' is fundamentally important. Second, the general ledger, from which the financial statements are derived, must include the complete financial picture.

The next step, therefore, is to open two new accounts in the general ledger to replace all of those accounts that were previously taken out and placed in separate ledgers. The two new accounts, given the names Accounts Receivable and Accounts Payable, are shown in Illustration C on page 98. Notice that the Accounts Receivable account in the general ledger is given a balance of $294.50 Dr. which is equal to the total

value of all the customers' accounts that it replaced. Similarly, the Accounts Payable account in the general ledger is given a balance of $262.90 Cr. which is equal to the total value of all the creditors' accounts that it replaced.

Each of the two new accounts in the general ledger is called a control account or controlling account, a term that will be defined later in this chapter.

The final appearance of the three-ledger system is shown in Illustration C.

## Subsidiary Ledger Defined

A **subsidiary ledger** is a separate ledger that contains a number of accounts of a similar nature; these several accounts make up the detailed information in respect to one particular control account in the general ledger.

*Illustration C. The simple three-ledger system.*

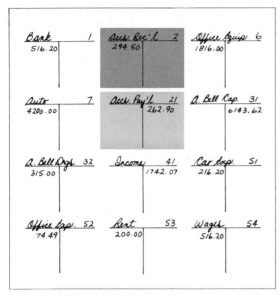

General ledger (in balance).

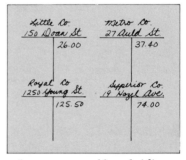

Accounts receivable subsidiary ledger (equal in value to its control account).

Accounts payable subsidiary ledger (equal in value to its control account).

## Control Account Defined

A **control account** is a general ledger account that shows the total value of a particular financial item, the details of which are maintained in a separate supporting subsidiary ledger.

## Accounts Receivable and Payable on the Balance Sheet

The person responsible for preparing the financial statements should do so only after the three ledgers are balanced. Only then can he be sure that the books of account are mechanically correct.

With the three-ledger system, it is no longer necessary to list the individual customers and creditors on the balance sheet. In fact, these individual accounts will not even appear on the work sheet, the source of information for statement preparation. Now the balance sheet will show the total of Accounts Receivable and the

total of Accounts Payable as illustrated by the partial balance sheet shown below.

**DR. P. R. PROCTOR**
**BALANCE SHEET**
**MARCH 31, 19–3**

ASSETS

*Current Assets*

| | | |
|---|---|---|
| Bank | $1 650.21 | |
| Accounts Receivable | 7 086.14 | |
| Supplies | 1 276.00 | $10 012.35 |

*Fixed Assets*

| | | |
|---|---|---|
| Equipment | $3 040.00 | |
| Automobile | 5 075.00 | 8 115.00 |
| | | $18 127.35 |

LIABILITIES

*Current Liabilities*

| | |
|---|---|
| Accounts Payable | $ 4 072.16 |

# Flowcharts

You should now have in mind a picture of the three-ledger system, although you do not as yet know how to operate it.

The operation of the three-ledger system cannot be separated from the rather involved matters of office procedures and clerical routines. It is only within the context of the whole office system that the operation of the three-ledger system can be adequately described.

One of the purposes of this textbook is to acquaint you with the important fundamental aspects of accounting systems, routines, and procedures. It has been found that the most suitable method of describing these accounting systems is by means of flowcharts and accompanying explanatory notes. Flowcharts are used extensively for this purpose throughout the remainder of this text. Therefore, before continuing with the study of subsidiary ledgers, let us break off briefly in order to examine the techniques of flowcharting as used in this text. Then, having accomplished this, we can take immediate advantage of this very useful accounting tool.

The flowcharting techniques used in this text describe office routines, systems, and procedures by means of diagrams and accompanying explanatory notes.

The flowcharting procedures described below are adapted from standard flowcharting techniques in order to illustrate more clearly the employees' functions within the organization:

1. Geometric symbols such as rectangles and squares are used to indicate various business documents, books, ledgers, forms, lists, etc. To assist him in drawing the symbols, a person usually has a flowcharting template such as the one illustrated below.

2. Solid lines with arrows are used to indicate the physical movement or path of the documents through the various stages of processing to their ultimate place of permanent storage (file). The chart is usually drawn so that the flow moves from left to right and from top to bottom.

3. Broken lines with arrows are used to indicate that information is taken from one document and is used to prepare another document, or to carry out an action (e.g. make a telephone call).

4. A triangle such as that shown below is used to represent a permanent storage file. Within the triangle, there appears the letter 'N', 'A', or 'D' which indicates respectively that the file is kept numerically, alphabetically, or by date.

5. The work locations (desks) of office employees are indicated by shaded green rectangles.

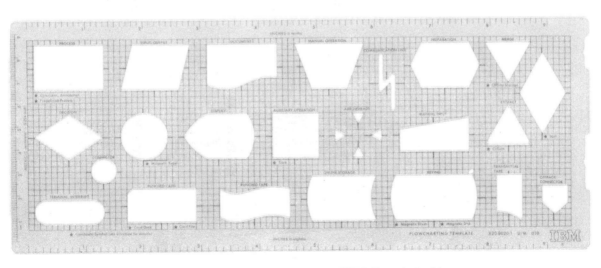

*Flowchart template (courtesy of IBM Canada Ltd.).*

6. The circled numerals refer to accompanying explanatory notes that provide the detailed information in respect to the various aspects of the business system being described.

## Basic Procedures for Accounts Receivable and Accounts Payable

On the next few pages, you will find flowcharts describing a basic accounts receivable procedure and a basic accounts payable procedure. It is your job to study these flowcharts together with the accompanying explanatory notes in order to acquire an understanding of these two important procedures. Do not presume that the procedures described here are followed precisely in every business office; this is not the case. An office manager may vary the basic procedure to suit his own special needs.

Primarily, flowchart #1 illustrates the following:

a. Certain business documents, known as **source documents**, play an important role in the accounting process and are the source of the accounting entries. In this particular procedure, the source documents are the copies of the sales invoices and the copies of the daily lists of cash receipts. These source docu-

---

**Flowchart 1  A Basic Accounts Receivable Procedure**

*Accounting Department*

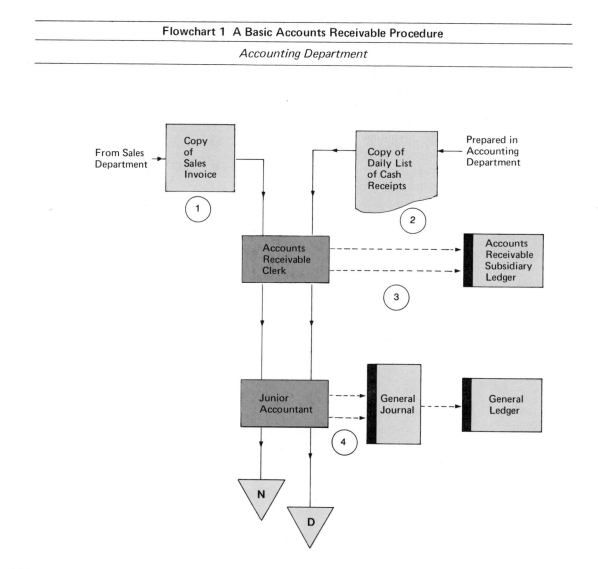

ments move from desk to desk during the accounting process; eventually, they are stored in permanent files.

b. A division of duties exists in a business office. In this particular case one employee maintains the accounts receivable ledger whereas a second employee prepares the general journal.

## Notes to Flowchart #1

① A multi-part sales invoice (see illustration on page 63) is prepared for each sale on account. (A full sales procedure flowchart is shown in Chapter 12.)

② Cheques received from customers are deposited in the bank each day. Before depositing them it is necessary to prepare a listing (in duplicate) as a permanent record of the pertinent information.

③ **Posting** It is the job of the accounts receivable clerk to keep the accounts receivable ledger up to date. This is accomplished by posting daily to the accounts in the ledger directly from the source documents that arrive on the desk of the accounts receivable clerk.

Posting, which was previously defined as the transferring of information to the ledger from the journal, must now be considered in a broader light to include also the transferring of information to the ledger directly from the source documents.

*Sales Invoices.* For each sales invoice a debit entry must be made to a customer's account. Once or twice each day a quantity of numbered sales invoices arrives at the desk of the accounts receivable clerk. This clerk places the pile of invoices before him and posts each one in turn to the appropriate customer's account. He records (a) the date, (b) the invoice number (in the Particulars column), (c) the debit amount, and (d) the new balance. To indicate that the posting of an invoice has been completed, the clerk places a check mark or his initials on the sales invoice as a final step. No cross-referencing is done, as it is for general ledger posting.

*Cash Receipts.* Each receipt from a customer represents a credit to the customer's account. On each business day, a copy of the daily list of cash receipts is forwarded to the desk of the accounts receivable clerk. He posts each receipt from a customer to the appropriate customer's account, showing the date, the credit amount, and the new balance. As each receipt is posted, it is checked off on the listing. No cross-referencing is necessary.

④ The junior accountant journalizes the routine transactions of the business in the general journal. A number of source documents arrives at his desk each day. Among these source documents are the copies of the sales invoices and the daily lists of cash receipts.

Journalizing is done as before except that transactions affecting customers' accounts must now be written in terms of the general ledger account for customers; namely, Accounts Receivable. For example, a sale on account is journalized as follows:

| | | | | | | | | | | |
|---|---|---|---|---|---|---|---|---|---|---|
| 16 | Accounts Receivable | | | | 164 | – | | | | |
| | Income | | | | | | | 164 | – | |
| | Invoice #216 to P. Norris | | | | | | | | | |

Similarly, a receipt on account is journalized as follows:

| | | | | | | | | | | |
|---|---|---|---|---|---|---|---|---|---|---|
| 19 | Bank | | | | 75 | 42 | | | | |
| | Accounts Receivable | | | | | | | 75 | 42 | |
| | Payment received from C. Watson | | | | | | | | | |

Primarily, flowchart #2 illustrates the following:

a. The business **source documents** in respect to the basic accounts payable procedure are (a) the matched sets of **purchase orders**, **receiving reports**, and **purchase invoices**, (b) the cheque copies. These source documents move from desk to desk during the accounting process. Eventually, they are filed in permanent storage.

b. The main division of duties is such that one employee maintains the accounts payable ledger and another employee prepares the general journal.

## Notes to Flowchart #2

① **Purchase Order** The Purchasing Department is responsible for the purchasing of goods and services. To order goods and services, a purchase order form showing all the pertinent details of the order is sent to the supplier. One copy is sent to the Accounting Department. (A full description of the purchasing function is described in Chapter 12.)

**Receiving Report** As goods are received by the business, they are counted and inspected by members of the Receiving Department. A receiving report is prepared

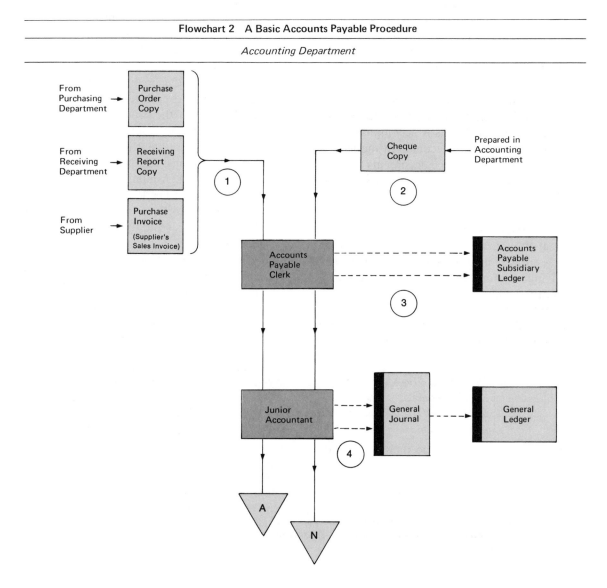

Flowchart 2   A Basic Accounts Payable Procedure

*Accounting Department*

which shows all of the important data in respect to the goods received. A copy of the receiving report is sent to the Accounting Department. (The receiving function is described in detail in Chapter 12.)

**Purchase Invoice** Whenever a business makes a sale on account it sends to the purchaser a sales invoice which shows the details of the transaction and requests payment. In the Accounting Department of the purchaser these suppliers' sales invoices are referred to as purchase invoices in order to distinguish them from the business's own sales invoices.

The first step in processing purchase invoices is to match the purchase order, the receiving report, and the purchase invoice. (These matched sets are then put through additional verifying steps which are described in Chapter 12.)

② Cheques are prepared and issued to the supplier a few days before payment is due. (Cheque preparation is described fully in Chapter 12.)

③ **Posting** The accounts payable clerk keeps the accounts payable ledger up to date by posting daily from the source documents that arrive at his desk.

*Purchase Invoices.* Each matched pur-chase invoice set requires that a credit entry be made to a supplier's account. The clerk posts from the matched set to the appropriate account, recording the date, the credit amount, and the new balance. After completing each posting he initials or places a check mark on the purchase invoice. No cross-referencing is done.

*Cheque Copies.* Each cheque copy (if it is paying an account payable) requires a debit entry to a supplier's account. The clerk posts the date, the debit amount, and records the new balance. He then initials or places a check mark on the cheque copy. No cross-referencing is done.

④ The junior accountant journalizes the routine transactions of the business in the general journal. A number of source documents arrives at his desk each day. Among these source documents are the purchase invoice matched sets and the cheque copies.

Journalizing is done as before except that transactions affecting creditors' accounts must now be written in terms of the general ledger account for creditors; namely, Accounts Payable. For example, a purchase of merchandise on account is journalized as follows:

| | 12 | Purchases | | | 275 | - | | | |
|---|---|---|---|---|---|---|---|---|---|
| | | Accounts Payable | | | | | 275 | - | |
| | | Merch. purchased from C. Stanby; P.I 1406 | | | | | | | |

Similarly, a payment on account is journalized as follows:

| | 29 | Accounts Payable | | | 64 | 20 | | | |
|---|---|---|---|---|---|---|---|---|---|
| | | Bank | | | | | 64 | 20 | |
| | | Cheque #156 issued to Warner's Hardware | | | | | | | |

## Posting to the General Ledger

The general ledger is posted in the usual manner with one exception. It is no longer necessary to keep it always up to date. Only the customers' and creditors' accounts must be posted daily.

Now that the customers' and creditors' accounts are kept separately, it is general practice to refrain from posting to the general ledger until the end of the month and then to do the posting in one concentrated effort. This is a far more efficient way of posting.

If it is found necessary to know the daily bank balance, it can be maintained in various ways other than by posting to the general ledger.

## Balancing the Ledgers

It is standard practice to balance all of the ledgers at the end of every month, after all postings have been completed.

To balance the general ledger, there is no change in the procedure already described. The most common method is to use an adding machine to total all of the account balances. The accounts with debit balances are entered as additions and the accounts with credit balances are entered as deductions. If the ledger is in balance, the total of the tape will be zero.

The procedure for balancing a subsidiary ledger is quite different and is described by means of the block flowchart at right. The balancing of a subsidiary ledger is usually the responsibility of the clerk in charge of the ledger. You must remember not to try to balance a subsidiary ledger until both the subsidiary ledger and the general ledger are posted up to date.

## Locating Errors when a Subsidiary Ledger does not Balance

As indicated by the flow in the top half of flowchart #3, the state of the subsidiary ledger is not acceptable until it is balanced with the control account. To be balanced, the sum of all its accounts must agree with the balance of its control account. Only then can the balancing procedure be brought to a conclusion.

When it is found that a subsidiary ledger does not balance, a search for the errors must be made. In conducting the search, let your guiding principle be this: whenever an amount is entered in any account in the subsidiary ledger, there must be an equivalent amount entered in the control account – and vice versa.

In your search for errors, there is no need to go back in the ledgers beyond the current month. The ledgers will have been balanced at the end of the previous month. The ledgers are balanced at the end of every month and there will be trial balance tapes on file as evidence. If errors exist in the accounts, you may rest assured that they were made in the current month.

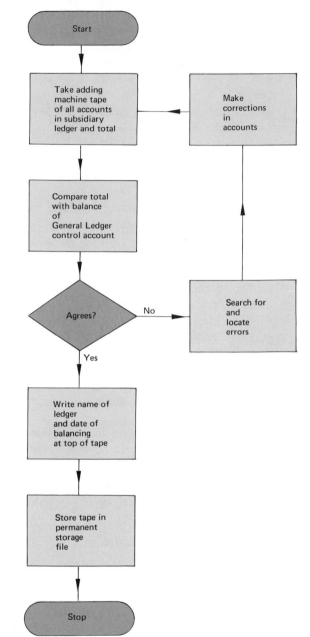

## Statement of Account

A **statement of account** is a record of a customer's account for a period of one month. It is standard practice to send a statement of account to each customer once a month. This informs him of the entries made to his account during the month and also of the balance owed. The

Arthur St.
Dial 999-6189

# McCAULEY'S LIMITED
## THUNDER BAY, ONTARIO
## P7E 5M9

Sold To

Mrs. G. Jones,
536 Cherrydale,
Thunder Bay, Ontario,
P7E 3N6

Importers and
Distributors

| Date | Particulars | Charges | Credits | Balance |
|------|-------------|---------|---------|---------|
| | | | Balance Brought Forward | 24.11 |
| NOV30 | PURSE | 17.35 | | 41.46 |
| DEC12 | 3175 | | 24.11 | 17.35 |

Interest Charged at 1% Per Month
If Not Paid During Month Following Purchase

*Statement of account – regular.*

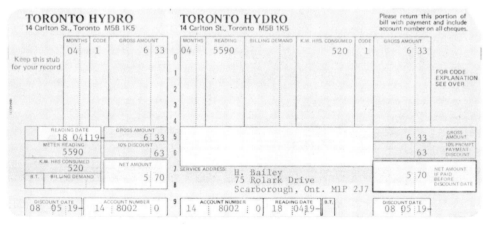

*Statement of account – punch card (courtesy of Toronto Hydro).*

customer can compare the statement with his own records to see if they are in agreement. A statement of account also serves as a subtle reminder to the customer that prompt payment of his account is expected.

In systems where the posting is done by machines, it is usual to use collated (partially matched) ledger accounts and statement. In this way, the ledger account and the statement can be prepared simultaneously.

## Non-Routine Entries to Subsidiary Ledgers

You have seen that accounting systems are designed so that the information flows to the office clerks by means of business source documents or vouchers. However, there are some transactions for which there are no source documents and which do not fit into the regular accounting routine. Transactions of this nature are not usually made known to the office clerks.

Consider the following:

J. Wiggins, a well-known and popular gentleman in a small community, owes a small disputed balance of $4.80 to Falls & Co. Suddenly Mr. Wiggins dies. The owner of Falls & Co., E. Falls, decides that it would be wise to pay the disputed

bill himself rather than to risk the chance of being a nuisance to the bereaved family and of possibly obtaining a bad reputation in the town. Accordingly, he instructs his accountant to write off the Wiggins balance and to charge it to his own (E. Falls) Drawings account.

Non-routine transactions are usually the full responsibility of the accountant alone. In addition to making the journal entry, he will also make any necessary postings to a subsidiary ledger. And he will do so promptly because the subsidiary ledger must be kept up to date.

The journal entry to write off the J. Wiggins account, after completing the posting of the subsidiary ledger, is as shown below, top.

Observe that completion of the posting to the subsidiary ledger is indicated by drawing a diagonal line through the Posting Reference column of the journal and placing a check mark in one of the halves. There is no source document to initial.

At the end of the month, this journal entry, along with all of the others for the month, is posted to the general ledger and cross-referenced in the usual manner. Observe that the $4.80 credit requires a double posting. The check mark indicates the posting to the subsidiary ledger; the numeral 2 indicates the posting to the Accounts Receivable account in the general ledger.

| | 14 | E. Falls Drawings | | | 4 80 | | |
| | | Accounts Receivable (J. Wiggins) | ✓ | | | | 4 80 |
| | | To write off the account of J. Wiggins, | | | | | |
| | | deceased, as instructed by E. Falls | | | | | |

| | 14 | E. Falls Drawings | 32 | | 4 80 | | |
| | | Accounts Receivable (J. Wiggins) | 2/✓ | | | | 4 80 |
| | | To write off the account of J. Wiggins, | | | | | |
| | | deceased, as instructed by E. Falls | | | | | |

# Bookkeeping and Accounting Terms

**Subsidiary Ledger** A separate ledger that contains a number of accounts of a similar nature. These several accounts make up the detailed

information in respect to one particular control account in the general ledger.

**Control Account** A general ledger account that

shows the total value of a particular financial item, the details of which are maintained in a separate supporting subsidiary ledger.

**Accounts Receivable Ledger** A book or file containing all the accounts of debtors (usually customers).

**Accounts Payable Ledger** A book or file containing all the accounts of creditors (usually suppliers).

**General Ledger** A book or file containing all the accounts of the business (other than those in subsidiary ledgers). It is these accounts that represent the complete financial position of the business or organization.

**Flowchart** A diagram or pictorial representation of a system or procedure.

**Cash Receipts** Cheques or cash received by the business, most commonly from customers paying their bills or from sales paid for in cash. Cash receipts are usually deposited in the bank on a daily basis.

**Customer's Statement of Account** A copy or duplicate record of the customer's account for a one-month period. Statements of account are sent to customers every month.

**Purchase Order** A business document prepared by the Purchasing Department detailing all pertinent information about an agreement to purchase goods or services.

**Receiving Slip** A business document prepared by the Receiving Department detailing all pertinent information in respect to a shipment of goods received into the business.

**Purchase Invoice** The manner of describing the supplier's sales invoice in the office of the purchaser to distinguish it from the purchaser's own sales invoice.

**Source Document** Any business form or paper of the type that gives rise to an accounting entry. (The source document will be the supporting voucher for the accounting entry.)

# Review Questions

1. Explain why only a few highly skilled persons are needed in an office.
2. What is meant by division of labor?
3. Describe briefly the way in which the accounts of a business grow.
4. In what ledger are the accounts of creditors kept? of debtors?
5. Give the names of the three ledgers in the three-ledger system.
6. Briefly describe flowcharting.
7. On a flowchart, what technique is used to indicate the flow of documents? of information?
8. Explain the purpose of the notes that accompany a flowchart.
9. Describe a sales invoice.
10. Explain what is meant by 'cash receipts'.
11. Posting is ordinarily performed by two methods. What are they?
12. What is a source document?
13. When posting directly from source documents, how does the clerk indicate that the posting has been completed?
14. In the accounts payable ledger, are purchase invoices posted as debits or credits?
15. Define 'control account'.
16. Define 'subsidiary ledger'.
17. Before attempting to balance the three ledgers, what must one be sure of?
18. When a subsidiary ledger does not balance with its control account, what procedure is followed?
19. In searching for errors, how far back in the records must one investigate?
20. What is a statement of account?
21. What is a purchase order?
22. Describe what is meant by matching.
23. Explain why non-routine transactions have to be handled differently.

# Exercises

1. The trial balance of Proctor's Pet Store is shown below.

PROCTOR'S PET STORE
TRIAL BALANCE
JUNE 30, 19—

| | | |
|---|---:|---:|
| Bank | $ 714 | |
| P. Smith | 35 | |
| J. Britt | 75 | |
| C. Powell | 102 | |
| D. Main | 56 | |
| W. Axwell | 27 | |
| Supplies | 250 | |
| Equipment | 1 575 | |
| Cleaners' Supply House | | $ 210 |
| Wendell's Store | | 57 |
| Arnwell Animal Hospital | | 135 |
| H. Proctor, Capital | | 2 442 |
| H. Proctor, Drawings | 5 000 | |
| Revenue | | 7 250 |
| Light and Heat Expense | 350 | |
| Miscellaneous Expense | 295 | |
| Rent Expense | 1 500 | |
| Telephone Expense | 115 | |
| | $10 094 | $10 094 |

Calculate the value of the accounts receivable accounts.

Calculate the value of the accounts payable accounts.

After H. Proctor changes over to a three-ledger system of accounting, with subsidiary ledgers and control accounts:

a. Show the general ledger trial balance.
b. Show the accounts receivable subsidiary ledger trial balance and agree it with the general ledger control account.
c. Show the accounts payable subsidiary ledger trial balance and agree it with the general ledger control account.

2. **H. Feebie decides to change his accounting system to a three-ledger system. On December 31, 19—, his trial balance is as shown below.**

FEEBIE'S REPAIR SERVICE
TRIAL BALANCE
DECEMBER 31, 19—

| | | |
|---|---:|---:|
| Bank | $ 1 420 | |
| N. Storey | 112 | |
| G. Walker | 75 | |
| P. Bush | 157 | |
| C. Danson | 35 | |
| Supplies | 1 057 | |
| Delivery Truck | 5 902 | |
| Tools and Equipment | 3 755 | |
| Watson Electric | | $ 265 |
| Jack's Machine Shop | | 315 |
| Pete's Welding | | 75 |
| City Gasolines | | 170 |
| H. Feebie, Capital | | 11 207 |
| H. Feebie, Drawings | 7 500 | |
| Revenue | | 10 055 |
| Delivery Expense | 257 | |
| Light and Heat | 195 | |
| Miscellaneous Expense | 105 | |
| Rent | 1 200 | |
| Wages | 317 | |
| | $22 087 | $22 087 |

**After the changeover, show:**

a. **The general ledger trial balance;**

b. **The accounts receivable subsidiary ledger trial balance, balanced with its control account in the general ledger;**

c. **The accounts payable subsidiary ledger trial balance, balanced with its control account in the general ledger.**

3. **This exercise is to be done in your workbook, or as directed by your teacher.**

**4.** This exercise is to be done in your workbook, or as directed by your teacher.

**5.** In your own words and in point form provide a simple explanation of each of the following flowchart segments based on the system established for this text on page 99.

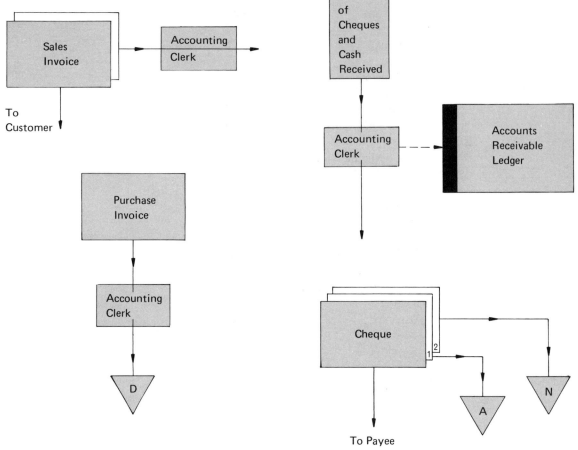

**6.** Among your office duties with the Quick Distributing Co. are those of the accounts receivable clerk. From business documents arriving on your desk you are to post daily to the customers' accounts.

On the morning of each working day, there arrive on your desk the following business documents:

a. Copies of all sales invoices issued on the previous working day by the Sales Department.

b. A listing of the day's cash receipts, prepared first thing each morning by the clerk who opens the mail.

Set up the accounts receivable ledger as of June 30, 19—, from the following detailed trial balance:

QUICK DISTRIBUTING CO.
ACCOUNTS RECEIVABLE TRIAL BALANCE
JUNE 30, 19—

| | | |
|---|---|---:|
| Adams Bros., 12 Mountain Avenue | Inv. No. 480 | $ 67.20 |
| | 507 | 94.20 |
| Defoe & Son, 620 Main Street | 512 | 75.65 |
| A. G. Farmer, 120A Blackwell Ave. | 514 | 315.62 |
| S. P. Handy, Ltd., 75 Porter Ave. | 484 | 216.25 |
| | 511 | 200.22 |
| R. Mortimer, 60 Hawley Crescent | 470 | 516.25 |
| | 496 | 621.90 |
| | 505 | 608.36 |
| Renforth Sales, 192 Dale Place | 510 | 137.62 |
| Vista Limited, 2001 Central Ave. | 515 | 50.00 |
| | | $2 903.27 |

From the following business papers, post to the customers' accounts daily:

| | | | | |
|---|---|---|---|---:|
| July 2 | Invoices | No. 516 Adams Bros. | | $59.24 |
| | | No. 517 Renforth Sales | | $145.50 |
| | Receipts | A. G. Farmer | No. 514 | $315.62 |
| | | S. P. Handy, Ltd. | No. 484 | $216.25 |
| 3 | Invoice | No. 518 Defoe & Son | | $75.85 |
| | Receipts | Nil | | |
| 4 | Invoices | No. 519 A. G. Farmer | | $217.90 |
| | | No. 520 The Williams Company | | |
| | | 417 Lake Street | | $150.00 |
| | Receipts | Adams Bros. | No. 480 | $67.20 |
| | | R. Mortimer  No. 470 & No. 496 | | $1 138.15 |
| 5 | Invoices | No. 521 Vista Limited | | $94.95 |
| | | No. 522 S. P. Handy, Ltd. | | $104.16 |
| | | No. 523 R. Mortimer | | $56.00 |
| | Receipt | Renforth Sales | No. 510 | $137.62 |
| 6 | Invoices | No. 524 Adams Bros. | | $167.07 |
| | | No. 525 The Williams Company | | $75.00 |
| | Receipts | Defoe & Son | No. 512 | $75.65 |
| | | Vista Limited | No. 515 | $50.00 |

Take off a trial balance of the subsidiary ledger as of July 6 and balance the subsidiary ledger with the control account. The senior accountant has arrived at a control account figure of $2 048.45.

**7.** On September 30, 19—, the detailed accounts payable trial balance of Magnetic Controls Company was as follows:

MAGNETIC CONTROLS COMPANY
ACCOUNTS PAYABLE TRIAL BALANCE
SEPTEMBER 30, 19—

| | | | |
|---|---|---|---|
| Daiton Enterprises | 106 Fleet Street, Barbary | 516 | $ 430.74 |
| Gordon & Associates | 7400 King Street, Oak City | B7407 | 216.92 |
| Henderson Bros. | Box 65, Welton | 16421 | 507.00 |
| | | 16907 | 615.00 |
| Kohler, R. M. | 141 Nixon Avenue, Barbary | 615 | 104.70 |
| North State Packaging | 1500 Middle Road, Lennox | 901 | 74.87 |
| Orenson & Sons | 560 The Eastway, Dayson | 1604 | 1 046.26 |
| | | 1809 | 516.15 |
| Riggs, J. B. | 75 Baxter Road, Estwing | 74621 | 502.00 |
| Smithers, P. R. | 106 Farr Street, Wibbling | 74 | 57.05 |
| Union Advertising | 7900 Primeau Avenue, | | |
| | Marks | 16352 | 436.21 |
| | | 17201 | 702.16 |
| | | 17306 | 518.90 |
| | | | $5 727.96 |

Set up the accounts payable ledger of Magnetic Controls Company.

From the business documents listed below, perform the duties of the accounts payable clerk by posting daily to the accounts payable ledger.

*Transactions*
October

1 *Purchase Invoices*
 —Smithers, P. R., No. 104, $151.89.
 —North State Packaging, No. 1046, $57.25.
 *Cheque Copies*
 —No. 65720, Union Advertising, on account, $800.
 —No. 65721, Henderson Bros., Inv. 16421, $507.

2 *Purchase Invoices*
 —Prouse & Reid, 14 Kay Street, Saxton, No. 597G, $316.29.
 —Union Advertising, No. 18002, $505.
 —Orenson & Sons, No. 1856, $216.
 *Cheque Copies*
 —No. 65722, Daiton Enterprises, Inv. 516, $430.74.
 —No. 65723, Orenson & Sons, on account, $500.

5 *Purchase Invoices*
 —Gordon & Associates, No. B7502, $315.20.
 —Kohler, R. M., No. 719, $174.90.
 —Riggs, J. B., No. 74998, $472.47.
 *Cheque Copies*
 —No. 65734, North State Packaging, Inv. 901, $74.87.
 —No. 65735, Union Advertising, balance of Inv. 17201, $338.37.

6 *Purchase Invoices*
 —Daiton Enterprises, No. 702, $375.62.
 —Henderson Bros., No. 17436, $1 746.21.
 *Cheque Copies*
 —No. 65739, Gordon & Associates, Inv. B7407, $216.92.

7 *Purchase Invoices*
 —Henderson Bros., No. 17807, $65.25.
 —Kohler, R. M., No. 792, $107.64.

–Prouse & Reid, No. 602B, $392.61.
*Cheque Copies*
–No. 65744, Henderson Bros., Inv. 16907, $615.
No. 65745, Orenson & Sons, balance of

Inv. 1604, $546.26.
–No. 65746, Prouse & Reid, Inv. 597G, $316.29.
–No. 65747, Smithers, P. R., Inv. 74, $57.05.

**Take off an accounts payable ledger trial balance and see that it agrees with the balance of the control account. The correct control account figure is $6 221.79.**

8.  **F. Bragg is a public accountant. On March 31, 19—, his general ledger trial balance is as follows:**

F. BRAGG

GENERAL LEDGER TRIAL BALANCE

MARCH 31, 19—

| No. | 1 | Bank | $ 516.20 | |
|---|---|---|---|---|
| | 2 | Accounts Receivable | 262.50 | |
| | 3 | Supplies | 375.00 | |
| | 4 | Office Equipment | 852.90 | |
| | 5 | Automobile | 4 751.65 | |
| | 21 | Accounts Payable | | $1 319.46 |
| | 31 | F. Bragg, Capital | | 3 181.23 |
| | 32 | F. Bragg, Drawings | 400.00 | |
| | 41 | Fees Income | | 4 075.62 |
| | 51 | Car Expenses | 196.50 | |
| | 52 | Light and Heat | 62.75 | |
| | 53 | Miscellaneous Expense | 47.51 | |
| | 54 | Rent | 375.00 | |
| | 55 | Telephone | 62.05 | |
| | 56 | Wages | 674.25 | |
| | | | $8 576.31 | $8 576.31 |

**Set up the general ledger accounts for F. Bragg as of March 31, 19—. (2 workbook ledger accounts are required for Bank.)**

**The accounts receivable ledger on March 31, 19—, contains the following accounts:**

| | | | |
|---|---|---|---|
| Blue Cab Company | 16 Fox Street | Inv. No. 74 | $110.00 |
| Champion Store | 175 Main Street | 75 | 37.50 |
| Oasis Restaurant | 325 Second Street | 76 | 75.00 |
| Village Restaurant | 400 Main Street | 77 | 40.00 |
| | | | $262.50 |

**Set up the accounts receivable ledger as of March 31, 19—. Observe that the total of the four accounts is equal to the balance of the control account in the general ledger.**

The accounts payable ledger on March 31, 19—, contains the following accounts:

| | | |
|---|---|---|
| M. Ball, Consultant | 430 Red Road, Bigtown | $ 200.00 |
| Queen Finance | 151 King Street | 1 047.21 |
| Stirling Company | 46 River Road | 42.65 |
| Tom's Garage | 705 Victoria Street | 29.60 |
| | | $1 319.46 |

Set up the accounts payable ledger as of March 31, 19—. Observe that the total of the four accounts is equal to the balance of the control account in the general ledger.

Each day you are to perform the duties of both the accounts receivable clerk and the accounts payable clerk. From the list of business transactions shown below, you are to post daily to any customers' or creditors' accounts affected. Although it will be necessary for you to post directly from the list of transactions, try to imagine that you are posting directly from the source documents themselves. Also, remember that not all business transactions affect the accounts of customers and creditors.

Each day you are to perform the duties of the junior accountant. Journalize each transaction in the two-column general journal. Do not post to the general ledger accounts until the end of April.

## Transactions
April
1 *Cheque Copy*
—No. 105, to P. Walters, $125, monthly rent.
3 *Sales Invoice*
—No. 78, to Blue Cab Company, $100.
5 *Cash Receipt*
—From Oasis Restaurant, $75, on account.
8 *Purchase Invoice*
—From Tom's Garage, $40.20, gasoline and oil.
9 *Cheque Copy*
—No. 106, to Queen Finance, $90, regular monthly payment.
12 *Sales Invoices*
—No. 79, to Champion Store, $175.
—No. 80, to Village Restaurant, $50.
15 *Cheque Copy*
—No. 107, to Municipal Telephone,

$20.50, telephone for month.
15 *Cash Receipt*
—From Blue Cab Company, $110, on account.
19 *Sales Invoice*
—No. 81, to Oasis Restaurant, $75.
22 *Purchase Invoice*
—From Stirling Company, $35, for supplies.
24 *Cheque Copies*
—No. 108, to M. Ball, $200, on account.
—No. 109, to Stirling Company, $42.65, on account.
30 *Cheque Copies*
—No. 110, to Municipal Hydro, $15, electricity for month.
—No. 111, to R. Carter, $200, part-time wages for month.

As the junior accountant, you are to post the general journal to the general ledger at the end of the month; then you are to take off a general ledger trial balance. It is your responsibility to see that the ledger balances.

As the accounts receivable clerk, you are to take off a trial balance of the accounts receivable ledger as of April 30, 19—. It is your responsibility to see that the accounts receivable ledger balances with the control account.

As the accounts payable clerk, you are to take off a trial balance of the accounts payable ledger as of April 30, 19—. See that this ledger balances with the control account.

9. On June 30, 19—, the general ledger trial balance of United Rental and Repair Service is as follows:

UNITED RENTAL AND REPAIR SERVICE
GENERAL LEDGER TRIAL BALANCE
JUNE 30, 19—

| No. | | | |
|---|---|---|---|
| 1 | Bank | $ 647.20 | |
| 2 | Accounts Receivable | 519.50 | |
| 3 | Supplies | 312.92 | |
| 4 | Equipment | 3 040.50 | |
| 5 | Delivery Truck | 3 500.00 | |
| 21 | Accounts Payable | | $ 665.50 |
| 31 | R. B. Jones, Capital | | 5 107.04 |
| 32 | R. B. Jones, Drawings | 3 600.00 | |
| 41 | Revenue | | 7 500.00 |
| 51 | Light and Heat Expense | 275.00 | |
| 52 | Miscellaneous Expense | 135.00 | |
| 53 | Rent Expense | 600.00 | |
| 54 | Telephone Expense | 75.40 | |
| 55 | Truck Expense | 567.02 | |
| | | $13 272.54 | $13 272.54 |

Set up the general ledger accounts as of June 30, 19—.
(2 workbook ledger accounts required for Bank.)

The accounts receivable ledger on June 30, 19—, is as follows:

| A. Barrett | 184 Jones Avenue | Inv. No. 50 | $142.50 |
|---|---|---|---|
| C. French | 314 Chestnut Street | 51 | 33.50 |
| J. Twiddle | 41 Guest Avenue | 52 | 125.90 |
| T. Walters | 90 Brooks Street | 53 | 217.60 |
| | | | $519.50 |

Set up the accounts receivable ledger as of June 30, 19—.

The accounts payable ledger as of June 30, 19—, is as follows:

| Able Finance Company | 3000 Belleview Avenue | $512.50 |
|---|---|---|
| General Supply Company | 50 James Street | 153.00 |
| | | $665.50 |

Set up the accounts payable ledger as of June 30, 19—.

Each day you are to perform the duties of both the accounts receivable clerk and the accounts payable clerk. From the list of business transactions that follows, you are to post daily to the accounts of customers and creditors affected by the transactions. Remember that not all of the business transactions affect the accounts of customers and creditors.

Each day you are to perform the duties of the junior accountant. Each source document is the source of a journal entry in the two-column general journal. Do not post to the general ledger accounts until the end of each month.

*Transactions*
July

1 *Sales Invoice*
   –No. 54, to J. Twiddle, $39.

3 *Cheque Copies*
   –No. 151, to Royal Realty, $100, for the rent for the month.
   –No. 152, to Able Finance, $56, monthly payment on the truck.

5 *Cheque Copy*
   –No. 153, to R. B. Jones, $100, personal withdrawal.

9 *Cash Receipt*
   –From J. Twiddle, $125.90, on account.

11 *Cheque Copy*
   –No. 154, to General Supply Company, $153, on account.

12 *Purchase Invoice*
   –From West Wind Oil, 1000 Bay Street, $67.50, for gas and oil used in the delivery truck.

16 *Purchase Invoice*
   –From General Supply Company, $350, for supplies.

19 *Sales Invoices*
   –No. 55, to C. French, $55.

   –No. 56, to T. Walters, $100.

20 *Cheque Copy*
   –No. 155, to Len's Hardware, $13.50, for miscellaneous items.

23 *Cash Receipt*
   –From A. Barrett, $100, on account.

24 *Cheque Copies*
   –No. 156, to City Telephone Co., $20, monthly telephone bill.
   –No. 157, to West Wind Oil, $67.50, on account.

25 *Cheque Copy*
   –No. 158, to R. B. Jones, $150, personal withdrawal.
   *Sales Invoice*
   –No. 57, to A. Barrett, $70.
   *Cash Receipt*
   –From C. French, $33.50, on account.

30 *Cheque Copy*
   –No. 159, to City Electric, $18, monthly hydro bill.

31 *Sales Invoice*
   –No. 58, to J. Twiddle, $40.

Acting as the junior accountant, post the general journal to the general ledger at the end of July. Then balance the general ledger.

Acting as the accounts receivable clerk take off a trial balance of the accounts receivable ledger as of July 31. Balance the accounts receivable ledger with the control account.

Acting as the accounts payable clerk, take off a trial balance of the accounts payable ledger as of July 31. Balance the accounts payable ledger with the control account.

10.   As the accountant for Willowvale Cartage, it is your responsibility to perform the accounting functions of a small business owned by B. G. Cook. Willowvale Cartage offers a cartage service on a cash basis as well as to a number of regular customers on a credit basis.

Set up the three ledgers of Willowvale Cartage from the following information:

a.

WILLOWVALE CARTAGE
CHART OF ACCOUNTS

| Bank | No. | 1 | Revenue | 41 |
|---|---|---|---|---|
| Accounts Receivable | | 2 | Gasoline and Oil | 51 |
| Office Supplies | | 3 | Insurance | 52 |
| Warehouse Supplies | | 4 | Light and Heat | 53 |
| Trucks | | 5 | Miscellaneous Expense | 54 |
| Bank Loan | | 21 | Rent | 55 |
| Accounts Payable | | 22 | Telephone | 56 |
| B. G. Cook, Capital | | 31 | Truck Expense | 57 |
| B. G. Cook, Drawings | | 32 | Wages | 58 |

**Note:** For the following general ledger accounts, provide workbook accounts as follows:

| | |
|---|---|
| Bank | 7 accounts |
| Accounts Receivable | 6 accounts |
| Accounts Payable | 3 accounts |
| Revenue | 4 accounts |

b.

WILLOWVALE CARTAGE
GENERAL LEDGER TRIAL BALANCE
JUNE 30, 19—

| | | |
|---|---|---|
| Bank | $  316.00 | |
| Accounts Receivable | 1 246.50 | |
| Office Supplies | 275.00 | |
| Warehouse Supplies | 114.00 | |
| Trucks and Equipment | 7 540.00 | |
| Bank Loan | | $1 000.00 |
| Accounts Payable | | 3 416.40 |
| B. G. Cook, Capital | | 5 075.10 |
| | $9 491.50 | $9 491.50 |

c.

WILLOWVALE CARTAGE
ACCOUNTS RECEIVABLE TRIAL BALANCE
JUNE 30, 19—

| | | | |
|---|---|---|---|
| Adelaide Sports | | | |
| 65 Brody St. | No. 204 | $ 212.00 | (2 workbook ledger accounts required.) |
| Best Drug Store | | | |
| 1210 Van Horne Ave. | No. 209 | 174.50 | (3 workbook ledger accounts required.) |
| Friday's Pharmacy | | | |
| Century Plaza | No. 186 | 319.20 | (2 workbook ledger accounts required.) |
| Murray's Auto Supply | | | |
| 100 William Street | No. 210 | 196.40 | (2 workbook ledger accounts required.) |
| Ward Millwork Ltd. | | | |
| 565 William Street | No. 201 | 344.40 | (3 workbook ledger accounts required.) |
| | | $1 246.50 | |

d.

WILLOWVALE CARTAGE
ACCOUNTS PAYABLE TRIAL BALANCE
JUNE 30, 19—

| | | | |
|---|---|---|---|
| Credit Finance Corp. | | | |
| 44 Rankin Street | Instalments | $2 986.55 | |
| Hatley Equipment | | | |
| 12 Rupert Avenue | No. 375 | 363.70 | |
| Westown Garage | | | |
| Century Plaza | No. 1047 | 66.15 | (2 workbook ledger accounts required.) |
| | | $3 416.40 | |

**From the following list of business documents, journalize the transactions in the general journal; post to the subsidiary ledgers daily; post to the general ledger at the end of the month.**

*Transactions*
July
1 *Sales Invoices*
   –No. 211, Murray's Auto Supply, $56.
   –No. 212, Ward Millwork Ltd., $35.
   *Purchase Invoice*
   –Hatley Equipment, No. 392, for warehouse supplies, $42.
   *Cash Sales Ticket*
   –No. 57, $25.
   *Cash Receipt*
   –Friday's Pharmacy, re No. 186, $319.20.
   *Cheque Copy*
   –No. 402, Credit Finance Corp., monthly instalment, $200.
2 *Sales Invoices*
   –No. 213, Best Drug Store, $104.

   –No. 214, Friday's Pharmacy, $74.
2 *Purchase Invoice*
   –Westown Garage, No. 1094, for truck repairs, $56.
   *Cash Receipts*
   –Ward Millwork Ltd., re No. 201, $344.40.
   –Adelaide Sports, re No. 204, $212.
   *Cheque Copy*
   –No. 403, to the accountant (you), for wages, $175.
5 *Sales Invoices*
   –No. 215, Adelaide Sports, $25.
   –No. 216, Ward Millwork Ltd., $16.
   –No. 217, Best Drug Store, $37.

*Cash Receipt*
—Murray's Auto Supply, re No. 210,
  $196.40.
*Cheque Copy*
—No. 404, Civic Hydro-Electric, for
  monthly electricity, $12.57.
6 *Sales Invoices*
—No. 218, Friday's Pharmacy, $65.
—No. 219, Murray's Auto Supply, $35.
*Cash Receipts*
—Best Drug Store, re No. 209, $174.50.
—Murray's Auto Supply, re No. 211, $56.
*Cheque Copy*
—No. 405, Hatley Equipment, on account
  re No. 375, $200.
7 *Sales Invoice*
—No. 220, Adelaide Sports, $19.
*Purchase Invoices*
—Mercury Sales, 19 Brent Ave., No. 74,
  for office supplies, $27.50.
—Westown Garage, No. 1103, for gasoline
  and oil, $114.16.
*Cash Sales Ticket*
—No. 58, $40.
*Cash Receipt*
—Ward Millwork Ltd., re No. 212, $35.
*Cheque Copy*
—No. 406, B. G. Cook, personal drawings,
  $100.
8 *Sales Invoices*
—No. 221, Best Drug Store, $24.
—No. 222, Ward Millwork Ltd., $32.
—No. 223, Murray's Auto Supply, $12.
9 *Sales Invoice*
—No. 224, Friday's Pharmacy, $23.
*Cash Receipts*
—Adelaide Sports, re No. 215, $25.
—Friday's Pharmacy, re No. 214, $74.
*Cheque Copy*
—No. 407, to the accountant, for wages,
  $175.
12 *Sales Invoices*
—No. 225, Best Drug Store, $36.
—No. 226, Adelaide Sports, $14.
*Cash Receipt*
—Best Drug Store, re No. 213, $104.
13 *Sales Invoices*
—No. 227, Ward Millwork Ltd., $15.
—No. 228, Friday's Pharmacy, $62.
—No. 229, Adelaide Sports, $75.

*Cash Receipt*
—Murray's Auto Supply, re No. 219,
  $35.
*Cheque Copy*
—No. 408, Westown Garage, re No. 1047,
  $66.15.
14 *Sales Invoices*
—No. 230, Murray's Auto Supply, $41.
—No. 231, Best Drug Store, $28.
—No. 232, Ward Millwork Ltd., $5.
*Purchase Invoice*
—Westown Garage, No. 1127, for gasoline
  and oil, $75.05.
*Cash Sales Ticket*
—No. 59, $36.
*Cash Receipts*
—Best Drug Store, re No. 217, $37.
—Ward Millwork Ltd., re No. 216, $16.
15 *Sales Invoice*
—No. 233, Adelaide Sports, $17.
*Cash Receipts*
—Adelaide Sports, re No. 220, $19.
—Friday's Pharmacy, re No. 218, $65.
*Cheque Copies*
—No. 409, Buff Insurance Agency,
  monthly insurance payment, $20.
—No. 410, Hatley Equipment, re balance
  of No. 375, $163.70.
*Miscellaneous*
—A debit memorandum was received from
  the bank stating that $7.54 had been
  deducted from the business bank account
  to pay for bank service charges.
16 *Sales Invoice*
—No. 234, Best Drug Store, $46.
*Cheque Copy*
—No. 411, to the accountant, for wages,
  $175.
19 *Sales Invoices*
—No. 235, Ward Millwork Ltd., $115.
—No. 236, Murray's Auto Supply, $201.
*Purchase Invoice*
—Westown Garage, No. 1174, for gasoline
  and oil, $75.16.
*Cash Receipts*
—Best Drug Store, re No. 221, $24.
—Murray's Auto Supply, re No. 223, $12.
20 *Sales Invoices*
—No. 237, Friday's Pharmacy, $47.
—No. 238, Ward Millwork Ltd., $41.

*Cash Sales Ticket*
—No. 60, $15.
*Cash Receipt*
—Adelaide Sports, re No. 226, $14.
*Cheque Copy*
—No. 412, B. G. Cook, for personal drawings, $150.

21 *Sales Invoice*
—No. 239, Adelaide Sports, $51.
*Cash Receipts*
—Ward Millwork Ltd., re No. 222, $32.
—Friday's Pharmacy, re No. 224, $23.
*Cheque Copy*
—No. 413, Receiver General of Canada, for postage stamps, $40.

22 *Sales Invoices*
—No. 240, Friday's Pharmacy, $18.
—No. 241, Best Drug Store, $43.
*Cheque Copy*
—No. 414, Magill's Office Supplies, for the cash purchase of office supplies, $16.20.

23 *Sales Invoice*
—No. 242, Ward Millwork Ltd., $19.
*Purchase Invoices*
—Westown Garage, No. 1204, for gasoline and oil, $74, for truck repairs, $116, total $190.
—Hatley Equipment, No. 419, for warehouse supplies, $59.
*Cash Sales Ticket*
—No. 61, $41.
*Cash Receipts*
—Best Drug Store, re No. 225, $36.
—Ward Millwork Ltd., re No. 227, $15.
*Cheque Copies*
—No. 415, Mercury Sales, re No. 74, $27.50.
—No. 416, to the accountant, for wages, $175.
—No. 417, A.P.M. Telephone Co., monthly bill, $15.25.

26 *Sales Invoices*
—No. 243, Murray's Auto Supply, $25.
—No. 244, Adelaide Sports, $29.
—No. 245, Ward Millwork Ltd., $10.

26 *Cash Receipts*
—Best Drug Store, re No. 231 and No. 234, $74.
—Ward Millwork Ltd., re No. 232, $5.
*Cash Sales Ticket*
—No. 62, $20.
*Cheque Copies*
—No. 418, Westown Garage, re No. 1094 and No. 1103, $170.16.
—No. 419, Hatley Equipment, re No. 392, $42.

27 *Sales Invoice*
—No. 246, Best Drug Store, $53.
*Cash Receipt*
—Ward Millwork Ltd., re No. 235 and No. 238, $156.

28 *Sales Invoices*
—No. 247, Adelaide Sports, $16.
—No. 248, Friday's Pharmacy, $40.
—No. 249, Murray's Auto Supply, $31.
—No. 250, Ward Millwork Ltd., $21.
*Purchase Invoice*
—Mercury Sales, No. 96, for office supplies, $114.20.
*Cash Receipts*
—Adelaide Sports, re No. 229 and No. 233, $92.
—Friday's Pharmacy, re No. 228, $62.
—Murray's Auto Supply, re No. 230, $41.

29 *Sales Invoice*
—No. 251, Adelaide Sports, $24.
*Purchase Invoice*
—Westown Garage, No. 1250, for gasoline and oil, $92.
*Cash Sales Ticket*
—No. 63, $56.
*Cash Receipt*
—Murray's Auto Supply, re No. 236, $201.

30 *Cash Receipt*
—Friday's Pharmacy, re No. 237, $47.
*Cheque Copy*
—Westown Garage, re No. 1127, $75.05.

31 *Sales Invoices*
—No. 252, Best Drug Store, $156.
—No. 253, Ward Millwork Ltd., $75.

**By means of trial balances:**
a. **Balance the general ledger.**
b. **Balance the subsidiary ledgers with their respective control accounts.**

11. Mr. E. W. Terry, an engineer, begins a small consulting business on a spare-time basis. He officially begins operations on July 1, 19—, with the following business assets: Bank Balance, $2 000; Office Furniture, $565; Automobile, $2 750; Equipment, $1 250. He has no business liabilities.

From the preceding information and the following chart of accounts set up the general ledger for E. W. Terry as of July 1, 19—. Journalize and post the opening entry.

E. W. TERRY
CHART OF ACCOUNTS

| Account | Number | | |
|---|---|---|---|
| Bank | 1 | E. W. Terry, Capital | 31 |
| Accounts Receivable | 2 | E. W. Terry, Drawings | 32 |
| Office Supplies | 3 | Fees Earned | 41 |
| Office Furniture | 4 | Car Expense | 51 |
| Automobile | 5 | Rent Expense | 52 |
| Equipment | 6 | Miscellaneous Expense | 53 |
| Accounts Payable | 21 | Telephone Expense | 54 |

**Note:** (3 workbook ledger accounts required for Bank; 2 accounts required for Accounts Receivable; 2 accounts required for Accounts Payable.)

Record the following transactions of the business in the general journal. Open subsidiary ledger accounts as necessary and post to them on a daily basis. Postings to the general ledger accounts are left until the end of the month.

*Transactions*
July
1 *Cheque Copy*
   –No. 1, Chambers Bros., advance payment for monthly rent, $140.
2 *Purchase Invoice*
   –Glen Printing, No. 651, for office supplies, $86.50.
4 *Sales Invoice*
   –No. 1, J. R. Greenley, for services rendered, $150.
5 *Sales Invoices*
   –No. 2, R. Grieve, for services rendered, $50.
   –No. 3, P. Webb, for services rendered, $35.
7 *Purchase Invoice*
   –Star Blueprinting, No. 370, for the printing of plans, $15.
8 *Purchase Invoice*

   –Dynamic Engineering, No. B126, for consultation, $26.
9 *Purchase Invoice*
   –McKay's Garage, No. B64, for gasoline and oil, $12.50.
10 *Sales Invoice*
   –No. 4, M. Page, for services rendered, $50.
   *Purchase Invoice*
   –Star Blueprinting, No. 397, for printing of plans, $26.
   *Cheque Copies*
   –No. 2, Glen Printing, re No. 651, $86.50.
   –No. 3, Star Blueprinting, re No. 370, $15.
   –No. 4, Dynamic Engineering, re No. B126, $26.
   –No. 5, McKay's Garage, re No. B64, $12.50.

11 *Cash Receipt*
  –J. R. Greenley, re No. 1, $150.
14 *Sales Invoice*
  –No. 5, R. Grieve, for services rendered, $20.
15 *Sales Invoice*
  –No. 6, J. R. Greenley, for services rendered, $40.
  *Purchase Invoice*
  –Automotive Electrical, No. 702, for repair to generator on car, $22.50.
16 *Sales Invoice*
  –No. 7, P. Webb, for services rendered, $16.
17 *Purchase Invoice*
  –Dynamic Engineering, No. B306, for consultation, $75.
18 *Cash Receipt*
  –R. Grieve, re No. 2, $50.
22 *Sales Invoice*
  –No. 8, M. Page, for services rendered, $18.
23 *Cash Receipt*
  –M. Page, re No. 4, $50.
  *Purchase Invoice*

McKay's Garage, No. B96, for gasoline and oil, $9.50.
24 *Cheque Copy*
  –No. 6, E. W. Terry, for personal drawings, $100.
25 *Cash Receipt*
  –J. R. Greenley, re No. 6, $40.
29 *Sales Invoice*
  –No. 9, J. R. Greenley, for services rendered, $20.
30 *Cheque Copies*
  –No. 7, Automotive Electrical, re No. 702, $22.50.
  –No. 8, Star Blueprinting, re No. 397, $26.
31 *Cash Receipt*
  –P. Webb, re No. 3, $35.
  *Cheque Copies*
  –No. 9, Township Hydro, for cash payment of hydro bill, $10.40.
  –No. 10, Municipal Telephone, for cash payment of telephone bill, $16.50.
  –No. 11, E. W. Terry, for personal drawings, $100.

**Post and balance the general ledger.**

**Take off subsidiary ledger trial balances and agree them with their respective control accounts.**

**12.  Discuss the flowchart shown opposite in terms of whether, by following the sequence of steps shown, every kind of trial balance error will be detected. Test the flowchart with different situations to see if it works in all cases.**

# Cases

### Case 1
Some commonly made errors are listed below. In each case state whether or not the error will throw the general ledger or subsidiary ledger trial balances out of balance.
1.  Failed to post $450.00 from the general journal to the accounts receivable ledger account of Wright & Howe.
2.  The balance of the Capital account was $67 208.21, but it was carried forward at the beginning of the new year as $62 708.21.
3.  A debit of $325.00 to accounts receivable was incorrectly posted to accounts payable.

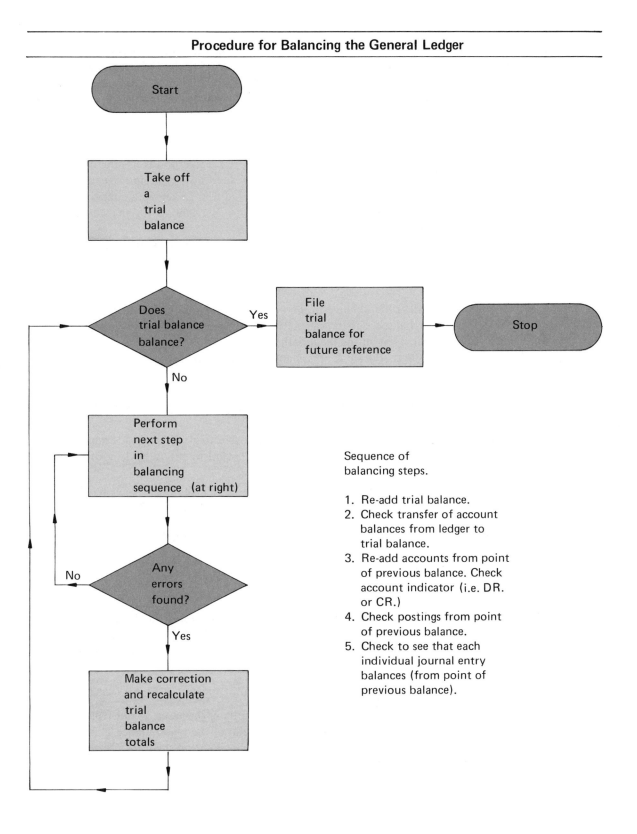

Sequence of balancing steps.

1. Re-add trial balance.
2. Check transfer of account balances from ledger to trial balance.
3. Re-add accounts from point of previous balance. Check account indicator (i.e. DR. or CR.)
4. Check postings from point of previous balance.
5. Check to see that each individual journal entry balances (from point of previous balance).

## Case 2

Jeff Brookes cannot understand why the debit balance in the Drawings account is extended to the Debit column of the balance sheet, instead of to the Debit column of the income statement, on the work sheet. He reasons that drawings is not an asset and that therefore it is not correct accounting to place it with the assets.

Do you agree with his reasoning? Explain.

## Case 3

W. Strongman is the proprietor of a retail shoe store. A successful advertising campaign has brought in new customers. The general ledger now contains over 300 customers' accounts. A friend of Strongman has advised him to set up a subsidiary ledger to handle all customers' accounts. Strongman is hesitant to do so because it will not cut down on his postings.

Prepare a written report outlining the advantages of using an accounts receivable ledger and an accounts receivable control account.

## Case 4

As of December 31, 19—, the balance in the accounts receivable control account is $12 685 and the total balance in the accounts receivable ledger is $13 158. The following errors have occurred during the month:

1. An invoice for $200 to Potter & Company is entered in the journal as $300. Posting to the subsidiary ledger is made directly from the invoice.
2. A sale for $715 is posted twice to T. Johnson's account.
3. An entry in the general journal recording the receipt of a cheque from S. Snider for $195 is not posted to the general ledger.
4. A cheque received from J. Thomas for $500 is posted to R. Gruen's account.
5. A cheque received from R. Bulson for $265 is posted to the debit side of his account.
6. The sale of $500 to Jung & Company is posted correctly to the general ledger, but is posted as $50 to the debit side of Jung & Company's account in the subsidiary ledger.
7. Cash received from K. Wright for $236.25 is entered correctly in the general journal, but is posted to the accounts receivable ledger as $263.25.

Calculate the correct balances.

## Case 5

Mr. Little of Little Hardware examines the accounts receivable trial balance. He sees that the total amount owed by his customers is $3 405.90. He wants to know when cheques are due from each of his customers. Where can he obtain this information?

## Case 6

The accounting clerk for the D. Mercer Finance Company prepares a trial balance of the accounts receivable ledger. He finds that the total of the trial balance is $300 less than the balance in the accounts receivable control account in the general ledger.

What kind of errors might have caused this difference?

## Case 7

As the owner of your own business, you have a habit of making deals with your customers about their accounts. On your own, without informing your accountant, you go to the subsidiary ledger records and make changes in the amounts. What problem have you caused the accountant? What should he do to overcome this problem?

## Case 8

As the accountant for J. Wing Co., you take over a new job and find it impossible to balance the accounts receivable and accounts payable ledgers. You discover that some older pages of the ledgers are lost. What should you do in an attempt to balance the subsidiary ledgers?

# 8 The Trading Business & the Synoptic Journal

## The Trading Business

You may have noticed that none of the examples or exercises used so far in this text have involved the buying or selling of merchandise. This omission has not been accidental. The author has intentionally used only service businesses – businesses that sell a service, not a commodity. The reason for this is to avoid, during the early stages of study, a certain minor accounting difficulty connected with the buying and selling of merchandise.

However, you are now ready to study the special accounting problems of 'trading businesses', that is, businesses that deal in merchandise. As you know, businesses of this type make up a large percentage of the business community.

## Merchandise Inventory

Businesses that buy goods for the purpose of selling them at a profit are known as trading businesses or merchandisers. The goods that they deal in are commonly called merchandise inventory, merchandise, stock-in-trade, or just stock.

The merchandise inventories of different businesses will consist of different types of goods. For instance, the merchandise inventory of a lumber company will consist of lumber and building materials; the merchandise inventory of a food retailer will consist of the food commodities that are ordinarily seen on the store shelves; the merchandise inventory of an automobile dealer will consist of new and used cars

as well as replacement parts.

There are two common methods of accounting for merchandise inventory. Of the two, the more complex method is the 'perpetual inventory method'. Under this method a record of all items in stock is kept up to date. This method is used by businesses that have a special need for such information. In many cases, these businesses are forced to purchase expensive automated equipment in order to produce the required information.

A simpler method of accounting for merchandise inventory is the 'periodic inventory method'. With this method, the up-to-date inventory figures are known only at the end of an accounting period. At that time, they are found by 'taking the inventory', that is, by actually counting and valuing the items in detail. This method is still used by many businesses today. The routines that are described in this chapter are based on the periodic inventory method.

### Balance Sheet Presentation

Because it usually must have the goods available to sell to the customer upon request, a trading business is obliged to keep a considerable inventory on hand. This inventory has a monetary value to the business and must, therefore, be included as an asset on the balance sheet. In particular, it will be listed as a current asset because in the ordinary course of business activity the inventory items will usually be sold and converted into cash within a year. An illustration of merchandise inventory on the balance sheet is shown in the illustration below.

Hardy's Hardware
*Balance Sheet*
*June 30, 19--*

Assets

*Current Assets*
| | | |
|---|---|---|
| Bank | $1 205.60 | |
| Accounts Receivable | 2 961.70 | |
| Merchandise Inventory | 8 059.00 | |
| Supplies | 316.00 | $12 542.30 |

*Fixed Assets*
| | | |
|---|---|---|
| Store Equipment | $13 964.00 | |
| Delivery Equipment | 14 050.00 | 28 014.00 |
| | | $40 556.30 |

Liabilities and Capital

*A partial balance sheet.*

## The Merchandise Inventory Account

Under the periodic inventory method, the merchandise of a business is kept in two accounts. One of these, the Merchandise Inventory account, is used only to show the correct inventory figure at the end of an accounting period. At that time, after 'taking the inventory', the account is adjusted to reflect the correct inventory figure. This periodic adjustment is the only accounting entry made to the Merchandise Inventory account and is the responsibility of a senior person in the office. More will be said of this 'adjustment' in Chapters 14 and 15.

You may find a Merchandise Inventory account appearing in many of your exercises. Do not be confused by this account. Just remember that the balance in the account represents the adjusted inventory figure at the end of the preceding fiscal period; or, what amounts to the same thing, at the beginning of the present fiscal period.

## Accounting for a Trading Business

Do not expect to learn everything about merchandise accounting in this chapter. You are not ready for it at this time. For now, you will be given just enough of the theory to enable you to do that which is important for you; namely, the handling of the day-to-day transactions of a trading business. The whole problem of merchandise inventory accounting will be clarified in Chapters 14 and 15.

In order to handle the day-to-day transactions of a trading business, you must become familiar with the accounting entries for two important aspects of the business; namely, **merchandise buying** and **merchandise selling**.

1. *Purchase of Merchandise.* During an accounting period, whenever merchandise intended for resale is purchased, the cost of the goods is debited to a new account called 'Purchases'. The name given to this new account is short for 'Purchases of Merchandise for Resale'.

If cash is paid for the merchandise, the accounting entry is:

| | |
|---|---|
| Dr. Purchases | $xxxx.xx |
| Cr. Bank | $xxxx.xx |

If the merchandise is bought on account, say from Victor Bros., the accounting entry is:

| | |
|---|---|
| Dr. Purchases | $xxxx.xx |
| Cr. Accounts Payable (Victor Bros.) | $xxxx.xx |

Not every item purchased is debited to the Purchases account. The Purchases account is used only for items of merchandise purchased with the intention of their being sold. For example, if a hardware store purchases a new delivery truck, the account to be debited is Delivery Truck. If the same hardware store purchases a shipment of hardware items to be put on sale, the account to be debited is Purchases. Similarly, if a tire dealer purchases some office supplies, the account to be debited is Office Supplies. But if the same tire dealer purchases a shipment of tires to be sold to the public, the account to be debited is Purchases.

2. *Sale of Merchandise.* Whenever merchandise is sold, the selling price of the goods is credited to an income account called 'Sales'.

When goods are sold for cash the accounting entry is:

| | |
|---|---|
| Dr. Bank | $xxxx.xx |
| Cr. Sales | $xxxx.xx |

When goods are sold on account, say to J. Fields, the accounting entry is:

| | |
|---|---|
| Dr. Accounts Receivable (J. Fields) | $xxxx.xx |
| Cr. Sales | $xxxx.xx |

During the accounting period, nothing is done to record the decrease in merchandise inventory that accompanies a sale. Whenever a sale is made the goods are eventually taken or delivered from the premises of the vendor. But under the periodic inventory method of inventory accounting, this decrease is not accounted for during the accounting period. This is another accounting situation where it is more expedient to allow certain records to become incorrect during the accounting period and to correct them at the end of the period. But more about that later.

## Freight-in and Delivery Expense

The accounting for a trading business usually involves two additional transactions that are new to you. These involve the accounts Freight-in and Delivery Expense. These two new accounts are debited with the costs of transporting or delivering the goods that a business deals in.

The **Freight-in** account is used to accumulate transportation charges pertaining to incoming merchandise. The **Delivery Expense** account is used to accumulate transportation charges pertaining to outgoing merchandise.

The charges for freight-in or delivery expense may originate from invoices of trucking companies, railway companies, or shipping companies. If a business has its own delivery equipment, these charges will originate from bills related to the running of the equipment, such as garage bills, repair bills, and bills for gasoline and oil.

You may wonder why two accounts so similar in nature are kept separately. The reason is that one of the accounts – Freight-in – has to do with the 'cost' of merchandise, and the other – Delivery Equipment – has to do with the 'sale' of merchandise. Owners, managers, and other senior officials are able to utilize this type of information in conducting the affairs of the business.

# The Synoptic Journal

You now have acquired a reasonably good appreciation of the accounting process. But it still needs to be refined and specialized to make it even more functional and more in tune with the real business world.

The **synoptic journal**, the topic of this section, is a many-columned journal that differs considerably from the two-column journal that you have been using. The new concept of 'having many columns' is an extremely important one. The principle is universally accepted, and many mechanical and electronic devices have been developed to take advantage of it.

This does not mean that the two-column journal is of no further use. On the contrary, it is still widely used today but usually not for ordinary routine transactions handled by office clerks. Routine transactions are usually recorded in a many-columned type of journal of which the synoptic journal is one.

## Journalizing in the Synoptic Journal

An illustration of one style of synoptic journal appears below. Observe the special money columns for Bank Dr., Bank Cr., Accounts Receivable Dr., Accounts Receivable Cr., Accounts

*The synoptic journal.*

Payable Dr., Accounts Payable Cr., Sales or Income Cr., Purchases Dr., and the blank column to be named by the accountant.

The theory of the synoptic journal is to accumulate similar items in special columns during the journalizing process. Later, when posting to the general ledger, it is the 'totals' of the special columns that are posted rather than the individual items contained within the columns. For each of the special columns, one posting is sufficient.

Theoretically, one could have a special column for every general ledger account. But in practice it is common to have special columns only for the items that occur frequently, and a general section for the remaining items. Otherwise, the journal page would be too wide.

Journalizing in the synoptic journal is easy. Obtain a sheet of 'synoptic' paper and try the following sample entries.

### Transaction 1
**May 4: Sold $56 of merchandise for cash; Sales Ticket No. 57.**

According to a recently learned rule, the accounting entry for this transaction is Dr. Bank, $56; Cr. Sales, $56. In the synoptic journal this entry is recorded as follows:

| SYNOPTIC JOURNAL | | | | | | | | | | | | | MONTH OF May, 19— | | | P. 42 | |
|---|---|---|---|---|---|---|---|---|---|---|---|---|---|---|---|---|---|
| Date 19— | Customer or Supplier or Explanation | # | Bank Dr. | Cr. | √ | Accounts Rec'l Dr. | Cr. | √ | Accounts Pay'l Dr. | Cr. | Sales or Income Cr. | Purch's Dr. | Other Accounts Account | PR | Dr. | Cr. |
| May 4 | Cash Sale | 57 | 56 — | | | | | | | | 56 — | | | | | |

### Transaction 2
**May 5: Sold $112 of merchandise to Paul Boxer on account. Invoice No. 165 was issued.**

The accounting entry for this transaction is Dr. Accounts Receivable (Paul Boxer), $112; Cr. Sales, $112. This entry follows the previous entry in the synoptic journal in the manner shown below. In respect to simple routine entries such as this, no explanations need to be written in.

Observe that in this particular design of synoptic journal there is only one column provided for reference numbers. Consequently, all reference numbers, whether for cheques issued, cash sales slips, sales invoices, or other source documents, are recorded in this single column.

Observe also that no check mark was placed in the '√' column beside Accounts Receivable to indicate that a posting to the subsidiary ledger was completed. This is because the system adopted here for posting to subsidiary ledgers is the one described in the previous chapter. You will recall that the postings to the customers' and creditors' accounts are made directly from the source documents. If the system used happens to be one in which the posting to the customers' and creditors' accounts is taken directly from the synoptic journal, then the '√' column is used to indicate that the postings are completed.

| SYNOPTIC JOURNAL | | | | | | | | | | | | | MONTH OF May, 19— | | | P. 42 | |
|---|---|---|---|---|---|---|---|---|---|---|---|---|---|---|---|---|---|
| Date 19— | Customer or Supplier or Explanation | # | Bank Dr. | Cr. | √ | Accounts Rec'l Dr. | Cr. | √ | Accounts Pay'l Dr. | Cr. | Sales or Income Cr. | Purch's Dr. | Other Accounts Account | PR | Dr. | Cr. |
| May 4 | Cash Sale | 57 | 56 — | | | | | | | | 56 — | | | | | |
| 5 | Paul Boxer | 165 | | | | 112 — | | | | | 112 — | | | | | |

## Transaction 3

**May 6: Purchased $316 of merchandise on account from Empire Wholesale; received their invoice.**

The accounting entry for this transaction, which you have recently learned, is Dr. Purchases, $316; Cr. Accounts Payable (Empire Wholesale), $316. The recording of this entry in the synoptic journal is shown below:

| SYNOPTIC JOURNAL | | | | | | | | | | | | MONTH OF *May, 19 —* | P. 42 | | | |
|---|---|---|---|---|---|---|---|---|---|---|---|---|---|---|---|---|
| Date 19— | Customer or Supplier or Explanation | # | Bank Dr. | Bank Cr. | Accounts Rec'l Dr. | Accounts Rec'l Cr. | V | Accounts Pay'l Dr. | Accounts Pay'l Cr. | Salesor Income Cr. | Purch's Dr. | Account | PR | Other Accounts Dr. | Cr. |
| May 4 | Cash Sale | 57 | 56 – | | | | | | | 56 – | | | | | |
| 5 | Paul Boxer | 165 | | | 112 – | | | | | 112 – | | | | | |
| 6 | Empire Wholesale | | | | | | | | 316 – | | 316 – | | | | |

## Transaction 4

**May 7: $37.20 of supplies is purchased and paid for with cheque No. 74 issued to Deluxe Stationers.**

The accounting entry for this transaction is Dr. Supplies, $37.20; Cr. Bank, $37.20. It is recorded in the synoptic journal in the manner shown below.

Notice that the accountant has used the blank column for 'Supplies'. It can be assumed from this that, for this business, Supplies is a frequently occurring item.

| SYNOPTIC JOURNAL | | | | | | | | | | | | | MONTH OF *May, 19 —* | P. 42 | | |
|---|---|---|---|---|---|---|---|---|---|---|---|---|---|---|---|---|
| Date 19— | Customer or Supplier or Explanation | # | Bank Dr. | Bank Cr. | Accounts Rec'l Dr. | Accounts Rec'l Cr. | V | Accounts Pay'l Dr. | Accounts Pay'l Cr. | Salesor Income Cr. | Purch's Dr. | Supplies Dr. | Account | PR | Other Accounts Dr. | Cr. |
| May 4 | Cash Sale | 57 | 56 – | | | | | | | 56 – | | | | | | |
| 5 | Paul Boxer | 165 | | | 112 – | | | | | 112 – | | | | | | |
| 6 | Empire Wholesale | | | | | | | | 316 – | | 316 – | | | | | |
| 7 | Deluxe Stationers | 74 | | 37 20 | | | | | | | | 37 20 | | | | |

## Transaction 5

**May 7: Issued cheque No. 75 in the amount of $200 to Arrow Realty in payment of the monthly rent.**

This accounting entry – Dr. Rent Expense, $200; Cr. Bank, $200 – is recorded in the synoptic journal as shown below:

Notice that there is not a special column for Rent Expense. The payment of the rent is a transaction that occurs only once a month and for that reason is recorded in the section headed 'Other Accounts'. Observe in this case that the amount is placed in the Debit column.

| SYNOPTIC JOURNAL | | | | | | | | | | | | | MONTH OF *May, 19 —* | P. 42 | | |
|---|---|---|---|---|---|---|---|---|---|---|---|---|---|---|---|---|
| Date 19— | Customer or Supplier or Explanation | # | Bank Dr. | Bank Cr. | Accounts Rec'l Dr. | Accounts Rec'l Cr. | V | Accounts Pay'l Dr. | Accounts Pay'l Cr. | Salesor Income Cr. | Purch's Dr. | Supplies Dr. | Account | PR | Other Accounts Dr. | Cr. |
| May 4 | Cash Sale | 57 | 56 – | | | | | | | 56 – | | | | | | |
| 5 | Paul Boxer | 165 | | | 112 – | | | | | 112 – | | | | | | |
| 6 | Empire Wholesale | | | | | | | | 316 – | | 316 – | | | | | |
| 7 | Deluxe Stationers | 74 | | 37 20 | | | | | | | | 37 20 | | | | |
| 7 | Arrow Realty | 75 | | 200 – | | | | | | | | | Rent Expense | | 200 – | |

## Additional Transactions

A number of additional transactions of a routine nature are listed below. Try to journalize them on your own before comparing your work with the synoptic journal entries on page 132.

6 May 10: Issued cheque No. 76 in the amount of $13.50 to A. Baldwin – a payment on account.

7 May 10: Issued cheque No. 77 in the amount of $46.20 to G. English & Co. – a payment on account.

8 May 11: Received a cheque for $16 from R. Smith on account.

9 May 11: Received a cheque for $375 from F. Jones on account.

10  May 13: Issued cheque No. 78 in the amount of $112 to M. Field in payment of his wages.

11  May 13: Issued cheque No. 79 in the amount of $135 to R. French in payment of his wages.

12  May 14: Issued Sales Invoice No. 166 for $250 to M. Birch.

13  May 14: Issued Sales Invoice No. 167 for $170 to Y. Ash.

14  May 17: Received an invoice from Continental Railway in the amount of $87.50 for freight charges on incoming merchandise.

15  May 18: Received an invoice from Budget Oil in the amount of $64.72. This invoice was for gasoline and oil used in the delivery truck.

16  May 19: Issued cheque No. 80 for $50 to G. Ripley, the proprietor, for his personal use.

17  May 20: Issued cheque No. 81 for $300 to Ideal Supply in payment of merchandise which was purchased for cash.

18  May 21: Received an invoice from Circle Supplies in the amount of $46; this invoice was in respect to the purchase of supplies on account.

19  May 21: Received an invoice from Deluxe Stationers in the amount of $420; this invoice was in respect to the purchase of a new office desk at a cost of $350 and some supplies at a cost of $70.

20  May 24: The owner of the business, G. Ripley, made an agreement with Crescent Bank to borrow $1 000. As a result of this agreement Crescent Bank deposited $1 000 in the business bank account and sent the business a notice to this effect.

21  May 25: Received a cheque for $62 from E. McRae on account.

22  May 26: Issued cheque No. 82 in the amount of $200 to Empire Wholesale on account.

23  May 26: Received an invoice from Prairie Manufacturing in respect to the purchase of merchandise on account; $160.

24  May 26: Received a cheque for $100 from R. Stoddard on account.

25  May 27: Issued cheque No. 83 for $112 to M. Field in payment of his wages.

26  May 27: Issued cheque No. 84 for $135 to R. French in payment of his wages.

SYNOPTIC JOURNAL                                                                 MONTH OF May, 19—                          P. 42

| Date 19— | Customer or Supplier or Explanation | # | Bank Dr. | Bank Cr. | V | Accounts Rec'l Dr. | Accounts Rec'l Cr. | V | Accounts Pay'l Dr. | Accounts Pay'l Cr. | Sales or Income Cr. | Purch's Dr. | Supplies Dr. | Other Accounts Account | PR | Other Dr. | Other Cr. |
|---|---|---|---|---|---|---|---|---|---|---|---|---|---|---|---|---|---|
| May 4 | Cash Sale | 51 | 56 — | | | | | | | | 56 — | | | | | | |
| 5 | Paul Boxer | 165 | | | | 112 — | | | | | 112 — | | | | | | |
| 6 | Empire Wholesale | | | | | | | | | 316 — | | 316 — | | | | | |
| 7 | Deluxe Stationers | 74 | | 37 20 | | | | | | | | | 37 20 | | | | |
| 7 | Arrow Realty | 75 | | 200 — | | | | | | | | | | Rent Expense | | 200 — | |
| 10 | A. Baldwin | 76 | | 13 50 | | | | | 13 50 | | | | | | | | |
| 10 | G. English + Co. | 77 | | 46 20 | | | | | 46 20 | | | | | | | | |
| 11 | R. Smith | | 16 — | | | | 16 — | | | | | | | | | | |
| 11 | F. Jones | | 375 — | | | | 375 — | | | | | | | | | | |
| 13 | M. Field | 78 | | 112 — | | | | | | | | | | Wages Expense | | 112 — | |
| 13 | R. French | 79 | | 135 — | | | | | | | | | | Wages Expense | | 135 — | |
| 14 | M. Birch | 166 | | | | 250 — | | | | | 250 — | | | | | | |
| 14 | Y. Ash | 167 | | | | 170 — | | | | | 170 — | | | | | | |
| 17 | Continental Rlwy | | | | | | | | | 87 50 | | | | Freight-in | | 87 50 | |
| 18 | Budget Oil | | | | | | | | | 64 72 | | | | Delivery Exp. | | 64 72 | |
| 19 | G. Ripley | 80 | | 50 — | | | | | | | | | | G. Ripley, Drawings | | 50 — | |
| 20 | Ideal Supply | 81 | | 300 — | | | | | | | | 300 — | | | | | |
| 21 | Circle Supplies | | | | | | | | | 46 — | | | 46 — | | | | |
| 21 | Deluxe Stationers | | | | | | | | | 420 — | | | 70 — | Office Equip. | | 350 — | |
| 24 | Crescent Bank | | 1 000 — | | | | | | | | | | | Bank Loan | | | 1 000 — |
| 25 | E. McRae | | 62 — | | | | 62 — | | | | | | | | | | |
| 26 | Empire Wholesale | 82 | | 200 — | | | | | 200 — | | | | | | | | |
| 26 | Prairie Manufacturing | | | | | | | | | 160 — | | 160 — | | | | | |
| 26 | R. Stoddard | | 100 — | | | | 100 — | | | | | | | | | | |
| 27 | M. Field | 83 | | 112 — | | | | | | | | | | Wages Expense | | 112 — | |
| 27 | R. French | 84 | | 135 — | | | | | | | | | | Wages Expense | | 135 — | |
| 31 | Purity Company | 168 | | | | 96 — | | | | | | 96 — | | | | | |
| 31 | G. Ripley | | 500 — | | | | | | | | | | | G. Ripley, Capital | | | 500 — |
| | | | 2 109 — | 1 340 90 | | 628 — | 553 — | | 259 70 | 1 094 22 | 484 — | 776 — | 133 20 | | | 1 246 22 | 1 500 — |

*Synoptic journal with entries for transactions 1 to 28.*

*27* May 31: Issued Sales Invoice No. 168 for $96 to Purity Company.

*28* May 31: G. Ripley, the owner, brought $500 of his personal funds into the business for the purpose of increasing his equity.

## Balancing the Columnar Journal

At the bottom of every page, and at the end of every month, a procedure called **cross balancing** is performed on the synoptic journal, or on any columnar journal. This procedure is often referred to as just 'balancing' the journal.

The steps in cross balancing a journal are described below. As you study these steps, refer to the illustration of the synoptic journal on page 132.

Step 1.  **Immediately beneath the last entry on the page, and in ink, draw a single ruled line across all money columns of the journal.**

Step 2.  **Separately, total (foot) each money column and write in the total in small pencil fig-** ures just beneath the single ruled line. You will recall that these small pencil figures are known as 'pencil footings' or 'pin totals'.

Step 3.  **Using an adding machine or a pencil and paper, separately add all of the pin totals of the debit columns and all of the pin totals of the credit columns; include all columns of the journal.** These two additions should produce the same grand total (i.e., a total of several totals). If the two sums are the same, the journal is 'in balance'. If the two sums are not the same, the journal is 'out of balance' or 'not in balance'.

A journal out of balance indicates that one or more errors have been made in its preparation. You may not proceed to the posting of the journal until the errors have been located and corrected.

Step 4.  **If step 3 indicates that the journal is in balance, write in the column totals in ink immediately beneath the pin totals.**

Step 5.  **In ink, draw a double ruled line across all money columns.**

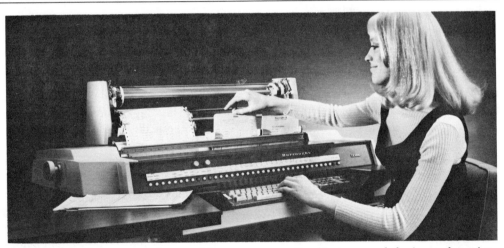

*With this modern accounting machine an operator is able to record the journal entries quickly, accurately, and neatly. A feature of the machine shown is its ability to handle both front-fed forms (ledger cards, single forms, multipart unit sets) and continuous preprinted stationery and journals (courtesy of Burroughs Business Machines Ltd.).*

## Forwarding in the Columnar Journal

Whenever a new journal page is started, and it is not the beginning of a month, it is customary to start the new page with the totals from the previous page. The totals at the end of one page are 'forwarded' to the beginning of the next.

At the end of a page, after balancing it in the manner already discussed in this chapter, it is merely necessary to write in 'Carried Forward' or just 'Forwarded' in the Explanation column. This is illustrated at the top of page 134. Remember that the journal is not posted until the end of the month.

| Date 19- | Customer or Supplier or Explanation | # | Bank Dr. | Bank Cr. | V | Accounts Rec'l Dr. | Accounts Rec'l Cr. | V | Accounts Pay'l Dr. | Accounts Pay'l Cr. | Salesor Income Cr. | Purch's Dr. | Wages Dr. | Drawings Dr. | Other Accounts Account | PR | Dr. | Cr. |
|---|---|---|---|---|---|---|---|---|---|---|---|---|---|---|---|---|---|---|
| 14 | C. Palmer | | 131 62 | | | | 131 62 | | | | | | | | | | | |
| 15 | D. Clarke | 106 | | | | 85 — | | | | | 85 — | | | | | | | |
| | Carried Forward | | 2 706 49 | 3 659 07 | | 4 091 07 | 3 967 02 | | 2 787 54 | 5 276 29 | 5 069 04 | 3 649 01 | 1 261 41 | 1 900 — | | | 1 620 90 | 45 — |

On the first line of the next page it is then necessary to —

1. Write in the date of the last entry made on the preceding page.
2. Write in 'Brought Forward' or just 'Forwarded' in the Explanation column.
3. Write in the column totals from the previous page.

These steps are illustrated below.

After these steps have been carried out, the journalizing process may be continued.

| Date 19- | Customer or Supplier or Explanation | # | Bank Dr. | Bank Cr. | V | Accounts Rec'l Dr. | Accounts Rec'l Cr. | V | Accounts Pay'l Dr. | Accounts Pay'l Cr. | Salesor Income Cr. | Purch's Dr. | Wages Dr. | Drawings Dr. | Other Accounts Account | PR | Dr. | Cr. |
|---|---|---|---|---|---|---|---|---|---|---|---|---|---|---|---|---|---|---|
| June 15 | Brought Forward | | 2 706 49 | 3 659 07 | | 4 091 07 | 3 967 02 | | 2 787 54 | 5 276 29 | 5 069 04 | 3 649 01 | 1 261 41 | 1 900 — | | | 1 620 90 | 45 — |

## Posting to the General Ledger

The procedure for posting from a columnar journal is different from that used to post from the two-column general journal. This new posting procedure can be nicely demonstrated by means of the synoptic journal.

In respect to the special columns of the synoptic journal, it is the 'column totals' that are posted and not the individual items contained in the columns. This is true for all columns except the two general columns in the Other Accounts section of the journal. Because these two general columns usually contain several items relating to a number of different general ledger accounts, the items in these two columns must be posted individually.

In detail, the procedure for posting a columnar journal is as follows:

1. Post the total of each special column to the account indicated in the column heading.
   a. Post to the debit or credit side of the account according to the column heading.
   b. In the account, date the entry with the last day of the month being posted.
   c. When cross referencing in the account, use Sn and the number of the journal page from which the postings are taken.
   d. When cross referencing in the journal, use the number of the account and place it in brackets beneath the column total.

2. Post each item individually in the two general columns of the Other Accounts section.
   a. Post the amount that appears in either of the two money columns.
   b. Post to the account named.
   c. Post to the debit or credit side of the account according to the heading of the column in which the amount appears.
   d. In the account, date the entry either with the last day of the month being posted, or with the day of the transaction.
   e. When cross referencing in the account, use Sn and the number of the journal page from which the postings are taken.
   f. When cross referencing in the journal, use the number of the account and place it in the Posting Reference (PR) column, on the same line as the amount being posted.

### Examples

In the following examples observe that each posting being studied is written on a white background for purposes of highlighting.

1. *Post the 'Bank Dr.' column —*
   a. In the account:

   (Notice that the account balance is not calculated at this time. Only after all postings are completed are the account balances usually determined. As a rule, they are found at that time with the help of an adding machine.)

| Account | Bank | | | | | | No. | 1 | |
|---|---|---|---|---|---|---|---|---|---|
| **Date** | | **Particulars** | **P.R.** | **Debit** | | **Credit** | **DR. CR.** | **Balance** | |
| mar 19— | 31 | Balance brought forward | — | | | | DR | 1 351 | 40 |
| Apr | 30 | | Sn41 | 1 630 | 20 | | | | |
| | 30 | | Sn41 | | | 1 264 19 | DR | 1 717 | 41 |
| May | 31 | | Sn42 | 2 109 | — | | | | |

b. In the synoptic journal:

SYNOPTIC JOURNAL     19—    P. 42

| Date 19— | | Customer or Supplier or Explanation | # | Bank Dr. | | Bank Cr. | | V | Accounts Dr. | | Accounts PR | Dr. | | Cr. | |
|---|---|---|---|---|---|---|---|---|---|---|---|---|---|---|---|
| May | 4 | Cash Sale | 57 | 56 | — | | | | | | | | | | |
| | 5 | Paul Boyer | 165 | | | | | | 112 | — | | | | | |
| | 6 | Empire Wholesale | | | | | | | | | | | | | |
| | 31 | Purity Company | 168 | | | | | | 96 | — | | | | | |
| | 31 | G. Ripley | | 500 | — | | | | | | l | | | 500 | — |
| | | | | 2 109 | — | 1 340 90 | | | 628 | — | | 1 246 22 | 1 500 | — | |
| | | | | 2 109 | — | 1 340 90 | | | 628 | — | | 1 246 22 | 1 500 | — | |
| | | | | (1) | | | | | | | | | | | |

2. *Post the 'Bank Cr.' column –*
   a. In the account:

| Account | Bank | | | | | | No. | 1 | |
|---|---|---|---|---|---|---|---|---|---|
| **Date** | | **Particulars** | **P.R.** | **Debit** | | **Credit** | **DR. CR.** | **Balance** | |
| mar 19— | 31 | Balance brought forward | — | | | | DR | 1 351 | 40 |
| Apr | 30 | | Sn41 | 1 630 | 20 | | | | |
| | 30 | | Sn41 | | | 1 264 19 | DR | 1 717 | 41 |
| May | 31 | | Sn42 | 2 109 | — | | | | |
| | 31 | | Sn42 | | | 1 340 90 | | | |

b. In the synoptic journal:

SYNOPTIC JOURNAL     19—    P. 42

| Date 19— | | Customer or Supplier or Explanation | # | Bank Dr. | | Bank Cr. | | V | Accounts Dr. | | Accounts PR | Dr. | | Cr. | |
|---|---|---|---|---|---|---|---|---|---|---|---|---|---|---|---|
| May | 4 | Cash Sale | 57 | 56 | — | | | | | | | | | | |
| | 5 | Paul Boyer | 165 | | | | | | 112 | — | | | | | |
| | 6 | Empire Wholesale | | | | | | | | | | | | | |
| | 31 | Purity Company | 168 | | | | | | 96 | — | | | | | |
| | 31 | G. Ripley | | 500 | — | | | | | | ..l | | | 500 | — |
| | | | | 2 109 | — | 1 340 90 | | | 628 | — | | 1 246 22 | 1 500 | — | |
| | | | | 2 109 | — | 1 340 90 | | | 628 | — | | 1 246 22 | 1 500 | — | |
| | | | | (1) | | (1) | | | | | | | | | |

3. *Post the item 'Rent Expense, $200'* –
    a. In the account:

| Account | Rent Expense | | | No. | 52 | |
|---------|--------------|-----|-------|-----|-----|---------|
| Date | Particulars | P.R. | Debit | Credit | DR. CR. | Balance |
| Apr 19— 30 | Balance brought forward | — | | | DR | 800 — |
| May 31 | | Sn42 | 200 — | | | |
| | | | | | | |
| | | | | | | |
| | | | | | | |
| | | | | | | |

    b. In the synoptic journal:

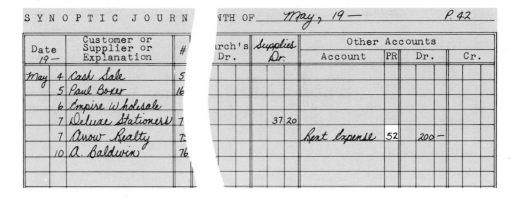

4. *Post the item 'G. Ripley, Capital, $500'* –
    a. In the account:

| Account | G. Ripley, Capital | | | No. | 31 | |
|---------|--------------------|-----|-------|-----|-----|---------|
| Date | Particulars | P.R. | Debit | Credit | DR. CR. | Balance |
| Apr 19— 30 | Balance brought forward | — | | | CR | 812 — |
| May 31 | | Sn42 | | 500 — | | |

    b. In the synoptic journal:

| SYNOPTIC JOURNAL | | | Bank | | h's | Other Accounts | | | |
|---|---|---|---|---|---|---|---|---|---|
| Date 19— | Customer or Supplier or Explanation | # | Dr. | Cr. | | Account | PR | Dr. | Cr. |
| May 4 | Cash Sale | 57 | 56 — | | | | | | |
| 31 | Purity Company | 168 | | | | | | | |
| 31 | G. Ripley | | 500 — | | | G. Ripley, Capital | 31 | | 500 — |
| | | | 2 109 — | 1 340 90 | | | | 1 246 22 | 1 500 — |
| | | | 2 109 — | 1 340 90 | | | | 1 246 22 | 1 500 — |
| | | | (1) | (1) | | | | | |

After being posted entirely, the synoptic journal appears as shown below:

| Date 19— | Customer or Supplier or Explanation | # | Bank Dr. | Bank Cr. | √ | Accounts Rec'l Dr. | Accounts Rec'l Cr. | √ | Accounts Pay'l Dr. | Accounts Pay'l Cr. | Salesor Income Cr. | Purch's Dr. | Supplies Dr. | Other Accounts Account | PR | Dr. | Cr. |
|---|---|---|---|---|---|---|---|---|---|---|---|---|---|---|---|---|---|
| May 4 | Cash Sale | 51 | 56 — | | | | | | | | 56 — | | | | | | |
| 5 | Paul Boxer | 165 | | | | 112 — | | | | | 112 — | | | | | | |
| 6 | Empire Wholesale | | | | | | | | 316 — | | | 316 — | | | | | |
| 7 | Deluxe Stationers | 74 | | 37 20 | | | | | | | | | 37 20 | | | | |
| 7 | Arrow Realty | 75 | | 200 — | | | | | | | | | | Rent Expense | 58 | 200 — | |
| 10 | Q. Baldwin | 76 | | 13 50 | | | | | 13 50 | | | | | | | | |
| 10 | H. English & Co. | 77 | | 46 20 | | | | | 46 20 | | | | | | | | |
| 11 | R. Smith | | 16 — | | | | 16 — | | | | | | | | | | |
| 11 | F. Jones | | 375 — | | | | 375 — | | | | | | | | | | |
| 13 | M. Field | 78 | | 112 — | | | | | | | | | | Wages Expense | 59 | 112 — | |
| 13 | R. French | 79 | | 135 — | | | | | | | | | | Wages Expense | 59 | 135 — | |
| 14 | M. Birch | 166 | | | | 250 — | | | | 250 — | | | | | | | |
| 14 | U. Ash | 167 | | | | 170 — | | | | 170 — | | | | | | | |
| 17 | Continental Rlwy. | | | | | | | | | 87 50 | | | | Freight-in | 54 | 87 50 | |
| 18 | Budget Oil | | | | | | | | | 64 72 | | | | Delivery Exp. | 52 | 64 72 | |
| 19 | G. Ripley | 80 | | 50 — | | | | | | | | | | G. Ripley, Drawings | 32 | 50 — | |
| 20 | Ideal Supply | 81 | | 300 — | | | | | | | | 300 — | | | | | |
| 21 | Circle Supplies | | | | | | | | | 46 — | | | 46 — | | | | |
| 21 | Deluxe Stationers | | | | | | | | | 420 — | | | 70 — | Office Equip. | 5 | 350 — | |
| 24 | Crescent Bank | | 1 000 — | | | | | | | | | | | Bank Loan | 22 | | 1 000 — |
| 25 | L. McRae | | 62 — | | | | 62 — | | | | | | | | | | |
| 26 | Empire Wholesale | 82 | | 200 — | | | | | 200 — | | | | | | | | |
| 26 | Prairie Manufacturing | | | | | | | | | 160 — | | 160 — | | | | | |
| 26 | R. Stoddard | | 100 — | | | | 100 — | | | | | | | | | | |
| 27 | M. Field | 83 | | 112 — | | | | | | | | | | Wages Expense | 59 | 112 — | |
| 27 | R. French | 84 | | 135 — | | | | | | | | | | Wages Expense | 59 | 135 — | |
| 31 | Purity Company | 168 | | | | 96 — | | | | 96 — | | | | | | | |
| 31 | G. Ripley | | 500 — | | | | | | | | | | | G. Ripley, Capital | 31 | | 500 — |
| | | | 2 109 — | 1 340 90 | | 628 — | 553 — | | 259 70 | 1 094 22 | 684 — | 776 — | 153 20 | | | 1 296 22 | 1 500 — |
| | | | (1) | (1) | | (2) | (2) | | (21) | (21) | (41) | (51) | (4) | | | | |

## Variations in Journalizing in the Synoptic Journal

1. Occasionally, you may want to record a transaction of a non-routine nature in the synoptic journal. It is permissible to do this provided that, if the accounting entry is not self-explanatory, an explanation is written (usually in parentheses). When writing explanations, it is permissible to write through the money columns. (See all three transactions illustrated below.)

2. Debit entries may be written in Credit columns or credit entries in Debit columns, provided that they are circled or written in red. This special designation of an entry indicates that its effect on the account is the opposite

to that specified in the column heading. When the column is totaled, the designated item must be subtracted in order that the column total, when posted, will have the proper effect on the account. (See the second transaction illustrated below.)

3. Although most accounting entries require only one line in the synoptic journal, there are times when two or more lines may be required. This situation arises when at least two of the accounts affected by a transaction need to be recorded in the Other Accounts section of the journal, or when an explanation is written on a separate line. (See the second and third transactions illustrated below.)

| Date 19— | Customer or Supplier or Explanation | # | Bank Dr. | Bank Cr. | √ | Accounts Rec'l Dr. | Accounts Rec'l Cr. | √ | Accounts Pay'l Dr. | Accounts Pay'l Cr. | Salesor Income Cr. | Purch's Dr. | Supplies Dr. | Wages Expense Dr. | Other Accounts Account | PR | Dr. | Cr. |
|---|---|---|---|---|---|---|---|---|---|---|---|---|---|---|---|---|---|---|
| Aug 3 | J. R. Proctor | 902 | | 150 — | | (Painting of office building) | | | | | | | | | Bldg. Maintenance | | 150 — | |
| 4 | M. Hicks | 903 | | 27 50 | | | | | | | (27 50) | | | | | | | |
| | (To refund amount overcharged on Sales Slip 174) | | | | | | | | | | | | | | | | | |
| 5 | Midwest Oil Co. | 904 | | 216 75 | | | | | | | | | | | Heat Expense | | 195 60 | |
| | (Heating fuel; part for oil delivered to home of proprietor) | | | | | | | | | | | | | | J. Roe, Drawings | | 21 15 | |

## Two-Journal System

Frequently, the synoptic journal and the two-column general journal are both used in a business. The synoptic journal is used to record the type of transaction for which it is most suitable; namely, routine transactions. Its preparation usually presents no difficulty for a junior employee. On the other hand, the two-column general journal is used by a senior accounting person to record entries of a non-routine and usually more complex nature. The basic structure of a two-journal system is illustrated below by means of a flowchart.

In a two-journal system, each journal is prepared independently of the other, and at the end of every month each of the journals is posted individually to the general ledger. If the general ledger is found to be out of balance after the postings have been completed, it is necessary to consider the possibility of errors existing in two journals. The procedure for finding errors when a trial balance does not balance (page 64) must be amended to include two separate journals.

### Flowchart 4  Basic Structure of a Two-Journal System

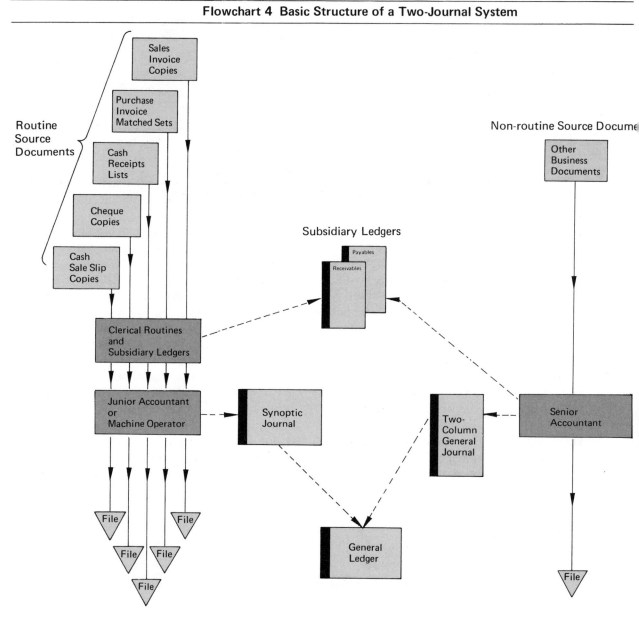

## General Journal Vouchers

A popular alternative to the general journal in the form of a book is a file of general journal vouchers. An example of a completed general journal voucher is shown below.

Unused journal vouchers are kept in the form of a pad at the desk of the person who is responsible for their preparation. As circumstances warrant, the general journal entries are written (usually one to a page), and the vouchers are filed in numerical order on a type of ring binder. The vouchers are numbered consecutively as they are written.

At the end of each month, the general journal vouchers for the month are posted to the general ledger. A minor difference in procedure is the use of the journal voucher number in cross referencing the journal entry in the account.

GENERAL JOURNAL VOUCHER

DATE: June 14 19 —          VOUCHER NO. 146

| Account | V | Subsidiary Ledger | PR | General Ledger Debit | General Ledger Credit |
|---|---|---|---|---|---|
| Sales | | | 41 | 230 95 | |
| Accounts Receivable | | | 2 | | 230 95 |
| Farrow Brothers | ✓ | 84 75 | | | |
| N. Robertson | ✓ | 90 00 | | | |
| S. Laing | ✓ | 56 20 | | | |
| | | 230 95 | | | |

EXPLANATION:
To cancel three Sales Invoices issued in error: #615; #616; #617.

*A completed general journal voucher.*

# Bookkeeping and Accounting Terms

**Trading Business** A business that deals in the buying and selling of merchandise. It buys the merchandise for the specific purpose of selling it at a profit.

**Merchandise Inventory** The goods that a trading business deals in. Also known as **stock-in-trade**.

**Purchases Account** The account that is charged with the cost of merchandise purchased for resale. 'Purchases' (the account name) is a short way of saying 'Purchases of Merchandise for Resale'.

**Freight-in** Transportation charges on incoming merchandise.

**Delivery Expense** Transportation charges on outgoing merchandise.

**Synoptic Journal** A multi-columned journal having a number of selected special columns and two general columns. The special columns are used to record the more frequently occurring items; the two general columns are used to record the less frequently occurring items. Each of the special columns is reserved for a specific type of entry as indicated in the column heading; no other type of entry may be recorded in the column. At posting time, it is the totals of the special columns that are posted to the general ledger, not the individual items contained in the columns.

**Cross Balancing** A procedure carried out in respect to columnar journals to find out if the journalizing is arithmetically correct. After totaling separately all of the columns of the journal, the sum of the Debit column totals should equal the sum of the Credit column totals. Also known as **balancing the journal**.

## Review Questions

1. What is a trading business?
2. What is merchandise inventory? Give examples of different types of merchandise inventory.
3. What is stock-in-trade?
4. Where is merchandise inventory shown on the balance sheet?
5. At the beginning of an accounting period, what does the balance in the merchandise inventory account represent?
6. Describe briefly what the Purchases account is used for.
7. Give the accounting entry for the purchase of merchandise, (a) for cash; (b) on account.
8. Give the accounting entry for the sale of merchandise, (a) for cash; (b) on account.
9. "Not every item purchased is debited to the Purchases account." Explain.
10. Explain the difference between Freight-in and Delivery Expense.

11. What is the principal difference between the synoptic journal and the two-column general journal?
12. For what type of transaction is the synoptic journal best suited?
13. In the synoptic journal, what is the purpose of the special columns?
14. In the synoptic journal, what is the purpose of the two general columns?
15. Why is it necessary to cross balance a columnar journal?
16. What is the major advantage of the synoptic journal?
17. When are explanations necessary in a synoptic journal?
18. Briefly describe the use of general journal vouchers.

## Exercises

1. At the end of July 19— the totals in a synoptic journal are as follows:

| SYNOPTIC JOURNAL | | | | | | | | | | | | | | | MONTH OF July, 19— | | | | |
|---|---|---|---|---|---|---|---|---|---|---|---|---|---|---|---|---|---|---|---|
| Date | Customer or Supplier or Explanation | # | Bank | | V | Accounts Rec'l | | V | Accounts Pay'l | | Sales or Income Cr. | Purch's Dr. | Supplies Dr | Wages Dr | Other Accounts | | | | |
| | | | Dr. | Cr. | | Dr. | Cr. | | Dr. | Cr. | | | | | Account | PR | Dr. | | Cr. |
| | | | 2 694 62 | 3 016 21 | | 3 096 17 | 2 546 21 | | 1 596 12 | 1 842 94 | 3 309 42 | 1 706 40 | 156 97 | 746 02 | | | 729 74 | | 11 26 |

Cross balance the synoptic journal.

## 2. At the end of June 19— the pin totals in a synoptic journal are as follows:

| | SYNOPTIC JOURNAL | | Bank | | | Accounts Rec'l | | | Accounts Pay'l | | Salesor Income | Purch's | Supplies | Wages | Other Accounts | | | |
|---|---|---|---|---|---|---|---|---|---|---|---|---|---|---|---|---|---|---|
| Date | Customer or Supplier or Explanation | # | Dr. | Cr. | √ | Dr. | Cr. | √ | Dr. | Cr. | Cr. | Dr. | Dr. | Dr. | Account | PR | Dr. | Cr. |
| | | | 6 092 10 | 5 961 02 | | 10 060 22 | 6 142 10 | | 4 092 17 | 9 402 19 | 10 104 11 | 7 574 80 | 356 51 | 3 023 65 | | | 409 97 | |

MONTH OF *June,* 19—

Cross balance the synoptic journal.

---

## 3. Journalize the following transactions in two-column general journal form for E & G TV and Stereo:

*Transactions*

Dec. 1 Received an invoice, #435, from Paramount Manufacturing for a shipment of television sets, $3 045.00.

2 Received an invoice, #B616, from Murray Transport Company for transportation charges on the above shipment of television sets, $435.

3 J. Moran has his own delivery service business. He provides a service to E & G TV and Stereo during peak periods. He has just completed a day's deliveries for E & G and personally presents his bill for the day to the accountant. Cheque #602 in the amount of $350 is issued immediately to J. Moran.

4 Received an invoice, #7042, from Swiss Stationers for a shipment of office forms and supplies to be used in the business, $136.

5 Issued Sales Invoice #789 to W. Parker for stereo speakers and electronic parts, $217.

5 Issued Cash Sales Slip, #143, for the cash sale of merchandise from the store, $52.

6 Received an invoice, #902, from Haniko Electric for a shipment of electronic parts, $2 678.

---

## 4. In a synoptic journal record the following transactions:

*Transactions*

March 4 Issued cheque #506 for $300 to Martin and Martin on account.

9 Issued Sales Invoice #5906 to O. P. Jones, $150.

10 Received Invoice #692 from Andrews Brothers for a shipment of merchandise, $450.

11 Received $500 on account from P. S. Ross.

11 Issued cheque # 507 for $65 to Municipal Telephone for the monthly phone bill.

Rule and balance the synoptic journal.

---

## 5. A notice is received from Carter Supply to the effect that they had overcharged by $50 on a previous invoice for merchandise. This notice requires an accounting entry as follows:

|  |  |
|---|---|
| Accounts Payable (Carter Supply)    50.00 |  |
| Purchases | 50.00 |

Show how you would record this entry in the synoptic journal using the circling technique in the Purchases column. Explain how, by using this technique, the correct balance is reached in the Purchases account.

---

6. This exercise is to be done in your workbook, or as directed by your teacher.

---

7. This exercise is to be done in your workbook, or as directed by your teacher.

---

8. This exercise is to be done in your workbook, or as directed by your teacher.

---

9. In the synoptic journal of P. D. R. Distributing Co., record the transactions listed below for August 19—. Use the spare column for 'Wages'. The chart of accounts for the business is as follows:

Account:
No. 1 Bank
2 Accounts Receivable
3 Merchandise Inventory
4 Supplies
5 Building
6 Furniture and Equipment
21 Accounts Payable
22 Bank Loan
23 Mortgage Payable
31 A. Orlando, Capital
32 A. Orlando, Drawings
41 Sales
51 Advertising
52 Building Repairs and Maintenance
53 Freight-in
54 Heat and Electricity
55 Miscellaneous Expense
56 Postage
57 Purchases
58 Telephone Expense
59 Wages

*Transactions*
August
2 *Cheque Copy*
   —No. 702, to D. Macdonald, $310, cash payment for painting the building occupied by the business.
3 *Invoice*
   —No. 210, to N. Rae, $34, for sale of goods.
   *Cash Receipt*
   —From B. Page, $100, on account.
5 *Cheque Copy*
   —No. 703, to E. Pickard, $190, for wages.
   *Cash Sales*
   —$151.75.
8 *Cheque Copy*
   —No. 704, to Receiver General of Canada, $20, for postage stamps.
**Note:** Cheques to the Government of Canada are made out to the Receiver General of Canada.
   *Invoice*
   —No. 211, to Atlas Stores, $502, for sale of goods.
9 *Purchase Invoice*
   —From Diamond Wholesalers, $325, for purchase of merchandise.
10 *Purchase Invoice*
   —From Continental Railway, $165, for freight charges on incoming merchandise.
11 *Cash Sales*
   —$74.
12 *Cheque Copies*
   —No. 705, to Vance Brothers, $300, on account.
   —No. 706, to E. Pickard, $190, for wages.
15 *Cheque Copies*
   —No. 707, to Century 21, $10, for newspaper advertising.

−No. 708, to A. Orlando, $100, for proprietor's personal use.
18 *Cash Sales*
 −$210.
19 *Cheque Copies*
 −No. 709, to Merry Manufacturing, $500, on account.
 −No. 710, to E. Pickard, $190, for wages.
 *Cash Receipt*
 −From G. Price, $140.25, on account.
22 *Cheque Copy*
 −No. 711, to Price-Vincent Ltd., $350, for mortgage instalment.
 *Sales Invoice*
 −No. 212, to T. Schmidt, $170, for sale of goods.
23 *Purchase Invoice*
 −From Deluxe Oil Company, $75, for gasoline used in the proprietor's automobile − $50 for business purposes, $25 for personal use.

24 *Bank Debit Slip*
 −From General Bank, $12, for bank service charges.
25 *Cheque Copy*
 −No. 712, to A. Orlando, $50, for proprietor's personal use.
26 *Cash Sales*
 −$70.
 *Cheque Copy*
 −No. 713, to E. Pickard, $190, for wages.
29 *Purchase Invoice*
 −From Federated Supply, $1 240, for the purchase of merchandise.
30 *Cheque Copy*
 −No. 714, to Public Utilities Commission, $45, electricity charges for light and heat.
31 *Sales Invoice*
 −No. 213, to R. Snell, $19, for sale of goods.
 *Cash Receipt*
 −From U. Stewart, $106, on account.

**After completing the journalizing of the above transactions, cross balance and rule the journal.**

---

**10.  From Exercise 9 above, summarize the postings that would be made to the general ledger. List the information in three columns: Account, Debit Amount, Credit Amount. Show that the postings are 'balanced' by totaling the two money columns.**

---

**11.  Record the following selected transactions in the synoptic journal of Howard Houghton Wholesaler. Use the spare column of the journal for Supplies, Dr. Since no chart of accounts is given for this exercise it will be necessary for you to make your own decisions in respect to the selection of accounts.**

*Transactions*
November
 1 *Sales Invoice*
 −Issued to O. Tyler, $84.50, for sale of goods.
 9 *Purchase Invoice*
 −From O.K. Office Supplies, $173.25, for new office chair, $68.95, and office supplies, $104.30.
15 *Correcting Entry*
 −Sales Invoice No. 50, which was issued to M. Stephens in the amount of $90, was journalized twice in error last month. Make the necessary correcting entry.
19 Howard Houghton, the owner, collected an account receivable from P. Anderson in the amount of $75. He did not turn the money into the business but kept it for his own personal use. However, he did inform you, the accountant, of the transaction and requested that you make the appropriate accounting entries.
22 Howard Houghton, the owner, purchased a first-aid kit for the business and paid for it out of his own pocket. He submitted the 'paid' bill for $15 to you and requested that you issue a cheque to reimburse him. Cheque No. 296 was issued by you.
29 Because of a period of heavy expenditures the business became short of funds. This

necessitated that the owner arrange a bank loan of $1 000 from The People's Bank. You were given a memo from the bank showing that the loan had been granted and that the $1 000 had been placed in the business bank account.

**Balance the synoptic journal.**

---

12. F. Dunn is the sole proprietor of Crest Hardware. He operates the store with the assistance of his wife and some occasional part-time help. Mrs. Dunn works in the store as well as being responsible for all direct aspects of accounting. The financial statements are prepared annually from her records by a professional accountant.

The books of account are very simple and consist of a general ledger, an accounts receivable ledger, an accounts payable ledger, and a synoptic journal. The last page used in the synoptic journal is page 72 and it shows that the spare column is used for General Expense.

Most of the sales of the business are cash sales or C.O.D. sales. The cash receipts are deposited in the bank on a daily basis. All payments are made by cheque.

The number of accounts in both subsidiary ledgers is very small. Mr. Dunn grants credit to only a few customers and buys his stock from only a few suppliers. Because of the small number of debtors and creditors the subsidiary ledger routine is very simple. All transactions are recorded in the synoptic journal and the postings to the subsidiary ledgers are made directly from the information in the journal and not from the source documents themselves. A check mark is placed in the '√' column in the journal to indicate that a subsidiary ledger posting has been completed.

Set up the three ledgers of Crest Hardware from the following trial balances:

CREST HARDWARE
GENERAL LEDGER TRIAL BALANCE
JANUARY 31, 19—

| | | | |
|---|---|---:|---:|
| 1 | Bank | $ 1 500.00 | |
| 2 | Accounts Receivable | 365.25 | |
| 3 | Merchandise Inventory | 8 090.20 | |
| 4 | Supplies | 395.00 | |
| 5 | Store Equipment | 4 906.21 | |
| 6 | Delivery Equipment | 3 500.00 | |
| 21 | Accounts Payable | | $ 1 404.00 |
| 22 | Federal Finance Co. | | 5 261.00 |
| 31 | F. Dunn, Capital | | 11 739.12 |
| 32 | F. Dunn, Drawings | 860.00 | |
| 41 | Sales | | 5 507.40 |
| 51 | Delivery Expense | 417.06 | |
| 52 | Freight-in | 269.50 | |
| 53 | General Expense | 164.10 | |
| 54 | Purchases | 3 064.20 | |
| 55 | Rent Expense | 300.00 | |
| 56 | Wages Expense | 80.00 | |
| | | $23 911.52 | $23 911.52 |

CREST HARDWARE
ACCOUNTS RECEIVABLE TRIAL BALANCE
JANUARY 31, 19—

| R. Dunlop (Invoice 1407) | $112.76 |
| G. Langford (Invoice 1431) | 157.06 |
| R. Potts (Invoice 1436) | 95.43 |
| | $365.25 |

CREST HARDWARE
ACCOUNTS PAYABLE TRIAL BALANCE
JANUARY 31, 19—

| City Hardware Supply (Their Invoice No. 17421) | $ 746.21 |
| Special Steel Products (Their Invoice No. 147A) | 657.79 |
| | $1 404.00 |

**In the synoptic journal, record the journal entries from the transactions listed below. Post to the subsidiary ledgers on a daily basis.**

*Transactions*
February

2 *Cash Sales*
 −$86.01.
 *Sales Invoice*
 − No. 1475, to R. Dunlop, $26.40, for sale of goods.
 *Purchase Invoice*
 −No. 18021, from City Hardware Supply, $264.25, for purchase of merchandise.
3 *Cash Sales*
 −$102.51.
 *Cash Receipt*
 −From R. Dunlop, $112.76, on account.
5 *Cash Sales*
 −$56.42.
6 *Cash Sales*
 −$109.75.
 *Cheque Copy*
 −No. 316, to R. Gamble, $28, wages for part-time help.
7 *Cash Sales*
 −$245.90.
 *Purchase Invoice*
 −No. 18340, from City Hardware Supply, $316.25, for purchase of merchandise.

7 *Cheque Copies*
 −No. 317, Special Steel Products, $500, on account.
 −No. 318, City Hardware Supply, $746.21, for No. 17421.
 −No. 319, F. Dunn, $150, drawings.
9 *Cash Sales*
 −$24.09.
10 *Cash Sales*
 −$47.98.
 *Sales Invoice*
 −No. 1476, to G. Langford, $59, sale of merchandise.
12 *Cash Sales*
 −$75.87.
 *Purchase Invoice*
 −No. 192A, Special Steel Products, $375.00, for purchase of merchandise.
 *Cheque Copy*
 −No. 320, to J. Moffat, $25, wages for part-time help.
13 *Cash Sales*
 −$152.06.

*Cheque Copy*

–No. 321, to Special Steel Products, $157.79, balance of 147A.

14 *Cash Sales*

–$310.02.

*Sales Invoice*

–No. 1477, to R. Potts, $243.67, sale of goods.

*Purchase Invoice*

–No. 1244, from Clix Oil Company, $23.75, for gasoline and oil used in the delivery truck.

*Cheque Copy*

–No. 322, F. Dunn, $150, drawings.

16 *Cash Sales*

–$32.86.

*Cash Receipt*

–From G. Langford, $157.06, in payment of invoice No. 1431.

17 *Cash Sales*

–$44.

*Purchase Invoice*

–No. 344, Joe Jay Transport, $76.45, charges for transportation on incoming merchandise.

19 *Cash Sales*

–$129.65.

*Cheque Copy*

–No. 323, to Oak Investments, $300, for the rent for the month.

20 *Cash Sales*

–$142.92.

21 *Cash Sales*

–$264.08.

*Cheque Copy*

–No. 324, to F. Dunn, $150, drawings.

23 *Cash Sales*

–$39.87.

*Sales Invoice*

–No. 1478, to R. Dunlop, $64.20, sale of goods.

*Cheque Copies*

–No. 325, to D. Parker, $29, part-time wages.

–No. 326, to Public Utilities Commission, $25.08, cash payment of electricity and water bills.

–No. 327, to City Telephone Company, $19.05, cash payment of telephone bill.

24 *Cash Sales*

–$44.60.

*Cash Receipt*

–From R. Dunlop, $26.40, invoice No. 1475.

26 *Cash Sales*

–$55.11.

*Cheque Copy*

–No. 328, to City Hardware Supply, $264.25, for invoice No. 18021.

27 *Cash Sales*

–$74.23.

28 *Cash Sales*

–$343.24.

*Cheque Copy*

–No. 329, to F. Dunn, $250, drawings.

*Purchase Invoice*

–No. 18472, from City Hardware Supply, $47.49, for store supplies.

**Balance the synoptic journal.**

**Post the synoptic journal to the general ledger.**

**Balance the general ledger.**

**Balance the subsidiary ledgers.**

**13.** The general ledger trial balance of Super Building Supplies on September 30, 19—, is as follows:

SUPER BUILDING SUPPLIES
GENERAL LEDGER TRIAL BALANCE
SEPTEMBER 30, 19—

| | | | |
|---|---|---|---|
| 1 | Bank | $ 1 276.41 | |
| 2 | Accounts Receivable | 3 561.85 | |
| 3 | Merchandise Inventory | 8 487.64 | |
| 4 | Office Supplies | 950.00 | |
| 5 | Delivery Equipment | 4 640.00 | |
| 6 | Office Equipment | 1 065.00 | |
| 21 | Accounts Payable | | $10 840.20 |
| 31 | D. K. Warren, Capital | | 9 395.88 |
| 32 | D. K. Warren, Drawings | 1 509.56 | |
| 41 | Sales | | 4 709.00 |
| 51 | Delivery Expense | 354.00 | |
| 52 | Miscellaneous Expense | 75.62 | |
| 53 | Purchases | 2 905.00 | |
| 54 | Rent Expense | 120.00 | |
| | | $24 945.08 | $24 945.08 |

The subsidiary ledger trial balances on September 30, 19—, are as follows:

*Accounts Receivable*

| | | |
|---|---|---|
| Arnprior Estates | 14 Brown's Place | $1 483.60 |
| Aurora Builders | 815 Keele Street | 900.00 |
| Consumers' Homes | 51 Albionville Road | 100.00 |
| Spartan Builders | 141 Wilson Avenue | 814.16 |
| Westwood Acres | 88 Finchwood Avenue | 264.09 |
| | | $3 561.85 |

*Accounts Payable*

| | | |
|---|---|---|
| General Tile Co. | 383 Hurst Street | $1 516.80 |
| King Crushed Stone | King | 3 161.10 |
| Mapleton Sand & Gravel | Mapleton | 2 658.19 |
| Marris Cement | Marris | 1 851.00 |
| Whyte's Hardware | Rexton | 1 653.11 |
| | | $10 840.20 |

Set up the three ledgers of Super Building Materials.

On page 19 of the synoptic journal, record the transactions for October. Post to the subsidiary ledgers daily from the entries in the synoptic journal. Use the spare column of the journal for Office Supplies.

*Transactions*

October

2 *Cash Sale*
 –To P. Marshall, $35.

5 *Cheque Copy*
 –No. 175, to Mapleton Sand & Gravel, $100, on account.

6 *Sales Invoice*
 –No. 151, to Consumers' Homes, $955, for sale of merchandise.

9 *Cash Receipt*
 –From Arnprior Estates, $1 000, on account.

11 *Purchase Invoice*
 –From Westing Stationers, Westing, $83.60, for office supplies.

15 *Cheque Copies*
 –No. 176, to C. O. Prentice, $120, for the rent for the month.
 –No. 177, to Grand & Son, $310, cash purchase of new office desk.

18 *Sales Invoice*
 –No. 152, to Spartan Builders, $152, for sale of merchandise.

20 *Cheque Copy*
 –No. 178, to Marris Cement, $750, on account.

21 The proprietor took home merchandise for his personal use, value $125.

**Note:** The proprietor must be charged with the value of the merchandise; furthermore, the decrease in merchandise is considered to be a decrease in 'purchases'.

25 *Cheque Copy*
 –No. 179, to Office Suppliers, $18, for cash purchase of stationery.
 *Purchase Invoice*
 –From General Tile, $432, purchase of tile.

28 *Cheque Copy*
 –No. 180, to Gray Lumber Co., $312, for the cash purchase of merchandise.
 *Sales Invoice*
 –No. 153, to Westwood Acres, $516, sale of goods.

29 *Purchase Invoice*
 –From Corgan Oil Limited, 40 Union Street, $157.50, for gas and oil used in the delivery truck.

30 *Cash Receipt*
 –From Spartan Builders, $500, on account.
 *Cash Sale*
 –To P. Percival, $50.

31 *Purchase Invoice*
 –From Marris Cement, $175, for cement.
 *Cheque Copy*
 –No. 181, to Local Telephone Co., $8.50, telephone bill.

**Balance the synoptic journal and post to the general ledger.**
**Balance the general ledger at October 31, 19—.**
**Balance the subsidiary ledgers at October 31, 19—.**

---

**14.  On March 20, 19—, P. Jackson sold a truck that was originally recorded in the Trucks account at $4 000. The truck was sold to J. Winters, a creditor, at a price of $1 200. Mr. Winters requested that the $1 200 be deducted from his account balance.**

  **Record the above transaction in the general journal voucher provided in the workbook.**

# Cases

### Case 1
W. Connor is the owner of Treadwell Shoe Company. Each time a shipment of shoes arrives from the wholesaler, he debits the Merchandise Inventory account. Explain why this is not good accounting practice. What account should he debit?

## Case 2

Mr. Snooks, owner of a shoe store, has been using a two-column general journal to record his daily transactions. What factors might influence Snooks to change to a synoptic journal?

## Case 3

In a cash transaction, F. Dunn, owner of Crest Hardware, sells a cash register that has been used in the store, and credits the Sales account. Is this procedure correct? Why? What effect would this entry have on the income statement?

## Case 4

J. Foster Co. has special columns in its synoptic journal for rent expense and telephone expense. Explain to Mr. Foster why it is not necessary to have a special column for rent or telephone expense.

## Case 5

On Snell Hardware's books all expenditures for the truck are charged to Delivery Expense. However, the truck is occasionally used to pick up merchandise inventory purchased. Mr. Snell estimates that the amount involved, recorded in Delivery Expense, should be charged elsewhere. Is this correct? Explain. What journal entry should be made?

## Case 6

Does a farmer have inventory? Explain.

## Case 7

In a ski resort the new accountant was confused as to what to include in inventory and what to exclude. Explain which of the following items should be inventory: skis, ski tow, ski jackets, chair lift, ski wax, coffee maker, tables and chairs, snow-making equipment. Explain the meaning of inventory to the new accountant.

## Case 8

W. Burgess, the bookkeeper for Murray's Auto Supplies, was introduced to the synoptic journal. He recorded the entries correctly in this journal, but when it came time to post, he posted every transaction as he had done before. Explain why this procedure accomplishes no saving compared to the two-column general journal.

## Case 9

The accountant who audits the books of a certain company suggests to the company bookkeeper that he use a synoptic journal instead of a two-column journal. The bookkeeper refuses and complains to his immediate superior about 'crazy' new ideas. What should the accountant say?

## Case 10

Two columns of a synoptic journal are totalled incorrectly, but the errors offset each other. The total of the Sales column is $2 000 more than it should be, and the total of the Accounts Receivable credit column is $2 000 less than it should be. What will be the effect on the accounts? on income? on total assets? How might the errors be detected?

# 9 The Five-Journal System

## Bank Debit and Credit Advices

The relationship between a bank and one of its depositors is basically this: the bank owes money to the depositor.

Suppose that Barrett Bros. has money on deposit with a bank. Both Barrett Bros. and the bank are obliged to keep track of this money. From Barrett Bros.' point of view the bank balance represents an asset, but from the bank's point of view it represents a liability.

Consider the following transactions.

1. Barrett Bros. makes a deposit of $100.
   a. Barrett Bros. will **debit** 'Bank' (to increase an asset).
   b. The bank will **credit** 'Barrett Bros.' (to increase a liability).
2. Barrett Bros. makes a withdrawal of $50.
   a. Barrett Bros. will **credit** 'Bank' (to decrease an asset).
   b. The bank will **debit** 'Barrett Bros.' (to decrease a liability).

Although both the bank and the depositor are following the same rules of debit and credit, it appears to some that they are directly opposed. New students of accounting are often troubled by this aspect of banking but only because they have had no light shed on the problem.

It is important that a business be able to calculate its bank balance at any time so that it does not issue cheques for more than the amount of its bank balance. To have this facility, a business must be aware of all entries affecting the bank balance. The entries that the business itself originates present no problem, but it must be notified by the bank of any entries that the bank originates.

When a bank initiates a change to a depositor's bank balance, it notifies him immediately by means of a **bank debit advice** or a **bank credit advice** (may be called bank debit memorandum

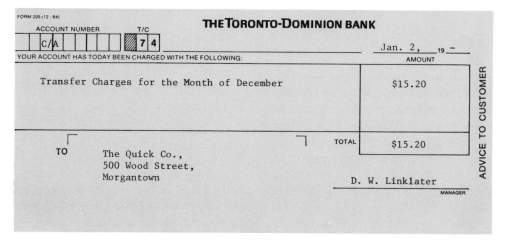

*A bank debit advice (courtesy of The Toronto-Dominion Bank).*

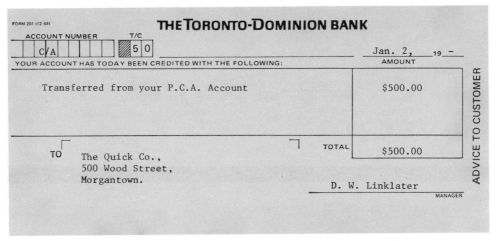

| FORM 201 (12-64) | | | **THE TORONTO-DOMINION BANK** | | |
|---|---|---|---|---|---|
| ACCOUNT NUMBER | T/C | | | | |
| C/A | 5 0 | | | Jan. 2, 19 – | |
| YOUR ACCOUNT HAS TODAY BEEN CREDITED WITH THE FOLLOWING: | | | | AMOUNT | |

Transferred from your P.C.A. Account $500.00

TO The Quick Co.,
500 Wood Street,
Morgantown.

TOTAL $500.00

D. W. Linklater
MANAGER

ADVICE TO CUSTOMER

*A bank credit advice (courtesy of The Toronto-Dominion Bank).*

or bank credit memorandum). The bank debit advice is associated with decreases to the account and the bank credit advice is associated with increases to the account. Examples of both forms are shown above.

The first form, the bank debit advice, informs the depositor that a bank service charge has been deducted from his account. When the depositor receives this notice he must make an appropriate accounting entry in his books of account. In this case the entry will probably be a debit to Bank Charges and a credit to Bank.

The bank credit advice shown above informs the depositor that a sum of money from his personal bank account has been transferred to the business bank account. The accounting entry that is appropriate for this transaction is a debit to Bank and a credit to the owner's Capital account.

# Sales Tax

You are probably well acquainted with sales tax. It is a popular method by means of which governments raise tax revenues. It is a tax related to the sale of goods and is calculated as a certain per cent of the selling price of the goods. The seller of the goods is obliged to be the collector of the sales tax; he collects it from his customers and periodically makes a remittance to the government.

Both the rates of tax and the various types of goods on which the tax is levied will depend on the laws of the country, province, or state in which the goods are sold. In every business, someone should be well informed about sales tax. He may obtain detailed information free of charge from the government offices responsible for the administering of the tax. In Canada, businessmen must be concerned with both federal sales tax and provincial sales tax.

## Accounting for Sales Tax

The simplest transaction involving sales tax is the cash sale. The seller of the goods calculates the amount of the tax or finds it from a tax table, adds the tax to the price of the goods, and collects the total amount from the customer. Because the tax portion must eventually be paid to the government, it represents a liability of the seller. Consider the following transaction:

**$40 of taxable merchandise is sold to R. Brown for cash. The rate of sales tax is 5 per cent.**

The accounting entry to record the transaction is:

| Dr. Bank | 42.00 | |
|---|---|---|
| Cr. Sales | | 40.00 |
| Cr. Sales Tax Payable | | 2.00 |

'Sales Tax Payable' is a liability account set up specially to accumulate sales tax. In an accounting system using a columnar journal, there will probably be a special column for Sales Tax Pay-

## SPORTS EQUIPMENT of Toronto Limited

490 Adelaide Street West, Toronto, Ontario
M5Z 1T3 Telephone 366-9666

## SALES INVOICE NO. 9621

Sold to: G. Watkins,
617 Central Place,
Marathon.
X5T U9N

Date: Nov. 16, 19--

P.O. No.: 4321

Terms: Net 30 Days

| Shipped by | Via | F.O.B. |
|---|---|---|
| C.P. Express | Rail | Toronto |

| Quantity | Description | Unit Price | Amount |
|---|---|---|---|
| 1 pr | O. H. A. Nets- Special | 28.00 | 28.00 |
| 1 only | P. B. M. Playball | 5.75 | 5.75 |
| 6 only | Hockey Sticks | 2.40 | 14.40 |
| 6 only | Bantam Hockey Sticks | 1.50 | 9.00 |
| | | | 57.15 |
| | 5% TAX | | 2.86 |
| ITEMS NOT EXTENDED OR SHIPPED WILL BE FORWARDED AS SOON AS POSSIBLE. NO GOODS RETURNABLE WITHOUT OUR WRITTEN PERMISSION. ALL CLAIMS FOR DAMAGES OR DEFICIENCY MUST BE MADE WITHIN FIVE DAYS FROM RECEIPT OF GOODS. | SHIPPING CHARGES | | |
| | TOTAL | | 60.01 |

*(Courtesy of Sports Equipment of Toronto Limited.)*

able because it is a frequently occurring item.

Goods sold on account also involve sales tax. Consider the above sales invoice on which a 5 per cent sales tax is charged.

The accounting entry to record this sales invoice is:

Dr. Accounts Receivable
  (G. Watkins)     60.01
Cr. Sales              57.15
Cr. Sales Tax Payable     2.86

### Remitting Sales Tax

Periodically, the seller must remit the accumulated sales tax to the government. This is usually done once a month. For example, the federal government of Canada requires that the sales tax collected during one month be sent to the government (to the Receiver General of Canada) by the fifteenth day of the following month. Taxes collected in January are due by the fifteenth of February, taxes collected in February are due by the fifteenth of March, and so on. Government auditors make periodic visits to businesses to ensure correctness of collections and remittances.

The accounting entry to record the cheque of remittance of sales tax to the government is:

Dr. Sales Tax Payable     xx.xx
Cr. Bank             xx.xx

## The Five-Journal System

The synoptic journal described in the previous chapter is suitable for only a very small business or organization. The fact that only one person at a time can work on it is a big disadvantage.

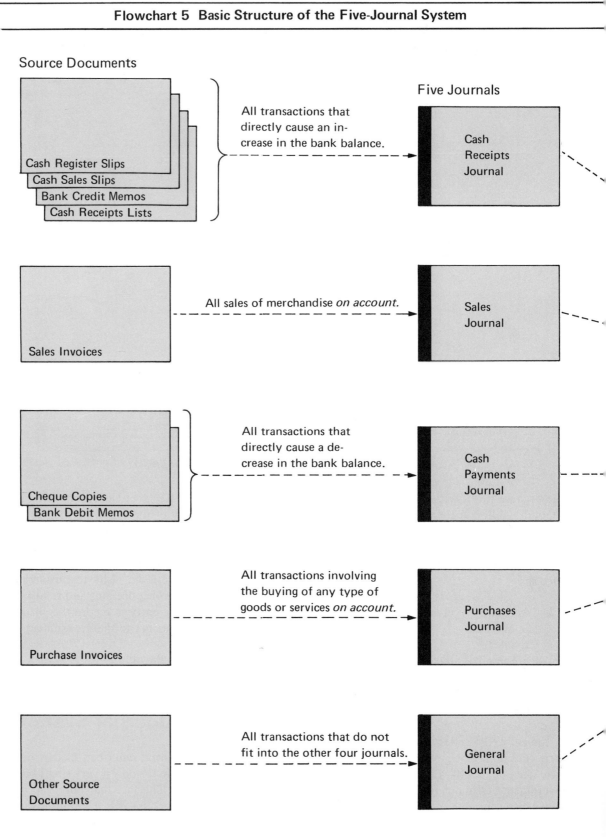

Source Documents

Cash Register Slips
Cash Sales Slips
Bank Credit Memos
Cash Receipts Lists

All transactions that directly cause an increase in the bank balance.

Five Journals

Cash Receipts Journal

Sales Invoices

All sales of merchandise *on account.*

Sales Journal

Cheque Copies
Bank Debit Memos

All transactions that directly cause a decrease in the bank balance.

Cash Payments Journal

Purchase Invoices

All transactions involving the buying of any type of goods or services *on account.*

Purchases Journal

Other Source Documents

All transactions that do not fit into the other four journals.

General Journal

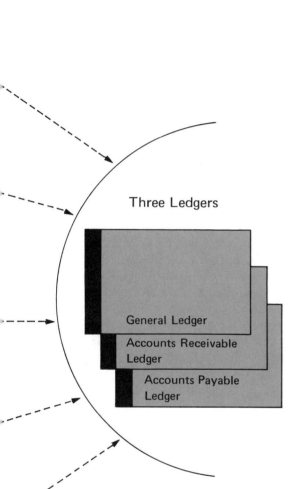

Three Ledgers

General Ledger

Accounts Receivable
Ledger

Accounts Payable
Ledger

Most businesses soon reach a point where they require more than one person to be independently involved in the journalizing process. To make this possible, systems using more than one journal have been developed. One such system is the **five-journal system**.

A system such as the five-journal system has two main advantages. First, it provides the conditions whereby five journals may be prepared independently. Secondly, it strongly influences the accounting system towards greater specialization of duties. The degree of specialization that develops will depend on the type of business, the volume of transactions, and other factors, but some specialization will take place.

The basic structure of the five-journal system is illustrated at left. The illustration shows that the accounting entries are channeled from the various source documents into the five separate journals, each of which is restricted to a particular type of transaction. Each of the special journals is posted individually to the three ledgers.

It should be apparent from the illustration how a number of specialists (or department heads) may come into existence in an accounting system. Large offices may require a specialist for each journal. Smaller offices often find that one man can specialize in the operation of two journals. For instance, there is a natural relationship between 'Sales' and 'Cash Receipts', and another natural relationship between 'Purchases' and 'Cash Payments'. Each of these pairs offers the possibility of making very effective combinations within the accounting department.

Learning to operate the five-journal system is not going to be difficult for you. You will find that the general journal, whether in the form of a book or journal vouchers, is used no differently than before. And each of the new journals is a columnar journal that follows very closely the techniques for using the synoptic journal. The only significant difference is that all of the routine transactions do not go into one journal; they must be directed to one of four special journals, as shown in the illustration.

## Cash Receipts Journal

**In the cash receipts journal are recorded the accounting entries for all transactions that directly cause an increase in the bank balance.**

| Date | Customer or Explanation | Other Accounts Cr. Account | PR | Amount | | | Sales Tax Pay'l Cr. | Sales Cr. | Acc'ts Rec'l Cr. | √ | Bank Dr | Amount of Deposit |
|---|---|---|---|---|---|---|---|---|---|---|---|---|
| Feb 4 | R. Smith #64 | | | | | | 2 38 | 47 50 | | | 49 88 | |
| 4 | P. Wylie #65 | | | | | | 1 32 | 26 37 | | | 27 69 | |
| 4 | D. Denison | | | | | | | | 65 29 | ✓ | 65 29 | |
| 4 | W. Scott | | | | | | | | 146 25 | ✓ | 146 25 | 289 11 |
| 5 | O. Miles #66 | | | | | | 1 40 | 27 90 | | | 29 30 | |
| 5 | J. Kelly | | | | | | | | 52 10 | ✓ | 52 10 | |
| 5 | S. Bruno | | | | | | | | 19 02 | ✓ | 19 02 | 100 42 |
| 5 | Centennial Bk Cr Memo | Interest Inc. | | 34 20 | | | | | | | 34 20 | 34 20 |

*A partially completed cash receipts journal.*

Every accounting entry in the cash receipts journal involves a debit to 'Bank'. The two most common transactions affecting the cash receipts journal are cash sales, and receipts on account from customers.

Illustrated above is a partially completed page from a typical cash receipts journal. It was prepared from the source documents listed below.
February

4 *Cash Sales Slip*
   –No. 64, to R. Smith, $47.50 plus sales tax of $2.38.

4 *Cash Sales Slip*
   –No. 65, to P. Wylie, $26.37 plus sales tax of $1.32.

4 *Cash Receipts*
   –D. Denison, $65.29, on account.
   –W. Scott, $146.25, on account.

5 *Cash Sales Slip*
   –No. 66, to O. Miles, $27.90 plus sales tax of $1.40.

5 *Cash Receipts*
   –J. Kelly, $52.10, on account.
   –S. Bruno, $19.02, on account.

5 *Bank Credit Advice*
   –From Centennial Bank, $34.20, for interest earned.

**Notes:**

1. Special columns are used for frequently occurring items; the 'Other Accounts Cr.' section is used for infrequently occurring items.
2. There are extra columns provided for use as necessary.
3. The √ column is used to indicate that postings to the accounts receivable ledger have been completed. All such postings from this journal will be credits to Accounts Receivable.
4. The little column to the right of the Bank Dr.

column is not used in this journal.

5. Because it is a columnar journal, the rules for columnar journals apply to the cash receipts journal. The column labeled 'Amount of Deposit' (explained below) does not form part of the balanced journal.
6. The 'Amount of Deposit' column is not a compulsory column. The cash receipts journal can be prepared without it. It is included only as a convenient way of tying in cash receipts with the record prepared by the bank. As you will see in a later chapter it is not always easy to make the records of the business agree with those of the bank. For this reason only, the 'Amount of Deposit' column has been included. This column does not form a part of the balanced accounting entries and must not be included when balancing or when posting the journal. The total of the 'Amount of Deposit' column will equal the total of the 'Bank' column.

## Sales Journal

**In the sales journal are recorded the accounting entries for all sales of merchandise on account.** Only one type of entry and one source document, the sales invoice, are involved with this journal.

At the top of the next page is an example of a partially completed sales journal. The illustration shows how our one style of columnar paper may be used as a sales journal. In the example, it is assumed that the rate of sales tax is 5 per cent.

**Notes:**

1. Only special columns are used in the sales journal. No provision is made for a general section.

*A partially completed sales journal.*

2. There are extra columns provided for use as necessary in the future.
3. The √ column is used to indicate that postings to the accounts receivable ledger have been completed. All such postings from this journal will be debits to Accounts Receivable.
4. Because it is a columnar journal, the rules for columnar journals apply to the sales journal.
5. All of the money columns must be included when balancing the journal.

## Cash Payments Journal (Cash Disbursements Journal)

**In the cash payments journal are recorded the accounting entries for all transactions that directly cause a decrease in the bank balance.** Every accounting entry in the cash payments journal involves a credit to 'Bank'. The most common type of transaction affecting the cash payments journal is the issuing of a cheque either as a payment on account or for a cash purchase of goods or services.

Shown below is an example of a partially completed cash payments journal. The illustration shows how our one style of columnar paper may be used as a cash payments journal. The journal was prepared from the source documents shown below.

February
3 *Cheque Copies*
  –No. 72, G. Collins Co., $56, on account.
  –No. 73, Taylor Bros., $75, on account.
4 *Bank Debit Advice*
  –$14.10, for bank service charges.
  *Cheque Copies*
  –No. 74, F. Downes, $150, for wages.
  –No. 75, K. Frost, $170, for wages.
5 *Cheque Copies*
  –No. 76, R. G. Hall, $120, for proprietor's personal use.
  –No. 77, Janson Trade Center, $26.50, for cash purchase of merchandise.
  –No. 78, Lumley's Limited, $50, for cash purchase of supplies.

**Notes:**
1. The cash payments journal is also commonly known as the cash disbursements journal.
2. Special columns are used for frequently occurring items; the general section is used for infrequently occurring items.
3. The √ column is used to indicate that the postings to the accounts payable ledger have

*A partially completed cash payments journal.*

been completed. All such postings from this journal will be debits to Accounts Payable.

4. Because it is a columnar journal, the rules for columnar journals apply to the cash payments journal.

5. All of the money columns must be included when balancing the journal.

## Purchases Journal

**In the purchases journal are recorded the accounting entries for all transactions involving the buying of any type of goods or services on account.** Every accounting entry in the purchases journal involves a credit to Accounts Payable. The source documents for these entries are the matched sets of purchase invoices.

There is shown below an example of a partially completed purchases journal. The illustration shows how our one style of columnar paper may be used as a purchases journal. The journal was prepared from the source documents shown below.

February

3 *Purchase Invoices*
  –Ref. No. 602, Williams' Equipment, $156, for repairs to equipment.
  –Ref. No. 603, P. R. Trotter, $15.80, for supplies.

4 *Purchase Invoices*
  –Ref. No. 604, Pascoe's, $6.40, miscellaneous expense.
  –Ref. No. 605, Reliable Trading, $171, for merchandise.

5 *Purchase Invoices*
  –Ref. No. 606, Mason & Mason, $12.04, for supplies.
  –Ref. No. 607, ABC Supply, $57, for merchandise.

–Ref. No. 608, N.S.E.W. Railway, $74, for transportation charges on incoming goods.
–Ref. No. 609, Hector Oil Co., $19.60, gas and oil for delivery truck.

**Notes:**

1. Special columns are used for frequently occurring items; the 'Other Accounts Dr' section is used for infrequently occurring items.

2. The $\sqrt{}$ column is used to indicate that the postings to the accounts payable ledger have been completed. All such postings from this journal will be credits.

3. Because it is a columnar journal, the rules for columnar journals apply to the purchases journal.

4. All of the money columns must be included when balancing the purchases journal.

5. Purchase invoice reference numbers are not used in all accounting systems. An accountant setting up a purchasing system has a choice of filing the purchase documents in either numeric or alphabetic order. If he chooses alphabetic order, no reference numbers are necessary. If he chooses numeric order, a reference number must be placed on each of the purchase document sets. It is usually easier and faster to locate purchase invoices that are filed in numeric order.

## Posting in the Five-Journal System

When the five-journal system is used, four of the journals are of the columnar type and must be 'balanced' before posting is started. The 'balancing' of these four journals is done in the same manner as that described on page 133 for the synoptic journal. Just remember to balance each

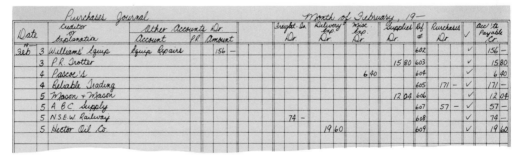

*A partially completed purchases journal.*

| Account | *Accounts Payable* | | | | | | | No. *21* | | | |
|---|---|---|---|---|---|---|---|---|---|---|---|
| Date | Particulars | P.R. | Debit | | Credit | | DR. CR. | Balance | | | |
| *19—* June 24 | *Balance Forwarded* | — | | | | | CR | 24 | 375 | 63 | |
| 30 | | P106 | | | 12 | 970 49 | | | | | |
| 30 | | CP57 | 15 906 26 | | | | CR | 22 | 039 | 86 | |
| | | | | | | | | | | | |
| | | | | | | | | | | | |
| | | | | | | | | | | | |

| Account | *Accounts Receivable* | | | | | | | No. *2* | | | |
|---|---|---|---|---|---|---|---|---|---|---|---|
| Date | Particulars | P.R. | Debit | | Credit | | DR. CR. | Balance | | | |
| *19—* Mar. 31 | *Balance Forwarded* | — | | | | | DR. | 6 | 474 | 07 | |
| 31 | | S67 | 13 047 25 | | | | | | | | |
| 31 | | CR74 | | | 12 096 40 | | | | | | |
| 31 | | J19 | | | 42 42 | | DR. | 7 | 382 50 | | |
| | | | | | | | | | | | |
| | | | | | | | | | | | |
| | | | | | | | | | | | |

of the journals separately.

You have known for some time how to post the general journal and have recently learned (page 134) how to post a columnar journal. This is practically all that you need to know in order to post in the five-journal system. Each journal is posted individually but the order in which they are posted does not matter. Only after all five of the journals have been posted should any attempt be made to balance the ledgers.

In the discussion of 'posting references in the accounts', on page 41, you were told to record the journal page number from which the entry is taken and to prefix it with a code letter; for example, J14. It was stated at that time that the journal code is necessary because several journals may be used simultaneously and the code is a means of identifying the specific journal with which the page number is associated. Now, perhaps, you can appreciate more fully the advantages of coding the posting references in the accounts and the need for additional codes for the four new journals. The new codes are as follows:

| Journal | Code |
|---|---|
| Cash Receipts Journal | CR |
| Cash Payments Journal | CP |
| Sales Journal | S |
| Purchases Journal | P |

The two sample accounts shown above illustrate the way in which the new coded posting references might appear.

## Mechanical Aids to Accounting

There are available a number of mechanical aids to accounting. Two mechanical aids that are widely used are: (1) the bookkeeping or accounting machine; and (2) the accounting pegboard, or 'one-write' system.

These two devices are illustrated below and on the next page.

*Bookkeeping or accounting machine (courtesy of Monroe International, Division of Litton Industries).*

*Accounting pegboard, or one-write board (courtesy of The McBee Company).*

Both the accounting machine and the accounting pegboards are designed to permit the simultaneous preparation by an operator of more than one business form, document, or record. This is achieved most commonly by the use of carbon paper and collated business forms. The concept of collated business forms is illustrated by means of the simple example shown below.

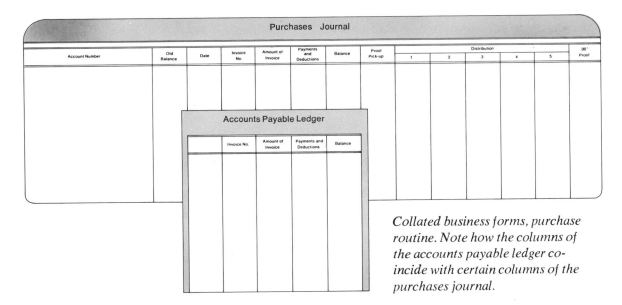

*Collated business forms, purchase routine. Note how the columns of the accounts payable ledger coincide with certain columns of the purchases journal.*

In this particular example, the two forms are made so that the five columns of the ledger card correspond exactly to five specific columns of the purchases journal. You can see that by placing the ledger card on top of the purchases journal with carbon paper interleaved and the forms properly aligned, anything that is written onto the ledger card will also come through onto the purchases journal page. This is the principle of one-write systems.

Other common one-write applications may be seen from the following illustrations:

**Cash Payments Routine**

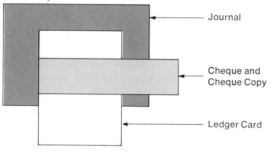

- Journal
- Cheque and Cheque Copy
- Ledger Card

**Sales Routine**

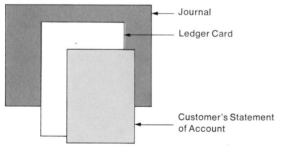

- Journal
- Ledger Card
- Customer's Statement of Account

**Cash Receipts Routine**

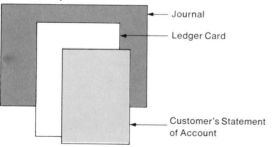

- Journal
- Ledger Card
- Customer's Statement of Account

# N.S.F. Cheques

Except for retail stores and their dealings with the general public, most goods and services are bought on account and paid for later by cheque. As a result, the use of cheques in our business economy is extensive.

A cheque, however, is not 'cash'. Ordinarily, the recipient of a cheque cannot be certain that it is valid. Usually, he must deposit it with his own bank and wait until it is cleared through the bank of the issuer. The decision as to whether a cheque is good or not is made by the bank of the issuer. The decision hinges on whether or not there is a sufficient balance in the issuer's bank account to cover the cheque.

A cheque received into your business will probably progress through the following stages:

1. Because most cheques are good ones, your actions whenever you receive a cheque are based on the optimistic assumption that all cheques are good. Therefore, you will (a) record the receipt of the cheque in the cash receipts journal as a debit to 'Bank' and a credit to some other account, and (b) deposit the cheque in your bank account. If the cheque happens to be a good one, that is probably the last that you will hear of it.

2. Your bank, also acting on the assumption that all cheques are good, increases the balance of your account accordingly. The cheque is then sent on, through the clearing house, to the bank of the person who wrote (or issued) the cheque.

3. The issuer's bank attempts to deduct the amount of the cheque from the issuer's account. If the balance of the account is large enough to cover the cheque, the deduction will be made. However, if the balance of the account is not large enough to cover the cheque, no deduction will be made. Instead, the bank will mark on the cheque 'Not Sufficient Funds' and will send it back to your bank. It is at this point that the cheque becomes 'dishonored' or 'N.S.F.' meaning 'not sufficient funds'. It is also referred to by many as having 'bounced'.

4. The dishonored cheque is then received by your bank. Since your bank account was

previously increased by the amount of what has turned out to be a worthless cheque, your bank exercises its right to even things out by making an offsetting deduction in the account. It does this promptly and then sends to you the dishonored cheque together with an explanatory debit advice. You will be informed as quickly as possible.

5. After receiving the 'bad news' from the bank, it is necessary for you to do two things:

a. Immediately try to contact the person who wrote the bad cheque, in an attempt to obtain proper payment. This may not be an easy matter.

b. In the cash payments journal, reverse the accounting entry that was previously made at the time of receiving the cheque. The required entry will be a credit to Bank and a debit to some other account.

## Bookkeeping and Accounting Terms

**Bank Advice** A notice sent by the bank to the depositor informing the depositor that the bank has initiated an entry to his bank account. The debit 'advice' is associated with a decrease to the account. The credit 'advice' is associated with an increase to the account. Also known as a **bank memorandum**.

**Sales Tax** A tax related to the sale of goods and calculated as a per cent of the selling price of the goods.

**Cash Receipts Journal** A special columnar journal in which are recorded the accounting entries for all transactions that directly cause an increase in the bank balance.

**Cash Payments Journal** A special columnar journal in which are recorded the accounting entries for all transactions that directly cause a decrease in the bank balance. Also known as

**cash disbursements journal**.

**Sales Journal** A special columnar journal in which are recorded the accounting entries for all sales of merchandise on account.

**Purchases Journal** A special columnar journal in which are recorded the accounting entries for all transactions involving the buying of any type of goods or services on account.

**One-Write System** An accounting technique that, by the use of collated business forms and carbon paper, permits the simultaneous preparation of more than one business paper.

**N.S.F. Cheque** A cheque which was not cashed when presented to the issuer's bank because there were not sufficient funds in the bank account to cover the amount of the cheque. Also known as a **dishonored cheque**.

## Review Questions

1. Explain the relationship between a bank and one of its depositors.
2. If both the bank and the depositor follow the same set of accounting rules, why does the bank's record of the depositor's money appear to be the opposite of the depositor's own record?
3. Why is it important that a business be able to calculate its bank balance at any time?
4. How is a depositor notified of changes in his bank balance that are initiated by the bank?
5. When a business receives a bank debit advice or a bank credit advice, what must be done in the books of account?
6. Briefly describe how sales tax works.
7. Where does one obtain information about sales tax?
8. Give three transactions that involve the account 'Sales Tax Payable'.

9. Why will there probably be a special column for Sales Tax Payable in a columnar journal?
10. When must sales tax be remitted to the government?
11. Name the five journals of the five-journal system.
12. What are the advantages of the five-journal system?
13. Name the two most common transactions recorded in a cash receipts journal.
14. In the cash receipts journal, what is the purpose of the column headed 'Amount of Deposit'?
15. What is the source document for entries recorded in the sales journal?
16. What type of entries are recorded in the cash payments journal?
17. Are the postings from the cash payments journal to the accounts payable subsidiary ledger debit postings or credit postings?
18. In what order are the five journals posted to the general ledger?
19. Give the abbreviation codes for the four special journals.
20. Describe what is meant by 'collated' business forms.
21. How does a 'one-write' system work?
22. Explain what is meant by an N.S.F. cheque.
23. How does a business learn of an N.S.F. cheque?
24. What two things must be done by an accountant who learns of an N.S.F. cheque?

# Exercises

**1. In a two-column general journal record the entries for the following transactions. Calculate sales tax at 5 per cent.**

*Transactions*

Aug. 7 Sold $150 of merchandise on account to F. Fulton, sales invoice #767.
    10 Sold $70 of merchandise for cash to J. Kaplan, cash sales ticket #402.
    11 Paid the monthly remittance for sales tax to the Receiver General, cheque #1751 for $675.02.

**2. For each of the transactions listed below, state in which of the five journals it would be recorded.**

*Transactions*
1. A cheque is issued to a supplier on account.
2. A purchase invoice is received from a supplier of merchandise.
3. A cheque is received on account from a customer.
4. A cash sale is made to a customer.
5. A sale on account is made to a customer.
6. A cheque is issued to the owner for his personal use.
7. A cheque is issued to pay the wages for the period.
8. A sales invoice is issued.
9. A correcting entry is made to transfer a debit amount from the Supplies account to the Miscellaneous Expense account.
10. A cheque is issued to pay for a cash purchase of merchandise.
11. A bank debit advice for service charge is received.
12. A cheque is issued to a supplier on account.
13. A cheque is issued to pay for the monthly rent.
14. A bank debit advice is received with

respect to an N.S.F. cheque.
15. A bank credit advice is received with respect to interest earned.
16. A new typewriter is purchased and a down payment is required. A cheque is issued.
17. The owner collects a debt from a customer but keeps the money for his personal use.
18. The owner spends a sum of money out of his own pocket for business purposes and is reimbursed by means of a cheque.

3. **Record the following transactions in a cash receipts journal.**
**Calculate sales tax at 5 per cent. Assume bank deposits are made at the end of each day.**

Dec. 1 The owner, P. Messer, increased his capital balance by depositing his personal cheque for $1 000 in the business bank account.
   3 $150 of merchandise was sold to H. Joseph for cash. Sales ticket #103.
   4 Received a cheque for $211 from S. Nolan on account.
   4 $75 of merchandise was sold to V. Kelly for cash. Sales ticket #104.
   5 Received a cheque for $165 from A. Cullen on account.

**Rule and balance the journal at this point.**

4. **Record the following sales invoices in a sales journal:**

Oct. 1 Sales invoice #70; goods $80; sales tax $4; total $84.
   2 Sales invoice #71; goods $140; sales tax $7; total $147.
   2 Sales invoice #72; goods $217; sales tax $10.85; total $227.85.
   3 Sales invoice #73; goods $596; sales tax $29.80; total $625.80.
   3 Sales invoice #74; goods $32.05; sales tax $1.60; total $33.65.

**Rule and balance the sales journal at this point.**

5. **Head up a cash payments journal as shown at the bottom of page 157 of your textbook. In this journal record the following transactions:**

*Transactions*

April 1 Issued cheque #40 to R. Morris for the cash purchase of supplies, $76.02.
   2 Issued cheque #41 to Cox Supply Co. for the cash purchase of merchandise, $361.40.
   3 Issued cheque #42 to Municipal Hydro in payment of the hydro for the previous month, $56.20.
   4 Issued cheque #43 to Franklin Wholesale on account, $300.
   4 Issued cheque #44 to C. Foster, the owner, for his personal use, $200.
   5 Received a debit memorandum from the City Bank to the effect that a $12.50 service charge had been made against the business's bank account.
   5 Issued cheque #45 to S. Main for weekly wages, $155.

**Rule and balance the journal at this point.**

6. **Head up a purchases journal as shown on page 158 of your textbook. In this journal record the following purchase invoices:**

Feb. 2  Received purchase invoice from Double Square Manufacturing for the purchase of merchandise, $110.38.

3  Received purchase invoice from North District Supply for the purchase of supplies, $67.20.

3  Received purchase invoice from Provincial Transfer Co. for freight charges on incoming merchandise, $147.50.

4  Received purchase invoice from Clarke's Service Station for gasoline and oil used in the delivery truck, $57.75.

5  Received purchase invoice from Circle Products for the purchase of merchandise, $525.

5  Received purchase invoice from Grant Auto Sales for the purchase of a new delivery truck, $5 259.45.

**Rule and balance the journal at this point.**

7.  For each of the selected transactions listed below, write down the accounting entry that is necessary. Use general journal form. Make your own choice of accounts.

Beside each entry, to the right, indicate in which journal the entry would be recorded if a five-journal system were used.

*Transactions*

1.  Issued cheque No. 65 to Morris and Hannah in payment of the rent for the month, $220.

2.  Receiver a purchase invoice for $540 from Grinnelco Ltd. for merchandise.

3.  Received a cheque from R. Jones, a customer, in part payment of his account, $60.

4.  A cash sale of $70 was made to A. Green. Add sales tax of 5 per cent.

5.  A withdrawal of $800, by means of cheque No. 76 made out to 'Cash', in order to pay the wages for the week.

6.  The proprietor, C. Jones, withdrew $100 cash for his personal use, cheque No. 91.

7.  Issued sales invoice No. 867 for $34.78 to C. Perry. Add sales tax of 5 per cent.

8.  The proprietor, C. Jones, took home merchandise valued at $48.39 for his personal use. Charge sales tax of 5 per cent.

9.  An error was discovered in the general ledger. An amount of $30 which had been debited to Miscellaneous Expense should have been debited to Supplies.

10.  Sold merchandise on account to Mercer & Company, invoice No. 911, $45. Add sales tax of 5 per cent.

11.  Issued cheque No. 105 for $120 to General Supply Company on account.

12.  Issued cheque No. 114 for $350.24 to the Receiver General in payment of the sales tax for the previous month.

13.  Made a cash purchase of merchandise in the amount of $100 from Pressed Fittings, cheque No. 121.

14.  Received a purchase invoice from Office Suppliers for an office desk, $350.

15.  Paid the telephone bill for the month, $10.75, cheque No. 139.

16.  An error was detected in the accounts receivable ledger. An amount of $12 which should have been credited to J. C. Walker's account was credited in error to P. M. Walker's account.

17.  Received a purchase invoice from J. R. Paulson for merchandise, $200.

18.  Purchased $35 of supplies from Baldwin's, cheque No. 154.

19.  Sold merchandise to P. Leonard for $150, invoice No. 946. Add sales tax of 5 per cent. Mr. Leonard made a down payment of $50.
    **Note:** An entry for this transaction is a combination of a sale for cash and a sale on account. As such, it theoretically fits two journals. However, it is customary to enter the whole entry in one journal, the cash receipts journal.

20. S. T. Anthony, a customer, came personally to the office to pay his account of $25. While he was there he also made a cash purchase of $15. Add sales tax of 5 per cent.

---

**8. For each of the selected transactions listed below, write down the accounting entry that is necessary. Use general journal form. Make your own choice of accounts. Add 5 per cent sales tax on all sales.**

**Beside each entry, to the right, indicate in which journal the entry would be recorded if a five-journal system were used.**

*Transactions*

1. Received an invoice from Continental Railway for transportation on purchases of merchandise, $96.40.
2. Received a bank debit advice from Royalty Bank in the amount of $19 for bank service charges.
3. The proprietor, A. Harvey, withdrew $250 for his personal use, cheque No. 204.
4. Cheque No. 215 was issued to C. Pearce on account, $84.
5. Invoice No. 86A was issued to Jenkins & Williams, $65.75.
6. Issued cheque No. 224 for $22.50 to the local telephone company in payment of the bill for the month.
7. Received a bank debit advice from Royalty Bank. The amount of the charge was $52 and was with respect to a cheque from W. Patterson which had been dishonored. The cheque had been given as payment for a cash sale.
8. The wages for the week amounted to $750. Cheque No. 231 for this amount was issued to C. Worth, the company paymaster, who took it to the bank and cashed it. He brought the money back to the office and gave it in turn to the proper employees.
9. Issued cheque No. 240 to Parker Investments in payment of the rent for the month, $300.
10. A cash sale of $42 was made to C. Donovan, cash sales slip No. 92.
11. Received a cheque for $75 from R. Grant, on account.

12. Received a purchase invoice from Jimpson's Garage for $157. Of the $157 charge, $124.70 was for gas, oil, and repairs for the delivery truck, and $32.30 was for gas and oil delivered to A. Harvey's (the proprietor's) summer cottage for use in a motor boat.
13. A. Harvey, the proprietor, collected a debt from a customer, E. Spence, in the amount of $40. He kept the money and used it for his own purposes. He requested the accountant to record the collection.
14. Received a purchase invoice for $25 for office supplies from Lailey & Co. Lailey & Co. is a customer of ours and has an account balance of $271.56, debit. The $25 is to be deducted from the amount owed to us by Lailey & Co.
15. Purchased a new typewriter from Embassy Typewriter Company at a cost of $325. A down payment of $150 was made, cheque No. 257.
16. Received a purchase invoice from O.K. Fabricators in the amount of $176. The invoice was with respect to the repair of the company building.
17. Issued cheque No. 260 to P. Lundy on account, $65.
18. Issued cheque No. 265 to Paramount Loan Company in payment of the monthly instalment on the automotive equipment, $310.
19. Sales Invoice No. 114A was issued to Provincial Processors, $23.45.
20. Issued cheque No. 271 to Imperial Office Supplies for the cash purchase of office supplies, $43.23.

**9. Head up a cash payments journal with the following special columns:**
Wages, Dr.; Drawings, Dr.; Supplies, Dr.; Purchases, Dr.; Accounts Payable,
Dr.; Bank, Cr.

From the following list of transactions select those that affect cash payments
and record the entries for these in the cash payments journal:

*Transactions*

Aug. 2 Issued cheque #400 to A. Wynn for the
rent for the month, $450.

2 Received a purchase invoice from
Sunny Products for the purchase of
merchandise, $375.

3 Issued sales invoices as follows:
#31, to P. Sandgate, $50 plus
5 per cent sales tax.
#32, to J. Ogilvie, $76.50 plus
5 per cent sales tax.

4 The owner, P. Mathews, contributed
$1 500 cash to the business, an increase
in his capital invested.

5 Received a purchase invoice from W.
Matheson for supplies, $74.75.

5 Issued cheque #401 to Manhattan
Wholesalers for the cash purchase of
merchandise, $650.

8 Received a cheque from C. Fairley
on account, $134.75.

9 Issued sales invoices as follows:
#33, to C. Mann, $70 plus 5 per cent
sales tax,
#34, to G. Lang, $325 plus 5 per
cent sales tax.

12 Received a bank debit memo from the
Guardian Bank indicating a decrease of
$18.40 in the bank balance because of
service charges.

12 Issued cheque #402 to Old Fashioned
Manufacturers for the cash purchase
of merchandise, $565.

13 Received a cheque from P. Ives for
$150 on account.

15 Issued cheques as follows:
#403, to A. Anderson, on account,
$378,
#404, to G. Jackson, on account,
$75,
#405, to B. Hutton, for wages, $375,
#406, to Z. Manson, for wages,
$425,
#407, to the owner, P. Mathews, for
his personal use, $500,
#408, to the Receiver General, for
sales tax due, $757.24.

17 Issued sales invoice #35 to D. French,
$60 plus 5 per cent sales tax.

19 Received $45 cash from P. Prince
on account.

22 Received a purchase invoice from
Maple Leaf Fabricators for the purchase of merchandise, $374.02.

23 Issued cheque #409 to Paul Harvey
Supplies for the cash purchase of
supplies, $257.24.

26 Issued cheque #410 to Ivory Producers
for the cash purchase of merchandise,
$845.

27 Issued cheque # 411 to Frank Wills
& Son on account, $200.

31 Issued cheque #412 to B. Hutton for
wages, $375.

31 Issued cheque #413 to Z. Manson
for wages, $425.

31 Issued cheque #414 to the owner, P.
Mathews, for his personal use, $600.

Rule and balance the journal.

10. Set up the general ledger of Bristol Appliances Company as of December 31, 19—.

On December 31, 19—, the combined chart of accounts and general ledger trial balance of Bristol Appliances Company was as follows:

| | | | |
|---|---|---|---|
| 1 | Bank | $ 813.12 | |
| 2 | Accounts Receivable | 2 471.49 | |
| 3 | Supplies | 312.50 | |
| 4 | Merchandise Inventory | 7 416.40 | |
| 5 | Store Equipment | 800.00 | |
| 6 | Delivery Truck | 2 200.00 | |
| 21 | Accounts Payable | | $1 941.60 |
| 22 | Bank Loan | | 8 000.00 |
| 23 | Sales Tax Payable | | 60.00 |
| 31 | S. C. Scales, Capital | | 4 011.91 |
| 32 | S. C. Scales, Drawings | | |
| 41 | Sales | | |
| 51 | Purchases | | |
| 52 | Rent | | |
| 53 | Salaries | | |
| 54 | Delivery Expense | | |
| 55 | Miscellaneous Expense | | |

Set up the subsidiary ledgers of Bristol Appliances Company as of December 31, 19—.

On December 31, 19—, the subsidiary ledger trial balances appeared as follows:

### ACCOUNTS RECEIVABLE TRIAL BALANCE
### DECEMBER 31, 19—

| | | |
|---|---|---|
| C. Booth, 129 James Street | Inv. No. 325 | $ 316.10 |
| M. Howard, 881 Wilson Avenue | 296 | 95.00 |
| J. Hudson, 14 Brook Drive | 306 | 912.75 |
| O. Langley, 65 Finch Avenue | 315 | 163.87 |
| T. Miles, 110 Church Street | 326 | 50.00 |
| S. Thorpe, 375 Beckett Drive | 217 | 135.00 |
| D. Wilkins, 70 Dixon Avenue | 331 | 500.00 |
| | 346 | 298.77 |
| | | $2 471.49 |

### ACCOUNTS PAYABLE TRIAL BALANCE
### DECEMBER 31, 19—

| | | |
|---|---|---|
| Stirling Company, 20 River Street | Ref. B245 | $ 560.20 |
| Triangle Electric, Roxborough | 4701 | 316.47 |
| Universal Vacuums, 20 Dexter Street | 6508 | 1 000.00 |
| Western Electric, 1000 Fleet Street | 246R | 64.93 |
| | | $1 941.60 |

In the journals of Bristol Appliances Company, record the transactions shown below. Bristol Appliances uses a five-journal system. The journals and the page numbers to be used are:

Cash Receipts Journal     Page  61
Cash Payments Journal     Page 117
Purchases Journal         Page  74
Sales Journal             Page  82
General Journal           Page  29

The subsidiary ledgers of Bristol Appliances are posted daily, directly from the source documents.

A 5 per cent sales tax is to be applied on all sales of merchandise.

## Transactions

January

2 *Cash Sales Slip*
   –No. 401, to T. Arthur, $125 plus sales tax.
   *Cash Receipt*
   –From C. Booth, $116.10, on account.
   *Cheque Copy*
   –No. 376, to J. C. Brown, $37.42, for the cash purchase of supplies.

3 *Purchase Invoice*
   –No. 1212, from Smith's Service Station, 3 Cary Street, $63.50, for gasoline and oil used in the delivery truck.
   *Cash Sales Slip*
   –No. 402, to R. Malone, $475 plus sales tax.

4 *Sales Invoice*
   –No. 347, to M. Howard, $310 plus sales tax.

5 *Cheque Copies*
   –No. 377, to Universal Vacuums, $500, on account.
   –No. 378, to 'Cash', $385, for the salaries for the week.

8 *Cash Receipt*
   –From T. Miles, $50, in full payment of account.
   *Correcting Entry*
   –An error was discovered in an entry made in December. An amount of $16.10 was debited incorrectly to Delivery Expense; it should have been debited to Miscellaneous Expense.

9 *Cash Sales Slip*
   –No. 403, to H. McPhee, $800 plus sales tax.

10 *Purchase Invoice*
   –No. 306R, from Western Electric, $630, for the purchase of merchandise.

10 *Cheque Copy*
   –No. 379, to Stirling Company, $712, for the cash purchase of merchandise.

11 *Sales Invoices*
   –No. 348, to O. Langley, $137.50 plus sales tax.
   –No. 349, to T. Miles, $200 plus sales tax.
   –No. 350, to S. Thorpe, $475.12 plus sales tax.

12 *Cash Receipt*
   –From Clover Stores, $105; because of a recent change in the system, certain supplies on hand were not usable and were sold for cash at a price of $105.
   *Cheque Copy*
   –No. 380, to 'Cash', $410, for the salaries for the week.

15 *Cheque Copies*
   –No. 381, to S. C. Scales, $300, for his personal use.
   –No. 382, to the Provincial Government, $60, for sales tax for the previous month.
   *Cash Receipts*
   –From C. Booth, $100; on account.
   –From J. Hudson, $512.75, on account.
   –From S. Thorpe, $135, invoice No. 217.
   –From D. Wilkins, $798.77, invoices No. 331 and 346.
   *Cash Sales Slips*
   –No. 404, to F. Lang, $480 plus sales tax.
   –No. 405, to K. Klein, $750 plus sales tax.

16 *Purchase Invoice*
   –No. 406, from Ritz Furniture, Melody

Road, $150, for the purchase of merchandise.

17 *Purchase Invoice*
—No. 708, from Super Stationers, $76.40, for supplies.

17 *Non-routine Transaction*
—The proprietor took an office typewriter home for his permanent personal use. The typewriter was included in the accounts at a value of $150. The transaction is subject to a 5 per cent sales tax.

18 *Cheque Copies*
—No. 383, to Triangle Electric, $316.47, paying invoice No. 4701.
—No. 384, to Stirling Company, $560.20, paying invoice No. B245.
—No. 385, to Western Electric, $64.93, paying invoice No. 246R.
—No. 386, to Smith's Service Station, $63.50; paying invoice No. 1212.

19 *Cheque Copy*
—No. 387, to 'Cash', $390, in payment of the weekly salaries.

22 *Sales Invoices*
—No. 351, to D. Wilkins, $300 plus sales tax.
—No. 352, to C. Booth, $281.63 plus sales tax.
—No. 353, to S. Thorpe, $31.12 plus sales tax.

23 *Purchase Invoice*
—No. 4912, from Triangle Electric, $65, for purchase of merchandise.

24 *Purchase Invoice*
—No. 842, from Super Stationers, $30, for supplies.

25 *Cheque Copy*
—No. 388, to local telephone company, $16.50, for monthly telephone bill.

26 *Cheque Copies*
—No. 389, to Boston Television Co., $112.60, for the cash purchase of merchandise.
—No. 390, to Admirable Company, $83, for the cash purchase of merchandise.
—No. 391, to 'Cash', $375, for the weekly salaries.
—No. 392, to Grayson Brothers, $250, for the rent for the month.

30 *Purchase Invoice*
—No. 864, from Super Stationers, $100, for supplies.

31 *Purchase Invoices*
—No. B319, from Stirling Company, $300, for merchandise.
—No. 6722, from Universal Vacuums, $261.81, for merchandise.
—No. 512, from Ritz Furniture, $86.40, for merchandise.

*Cash Sales Slip*
—No. 406, to M. Morse, $906.50 plus sales tax.

*Sales Invoices*
—No. 354, to J. Hudson, $1 200 plus sales tax.
—No. 355, to M. Howard, $12.08 plus sales tax.
—No. 356, to S. Thorpe, $19.65 plus sales tax.

*Cheque Copy*
—No. 393, to local hydro, $16.40, for hydro for the month.

Balance the special journals and post the five journals to the general ledger.

Balance the general ledger as of January 31.

Balance the subsidiary ledgers as of January 31.

---

11.  C. D. Mould is the proprietor of Husky Hardware. He uses five journals and three ledgers in his accounting system. He posts the subsidiary ledgers daily, directly from the source documents. In his locality there is a 3 per cent sales tax on all sales.

The chart of accounts for Husky Hardware is shown below:

HUSKY HARDWARE
CHART OF ACCOUNTS

| | |
|---|---|
| 1 Bank | 31 C. D. Mould, Capital |
| 2 Accounts Receivable | 32 C. D. Mould, Drawings |
| 3 Merchandise Inventory | 41 Sales |
| 4 Supplies | 51 Purchases |
| 5 Store Equipment | 52 Rent |
| 6 Delivery Equipment | 53 Miscellaneous Expense |
| 21 Accounts Payable | 54 Wages |
| 22 Sales Tax Payable | |

The general ledger trial balance of Husky Hardware as of June 30, 19—, is as follows:

HUSKY HARDWARE
GENERAL LEDGER TRIAL BALANCE
JUNE 30, 19—

| | | |
|---|---|---|
| Bank | $ 2 614.20 | |
| Accounts Receivable | 412.50 | |
| Merchandise Inventory | 4 095.12 | |
| Supplies | 300.00 | |
| Store Equipment | 2 675.00 | |
| Delivery Equipment | 3 500.00 | |
| Accounts Payable | | $ 5 063.94 |
| Sales Tax Payable | | 108.52 |
| C. D. Mould, Capital | | 7 864.36 |
| C. D. Mould, Drawings | 5 876.34 | |
| Sales | | 19 800.00 |
| Purchases | 9 500.00 | |
| Rent | 1 800.00 | |
| Miscellaneous Expense | 216.41 | |
| Wages | 1 847.25 | |
| | $32 836.82 | $32 836.82 |

The subsidiary ledger trial balances are as follows:

HUSKY HARDWARE
ACCOUNTS RECEIVABLE TRIAL BALANCE
JUNE 30, 19—

| | | | |
|---|---|---|---|
| J. Barkley, 260 Western Avenue | No. 490 | $92.46 | |
| | 496 | 15.02 | |
| | 503 | 60.10 | $167.58 |
| T. Fairley, 300 Center Road | 501 | | 56.42 |
| S. Harvey, 466 Keeley Street | 502 | | 76.50 |
| R. Taylor, 588 Truway Drive | 498 | | 112.00 |
| | | | $412.50 |

HUSKY HARDWARE
ACCOUNTS PAYABLE TRIAL BALANCE
JUNE 30, 19—

| | | |
|---|---|---|
| Household Utensils Company | Inv. No. 52 | $1 067.50 |
| 487 Faith Avenue | | |
| J. & A. Hardware Supply | 596 | 505.25 |
| 600 Young Street | | |
| Learner Bros. | 141 | 3 067.20 |
| 5012 Direct Avenue | | |
| Specialty Manufacturing Co. | 163 | 423.99 |
| Barbary | | |
| | | $5 063.94 |

**Set up the three ledgers of Husky Hardware as of June 30, 19—.**

**Journalize the transactions listed below in the five journals of Husky Hardware. Use the following page numbers:**

| | |
|---|---|
| Cash Receipts Journal | Page 42 |
| Cash Payments Journal | Page 93 |
| Sales Journal | Page 56 |
| Purchases Journal | Page 85 |
| General Journal | Page 16 |

## Transactions

July

2 *Cheque Copy*
–No. 187, to D. C. Harper, $300, for the rent for July.
*Purchase Invoice*
–From Household Utensils Company, No. 87, $184.50, for the purchase of merchandise.

3 *Sales Invoices*
–No. 504, to S. Harvey, $50 plus sales tax.
–No. 505, to R. Taylor, $26.85 plus sales tax.
–No. 506, to T. Fairley, $12.85 plus sales tax.
–No. 507, to J. Barkley, $64 plus sales tax.

4 *Cash Receipt*
–From the owner C. D. Mould, $1 000, for the purpose of increasing his investment in the business.

5 *Purchase Invoice*
–From Learner Brothers, No. 206, $35.60, for supplies.
*Cheque Copy*
–No. 188, to Federal A–1 Supply House, $146, for the cash purchase of merchandise.
*Cash Register Slips*
–$846.81. The cash sales for the week amounted to $822.15 plus sales tax of $24.66.

8 *Cash Receipt*
–From T. Fairley, $56.42, paying invoice No. 501.

9 *Sales Invoices*
–No. 508, to L. Peck, $41 plus sales tax.
–No. 509, to S. Harvey, $18 plus sales tax.
–No. 510, to T. Fairley, $25.50 plus sales tax.

10 *Purchase Invoice*
–From J. & A. Hardware Supply, $312, for a shipment of hammers, saws and other tools.

12 *Cash Register Slips*

–$964.08. The cash sales for the week amounted to $936 plus sales tax of $28.08.

*Bank Debit Memo*

–From Sovereign Bank, $10.20, bank account decreased because of bank service charge.

*Cheque Copy*

–No. 189, to Modern Manufacturing Company, $265, for the cash purchase of merchandise.

13 *Cash Receipts*

–From S. Harvey, $128, paying invoices No. 502 and No. 504.

–From J. Barkley, $107.48, paying invoices No. 490 and No. 496.

15 *Cheque Copies*

–No. 190, to Learner Brothers, $1 500, on account.

–No. 191, to Household Utensils Company, $500, on account.

–No. 192, to B. Wiley, $400, wages for the first half of the month.

–No. 193, to W. Brown, $425, wages for the first half of the month.

–No. 194, to C. D. Mould, $500, personal withdrawal by proprietor.

–No. 195, to the Provincial Government, $108.52, sales tax for the previous month.

17 *Sales Invoices*

–No. 511, to V. Parker, 466 Janes Road, $75 plus sales tax.

–No. 512, to L. Peck, $45 plus sales tax.

–No. 513, to S. Harvey, $19.50 plus sales tax.

*Cash Receipt*

–From R. Taylor, $112, paying invoice No. 498.

18 *Non-routine Transaction*

–The proprietor submits bills amounting to $24.08 for miscellaneous expenses which he has paid out of his own pocket.

He asks that his Drawings account be credited.

19 *Cash Register Slips*

–$881.68. The cash sales for the week amounted to $856 plus $25.68 sales tax.

*Cash Receipts*

–From S. Harvey, $38.63, paying his account in full.

–From T. Fairley, $13.24, paying invoice No. 506.

–From L. Peck, $42.23, paying invoice No. 508.

22 *Purchase Invoice*

–From Maple Feed Company, Maple, No. 996, $600, for the purchase of merchandise.

23 *Purchase Invoice*

–From Household Utensils Company, No. 156, $412.65, for the purchase of merchandise.

26 *Cash Register Slips*

–$1 096.95. The cash sales for the week amounted to $1 065 plus sales tax of $31.95.

*Cheque Copy*

–No. 196, to Learner Brothers, $263, for the cash purchase of merchandise.

29 *Cheque Copies*

–No. 197, to Household Utensils Company, $567.50, paying the balance of invoice No. 52.

–No. 198, to J. & A. Hardware Supply, $505.25, paying invoice No. 596.

–No. 199, to Specialty Manufacturing Company, $423.99, paying invoice No. 163.

31 *Cheque Copies*

–No. 200, to B. Wiley, $400, wages for the last half of the month.

–No. 201, to W. Brown, $425, wages for the last half of the month.

–No. 202, to C.D. Mould, $500, for his personal use.

**Balance and post the journals to the general ledger.**
**Balance the general ledger.**
**Balance the subsidiary ledgers.**

12. Travel Trailers is a business owned and operated by Charles Fowler. The business earns its income from the selling and servicing of mobile homes and trailers. All sales and service transactions are subject to a 5 per cent sales tax.

Because of a special arrangement with an independent finance company, Travel Trailers is able to treat every trailer sale as a cash transaction. This is possible because the finance company pays Travel Trailers in full for any trailer sold and then collects from the customer on an instalment basis including interest charges.

From the following combined chart of accounts and general ledger trial balance, set up the general ledger of Travel Trailers as of May 31, 19—.

TRAVEL TRAILERS
GENERAL LEDGER TRIAL BALANCE
MAY 31, 19—

| | | | |
|---|---|---:|---:|
| 1 | Bank | $ 1 751.75 | |
| 2 | Accounts Receivable | 1 166.97 | |
| 3 | Supplies | 151.00 | |
| 4 | Inventory-Trailers | 19 476.42 | |
| 5 | Inventory-Parts | 5 946.90 | |
| 6 | Equipment | 8 472.94 | |
| 7 | Delivery Truck | 3 000.00 | |
| 21 | Accounts Payable | | $ 4 987.50 |
| 22 | Bank Loan | | 20 000.00 |
| 23 | Sales Tax Payable | | 817.40 |
| 31 | C. Fowler, Capital | | 9 253.37 |
| 32 | C. Fowler, Drawings | 4 374.00 | |
| 41 | Sales | | 49 373.51 |
| 51 | Purchases-Trailers | 29 940.70 | |
| 52 | Purchases-Parts | 2 641.05 | |
| 53 | Bank Interest Expense | 516.50 | |
| 54 | Delivery Expense | 174.72 | |
| 55 | Miscellaneous Expense | 94.72 | |
| 56 | Rent Expense | 1 000.00 | |
| 57 | Wages Expense | 5 724.11 | |
| | | $84 431.78 | $84 431.78 |

From the information shown below set up the accounts receivable ledger of Travel Trailers as of May 31, 19—.

| Customer | Address | Invoice | | Amount |
|---|---|---|---|---:|
| B. Fraser | 15 Gay Street | Re Invoice No. 634 | | $ 330.75 |
| W. Hoyle | 49 First Street | | 635 | 77.70 |
| A. Newman | 250 Fort Road | | 629 | 225.75 |
| Schell Brothers | 96 Garrison Avenue | | 633 | 204.75 |
| N. Thompson | 20 Wilson Avenue | | 630 | 315.00 |
| L. Walker | 4 Dennis Avenue | | 631 | 13.02 |
| | | | Total | $1 166.97 |

From the following information set up the accounts payable ledger of
Travel Trailers as of May 31, 19—.

| Supplier | Address | Invoice | Amount |
|---|---|---|---|
| Double-G Industries | Manortown | Inv. No. 420 | $1 575.00 |
| Modern Mobile Homes | West City | 2213 | 2 100.00 |
| National Hardware | 64 Venture St. | 2309 | 787.50 |
| Windsor Manufacturing Co. | Windsor | 404 | 525.00 |
| | | Total | $4 987.50 |

Travel Trailers uses five journals in its accounting system. Set up the five
journals for June as shown below.

**Sales Journal** — Page 19

| Date | Name | | | | | INV. NO. | Accounts Rec'l DR. | ✓ | Sales Tax Pay'l CR | Sales CR |
|---|---|---|---|---|---|---|---|---|---|---|

**Purchases Journal** — Page 74

| Date | Name | Other Accounts DR | | | Delivery Expense DR | Supplies DR | Purch's Parts DR | Purch's Trailers DR | ✓ | Acc'ts Pay'l CR |
|---|---|---|---|---|---|---|---|---|---|---|
| | | Account | PR | Amount | | | | | | |

**Cash Receipts Journal** — Page 37

| Date | Name | Other Accounts CR | | | Sales Tax Payable CR | Sales CR | Acc'ts Rec'l CR | Bank DR | |
|---|---|---|---|---|---|---|---|---|---|
| | | Account | PR | Amount | | | | | |

**Cash Payments Journal** — Page 84

| Date | Name | Other Accounts DR | | | Wages DR | Drawings DR | Supplies DR | Purch's Parts DR | Purch's Trailers DR | Acc'ts Pay'l DR | CH # | Bank CR |
|---|---|---|---|---|---|---|---|---|---|---|---|---|
| | | Account | PR | Amount | | | | | | | | |

**General Journal** — Page 5

| Date | Particulars | PR. | Debit | Credit |
|---|---|---|---|---|

Journalize the following transactions for June. Post to the subsidiary ledgers
daily.

## Transactions
June

1 *Sales Invoice*
 —No. 636, to A. Newman, $190 plus 5 per
cent sales tax, for repairs to trailer.

*Cheque Copy*
—No. 755, issued to General Real Estate,
$300, for the monthly rent.

2 *Sales Invoice*
  –No. 637, to L. Walker, $300 plus 5 per
  cent sales tax, for sale of trailer parts.
  *Cheque Copy*
  –No. 756, issued to Double-G Industries,
  $300, on account.
3 *Purchase Invoices*
  –From Parker Manufacturing, 10 Bergen
  Street, No. 40, $135, for supplies.
  –From Double-G Industries, No. 472,
  $551.20, for trailer parts.
4 *Cash Receipts*
  –Received from W. Hoyle, $77.70, in
  payment of account.
  –Received from Federated Finance Com-
  pany, $5 985 cash, for sale of trailer,
  selling price $5 700, sales tax $285.
  *Bank Debit Advice*
  –From Central Bank, $120, for interest
  charged on bank loan.
5 *Cheque Copies*
  –No. 757, issued to C. Fowler, $400,
  owner's personal use.
  –No. 758, made out to Cash, $475 for the
  wages for the week.
  *Sales Invoice*
  –No. 638, to N. Thompson, $370 plus
  sales tax, for trailer repairs and parts.
8 *Cheque Copy*
  –No. 759, to J. C. Pat Supply, $76.62, for
  cash purchase of supplies, $43.50, and
  miscellaneous expense, $33.12.
  *Non-routine Item*
  –Correction required. $12.50 item was
  charged incorrectly to Delivery Expense;
  it should be charged to Miscellaneous
  Expense.
9 *Cash Receipt*
  –From A. Newman, $225.75, on account.
  *Purchase Invoices*
  –From Windsor Manufacturing, No. 452,
  $420, for trailer parts.
  –Maynard's Garage, 49 Larry's Lane,
  No. 64; $67.50, for gasoline and oil used
  in delivery truck.
10 *Bank Debit Advice*
  –From Central Bank, $1 000, to reduce
  the bank loan.
  *Sales Invoice*
  –No. 639, to B. Fraser, $450 plus 5 per

cent sales tax, for trailer parts.
  *Cheque Copies*
  –No. 760, to Modern Mobile Homes,
  $1 000, on account.
  –No. 761, to Double-G Industries, $500,
  on account.
  *Purchase Invoice*
  –From Windsor Manufacturing Co., No.
  481, $4 575, for one new trailer.
11 *Sales Invoice*
  –No. 640, to Schell Brothers, $575 plus
  5 per cent sales tax, for trailer parts and
  service.
  *Cheque Copy*
  –No. 762, to C. Fowler, $400, owner's
  personal use.
12 *Cash Receipts*
  –From Schell Brothers, $204.75, on account.
  –From B. Fraser, $330.75, on account.
  –From N. Thompson, $315, on account.
  *Cheque Copy*
  –No. 763, made out to Cash, $501, weekly
  wages.
15 *Cash Receipt*
  –From Federated Finance Company,
  $5 355, cash for sale of trailer, selling
  price, $5 100, sales tax $255.
  *Cheque Copies*
  –No. 764, to Provincial Government,
  $817.40, paying sales tax collected in May.
  –No. 765, to Double-G Industries, $775,
  paying the balance of invoice No. 420.
  *Purchase Invoice*
  –From Maynard's Garage, No. 82, $142,
  for repairs to delivery truck.
16 *Purchase Invoices*
  –From National Hardware, No. 2412,
  $92.50, for supplies.
  –From Double-G Industries, No. 515,
  $7 680, for one new trailer.
  –From Windsor Manufacturing Co., No.
  499, $270, for trailer parts.
17 *Sales Invoice*
  –No. 641, to W. Hoyle, $110 plus sales
  tax, for trailer service.
  *Cheque Copy*
  –No. 766, to Emerald Store, $10.50, for the
  cash purchase of miscellaneous items.
18 *Cheque Copies*
  –No. 767, to C. Fowler, $200, owner's

drawings.

–No. 768, to National Hardware, $787.50, on account.

–No. 769, to Modern Mobile Homes, $1 100, on account.

19 *Purchase Invoice*

–From National Hardware, No. 2480, $409.50, for trailer parts.

*Cheque Copy*

–No. 770, made out to Cash, $460, for the wages for the week.

22 *Sales Invoice*

–No. 642, to L. Walker, $290 plus sales tax of 5 per cent, for trailer parts and service.

*Purchase Invoice*

–From Parker Manufacturing, No. 90, $56, for supplies.

*Non-routine Transaction*

–The owner collected $13.02 from L. Walker (for invoice No. 631) but he kept the money for his own use. (Debit his Drawings account.)

24 *Cash Receipt*

–Received from Federated Finance Company, $2 047.50 cash, for sale of trailer, selling price $1 950, sales tax $97.50.

25 *Cheque Copy*

–No. 771, to C. Fowler, $350, personal drawings.

26 *Sales Invoice*

–No. 643, to A. Newman, $236 plus sales tax, for trailer repairs.

*Cheque Copies*

–No. 772, to Windsor Manufacturing, $945.00, on account.

–No. 773, made out to Cash, $498, for the wages for the week.

29 *Cash receipts*

–From B. Fraser, $472.50, on account.

–From Schell Brothers, $603.75, on account.

*Purchase Invoices*

–From Modern Mobile Homes, No. 2409, $3 050, for new trailer unit.

–From National Hardware, No. 2561, $93, for supplies.

30 *Sales Invoice*

–No. 644, to W. Hoyle, $230 plus sales tax, for trailer servicing.

**Balance the special journals.**
**Post the five journals to the general ledger.**
**Balance the general ledger as of June 30.**
**Balance the subsidiary ledgers as of June 30.**

# Cases

### Case 1

The Ross Paper Box Company was a well-established business which sold a limited line of higher priced, but profitable merchandise to an exclusive clientele. The books of account consisted of a two-column general journal and a general ledger. The accountant, J. Thomas, who did things his own way, had been with the company for 25 years and provided accurate and timely statements every month. The firm hired a recent graduate in accounting and marketing as the general manager. He was very aggressive and wanted to see the business increase its sales. Within six months he introduced new lines of merchandise which added numerous customers. The volume of transactions increased from 200 to 3 000 per month. It became necessary for Thomas to take the books home and work on them at night. At the end of December, with the accounting statements for October 31 still not completed, Thomas resigned.

1. What do you think caused Thomas to quit after 25 years with the company?
2. If you had been the accountant during the period of increased sales what changes would you have made in the accounting system?

## Case 2

R. Newman, owner of a wholesale business, has his accountant set up special journals to meet his particular needs. The accountant uses the following books of original entry:

Cash Receipts Journal
Cash Payments Journal
Purchases Journal
Sales Journal
General Journal

Mr. Newman does not understand why a general journal is necessary. Explain the need for a general journal and list the entries one would expect to find there.

## Case 3

A business which has approximately 1 000 charge customers has always used the manual system to maintain the accounts receivable ledger. It is now considering using a bookkeeping machine.
1. Will the machine improve the accuracy of posting? Explain.
2. What other advantages is the posting machine likely to provide?

## Case 4

Shoe store owner D. Hermiston made approximately 300 credit sales and 100 credit purchases each month. Mr. Hermiston recorded all these sales and purchases in a general journal. A friend asked him why he did not use a sales journal and a purchases journal. Mr. Hermiston replied that he did not understand their use. He believed that they simply divided the work among several people. Since he did his own accounting, he had no need for these special journals.

Is division of labor the only reason for using special journals? Explain.

## Case 5

S. Matt has received notice from his bank that a cheque for $50 received from J. Mullen has been marked N.S.F. Matt prepares the following journal entry:

Bad Debt Expense                     $50–
    Accounts Receivable/J. Mullen        $50–

1. What procedure should Matt have followed when he received the bank debit memorandum?
2. When, and only when, would the above journal entry be recorded in the books?

## Case 6

Bob Jarvis, the accountant for Wright Brothers, sets up an accounting system to eliminate the accounts receivable and accounts payable ledgers. All invoices owing to creditors and all invoices due from customers are kept in separate file folders until paid. When invoices are paid, they are removed from the customers' and creditors' files and placed in a file for paid invoices. At the end of the month the unpaid files are totalled and these totals agreed with the balances in the control accounts in the general ledger.

What advantages and disadvantages are there to such a system?

## Case 7

N. Howard conducts a small retail business. At the time of a sale she collects the tax from the customer but makes no attempt to distinguish on her books between the amount of the sale and the amount of the sales tax. In her entries involving cash sales she debits Cash and credits Sales for the total amount.

1. If Howard's total sales for the month amounted to $52 500, how much sales tax would she remit to the provincial treasurer if the rate of tax is 5%? Assume that all sales are taxable.
2. What entry would be made to record the sales tax?

## Case 8

A review of the accounting records of Nixon Co. disclosed the following errors:

1. Cash received from H. Latimer for $285.00 has been entered correctly in the cash receipts journal, but posted to the accounts receivable ledger as $258.00.
2. An invoice for 45 cartons at $1.75 each shipped to Best Drug Store has been extended and entered in the sales journal as $87.75.
3. Cash of $65.00 has been entered correctly in the cash receipts journal as received from M. Smith, but has been posted in the accounts receivable ledger to the account of M. Smythe.
4. The footings of the 'Purchases' column in the cash payments journal has been overstated by $100.
5. A cheque for $150 payable to G. Graham for legal fees was entered incorrectly in the cash payments journal as $160. The journal has not yet been posted.

Show how these errors should be corrected, giving journal entries where applicable.

## Case 9

The bank sends a debit memorandum for interest on a loan, but the company has no loan. An employee suggests that the charge be accepted, claiming that banks never make errors. What is your opinion? Explain.

## Case 10

M. Lunney Co. has two bank accounts, one with a balance on deposit of $100 000 and one which is overdrawn by $5 000. The bank charges interest on the $5 000. Is this fair? Explain.

## Case 11

Someone suggests that the purchases journal should also be used to record the subsequent payments. Is this possible?

## Case 12

During a company audit, an auditor had sealed one of the journals. An employee who needed to journalize in this book broke the seal and used the books. What problems has he caused?

## Case 13

Before posting to the general ledger, the equality of the Debit and Credit column totals in the journals should be proved. Suppose that this was not done, and that the total of a column in the cash receipts journal was incorrectly added by $100.

1. How would this error first be discovered?
2. What steps would normally be followed to find the cause of the error?

# 10 Special Transactions

Certain transactions, although not as simple as those you have already studied, are still classed as being 'routine'. Because they occur with considerable frequency, they are considered to be 'everyday' transactions and as such require your close attention.

## Cash Discounts

Perhaps you are already acquainted with 'cash discounts'. They are usually offered on water, hydro, and similar bills that come into the home from the offices of municipalities.

A cash discount is a reduction that may be taken in the amount of a bill, provided that it is paid before a certain date stipulated on the bill. The purpose of a cash discount is to encourage the customer to pay promptly. Many businesses, as well as municipalities, offer cash discounts to their customers.

### Terms of Sale

Every seller of goods or services makes certain arrangements with his customers as to when the goods or services are to be paid for and whether a cash discount is to be offered. These arrange-

ments are commonly known as the 'terms of sale'.

The terms of sale can be anything that the seller and buyer agree to but most often the terms are standard ones such as those listed on the next page.

The terms of sale to a customer will depend on his reputation for reliability in paying, particularly as evidenced by past experience with him. A reliable customer of long standing will probably be granted very favorable terms, whereas a new customer about whom there is little information available will probably be required to pay cash on delivery, at least for a short time.

The terms of every sale are recorded on the sales invoice (see illustration page 182). Each time the customer makes a purchase he is, therefore, reminded of the arrangements for making payment.

Once the terms of sale for a particular customer have been decided on, they will likely remain unchanged for some time. It is, therefore, a simple matter to record the customer's usual terms on his account card as illustrated below. This provides very helpful information to the credit manager, the man who is responsible for collecting the debts.

| ACCOUNT | | | | |
|---|---|---|---|---|
| Customer's Name *Baxter & Son* | | | Account No. — | |
| Address *15 Deacon Street* | | | Terms of Sale *2/10, n/30* | |
| *Mayville Z4T 9Y2* | | | Credit Limit *$600.* | |
| Date | Reference | Debit | Credit | Balance |
| *June 10, 19-5* | *429* | *50.00* | | *DR. 50.00* |

*Account card showing terms of sale.*

## Standard Terms of Sale

*Terms and Explanation*

**1. C.O.D.** Cash on Delivery. The goods must be paid for at the time they are delivered.

**2. On Account or Charge.** The full amount of the invoice is due at the time the invoice is received but usually a brief time, 10 to 15 days, is given to make payment.

**3. 30 Days or Net 30** The full amount of the invoice is due 30 days after the date of the invoice.

**60 Days or Net 60** The full amount of the invoice is due 60 days after the date of the invoice.

**4. 2/10,n/30** This is read as '2 per cent, 10; net, 30'. If the bill is paid within 10 days from the invoice date, a cash discount of 2 per cent may be taken. Otherwise, the full amount of the invoice is due 30 days after the invoice date.

**1/15,n/60** If the bill is paid within 15 days from the invoice date, a cash discount of 1 per cent may be taken. Otherwise, the full amount of the invoice is due 60 days after the invoice date.

## Accounting for Cash Discount

Accounting for cash discount begins at the time a credit sale is made to a customer and an invoice offering a cash discount is issued. Examine the invoice shown below.

---

### STAR ✳ SUPPLY

*419 Mill's Gate, Oak City*

SOLD TO   W. Hay,
16 Mark's Road,
Oak City.   P8F 4R2

INVOICE NUMBER  971

DATE   March 15, 19--

TERMS  3/10,N/30

| Quantity | Description | Unit Price | Amount |
|----------|-------------|------------|--------|
| 6 Pkg. | Typewriting paper | $7.50 | $45.00 |
| | 5% Sales Tax | | 2.25 |
| | | | $47.25 |

---

## IN THE BOOKS OF STAR SUPPLY (THE SELLER)

From a copy of the sales invoice the seller makes the following accounting entry in the sales journal:

SALES JOURNAL

| DATE | CUSTOMER | SALES CR | SALES TAX PAY'L CR | ACC'S REC'L DR |
|------|----------|----------|--------------------|----------------|
| Mar 15 | W. Hay | 45.00 | 2.25 | 47.25 |

## IN THE BOOKS OF W. HAY (THE BUYER)

The accounting entries in the books of the buyer will depend on his accounting system. Assuming that he records the purchase invoice (Star Supply's sales invoice) in his purchases journal as soon as it arrives in the mail (say March 17), the accounting entry will appear as follows:

PURCHASES JOURNAL

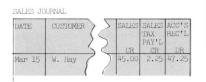

| DATE | CREDITOR | SUP-PLIES DR | PUR-CHASES DR | ACC'S PAY'L CR |
|------|----------|--------------|---------------|----------------|
| Mar 17 | Star Supply | 47.25 | | 47.25 |

## IN THE BOOKS OF STAR SUPPLY (THE SELLER)

One or more copies of the sales invoice will be sent by mail to the buyer, W. Hay.

The theoretical effect of the transaction is shown below:

When Mr. Hay's cheque is received by Star Supply, it will be absorbed into the system. Of special interest to us now is the fact that the details of the cheque will be included on the daily cash receipts listing which is forwarded to the accounts receivable clerk for posting to the subsidiary ledger. As part of his regular duties, this clerk will be required to verify any cash discounts that have been taken and to write on the listing the amount of any discount as well as the gross amount of the payment (i.e., the amount before the deduction for discount). In cases where there are discounts, the clerk will post the *gross amount* to the customer's account.

After being journalized in the cash receipts journal by a second clerk, the accounting entry recording the cheque of W. Hay appears as follows:

CASH RECEIPTS JOURNAL

| DATE | CUSTOMER | DISCOUNTS ALLOWED DR | ACC'S REC'L CR | BANK DR |
|------|----------|----------------------|----------------|---------|
| Mar 26 | W. Hay | 1.42 | 47.25 | 45.83 |

## IN THE BOOKS OF W. HAY (THE BUYER)

Observe that it is not necessary for a buyer of goods to do any accounting for sales tax on the goods purchased. The theoretical effect of the transaction is shown below:

In the accounting department of the buyer, someone will have the responsibility of checking each purchase invoice to see if a discount is offered. Where discounts are offered, special treatment is necessary to ensure that payment is made within the allotted time. This special treatment may take several forms. Assume in this case that a cheque to pay the invoice is prepared immediately, but is dated March 25 (10 days after the invoice date), and is held in the office for release one day before the date on the cheque. The cheque will be made out for $45.83. This amount is arrived at by deducting the 3 per cent discount ($1.42) from the amount of the invoice ($47.25). The cheque will carry an explanation that it is in payment of Invoice No. 971.

On March 25 an accounting entry will be recorded in the cash payments journal from the details shown on the copy of the cheque now released. The effect of the entry is to –

1. Decrease Bank by $45.83, the amount of the cheque.
2. Eliminate the debt of $47.25 to Star Supply. (It was agreed between the two parties that a cheque of $45.83 within 10 days would be sufficient to pay off the full debt of $47.25.)
3. Record the discount of $1.42 that was earned on the transaction.

The accounting entry as it appears in the cash payments journal is shown below:

CASH PAYMENTS JOURNAL

| DATE | CREDITOR | ACC'S PAY'L DR | DISCOUNTS EARNED CR | BANK CR |
|------|----------|----------------|---------------------|---------|
| Mar 25 | Star Supply | 47.25 | 1.42 | 45.83 |

## IN THE BOOKS OF STAR SUPPLY (THE SELLER)

The effect of the above accounting entry is to—
1. Increase Bank by the amount of the cheque, $45.83.
2. Eliminate the $47.25 debt of W. Hay.
3. Record the discount of $1.42 that was allowed on the transaction.

The theoretical effect of the two transactions is shown below:

| Acc's Rec'l (W. Hay) | Sales | Sales Tax Payable | Discounts Allowed | Bank |
|---|---|---|---|---|
| 47.25 \| 47.25 | \| 45.00 | \| 2.25 | 1.42 \| | 45.83 \| |

Take note that the Discounts Allowed account is an expense account.

## IN THE BOOKS OF W. HAY (THE BUYER)

The theoretical effect of the two transactions is shown below:

| Supplies | Acc's Pay'l (Star Supply) | Discounts Earned | Bank |
|---|---|---|---|
| 47.25 \| | 47.25 \| 47.25 | \| 1.42 | \| 45.83 |

Take note that the Discounts Earned account is an income account.

---

There are still a few facts to learn about cash discounts.

1. You have probably wondered what is done when a customer takes a late discount. In other words, what is done when a customer still takes the discount after the discount period has expired. A wise businessman will be reasonable in his handling of such situations, remembering that there may be postal tie-ups or other legitimate delays. He wants to avoid acquiring a reputation for being niggardly, but at the same time, he does not want to let his customers take advantage of him.

   If it is decided to disallow a late discount, the usual practice is to cash the customer's deficient cheque; credit the customer's account by the amount of the deficient cheque; write to the customer requesting politely that he make up the deficiency in the payment.

2. The Discounts Earned account is often referred to as the Discount off Purchases account. The Discounts Allowed account is often referred to as the Discount off Sales account.

3. Every business will try to take advantage of cash discounts offered by its suppliers. Therefore, entries to Discounts Earned account can be expected to occur frequently and will normally require a special column in the cash payments journal of every business.

   Not all businesses will require a Discounts Allowed account – only those that offer cash discounts to customers. Businesses that do offer cash discounts will need to set up a special column for Discounts Allowed in the cash receipts journal.

## Returns and Allowances

You have probably had the experience of purchasing an item only to find out later that there is something wrong with it. Do you recall how anxious and impatient you were for the store to make matters right?

This same kind of transaction occurs time and time again in business and gives rise to a number of different accounting situations, each requiring special treatment. Consider the following cases (pages 185 to 190).

## Case 1.   Replacement of Goods

Star Supply issues the following invoice as a result of a sale to J. Morris:

---

### STAR ✳ SUPPLY
#### 419 Mill's Gate, Oak City

| SOLD TO | J. Morris,<br>85 Brown Avenue,<br>Oak City. T7Y 8G4 | INVOICE NUMBER | 984 |
|---|---|---|---|
| DATE | March 19, 19-- | TERMS | Net 30 |

| Quantity | Description | Unit Price | Amount |
|---|---|---|---|
| 2 Gross | Black and Red Typewriter Ribbons | $15.00 | $30.00 |
| | 5% Sales Tax | | 1.50 |
| | | | $31.50 |

---

## IN THE BOOKS OF STAR SUPPLY (THE SELLER)

The journal entry is:

SALES JOURNAL

| DATE | CUSTOMER | SALES<br><br>CR | SALES<br>TAX<br>PAY'L<br>CR | ACC'S<br>REC'L<br><br>DR |
|---|---|---|---|---|
| Mar 19 | J. Morris | 30.00 | 1.50 | 31.50 |

The theoretical effect of the transaction is:

| ACC'S REC'L<br>(J. MORRIS) | SALES | SALES TAX<br>PAYABLE |
|---|---|---|
| 31.50 | 30.00 | 1.50 |

Provided that the returned goods are put back in stock, no accounting entries are necessary for the exchange. However, because of the delay, through no fault of the purchaser, it is understood that payment will not be expected until 30 days after the delivery of the proper goods.

## IN THE BOOKS OF J. MORRIS (THE BUYER)

Upon receipt of the invoice and the goods which appear to be satisfactory, the journal entry is:

PURCHASES JOURNAL

| DATE | CREDITOR | SUP-<br>PLIES<br>DR | PUR-<br>CHASES<br>DR | ACC'S<br>PAY'L<br>CR |
|---|---|---|---|---|
| Mar 20 | Star Supply | 31.50 | | 31.50 |

The theoretical effect of the transaction is:

| SUPPLIES | ACC'S PAY'L<br>(STAR SUPPLY) |
|---|---|
| 31.50 | 31.50 |

When the package of typewriting ribbons is opened by the employees of J. Morris, it is found that the ribbons are all black, and not red and black as ordered. A phone call is put through to the office of Star Supply and a complaint registered. Star Supply agrees to make good on the order. A short time later, the correct goods are delivered and the incorrect goods are picked up.

No accounting entries are necessary for this exchange.

## Case 2.  Return of Goods

Star Supply issues the following invoice as a result of a sale to Super Stationery.

---

## STAR ✺ SUPPLY

### 419 Mill's Gate, Oak City

| SOLD TO | Super Stationery,<br>51 McLeod Avenue,<br>Oak City. T7Y 7A1 | INVOICE NUMBER | 997 |
|---------|------------------------------|----------------|-----|
| DATE | March 22, 19— | TERMS | Net 30 |

| Quantity | Description | Unit Price | Amount |
|----------|-------------|------------|--------|
| 8 Doz. | "Fabulous" Ball Pens | $1.50 | $12.00 |
| | 5% Sales Tax | | .60 |
| | | | $12.60 |

---

## IN THE BOOKS OF STAR SUPPLY (THE SELLER)

The journal entry and the theoretical effect of the transaction are:

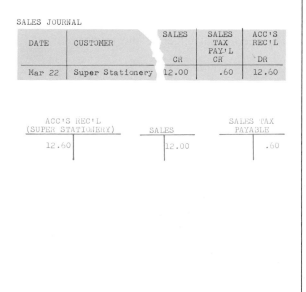

SALES JOURNAL

| DATE | CUSTOMER | SALES CR | SALES TAX PAY'L CR | ACC'S REC'L DR |
|------|----------|----------|--------------------|----------------|
| Mar 22 | Super Stationery | 12.00 | .60 | 12.60 |

ACC'S REC'L (SUPER STATIONERY)   12.60 |

SALES   | 12.00

SALES TAX PAYABLE   | .60

## IN THE BOOKS OF SUPER STATIONERY (THE BUYER)

Upon receipt of the invoice and the goods, the journal entry and the theoretical effect in the accounts are as shown below. Because Super Stationery purchased the ball point pens for re-sale, the debit entry is to Purchases account.

PURCHASES JOURNAL

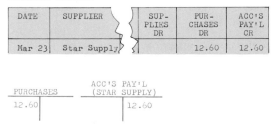

| DATE | SUPPLIER | SUP-PLIES DR | PUR-CHASES DR | ACC'S PAY'L CR |
|------|----------|--------------|---------------|----------------|
| Mar 23 | Star Supply | | 12.60 | 12.60 |

PURCHASES   12.60 |

ACC'S PAY'L (STAR SUPPLY)   | 12.60

When the ball point pens are used, Super Stationery discovers that they are defective. Contact is made with Star Supply and a complaint is registered. The outcome of the discussion is that the goods are to be returned (picked up by the vendor) and not to be replaced. Of course, Super Stationery is not expected to pay for them.

No accounting entry is made at this time.

# FACTS ABOUT CREDIT INVOICES

When the goods are received back from Super Stationery, the sale has in fact been canceled and action must be taken by Star Supply to correct the accounts. Of prime concern is the customer; his account must be reduced by a **credit** entry and he must be informed that the reduction has been made.

The accounting entry to record the return of goods, and the **credit** to the customer's account in particular, is begun by the issuing of a **credit invoice** by the vendor. A credit invoice (also known by the names **credit note** and **credit memo**) is in reality a minus invoice, having precisely the opposite effect of a regular invoice.

Star Supply's credit invoice crediting the account of Super Stationery for the return of the ball point pens is shown below and is a typical example of a credit invoice.

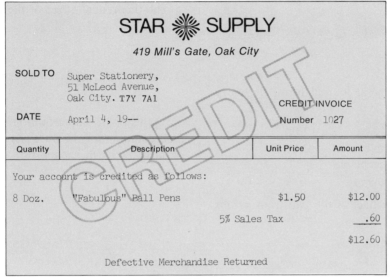

*Credit invoice.*

1. In the accounts, the effect of a credit invoice is opposite to that of a regular sales invoice.
2. The credit invoice is also known by the names credit note and credit memo.
3. For any one business, the credit invoice is usually of the same basic design and appearance as the regular sales invoice form.
4. The word 'Credit' is prominently displayed on the form.
5. The credit invoice form is usually either (i) printed on pink paper, or (ii) printed on white paper using red ink.
6. Credit invoices may be numbered in sequence with the regular invoices or they may be given their own sequence of numbers.
7. The path of a credit invoice is the same as that of a regular sales invoice. See page 100.

---

## IN THE BOOKS OF STAR SUPPLY

Credit invoices are most efficiently recorded through the sales journal (although they may be handled through the general journal). However, since a credit invoice has the opposite effect of a regular sales invoice, the amounts entered from the credit invoice must be individually circled in the journal. For a review of this technique, refer to page 137.

## IN THE BOOKS OF SUPER STATIONERY

When received by Super Stationery, the credit invoice of Star Supply will follow the routine established for purchase invoices. However, since the effect of a credit invoice is opposite to that of a regular sales invoice, care must be taken to circle individually the amounts entered in the purchases journal from the credit invoice. The accounting entry to record the credit invoice in

# IN THE BOOKS OF STAR SUPPLY

The way in which the credit invoice is recorded in the sales journal is illustrated below (fifth line):

SALES JOURNAL

| DATE | CUSTOMER | SALES CR | SALES TAX PAY'L CR | INV. NO. | ACC'S REC'L DR |
|------|----------|----------|--------------------|----------|----------------|
| Apr 3 | Delsey's | 24.00 | 1.20 | 1023 | 25.20 |
| 3 | R. Brown | 10.00 | .50 | 1024 | 10.50 |
| 4 | J. Jones | 18.00 | .90 | 1025 | 18.90 |
| 4 | A & A Printing | 15.00 | .75 | 1026 | 15.75 |
| 4 | Super Stationery | 12.00 | .60 | 1027 | 12.60 |
| 4 | Heart Hair | 20.00 | 1.00 | 1028 | 20.10 |

If written in general journal form, the entry would be:

Dr. Sales                    12.00
Dr. Sales Tax Payable       .60
    Cr. Accounts Receivable
        (Super Stationery)         12.60

The theoretical effect of the two transactions is:

```
ACC'S REC'L
(SUPER STATIONERY)          SALES              SALES TAX
                                               PAYABLE
12.60 |                          | 12.00              | .60
      | 12.60      12.00 |                    .60 |
      |                  |                        |
```

At this point, Star Supply has completed its accounting for the sale of and the return of the defective merchandise.

# IN THE BOOKS OF SUPER STATIONERY

the purchases journal is shown below. Observe that the credit entry is to Purchases account since that is the account that was previously debited.

PURCHASES JOURNAL

| DATE | SUPPLIER | SUP-PLIES DR | PUR-CHASES DR | ACC'S PAY'L CR |
|------|----------|--------------|---------------|----------------|
| Apr 6 | Star Supply | | 12.60 | 12.60 |

The theoretical effect of the two transactions is:

```
PURCHASES                   ACC'S PAY'L
                           (STAR SUPPLY)
12.60 |                               | 12.60
      | 12.60        12.60 |
```

At this point, Super Stationery has completed its accounting for the purchase of and the return of the defective merchandise.

# Case 3. Allowance for Goods

Star Supply issues the following invoice as a result of a sale to P. & Q. Garage.

## STAR ✳ SUPPLY

*419 Mill's Gate, Oak City*

| SOLD TO | P. & Q. Garage,<br>95 Sentinel Street,<br>Tidings Corner. L9F 3D9 | | INVOICE NUMBER | 1008 |
| --- | --- | --- | --- | --- |
| DATE | March 24, 19-- | | TERMS | 2/10,N/30 |

| Quantity | Description | Unit Price | Amount |
| --- | --- | --- | --- |
| 4 Pkgs. | Invoice Forms | $12.00 | $48.00 |
| | 5% Sales Tax | | 2.40 |
| | | | $50.40 |

## IN THE BOOKS OF STAR SUPPLY (THE SELLER)

The journal entry is recorded as for the two previous cases.

The theoretical effect of the transaction is:

## IN THE BOOKS OF P. & Q. GARAGE (THE BUYER)

The journal entry is recorded as for the two previous cases with Supplies being the account debited.

The theoretical effect of the transaction is:

At the time the goods are inspected, it is found that the four packages of invoice forms are not printed according to the instructions given to Star Supply. A complaint is made to Star Supply and a compromise is made between the two companies as follows: P. & Q. Garage is persuaded to keep and use the invoice forms, and Star Supply agrees to give an allowance of 50 per cent off the price of the goods.

# CREDIT INVOICE OF VENDOR

As was shown in Case 2, the making right of the accounting for such a situation is begun by the vendor company which issues a credit invoice.

Accordingly, Star Supply issues the credit invoice shown below.

## STAR ✳ SUPPLY

*419 Mill's Gate, Oak City*

SOLD TO    P. & Q. Garage,
           95 Sentinel Street,
           Tidings Corner. L9F 3D9          **CREDIT INVOICE**

DATE       April 7, 19--                     Number  1036

| Quantity | Description | Unit Price | Amount |
|----------|-------------|------------|--------|
| Your account is credited as follows: | | | |
| 50% Allowance for merchandise on invoice #1008, goods incorrectly printed: | | | |
| 4 Pkgs. | Invoice Forms | $6.00 | $24.00 |
| | 5% Tax | | 1.20 |
| | | | $25.20 |

---

## IN THE BOOKS OF STAR SUPPLY

The journal entry recording the credit invoice is:

SALES JOURNAL

| DATE | CUSTOMER | SALES CR | SALES TAX CR | ACC'S REC'L DR |
|------|----------|----------|--------------|----------------|
| Apr 7 | P & Q Garage | 24.00 | 1.20 | 25.20 |

The theoretical effect of the two transactions is:

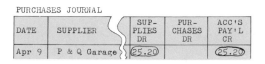

| ACC'S REC'L (P. & Q. GARAGE) | SALES | SALES TAX PAYABLE |
|---|---|---|
| 50.40 | | |
| 25.20 | 24.00 | 48.00 |
| | | 1.20 | 2.40 |

At this point, Star Supply has completed its accounting for the sale of and the allowance for the defective merchandise.

## IN THE BOOKS OF P. & Q. GARAGE

The credit invoice is accepted and processed in the normal way. The journal entry recording the transaction is:

PURCHASES JOURNAL

| DATE | SUPPLIER | SUP-PLIES DR | PUR-CHASES DR | ACC'S PAY'L CR |
|------|----------|--------------|----------------|----------------|
| Apr 9 | P & Q Garage | 25.20 | | 25.20 |

The theoretical effect of the two transactions is:

| SUPPLIES | ACC'S PAY'L (STAR SUPPLY) |
|---|---|
| 50.40 | |
| 25.20 | 50.40 |
| 25.20 | |

At this point, the accounting for the sale of and the allowance for the defective merchandise is complete.

# Cash Refund

The cash sale is a very common business transaction. But dissatisfaction can occur with cash sales as well as with sales on account. When a buyer pays cash for goods and later finds them to be unsatisfactory, he usually demands and gets his money back – in other words, he obtains a **cash refund**. The accounting for cash refunds takes place as follows:

TRANSACTION

On May 16, 19—, Star Supply makes a cash purchase of a new battery from Cut-Rate Auto Parts. The cost of the battery is $25 plus sales tax of 5 per cent. A cheque is issued by Star Supply to pay for the goods.

## BOOKS OF SELLER

Journal entry is:

The theoretical effect is:

## BOOKS OF BUYER

Journal entry is:

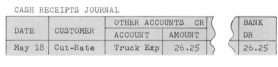

The theoretical effect is:

| TRUCK EXPENSE | | BANK | |
|---|---|---|---|
| 26.25 | | | 26.25 |

TRANSACTION

On May 18, 19—, at the time the battery is being installed, the mechanic finds that it is cracked. It is, therefore, returned to Cut-Rate Auto Parts and a refund cheque for the full amount is obtained. The refund cheque is included in the day's cash receipts.

## BOOKS OF SELLER

Journal entry is:

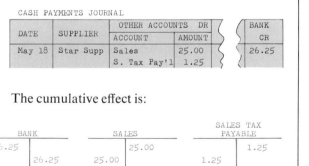

The cumulative effect is:

| BANK | | SALES | | SALES TAX PAYABLE | |
|---|---|---|---|---|---|
| 26.25 | | | 25.00 | | 1.25 |
| | 26.25 | 25.00 | | 1.25 | |

## BOOKS OF BUYER

Journal entry is:

The cumulative effect is:

| TRUCK EXPENSE | | BANK | |
|---|---|---|---|
| 26.25 | | | 26.25 |
| | 26.25 | 26.25 | |

**Note**: Rather than give a refund to a cash customer, many businesses prefer to issue a credit note. The issuing of a credit note sets up an account for the customer in which there is a credit balance. The customer is thus encouraged to make purchases from the business which are to be paid for out of the credit balance. He is also discouraged from spending the refund at another place of business.

## Cash Discount Combined with a Return or Allowance

If an invoice is received on which there is a cash discount, and some time before the discount date a portion of the goods is returned or an allowance is obtained, the discount may be taken only on the net cost of the goods. The net cost is found by deducting the amount of the credit note from the amount of the sales invoice. In such cases, it is wise to make certain of the discount date by discussing it with the vendor. Because of the circumstances, the discount date will probably be moved ahead, perhaps to the date of the credit note.

## Sales Returns and Allowances Account

The previous sections indicated that the accounts involved in the accounting for returns, allowances, or cash refunds are the same (except used in reverse) as those used for the original sale. This is correct accounting practice and is adopted extensively in the business community.

However, there are some businesses, large department stores for example, that require more specific information in respect to returns, allowances, and refunds. They want to know what proportion of the goods sold is returned to them. They obtain this information by using a separate account in which to accumulate sales returns and allowances.

Consider the following transactions:

TRANSACTION

Simplex Co. sells $50 of goods to A. Moss. An invoice is issued for the sale on November 12, 19—.

The journal entry for the transaction in the books of Simplex Co. is:

SALES JOURNAL

| DATE | CUSTOMER | SALES RETURNS ALLOW'S DR | SALES CR | SALES TAX PAY'L CR | ACC'S REC'L DR |
|------|----------|------|------|------|------|
| Nov 12 | A. Moss | | 50.00 | 2.50 | 52.50 |

The effect in the accounts is:

| ACC'S REC'L (A. MOSS) | SALES TAX PAYABLE | SALES |
|------|------|------|
| 52.50 | 2.50 | 50.00 |

TRANSACTION

Because a portion of the goods sold to A. Moss is defective and returned, Simplex Co. issues a credit invoice for $18 plus tax on November 18, 19—. (Simplex Co. uses a Sales Returns and Allowances account.)

The journal entry for the transaction in the books of Simplex Co. is:

SALES JOURNAL

| DATE | CUSTOMER | SALES RETURNS ALLOW'S DR | SALES CR | SALES TAX PAY'L CR | ACC'S REC'L DR |
|------|----------|------|------|------|------|
| Nov 18 | A. Moss | 18.00 | | .90 | 18.90 |

Observe that —
1. Because Simplex Co. accumulates returns and allowances separately, there is a special column provided for a Sales Returns and Allowances account in the sales journal.
2. The Sales Returns and Allowances column is a debit column because entries to the Sales Returns and Allowances account are normally debits.

The cumulative effect in the account is:

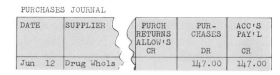

These two accounts together show the true 'Sales' figure, called 'Net Sales'. In this case the net sales figure is $32.

---

## Purchases Returns and Allowances Account

There are certain businesses that consider it necessary to know the total amount of returns and allowances for merchandise purchased. They want to know what proportion of the merchandise purchased by them is returned to their suppliers. They obtain this information by using a separate account in which to accumulate purchases returns and allowances. (Note that this includes only items of merchandise inventory that are purchased and later returned. It does not include items such as supplies or expense items such as truck parts. These latter items are handled by means of a direct credit to the account involved.)

Consider the following transactions:

---

### TRANSACTION

On June 12, 19—, Baytown Drug Market receives a shipment of drugs and the sales invoice for them from Drug Wholesale Company. The total of the invoice is $147.

The journal entry for the transaction in the books of Baytown Drug Market is:

PURCHASES JOURNAL

| DATE | SUPPLIER | PURCH RETURNS ALLOW'S CR | PUR- CHASES DR | ACC'S PAY'L CR |
|------|----------|----------|----------|----------|
| Jun 12 | Drug Whols | | 147.00 | 147.00 |

---

The effect in the accounts is:

---

### TRANSACTION

On June 14, Baytown Drug Market notices that a number of the packages received from Drug Wholesale Company are damaged. The damaged goods are returned for credit and a credit note for $48.30 is received on June 16. (Baytown Drug Market uses a Purchases Returns and Allowances account.)

The journal entry for the transaction in the books of Baytown Drug Market is:

PURCHASES JOURNAL

| DATE | SUPPLIER | PURCH RETURNS ALLOW'S CR | PUR- CHASES DR | ACC'S PAY'L CR |
|------|----------|----------|----------|----------|
| June 16 | Drug Whols | 48.30 | | (48.30) |

Observe the use of a Purchases Returns and Allowances credit column in the purchases journal.

The cumulative effect in the accounts is:

These two accounts together show the true 'Purchases' figure, called 'Net Purchases'. In this case, the net purchases figure is $98.70.

# Petty Cash Fund

The most common method of making payment for expenditures is by cheque. However, every business must continually face the situation where it is not convenient to issue a cheque and where 'cash' is the expected thing. Consider the following transactions:

1. The janitor requires some electrical fuses and during his lunch period he purchases with his own money a quantity of fuses from the local hardware store. He then submits the cash register slip for $1.50 to the accounting department so that he may be reimbursed.
2. Two salaried employees are asked to work overtime in order to complete a special job. As a favor, they are each given $3 for supper money.
3. A parcel is delivered by an express company for which express charges of $2.50 must be paid immediately.

The most efficient way to pay for small expenditures of this type is with cash. For this reason a small quantity of cash, usually no more than $100, is kept in the office. It is called the **petty cash fund**.

## Establishing a Petty Cash Fund

To establish a petty cash fund it is merely necessary to withdraw a sum of money from the bank account and to put it in the care of some person in the office. More precisely, a cheque is issued (made out to Petty Cash usually) and given to the person chosen to be in charge of petty cash; this person cashes the cheque and brings the money (in the form of small bills and coins) back to the office. The petty cash fund is usually kept in a metal cash box (with lock) and, outside of office hours, the box is usually kept in the company safe or vault. Naturally, the keeper of the petty cash is instructed as to the type of expenditure that may be made out of petty cash funds.

The accounting entry to establish a petty cash fund is shown by the following:

It is decided to establish a petty cash fund of $50. A cheque, dated September 20, 19—, in the amount of $50 is made out to Petty Cash and is given to the person chosen to keep the petty cash.

The journal entry to record the transaction is:

The effect in the accounts is:

| PETTY CASH | | BANK | |
|---|---|---|---|
| 50.00 | | | 50.00 |

At this time, after the cheque is cashed, the petty cash box will contain $50 in cash.

## Operating the Petty Cash Fund

The keeper of the petty cash fund is authorized to make small payments out of the fund from time to time. But for every amount paid out of the fund, a bill for the expenditure (submitted by the recipient of the money) must be put in. If a bill is not available, the recipient of the money must fill out a petty cash voucher such as the one shown on page 195. The petty cash voucher is then placed in the box. A supply of unused petty cash vouchers (also known as petty cash slips) is kept with the petty cash fund.

At any time, the total of the bills, vouchers, and cash in the petty cash box should be equal to the petty cash fund. The keeper of the fund is responsible for seeing that this is so.

The accounting for this aspect of petty cash is easy because no entry is made. It is one of those accounting situations where it is advantageous to allow the records to become temporarily incorrect. This method of handling petty cash is known as the **imprest method**.

A petty cash voucher.

## Replenishing Petty Cash

As time passes, of course, the cash in the petty cash box will diminish as the bills and vouchers are paid. A point will be reached where there may not be enough cash in the fund to pay the next bill or voucher. To prevent this, a lower limit is usually placed on the fund. When this point is reached, the fund must be replenished.

To show the accounting for replenishing petty cash, let us continue the example begun previously.

---

TRANSACTION

On October 2, the contents of the petty cash box are as shown at the top of the next column.

| Cash | $ 4.15 |
|---|---|
| Bills and Vouchers | 45.85 |
| Total | $50.00 |

The breakdown of the bills and vouchers by account charged is as follows:

*Vouchers*

| | | |
|---|---|---|
| 1. | Miscellaneous Expense | $ 2.59 |
| 2. | Postage | 4.00 |
| 3. | Miscellaneous Expense | 3.75 |
| 4. | Building Maintenance | 1.56 |
| 5. | Donations | 5.00 |
| 6. | Building Maintenance | 4.75 |
| 7. | Truck Expense | 5.15 |
| 8. | Miscellaneous Expense | 6.00 |
| 9. | Postage | 4.00 |
| 10. | Supplies | 9.05 |
| | Total | $45.85 |

The lower limit of the petty cash fund is set at $5.

Because the amount of cash in the petty cash box is less than the lower limit of $5, it is necessary to replenish the petty cash fund. The first step is for the keeper of the fund to prepare a summary of the charges from the bills and vouchers in the box. There is no definite form in which the summary must be prepared. The summary might appear as shown below.

To this summary are attached the bills and vouchers from which the summary was prepared.

The second step in replenishing the petty cash fund is for the keeper of the fund to obtain a cheque with which to replace the cash that has been expended out of the fund. He does this by (1) submitting the summary, together with the bills and vouchers, to the department that issues cheques, and (2) by receiving a cheque, made out to petty cash, for an amount equal to the total shown on the summary (in this example, $45.85). The summary and the supporting papers are accepted as the source document for the cheque.

When the cheque is cashed and the money placed in the petty cash box (along with the $4.15 already there), the fund is restored to its original amount of $50 cash. It is then ready to begin another cycle.

Under the imprest method of handling petty cash, the accounting entry to record the issuing of the replenishing cheque is as follows:

CASH PAYMENTS JOURNAL

| DATE | NAME | OTHER ACC'S DR | | BANK CR |
|------|------|----------------|--------|---------|
| | | ACCOUNT | AMOUNT | |
| Oct 2 | Petty Cash | Bldg Mntc | 6.31 | 45.85 |
| | | Donations | 5.00 | |
| | | Misc. Exp | 12.34 | |
| | | Postage | 8.00 | |
| | | Supplies | 9.05 | |
| | | Truck Exp | 5.15 | |

Observe that the accounting entry is one that –
1. Debits a number of accounts in exact accordance with the petty cash summary of charges.

2. Credits Bank with the amount of the replenishing cheque.

**Note:** The above entry is in effect a consolidation of more than one entry; namely, (1) those that require a charge to an expense or asset account and a decrease to Petty Cash, and (2) the one that requires an increase to Petty Cash and a decrease to Bank.

In the accounts, the cumulative effect of the two entries, i.e. (1) the entry to establish the fund, and (2) the replenishing entry, is:

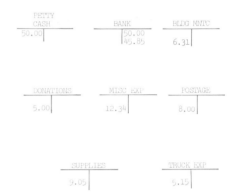

The above accounts reflect the two usual types of accounting entries that are necessary when the imprest method of petty cash is used. These are –
1. The entry to establish the fund, or, what amounts to the same thing, to increase the fund.
2. The replenishing entry that records the credit to Bank and distributes the charges to the various accounts.

# Bookkeeping and Accounting Terms

**Cash Discount** A reduction that may be taken in the amount of a bill provided that the bill is paid within the discount period shown on the bill.
**Terms of Sale** The conditions agreed to at the time of sale, between the buyer and the seller, in respect to the length of time allowed for payment and whether a cash discount may be taken.
**Discounts Earned** Income acquired by a busi- ness that takes advantage of cash discounts offered by its suppliers. Also known as **discount off purchases**.
**Discounts Allowed** Expense incurred by a business that offers a cash discount to its customers who take advantage of the offer. Also known as **discount off sales**.
**Sales Return and Purchase Return** The result of

the buyer of goods returning them to the seller either for a credit note or for replacement, the goods being returned because in some way they were deficient. From the seller's position, this is a 'sales return'; from the buyer's position, this is a 'purchase return'.

**Sales Allowance and Purchase Allowance** The result of an agreement between the seller of deficient goods and the buyer to the effect that the goods will not be returned but that the price will be decreased by means of a credit note. From the seller's position, this is a 'sales allowance'; from the buyer's position, this is a 'purchase allowance'.

**Cash Refund** The result of the buyer of goods having his money returned by the seller in respect to deficient goods that have been paid for.

**Credit Invoice** A business document, the purpose of which is to initiate a reduction in a customer's account. The reason for the reduction is explained in detail on the credit invoice form. A credit invoice is really a negative sales invoice. Also known as **credit note** or **credit memo**.

**Net Sales** The figure obtained by subtracting the balance of the Sales Returns and Allowances account from the balance of the Sales account.

**Net Purchases** The figure obtained by subtracting the balance of the Purchases Returns and Allowances account from the balance of the Purchases account.

**Petty Cash** A small amount of money, usually $100 or less, kept in the office for the convenience of paying cash for small bills and expenditures.

# Review Questions

1. What is a cash discount?
2. What is the purpose of a cash discount?
3. Explain the meaning of 'terms of sale'.
4. Explain the meaning of C.O.D.; Net 30; 2/15,n/30.
5. Where may the terms of sale be seen?
6. Under what circumstances might a customer be requested to pay C.O.D.?
7. Of what value is it to record a customer's usual terms of sale on his account card?
8. In the office of the buyer, what is done with a purchase invoice on which a cash discount is offered?
9. Calculate the discount and the net amount of an invoice for $52.50 if the rate of discount is 3 per cent.
10. If J. Jones pays a bill of $50 by means of a cheque for $49 because he was entitled to a 2 per cent discount, what is the amount of the entry made to his account in the books of the seller?
11. Are discounts earned associated with the buyer or the seller?
12. What is usually done when a customer takes a late discount?
13. What is another name for Discounts Allowed? for Discounts Earned?
14. Nearly all businesses have a Discounts Earned account, but not all businesses have a Discounts Allowed account. Explain.
15. Explain the difference between a 'sales return' and a 'sales allowance'.
16. When goods are purchased and later returned for credit, under what circumstances in the books of the buyer will the credit entry be to Purchases account (or Purchase Returns and Allowances account)?
17. In your own words, explain why you think the term credit invoice was chosen.
18. How can you usually distinguish between a regular sales invoice and a credit invoice?
19. When you journalize a credit invoice in the sales journal, what must you be careful to do?
20. Under what circumstances would a buyer want a cash refund?
21. Explain how a cash discount is calculated when a return or allowance is involved in the transaction.
22. Under what circumstances does a business maintain a separate account for sales returns and allowances?

23. Why is it necessary to have a petty cash fund in a business office?

24. State the rule that the keeper of the fund must follow when expenditures from the fund are made.

25. How often is the petty cash fund replenished?

26. Give the accounting entry to establish a petty cash fund.

## Exercises

1. Complete the following schedule by calculating the amount of the payment that is necessary in each case. Where credit notes are involved assume that the discount period is adjusted to start from the date on the credit note.

| Date of Invoice | Amount of Invoice | Terms of Sales | Amount of Credit Note | Date of Credit Note | Date Payment is Made | Amount of Payment Required |
|---|---|---|---|---|---|---|
| Mar 12 | $52.50 | 2/10,N/30 | – | – | Mar 20 | |
| May 18 | 47.25 | Net 30 | – | – | May 27 | |
| Sep 4 | 115.50 | 3/15,N/60 | – | | Oct 10 | |
| Feb 6 | 1 050.00 | 1/20,N/60 | $126.00 | Feb 18 | Mar 6 | |
| Oct 19 | 588.00 | 2/10,N/30 | 42.00 | Nov 5 | Nov 27 | |
| Aug 27 | 882.00 | 2/15,N/60 | 168.00 | Sep 7 | Sep 10 | |

2. (a) (i) In two-column general journal form record the accounting entry for the invoice shown below in the books of Circle Supply.

900 Park Street                                               Maple City

# Circle O Supply

SOLD TO: Watson Construction
1500 Randell Road
Maple City X3Y 7N5          INVOICE NUMBER 715

DATE     August 3, 19--          TERMS 2/10,N/30

| Quantity | Description | Unit Price | Amount |
|---|---|---|---|
| 10 boxes | #10 Woodscrews | $5.50 | $55.00 |
| 2 | Standard Crowbars | 4.10 | 8.20 |
| | | | $63.20 |
| | | 5% Sales Tax | 3.16 |
| | | | $66.36 |

(ii) On August 12 a cheque in the amount of $65.03 is received from Watson Construction. In two-column general journal form show the accounting entry to be recorded in the books of Circle Supply.

(b) If Watson Construction charges the merchandise shown on the above invoice to an account called Small Tools and Supplies, show the journal entries for the above two transactions that would be made in the books of Watson Construction. Use appropriate dates.

3. (a) In the books of Circle Supply, in two-column general journal form, record the accounting entry for the following invoice.

| 900 Park Street | | | Maple City |
|---|---|---|---|

**Circle ◯ Supply**

SOLD TO: Kitchen Cabinets
East Side Road
Maple City  X3Y 4H2   INVOICE NUMBER  802

DATE  August 9, 19--   TERMS  2/10,N/30

| Quantity | Description | Unit Price | Amount |
|---|---|---|---|
| 10 | Contact Cement, Large | $7.85 | $78.50 |
| | 5% Sales Tax | | 3.93 |
| | | | $82.43 |

(b) On August 24 a cheque is received from Kitchen Cabinets for $80.78, the amount of the invoice less the discount. Circle Supply decided to disallow the discount. Record the receipt of the cheque in the general journal of Circle Supply.

(c) Explain what additional step should be taken.

4. (a) In the books of Circle Supply, in two-column general journal form, record the accounting entry for the following invoice.

| 900 Park Street | | | Maple City |
|---|---|---|---|

**Circle ◯ Supply**

SOLD TO: Motor Electric Service
400 Northline
Abbotsville  W4P 3R9   INVOICE NUMBER  832

DATE  August 15, 19--   TERMS  2/10,N/30

| Quantity | Description | Unit Price | Amount |
|---|---|---|---|
| 1 Carton | #35 Copper Wire | $65.00 | $65.00 |
| 24 | Propane Torch Refills | 4.20 | 100.80 |
| | | | $165.80 |
| | 5% Sales Tax | | 8.29 |
| | | | $174.09 |

(b) When the goods were unpacked by Motor Electric Service it was found that propane torch nozzles had been sent in error instead of propane torch refills. Circle Supply corrected the situation by delivering the correct items and picking up the incorrect items for return to the stock room. In the books of Circle Supply record the necessary accounting entries.

---

5. (a) (i) In the books of Circle Supply, in two-column general journal form, show the accounting entry to be recorded for the invoice below.

| 900 Park Street | | | Maple City |
|---|---|---|---|

**Circle ⬭ Supply**

SOLD TO: Jackson and Jackson
Marmora Road
Maple City  X3Y 6T8    INVOICE NUMBER    873

DATE    September 3, 19--    TERMS  2/10,N/30

| Quantity | Description | Unit Price | Amount |
|---|---|---|---|
| 100 | General Purpose Connectors | $1.00 | $100.00 |
| | 5% Sales Tax | | 5.00 |
| | | | $105.00 |

(ii) The goods are found to be inadequate for the work intended and are returned for credit. The following credit invoice is issued. Show the accounting entry to record this credit invoice in the books of Circle Supply.

| 900 Park Street | | | Maple City |
|---|---|---|---|

**Circle ⬭ Supply**

SOLD TO: Jackson and Jackson
Marmora Road
Maple City  X3Y 6T8    CREDIT INVOICE
NUMBER  891

DATE    September 9, 19--

| Quantity | Description | Unit Price | Amount |
|---|---|---|---|
| 100 | General Purpose Connectors (Ordered on invoice #873) | $1.00 | $100.00 |
| | 5% Sales Tax | | 5.00 |
| | | | $105.00 |

(b) For the above transactions record the accounting entries to be made in the books of Jackson and Jackson. Use appropriate dates. The goods affect the Supplies account.

6. (a) (i) The invoice shown below was issued by Circle Supply to Crown Metal and Machines. In two-column general journal form show the accounting entry to record the invoice in the books of Circle Supply.

| 900 Park Street | | | Maple City |
|---|---|---|---|

**Circle O Supply**

SOLD TO: Crown Metals and Machines
150 Cherry Road
McCarten   W4R 2M2        INVOICE NUMBER  851

DATE        August 21, 19--            TERMS 2/10,N/30

| Quantity | Description | Unit Price | Amount |
|---|---|---|---|
| 40 meters | 1 cm  Steel Pipe | $ .72 | $ 28.80 |
| 150 meters | 2 cm  Steel Pipe | 1.95 | 292.50 |
| 3 doz. | All-purpose Metal Turnbuckles 6.00 | | 18.00 |
| | | | $339.30 |
| | 5% Sales Tax | | 16.97 |
| | | | $356.27 |

(ii) Because the 3 dozen all-purpose metal turnbuckles proved to be defective, the following credit invoice was issued.

| 900 Park Street | | | Maple City |
|---|---|---|---|

**Circle O Supply**

SOLD TO: Crown Metals and Machines
150 Cherry Road
McCarten   W4R 2M2        CREDIT INVOICE
NUMBER  869

DATE        August 25, 19--

| Quantity | Description | Unit Price | Amount |
|---|---|---|---|
| 3 doz. | All-purpose Metal Turnbuckles (Defective) | $6.00 | $18.00 |
| | 5% Sales Tax | | .90 |
| | | | $18.90 |

In the books of Circle Supply record the accounting entry for the credit invoice.

(iii) On September 2 a cheque is received by Circle Supply from Crown Metals and Machines in full payment of Invoice #851 and Credit Invoice #869 less the cash discount. Calculate the amount of the cheque.

(iv) In the books of Circle Supply record the receipt of the above cheque.

(b) For the above sequence of transactions, record the accounting entries to be made in the books of Crown Metals and Machines. Use appropriate dates. The account to be charged with the goods is Property Maintenance.

---

7. On March 16, 19—, after a bill of $12.16 is paid, the contents of a petty cash fund having a lower limit of $5 are as follows:

| | | | |
|---|---|---|---|
| Cash | $ 1.68 | Building Expense | 10.50 |
| *Bills and Vouchers* | | Miscellaneous Expense | 2.05 |
| Miscellaneous Expense | 6.04 | Postage | 9.00 |
| Miscellaneous Expense | 1.25 | Miscellaneous Expense | 4.15 |
| Sales Promotion | 3.17 | Building Expense | 12.16 |

Prepare the summary of charges necessary to replenish the fund.

In general journal form, write out the accounting entry necessary to replenish the fund.

---

8. On June 10, 19—, a $25 petty cash fund, having a lower limit of $2, is in the following condition:

| | | | |
|---|---|---|---|
| Cash | $ .54 | Office Expense | 2.14 |
| *Bills and Vouchers* | | P. Martin, Drawings | 10.00 |
| Office Expense | 5.02 | Office Expense | 1.20 |
| Office Supplies | .75 | Office Expense | 2.00 |
| Advertising | 2.00 | Office Supplies | 1.35 |

Prepare the summary of charges necessary to replenish the fund.

In general journal form, write out the required accounting entry to replenish the fund.

---

9. Record the following 'selected' transactions of the Canadian Copper Company in general journal form.

*Transactions*

October

1 *Purchase Invoice*
—No. 6457, from Dominion Nickel Company, dated September 29, amount, $11 760, terms, Net 30 days, for a shipment of copper.

3 *Cheque Copy*
—No. 750, to Petty Cash, $25, to increase petty cash fund from $25 to $50.

7 *Purchase Invoice*
—No. 354, from Continental Railway Company, $762.12, in respect to the

shipment of copper from Dominion Nickel Company.

8 *Cheque Copy*
–No. 765, to Mallory & Co., $353.99, in payment of their sales invoice No. 6421 for $361.21 less a 2 per cent discount.

11 *Cheque Copy*
–No. 784, to Ewing & Barlock, $51.62; cash refund for defective copper bars returned. (Canadian Copper Company does not keep separate accounts for returns and allowances.)

12 *Cash Receipt*
–Cheque from Kirby Brothers, $116.62, in payment of sales invoice No. 692, dated September 30, having terms of 2/15,n/30.

17 *Cheque Copy*
–No. 801, to Petty Cash, $48.68; replenishing cheque for the following charges: Office Supplies, $17.14; Miscellaneous Expense, $23.22; Delivery Expense, $1.35; Freight-in, $6.97.

25 *Cheque Copy*
–No. 814, to Pearson Bros., $12.14; for the cash purchase of office supplies.

26 *Sales Invoice*
–No. 751, to Toro Fixtures, $643; sale of goods on account; terms of sale, Net 30 days; sales tax 3 per cent to be added.

27 *Cheque Copy*
–No. 827, to Commercial Cartage, $412; cash payment for delivery service for the month of September.

30 *Credit Note Received*
–No. 6529, from Dominion Nickel Company, $900; allowance for defective goods on invoice No. 6457.

---

**10.** Record the following 'selected' transactions of Wholesale Food Distributors in general journal form. In working out your answers, bear in mind the following:

a. A few of the transactions are dependent on previous ones.

b. Wholesale Food Distributors maintains separate accounts for both Purchases Returns and Allowances, and Sales Returns and Allowances.

c. The amounts of certain cheques (receipts and expenditures) have been left for you to decide.

*Transactions*

November

3 *Sales Invoices*
–No. 962, Palmer's Grocery, $496.26; terms, 2/10,n/30; add 5 per cent sales tax.
–No. 963, Grey's Market, $376.14; terms, 2/10,n/30; add 5 per cent sales tax.
–No. 964, Alec's Groceteria, $197.26; terms, 2/10,n/30; add 5 per cent sales tax.

4 *Cheque Copy*
–No. 404, to D. K. Knight, $100, loan to an employee to help him overcome a personal hardship.

5 *Purchase Invoice*
–No. 213, from Gordon Canners, $1 260, dated Nov. 2; terms 3/20,n/60, for merchandise purchased.
*Bank Debit Note*
–From City Bank, $75.10, cheque returned N.S.F. from Doyle's Grocery.

7 *Cheque Copy*
–No. 412, to Outboard Motor Sales, $425; instructions from J. D. Doan, the owner, to pay for a new outboard motor delivered to his cottage for his personal use.

8 *Purchase Invoice*
–No. 5698, from Elmer Canners, $1 050; for merchandise purchased; terms, Net 60 days, dated Nov. 6.

10 *Credit Note Received*
–No. 445, from Gordon Canners, $147, dated Nov. 9; allowance granted on invoice No. 213 for incorrect goods.

10 *Cheque Copy*
–No. 443, to Petty Cash, to replenish petty cash as per the following summary of charges:

| | |
|---|---|
| Travelling Expenses | $12.92 |
| Delivery Expense | 40.89 |

Building Maintenance 26.14
Miscellaneous Expense 16.19

11 *Cheque Copy*
—No. 447, to Brown Brothers, $475, to pay for C.O.D. delivery of a new office desk.

12 *Cash Receipt*
—Cheque of Grey's Market, paying sales invoice No. 963.

*Credit Note Issued*
—No. 1007, to Palmer's Grocery, $56.70 including 5 per cent sales tax, for defective merchandise returned; discount period adjusted to begin on November 12.

14 *Credit Note Received*
—No. 565, from Burlington Fruit Growers Association, $2 332.80, correcting their invoice No. 412, which was issued incorrectly in the amount of $2 592 instead of $259.20. (**Note**: This is neither a 'return' nor an 'allowance'.)

18 *Cheque Copy*
—No. 474, to G. Simcoe, $47.25; cash refund for defective merchandise that had been returned, $45; sales tax, $2.25.

22 *Cash Receipt*
—Cheque from Palmer's Grocery, paying invoice No. 962 and credit note No. 1007 less discount.

25 *Cheque Copy*
—No. 491, to Gordon Canners, paying sales invoice No. 213 and credit note No. 445 less discount.

26 *Cheque Copy*
—No. 497, to Elmer Canners, paying invoice No. 5698.

30 *Cash Receipt*
—Cheque from Alec's Groceteria, paying sales invoice No. 964.

---

**11.  T. O. Sprague is the sole proprietor of Best Wholesale Confectionery, a business that has been in operation for a number of years.**

On August 31, 19—, the accounts receivable ledger contains the following accounts:

| Customer Name | Address | Invoice Number | Invoice Date | Amount |
|---|---|---|---|---|
| Dick's Confectionery | 16 Brown Street | 703 | Aug. 27 | $ 57.75 |
| G.E.S. Smoke & Gift Shop | 702 Dan Avenue | 704 | Aug. 27 | 73.50 |
| Haddy's Variety Store | 49 Porterfield Road | 700 | Aug. 27 | 94.50 |
| Harry's Cigarette Store | 156 Main Street | 690 | Aug. 15 | 42.00 |
| Howie's Sweets | 27 Lake Street | 696 | Aug. 20 | 157.50 |
| Jim's Snack Bar | 35 College Street | 701 | Aug. 27 | 26.25 |
| M. D. Sundries | 516 Franklin Avenue | 702 | Aug. 27 | 63.00 |
| | | | | $514.50 |

All sales made by Best Wholesale Confectionery are on terms of 2/10,n/30. It is a policy of the business to allow its customers to be one day late in respect to discounts; the customer's cheque must arrive by the eleventh day to be eligible for the discount.

Sales tax in this locality is at the rate of 5 per cent.

On August 31, 19—, the accounts payable ledger contains the following accounts:

| Supplier Name | Address | Invoice Number | Invoice Date | Terms | Amount |
|---|---|---|---|---|---|
| City Confections | 65 Monarch Drive | 492 | July 30 | Net 60 | $1 060.50 |
| Famous Candy Co. | 72 Queen's Place | 565 | Aug 4 | Net 30 | 1 312.50 |
| Memory Novelties | 100 Regal Lane | 209 | Aug 22 | 3/20,n/60 | 525.00 |
| Paramount Tobacco | 46 Park Street | 1756 | July 30 | Net 60 | 236.25 |
| Winner Supplies | 52 River Drive | 974 | Aug 29 | 2/15,n/30 | 183.75 |
| | | | | | $3 318.00 |

The combined general ledger trial balance and chart of accounts of Best Wholesale Confectionery as of August 31, 19—, is shown below.

BEST WHOLESALE CONFECTIONERY
GENERAL LEDGER TRIAL BALANCE
AUGUST 31, 19—

| | | | |
|---|---|---|---|
| 1 | Petty Cash | $ 50.00 | |
| 2 | Bank | 3 062.50 | |
| 3 | Accounts Receivable | 514.50 | |
| 4 | Merchandise Inventory | 5 100.00 | |
| 5 | Supplies | 125.00 | |
| 6 | Delivery Equipment | 6 040.00 | |
| 7 | Warehouse Equipment | 2 984.00 | |
| 101 | Accounts Payable | | $ 3 318.00 |
| 102 | Sales Tax Payable | | 201.00 |
| 201 | T. O. Sprague, Capital | | 12 453.63 |
| 202 | T. O. Sprague, Drawings | 6 425.00 | |
| 301 | Sales | | 28 875.00 |
| 401 | Bank Charges | 36.70 | |
| 402 | Delivery Expense | 516.90 | |
| 403 | Discounts Allowed | 572.00 | |
| 404 | Discounts Earned | | 119.12 |
| 405 | Light and Heat | 275.00 | |
| 406 | Maintenance Expense | 174.50 | |
| 407 | Office Expense | 151.20 | |
| 408 | Purchases | 14 975.25 | |
| 409 | Rent | 2 100.00 | |
| 410 | Telephone | 184.20 | |
| 411 | Wages | 1 680.00 | |
| | | $44 966.75 | $44 966.75 |

Best Wholesale Confectionery tries to take advantage of discounts offered by its suppliers. Its policy is to pay invoices having discounts on the day before the discount expires – provided, of course, that there is a sufficient balance in the bank account to cover the cheques. To avoid the possible embarrassment of issuing a bad cheque, the accountant is responsible for calculating the bank balance at the end of each day. He does this by adding the day's cash receipts and subtracting the day's cash payments from the calculated bank balance of the previous day.

Best Wholesale Confectionery uses a five-journal system. The journals and the next unused page numbers are:

| | |
|---|---|
| Cash Receipts Journal | Page 76 |
| Cash Disbursements Journal | Page 94 |
| Sales Journal | Page 67 |
| Purchases Journal | Page 85 |
| General Journal | Page 24 |

The owner of the business, T. O. Sprague, does not consider it worthwhile to have separate accounts for returns and allowances, and consequently he does not have them.

The subsidiary ledgers of the business are posted directly from the source documents rather than from the journals themselves. Mr. Sprague prefers this method.

**Set up the three ledgers of Best Wholesale Confectionery as of August 31, 19—. Prepare the five journals of Best Wholesale Confectionery for the September transactions.**

**Journalize the transactions for the month of September listed below. Post to the subsidiary ledgers daily.**

## Transactions

September

3 *Sales Invoices*
 –No. 705, to Jim's Snack Bar, $620 plus $31 sales tax, for sale of goods.
 –No. 706, to Howie's Sweets, $400 plus $20 sales tax, for sale of goods.
 *Cheque Copy*
 –No. 442, to Amber & Green, $300, rent for September.

4 *Cash Receipts*
 –Cheque of Harry's Cigarette Store, $42, in full of account.
 –Cheque of P. Watson, $63, cash sale, $60 plus 5 per cent sales tax.
 *Purchase Invoices*
 –From Famous Candy Co., No. 615, $262.50, dated Sept. 2; terms, Net 30, for merchandise.
 –From Winner Supplies, No. 1004, $52.50, dated Sept. 1; terms, 2/15,n/30, for supplies (assume goods are satisfactory).

5 *Bank Credit Note*
 –From Cliffside Bank, $1 000; because Famous Candy Co.'s invoice of August 4 was overdue, Mr. Sprague borrowed $1 000 from the bank.

*Cheque Copies*
 –No. 443, to Famous Candy Co., $1 312.50; paying invoice No. 565.
 –No. 444, to Petty Cash, $47.20; replenishing cheque for the following summary of charges:

| | |
|---|---|
| Office Expense | $24.02 |
| Delivery Expense | 8.18 |
| Drawings | 15.00 |

*Credit Note Issued*
 –No. 707, to Dick's Confectionery, $8 plus 40¢ sales tax; allowance for defective merchandise; discount date adjusted to date of credit note.

6 *Cash Receipts*
 –Cheque of G.E.S. Smoke & Gift Shop, $72.03, in payment of invoice No. 704 less $1.47 cash discount.
 –Cheque of Haddy's Variety Store, $92.61, in payment of invoice No. 700 less $1.89 cash discount.
 –Cheque of Jim's Snack Bar, $25.72; in payment of invoice No. 701 less 53¢ cash discount.
*Credit Note Received*
 –From City Confections, No. 540, $94.50;

dated Sept. 4; no discount date adjustment;
correction in price charged for goods.

7 *Purchase Invoice*
–From Wonderful Cartage Co., 8 Elm
Street, No. 402, $64.15; terms Net 30;
dated Sept. 6; for delivery services per-
formed for the month of August.
*Cheque Copy*
–No. 445, to 'Cash', $550, for the wages of
employees for the week just ended.

10 *Sales Invoices*
–No. 708, to G.E.S. Smoke & Gift Shop,
$640 plus $32 sales tax; sale of merchandise.
–No. 709, to M. D. Sundries, $765 plus
$38.25 sales tax; sale of merchandise.

11 *Cash Receipts*
–Cheque of Howie's Sweets, $157.50, paying
invoice No. 696.
–Cheque of M. D. Sundries, $61.74, paying
invoice No. 702 less $1.26 cash discount.
*Cheque Copy*
–No. 446, to Memory Novelties, $509.25,
paying invoice No. 209 less $15.75 cash
discount.
*Purchase Invoice*
–From Paramount Tobacco, No. 1803,
$157.50, dated Sept. 10; terms, Net 60;
for merchandise.

12 *Cheque Copy*
–No. 447, to Municipal Telephone Co.,
$16.15, cash payment of telephone bill for
September.
*Purchase Invoice*
–From Memory Novelties, No. 305,
$325.50, dated Sept. 11; terms 3/20,n/60;
for merchandise.

13 *Cash Receipts*
–Cheque of Howie's Sweets, $411.60,
paying invoice No. 706 less $8.40 cash
discount.
–Cheque of Jim's Snack Bar, $637.98,
paying invoice No. 705 less $13.02 cash
discount.
*Purchase Invoice*
–From Winner Supplies, No. 1111,
$152.25, dated Sept. 12; terms, 2/15,n/30;
for supplies.
*Cheque Copy*
–No. 448, to Winner Supplies, $180.07,

paying invoice No. 974 less $3.68 cash
discount.

14 *Cheque Copies*
–No. 449, to 'Cash', $570; for the wages
for the week.
–No. 450, to T. O. Sprague, $500; drawings
for personal use.
–No. 451, to Provincial Government, $201;
paying the sales tax collected for the
previous month.
–No. 452, to Municipal Electric, $45.02;
cash payment for electricity used for the
month of August.

17 *Cash Receipts*
–Cheque of Dick's Confectionery, $48.36,
paying invoice No. 703 and credit note
No. 707 less 99¢ cash discount.
–Cheque of W. Symons, $183.75, cash sale
of $175 plus $8.75 sales tax.
*Sales Invoices*
–No. 710, to Haddy's Variety Store, $310
plus $15.50 sales tax, sale of merchandise.
–No. 711, to Harry's Cigarette Store, $307
plus $15.35 sales tax, sale of merchandise.
–No. 712, to Jim's Snack Bar, $767 plus
$38.35 sales tax, sale of merchandise.
*Credit Note Received*
–From Paramount Tobacco, No. 1851,
$52.50, dated Sept. 16; terms, adjusted to
start from date of credit note; allowance
on invoice No. 1756 for inferior merchandise.
*Cheque Copy*
–No. 453, to Winner Supplies, $51.45,
paying invoice No. 1004 less $1.05 cash
discount.

18 *Cash Receipts*
–Cheque of G.E.S. Smoke & Gift Shop,
$658.56, paying invoice No. 708 less
$13.44 cash discount.
–Cheque of M. D. Sundries, $787.18,
paying invoice No. 709 less $16.07 cash
discount.
*Cheque Copies*
–No. 454, to City Confections, $966,
paying invoice No. 492 and credit note
No. 540.

19 *Purchase Invoices*
–From Famous Candy Co., No. 719, $588,
dated Sept. 18; terms, Net 30; for purchase

of merchandise.

–From City Confections, No. 588, $105, dated Sept. 17; terms, Net 60; for purchase of merchandise.

–From Memory Novelties, No. 351, $210, dated Sept. 18; terms, 3/20,n/60; for purchase of merchandise.

19 *Cheque Copy*

–No. 455, to W. Symons, $15.75, cash refund for inferior goods, $15 plus 75¢ sales tax.

20 *Bank Debit Memo*

–From Cliffside Bank, $12.50, bank service charge.

21 *Cheque Copies*

–No. 456, to 'Cash', $556, wages for the week.

–No. 457, to T. O. Sprague, $400, personal drawings.

24 *Sales Invoices*

–No. 713, to Dick's Confectionery, $240 plus $12 sales tax, sale of merchandise.

–No. 714, to Howie's Sweets, $147 plus $7.35 sales tax, sale of merchandise.

25 No transactions.

26 *Purchase Invoice*

–From Winner Supplies, No. 1190, $78.75, dated Sept. 25; terms, 2/15,n/30; purchase of supplies.

27 *Cheque Copy*

–No. 458, to Winner Supplies, $149.20, paying invoice No. 1111 less $3.05 cash discount.

*Cash Receipts*

–Cheque of Jim's Snack Bar, $789.24, paying invoice No. 712 less $16.11 cash discount.

–Cheque of Harry's Cigarette Store, $315.90, paying invoice No. 711 less $6.45 cash discount.

28 *Purchase Invoice*

–From Paramount Tobacco, No. 1892, $199.50, dated Sept. 26; terms, Net 60; for merchandise purchased.

*Cheque Copies*

–No. 459, to 'Cash', $590, wages for the week.

–No. 460, to T. O. Sprague, $600, personal drawings.

–No. 461, to Petty Cash, $47.51; to replenish the fund for the following summary of charges:

| | |
|---|---|
| Office Expense | $15.00 |
| Maintenance Expense | 18.42 |
| Delivery Expense | 14.09 |

**Balance the journals as necessary.**

**Post the journals to the general ledger.**

**Balance the general ledger and the two subsidiary ledgers.**

# Cases

### Case 1

On March 31, the accountant of the Routledge Company prepared a balance sheet showing as a current asset the $200 original amount of the imprest petty cash fund. At that date, however, the fund contained petty cash vouchers in the amount of $175.

1. What is wrong with this procedure?
2. How should it be handled?

## Case 2

By preparing several accounting records at one writing, the accountant can save time and minimize errors in the records. Explain how this can be done in connection with the accounts receivable of a small company which does not own an accounting machine.

## Case 3

Randy Timmins, a high school student who had studied the theory behind cash discounts, works at H. R. Robbins Co. He told Mr. Slow, the manager, how the company could save money by ensuring that clerks did not overlook discounts. Mr. Slow stated that because of the volume of invoices and lack of sufficient cash, they could not take advantage of all discounts. Describe a system that would ensure that all discounts would be taken. What should be done about insufficient cash?

## Case 4

Below is the comparative income statement for Scott's Bakery. It contains information for three consecutive accounting periods. The accounting period is for four months or one third of the fiscal year.

SCOTT'S BAKERY
COMPARATIVE INCOME STATEMENT
DECEMBER 31, AUGUST 31, APRIL 30, 19–1

|  | | *Last Period* | *Second Period* | *First Period* |
|---|---|---|---|---|
| *Revenue:* | | | | |
| Sales | | $64 400 | $55 500 | $52 800 |
| *Expenses:* | | | | |
| Baking Supplies | $12 000 | | $10 100 | $ 8 200 |
| Advertising | 5 200 | | 3 500 | 3 600 |
| Labor | 31 000 | | 30 400 | 30 000 |
| Miscellaneous Expense | 500 | | 400 | 450 |
| Delivery | 3 000 | | 2 400 | 2 300 |
| Building Rental | 500 | | 500 | 500 |
| Rental of Machines | 1 200 | | 1 200 | 1 200 |
| Total Expenses | | 53 400 | 48 500 | 46 250 |
| *Net Income* | | $11 000 | $ 7 000 | $ 6 550 |

1. The profits for each period have shown a steady increase. What is the major factor that has contributed to this increase?
2. Late in August at the end of the second period the company decided to increase its advertising. What effect has this policy had upon the business?
3. The bakery is contemplating going into the home delivery service. The delivery expense will be an additional $2 500 each four-month period. Is this home delivery service a good idea?
4. What is your general opinion of the results of company operations as shown on the comparative income statement?

## Case 5

Select the items below which would be posted to the control accounts. Set up control accounts in general ledger form and post those amounts. Indicate in a posting reference the book of original entry from which the items would be obtained. Calculate the final balances in the control accounts.

Beginning balances are:

| | | |
|---|---|---|
| Accounts Receivable | $116 500 | |
| Accounts Payable | 73 870 | |

| | | |
|---|---|---|
| 1. | Collections received from customers | $250 348.60 |
| 2. | Payments to suppliers | 267 840.00 |
| 3. | Credit Sales | 328 000.00 |
| 4. | Merchandise returned to suppliers | 4 100.00 |
| 5. | Purchases (other than for cash) | 274 000.00 |
| 6. | Returned Sales & Allowances | 725.00 |
| 7. | Credit Sale to J. Darin posted in error to account of S. McLean | 345.00 |
| 8. | Cheque received from customer and deposited in the bank was returned N.S.F. | 50.00 |
| 9. | Cash refunds to customers for returned goods | 1 750.00 |
| 10. | Refunds received from creditors for return of damaged merchandise | 600.00 |

## Case 6

Wholesale Food Distributors sold merchandise on account to Palmer's Grocery on December 15. The amount of the invoice was $10 000. Terms of the sale were 2/10,n/30. Wholesale Food Distributors received a cheque for $9 800 as payment in full. A few days later Palmer's Grocery returned $2 000 worth of the shipment because it was defective. Wholesale Food Distributors issued a credit memorandum on December 31.

1. For how much should the credit memo be issued? Explain.
2. Write the accounting entry for the transaction on the books of each company.

## Case 7

T. Sprague, the proprietor of Best Wholesale Confectionery, purchased three type-writers for use in his business. One typewriter proved defective and was returned to the supplier, Acme Office Supplies. The accounting clerk debited Accounts Payable/Acme Office Supplies and credited Purchase Returns and Allowances.

1. Was it wrong for the accounting clerk to credit Purchase Returns and Allowances? Why?
2. What effect would this error have on the net income and on the assets if no correction were made?

## Case 8

Bristol Appliances Company has been using the circle method to handle merchandise returned from customers, recording them as a direct reduction to sales. In recent months there has been an increase in the amount of returns. The accountant decides to set up a separate column for sales returns and allowances, and the circle method is abandoned. The increase in returns was one reason for the change in the accounting system. State three additional reasons why the accountant might keep a separate column for sales returns and allowances.

## Case 9

You are placed in charge of a $100 petty cash fund. As of December 31, 19–7, the end of a fiscal period, you have neglected to have it replenished because there was still currency and coin totalling $15 in the fund on that date. Most of the expenditures from the fund have been for office supplies and delivery expense items. The fund was next replenished on January 6, 19–8, when cash in the fund was only $2.

1. What errors, if any, were there in the 19–7 financial statements?
2. What errors, if any, would there be in the 19–8 financial statements if the January 6 replenishment is recorded in the usual way?

## Case 10

A cheque for $1 176 was received from a customer within 10 days from the date of sending him a sales invoice for $1 200 with terms of 2/10,n/30. In recording the receipt of the cheque, the accounting clerk entered $1 176 in the Cash column and $1 200 in the Accounts Receivable column of the cash receipts journal. He made no entry in the Discounts Allowed column. What procedure will bring this error to light?

# 11 Cash and Banking Activities

The word 'cash' is used in both a narrow and a broad sense. In its narrow sense, cash means dollar bills and coins. In its broad sense, cash includes not only dollar bills and coins but also cheques, bank balances, and certain other items such as money orders. In most cases, the context of the sentence will tell which of the two meanings is intended.

The acquisition of cash is a major pursuit of a business. The principal objective of a business is to earn a profit. But it is equally important to have this profit available in the form of cash. It is only in the form of cash that a business can use its profits to pay its bills, to meet its expenses, to give to the owners, and so on.

Because of its importance in business, there is usually a quantity of cash (in addition to petty cash) on hand in the office each day. For the most part, this cash is received from customers – either in the form of cheques sent through the mails to pay their accounts, or in the form of cash collected in a store or other retail outlet.

## Internal Control

Cash is the single item most likely to be stolen outright by employees or to tempt employees to embezzle; that is, to steal money and to try to cover up the theft by falsifying the accounting records. This characteristic of cash leads us to another aspect of accounting called **internal control**.

Internal control has to do with the ability of the accounting system to compel the employees to be correct and to be honest. In very small businesses where the owner is able to exercise control personally, no internal control is necessary. But as soon as employees are brought into

the business, internal control becomes a factor to be considered. And where there are numerous employees, internal control is essential. No matter that most employees are honest; it takes only one thief or incompetent to give a business a problem that sometimes leads to the death of the business through insolvency (inability of a business to pay its debts). It is too great a risk for a businessman to rely solely on the honesty and the ability of his employees. He is forced to administer accounting controls. A wise businessman will establish the best internal control that is practicable in his business.

The most important elements of good internal control are –

1. Where accounting records and documents are prepared, the system, where possible, should be designed so that the work of one person must agree with the work of another person whose work is created independently.
2. The person whose function it is to record transactions or prepare accounting records should not also have the function of handling or controlling assets.
3. All assets should physically be kept in a safe place. For negotiable assets (those that can be easily converted into cash) it should be required that two authorized persons be present before access to the assets is allowed.
4. Powers of approval and authorization should be restricted to a few key employees.
5. Periodically there should be an audit to ensure that the accounting system is being followed in the prescribed manner.

In this and future chapters, you will see various aspects of the total accounting system. Be alert to the elements of good internal control that are present.

# Cash Registers

No doubt you are familiar with businesses that have a cash register. You are probably also aware that these are businesses that take in considerable amounts of cash, usually from the general public through retail outlets. However, unless you have had the opportunity to use a cash register, you probably know no more about it than the average customer. Let us look then at what a cash register can do for an owner or manager.

By visiting any sales office of a manufacturer of cash registers, you will quickly learn that there is a wide selection of cash registers to choose from. They are manufactured in a variety of models with capabilities ranging from simple to complex. They will not all be discussed here. Only the basic features of an intermediate level machine will be considered.

A National Cash Register machine is shown below; it is an intermediate level machine. For

*Cash register (courtesy of The National Cash Register Company of Canada Limited).*

an owner or a manager it does the following:
1. It provides a cash drawer in which money may be conveniently stored in an orderly way and in relative safety.
2. It displays the type and amount of the transaction in the glass window at the top of the machine. This is called the **indication.** The displaying of this information in full view of the customer has the effect of discouraging dishonesty on the part of the cashier.
3. It provides for the customer an itemized re-

ceipt, often referred to as the cash register slip.
4. If required, it prints the details of transactions on the customer's bill or sales slip which may be inserted in an opening in the machine.
5. It provides a detailed record of all transactions, stored internally on a continuous paper tape. This record is usually referred to as the **audit strip**, or in some cases the 'sales journal'. At the end of each day, the used portion of the paper tape audit strip is torn off, to be used for accounting purposes.

A sample audit strip is shown below. Observe the detailed information and the coding provided by the machine.

The audit strip may be locked inside the machine. A key, usually kept by the manager, is required to unlock the machine and gain access to the audit strip. This is an important control feature of the cash register.

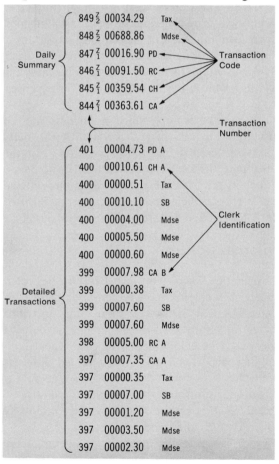

*Cash register audit strip.*

6. At the end of each business day, as a result of certain cash register keys being depressed, it prints a summary of the totals for the day on the audit strip. As the total for each type of transaction is printed by the machine it is also displayed visibly in the indication window. In this way the clerk operating the cash register can obtain the summary totals without gaining access to the audit strip.

An example of an audit strip summary is shown on page 214.

A very important control feature provided by the machine is that the summarizing operation cannot be performed unless a special key (proprietor's reset key) is inserted into the machine. This key is usually kept in the custody of the manager, and as a result the totals are locked in the mechanism of the register until the manager wishes them to be released.

7. By means of 'activity counters', it provides a count of such things as the number of sales made by each clerk, the number of sales made by each department, and the total number of sales.

8. It permits the operator to subtotal the purchases for any single transaction so that the sales tax may be ascertained from a tax schedule (usually attached to the machine with tape). The amount of the sales tax may then be entered into the cash register and added on to the amount of the customer's purchases.

## Using the Cash Register

It is not a purpose of this book to teach you the detailed operation of a cash register. That information may be obtained from the manufacturer. The objective here is to acquaint you with certain basic features of the machine that are essential to an understanding of cash register accounting.

## Change Fund

At the beginning of each day, a quantity of money, called a **change fund**, is placed in the cash drawer of the cash register. This change fund is made up of a mixture of bills and coins and usually is in the amount of twenty or twenty-

five dollars. It is customary to make it the same amount each day.

## Cash Sale

The simplest and most common type of transaction is the **cash sale**. With the cash sale, it is merely necessary for the clerk to record into the cash register the amounts of the individual items purchased, take a subtotal, add in the sales tax, code the transaction 'cash' by depressing the 'cash' key, and take a final total. (**Note:** When some of the items are taxable and some are non-taxable, a variation of this procedure is necessary.) The cash received from the customer is placed in the cash drawer. Transaction 397 on the audit strip shown on the previous page is an example of this type of transaction. (Observe that the audit strip must be read from bottom to top.)

## Charge Sale

In addition to being recorded through the cash register, a **charge sale** requires the preparation of a sales slip similar to the one shown below.

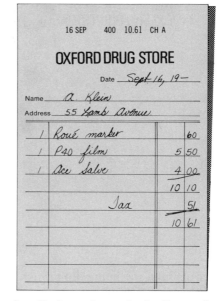

| | 16 SEP | 400 | 10.61 | CH A | |
|---|---|---|---|---|---|

OXFORD DRUG STORE

Date Sept 16, 19—

Name  a. Klein

Address  55 Lamb Avenue

| 1 | Roué marker | | 60 |
| 1 | P40 film | 5 | 50 |
| 1 | Ace Salve | 4 | 00 |
| | | 10 | 10 |
| | Tax | | 51 |
| | | 10 | 61 |

The sales slip is made out in duplicate: the original is for the customer; the copy is used as the source document for a debit entry to the accounts receivable ledger. The procedure, which may vary from system to system, is approximately as follows:

1. Prepare the sales slip in duplicate.
2. Enter each of the items purchased in the

cash register.

3. Take a subtotal.
4. Add on the sales tax.
5. Place the sales slip in the slip printer device of the machine.
6. Take a total, using the 'charge' key; details of the transaction are printed at the top of the sales slip (see example below).
7. Give original of sales slip to customer.
8. Place copy of sales slip in cash drawer for posting to customer's account.

**Note:** No money is received as a part of a charge sale transaction. On the audit strip on page 214, transaction 400 illustrates a charge sale.

## Receipt on Account

The procedure for recording a **receipt on account** is approximately as follows:

1. Prepare in duplicate a sales slip such as the one shown below.

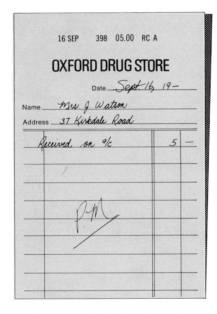

2. Place the sales slip in the slip printer, so that it will be register printed.
3. Enter the amount of the transaction in the cash register; code the transaction 'received'; press the 'Total' key.
4. Give the original of the sales slip to the customer.
5. Place the copy of the sales slip in the cash register drawer for posting to the customer's account.

6. Place the money received in the cash drawer.

See transaction 398 on the audit strip shown on page 214.

## Paid Out

In stores having a cash register it is generally not customary to have a petty cash fund. Small expenditures that would normally be paid out of a petty cash fund can be paid out of the cash register. The procedure for recording a **paid out** is approximately as follows:

1. Obtain a bill or voucher for the expenditure to be made. If the expenditure is for goods or services, the supplier's sales invoice must be obtained. However, if the expenditure is for a sales refund, it will be necessary to prepare a sales slip form in the manner shown below.

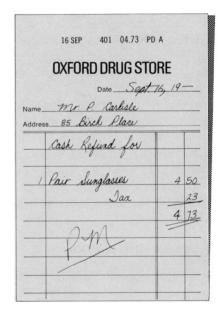

Observe that it is necessary to show the amount of the sales tax.

2. Place the bill or sales slip in the printer so that it will be register printed.
3. Enter the amount of the transaction in the cash register; code it 'Paid Out'; press the 'Total' key.
4. Pay out the required sum of money.
5. Place the bill or sales slip in the cash register drawer to be used later for accounting purposes.

See transaction 401 on the audit strip.

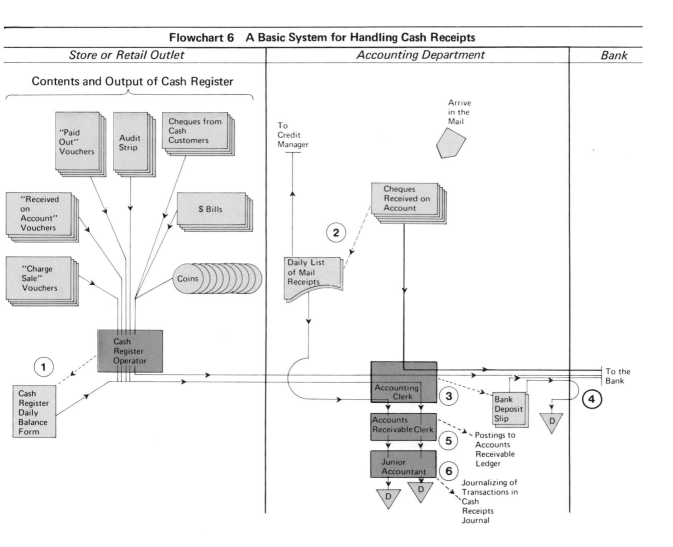

# Basic Cash Receipts System

The flowchart above and its explanatory notes which follow describe a basic system for handling and recording cash register receipts and mail receipts.

## Notes to Flowchart #6

① **End-of-Day Procedure – Cash Register Operator.** At the end of each business day, the operator of each cash register must count the cash in the register and prepare a summary of the day's activity on a form to be used by the accounting department. In this text, the

form shown on page 218 is used; it is called a **cash register daily balance form** and is designed especially for students using this text. In actual practice, you will find a variety of designs and form names in use.

The steps required to fill in this form are as follows:

a. Obtain the cash register summary totals from the cash register using the proprietor's reset key. The cash register system used here produces the type of summary shown on page 214 and explained below:

| Figures | Code | Explanation |
|---------|------|-------------|
| 34.29 | TAX | The total sales tax on all sales. |
| 688.86 | MDSE | The total sales figure, for both charge sales and cash sales, but not including sales tax. |
| 16.90 | PD | The total cash paid out, for which there should be equivalent vouchers in the cash register drawer. |
| 91.50 | RC | The total cash received on account from customers for which there should be equivalent vouchers in the drawer. |
| 359.54 | CH | The total charge sales including sales tax, for which there should be equivalent vouchers in the drawer. |
| 363.61 | CA | The total cash sales including sales tax. |

---

CASH REGISTER    DAILY BALANCE FORM              DATE *September 16* 19—

**SUMMARY OF CASH**

| | | | |
|---|---|---|---|
| Cash Sales Total * | 363 | 61 | 1 |
| Received on Account Total * | 91 | 50 | 2 |
| Add | 455 | 11 | 3 |
| Less:  Paid Out Total * | 16 | 90 | 4 |
| Total Cash Called For | 438 | 21 | 5 |
| Actual Cash in Drawer | 435 | 21 | 6 |
| Cash Short | 3 | 00 | 7 |
| Cash Over | | | 8 |

**BREAKDOWN OF PAID OUTS**

| | | | |
|---|---|---|---|
| Cash Refunds - Merchandise | 4 | 50 | 9 |
| - Sales Tax | | 23 | 10 |
| Total Refunds | 4 | 73 | 11 |
| Other a/c's - *Misc. Exp.* | 7 | 50 | 12 |
| - *Supplies* | 4 | 67 | 13 |
| - | | | 14 |
| Paid Out Total       4 | 16 | 90 | 15 |

**SUMMARY OF SALES**

| | | | |
|---|---|---|---|
| Merchandise Total * | 688 | 86 | 16 |
| Less: Merchandise Refunded 9 | 4 | 50 | 17 |
| Net Sales | 684 | 36 | 18 |

**SUMMARY OF SALES TAX PAYABLE**

| | | | |
|---|---|---|---|
| Sales Tax Total * | 34 | 29 | 19 |
| Less: Sales Tax on Refunds 10 | | 23 | 20 |
| Net Sales Tax Payable | 34 | 06 | 21 |

**ACCOUNTING SUMMARY**

| | | DEBIT | | CREDIT | |
|---|---|---|---|---|---|
| DEBITS: Bank | 6 | 435 | 21 | | |
| Acc's Rec'l (Charge Sales) * | | 359 | 54 | | |
| Other a/c's - *Misc. Exp.* 12 | | 7 | 50 | | |
| - *Supplies* 13 | | 4 | 67 | | |
| - 14 | | | | | |
| Cash Short and Over | 7 | 3 | 00 | | |
| CREDITS: Accounts Receivable | 2 | | | 91 | 50 |
| Sales | 18 | | | 684 | 36 |
| Sales Tax Payable | 21 | | | 34 | 06 |
| Cash Short and Over | 8 | | | | |
| BALANCING TOTALS | | 809 | 92 | 809 | 92 |

* Pick up from Audit Strip Summary

Clerk *M Fowler*

b. On the cash register daily balance form, write in the six totals from the audit strip summary. The appropriate places on the daily balance form are marked with an asterisk, (*). It is not difficult to decide where each total goes.

c. (i) Remove the cash and vouchers from the cash register drawer.

   (ii) Separate the cash from the vouchers and sort the vouchers into three groups: PDs, RCs, and CHs. For each of these three groups, see that the total of the vouchers agrees with the figure shown on the audit strip summary.

   (iii) Count out (in the desired mixture) the amount of the change fund with which the day was started. Put it in a safe place overnight. It will be used to begin business on the next business day.

   (iv) Count the remaining cash (be sure to double check) and record the amount on line 6 of the daily balance form.

   (v) Complete the 'Summary of Cash' portion of the form.
**Note:** If line 5 is greater than line 6, there will be a cash shortage; if line 5 is less than line 6, there will be a cash overage; if line 5 is equal to line 6, there will be neither an overage nor a shortage.

d. Analyse the paid out vouchers and complete the 'Breakdown of Paid Outs' portion of the daily balance form.

e. Complete the 'Summary of Sales' portion and the 'Summary of Sales Tax Payable' portion of the daily balance form. Observe that the figure to be entered on line 17 is obtained from line 9, and the figure to be entered on line 20 is obtained from line 10 and so on. This is a technique used throughout the form.

f. Complete the 'Accounting Summary' portion of the daily balance form. The two balancing totals must agree if the work has been done correctly.

g. Date and sign the cash register daily balance form and deliver it to the accounting department together with the money and the three groups of vouchers.

CASH SHORT AND OVER. Businesses that deal with the general public for cash are subject to cash shortages and overages due to errors made by their clerks. The way in which a shortage or overage is calculated was discussed in the preceding section.

It is the policy of some businesses to hold their clerks responsible for shortages and overages. That is, the clerks may keep any overages, but must make up any shortages out of their own pockets. In such a business, it is not necessary to record the shortages or overages in the books of account.

Other businesses take a more liberal attitude and accept the shortages and overages themselves. In this type of business, it is necessary to record the overages and shortages in the books of account. During the accounting period, they are accumulated in an account called 'Cash Short and Over'. The shortages go into the account as debits since they are losses or decreases in equity. The overages go in as credits since they are gains or increases in equity. At any particular time the balance in the account will represent either expense or income depending on whether it has a debit balance or a credit balance. A debit balance means that the shortages have exceeded the overages and a credit balance means that the overages have exceeded the shortages.

② Each day a list is prepared of the cheques that arrive in the day's mail. It is necessary to prepare the list because the cheques themselves cannot be kept but must be deposited in the bank. The listing is illustrated below.

OXFORD DRUG STORE
MAIL RECEIPTS
SEPT. 16, 19—

| Customer | Cheque Date | Invoice Number | Amount |
|---|---|---|---|
| P. Bourne | Sept. 14 | 3154 | $ 64.10 |
| R. Walsh | Sept. 15 | — | 75.00 |
| | | | $139.10 |

③ The preparation of the bank deposit is an important duty in a business office and is entrusted to an experienced employee. The flowchart on page 217 shows the cash, cheques, and the supporting documents being channeled to the desk of this clerk. After they have all arrived, this clerk will prepare the bank deposit by performing the steps below. As you read these steps, refer to the sample deposit slip shown below.

*(Courtesy of The Toronto-Dominion Bank.)*

a. Obtain a bank deposit slip form (to be prepared in duplicate by using carbon paper). A supply of these forms is usually kept in the office.

b. Count the currency by the various denominations and write the number of each type of bill and the corresponding value on the bank deposit slip in the appropriate spaces.

c. Count the coin and write the total amount in the proper space on the bank deposit slip. Coins should be wrapped in coin wrappers if there are sufficient quantities. (50 pennies; 40 nickels; 50 dimes; 40 quarters.)

d. Examine the cheques from customers to ensure that they have been made out properly. Then endorse each cheque on the reverse side.

**Note:** Although there are a number of different ways to endorse a cheque, businesses usually just rubber stamp them in the manner shown below.

FOR DEPOSIT ONLY
TO THE CREDIT OF
WILBY SALES LIMITED

FOR DEPOSIT ONLY
TO THE CREDIT OF
DR. J. P. SMITH

When the depositor deposits a cheque, he gets money (in the form of an increase in his bank balance) in return from the bank. By endorsing the cheque he is guaranteeing it. If for any reason the cheque is not good, the depositor has agreed to repay the bank.

e. List the cheques by name and amount in the appropriate section of the deposit slip. Total the cheques and transfer the totals as indicated on the slip. Complete the deposit slip.

f. Make sure that the deposit slip total is equal to the sum of (1) the daily list of mail receipts, plus (2) the cash register daily balance form (line 6).

④ The cash, cheques, and the deposit slip are placed in an envelope or cloth bag to be taken to the bank. This is done daily, as it is dangerous to keep any sizable sum of money on the premises. Deposits may be taken to the bank even after banking hours by using what is called the night depository.

The bank's clerk will check the accuracy of the deposit slip preparation. If he finds it in order he will place the bank's stamp on all copies of the deposit slip. One copy will be returned to the business where it is filed in the accounting department.

If all is not found to be in order, the bank will not process the deposit until the matter is discussed and corrected.

5. From the listing of mail receipts and the cash register vouchers that arrive on her desk the accounts receivable clerk posts to the accounts receivable ledger as necessary.

   a. Each cash register 'charge sale' voucher requires a debit posting to a customer's account.

   b. Each cash register 'received on account' voucher requires a credit posting to a customer's account.

   c. Each receipt from a customer listed on the daily list of mail receipts requires a credit posting to a customer's account.

As each posting is completed a check mark or the clerk's initials must be placed on the voucher or list, usually beside the amount that was posted. The cash register vouchers are then stapled to the cash register daily balance form.

6. It is the responsibility of the junior accountant to record the accounting entries for each of the two types of cash receipts.

   a. *Mail Receipts.* The source document for mail receipts is the daily list of mail receipts. The necessary accounting entry is recorded in the cash receipts journal. This entry may be written in detail, showing the receipt from each customer separately, as in Example A shown below, or it may be written in summary form showing only the totals, as in Example B below. When the latter method is used and it is found necessary to check back on a transaction, one must refer to the mail receipts lists for the detailed information. These are kept on file.

   b. *Cash Register Receipts.* The accounting entry to record the cash register receipts is picked up directly from the 'Accounting Summary' section of the cash register daily balance form. The data is merely transferred from the daily balance form to the cash receipts journal as shown in the illustration below of the journalizing required for the daily balance form on page 218.

Observe:

1. The circled amounts in Credit columns are treated as debits when totaling a column or when posting.
2. The amount of deposit, $574.31, includes both the mail receipts and the cash register receipts.
3. If it is necessary to check back on any individual receipt, it will have to be done by referring back to the individual vouchers attached to the daily balance form.
4. Postings to customers' accounts will be made directly from the cash register vouchers.

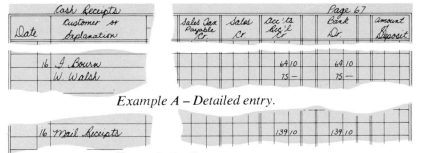

*Example A – Detailed entry.*

*Example B – Summary entry.*

*Cash receipts journal.*

# The Banking Relationship

The relationship between a bank and a business (depositor) was explained in a previous chapter (see page 151). Several important facts about this relationship were pointed out. You were told that both the bank and the business are obliged to keep track of the business's money kept on deposit at the bank. You were also told that the record prepared by the bank appears to be the opposite of the record prepared by the business. This is so because the business considers the money to be an asset whereas the bank considers it to be a liability. Also, you have learned that most of the transactions affecting the bank balance are originated by the business – through the making of deposits and the issuing of cheques. And whenever the bank finds it necessary to originate an entry to its customer's account, it informs him promptly by sending a debit memo or a credit memo.

## Current Bank Account

A bank provides various types of deposit accounts to meet the special needs of its customers. Especially for businesses, it provides the 'current' bank account. The special features of a current bank account are –

1. No interest is allowed on the account balance (as there is on a 'savings' account).
2. Once a month the bank sends to the depositor a copy of all debit and credit memos issued during the month and all of the cheques cashed during the month. These cheques are known as the 'paid' cheques.
3. Once a month also, the bank sends to the depositor a carbon copy of its ledger account for him. This form is known as the **bank statement** and is illustrated below.
4. The service charge required for the cashing and handling of cheques is left to the discretion of the bank manager. His decision is affected by such things as the number of

*Bank statement (courtesy of The Toronto-Dominion Bank).*

cheques cashed, the average bank balance, the amount of any bank loan, and so on.

## Bank Reconciliation

Since both the bank and the business keep track of the same funds, you might expect the month-end balance shown by the bank statement to agree with the month-end balance shown by the general ledger Bank account. This is rarely the case. Usually, when the bank statement is received, it is found to have a 'balance' different from that of the general ledger Bank account.

Since the bank statement usually shows a balance that is different from the Bank account in the general ledger, how can the accountant be certain that either record is correct? He accomplishes this by 'reconciling the bank account'. At the end of each month, he conducts a thorough investigation of the two sets of records in order to ascertain precisely the reasons for the difference. When this is done, he then formally documents the evidence by preparing a **bank reconciliation statement.**

An example of a bank reconciliation statement is shown below.

The steps in reconciling a bank account are:

1. Have the following records available: (a) the bank statement and related vouchers received from the bank; (b) the bank reconciliation statement for the previous month end; (c) the general ledger, the cash receipts journal, the cash payments journal, and the general journal.

2. On proper paper, write the heading Bank Reconciliation Statement.

3. On one side of the page, enter the balance per bank statement figure, which will be the final amount in the 'balance' column of the bank statement. On the other side of the page, enter the balance per general ledger figure, which will be the final balance in the Bank account (after the general ledger is posted and balanced).

4. Search for the items causing the difference between the two balances. This is the most difficult and most important part of a reconciliation. It involves comparing in detail the bank's record against the business's record. You are looking for items that are not recorded equally in both records. Techniques

| Boxwell and Company Bank Reconciliation Statement March 31, 19-- | | | | | |
|---|---|---|---|---|---|
| Balance per Bank Statement | 1 204 90 | Balance per General Ledger | | 1 147 76 |
| Add: | | Deduct: | | |
| Outstanding Deposit | 300 51 | Amount of error in | | |
| | 1 505 41 | recording cheque #697 | | |
| | | Was recorded as $5.60 | | |
| Deduct: | | Should have been $6.50 | | |
| Outstanding Cheques | | Difference 90¢ | | 90 |
| #702 $60.00 | | | | 1 146 86 |
| #705 72.40 | | | | |
| #709 51.90 | | Deduct: | | |
| #710 175.00 | | Bank Service Charges | | |
| #711 2.75 | 362 05 | deducted on bank | | |
| | | statement but not | | |
| | | recorded in company | | |
| | | books in same month | | 3 50 |
| True Balance | 1 143 36 | True Balance | | 1 143 36 |

for doing this are explained more fully below in the section headed 'Locating the Items of Disagreement'.

5. Record the items of disagreement on the reconciliation statement, adding or subtracting them as necessary until the two balances are shown to be equal. This step is explained in detail below in the section headed 'Recording the Items of Disagreement'. You cannot consider the job completed until the point of balance is reached.

6. Record in the books of the business the items of disagreement that are listed on the general ledger side of the reconciliation statement. These represent items that have already been recorded by the bank and which must also be recorded by the business.

LOCATING THE ITEMS OF DISAGREEMENT

Locating the items of disagreement usually requires a well-organized and skilful approach. The general suggestions given below will be of help to you, but the actual experience of solving the problems at the end of the chapter will benefit you the most.

1. When comparing the two sets of records, it is never necessary to go back in the books beyond one month. Any differences that occurred before then will be listed on the previous reconciliation statement.

2. The bank's record must be compared in detail against the business's record. When items are found to correspond exactly, they are marked in some way with a colored pencil. After the comparison is over, the items without the colored marks are the significant ones. They are the items of disagreement.

3. The most common source of disagreement between the two sets of records is the quantity of uncashed cheques commonly known as the 'outstanding cheques'. When a cheque is issued by a business, it is recorded promptly in the books of the business, but it is not recorded in the records of the bank until the time it is cashed. In many cases, this is after some time has elapsed.

4. A less frequently occurring but fairly common source of disagreement between the two records is the 'outstanding deposit'. An outstanding deposit is one that is recorded in the

books of the business during a certain month but which is not deposited in the bank until the following month. This usually occurs on the last day of the month in businesses that have a one-day delay in the depositing of cash receipts. (The outstanding deposit will appear on the bank statement of the following month, usually as the first item in the Deposit column.)

5. There are numerous other possible items of disagreement. One of these would be an error made by either a bank employee or a company employee. Another would be a bank service charge that has not yet been recorded in the books of the company.

6. When comparing the records, it is important not to forget the items of disagreement that appear on the previous reconciliation statement. During the current month, most of these items will cease to be items of disagreement. For example, a cheque outstanding on the April 30 reconciliation statement, if cashed during May, will not be an item of disagreement on the May 31 reconciliation statement.

Some items, however, may not be cleared up in the current month and will have to be carried forward to the new reconciliation. For example, an outstanding cheque appearing on the April reconciliation, if not cashed during the month of May, will continue to be outstanding and must appear also on the May reconciliation.

RECORDING THE ITEMS OF DISAGREEMENT

The items of disagreement must be recorded on the bank reconciliation statement.

1. All items of disagreement must be included. It is often advisable to group items of a similar nature, e.g., outstanding cheques.

2. Each item must be recorded on one side of the reconciliation statement only; that is, either on the bank statement side or on the general ledger side. You must follow this rule: choose the side where the item has not been seen or recorded as of the reconciliation date. For example, an outstanding cheque, because it represents an item not seen by the bank, would be recorded on the bank statement side. Similarly, an outstanding bank

service charge, because it represents an item not recorded in the company records, would be entered on the general ledger side.

3. Each item represents either an increase or a decrease to the balance. Your common sense should tell you which it is. Just decide what effect the item has on the bank balance and act accordingly. For example, cheques and service charges represent decreases to the bank balance and are therefore treated as

deductions on the reconciliation. Similarly, deposits increase the bank balance and are therefore treated as additions on the reconciliation.

4. If all of the items of disagreement are found and entered correctly, the two sides of the reconciliation statement will balance. If not, then it will be necessary for you to repeat the process. The reasons for the difference must be found.

# Bookkeeping and Accounting Terms

**Internal Control** The plan of organization and all the coordinated methods and measures adopted to safeguard assets, ensure the accuracy and reliability of the accounting data, promote operational efficiency, and maintain adherence to prescribed policies.

**Current Bank Account** A type of deposit ac-

count and related service provided by the bank specifically to meet the needs of businesses.

**Bank Reconciliation** A routine procedure to ascertain the reasons for the difference between the balance on deposit as shown by the bank and the balance on deposit as shown by the business or individual.

# Review Questions

1. The word 'cash' is used in both a narrow and a broad sense. Explain.
2. Briefly, what is internal control?
3. In very small businesses, why are accounting controls usually not necessary?
4. At what stage in the development of a business is it necessary to introduce some accounting controls?
5. Name the first element of internal control.
6. What is the purpose of the cash register indication window?
7. Explain the purpose of the cash register slip.
8. Briefly, what is the audit strip?
9. What accounting controls are provided by the cash register?
10. How does a cash register assist the operator in calculating sales tax?
11. What information is printed on the 'daily summary' section of the audit strip?
12. List four types of transactions that can be handled by means of a cash register.

13. Briefly describe the balancing procedure of the cash register operator.
14. What is the purpose of the cash receipts daily balance form?
15. Explain how the cash register change fund works.
16. Give the accounting entry for a cash shortage of $5.
17. Who prepares the bank deposit slip?
18. Give an example of the most common type of endorsement used by businesses.
19. What is the purpose of endorsing a cheque?
20. What are the source documents for the accounting entries for cash receipts?
21. Name a special feature of a current bank account.
22. Explain briefly the need for reconciling a bank account.
23. What is an outstanding cheque? an outstanding deposit?
24. Why is it necessary to prepare a bank reconciliation statement?

# Exercises

1. **Miss Murphy is a cash register operator at Loew's Book Supply. At the end of the March 20 business day the contents of her cash register are as follows:**

a. *Dollar Bills* – $20 × 6
   – $10 × 14
   – $5 × 6
   – $2 × 14
   – $1 × 78
b. *Coin* – $8.19
c. *'Paid Out' Vouchers*
   (i) A bill for the cash purchase of supplies, $6.90
   (ii) A cash refund for $10.50, including 50¢ sales tax

d. *'Received' Vouchers*
   (i) R. B. Morrow – $75.00
   (ii) J. N. Perroux – $50.00
   (iii) M. Rogers – $50.00

e. *'Charge' Vouchers*
   (i) B. Anderson – $57.75
   (ii) M. N. Brown – $18.38
   (iii) C. Carter – $97.60
   (iv) O. Orville – $78.54
   (v) A. Farrow – $52.45

**The summary of the day's transactions as shown by the cash register audit strip is as follows:**

| | | | |
|---|---|---|---|
| Tax | $ 25.32 | RC | 175.00 |
| Mdse | 506.24 | CH | 304.72 |
| PD | 17.40 | CA | 226.84 |

The amount of the change fund given to Miss Murphy at the beginning of each day is $20. At the end of each day, $20 is taken out of the contents of the cash drawer to be used to start with on the next business day. On this particular day Miss Murphy removes $8 in coin and 12 one-dollar bills.

**Prepare the cash register daily balance form.**

2. **You are a clerk at Loew's Book Supply. One of your duties is the preparation of the bank deposit. Each day you receive (a) a copy of the daily list of mail receipts together with the customers' cheques, and (b) the cash register daily balance form together with the related vouchers.**

   **On March 20, you receive the cash register daily balance form and the related vouchers of Exercise 1. You also receive the daily list of mail receipts shown below together with the accompanying cheques.**

LOEW'S BOOK SUPPLY
MAIL RECEIPTS
MARCH 20, 19—

| | | |
|---|---|---|
| J. Stinson | on account | $ 50.00 |
| W. Walker | on account | 100.00 |
| | | $150.00 |

Prepare the deposit slip for the cash receipts of Loew's Book Supply for March 20.

3. As the junior accountant for Loew's Book Supply, record the accounting entries for Exercises 1 and 2 in the cash receipts journal.

4. At the end of the next business day the contents of Miss Murphy's cash register are:

a. *Currency*
   $20 × 10
   $10 × 9
   $5 × 11
   $2 × 31
   $1 × 5
   Cheque from J. Gorman, $10.00

b. *Coin*      $19.38

c. *'Paid Out' Vouchers*
   (i)   Cash purchase of supplies        $ 4.50
   (ii)  Cash payment for delivery
         charges                            2.50
   (iii) Cash refund including 30¢
         sales tax                          6.25
   (iv)  Cash refund including 78¢
         sales tax                         16.28
                                          _____
                                          $29.53
                                          =======

d. *'Received' Vouchers*
   (i)   P. Tilson                        $37.50
   (ii)  D. Wilson                         19.25
                                          _____
                                          $56.75
                                          =======

e. *'Charge' Vouchers*
   (i)   C. Cox                           $ 63.00
   (ii)  T. Franks                         147.00
   (iii) M. Nelson                          26.25
   (iv)  G. Tutt                            73.50
                                          _____
                                          $309.75
                                          =======

The summary of the day's transactions as shown by the audit strip is:

| Tax  | $ 33.46 | RC | 56.75  |
|------|---------|----|--------|
| Mdse | 669.20  | CH | 309.75 |
| PD   | 29.53   | CA | 392.91 |

Prepare the cash register daily balance form.

5. If Miss Murphy keeps $10 in coin, 4 two-dollar bills, and 2 one-dollar bills to make up her change fund for the next day, and if there are no mail receipts, prepare the bank deposit slip for March 21.

6. Journalize the cash receipts for Loew's Book Supply for March 21.

7. The following is a summary of the accounts receivable ledger of Select Sales Company on June 1, 19—:

| Customer | Address | Sales Slip | Amount | Balance |
|----------|---------|------|--------|---------|
| P. J. Carey | 88 Kenneth Ave. | 141 | | $ 48.30 |
| M. P. Dewar | 94 Belair Drive | 151 | | 105.00 |
| D. E. Gale | 400 Brewster Street | 147 | | 89.25 |
| R. B. Hancock | 41 Bisher Avenue | 146 | | 31.50 |
| F. Lipton | 900 Mandor Drive | 99 | | 42.00 |
| G. McDonald | 102 Mid-Land Blvd. | 96 | $21.00 | |
| | | 157 | 52.50 | 73.50 |
| W. Pimm | 16 Brent Road | 132 | | 63.00 |
| F. Slater | 12 Hastings Avenue | 104 | $15.75 | |
| | | 125 | 26.25 | |
| | | 162 | 94.50 | 136.50 |
| | | | | $589.05 |

**Set up the accounts receivable ledger of Select Sales Company as of June 1.**

**From the following transactions post to the subsidiary ledger accounts as required. The system adopted by Select Sales Company is that of posting directly from the source documents to the subsidiary ledgers.**

*Transactions*
June 2 *Partial Cash Register Daily Balance Form*

| ACCOUNTING SUMMARY | | DEBIT | CREDIT |
|--------------------|---|-------|--------|
| DEBITS: Bank | 6 | 641 15 | |
| Acc's Rec'l (Charge Sales)* | | 347 55 | |
| Other a/c's - | 12 | | |
| - | 13 | | |
| - | 14 | | |
| Cash Short and Over | 7 | 1 00 | |
| CREDITS: Accounts Receivable | 2 | | 195 30 |
| Sales | 18 | | 756 50 |
| Sales Tax Payable | 21 | | 37 90 |
| Cash Short and Over | 8 | | |
| BALANCING TOTALS | | 989 70 | 989 70 |

*'Charge' Vouchers*

| | | |
|---|---|---|
| Sales slip 163 | P. J. Carey | $ 47.25 |
| Sales slip 164 | W. Pimm | 65.10 |
| Sales slip 165 | D. E. Gale | 119.70 |
| Sales slip 166 | M. P. Dewar | 115.50 |
| | | $347.55 |

*'Received' Vouchers*

| | | |
|---|---|---|
| On sales slip 167 from P. J. Carey | Re 141 | $ 48.30 |
| On sales slip 168 from F. Slater | Re 104, 125 | 42.00 |
| On sales slip 169 from M. P. Dewar | Re 151 | 105.00 |
| | | $195.30 |

June 2 *Daily List of Mail Receipts*

        Cheque from R. B. Hancock      Paying sales slip 146     $31.50

June 3 *Partial Cash Register Daily Balance Form*

| ACCOUNTING SUMMARY | | DEBIT | | CREDIT | |
|---|---|---|---|---|---|
| DEBITS:Bank | 6 | 373 | 25 | | |
| Acc's Rec'l (Charge Sales)* | | 194 | 25 | | |
| Other a/c's - | 12 | 10 | 00 | | |
| - | 13 | | | | |
| - | 14 | | | | |
| Cash Short and Over | 7 | | | | |
| CREDITS:Accounts Receivable | 2 | | | 94 | 50 |
| Sales | 18 | | | 460 | 00 |
| Sales Tax Payable | 21 | | | 23 | 00 |
| Cash Short and Over | 8 | | | | |
| BALANCING TOTALS | | 577 | 50 | 577 | 50 |

*'Charge' Vouchers*

| | | |
|---|---|---|
| Sales slip 170 | F. Lipton | $ 78.75 |
| Sales slip 171 | G. McDonald | 115.50 |
| | | $194.25 |

*'Received' Vouchers*

  On sales slip 172 from F. Slater   Re 162     $94.50

June 4 *Partial Cash Register Daily Balance Form*

| ACCOUNTING SUMMARY | | DEBIT | | CREDIT | |
|---|---|---|---|---|---|
| DEBITS:Bank | 6 | 466 | 35 | | |
| Acc's Rec'l (Charge Sales)* | | 135 | 50 | | |
| Other a/c's - | 12 | | | | |
| - | 13 | | | | |
| - | 14 | | | | |
| Cash Short and Over | 7 | | | | |
| CREDITS:Accounts Receivable | 2 | | | 63 | 00 |
| Sales | 18 | | | 512 | 00 |
| Sales Tax Payable | 21 | | | 25 | 60 |
| Cash Short and Over | 8 | | | 1 | 25 |
| BALANCING TOTALS | | 601 | 85 | 601 | 85 |

*'Charge' Vouchers*

| | | |
|---|---|---|
| Sales slip 173 | F. Slater | $52.50 |
| Sales slip 174 | W. Pimm | 83.00 |
| | | $135.50 |

*'Received' Vouchers*

  On sales slip 175 from W. Pimm   Re 132     $63.00

June 4  *Daily List of Mail Receipts*

| | | |
|---|---|---|
| Cheque from F. Lipton | Paying sales slip 99 | $42.00 |
| Cheque from G. McDonald | Paying sales slip 96 | 21.00 |
| | | $63.00 |

**Prepare a subsidiary ledger trial balance as of June 4.**

---

**8.   In a large department store cash registers are used extensively. Give reasons why cash registers are essential in such circumstances.**

---

**9.   Explain why it is uncommon to find a petty cash fund in a store which has a cash register.**

---

**10.   Study the flowchart on page 217 to answer the following questions:**
1.   Who prepares the cash register daily balance form?
2.   What do the contents of the cash register consist of?
3.   Where do the cheques received on account eventually go?
4.   The bank deposit slip is prepared in duplicate. State what happens to each copy.
5.   In what department is the daily list of mail receipts filed, and is it filed by date, by number, or alphabetically?

---

**11.   From the following information prepare a bank reconciliation statement for P. F. Faulkner as of June 30, 19—:**
1.   The balance per the general ledger is $1 291.60.
2.   The balance per the bank statement is $1 118.34.
3.   There is an outstanding deposit of $402.91.
4.   There are four outstanding cheques: #65 for $72.00; #74 for $35.00; #77 for $12.50; and #83 for $117.40.
5.   There is a bank service charge shown on the bank statement for $7.25. This was not recorded in the business books.

---

**12.   The Bank account in the general ledger of J. C. Waters shows a balance of $1 267.91 DR. at March 31, 19—. On that same date, the bank statement shows a balance of $672.88 CR. The following items were found to be the items of difference.**

a.  Outstanding deposit of $516.13.
b.  Outstanding cheques of $112.40, $70.23, $16.21, and $19.40.
c.  A cheque of $166.20 which had been cashed by the bank but which had mistakenly not been recorded in the cash payments journal.
d.  A cheque of $29.06 which had been cashed by the bank for $29.60 and charged by them as $29.60.
e.  Bank service charge of $1.40 recorded on the bank statement on the last day of the month.
f.  An N.S.F. cheque for $129 shown on the bank statement on the last day of the month.

**Prepare a bank reconciliation statement.**

In general journal form, show the journal entries required in the books of the company.

---

13.  Shown below are all of the records that you will need to reconcile the current bank account of Proctor & Kemp at July 31, 19—.

**Note:** Normally the bank returns all of the 'paid' cheques to the business along with the bank statement. This cannot be done in a textbook. Instead, on the bank statement in brackets beside each amount in the Cheques column is either an explanation of the charge or the cheque number.

a.  Bank reconciliation statement for the previous month end, shown below.

b.  'Amount of Deposits' column of cash receipts journal for July, page 14.

| |
|---|
| 262.75 |
| 312.70 |
| 274.19 |
| 161.40 |
| 700.20 |
| 265.92 |
| 400.61 |
| 396.21 |
| 316.40 |
| 3 090.38 |

Proctor & Kemp
Bank Reconciliation Statement
June 30, 19—

| | | | | |
|---|---|---|---|---|
| Balance per Bank Statement | 1 406 03 | Balance per General Ledger | | 773 28 |
| Add: Outstanding Deposit | 551 00 | Deduct: Bank Charges | | |
| | 1 957 03 | not entered in books | | |
| Deduct: Outstanding Cheques | | of company | | |
| #83 $5.10 | | (1) Service Charge $16.50 | | |
| 780 71.03 | | (2) Loan Interest 33.50 | 50 00 | |
| 828 400.00 | | | | |
| 846 96.02 | | | | |
| 852 123.50 | | | | |
| 860 15.00 | | | | |
| 871 16.01 | | | | |
| 873 17.50 | | | | |
| 881 33.60 | | | | |
| 886 121.47 | | | | |
| 889 60.00 | | | | |
| 890 170.00 | | | | |
| 891 31.94 | | | | |
| 892 27.61 | | | | |
| 894 13.82 | | | | |
| 898 12.50 | | | | |
| 899 18.65 | 1 233 75 | | | |
| True Balance | 723 28 | True Balance | | 723 28 |

c. Excerpts from cash payments journal for
July, page 18.

| Explanation | Chq. No. | Bank Credit |
|---|---|---|
| | 900 | 100.00 |
| | 901 | 171.31 |
| | 902 | 142.19 |
| Loan Interest June | | 33.50 |
| Service Charge June | | 16.50 |
| | 903 | 16.41 |
| | 904 | 17.50 |
| | 905 | 10.00 |
| | 906 | 12.40 |
| | 907 | 19.61 |
| | 908 | 31.40 |
| | 909 | 76.39 |
| | 910 | 65.20 |
| | 911 | 500.00 |
| | 912 | 216.75 |
| | 914 | 8.21 |
| | 915 | 2.60 |
| | 916 | 9.40 |
| | 917 | 50.00 |
| | 918 | 50.00 |
| | 919 | 33.19 |
| | 920 | 29.33 |
| | 921 | 65.00 |
| | 922 | 25.00 |
| | 923 | 25.00 |
| | 924 | 419.63 |
| | 925 | 372.60 |
| | 926 | 900.00 |
| | | 3 419.12 |

d. July general journal entry affecting 'Bank',
page 9.

| | | |
|---|---|---|
| Bank | 5.10 | |
| Miscellaneous Income | | 5.10 |

To cancel outstanding cheque
No. 83 issued June 19—

e. Partial general ledger Bank account.

| DATE | | PARTICULARS | P.R. | DEBIT | CREDIT | BALANCE | DR CR |
|---|---|---|---|---|---|---|---|
| 19-- | | | | | | | |
| June | 30 | | | | | 773.28 | DR |
| July | 31 | | CR14 | 3090.38 | | | |
| | 31 | | CP18 | | 3419.12 | | |
| | 31 | | J9 | 5.10 | | 449.64 | DR |

f. July bank statement.

| CHEQUES | | | | DEPOSITS | DATE | BALANCE |
|---|---|---|---|---|---|---|
| | | | | | June 30 | 1 406.03 |
| 18.65 | (899) | 31.94 | (891) | 551.00 | July 2 | 1 906.44 |
| 121.47 | (886) | | | | 3 | 1 784.97 |
| 100.00 | (900) | 96.02 | (846) | 262.75 | 5 | 1 851.70 |
| 12.50 | (898) | | | | 5 | 1 839.20 |
| 71.03 | (780) | 27.61 | (892) | | 6 | 1 740.56 |
| 142.19 | (902) | | | | 6 | 1 598.37 |
| 400.00 | (828) | | | 312.70 | 8 | 1 511.07 |
| 15.00 | (860) | 13.82 | (894) | | 9 | 1 482.25 |
| 16.01 | (871) | 171.31 | (901) | | 10 | 1 294.93 |
| 17.50 | (904) | | | | 10 | 1 277.43 |
| 10.00 | (905) | | | 274.19 | 11 | 1 541.62 |
| 500.00 | (911) | | | | 12 | 1 041.62 |
| 33.60 | (N.S.F. cheque of R.C. Jones) | | | 161.40 | 15 | 1 169.42 |
| 50.00 | (913) | | | | 16 | 1 119.42 |
| 170.00 | (890) | 12.40 | (906) | | 17 | 937.02 |
| 76.39 | (909) | | | | 19 | 860.63 |
| 31.40 | (908) | | | 700.20 | 22 | 1 529.43 |
| 9.40 | (916) | 19.61 | (907) | | 23 | 1 500.42 |
| 2.60 | (915) | | | | 23 | 1 497.82 |
| | | | | 265.92 | 25 | 1 763.74 |
| 33.19 | (919) | | | 400.61 | 26 | 2 131.16 |
| 17.50 | (873) | | | | 27 | 2 113.66 |
| 50.00 | (917) | | | 396.21 | 30 | 2 459.87 |
| 25.00 | (922) | 419.63 | (924) | | 31 | 2 015.24 |
| 165.00 | (Promissory Note paid to Arno Bros.) | | | | 31 | 1 850.24 |
| 29.00 | (Interest on Loan) | | | | 31 | 1 821.24 |
| 12.60 | (Service Charge) | | | | 31 | 1 808.64 |

 Reconcile the bank and make the necessary accounting entries in the books of
the company.

**14.** From the following records, reconcile the bank account of Baker and Baker as of April 30, 19—.

a. Previous bank reconciliation statement.

| Baker and Baker | | | | | | |
|---|---|---|---|---|---|---|
| Bank Reconciliation Statement | | | | | | |
| March 31, 19— | | | | | | |
| Balance per Bank Statement | | 943 | 80 | Balance per General Ledger | 305 | 08 |
| Add: Outstanding Deposit | | 216 | 50 | | | |
| | | 1 160 | 30 | | | |
| Deduct: Outstanding Cheques | | | | | | |
| #1207 | $23.01 | | | | | |
| #1361 | 14.16 | | | | | |
| #1390 | 17.50 | | | | | |
| #1406 | 36.71 | | | | | |
| #1409 | 19.40 | | | | | |
| #1415 | 141.72 | | | | | |
| #1420 | 13.16 | | | | | |
| #1425 | 51.61 | | | | | |
| #1426 | 36.44 | | | | | |
| #1428 | 18.19 | | | | | |
| #1431 | 76.42 | | | | | |
| #1432 | 19.36 | | | | | |
| #1433 | 14.40 | | | | | |
| #1434 | 85.19 | | | | | |
| #1435 | 19.65 | | | | | |
| #1436 | 116.40 | | | | | |
| #1438 | 78.90 | | | | | |
| #1439 | 25.00 | | | | | |
| #1440 | 50.00 | 857 | 22 | | | |
| | | 303 | 08 | | | |
| Add: Correction of bank error | | | | | | |
| Cheque #1416 for $110.00 was | | | | | | |
| cashed for $112.00 and | | | | | | |
| charged to account for | | | | | | |
| $112.00 | | 2 | 00 | | | |
| True Balance | | 305 | 08 | True Balance | 305 | 08 |

b. Partial cash payments journal for April, page 17.

| Date | | Chq. No. | | | Bank CR |
|---|---|---|---|---|---|
| 19--<br>APRIL | 1 | 1441 | | | 75.92 |
| | 2 | 1442 | | | 80.00 |
| | 2 | 1443 | | | 120.00 |
| | 4 | 1444 | | | 33.71 |
| | 5 | 1445 | | | 10.00 |
| | 8 | 1446 | | | 17.50 |
| | 9 | 1447 | | | 20.10 |
| | 9 | 1448 | | | 10.00 |
| | 9 | 1449 | | | 125.00 |
| | 10 | 1450 | | | 300.00 |
| | 11 | 1451 | | | 14.77 |
| | 12 | 1452 | | | 84.33 |
| | 15 | 1453 | | | 19.06 |
| | 15 | 1454 | | | 69.50 |
| | 15 | 1455 | | | 20.00 |
| | 16 | 1456 | | | 5.61 |
| | 18 | 1457 | | | 3.20 |
| | 19 | 1458 | | | 42.75 |
| | 20 | 1459 | | | 41.00 |
| | 20 | 1460 | | | 18.30 |
| | 23 | 1461 | | | 19.00 |
| | 23 | 1462 | | | 80.00 |
| | 24 | 1463 | | | 100.00 |
| | 24 | 1464 | | | 64.70 |
| | 25 | 1465 | | | 30.00 |
| | 26 | 1466 | | | 10.00 |
| | 27 | 1467 | | | 4.50 |
| | 27 | 1468 | | | 3.50 |
| | 27 | 1469 | | | 12.00 |
| | 30 | 1470 | | | 19.00 |
| | 30 | 1471 | | | 36.00 |
| | 30 | 1472 | | | 7.85 |
| | | | | | 1497.30 |

c. 'Amount of Deposit' column of cash receipts journal for April, page 8.

| April | 4 | 216.50 |
|---|---|---|
| | 10 | 171.41 |
| | 15 | 94.80 |
| | 20 | 156.80 |
| | 24 | 363.85 |
| | 27 | 410.00 |
| | 30 | 94.00 |
| | | 1507.36 |

d. April general journal entry affecting Bank, page 9.

| Bank | 42.75 | |
|---|---|---|
| Accounts Payable – C. Brown | | 42.75 |

To cancel cheque No. 1458
which was issued in error.

e. Partial general ledger Bank account.

| | | BANK | | | | | | | No.1 | | |
|---|---|---|---|---|---|---|---|---|---|---|---|
| DATE | | PARTICULARS | P.R. | DEBIT | | | CREDIT | | BALANCE | | DR CR |
| March | 31 | | | | | | | | 305 | 08 | DR |
| April | 30 | | CR8 | 1 507 | 36 | | | | | | |
| | 30 | | CP17 | | | | 1 497 | 30 | | | |
| | 30 | | J9 | 42 | 75 | | | | 357 | 89 | DR |

f. April bank statement.

| CHEQUES | | | | DEPOSITS | DATE | BALANCE |
|---|---|---|---|---|---|---|
| | | | | | Mar 31 | 943.80 |
| | | | | 216.50 | Apr 1 | 1160.30 |
| 116.40 | (#1436) | 13.16 | (#1420) | | 2 | 1030.74 |
| 75.92 | (#1441) | 17.50 | (#1390) | 216.50 | 4 | |
| 76.42 | (#1431) | | | | 4 | 1077.40 |
| 19.40 | (#1409) | 85.19 | (#1434) | | 5 | |
| 10.00 | (#1445) | | | | 5 | 962.81 |
| 18.19 | (#1428) | | | | 8 | 944.62 |
| 36.71 | (#1406) | 50.00 | (#1440) | 171.41 | 10 | |
| 25.00 | (#1439) | 120.00 | (#1443) | | 10 | |
| 300.00 | (#1450) | | | | 10 | 584.32 |
| 14.40 | (#1433) | | | | 11 | 569.92 |
| 78.90 | (#1438) | 80.00 | (#1442) | | 15 | |
| 20.00 | (#1455) | 20.10 | (#1447) | | 15 | 370.92 |
| 141.72 | (#1415) | | | 94.80 | 16 | 324.00 |
| 51.61 | (#1425) | 125.00 | (#1449) | | 18 | 147.39 |
| | | | (Correct March Error) | 2.00 | 19 | 149.39 |
| | | | | 156.80 | 20 | 306.19 |
| 36.44 | (#1426) | 84.33 | (#1452) | | 23 | |
| 18.30 | (#1460) | | | | 23 | 167.12 |
| 100.00 | (#1463) | | | 363.85 | 24 | 430.97 |
| 19.65 | (#1435) | 16.09 | (#1453) | | 25 | 395.23 |
| | | | | 410.00 | 27 | 805.23 |
| DM 5.60 | (Service Charge) | | | | 27 | 799.63 |
| INT 36.00 | (Interest on Loan) | | | | 30 | 763.63 |
| DM 250.00 | (Loan Reduction) | | | | 30 | 513.63 |
| | | (Note Collected, R.Smith) | | 100.00 | 30 | 613.63 |
| 3.20 | (#1457) | 4.50 | (#1467) | | | |
| | | | | | 30 | 605.93 |

**Record the necessary accounting entries in the books of the business.**

---

**15.   From the following records, prepare the bank reconciliation statement for Madison Company as of October 31, 19—.**

a.  Previous bank reconciliation statement.

Madison Company
Bank Reconciliation Statement
September 30, 19—

| Bal. per Bk. Statement | | 2 102 69 | Bal. per General Ledger | | 1 652 95 |
|---|---|---|---|---|---|
| Deduct: Outstanding Chqs. | | | Deduct: | | |
| #519 | $20.00 | | Service Charge $12.50 | | |
| #526 | 37.50 | | Loan Interest 36.25 | | 48 75 |
| #528 | 105.00 | | | | |
| #529 | 2.70 | | | | |
| #531 | 5.19 | | | | |
| #532 | 74.10 | | | | |
| #533 | 112.02 | | | | |
| #534 | 56.94 | | | | |
| #535 | 85.04 | 498 49 | | | |
| True Balance | | 1 604 20 | True Balance | | 1 604 20 |

b. October general journal entry affecting Bank.

| | General Journal | | Page 64 | | | | |
|---|---|---|---|---|---|---|---|
| Date | Particulars | P.R. | Debit | | Credit | | |
| Oct 4 | Bank Charges | 54 | 12 | 50 | | | |
| | Bank Interest | 56 | 36 | 25 | | | |
| | Bank | 1 | | | 48 | 75 | |
| | To record charges picked up | | | | | | |
| | from September bank statement | | | | | | |

c. Partial cash payments journal.

Page 174

| Date | Chq. No | Bank Cr | |
|---|---|---|---|
| Oct 1 | 536 | 19 | 05 |
| 1 | 537 | 164 | 02 |
| 2 | 538 | 73 | 74 |
| 3 | 539 | 27 | 60 |
| 3 | 540 | 1 | 95 |
| 4 | 541 | 365 | 12 |
| 5 | 542 | 92 | 06 |
| 8 | 543 | 74 | 09 |
| 8 | 544 | 19 | 65 |
| 10 | 545 | 74 | 02 |
| 11 | 546 | 76 | 75 |
| 12 | 547 | 56 | 21 |
| 12 | 548 | 42 | 96 |
| 15 | 549 | 33 | 21 |
| 17 | 550 | 24 | 02 |
| 19 | 551 | 88 | 61 |
| 22 | 552 | 58 | 36 |
| 22 | 553 | 19 | 05 |
| 23 | 554 | 91 | 50 |
| 24 | 555 | 13 | 30 |
| 24 | 556 | 17 | 50 |
| 26 | 557 | 8 | 61 |
| 29 | 558 | 1 047 | 65 |
| 29 | 559 | 319 | 02 |
| 30 | 560 | 1 | 75 |
| 31 | 561 | 2 | 50 |
| 31 | 562 | 19 | 41 |
| | | 2 831 | 71 |

d. Partial cash receipts journal.

Page 147

| Date | Bank Dr | | Amount Deposit | |
|---|---|---|---|---|
| Oct 3 | 16 | 50 | | |
| 3 | 25 | 02 | | |
| 3 | 516 | 95 | 558 | 47 |
| 8 | 104 | 20 | | |
| 8 | 756 | 12 | | |
| 8 | 56 | 12 | | |
| 8 | 96 | 02 | 1 012 | 46 |
| 11 | 33 | 40 | 33 | 40 |
| 15 | 17 | 50 | | |
| 15 | 12 | 09 | 29 | 59 |
| 22 | 19 | 06 | | |
| 22 | 502 | 00 | 521 | 06 |
| 24 | 12 | 06 | | |
| 24 | 13 | 50 | | |
| 24 | 91 | 02 | | |
| 24 | 16 | 51 | 133 | 09 |
| 29 | 56 | 93 | | |
| 29 | 83 | 16 | | |
| 29 | 102 | 52 | | |
| 29 | 127 | 06 | | |
| 29 | 31 | 50 | 401 | 17 |
| 31 | 167 | 75 | | |
| 31 | 138 | 44 | 306 | 19 |
| | 2 995 | 43 | 2 995 | 43 |
| | (1) | | | |

e. Bank statement for October.

| CHEQUES | | | | DEPOSITS | DATE | BALANCE |
|---|---|---|---|---|---|---|
| | | | | | Sep 30 | 2 102.69 |
| 37.50 | (526) | | | | Oct 2 | 2 065.19 |
| | | | | 558.47 | 3 | 2 623.66 |
| 2.70 | (529) | 85.04 | (535) | | 4 | 2 535.92 |
| 19.05 | (536) | | | | 5 | 2 516.87 |
| 74.10 | (532) | 105.00 | (528) | | 8 | 2 337.77 |
| 73.74 | (538) | | | 1 012.46 | 9 | 3 276.49 |
| 5.19 | (531) | 27.60 | (539) | | 10 | 3 243.70 |
| 56.94 | (534) | | | | 11 | 3 186.76 |
| 74.09 | (543) | 112.02 | (533) | 33.40 | 15 | 3 034.05 |
| 96.02 | (N.S.F. cheque of J. Marble) | | | | 15 | 2 938.03 |
| 164.02 | (537) | | | | 16 | 2 774.01 |
| 33.21 | (549) | 19.65 | (544) | 29.59 | 17 | 2 750.74 |
| 365.12 | (541) | | | | 18 | 2 385.62 |
| 76.75 | (546) | | | 521.06 | 22 | 2 829.93 |
| 1.95 | (540) | 58.36 | (552) | | 23 | 2 769.62 |
| 42.96 | (548) | | | | 24 | 2 726.66 |
| | | | | 133.09 | 25 | 2 859.75 |
| 88.61 | (551) | | | | 26 | 2 771.14 |
| 91.50 | (554) | | | | 29 | 2 679.64 |
| 13.30 | (555) | | | 401.17 | 30 | 3 067.51 |
| 8.61 | (557) | 1 047.65 | (558) | | 31 | 2 011.25 |
| 15.20 | (Int) | 30.20 | (Service Charges) | | 31 | 1 965.85 |

f. General ledger account showing October figures.

| Account | Bank | | | | | | No. | 1 | |
|---|---|---|---|---|---|---|---|---|---|
| Date | Particulars | P.R. | Debit | Credit | DR. CR. | Balance | | | |
| 19— | | | | | | | | | |
| Sept 30 | | — | | | DR | 1 652 95 | | | |
| Oct 4 | | J 64 | | 48 75 | | | | | |
| 31 | | CP174 | | 2 831 71 | | | | | |
| 31 | | CR147 | 2 995 43 | | DR | 1 767 92 | | | |

# Cases

## Case 1

Upon graduation you have accepted a position as an accounting clerk for Superior Ace Company. Mr. Day, your immediate superior, has never insisted on the preparation of bank reconciliation statements. He claims that he has faith in his bankers and the employees he has trained. What arguments should you put forth on the validity of bank reconciliation statements?

## Case 2

The D. Trivett & Son supermarket is open from 9 a.m. to 10 p.m. six days a week. The daily cash receipts amount to several thousand dollars and are placed in an office safe at the end of the day. The receipts are then deposited in the bank the next morning. The receipts for Friday and Saturday, usually totalling $10 000 to $12 000, are banked on Monday morning.
1. Is this policy a wise one? Explain.
2. If you were the manager of the supermarket what procedures might you take to protect cash receipts?

## Case 3

The Pizza Parlour is owned by Mr. Lombardi. Mr. Lombardi has both table and take-out service. Orders for the take-out service are written on plain colored pads purchased from the corner variety store. Dining room orders are written on pre-numbered business forms. Any expenses incurred during business hours are paid out of the cash register drawer. A memo stating the amount and item is written up on the same colored paper used for take-out orders. This slip is then put under the change compartment in the cash register. Any waitress can receive cash from customers. Mr. Lombardi often finds that there is cash missing from the cash register at the end of the day. Usually Mr. Lombardi will carry around the day's cash receipts in his pocket until his bank informs him that one of the cheques he has written has come through to his account. Of course he must take the amount to the bank to cover the cheque before it can be paid.

1. State the weaknesses in Mr. Lombardi's cash control system.
2. List the changes you would make in the system and your reasons for making them.

## Case 4

John V. Slippery has been hired to act as cashier and general accountant. Both receipts and payments are entered in the cash books by the cashier, who makes deposits and writes up cheques. All cheques are signed by the treasurer. Slippery, in need of funds, withholds from deposits over a period of months an amount of $4 000. Since he is not responsible for posting to the accounts receivable ledger, the collections are properly entered in the cash receipts journal and posted to the various customers' accounts by the accounting clerk. At the end of the month, to cover up the cash shortage, Slippery processes a cheque to pay a phony purchase invoice by cash. This cheque, when entered in the cash payments journal, offsets the $4 000 which has been withheld from the bank. The cheque is not mailed to the creditor, is destroyed by Slippery, and checked off as a cancelled cheque. Similarly, it is omitted as an outstanding cheque in the monthly reconciliation of the bank statement.

1. Will this shortage of $4 000 ever be discovered? Explain.
2. What recommendations would you make to management to provide an internal control system to prevent the occurrence of such fraud?

## Case 5

Stein Store uses a cash register to record all cash sales. On a certain day the cash count at the close of the business indicated $15.00 less cash than was shown by the totals on the cash register tapes.

1. In what account would this cash shortage be recorded? Would the account be debited or credited?
2. If you were the employer of this store, would you demand that your employee make up any cash difference?

## Case 6

A cheque for $675 issued in payment of a typewriter for the business was erroneously recorded in the cash payments journal as $765.

1. When would this error be detected?
2. Record the journal entry to correct the accounts.

## Case 7

On December 31, 19—, the S. Wilson Company receives the monthly statement from the City Bank. The statement shows a balance of cash of $28 495.70. The balance shown in the Cash account amounts to $23 079.15. How is the difference between the two balances to be accounted for? If you were the accountant for this company, how would you proceed?

## Case 8

J. C. WATERS

BANK RECONCILIATION STATEMENT

MARCH 31, 19—

| | | |
|---|---:|---:|
| Balance per bank statement | | $2 046.75 |
| Add late deposit, March 31 | | 271.50 |
| | | $2 318.25 |
| Less outstanding cheques | | |
| #418 | $ 62.80 | |
| 522 | 103.40 | |
| 523 | 41.90 | 208.10 |
| True balance | | $2 110.15 |
| Balance per Cash account | | $2 186.85 |
| Less bank charges | $ 5.40 | |
| N.S.F. cheque – Walker | 71.30 | 76.70 |
| True balance | | $2 110.15 |

Answer the following questions about J. C. Waters's bank reconciliation statement as shown above:

1. Does the $2 046.75 represent the bank balance at the beginning or at the end of the month?
2. Why do you think the March 31 deposit was not included in the bank balance?
3. How does Waters know that there are three cheques outstanding? Why are they subtracted?
4. Is $2 186.85 the cash balance at the beginning or at the end of the month?
5. What is an N.S.F. cheque? Why is it subtracted from the balance per books?
6. A certified cheque for $200 payable to R. Smit is still outstanding. Why is it not part of the outstanding cheques on the bank reconciliation statement?

## Case 9

Mr. Wilson has two bank balances in his business, a current account and a savings account. When he deposited his receipts for the day he made a mistake and prepared a deposit slip for his savings account instead of for his current account. When will Mr. Wilson discover this error and what should he do about it?

## Case 10

T. Coates, accountant for Graham & Son, found it necessary to have a cheque for $2 000 certified by the bank. The date on this cheque is November 25. This cheque was held by the payee for several weeks before he took any action. Should the certified cheque appear on the November 30 bank reconciliation statement prepared by Coates? Explain.

# Supplement to Chapter 11

## Green Thumb Garden Center Exercise

### Introductory Information

The Green Thumb Garden Center is a business owned and operated by Mr. G. O. Emms. It is a seasonal business which the owner closes down each year from November 1 to March 31. During the season that the business is open, it is operated seven days a week. The most profitable business days are Saturdays and Sundays.

The Green Thumb Garden Center sells a variety of goods and services. Among these are the following: shrubs, bushes, trees, plants, fertilizers, seeds, bulbs, insecticides, sod, loam, soil, concrete products, and landscaping. All goods and services sold by the business are subject to a 5 per cent government sales tax.

Mr. Emms employs a number of workers to assist him. Most of these are hired on a part-time basis as they are needed. Once each week Mr. Emms withdraws from the bank (by means of a cheque made out to Cash) sufficient cash to pay the employees.

Most of the sales of the business are on a cash basis. As a result, the accounting system of the business is geared towards the cash register. In addition to the cash sales, all charge sales and receipts from customers are processed through the cash register. There are relatively few charge customers.

At the close of each day's business, a cash register balancing procedure is performed and an accounting summary prepared. A bank deposit is made each day by using a night depository service.

Small expense items are not paid for out of the cash register funds. Mr. Emms maintains a petty cash fund of $100 for this purpose.

The business accounting system utilizes three special journals as follows:

|  |  |  |  |  |  |  | Page 77 |
|---|---|---|---|---|---|---|---|
| Date | Name | Other Accounts Dr. | Truck Expense Dr. | Soil Prep. & Mtce. Dr. | Equipment Expense Dr. | Purchases Dr. | Accounts Payable Cr. |

*Purchases Journal*

|  |  |  |  |  |  |  |  | Page 47 |
|---|---|---|---|---|---|---|---|---|
| Date | Name | Other Accounts Dr. | Wages Dr. | G.O.E. Drawings Dr. | Soil Prep. & Mtce. Dr. | Discounts Earned Cr. | Accounts Payable Dr. | Bank Cr. |

*Cash Payments Journal*

|  |  |  |  |  |  |  | Page 65 |
|---|---|---|---|---|---|---|---|
| Date | Name | Other Accounts Cr. | Cash Short & Over Dr. | Discounts Allowed Dr. | Sales Tax Payable Cr. | Sales Cr. | Accounts Receivable Cr. | Bank Dr. |

*Cash Receipts Journal*

The business does not keep perpetual inventory records.

GREEN THUMB GARDEN CENTER
GENERAL LEDGER TRIAL BALANCE
MAY 31, 19—

| No. | Account | Dr. | Cr. |
|---|---|---|---|
| 1. | Petty Cash | $ 100.00 | |
| 2. | Bank | 3 527.24 | |
| 3. | Accounts Receivable | 2 469.91 | |
| 4. | Inventory – Merchandise and Nursery Stock | 10 746.53 | |
| 5. | Supplies | 595.00 | |
| 6. | Land | 48 000.00 | |
| 7. | Buildings | 23 500.00 | |
| 8. | Trucks and Tractors | 27 500.00 | |
| 21. | Bank Loan | | $ 20 000.00 |
| 22. | Mortgage Payable | | 22 500.00 |
| 23. | Accounts Payable | | 7 861.87 |
| 24. | Sales Tax Payable | | 160.45 |
| 31. | G. O. Emms, Capital | | 66 175.94 |
| 32. | G. O. Emms, Drawings | 5 654.60 | |
| 41. | Sales | | 25 042.19 |
| 51. | Bank Charges | 547.53 | |
| 52. | Building Repairs | 146.51 | |
| 53. | Cash Short and Over | 10.04 | |
| 54. | Discounts Allowed | 95.75 | |
| 55. | Discounts Earned | | 316.70 |
| 56. | Equipment Expense | 506.86 | |
| 57. | Freight-in | 256.50 | |
| 58. | Light, Heat, and Power | 306.75 | |
| 59. | Miscellaneous Expense | 92.41 | |
| 60. | Purchases | 10 001.05 | |
| 61. | Soil Preparation and Maintenance | 2 001.15 | |
| 62. | Telephone | 519.42 | |
| 63. | Truck Expense | 1 104.40 | |
| 64. | Wages | 4 375.50 | |
| | | $142 057.15 | $142 057.15 |

GREEN THUMB GARDEN CENTER
ACCOUNTS RECEIVABLE LEDGER
MAY 31, 19—

| Customer | Address | Usual Terms | Inv. Date | Inv. No. | Amount |
|---|---|---|---|---|---|
| P. Barker | 16 Ava Street | Net 30 | May 16 | 398 | $ 131.25 |
| J. Bowen | 42 Woodlawn Ave. | Net 30 | May 14 | 394 | 78.75 |
| F. Carson & Sons | 165 Pleasant Road | 2/10,n/30 | May 30 | 408 | 541.80 |
| N. Everist | 46 Hart Street | Net 30 | May 4 | 375 | 56.70 |
| O. Harrison | 96 Brock Road | Net 30 | May 5 | 377 | 63.00 |
| P. Pierce | 205 Ford Street | Net 30 | May 6 | 379 | 36.53 |
| A. Renforth | 90 Oak Lane | Net 30 | May 12 | 390 | 178.50 |
| C. Swinton | 27 North Cr. | 2/10,n/30 | May 26 | 407 | 1 094.63 |
| Varga Brothers | 55 Sharp Drive | 2/10,n/30 | May 24 | 402 | 288.75 |
| | | | | | $2 469.91 |

GREEN THUMB GARDEN CENTER
ACCOUNTS PAYABLE LEDGER
MAY 31, 19—

| Supplier | Address | Terms | Inv. No. | Inv. Date | Amount | Account Balance |
|---|---|---|---|---|---|---|
| Acorn Seed Company | 10 Lynn Road | 2/15,n/30 | 654 | May 18 | $147.00 | |
| | | | 672 | May 21 | 317.10 | $ 464.10 |
| Clay Ceramic Co. | 74 Pine Street | Net 45 | 1701 | Apr. 24 | | 540.75 |
| Canada Products | 100 Willow Ave. | Net 30 | B160 | May 4 | $ 58.80 | |
| | | | B188 | May 12 | 98.91 | |
| | | | B249 | May 30 | 35.91 | 193.62 |
| Kemp Haulage | Summerside | 1/10,n/30 | 747 | May 23 | $ 52.50 | |
| | | | 754 | May 23 | 52.50 | |
| | | | 760 | May 23 | 52.50 | |
| | | | 772 | May 27 | 52.50 | |
| | | | 795 | May 31 | 78.75 | 288.75 |
| M & M Chemicals | 500 Grand St. | Net 60 | 1046 | Apr. 9 | | 1 932.00 |
| Poplar Finance | 200 Crest Rd. | Per Contract | | | | 2 560.00 |
| Sylvester Concrete | 482-4 Delta Rd. | Net 30 | 446 | May 5 | | 783.51 |
| Triangle Sod | 4th Side Road | Net 30 | 374 | May 22 | | 1 099.14 |
| | | | | | | $7 861.87 |

Set up the three ledgers of the Green Thumb Garden Center as of May 31, 19—.

Set up a cash receipts journal (page 65), a cash payments journal (page 47), and a purchases journal (page 77) for the Green Thumb Garden Center for June 19—.

Journalize the transactions listed below. Post daily to the subsidiary ledgers, directly from the source documents.

## Transactions

June 1 *Cash Register Summary*

| ACCOUNTING SUMMARY | DEBIT | CREDIT |
|---|---|---|
| DEBITS: Bank | 160 05 | |
| Acc's Rec'l (Charge Sales) | | |
| Cash Short and Over | 2 00 | |
| CREDITS: Accounts Receivable | | |
| Sales | | 154 33 |
| Sales Tax Payable | | 7 72 |
| Cash Short and Over | | |
| BALANCING TOTALS | 162 05 | 162 05 |

*Purchase Invoice*
–From Canada Products, No. B261, $372.75, dated May 31; terms Net 30; for fertilizer for resale.

June 2 *Cash Register Summary*

| ACCOUNTING SUMMARY | DEBIT | CREDIT |
|---|---|---|
| DEBITS: Bank | 551 98 | |
| Acc's Rec'l (Charge Sales) | | |
| Discounts Allowed | 5 78 | |
| Cash Short and Over | | |
| CREDITS: Accounts Receivable | | 288 75 |
| Sales | | 256 20 |
| Sales Tax Payable | | 12 81 |
| Cash Short and Over | | |
| BALANCING TOTALS | 557 76 | 557 76 |

*'Received' Voucher*
–Voucher No. 416 to Varga Brothers, paying Invoice No. 402 for $288.75 less 2 per cent discount; net amount $282.97.

*Purchase Invoice*

–From Triangle Sod, No. 406, $312.90, dated June 1; terms Net 30; for sod for resale (assume goods satisfactory for all purchases).

*Cheque Copies*

–No. 661, to Acorn Seed Company, $?, paying Invoice No. 654 less 2 per cent cash discount.

–No. 662, to Kemp Haulage, $?, paying Invoices No. 747, No. 754, No. 760 less 1 per cent cash discount.

June 3 *Cash Register Summary*

| ACCOUNTING SUMMARY | | DEBIT | CREDIT |
|---|---|---|---|
| DEBITS: Bank | | 247 20 | |
| Acc's Rec'l (Charge Sales) | | | |
| | | | |
| Cash Short and Over | | | |
| CREDITS: Accounts Receivable | | | 56 70 |
| Sales | | | 180 00 |
| Sales Tax Payable | | | 9 — |
| Cash Short and Over | | | 1 50 |
| BALANCING TOTALS | | 247 20 | 247 20 |

*'Received' Voucher*

–Voucher No. 417 to N. Everist, paying Invoice No. 375 for $56.70.

*Cheque Copy*

–No. 663, to Petty Cash, $?, to reimburse petty cash fund with respect to the following summary:

| Petty Cash Summary | |
|---|---|
| June 3, 19- | |
| Building Repairs | $14.10 |
| Equipment Expense | 2.50 |
| Soil Preparation & Maint. | 35.50 |
| Truck Expense | 17.70 |
| Miscellaneous Expense | 26.75 |

June 4 *Cash Register Summary*

| ACCOUNTING SUMMARY | | DEBIT | CREDIT |
|---|---|---|---|
| DEBITS: Bank | | 100 38 | |
| Acc's Rec'l (Charge Sales) | | 330 75 | |
| | | | |
| Cash Short and Over | | | |
| CREDITS: Accounts Receivable | | | |
| Sales | | | 410 60 |
| Sales Tax Payable | | | 20 53 |
| Cash Short and Over | | | |
| BALANCING TOTALS | | 431 13 | 431 13 |

*'Charge' Voucher*

–Voucher No. 418 to Varga Brothers for the sale of merchandise, $315.00 plus 5 per cent sales tax; terms, 2/10,n/30; total $330.75.

*Purchase Invoices*

–From Clay Ceramic Co., No. 1916, $1 003.80, dated June 3; terms, Net 45; flower pots and ornamental garden items (merchandise for resale).

–From M. & M. Chemicals, No. 1193, $784, dated June 3; terms, Net 60; for insecticides etc., for resale.

*Cheque Copies*

–No. 664, to Sylvester Concrete, $?, paying Invoice No. 446.

–No. 665, to Public Utilities Commission, $14.85, for electricity for the month of May. (Note: As soon as this bill was received cheque No. 665 was prepared.)

*Bank Statement and Vouchers*

–The bank statement and related vouchers and paid cheques arrived from the bank. Included in the vouchers was a debit note for bank charges in the amount of $41.50 for May; this was the first notice for these charges.

At this time, the following bank reconciliation statement was prepared. You will require this statement in order to prepare the reconciliation statement at the end of June.

| Green Thumb Garden Center Bank Reconciliation Statement May 31, 19— | | | | |
|---|---|---|---|---|
| Balance per Bk. Statement | 3 406 15 | Balance per Gen. Ledger | | 3 527 24 |
| Add: Outstanding Deposit | 516 31 | Deduct: Bank Interest | | |
| | 3 922 46 | and Service Charge | | 41 50 |
| Deduct: Outstanding Cheques | | | | |
| #641 $74.00 | | | | |
| #650 36.50 | | | | |
| #654 29.12 | | | | |
| #655 116.26 | | | | |
| #657 37.40 | | | | |
| #658 42.15 | | | | |
| #659 95.14 | | | | |
| #660 6.15 | 436 72 | | | |
| True Balance | 3 485 74 | True Balance | | 3 485 74 |

June 5 *Cash Register Summary*

| ACCOUNTING SUMMARY | | DEBIT | CREDIT |
|---|---|---|---|
| DEBITS: Bank | | 1 669 90 | |
| Acc's Rec'l (Charge Sales) | | | |
| | | | |
| Discounts Allowed | | 21 89 | |
| Cash Short and Over | | 1 23 | |
| CREDITS: Accounts Receivable | | | 1 194 16 |
| Sales | | | 475 10 |
| Sales Tax Payable | | | 23 76 |
| Cash Short and Over | | | |
| BALANCING TOTALS | | 1 693 02 | 1 693 02 |

*'Received' Vouchers*

–Voucher No. 419, to C. Swinton, paying Invoice No. 407 in the amount of $1 094.63 less a 2 per cent cash discount; net amount $1 072.74.

–Voucher No. 420, to O. Harrison, paying Invoice No. 377 in the amount of $63.

–Voucher No. 421, to P. Pierce, paying Invoice No. 379 in the amount of $36.53.

## Cheque Copies

–No. 666 to Cash, $604.16, wages for the week.

–No. 667, to G. O. Emms, $440, personal drawings of owner.

–No. 668, to Acorn Seed Company, $?, paying Invoice No. 672 less a 2 per cent cash discount.

### June 6  Cash Register Summary

| ACCOUNTING SUMMARY | | DEBIT | CREDIT |
|---|---|---|---|
| DEBITS: | Bank | 847 44 | |
| | Acc's Rec'l (Charge Sales) | 852 15 | |
| | | | |
| | Cash Short and Over | | |
| CREDITS: | Accounts Receivable | | |
| | Sales | | 1 618 66 |
| | Sales Tax Payable | | 80 93 |
| | Cash Short and Over | | |
| BALANCING TOTALS | | 1 699 59 | 1 699 59 |

### 'Charge' Vouchers

–Voucher No. 422, to C. Swinton, $516.07 plus 5 per cent sales tax, for sale of merchandise; terms, 2/10,n/30; total $541.87.

–Voucher No. 423, to A. Renforth, $295.50 plus 5 per cent sales tax, for sale of merchandise; terms, Net 30; total $310.28.

### Purchase Invoices

–From Equipment Repair and Supply, 16 Barr St., No. 21, $157.50, dated June 5; terms, Net 30; for repairs to equipment.

–From Canada Products, No. B295, $997.50, dated June 4; terms, Net 30; for fertilizers and chemicals for soil to be charged as follows: Purchases, $871.50; Soil Preparation & Maintenance, $126.

### Cheque Copies

–No. 669, to Clay Ceramic Co., $540.75, paying Invoice No. 1701.

–No. 670, to Kemp Haulage, $?, paying Invoice No. 772 less 1 per cent cash discount.

–No. 671, to Canada Products, $58.80, paying Invoice No. B160.

### June 7  Cash Register Summary

| ACCOUNTING SUMMARY | | DEBIT | CREDIT |
|---|---|---|---|
| DEBITS: | Bank | 941 83 | |
| | Acc's Rec'l (Charge Sales) | | |
| | | | |
| | Cash Short and Over | 10 00 | |
| CREDITS: | Accounts Receivable | | |
| | Sales | | 906 50 |
| | Sales Tax Payable | | 45 33 |
| | Cash Short and Over | | |
| BALANCING TOTALS | | 951 83 | 951 83 |

### Cheque Copy

–No. 672, to Public Utilities Commission, $27.50, cash payment of water bill (charge Soil Preparation & Maintenance).

### June 8  Cash Register Summary

| ACCOUNTING SUMMARY | | DEBIT | CREDIT |
|---|---|---|---|
| DEBITS: | Bank | 611 18 | |
| | Acc's Rec'l (Charge Sales) | | |
| | | | |
| | Discounts Allowed | 10 84 | |
| | Cash Short and Over | | |
| CREDITS: | Accounts Receivable | | 541 80 |
| | Sales | | 76 40 |
| | Sales Tax Payable | | 3 82 |
| | Cash Short and Over | | |
| BALANCING TOTALS | | 622 02 | 622 02 |

### 'Received' Voucher

–Voucher No. 424, to F. Carson & Sons, paying Invoice No. 408 for $541.80 less 2 per cent cash discount; net amount $530.96.

### Cheque Copies

–No. 673, to M. & M. Chemicals, $1 932, paying Invoice No. 1046.

–No. 674, to Poplar Finance, $175, regular monthly payment on truck.

### June 9  Cash Register Summary

| ACCOUNTING SUMMARY | | DEBIT | CREDIT |
|---|---|---|---|
| DEBITS: | Bank | 117 60 | |
| | Acc's Rec'l (Charge Sales) | 71 40 | |
| | | | |
| | Cash Short and Over | | |
| CREDITS: | Accounts Receivable | | |
| | Sales | | 180 00 |
| | Sales Tax Payable | | 9 00 |
| | Cash Short and Over | | |
| BALANCING TOTALS | | 189 00 | 189 00 |

### 'Charge' Voucher

–Voucher No. 425, to O. Harrison, $68 plus 5 per cent sales tax; terms, Net 30; for sale of merchandise; total $71.40.

### Purchase Invoices

–From City Gas & Oil Co., 15 Boa Street, No. 1651, $135.68, dated June 8; terms, Net 30; for gasoline and oil used in the trucks and equipment as follows: Trucks, $94.67; Equipment, $41.01.

–From Kemp Haulage, No. 822, $231, dated June 7; terms, 1/10,n/30; topsoil for resale.

### June 10  Cash Register Summary

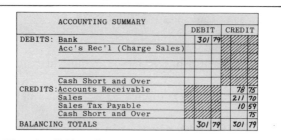

| ACCOUNTING SUMMARY | | DEBIT | CREDIT |
|---|---|---|---|
| DEBITS: | Bank | 301 79 | |
| | Acc's Rec'l (Charge Sales) | | |
| | | | |
| | Cash Short and Over | | |
| CREDITS: | Accounts Receivable | | 78 75 |
| | Sales | | 211 70 |
| | Sales Tax Payable | | 10 59 |
| | Cash Short and Over | | 75 |
| BALANCING TOTALS | | 301 79 | 301 79 |

### 'Received' Voucher

–Voucher No. 426, to J. Bowen; paying Invoice No. 394.

**June 10** *Cheque Copies*

–No. 675, to Northwestern Telephone Company, $25.20, cash payment of telephone bill.

–No. 676, to Kemp Haulage, $?, paying Invoice No. 795 less 1 per cent cash discount.

**June 11** *Cash Register Summary*

| ACCOUNTING SUMMARY | | DEBIT | CREDIT |
|---|---|---|---|
| DEBITS: | Bank | 137 66 | |
| | Acc's Rec'l (Charge Sales) | 131 25 | |
| | Cash Short and Over | | |
| CREDITS: | Accounts Receivable | | |
| | Sales | | 256 10 |
| | Sales Tax Payable | | 12 81 |
| | Cash Short and Over | | |
| BALANCING TOTALS | | 268 91 | 268 91 |

*'Charge' Voucher*

–Voucher No. 427, to P. Pierce, for the sale of merchandise, $125 plus 5 per cent sales tax; terms, Net 30; total $131.25.

*Purchase Invoice*

–From M. & M. Chemicals, No. 1221, $781.90, dated June 10; terms, Net 60; to be charged to Soil Preparation & Maintenance.

*Cheque Copy*

–No. 677, to Canada Products, $98.91, paying Invoice No. B188.

**June 12** *Cash Register Summary*

| ACCOUNTING SUMMARY | | DEBIT | CREDIT |
|---|---|---|---|
| DEBITS: | Bank | 594 21 | |
| | Acc's Rec'l (Charge Sales) | 278 25 | |
| | Cash Short and Over | 09 | |
| CREDITS: | Accounts Receivable | | 178 50 |
| | Sales | | 661 00 |
| | Sales Tax Payable | | 33 05 |
| | Cash Short and Over | | |
| BALANCING TOTALS | | 872 55 | 872 55 |

*'Received' Voucher*

–Voucher No. 428, to A. Renforth, $178.50, paying Invoice No. 390.

*'Charge' Voucher*

–Voucher No. 429, to F. Carson & Sons, for the sale of merchandise; terms 2/10,n/30; $265 plus 5 per cent sales tax; total $278.25.

*Cheque Copies*

–No. 678, to Cash, $705.19, for the wages for the week.

–No. 679, to G. O. Emms, $350, owner's personal drawings.

–No. 680, to Foster Bros., $44.21, for the cash purchase of miscellaneous items to be charged to Miscellaneous Expense.

**June 13** *Cash Register Summary*

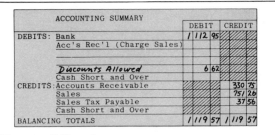

| ACCOUNTING SUMMARY | | DEBIT | CREDIT |
|---|---|---|---|
| DEBITS: | Bank | 669 06 | |
| | Acc's Rec'l (Charge Sales) | | |
| | Cash Short and Over | 21 | |
| CREDITS: | Accounts Receivable | | |
| | Sales | | 637 40 |
| | Sales Tax Payable | | 31 87 |
| | Cash Short and Over | | |
| BALANCING TOTALS | | 669 27 | 669 27 |

*Purchase Invoice*

–From Acorn Seed Company, No. 756, $82.43, dated June 12; terms, 2/15,n/30; for merchandise for resale.

**June 14** *Cash Register Summary*

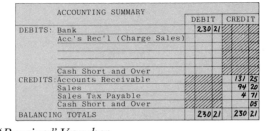

| ACCOUNTING SUMMARY | | DEBIT | CREDIT |
|---|---|---|---|
| DEBITS: | Bank | 1 112 95 | |
| | Acc's Rec'l (Charge Sales) | | |
| | *Discounts Allowed* | 6 62 | |
| | Cash Short and Over | | |
| CREDITS: | Accounts Receivable | | 330 75 |
| | Sales | | 751 26 |
| | Sales Tax Payable | | 37 56 |
| | Cash Short and Over | | |
| BALANCING TOTALS | | 1 119 57 | 1 119 57 |

*'Received' Voucher*

–Voucher No. 430, to Varga Brothers, $324.13, paying Invoice No. 418 less 2 per cent cash discount.

*Purchase Invoice*

–From Triangle Sod, No. 452, $787.50, dated June 12; terms, Net 30; for purchase of sod for resale.

*Bank Debit Advice*

This debit note from Central Bank stated that $2 000 had been deducted from the business bank account for the purpose of reducing the bank note. Mr. Emms had instructed the bank to make the deduction.

**June 15** *Cash Register Summary*

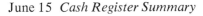

| ACCOUNTING SUMMARY | | DEBIT | CREDIT |
|---|---|---|---|
| DEBITS: | Bank | 230 21 | |
| | Acc's Rec'l (Charge Sales) | | |
| | Cash Short and Over | | |
| CREDITS: | Accounts Receivable | | 131 25 |
| | Sales | | 94 20 |
| | Sales Tax Payable | | 4 71 |
| | Cash Short and Over | | 05 |
| BALANCING TOTALS | | 230 21 | 230 21 |

*'Received' Voucher*

–Voucher No. 431, to P. Barker, $131.25, paying Invoice No. 398.

*Cheque Copies*

–No. 681, to Government Treasurer, $?, paying the sales tax for the previous month.

–No. 682, to Proud Insurance Company, $278.50, regular monthly mortgage payment.

## June 16 Cash Register Summary

| ACCOUNTING SUMMARY | DEBIT | CREDIT |
|---|---|---|
| DEBITS: Bank | 75 60 | |
| Acc's Rec'l (Charge Sales) | 26 93 | |
| | | |
| Cash Short and Over | | |
| CREDITS: Accounts Receivable | | |
| Sales | | 97 65 |
| Sales Tax Payable | | 4 88 |
| Cash Short and Over | | |
| BALANCING TOTALS | 102 53 | 102 53 |

*'Charge' Voucher*
–Voucher No. 432, to P. Barker, for sale of merchandise; terms, Net 30; $25.65 plus 5 per cent sales tax.

*Cheque Copies*
–No. 683, to Central Supply, $39.38, for the cash purchase of supplies.
–No. 684, to Mainline Express, $65.85, for the cash payment of express charges, to be charged to Freight-in.

## June 17 Cash Register Summary

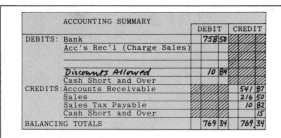

| ACCOUNTING SUMMARY | DEBIT | CREDIT |
|---|---|---|
| DEBITS: Bank | 758 50 | |
| Acc's Rec'l (Charge Sales) | | |
| | | |
| Discounts Allowed | 10 84 | |
| Cash Short and Over | | |
| CREDITS: Accounts Receivable | | 541 87 |
| Sales | | 216 50 |
| Sales Tax Payable | | 10 82 |
| Cash Short and Over | | 15 |
| BALANCING TOTALS | 769 34 | 769 34 |

*'Received' Voucher*
–Voucher No. 433, to C. Swinton, $531.03, paying Invoice No. 422 less 2 per cent cash discount. Although the payment was received after the discount period it was decided to allow the customer the discount.

*Purchase Invoices*
–From Equipment Repair and Supply, No. 40, $201.60, dated June 15; terms, Net 30; for truck repairs.
–From Kemp Haulage, No. 856, $211.05, dated June 16; terms, 1/10,n/30; topsoil and fertilizer to improve the condition of the soil on the business's property, to be charged to Soil Preparation & Maintenance.

*Cheque Copy*
–No. 685, to Kemp Haulage, $?, paying Invoice No. 822 less the cash discount.

## June 18 Cash Register Summary

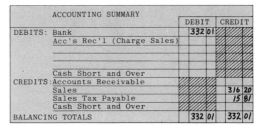

| ACCOUNTING SUMMARY | DEBIT | CREDIT |
|---|---|---|
| DEBITS: Bank | 321 51 | |
| Acc's Rec'l (Charge Sales) | 420 00 | |
| | | |
| Cash Short and Over | | |
| CREDITS: Accounts Receivable | | 52 50 |
| Sales | | 656 20 |
| Sales Tax Payable | | 32 81 |
| Cash Short and Over | | |
| BALANCING TOTALS | 741 51 | 741 51 |

*'Charge' Voucher*
–Voucher No. 434, to Varga Brothers, for the sale of merchandise; terms, 2/10,n/30; $400 plus 5 per cent sales tax; total $420.

*'Credit Note' Voucher*
–Voucher No. 435, to P. Pierce, to credit the customer's account for defective merchandise, $50 plus 5 per cent sales tax.

*Cheque Copy*
–No. 686, to The Business House, $15.75, for the cash purchase of items to be charged to Miscellaneous Expense.

## June 19 Cash Register Summary

| ACCOUNTING SUMMARY | DEBIT | CREDIT |
|---|---|---|
| DEBITS: Bank | 332 01 | |
| Acc's Rec'l (Charge Sales) | | |
| | | |
| Cash Short and Over | | |
| CREDITS: Accounts Receivable | | |
| Sales | | 316 20 |
| Sales Tax Payable | | 15 81 |
| Cash Short and Over | | |
| BALANCING TOTALS | 332 01 | 332 01 |

*Purchase Invoice*
–From Sylvester Concrete, No. 491, $1 236.25, dated June 17; terms, Net 30; patio stones for resale.

*Cheque Copies*
–No. 687, to Cash, $567.25, wages for the week.
–No. 688, to G. O. Emms, $450, owner's personal drawings.

## June 20 Cash Register Summary

| ACCOUNTING SUMMARY | DEBIT | CREDIT |
|---|---|---|
| DEBITS: Bank | 545 03 | |
| Acc's Rec'l (Charge Sales) | | |
| | | |
| Cash Short and Over | | |
| CREDITS: Accounts Receivable | | |
| Sales | | 519 05 |
| Sales Tax Payable | | 25 98 |
| Cash Short and Over | | |
| BALANCING TOTALS | 545 03 | 545 03 |

*Purchase Invoice*
–From Triangle Sod, No. 474, $558.08, dated June 19; terms, Net 30; sod for resale.

## June 21  *Cash Register Summary*

| ACCOUNTING SUMMARY | | DEBIT | CREDIT |
|---|---|---|---|
| DEBITS: | Bank | 784 71 | |
| | Acc's Rec'l (Charge Sales) | | |
| | | | |
| | Cash Short and Over | 9 40 | |
| CREDITS: | Accounts Receivable | | |
| | Sales | | 756 25 |
| | Sales Tax Payable | | 37 86 |
| | Cash Short and Over | | |
| BALANCING TOTALS | | 794 11 | 794 11 |

*Cheque Copies*

–No. 689, to Petty Cash, $?, reimbursement with respect to following summary:

| Petty Cash Summary | |
|---|---|
| June 21, 19- | |
| Soil Preparation & Maintenance | $26.15 |
| Sales | 35.00 |
| Sales Tax Payable | 1.75 |
| Miscellaneous Expense | 35.01 |

–No. 690, to Triangle Sod, $?, paying Invoice No. 374.

## June 22  *Cash Register Summary*

| ACCOUNTING SUMMARY | | DEBIT | CREDIT |
|---|---|---|---|
| DEBITS: | Bank | 432 78 | |
| | Acc's Rec'l (Charge Sales) | 2 159 50 | |
| | | | |
| | *Discounts Allowed* | 5 57 | |
| | Cash Short and Over | | |
| CREDITS: | Accounts Receivable | | 278 25 |
| | Sales | | 2 209 14 |
| | Sales Tax Payable | | 110 46 |
| | Cash Short and Over | | |
| BALANCING TOTALS | | 2 597 85 | 2 597 85 |

*'Charge' Voucher*

–Voucher No. 436, to C. Swinton, for the sale of merchandise; terms, 2/10,n/30; $2 056.67 plus 5 per cent sales tax; total $2 159.50.

*'Received' Voucher*

–Voucher No. 437, to F. Carson & Sons, $272.68, paying Invoice No. 429 less 2 per cent cash discount.

## June 23  *Cash Register Summary*

| ACCOUNTING SUMMARY | | DEBIT | CREDIT |
|---|---|---|---|
| DEBITS: | Bank | 136 77 | |
| | Acc's Rec'l (Charge Sales) | | |
| | | | |
| | Cash Short and Over | | |
| CREDITS: | Accounts Receivable | | 100 00 |
| | Sales | | 35 02 |
| | Sales Tax Payable | | 1 75 |
| | Cash Short and Over | | |
| BALANCING TOTALS | | 136 77 | 136 77 |

*'Received' Voucher*

–Voucher No. 438, to A. Renforth, $100, on account.

## June 24  *Cash Register Summary*

| ACCOUNTING SUMMARY | | DEBIT | CREDIT |
|---|---|---|---|
| DEBITS: | Bank | 107 00 | |
| | Acc's Rec'l (Charge Sales) | | |
| | | | |
| | Cash Short and Over | 10 | |
| CREDITS: | Accounts Receivable | | |
| | Sales | | 102 00 |
| | Sales Tax Payable | | 5 10 |
| | Cash Short and Over | | |
| BALANCING TOTALS | | 107 10 | 107 10 |

*Purchase Invoices*

–From Acorn Seed Company, No. 801, $813.75, dated June 23; terms, 2/15,n/30; merchandise for resale.

–From Clay Ceramic Co., No. 2016, $136.50, dated June 22; terms, Net 45; merchandise for resale.

## June 25  *Cash Register Summary*

| ACCOUNTING SUMMARY | | DEBIT | CREDIT |
|---|---|---|---|
| DEBITS: | Bank | 126 47 | |
| | Acc's Rec'l (Charge Sales) | 97 23 | |
| | | | |
| | Cash Short and Over | | |
| CREDITS: | Accounts Receivable | | |
| | Sales | | 213 05 |
| | Sales Tax Payable | | 10 65 |
| | Cash Short and Over | | |
| BALANCING TOTALS | | 223 70 | 223 70 |

*'Charge' Voucher*

–Voucher No. 439, to A. Renforth, for sale of merchandise; terms, Net 30; $92.60 plus 5 per cent sales tax; total $97.23.

*Cheque Copy*

–No. 691, to Poplar Finance Co., $182, regular finance payment on tractor.

## June 26  *Cash Register Summary*

| ACCOUNTING SUMMARY | | DEBIT | CREDIT |
|---|---|---|---|
| DEBITS: | Bank | 436 13 | |
| | Acc's Rec'l (Charge Sales) | | |
| | | | |
| | Cash Short and Over | | |
| CREDITS: | Accounts Receivable | | |
| | Sales | | 412 50 |
| | Sales Tax Payable | | 20 63 |
| | Cash Short and Over | | 3 00 |
| BALANCING TOTALS | | 436 13 | 436 13 |

*Cheque Copies*

–No. 692, to Acorn Seed Co., $?, paying Invoice No. 756 less 2 per cent cash discount.

–No. 693, to Cash, $505.60, wages for the week.

–No. 694, to G. O. Emms, $400, owner's personal drawings.

**June 27** *Cash Register Summary*

| ACCOUNTING SUMMARY | | DEBIT | CREDIT |
|---|---|---|---|
| DEBITS: | Bank | 1 436 29 | |
| | Acc's Rec'l (Charge Sales) | | |
| | Discounts Allowed | 8 40 | |
| | Cash Short and Over | | |
| CREDITS: | Accounts Receivable | | 491 40 |
| | Sales | | 907 90 |
| | Sales Tax Payable | | 45 39 |
| | Cash Short and Over | | |
| BALANCING TOTALS | | 1 444 69 | 1 444 69 |

*'Received' Vouchers*

–Voucher No. 440, to O. Harrison, $71.40; paying Invoice No. 425.

–Voucher No. 441, to Varga Brothers, $411.60; paying Invoice No. 434 less 2 per cent discount.

*Purchase Invoice*

–From Canada Products, No. B340, $330.75, dated June 25; terms, Net 30; for merchandise for resale.

**June 28** *Cash Register Summary*

| ACCOUNTING SUMMARY | | DEBIT | CREDIT |
|---|---|---|---|
| DEBITS: | Bank | 730 00 | |
| | Acc's Rec'l (Charge Sales) | | |
| | Cash Short and Over | | |
| CREDITS: | Accounts Receivable | | |
| | Sales | | 695 21 |
| | Sales Tax Payable | | 34 76 |
| | Cash Short and Over | | 03 |
| BALANCING TOTALS | | 730 00 | 730 00 |

**June 29** *Cash Register Summary*

| ACCOUNTING SUMMARY | | DEBIT | CREDIT |
|---|---|---|---|
| DEBITS: | Bank | 59 01 | |
| | Acc's Rec'l (Charge Sales) | 105 00 | |
| | Cash Short and Over | | |
| CREDITS: | Accounts Receivable | | |
| | Sales | | 156 20 |
| | Sales Tax Payable | | 7 81 |
| | Cash Short and Over | | |
| BALANCING TOTALS | | 164 01 | 164 01 |

*'Charge' Vouchers*

–Voucher No. 442, to J. Bowen, for sale of merchandise; terms, Net 30; $30 plus 5 per cent sales tax; total $31.50.

–Voucher No. 443, to P. Pierce, for sale of merchandise; terms, Net 30; $70 plus 5 per cent sales tax; total $73.50.

*Cheque Copies*

–No. 695, to Canada Products, $35.91, paying Invoice No. B249.

–No. 696, to First-Rate Repair Service, $233.10, cash payment to be charged to Equipment Expense.

*Credit Note Received*

–From Triangle Sod, No. 509, $183.75, with respect to inferior goods shipped on Invoice No. 474.

**June 30** *Cash Register Summary*

| ACCOUNTING SUMMARY | | DEBIT | CREDIT |
|---|---|---|---|
| DEBITS: | Bank | 88 20 | |
| | Acc's Rec'l (Charge Sales) | | |
| | Cash Short and Over | | |
| CREDITS: | Accounts Receivable | | |
| | Sales | | 84 00 |
| | Sales Tax Payable | | 4 20 |
| | Cash Short and Over | | |
| BALANCING TOTALS | | 88 20 | 88 20 |

**Balance the journals and post to the general ledger.**

**Balance the general ledger, the accounts receivable ledger, and the accounts payable ledger.**

**On July 3, the bank statement and related vouchers arrive from the bank. The bank statement appears below. Reconcile the bank account of Green Thumb Garden Center as of June 30.**

THE CENTRAL BANK

In
Account    Green Thumb Garden Center,
With      Concord Highway.

| Cheques and Debits | | | | Deposits | Date | Balance |
|---|---|---|---|---|---|---|
| | | Balance Brought Forward | | | May 31 | 3 406.15 |
| (#650) | 36.50 | (#660) | 6.15 | 516.31 | June 1 | 3 879.81 |
| (#659) | 95.14 | | | 160.05 | June 2 | 3 944.72 |
| (#661) | 144.06 | | | 551.98 | June 3 | 4 352.64 |
| | | | | 247.20 | June 4 | 4 599.84 |
| (#662) | 155.92 | (#663) | 96.55 | 100.38 | June 5 | 4 447.75 |
| (#665) | 14.85 | | | | June 5 | 4 432.90 |
| (#657) | 37.40 | | | 1 669.90 | June 8 | 6 065.40 |
| | | | | 847.44 | June 8 | 6 912.84 |
| | | | | 941.83 | June 8 | 7 854.67 |
| (#666) | 604.16 | | | 611.18 | June 9 | 7 861.69 |
| | | | | 117.60 | June 10 | 7 979.29 |
| (#667) | 440.00 | (#668) | 310.76 | 301.79 | June 11 | 7 530.32 |
| ( DM ) | 2 000.00 | (Loan Reduction) | | 137.66 | June 12 | 5 667.98 |
| (#658) | 42.15 | (#669) | 540.75 | 594.21 | June 15 | 5 679.29 |
| (#681) | 160.45 | | | 669.06 | June 15 | 6 187.90 |
| | | | | 1 112.95 | June 15 | 7 300.85 |
| | | | | 230.21 | June 16 | 7 531.06 |
| (#641) | 74.00 | (#670) | 51.97 | 75.60 | June 17 | 7 480.69 |
| (#671) | 58.80 | (#677) | 98.91 | 758.50 | June 18 | 8 081.48 |
| (#682) | 278.50 | (#685) | 228.69 | 321.51 | June 19 | 7 895.80 |
| (#655) | 116.26 | (#686) | 15.75 | 332.01 | June 19 | 8 095.80 |
| | | | | 545.03 | June 20 | 8 640.83 |
| | | | | 784.71 | June 22 | 9 425.54 |
| (#673) | 1 932.00 | (#684) | 65.85 | 432.78 | June 23 | 7 860.47 |
| (#675) | 25.20 | (#678) | 705.19 | 136.77 | June 24 | 7 266.85 |
| (#679) | 350.00 | (#687) | 567.25 | 107.00 | June 25 | 6 456.60 |
| (#676) | 77.96 | | | 126.47 | June 26 | 6 505.11 |
| (#654) | 29.12 | | | 436.13 | June 26 | 6 912.12 |
| | | | | 1 436.29 | June 26 | 8 348.41 |
| | | | | 730.00 | June 29 | 9 078.41 |
| (#688) | 450.00 | (#691) | 182.00 | 59.01 | June 30 | 8 505.42 |
| (#690) | 1 099.14 | | | | June 30 | 7 406.28 |
| ( DM ) | 101.10 | (Bank Interest) | | | June 30 | 7 305.18 |

*Bank statement of Green Thumb Garden Center.*

# 12 Basic Accounting Systems and Procedures

It is important that students of accounting have an appreciation of the various activities and procedures that occur in business offices. The purpose of this chapter is to help you acquire this appreciation by describing a number of office routines by means of flowcharts and supporting notes. You must keep in mind, of course, that the routines shown here are very simple ones illustrating basic ideas. The routines found in the real business world will be variations of those shown here.

## A Basic Purchasing Routine

The buying of materials, parts, and services is something that all businesses must do. In some

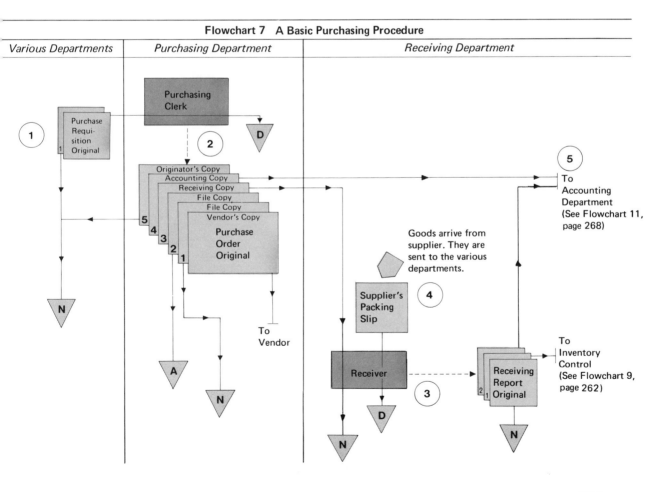

**Flowchart 7   A Basic Purchasing Procedure**

| Various Departments | Purchasing Department | Receiving Department |

businesses, such as the office of a public accountant for example, purchasing is a minor, relatively unimportant function. But in other businesses, such as manufacturing companies and large department stores, the purchasing function is a matter of considerable importance and requires special attention.

The flowchart on page 251 and the accompanying explanatory notes describe a basic purchasing routine.

## Notes to Flowchart #7

① In most businesses, there are key persons who have the authority to initiate the making of purchases. These are usually department heads or other persons of authority. Under their direction, the first step in the purchase routine is taken. This first step is the preparation of a business document called a **purchase requisition**. An illustration of a purchase requisition appears below.

A purchase requisition is a business form requesting the Purchasing Department to order certain goods or services according to the information and instructions recorded on the form. One copy of each purchase requisition is sent to the Purchasing Department.

| PURCHASE REQUISITION | | NO. 1354 | |
|---|---|---|---|
| DATE: *March 15, 19—* | | | |
| DEPARTMENT: *Production* | | | |
| APPROVED BY: *P. Hewitt* | | | |
| Quantity | Stock Number | Description | Suggested Price |
| *15* | *C-54* | *Belting – 6 m long – 12 cm wide* | *2.50 ea.* |

**SPECIAL INSTRUCTIONS**

| | |
|---|---|
| Order from: *Mercury Belting* | |
| Date required: *April 15* | |
| Ship via: *cheapest* | Purchase Order Number |
| Destination: *main plant* | |

② It is the responsibility of the Purchasing Department (under the direction of the purchasing agent) to be expert in matters related to purchasing. This department keeps available the latest information in respect to such things as sources of supply, new products, latest prices, quality suppliers, means of transportation, and so on.

When the Purchasing Department receives a purchase requisition it proceeds to order the goods. On the basis of past experience, the instructions of the requisitioner, and the information that it has available, a supplier is selected. The order is formally placed by means of a **purchase order** form which authorizes the supplier to send the goods and to bill the purchaser. The purchase order form, such as the one illustrated on page 253, specifies all information necessary to the purchase, including quantity, price, part number, description, delivery date, method of shipment, and so on.

Several copies of the purchase order form are prepared. The flowchart indicates the use to which each copy is put.

## JOHN F. GILL SUPPLY LTD.

Telephone 634-4186

"Gill" Quality Industrial Supplies
347 William Dr.  Winona
F4I 2T5

# PURCHASE ORDER  NO. 609

TO

Mercury Belting Company Limited,
4001 Monarch Drive,
Winnipeg, Manitoba.
T7R 4P3

| Quantity | Stock Number | Description | Unit Price |
|----------|--------------|-------------|------------|
| 15 | B 65 | Belting – 6m long – 12 cm wide | $2.50 |

| Date Ordered | Date Required | Shipping Instructions |
|--------------|---------------|------------------------|
| March 16, 19-- | April 15, 19-- | Via Express          FOB   Winona |

John F. Gill Supply Ltd.

Per *R. Larson*

Purchasing Agent

---

③ One copy of the purchase order is forwarded to the Receiving Department to assist the receiver in the checking of the goods when they arrive. The receiver will not accept goods for which he has not received a purchase order, nor will he accept goods that he can see are in poor condition.

After checking the goods against the supplier's packing slip and the purchase order, the receiver writes up a **receiving report.** This business form, illustrated on page 254, provides all the pertinent details with respect to the goods received.

④ A **packing slip** is enclosed with the goods by the supplier for the convenience of the buyer in identifying the goods. It is a business paper providing a description of the goods and showing the quantities but not the prices. In many instances, the packing slip is merely a carbon copy of the supplier's sales invoice with the prices blocked out.

⑤ One copy of the purchase order and one copy of the receiving report are sent to the Accounting Department where they are matched with the supplier's sales invoice as part of the accounts payable routine. The accounts payable routine is described by means of the flowchart and explanatory notes on page 268.

## RECEIVING REPORT    NO. 211

| Date Goods Received | | P.O. No. | |
|---|---|---|---|
| *April 12, 19—* | | *609* | |

**Goods Received From**

*Mercury Belting Co. Ltd.,*
*4001 Monarch Drive,*
*Winnipeg, Manitoba*
*T7R 4P3*

| Quantity | Stock Number | Description | Unit Price |
|---|---|---|---|
| *15* | *B65* | *6 m lengths of belting* *—12 cm wide* | *2.50* |

| No. Packages | Weight |
|---|---|
| *1* | *35#* |

| Del'd By | Via |
|---|---|
| *Nairn Transport* | *Truck Express* |

| Rec'd By | Checked By |
|---|---|
| *Sparks* | *Sparks* |

# Bookkeeping and Accounting Terms

**Purchase Requisition** A business form requesting the Purchasing Department to order certain goods or services in accordance with the information and instructions recorded on the form. Only key personnel, such as department heads, are usually authorized to issue purchase requisitions.

**Purchase Order** A business form initiated by the Purchasing Department authorizing the supplier to ship certain goods or to perform certain services as detailed on the purchase order, and to send a bill for these goods or services.

**Receiving Report** A business form initiated by the Receiving Department on which is recorded detailed information with respect to goods received by the business.

**Packing Slip** A business paper providing a description of the goods and of the quantities shipped but not of prices. In many instances, the packing slip is merely a carbon copy of the sales invoice with the prices and dollar amounts blocked out. The packing slip is enclosed with the goods by the supplier for the convenience of the purchaser's employees in identifying the goods.

# Review Questions

1. Name two specific local businesses in which purchasing is an important function. Explain the reasons for your selection.
2. Give the name of the business document that is used to initiate a purchase of goods or services.
3. What persons in a business are given the authority to initiate purchase requisitions? Give five specific examples from businesses in your community.
4. Only certain employees are allowed to initiate purchase requisitions. Why?
5. Where is the original purchase requisition filed? where is the copy filed?
6. Where does the Purchasing Department obtain the information necessary to prepare the purchase order form? List the key items of information shown on the purchase order.
7. Trace the path of each copy of the purchase order and state the purpose of each copy and of the original.
8. Where is the receiving copy of the purchase order eventually filed? To what use is it put before it is filed?
9. The 'accounting' copy of the purchase order is forwarded to the Accounting Department. Examine flowchart #11 on page 268 and state briefly the use to which this copy is put.
10. Why is the use of a purchase requisition an element of internal control? Explain briefly.
11. Explain the purpose of the supplier's packing slip.
12. When goods arrive at the Receiving Department what procedure is followed? Explain in your own words.
13. Why are two copies of the receiving report required (in addition to the original)?
14. Both the purchase order forms and the receiving report forms are numbered in sequence. Why do you think this is done?
15. By having a Receiving Department that is independent of the Purchasing Department a degree of internal control is exercised. Give an example of how a fraud could be committed more easily if the Purchasing Department had control over the receiving of goods.
16. A copy of the receiving report is forwarded to the inventory control section. Examine flowchart #9 on page 262 and state briefly the use to which it is put.

---

## Individual Projects

1. Write a brief report explaining the methods used by a Purchasing Department to keep up to date and expert in regard to the procurement of goods and services. The information for your report should be obtained from the manager of the Purchasing Department of a local business.
2. By visiting the Purchasing Department of a local business, find out what factors are taken into consideration when selecting a supplier. Write a brief report.
3. Ask the manager of the Purchasing Department of a local business to help you prepare a flowchart of the purchasing routine for his business.

## Class Project

Collect samples of purchase requisitions, purchase orders, and receiving reports from a number of businesses. Each member of the class should be responsible for writing a letter of request to the Purchasing Department of a large or medium-sized company.

Prepare a bulletin board display.

# A Basic Sales Procedure

A basic sales routine is described by means of the flowchart shown below and the accompanying explanatory notes. Again, it is necessary to explain that the system described is a basic one only and that in actual practice it would be adapted with variations to suit particular businesses.

## Notes to Flowchart #8

1. Orders from customers may be received in the following ways:
   a. By mail, either in the form of a letter or a purchase order.
   b. By telephone.
   c. By salesmen.

On a multiple-copy form known as the **sales order** (or **shipping order**), the order clerk types or writes the information necessary to the sale. The sales order form is not completely filled in at this time. Certain items of information are supplied by other employees later in the routine. An example of a sales order is shown on page 257.

2. Before any other step is taken, if the customer requires credit, the approval of the credit manager must be obtained. For regular customers of proven reliability credit approval is given easily. However, for new customers or for those whose reputation is poor, the credit manager has work to do. He must investigate the customer's credit history

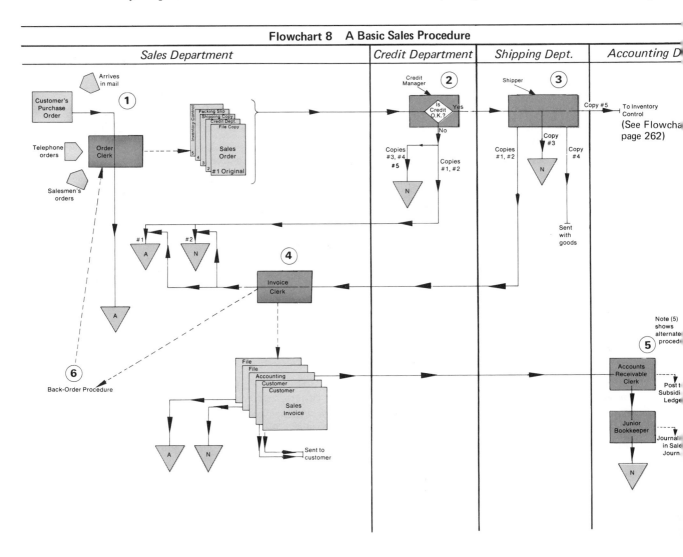

**Flowchart 8   A Basic Sales Procedure**

## THE QUICK CO.
500 Wood Street
Morgantown
W2C 8F4

## SALES ORDER
## NO. 1168

| Date | May 12, 19— | | Salesman | J. Green |
|---|---|---|---|---|
| Sold to | Irving Frank & Co. | | Ship To | Same |
| Address | 21 James Street | | Address | |
| City | Morgantown W2C 3X9 | | City | |
| P.O. No. | 69 | Terms Net 30 days | Date Req. | May 31 |

| Quantity | Stock No. | Description | Unit Price | Quantity Shipped | Quantity Back Ordered |
|---|---|---|---|---|---|
| 15 | H96 | Hammers | 2.49 | | |
| 24 | H16 | Saw Blades | .51 | | |
| 3 | D40 | 100m 1cm hose | 12.75 | | |
| | | | | | |
| | | | | | |
| | | | | | |
| | | | | | |
| | | | | | |
| | | | | | |

| Via | Our truck | F.O.B. | Frank & Co. | Shipper |
|---|---|---|---|---|
| Credit Approved | | | | |

and credit rating and will probably discuss the terms of sale with him. Before approving credit, he must be satisfied that no difficulty will be encountered in collecting from the customer.

Eventually, on the basis of his investigation, the credit manager will either grant or refuse credit to the customer. If he refuses credit, and the customer will not agree to pay cash, then that particular sales transaction is stopped and the copies of the sales order are filed. If he approves credit, the sales order is signed by him and forwarded intact to the Shipping Department.

③ For each sales order that it receives, the Shipping Department prepares the goods for shipment. This involves (a) obtaining the goods from the stockkeeper, (b) packaging and wrapping the goods if necessary, (c) addressing the goods, (d) completing the shipper's portion of the sales order form, separating the copies of the form and enclosing the packing slip copy, (e) loading the goods for delivery.

The relationship between the Shipping Department and the stockroom must of necessity be a close one and in many businesses, the stockroom comes under the jurisdiction of the Shipping Department. In most cases, the stockroom is located close to the shipping facilities. This is an efficient arrangement because it enables the shipping room employees to learn quickly what goods are in stock, and it also speeds up delivery.

The shipping room and the stockroom are two areas of a business that require strict accounting controls. This is especially true of businesses that deal in such goods as hardware items, radios, clothing, etc., that may be tempting to steal, easy to dispose of for cash, and difficult to identify. Flowchart #8 describes a system that has the following accounting controls:

a. No one except the stockkeeper and his assistants is allowed into the stockroom.

b. No goods may be released from the stockroom for shipment unless a proper sales order (copy #3 in this case) is presented.

**SALES ORDER NO. 1168**

| Date | May 12, 19— | Salesman | J. Green |
|---|---|---|---|
| Sold to | Irving Frank & Co. | Ship To | Same |
| Address | 21 James Street | Address | |
| City | Morgantown W2C 3X9 | City | |

| P.O. No. | 69 | Terms | Net 30 days | Date Req. | May 31 |
|---|---|---|---|---|---|

| Quantity | Stock No. | Description | Unit Price | Quantity Shipped | Quantity Back Ordered |
|---|---|---|---|---|---|
| 15 | H96 | Hammers | 2.49 | 15 | |
| 24 | H16 | Saw Blades | .51 | 20 | 4 |
| 3 | D40 | 100 m 1 cm hose | 12.75 | 3 | |

| Via | Our truck | F.O.B. | Frank & Co. | Shipper | |
|---|---|---|---|---|---|
| Credit Approved | R. B. Hamilton | | | | |

c. The sales order forms are serially numbered and kept under the control of the sales order clerk.

d. No goods may be shipped without there being a packing slip (copy #4) sent with them.

e. Copy #5 of the sales order is forwarded to the inventory control section where the quantities of all goods are kept track of and periodically checked against the actual goods on hand.

The shipper must complete the shipper's portion of the sales order form. He does this by (a) writing in the quantity shipped, (b) writing in the quantity back-ordered*, (c) signing his name in the appropriate place on the form, and (d) if the method of shipment is changed from that shown on the form, changing the information on the form. See the illustration above.

④ The primary function of the invoice clerk is to prepare the typewritten sales invoice (except where the system is automated). Once prepared, the copies of the sales invoice are separated and started on their special ways. All the information necessary for the preparation of the sales invoice, except the sales tax which must be calculated, is to be found on the sales order copies. Only goods actually shipped are invoiced. An example of a completed sales invoice appears on page 259.

⑤ The flowchart illustrates a simple and common method of handling the accounting entries for sales invoices. With this method, each invoice is used first as the source of an entry to the accounts receivable ledger and second as the source of an entry in the sales journal. However, this is not the only method

---

* If the business is short of a particular item and is unable to fill the customer's order for that item entirely, the shipper ships as many of the item as he has on hand. He records this under 'Quantity Shipped'. At the same time, he finds out if the short item is in the process of being re-stocked. If the answer is 'yes', he records the quantity that was short in the section headed 'Back-Ordered'. This action initiates a new order for the quantity that was short-shipped (see Note 6).

```
THE QUICK CO.                          SALES INVOICE
        500 Wood Street                          NO. 510
        Morgantown
        W2C 8F4


Sold to: Irving Frank & Co.              Date:    May 15, 19--
         21 James Street
         Morgantown                      P.O. No.: 69
         W2C 3X9
                                         Terms:   Net 30 days

Shipped by          Via                F.O.B.
         Truck              Our Truck           Frank & Co.

Quantity          Description        Unit Price      Amount

   15     H 96    Hammers             $2.49        $37.35

   20     H 16    Saw Blades            .51         10.20

    3     G 40    100 m   1cm  hose   12.75         38.25

                                                   $85.80

                  5 Per Cent Sales Tax              4.29

                                      Total        $90.09
```

available to the accountant. Two common alternatives are described below:

*Alternative 1*

a. Make the postings to the accounts receivable ledger from the individual invoice copies as shown in the flowchart.

b. Do not journalize each individual invoice in the sales journal as shown in the flowchart. Instead, accumulate the sales invoices for each month in a binder. At the end of each month, using an adding machine, summarize these sales invoices to find the cumulative accounting entry for the month. Journalize this accounting entry in the general journal. With this system, the accounting entry will be the same as when a sales journal is used, but there will be no actual sales journal. The sales journal for any month is replaced by a binder containing all the sales invoices for that month.

*Alternative 2*

a. Request that two copies of the sales invoices be sent to the Accounting Department.

b. Do not have the conventional type of subsidiary ledger for accounts receivable (i.e., account pages or account cards). Instead, let the sales invoice copies (one of the two copies received) form the accounts receivable ledger. As the sales invoice copies are received they are placed in an 'Unpaid Invoices' file. As the invoices are paid they are taken out of the 'Unpaid Invoices' file and are placed in a 'Paid Invoices' file. When an invoice is partially paid the amount of the partial payment is noted on the invoice copy which remains in the 'unpaid' file until it is fully paid. The invoices remaining in the 'unpaid' file represent the accounts receivable of the business.

Although theoretically simple, this system requires strong accounting controls. Only authorized personnel may have access to the files. The difficulty lies in the danger of invoice copies being removed from the files by non-authorized persons and of the copies not being returned or of their being placed back in a wrong file.

c. The second invoice copy is used by the junior accountant as the source document for the journal entries. Either of the two methods shown above may be selected; that is, the method shown on the flowchart or the method described in alternative 1.

(6) *Back-Order Procedure*

You have already seen that when an order can be only partially filled the goods that are available are shipped and billed (i.e., an invoice is issued to the customer). This allows the customer to have immediately those goods that are available.

When the invoice clerk receives sales orders showing that certain items have been back-ordered, in addition to performing the normal routine, he or she also prepares a new sales order for the goods that are back-ordered. In this respect, the invoice clerk works under the control and supervision of the order clerk.

These new sales orders are processed in the usual manner except that when they arrive at the Shipping Department they will be set aside awaiting the arrival of the merchandise to be shipped.

# Bookkeeping and Accounting Terms

**Shipping Order** A business form originated by the Order Department (a division of the Sales Department) on which is recorded detailed information in respect to goods or services requested for purchase by customers. Also known as **sales order**.

# Review Questions

1. Would all businesses receive orders from customers in the three ways indicated on the flowchart; i.e., by mail, by telephone, and by salesmen? Explain.
2. With what business form is the sales routine started? List the key pieces of information shown on this form.
3. Why is it important that a customer's credit be approved by the Credit Department?
4. In your opinion why do the sales orders go first to the Credit Department?
5. If credit is approved, what happens next to the sales order set?
6. If credit is not granted on an order, what happens to copy #1 and copy #2 of the sales order? Explain why this procedure is followed.
7. If a customer's credit is not good, what alternatives does the credit manager have?
8. Explain the function of the Shipping Department.
9. Describe the steps necessary to get goods ready for shipment.
10. Give another name for copy #4 of the sales order. What is its purpose?
11. Explain why the stockroom is usually close to the shipping room.
12. Why are strict controls necessary in the shipping room and the stockroom?
13. Name the five steps of internal control in the stockroom. Discuss the merits of each step.
14. Explain back-ordering.
15. How does the invoice clerk obtain the information necessary to prepare the sales invoices?
16. Why is there both a numerical and an alphabetical file of sales order copies?
17. How does the invoice clerk know when to follow the back-order procedure?

18. What key information is shown on the sales invoice?
19. What is the source document for debit entries to the accounts receivable ledger?
20. From the flowchart, give an example of how an internal control is effected by a separation of duties; that is, by not allowing one department to have complete control.
21. Where would you go to find a copy of a sales invoice if the only information you had was its number?
22. Copy # 5 of the sales order is forwarded to the inventory control section. Examine flowchart #9 on page 262 and then state briefly the use to which this copy is put.

## Individual Projects

1. Write a brief report explaining the methods used by a credit department to find out about the credit reputation of its customers and potential customers. The information for this report is best obtained by contacting directly the credit manager of a local business.

2. Ask the office manager of a local business to assist you in preparing a flowchart of the sales routine for his business.

## Class Project

Collect samples of sales orders and sales invoices from a number of businesses. Display these forms on the bulletin board.

# Inventory Control for a Trading Company (Manual Perpetual Inventory System)

For many businesses, the keeping of accurate and up-to-date information about inventories is an essential requirement. Manufacturers must avoid stoppages in production due to lack of parts or materials; wholesalers must maintain adequate supplies of merchandise to meet the needs of their customers. Therefore, these and other businesses must keep on hand certain minimum quantities of all inventory items. And to be able to do this they must know what quantities they have on hand.

A very common way of keeping track of the many inventory items is by means of a card record called a **perpetual inventory** file. A flowchart describing a perpetual inventory system (manual method) is shown at the top of page 262. Along with its accompanying notes it describes a typical manual system.

## Notes to Flowchart #9

① A perpetual inventory file is made up of a number of cards such as the one shown on page 262. One card is included for each individual item kept in stock.

In the top portion of an inventory card (stock card), the following information is recorded:

a. The stock number. In a handwritten system, the stock number is used for accurate and easy reference. However, in modern automated systems, the stock number is of far greater importance. Some manual systems include a stock number only because they expect to make a change to an automated system in the near future, and by already having the stock numbers in use the transition from a manual to an automated system may be made more easily.

b. A general description of the merchandise.

c. The location of the merchandise in the warehouse.

d. The maximum and minimum quantities to be kept in stock. The purpose of setting a maximum figure is to avoid having any more funds tied up in inventory than is necessary. The purpose of setting a minimum figure is to avoid running short of any item and therefore being unable to supply a customer.

These maximum and minimum quantities are decided upon by management on the basis of factors such as (1) sales statistics, (2) seasonal nature of the in-

*Stockkeeping Department*

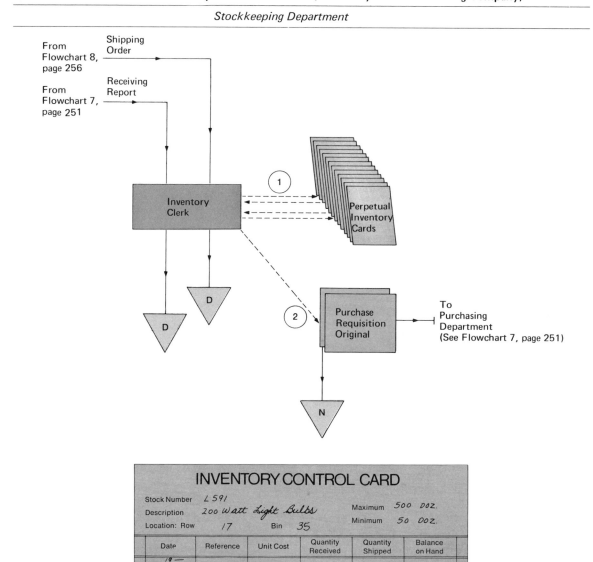

INVENTORY CONTROL CARD

Stock Number    *L 591*
Description    *200 Watt Light Bulbs*          Maximum    *500 DOZ.*
Location: Row    *17*          Bin    *35*          Minimum    *50 DOZ.*

| Date | Reference | Unit Cost | Quantity Received | Quantity Shipped | Balance on Hand |
|------|-----------|-----------|-------------------|------------------|-----------------|
| *19 —* | | | | | |
| *Nov. 5* | *Balance forward* | | | | *216* |
| *11* | *S.O. 436* | | | *100* | *116* |
| *14* | *S.O. 501* | | | *40* | *76* |
| *19* | *S.O. 530* | | | *35* | *41* |
| *21* | *S.O. 539* | | | *20* | *21* |
| *22* | *R.R. 1074* | *41¢* | *450* | | *471* |
| *25* | *S.O. 561* | | | *75* | *396* |
| | | | | | |
| | | | | | |
| | | | | | |
| | | | | | |
| | | | | | |
| | | | | | |

ventory item, (3) nearness to a source of supply, and (4) expected changes in the market. From time to time they are reviewed and changed if necessary.

For each inventory item, there is an inventory card. The main body of the card is used to keep track of the quantity of the item in stock. Changes in the quantities result from goods being shipped out to customers or being received in from suppliers or returned from customers. The inventory clerk learns of these transactions by means of the shipping orders (sales orders) and the receiving reports that come to him. Each shipping order represents a shipment of goods out of the plant and must be recorded on the appropriate card as a decrease. Each receiving report represents a receipt of goods into the plant and must be recorded on the appropriate card as an increase.

Observe that each time a new supply of an item is purchased the unit cost is recorded on the inventory card as well as the quantity. This unit cost is used at the end of the fiscal period when the merchandise inventory is evaluated for the financial statements.

② In addition to keeping the perpetual inventory cards up to date, the inventory clerk is responsible for initiating the purchase requisition required to order the additional goods that may be necessary. Each time a

shipment is recorded he must compare the 'balance on hand' figure with the 'minimum' figure shown at the top of the card. If the balance on hand is equal to or lower than the minimum suggested, the inventory clerk must write up a purchase requisition ordering a sufficient quantity of the goods to bring the balance on hand up to the suggested maximum figure.

## Taking Inventory—Adjusting Perpetual Inventory

The file of inventory control cards theoretically agrees with the actual inventory; that is, the count of all the merchandise actually on hand in the stockroom. But, as time passes, it is found that the theoretical figures from the cards do not always agree with the count of goods actually on hand. These discrepancies are caused by unreported loss, theft, and damage and removal of the physical goods.

Periodically (one or more times a year) a physical inventory must be taken. That is, the goods on hand must be actually counted and listed. In this way the discrepancies become known and the inventory control cards are adjusted by means of an entry on the cards which brings their balance on hand figures into agreement with the figures on the count sheets.

## Bookkeeping and Accounting Terms

**Perpetual Inventory** An inventory system in which a detailed record for each inventory item is kept showing the quantity of the item on hand and the unit cost of the item.

## Review Questions

1. Name three businesses for which inventory control is essential. Give reasons for your choices.
2. Name three businesses for which inventory control is not essential. Give reasons for

your choices.
3. A business should carry as small an inventory as it effectively can. Explain the disadvantage of carrying too much inventory.
4. What information is shown on a perpetual

inventory card?

5. Explain the use and importance of stock numbers.

6. Name the two source documents for entries to the perpetual inventory.

7. The inventory clerk has two main responsibilities. Describe them briefly.

8. How does the inventory clerk know when it is necessary to order an inventory item?

9. How does the inventory clerk arrive at the quantity of an item to be ordered?

10. Invariably, for some of the inventory items, the physical quantity actually on hand will disagree with the quantity shown on the inventory card. Explain the factors that could cause this.

11. Periodically, the perpetual inventory cards are all made correct. How is this accomplished?

12. Explain how the maximum and the minimum figures are arrived at.

13. Explain the purpose of recording the unit cost on the inventory cards.

14. Trace the shipping order copy and the receiving report copy back to their sources on flowchart #7 and flowchart #8. State the copy number of each that comes to the stockkeeping section.

15. Explain the basic meaning of the dotted lines on the flowchart.

16. Are the 'balances' on the inventory cards always accurate? Explain.

## Individual Project

Arrange to visit a company that has a perpetual inventory of parts and materials to be used by the business (for example, a manufacturing company). Find out how this type of perpetual inventory differs from the one described in this text for a trading company. Write a brief report.

## Class Project

Arrange to visit a business to view the shipping and stockroom facilities. Write a brief report. In your report, explain the accounting controls that are used.

# Inventory Control for a Trading Company (Automated System Using Punched Cards)

In larger businesses where the number of transactions is very high and where more and faster information is demanded, inventories are usually maintained by means of automated equipment such as a computer. The flowchart on page 265 together with its accompanying notes describes such a system.

## Notes to Flowchart #10

① As in the manual method, the shipping orders and the receiving reports are the source documents representing changes in the inventory. In an automated system, these source documents are forwarded to a keypunch operator in the Data Processing Department. For each different inventory item

on each source document the keypunch operator prepares a punched card that contains the essential details of the transaction in coded form (using combinations of punched holes). This card is known as the 'transaction' card. All of the transaction cards together are known as the **transaction file**. A transaction card is shown on page 265. Examine it to see the type of data it contains.

② Each week (or each day in some businesses) the entire inventory records are updated by the computer (or other automated equipment) and produced in printed and punched card form. One card is produced for each inventory item. All of the inventory cards together are known as a **master file**. The most recent master file is called the new master file; the next to most recent one is called the old master file. An example of an inventory master file card is shown at the top of page 266. Examine the column headings on this card.

③ The old master file and the inventory transaction file are fed into the computer, which is programmed to update the inventory. Among those things produced will be a new master file of punched cards and an inventory status report. A sample page of a computer-produced inventory status report is shown on page 266.

④ The inventory status report is designed for easy analysis by the stockkeeper. In analysing the report, he looks in particular to see which items are in short supply and therefore need to be restocked. For any item which shows a balance on hand lower than the suggested minimum, he will write up a purchase requisition to initiate the ordering of additional stock.

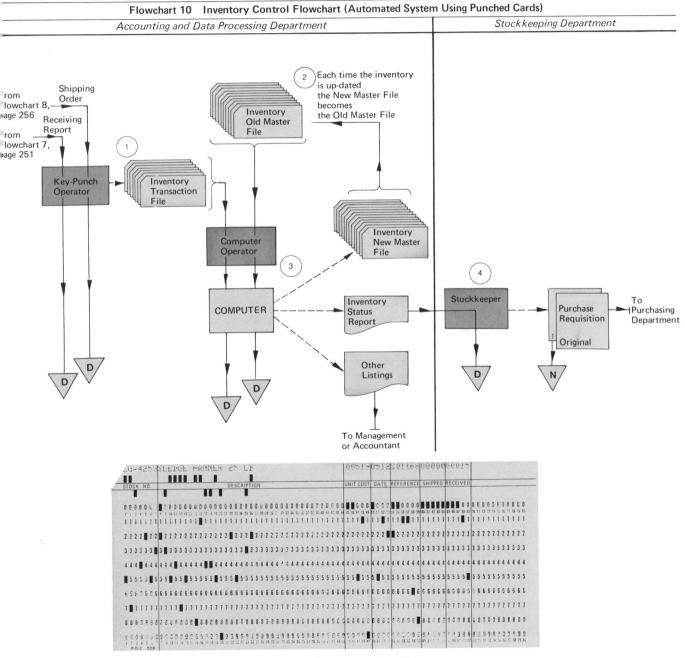

*Inventory card – transaction file.*

*Inventory card – master file.*

| STOCK NUMBER | DESCRIPTION | OLD BALANCE | QUANTITY RECEIVED | QUANTITY SHIPPED | NEW BALANCE | MAXIMUM | MINIMUM |
|---|---|---|---|---|---|---|---|
| | INVENTORY STATUS REPORT | | | | | | |
| EH-3703 | BALL HAMMER 8 OZ | 74 | 0 | 33 | 41 | 100 | 40 |
| EH-3704 | BALL HAMMER 16 OZ | 52 | 50 | 26 | 76 | 100 | 25 |
| EH-3705 | BALL HAMMER 24 OZ | 24 | 170 | 19 | 175 | 200 | 25 |
| EH-3707 | BALL HAMMER 32 OZ | 36 | 150 | 170 | 16 | 200 | 25 |
| EH-3709 | BALL HAMMER 40 OZ | 47 | 0 | 6 | 41 | 200 | 25 |
| EG-4119 | CLAW HAMMER 13 OZ | 12 | 35 | 1 | 46 | 50 | 15 |
| EG-4126 | CLAW HAMMER 16 OZ | 74 | 0 | 32 | 42 | 200 | 50 |
| EG-4131 | CLAW HAMMER 16 OZ (STANLEY) | 156 | 0 | 53 | 103 | 300 | 100 |
| EG-4132 | CLAW HAMMER 16 OZ (NEOPHRENE HANDLE) | 13 | 0 | 5 | 8 | 25 | 10 |
| EG-4135 | CLAW HAMMER 16 OZ (LEATHER HANDLE) | 90 | 200 | 5 | 285 | 300 | 100 |
| EG-4108 | TACK HAMMER 8 OZ | 54 | 95 | 3 | 146 | 150 | 50 |
| EH-3725 | BRICK HAMMER | 12 | 60 | 2 | 70 | 75 | 25 |
| BE-5263 | RUBBER MALLET 14 OZ | 32 | 0 | 12 | 20 | 100 | 25 |
| BE-5266 | RUBBER MALLET 28 OZ | 27 | 70 | 13 | 84 | 100 | 25 |
| EH-3753 | SLEDGE HAMMER 6 LB | 40 | 0 | 20 | 20 | 100 | 25 |
| EH-3755 | SLEDGE HAMMER 8 LB | 11 | 90 | 3 | 98 | 100 | 25 |
| EH-3757 | SLEDGE HAMMER 10 LB | 5 | 45 | 3 | 47 | 50 | 10 |
| EG-3203 | HAND DRILL 1/4 INCH | 37 | 0 | 13 | 24 | 100 | 25 |
| EG-3206 | HAND DRILL 1/4 INCH HEAVY DUTY | 46 | 0 | 15 | 31 | 100 | 25 |
| EG-3224 | AUTOMATIC PUSH DRILL (8 BITS) | 56 | 0 | 27 | 29 | 100 | 25 |

*(Courtesy of IBM Canada Ltd.)*

# Review Questions

1. What types of businesses require automated inventory control systems?
2. Name the source document for an increase in inventory.
3. Name the source document for a decrease in inventory.
4. Explain what happens to the two source documents.
5. What does a keypunch operator do?
6. What is a transaction card?
7. How many transaction cards are prepared from the information on one sales order?
8. What is a transaction file?
9. Explain the difference between the new master file and the old master file.
10. What is the 'input' to the computer?
11. What is the 'output' of the computer?
12. Who receives the inventory status report?

For what purpose does he use it?

13. List the key information that appears on the inventory status report.
14. "The master file is updated." Explain.
15. How often is a master file updated?
16. How does the new master file become the old master file?
17. What is the purpose of the purchase requisition?
18. Explain the basic difference between the

automated and the manual inventory systems, apart from their method of preparation.

19. In the automated inventory system, in what form does the computer accept data?
20. In the manual inventory system, information flows directly from the source documents to the inventory file. Explain how the automated system is different in this regard.

## Individual Project

Visit a computer installation to view an inventory updating procedure. Observe both the differences and the similarities between the system you observe and the one described in this chapter. Summarize your findings.

# Basic Procedure for Accounts Payable and Cheque Preparation

Flowchart #11 on page 268 illustrates a basic procedure for the processing of purchase invoices and for the preparation of the cheques to pay them. Study this flowchart and the accompanying notes carefully.

## Notes to Flowchart #11

①  The sales invoice is a business form prepared by the seller of goods or services whenever he makes a sale on account. Two copies of the sales invoice are sent to the purchaser.

In the Accounting Department of the purchaser the suppliers' sales invoices are referred to as 'purchase invoices' in order to distinguish them from the business's own sales invoices.

②  The processing of a purchase invoice begins at the desk of a junior clerk. As you can see from the flowchart, this clerk receives a copy of the purchase order and a copy of the purchase invoice. Among this clerk's various duties are the following:

a. To mark (using a rubber stamp and ink pad) the purchase invoice with an **author-**

**izations stamp** such as the one shown below.

| AUTHORIZATIONS | |
| --- | --- |
| AGREED WITH PURCHASE ORDER | *PK* |
| EXTENSIONS AND ADDITIONS | *PK* |
| GOODS RECEIVED | *Q.* |
| ACCOUNTS TO BE CHARGED | 51 |
| APPROVED FOR PAYMENT | M.T. |

b. To check the extensions (quantity times price) and the additions on the purchase invoice.
c. To compare the purchase order with the purchase invoice to ensure that the details (quantities, prices, part numbers, etc.) are in agreement.

If everything is in order the clerk initials the purchase invoice in the appropriate sections of the 'Authorizations' stamp. The purchase invoice and the purchase order copy are clipped together and forwarded to another clerk for further processing. Purchase invoices that are not correct in all respects are separated from the others and given to a senior person for investigation and clarification.

③  All purchase invoice-purchase order matched sets arrive at the desk of a second junior

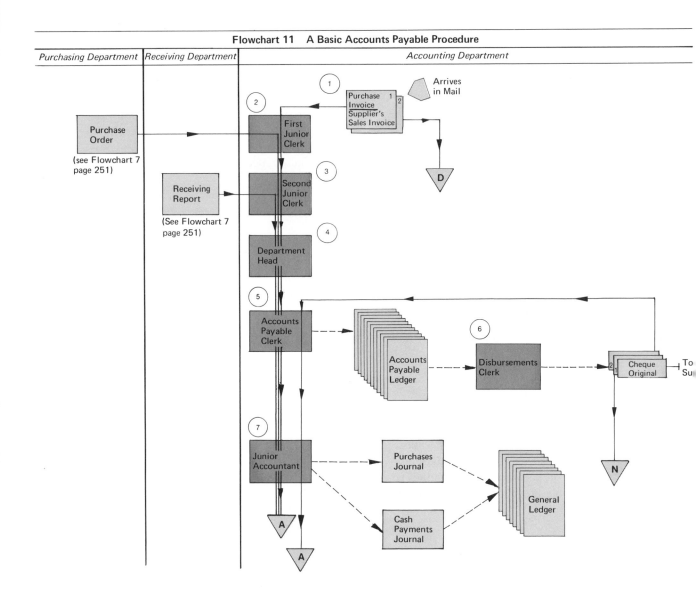

clerk. This clerk also receives the copies of all receiving reports. It is the responsibility of this clerk to match the receiving reports with the purchase invoice-purchase order combinations. Matched documents are attached together, initialed by the clerk in the appropriate section of the 'Authorizations' stamp, and forwarded for additional processing. Unmatched forms stay at the desk of the clerk awaiting a match. After a reasonable period of time, those that do not match are given to a senior person for special attention.

④ The final step in the verification of the pur-

chase documents is the scrutiny and approval by the department head. He initials the matched set of purchase documents if he is satisfied that all aspects of the accounting routine have been carried out properly. His initials indicate that the purchase invoice is approved for payment.

⑤ The accounts payable clerk posts directly from the source documents to the individual accounts in the accounts payable ledger. The purchase invoice matched sets are posted as credits; the cheque copies, if they affect the customers' accounts, are posted as debits. The posting process may be done manually or by means of a posting machine.

⑥ The disbursements clerk is responsible for preparing all cheques as required and for having them mailed to the intended recipients. Most cheques issued are for goods and services received from suppliers, and consequently the information for the preparation of these cheques comes from the accounts payable ledger. Periodically, the clerk examines the accounts in the ledger and decides who should be paid and how much they should receive. The cheques are prepared, approved, and signed by company officials, and sent on their way.

The information for every cheque is not obtained from the accounts payable ledger.

Many cheques are issued merely on the instructions of the disbursement clerk who is completely familiar with all business activities that require the issuing of cheques. For example, he knows of all contracts, loan agreements, instalment purchases, and so on, entered into by the business. He will originate some cheques merely upon the receipt of a written memorandum from a senior company officer.

⑦ The purchase invoice matched sets are the source documents for the accounting entries to the purchases journal. The cheque copies are the source documents for the accounting entries to the cash payments journal.

# Review Questions

1. Explain the difference between a sales invoice and a purchase invoice.
2. Briefly describe the duties of the first junior clerk.
3. Explain the purpose of the authorizations stamp.
4. Explain the meaning of the term 'matching'.
5. Which documents match? Explain.
6. Briefly describe the duties of the second junior clerk.
7. Will there be a receiving report to match every purchase invoice? Explain.
8. When all of the authorizations are completed, what is the status of the purchase invoice?
9. Name the source document for debit entries to the accounts payable ledger.
10. Name the source document for entries in the purchases journal.
11. Name the source document for credit entries to the accounts payable ledger.
12. Name the source document for entries to

the cash payments journal.
13. Briefly explain the duties of the disbursements clerk.
14. Do you think that the work of the disbursements clerk is important? Explain.
15. How does the disbursements clerk know what cheques should be issued?
16. From the flowchart, give an example of internal control being effected by not allowing persons who prepare accounting records to also handle or control assets.
17. From the flowchart, give an example of internal control being effected by having the work of one person agree with the work of another person whose work is created independently.
18. In flowchart #11 who do you think is the most important employee in regard to internal control? Explain briefly.
19. In flowchart #11 do you think that internal control is strong or weak? Explain briefly.

## Individual Project

Write a report describing the aspects of internal control that are present in the accounts payable routine.

*Accounting Department*

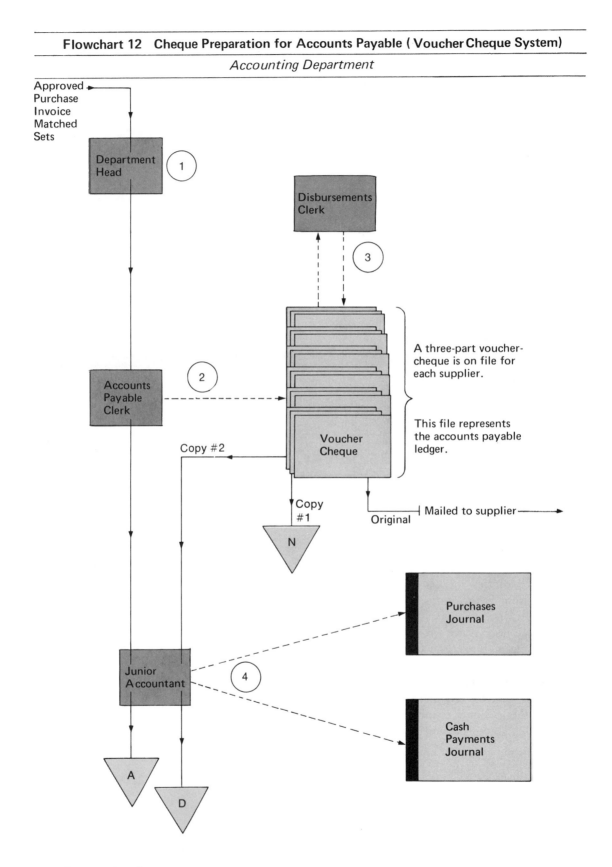

Approved
Purchase
Invoice
Matched
Sets

Department
Head ①

Disbursements
Clerk

③

A three-part voucher-
cheque is on file for
each supplier.

Accounts
Payable
Clerk ②

This file represents
the accounts payable
ledger.

Copy #2

Voucher
Cheque

Copy
#1

N

Original   Mailed to supplier ⟶

Purchases
Journal

Junior
Accountant ④

Cash
Payments
Journal

A

D

# Cheque Preparation for Accounts Payable (Voucher Cheque System)

An alternate method of preparing cheques is described by means of the flowchart on page 270 and the accompanying explanatory notes.

## Notes to Flowchart #12

① As in the previous system, the purchase invoice matched sets undergo a series of verifying steps. The final step is the authorization by the department head.

② The heart of this system is the voucher cheque, shown below.

In addition to serving as the cheque with which payment is made to the supplier, the voucher cheque also serves as a form of accounts payable account. There is kept on file a voucher cheque for each supplier. The supplier's name is the first item of information that is placed on the cheque. The file of cheques represents the accounts payable ledger. As approved purchase invoices (or credit notes representing adjustments to previous purchase invoices) are received by the accounts payable clerk, they are recorded in the voucher section of the appropriate suppliers' cheques.

The voucher section of the cheque is designed for the accumulation of several purchase invoices. The cheque shown below has four entries on it, three charges and one credit. Although the balance owing to the supplier is not shown, it can be found readily by means of an adding machine.

③ The disbursements clerk has the responsibility of authorizing payments to be made to suppliers. To carry out this responsibility it is necessary for him to be thoroughly familiar with the file of voucher cheques, the suppliers' terms of sale, and the due dates and the discount dates of the invoices.

When he decides that a certain supplier should be paid, he instructs a subordinate clerk to total the purchase invoices listed on the voucher section of the cheque (Net Amount column) and to complete the cheque section of the form. The cheque is then

*Partially completed voucher cheque.*

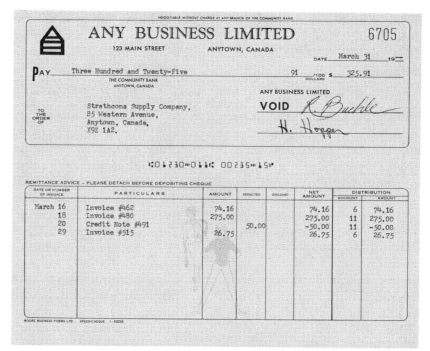

The voucher cheque (top portion):

**ANY BUSINESS LIMITED** — 6705

123 MAIN STREET  ANYTOWN, CANADA

DATE March 31  19—

PAY Three Hundred and Twenty-Five  91 /100 $ 325.91

THE COMMUNITY BANK
ANYTOWN, CANADA

ANY BUSINESS LIMITED

TO THE ORDER OF  Strathcona Supply Company,
85 Western Avenue,
Anytown, Canada,
X9Z 1A2.

VOID

REMITTANCE ADVICE – PLEASE DETACH BEFORE DEPOSITING CHEQUE

| DATE OR NUMBER OF INVOICE | PARTICULARS | AMOUNT | DEDUCTED | DISCOUNT | NET AMOUNT | DISTRIBUTION ACCOUNT | DISTRIBUTION AMOUNT |
|---|---|---|---|---|---|---|---|
| March 16 | Invoice #462 | 74.16 | | | 74.16 | 6 | 74.16 |
| 18 | Invoice #480 | 275.00 | | | 275.00 | 11 | 275.00 |
| 20 | Credit Note #491 | | 50.00 | | -50.00 | 11 | -50.00 |
| 29 | Invoice #515 | 26.75 | | | 26.75 | 6 | 26.75 |

*Completed voucher cheque (courtesy of Moore Business Forms Ltd.).*

signed by an officer of the company and the three parts are sent on their respective ways. Before being mailed, the completed cheque appears as shown above.

(4) The junior accountant journalizes from the purchase invoices to the purchases journal and from the cheque copies to the cash payments journal.

With this particular system, it is not necessary to use a cash payments journal although one may choose to do so. Instead, the following alternate procedure may be used:

a. During each month, accumulate in a binder all the *accounting* copies of the voucher cheques.

b. At the end of each month, summarize these voucher cheque copies to determine the required accounting entry for the month. To do this it is necessary to go through the vouchers several times using an adding machine to accumulate the total charges to each of the various accounts listed in the section of the cheque headed 'Distribution'. The credit to Bank is obtained by totaling all of the cheques for the period. The accounting entry for the month will be the same as if a cash payments journal had been used. The accounting entry is journalized in the general journal with this system.

## Review Questions

1. The voucher cheque has two major parts. Explain what they are.
2. Explain briefly how the voucher cheque is used to accumulate the liability to a supplier.
3. Explain how the voucher cheque is used to pay a debt.
4. Explain the work of the disbursements clerk.
5. Briefly explain the alternate procedure to using a cash payments journal. What are the advantages and the disadvantages?
6. Explain the difference between this system

and the previous one in respect to: (i) cheque copy #2; (ii) the make-up of the accounts payable ledger.

7. Explain the purpose of having an outside audit performed – for any system.

## Class Project

Obtain samples and literature from a manufacturer of voucher cheques. Prepare a bulletin board display.

# Cases

### Case 1

J. Richards does not use a sales journal in his business, and posts from the sales invoices directly to the customers' accounts in the accounts receivable ledger.

Describe how this system would operate by answering the following questions:

1. How many copies of the sales invoices are needed and how would they be filed?
2. How would you show that the sales invoices have been posted to the accounts receivable ledger?
3. What would be the posting reference in the customers' accounts?
4. How would you determine the total sales for the month? What entry would you make in the books?
5. What are the advantages, if any, of this system over that of keeping a sales journal?

### Case 2

Because of the volume of business transactions affecting the cash accounts, more attention is usually given to internal control of cash than to any other area.

1. Select a business concern (drugstore, dentist, doctor, department store, supermarket, restaurant, bank, service station, dry cleaners, etc.) and inquire about the internal control methods used for cash in regard to cash receipts and cash disbursements.
2. Submit a report outlining the controls employed, and explaining why these controls are used.
3. Prepare a list of questions on cash control to assist you in your report; for example, "Are all disbursements made by prenumbered cheques?"

### Case 3

You have been hired as an accounting clerk by a local wholesaler engaged in a novelties line.

To date, you find that the owner has always kept track of his inventory by taking a weekly walk down the rows in his store and recording the items he considers are low in quantity or out of stock and which should be replenished.

He then proceeds to order enough goods to bring his inventory up to what he considers a normal operating level.

1. What are the main disadvantages of this method of inventory control?
2. Describe a method of inventory control that would overcome these disadvantages.

### Case 4

Don Jonescu operates a small variety store and hires you on a part-time basis. For an extra 50 cents an hour, you offer to keep formal accounting records for him.

He replies that since he is in close contact with the business he has no need for records. He relies on the bank records, invoices issued and received, and an annual physical inventory. He feels that this is sufficient. What would you say to Mr. Jonescu to convince him that he should have a more formal accounting system?

## Case 5
In most large businesses the mail clerk opens the mail and lists cash remittances in triplicate, giving the names and amounts. He has no access to the accounting records.
1. Are there any circumstances under which he could take money without being detected?
2. If so, how would you prevent it?

## Case 6
J. Pope is a shipping clerk for the H. S. Davidson Company. It is his duty to ship goods to customers as called for on the sales orders. On several occasions he has packaged goods and mailed them to a friend to be sold later. What controls should be set up to prevent Pope from carrying out his plans to steal from the company?

## Case 7
It is the practice of A. Andrews to take physical inventory only at the end of each fiscal year. It is becoming all too common in his business to be out of items in demand. Loss of income results. What recommendations would you suggest to management to make sure sufficient stock is always on hand?

## Case 8
Fine Oil Co. operates a 24-hour gas station. It has a mechanic shop, four gas pumps, and a merchandise area. The gross sales are approximately $25 000 a month. Lately, the monthly net income has been decreasing to 1 per cent of gross sales. What are some of the factors that you, as the new manager, would investigate regarding the decrease in net income?

## Case 9
R. C. Cooper Company has set up a perpetual inventory system to maintain control over its inventory. At the end of the year, a physical inventory is taken and the amount of inventory is determined to be less than that called for by the inventory cards. Explain why the physical inventory can differ from the perpetual inventory cards. Should a business wait a year to discover these differences?

## Case 10
Preparation of cheques, recording of payments and reconciling of the bank account are all handled by Mr. MacQuarrie of Typewriters Limited. Mr. MacQuarrie notes that a cheque for $200 has been outstanding for over a year and probably will not be cashed. He therefore writes a cheque for $200 payable to himself, forges the treasurer's signature, cashes the cheque, makes no entry in the cash payments journal, conceals the disbursement by omitting the long-outstanding item from the list of outstanding cheques on the bank reconciliation, and destroys the fraudulent cheque.

What weaknesses are evident in Typewriters Limited that create this opportunity for MacQuarrie?

## Case 11

Cash is the one item most likely to be stolen outright by employees or to tempt employees to embezzle; that is, to steal money and to try to cover up the theft by falsifying the accounting records. Explain how the following can contribute to the internal control of cash:

1. Cash registers which print receipts.
2. Printed prenumbered slips for recording cash sales.
3. A petty cash system.
4. Requirement of two signatures on cheques.
5. A bank reconciliation statement.

## Case 12

A.B.C. Supply makes 500 sales on account in an average month. Each sale is recorded in the sales journal, from which the accounting clerk posts to the accounts receivable ledger and to the general ledger.

1. How much work might be saved by posting directly from the sales invoices to the customers' accounts in the subsidiary ledger?
2. How should total sales be recorded if this method is followed?

# 13 Payroll Accounting

The term **payroll** is used to refer to that portion of the accounting process which deals specifically with the salaries and wages paid to employees for a certain period of time. This certain period of time, referred to as the pay period, may be a weekly, biweekly (every two weeks), semimonthly (every ½ month), or monthly pay period. The federal government, through legislation such as the Income Tax Act, the Unemployment Insurance Act, and the Canada Pension Plan Act, requires the employer to keep accurate records of all salaries and wages paid to each employee for each pay period.

## Excerpt from the Income Tax Act

**185.** (1) Every person carrying on business and every person who is required, by or pursuant to this Act, to pay or collect taxes or other amounts shall keep records and books of account (including an annual inventory kept in prescribed manner) at his place of business or residence in Canada or at such other place as may be designated by the Minister, in such form and containing such information as will enable the taxes payable under this Act or the taxes or other amounts that should have been deducted, withheld or collected to be determined.

(2) Every registered Canadian charitable organization shall keep records and books of account (including a duplicate of each receipt containing prescribed information for a donation received by it) at an address in Canada recorded with the Minister or designated by the Minister in such form and containing such information as will enable the donations to it that are deductible under this Act to be verified.

(3) Where a person has failed to keep adequate records and books of account for the purposes of this Act, the Minister may require him to keep such records and books of account as he may specify and that person shall thereafter keep records and books of account as so required.

(4) Every person required by this section to keep records and books of account shall, until written permission for their disposal is obtained from the Minister, retain every such record or book of account and every account or voucher necessary to verify the information in any such record or book of account. R.S., c. 148, s. 125; 1966-67, c. 47, s. 15.

## Excerpt from the Canada Pension Plan Act

**25.** (1) Every employer paying remuneration to an employee employed by him in pensionable employment shall keep records and books of account at his place of business or residence in Canada, or at such other place as may be designated by the Minister, in such form and containing such information as will enable any contributions payable under this Act or any contributions or other amounts that should have been deducted or paid to be determined, and where any such employer has failed to keep adequate records and books of account, the Minister may require him to keep such records and books of account as he may specify, and the employer shall thereafter keep records and books of account as so required.

(2) Every employer required by this section to keep records and books of account shall, until written permission for their disposal is obtained from the Minister, retain every such record or book of account and every account or voucher necessary to verify the information contained therein. 1964-65, c. 51, s. 25.

### Excerpt from the Unemployment Insurance Act

**97.** (1) The Commission may require any person to keep such books, records and accounts as the Commission directs and may require any person to make written returns of information deemed by the Commission to be necessary for the purposes of this Act, and failure to comply with any such direction or requirement is an offence against this Act.

(2) The powers and functions of the Commission under this section may be exercised by any officer appointed pursuant to this Act and authorized in that behalf by general or special directions of the Commission.

(3) No person shall, with intent to evade any of the provisions of this Act or the regulations, destroy, alter, mutilate or secrete any records or books or make or counsel or procure the making of any false or fraudulent entries in records or books, or omit or concur in omitting to enter any material particular in records or books. 1955, c. 50, s. 97.

It is important that care be taken in preparing the payroll. All the payroll data must be col-lected carefully and accurately in order that calculations resulting in the proper pay for each employee may be made. Once the payroll is prepared, the data are used to record the appropriate accounting entries. Also, as previously mentioned, the government requires accurate payroll records to determine the employees' and employer's liabilities for taxes, pension premiums, and unemployment insurance premiums.

## Methods of Paying Employees

There are three basic methods of calculating the pay for employees. Employees are paid either a salary, a wage, or a commission.

### Salaries

**Salaries** are paid to office workers, teachers, supervisors, executives, and civil servants. Salaries are usually determined on a yearly basis with equal payments being made each pay period. For example, consider the case of Harold Evans, who is employed by Nor-Can Grocers Limited, a food wholesaler. Mr. Evans receives an annual salary of $16 770 and is paid every two weeks (biweekly). His pay for each pay period is calculated as follows:

$$\underbrace{\$16\,770.00}_{\text{annual salary}} \div \underbrace{26}_{\text{pay periods per year}} = \underbrace{\$645.00}_{\text{per pay period}}$$

### Wages

**Wages** are paid to workers in large factories and shops. A person paid on a wage basis receives a certain amount of pay for each hour worked, with payments being made some time after the completion of the pay period. In some industries, a wage-earner may be paid on a piece-work basis so that his wage is measured by how much production he turns out. Some businesses pay a certain minimum amount based on the hours worked plus a piece-work bonus for extra quantities produced over and above a stated amount per day or per week.

## Time clocks and timecards

Where the amount of an employee's pay depends on the number of hours he has worked, a method is needed to record (a) the time that each employee starts work each morning, afternoon, and evening; (b) the time that each employee leaves work each morning, afternoon, and evening.

This record permits the Payroll Department to calculate the total hours worked by each employee for each pay period. A mechanical device that is widely used to accumulate this information is the time clock. The time clock is used with timecards.

When a timecard is inserted into the time clock, the mechanism of the clock automatically imprints the time at which the employee is entering or leaving work. Time clocks are usually located near the employees' entrance to the plant, and are in such a position that they can be viewed by a foreman or supervisor to prevent improper use. The timecard shown below is for a one-week period. The times are automatically recorded by the clock in one of six positions: Morning In, Morning Out, Afternoon In, Afternoon Out, Extra In, Extra Out.

*Time clock (courtesy of Simplex International Time Equipment Co. Ltd.).*

## Completing the timecard

At the end of each pay period the payroll clerk completes the timecards for all of the employees. For each card he must:
1.  Calculate the number of hours worked each day (both regular and overtime).
    **Notes:**
    a.  For this particular business the regular work week consists of a five-day week of eight hours per day. Any time worked after 5:00 p.m., or on Saturday and Sunday, is to be considered as overtime.
    b.  Most business firms have some rules with respect to employees who are late coming to work. We will assume that employees are penalized 15 minutes if they are late by one to 15 minutes, 30 minutes if they are late 16 to 30 minutes, and so on.
2.  Total the number of regular hours.
3.  Total the number of overtime hours.
4.  Complete the bottom section of the card. There is space provided to multiply the regular hours by the regular rate, and the overtime hours by the overtime rate. Then, the regular earnings and the overtime earnings are added together to obtain the gross earnings for the employee.

| Time Card | | | | | | | |
|---|---|---|---|---|---|---|---|
| Week Ended September 14 19-- | | | | | | | |
| Social INS. No. 603 456 667 | | | | | | | |
| Name | | | | Burns, Joseph | | | |
| Day | Morning In | Out | Afternoon In | Out | Extra In | Out | Total Hours |
| M | 7:58 | 12:01 | 12:59 | 5:01 | | | 8 |
| T | 7:56 | 12:01 | 12:58 | 5:02 | | | 8 |
| W | 8:03 | 12:00 | 12:58 | 5:01 | | | 7¾ |
| T | 7:58 | 12:01 | 12:59 | 5:01 | | | 8 |
| F | 7:59 | 12:01 | 12:57 | 5:00 | 5:57 | 7:02 | 8/1 |
| S | 7:59 | 12:02 | | | | | /4 |
| S | | | | | | | |

| | Hours | Rate | Earnings |
|---|---|---|---|
| Regular Time | 39¾ | 6.80 | 270.30 |
| Overtime | 5 | 10.20 | 51.00 |
| Gross Pay | | | 321.30 |

## Commission

**Commission** is paid to salesmen, sales clerks, and sales agents. Commission is a stated percentage of the dollar value of sales made by the employee. In most cases, however, a basic salary is paid to the employee in addition to the commission to provide him with at least a minimum income during difficult periods. To illustrate how this affects a particular employee, consider Rod Ferguson, a salesman for Nor-Can Grocers Limited, who receives $195 per week and a commission equal to one half per cent of the net sales made by him. During the last two weeks Mr. Ferguson has sold $29 000 worth of merchandise.

Calculation:

| | |
|---|---|
| Basic Salary (2 weeks × $195.00) = | $390.00 |
| Commission (½% of $29 000.00) = | $145.00 |
| Total Earnings for two weeks    = | $535.00 |

## Payroll Deductions

You are probably aware of the factors involved in the preparation of a pay cheque. Employees are hired with the understanding that they will be paid a certain amount per hour, week, or year. You will recall that Harold Evans receives an annual salary of $16 770 payable every two weeks in equal portions of $645. When Evans received his last pay cheque, it was made out in the amount of $473.27. The difference between the $645 and the $473.27 he received is $171.73. Harold Evans was not short-changed. The $171.73 represents various deductions made.

The $645 is referred to as the **gross pay** while the $473.27 is referred to as the **net pay**. The payroll equation, therefore, is as follows:

For Harold Evans:

GROSS PAY − DEDUCTIONS = NET PAY
$645.00    −    $171.73    =    $473.27

The calculations that are necessary in order to arrive at the net pay for Harold Evans were made on a special columnar paper called a **payroll journal**, **payroll summary** or **payroll register**. Nor-Can Grocers Ltd., the wholesaling firm which employs Evans, uses the payroll journal illustrated below.

## Social Insurance Number

As was previously mentioned, the employer is required to withhold a portion of the employee's pay from this pay cheque because of government regulations. These deductions include Canada Pension or Quebec Pension, personal income taxes, and Unemployment Insurance. Naturally, care must be taken to see that each employee is credited properly for his contributions. To assist in this respect the federal government requires each employee to apply for a Social Insurance Number (SIN) as soon as he starts to work. This is his permanent identification number. With the increasing use of computers to process information, the Social Insurance Number becomes very important. It should be noted that no benefits are paid out by the federal government unless the claimant has a SIN number. At the top of the next column is an illustration of the social insurance card, showing the nine-digit number.

PAYROLL JOURNAL     For the _____ ended _____ 19__

| Employee | Net Claim Code | Earnings | | | C.P.P. | U.I. Premium | R.R.P. | Income Tax | | Health Ins. | Union Dues | Group Life | | Total Ded'ns | Net Pay |
|---|---|---|---|---|---|---|---|---|---|---|---|---|---|---|---|
| | | Regular | Extra | Gross | | | | Taxable Income | Ded'n | | | | | | |
| | | | | | | | | | | | | | | | |
| | | | | | | | | | | | | | | | |

## Canada Pension Plan and Quebec Pension Plan

The first deduction we shall examine is the **Canada Pension Plan** and **Quebec Pension Plan**. There are many people who are unable, during their productive working years, to accumulate enough savings for those days when they will no longer be able to work. Pension plans are designed to provide an income for people after retirement, or for those who have to stop working because of disabilities. They also provide an income for a wife if she is widowed.

The federal government instituted a pension plan for the Canadian worker which became effective January 1, 1966. This plan, which is named the Canada Pension Plan, is called the Quebec Pension Plan in the Province of Quebec and is administered there by the provincial government, but elsewhere by the federal government. Both plans are portable, as explained below.

The following are extracts from a booklet on the Canada Pension Plan prepared by the Department of National Health and Welfare, Canada.

"The Plan operates in all parts of the country except where a province establishes its own comparable program. The Province of Quebec is doing so. The two Plans are to be closely coordinated.

"This means that if your place of employment is changed to Quebec or if as a self-employed person you move your residence to Quebec, your contributions to the Quebec Pension Plan will produce the same benefits as are described in this booklet. The reverse also applies. Anyone who is now in Quebec, but later moves to take up work in any other part of the country, will get the same benefits as if he had contributed to one Plan throughout.

"Benefits are portable. Once you have contributed to the Plan, you cannot lose the right to the retirement pension based on those years of contribution. If you change jobs in Canada, your pension rights are the same as if you had been in one job all the time. If you leave Canada, you retain your right to the pension you earned before you left. The same rules apply to the other benefits, provided that you meet the qualifying conditions. . . .

"Benefit amounts are not fixed once and for all. They will be increased in line with rises in the cost of living."*

The Plan covers on a compulsory basis most types of employment. To be covered for a particular year, an employee must be between the ages of 18 and 70 and earn more than $800 in that year.

## Employee Contributions

The maximum earnings on which contributions must be made are $8 300 less an annual basic exemption of $800, or $7 500. The rate of contribution is 1.8 per cent. Therefore, the maximum deduction for any employee is $7 500 $\times$ $\frac{1.8}{100}$ = $135.00 for the year. It has been a trend to amend the maximum earnings on which contributions are made but the rate has remained the same.

To avoid the necessity of making individual calculations for each employee, the Department of National Revenue, Taxation Division publishes a booklet of tables for determining the amount of deduction to be made from each gross pay. Included in this booklet is a set of deduction tables for every possible payroll plan. The most common plans are for pay periods that are weekly, biweekly, semimonthly, or monthly. Each table shows the correct deduction to be made for a wide range of gross earnings. The illustrations on pages 282 and 283 show two of the pages from a contemporary booklet for the biweekly pay period.

---

* Department of National Health and Welfare, *The Canada Pension Plan* (Ottawa: Queen's Printer, 1965), p. 7.

BIWEEKLY PAY PERIOD — *PÉRIODE DE PAIE DE DEUX SEMAINES*
$270.49 — $390.48

| Remuneration / *Rémunération* | | C.P.P. R.P.C. | U.I. Premium *Prime d'a.-c.* | Remuneration / *Rémunération* | | C.P.P. R.P.C. | U.I. Premium *Prime d'a.-c.* | Remuneration / *Rémunération* | | C.P.P. R.P.C. | U.I. Premium *Prime d'a.-c.* |
|---|---|---|---|---|---|---|---|---|---|---|---|
| From-*de* | To-*à* | | | From-*de* | To-*à* | | | From-*de* | To-*à* | | |
| $ 270.49 – | 271.03 | 4.32 | 4.47 | $ 310.49 – | 311.03 | 5.04 | 5.13 | $ 350.49 – | 351.03 | 5.76 | 5.79 |
| 271.04 – | 271.59 | 4.33 | 4.48 | 311.04 – | 311.59 | 5.05 | 5.14 | 351.04 – | 351.59 | 5.77 | 5.80 |
| 271.60 – | 272.14 | 4.34 | 4.49 | 311.60 – | 312.14 | 5.06 | 5.15 | 351.60 – | 352.14 | 5.78 | 5.81 |
| 272.15 – | 272.70 | 4.35 | 4.49 | 312.15 – | 312.70 | 5.07 | 5.15 | 352.15 – | 352.70 | 5.79 | 5.81 |
| 272.71 – | 273.25 | 4.36 | 4.50 | 312.71 – | 313.25 | 5.08 | 5.16 | 352.71 – | 353.25 | 5.80 | 5.82 |
| 273.26 – | 273.81 | 4.37 | 4.51 | 313.26 – | 313.81 | 5.09 | 5.17 | 353.26 – | 353.81 | 5.81 | 5.83 |
| 273.82 – | 274.37 | 4.38 | 4.52 | 313.82 – | 314.37 | 5.10 | 5.18 | 353.82 – | 354.37 | 5.82 | 5.84 |
| 274.38 – | 274.92 | 4.39 | 4.53 | 314.38 – | 314.92 | 5.11 | 5.19 | 354.38 – | 354.92 | 5.83 | 5.85 |
| 274.93 – | 275.48 | 4.40 | 4.54 | 314.93 – | 315.48 | 5.12 | 5.20 | 354.93 – | 355.48 | 5.84 | 5.86 |
| 275.49 – | 276.03 | 4.41 | 4.55 | 315.49 – | 316.03 | 5.13 | 5.21 | 355.49 – | 356.03 | 5.85 | 5.87 |
| 276.04 – | 276.59 | 4.42 | 4.56 | 316.04 – | 316.59 | 5.14 | 5.22 | 356.04 – | 356.59 | 5.86 | 5.88 |
| 276.60 – | 277.14 | 4.43 | 4.57 | 316.60 – | 317.14 | 5.15 | 5.23 | 356.60 – | 357.14 | 5.87 | 5.89 |
| 277.15 – | 277.70 | 4.44 | 4.58 | 317.15 – | 317.70 | 5.16 | 5.24 | 357.15 – | 357.70 | 5.88 | 5.90 |
| 277.71 – | 278.25 | 4.45 | 4.59 | 317.71 – | 318.25 | 5.17 | 5.25 | 357.71 – | 358.25 | 5.89 | 5.91 |
| 278.26 – | 278.81 | 4.46 | 4.60 | 318.26 – | 318.81 | 5.18 | 5.26 | 358.26 – | 358.81 | 5.90 | 5.92 |
| 278.82 – | 279.37 | 4.47 | 4.60 | 318.82 – | 319.37 | 5.19 | 5.26 | 358.82 – | 359.37 | 5.91 | 5.92 |
| 279.38 – | 279.92 | 4.48 | 4.61 | 319.38 – | 319.92 | 5.20 | 5.27 | 359.38 – | 359.92 | 5.92 | 5.93 |
| 279.93 – | 280.48 | 4.49 | 4.62 | 319.93 – | 320.48 | 5.21 | 5.28 | 359.93 – | 360.48 | 5.93 | 5.94 |
| 280.49 – | 281.03 | 4.50 | 4.63 | 320.49 – | 321.03 | 5.22 | 5.29 | 360.49 – | 361.03 | 5.94 | 5.95 |
| 281.04 – | 281.59 | 4.51 | 4.64 | 321.04 – | 321.59 | 5.23 | 5.30 | 361.04 – | 361.59 | 5.95 | 5.96 |
| 281.60 – | 282.14 | 4.52 | 4.65 | 321.60 – | 322.14 | 5.24 | 5.31 | 361.60 – | 362.14 | 5.96 | 5.97 |
| 282.15 – | 282.70 | 4.53 | 4.66 | 322.15 – | 322.70 | 5.25 | 5.32 | 362.15 – | 362.70 | 5.97 | 5.98 |
| 282.71 – | 283.25 | 4.54 | 4.67 | 322.71 – | 323.25 | 5.26 | 5.33 | 362.71 – | 363.25 | 5.98 | 5.99 |
| 283.26 – | 283.81 | 4.55 | 4.68 | 323.26 – | 323.81 | 5.27 | 5.34 | 363.26 – | 363.81 | 5.99 | 6.00 |
| 283.82 – | 284.37 | 4.56 | 4.69 | 323.82 – | 324.37 | 5.28 | 5.35 | 363.82 – | 364.37 | 6.00 | 6.01 |
| 284.38 – | 284.92 | 4.57 | 4.70 | 324.38 – | 324.92 | 5.29 | 5.36 | 364.38 – | 364.92 | 6.01 | 6.02 |
| 284.93 – | 285.48 | 4.58 | 4.71 | 324.93 – | 325.48 | 5.30 | 5.37 | 364.93 – | 365.48 | 6.02 | 6.03 |
| 285.49 – | 286.03 | 4.59 | 4.72 | 325.49 – | 326.03 | 5.31 | 5.38 | 365.49 – | 366.03 | 6.03 | 6.04 |
| 286.04 – | 286.59 | 4.60 | 4.72 | 326.04 – | 326.59 | 5.32 | 5.38 | 366.04 – | 366.59 | 6.04 | 6.04 |
| 286.60 – | 287.14 | 4.61 | 4.73 | 326.60 – | 327.14 | 5.33 | 5.39 | 366.60 – | 367.14 | 6.05 | 6.05 |
| 287.15 – | 287.70 | 4.62 | 4.74 | 327.15 – | 327.70 | 5.34 | 5.40 | 367.15 – | 367.70 | 6.06 | 6.06 |
| 287.71 – | 288.25 | 4.63 | 4.75 | 327.71 – | 328.25 | 5.35 | 5.41 | 367.71 – | 368.25 | 6.07 | 6.07 |
| 288.26 – | 288.81 | 4.64 | 4.76 | 328.26 – | 328.81 | 5.36 | 5.42 | 368.26 – | 368.81 | 6.08 | 6.08 |
| 288.82 – | 289.37 | 4.65 | 4.77 | 328.82 – | 329.37 | 5.37 | 5.43 | 368.82 – | 369.37 | 6.09 | 6.09 |
| 289.38 – | 289.92 | 4.66 | 4.78 | 329.38 – | 329.92 | 5.38 | 5.44 | 369.38 – | 369.92 | 6.10 | 6.10 |
| 289.93 – | 290.48 | 4.67 | 4.79 | 329.93 – | 330.48 | 5.39 | 5.45 | 369.93 – | 370.48 | 6.11 | 6.11 |
| 290.49 – | 291.03 | 4.68 | 4.80 | 330.49 – | 331.03 | 5.40 | 5.46 | 370.49 – | 371.03 | 6.12 | 6.12 |
| 291.04 – | 291.59 | 4.69 | 4.81 | 331.04 – | 331.59 | 5.41 | 5.47 | 371.04 – | 371.59 | 6.13 | 6.13 |
| 291.60 – | 292.14 | 4.70 | 4.82 | 331.60 – | 332.14 | 5.42 | 5.48 | 371.60 – | 372.14 | 6.14 | 6.14 |
| 292.15 – | 292.70 | 4.71 | 4.82 | 332.15 – | 332.70 | 5.43 | 5.48 | 372.15 – | 372.70 | 6.15 | 6.14 |
| 292.71 – | 293.25 | 4.72 | 4.83 | 332.71 – | 333.25 | 5.44 | 5.49 | 372.71 – | 373.25 | 6.16 | 6.15 |
| 293.26 – | 293.81 | 4.73 | 4.84 | 333.26 – | 333.81 | 5.45 | 5.50 | 373.26 – | 373.81 | 6.17 | 6.16 |
| 293.82 – | 294.37 | 4.74 | 4.85 | 333.82 – | 334.37 | 5.46 | 5.51 | 373.82 – | 374.37 | 6.18 | 6.17 |
| 294.38 – | 294.92 | 4.75 | 4.86 | 334.38 – | 334.92 | 5.47 | 5.52 | 374.38 – | 374.92 | 6.19 | 6.18 |
| 294.93 – | 295.48 | 4.76 | 4.87 | 334.93 – | 335.48 | 5.48 | 5.53 | 374.93 – | 375.48 | 6.20 | 6.19 |
| 295.49 – | 296.03 | 4.77 | 4.88 | 335.49 – | 336.03 | 5.49 | 5.54 | 375.49 – | 376.03 | 6.21 | 6.20 |
| 296.04 – | 296.59 | 4.78 | 4.89 | 336.04 – | 336.59 | 5.50 | 5.55 | 376.04 – | 376.59 | 6.22 | 6.21 |
| 296.60 – | 297.14 | 4.79 | 4.90 | 336.60 – | 337.14 | 5.51 | 5.56 | 376.60 – | 377.14 | 6.23 | 6.22 |
| 297.15 – | 297.70 | 4.80 | 4.91 | 337.15 – | 337.70 | 5.52 | 5.57 | 377.15 – | 377.70 | 6.24 | 6.23 |
| 297.71 – | 298.25 | 4.81 | 4.92 | 337.71 – | 338.25 | 5.53 | 5.58 | 377.71 – | 378.25 | 6.25 | 6.24 |
| 298.26 – | 298.81 | 4.82 | 4.93 | 338.26 – | 338.81 | 5.54 | 5.59 | 378.26 – | 378.81 | 6.26 | 6.25 |
| 298.82 – | 299.37 | 4.83 | 4.93 | 338.82 – | 339.37 | 5.55 | 5.59 | 378.82 – | 379.37 | 6.27 | 6.25 |
| 299.38 – | 299.92 | 4.84 | 4.94 | 339.38 – | 339.92 | 5.56 | 5.60 | 379.38 – | 379.92 | 6.28 | 6.26 |
| 299.93 – | 300.48 | 4.85 | 4.95 | 339.93 – | 340.48 | 5.57 | 5.61 | 379.93 – | 380.48 | 6.29 | 6.27 |
| 300.49 – | 301.03 | 4.86 | 4.96 | 340.49 – | 341.03 | 5.58 | 5.62 | 380.49 – | 381.03 | 6.30 | 6.28 |
| 301.04 – | 301.59 | 4.87 | 4.97 | 341.04 – | 341.59 | 5.59 | 5.63 | 381.04 – | 381.59 | 6.31 | 6.29 |
| 301.60 – | 302.14 | 4.88 | 4.98 | 341.60 – | 342.14 | 5.60 | 5.64 | 381.60 – | 382.14 | 6.32 | 6.30 |
| 302.15 – | 302.70 | 4.89 | 4.99 | 342.15 – | 342.70 | 5.61 | 5.65 | 382.15 – | 382.70 | 6.33 | 6.31 |
| 302.71 – | 303.25 | 4.90 | 5.00 | 342.71 – | 343.25 | 5.62 | 5.66 | 382.71 – | 383.25 | 6.34 | 6.32 |
| 303.26 – | 303.81 | 4.91 | 5.01 | 343.26 – | 343.81 | 5.63 | 5.67 | 383.26 – | 383.81 | 6.35 | 6.33 |
| 303.82 – | 304.37 | 4.92 | 5.02 | 343.82 – | 344.37 | 5.64 | 5.68 | 383.82 – | 384.37 | 6.36 | 6.34 |
| 304.38 – | 304.92 | 4.93 | 5.03 | 344.38 – | 344.92 | 5.65 | 5.69 | 384.38 – | 384.92 | 6.37 | 6.35 |
| 304.93 – | 305.48 | 4.94 | 5.04 | 344.93 – | 345.48 | 5.66 | 5.70 | 384.93 – | 385.48 | 6.38 | 6.36 |
| 305.49 – | 306.03 | 4.95 | 5.05 | 345.49 – | 346.03 | 5.67 | 5.71 | 385.49 – | 386.03 | 6.39 | 6.37 |
| 306.04 – | 306.59 | 4.96 | 5.05 | 346.04 – | 346.59 | 5.68 | 5.71 | 386.04 – | 386.59 | 6.40 | 6.37 |
| 306.60 – | 307.14 | 4.97 | 5.06 | 346.60 – | 347.14 | 5.69 | 5.72 | 386.60 – | 387.14 | 6.41 | 6.38 |
| 307.15 – | 307.70 | 4.98 | 5.07 | 347.15 – | 347.70 | 5.70 | 5.73 | 387.15 – | 387.70 | 6.42 | 6.39 |
| 307.71 – | 308.25 | 4.99 | 5.08 | 347.71 – | 348.25 | 5.71 | 5.74 | 387.71 – | 388.25 | 6.43 | 6.40 |
| 308.26 – | 308.81 | 5.00 | 5.09 | 348.26 – | 348.81 | 5.72 | 5.75 | 388.26 – | 388.81 | 6.44 | 6.41 |
| 308.82 – | 309.37 | 5.01 | 5.10 | 348.82 – | 349.37 | 5.73 | 5.76 | 388.82 – | 389.37 | 6.45 | 6.42 |
| 309.38 – | 309.92 | 5.02 | 5.11 | 349.38 – | 349.92 | 5.74 | 5.77 | 389.38 – | 389.92 | 6.46 | 6.43 |
| 309.93 – | 310.48 | 5.03 | 5.12 | 349.93 – | 350.48 | 5.75 | 5.78 | 389.93 – | 390.48 | 6.47 | 6.44 |

To determine the deduction for an employee, look down the 'Remuneration' column until you find the bracket containing the employee's gross pay. You will recall that Harold Evans has a biweekly salary of $645.00. This falls in the bracket of $641.04 – 646.03. The deduction of $11.03 is indicated to the immediate right of the remuneration bracket in the column headed 'C.P.P.'. This deduction is then recorded in the payroll journal in the C.P.P. column opposite Evans's name, as shown at the bottom of page 283.

At this point, it needs to be pointed out that the employer is required to contribute an amount equal to that contributed by the employee. We will show how this is accounted for later in the chapter. Note also that by using the tables to determine the $11.03 as a deduction, Harold Evans will reach the maximum annual contribution of $135.00 in the thirteenth pay period at which time only $2.64 will be deducted. The following calculation shows this:

    a. 12 pay periods of $11.03 for each pay period equals a total deduction to date of

### BIWEEKLY PAY PERIOD — *PÉRIODE DE PAIE DE DEUX SEMAINES*
#### $390.49 — $1,091.03

| Remuneration *Rémunération* From-*de* | To-*à* | C.P.P. R.P.C. | U.I. Premium *Prime d'a.-c.* | Remuneration *Rémunération* From-*de* | To-*à* | C.P.P. R.P.C. | U.I. Premium *Prime d'a.-c.* | Remuneration *Rémunération* From-*de* | To-*à* | C.P.P. R.P.C. | U.I. Premium *Prime d'a.-c.* |
|---|---|---|---|---|---|---|---|---|---|---|---|
| $ 390.49 – | 391.03 | 6.48 | 6.45 | $ 430.49 – | 431.03 | 7.20 | 6.60 | $ 786.04 – | 791.03 | 13.64 | 6.60 |
| 391.04 – | 391.59 | 6.49 | 6.46 | 431.04 – | 436.03 | 7.25 | 6.60 | 791.04 – | 796.03 | 13.73 | 6.60 |
| 391.60 – | 392.14 | 6.50 | 6.47 | 436.04 – | 441.03 | 7.34 | 6.60 | 796.04 – | 801.03 | 13.82 | 6.60 |
| 392.15 – | 392.70 | 6.51 | 6.47 | 441.04 – | 446.03 | 7.43 | 6.60 | 801.04 – | 806.03 | 13.91 | 6.60 |
| 392.71 – | 393.25 | 6.52 | 6.48 | 446.04 – | 451.03 | 7.52 | 6.60 | 806.04 – | 811.03 | 14.00 | 6.60 |
| 393.26 – | 393.81 | 6.53 | 6.49 | 451.04 – | 456.03 | 7.61 | 6.60 | 811.04 – | 816.03 | 14.09 | 6.60 |
| 393.82 – | 394.37 | 6.54 | 6.50 | 456.04 – | 461.03 | 7.70 | 6.60 | 816.04 – | 821.03 | 14.18 | 6.60 |
| 394.38 – | 394.92 | 6.55 | 6.51 | 461.04 – | 466.03 | 7.79 | 6.60 | 821.04 – | 826.03 | 14.27 | 6.60 |
| 394.93 – | 395.48 | 6.56 | 6.52 | 466.04 – | 471.03 | 7.88 | 6.60 | 826.04 – | 831.03 | 14.36 | 6.60 |
| 395.49 – | 396.03 | 6.57 | 6.53 | 471.04 – | 476.03 | 7.97 | 6.60 | 831.04 – | 836.03 | 14.45 | 6.60 |
| 396.04 – | 396.59 | 6.58 | 6.54 | 476.04 – | 481.03 | 8.06 | 6.60 | 836.04 – | 841.03 | 14.54 | 6.60 |
| 396.60 – | 397.14 | 6.59 | 6.55 | 481.04 – | 486.03 | 8.15 | 6.60 | 841.04 – | 846.03 | 14.63 | 6.60 |
| 397.15 – | 397.70 | 6.60 | 6.56 | 486.04 – | 491.03 | 8.24 | 6.60 | 846.04 – | 851.03 | 14.72 | 6.60 |
| 397.71 – | 398.25 | 6.61 | 6.57 | 491.04 – | 496.03 | 8.33 | 6.60 | 851.04 – | 856.03 | 14.81 | 6.60 |
| 398.26 – | 398.81 | 6.62 | 6.58 | 496.04 – | 501.03 | 8.42 | 6.60 | 856.04 – | 861.03 | 14.90 | 6.60 |
| 398.82 – | 399.37 | 6.63 | 6.58 | 501.04 – | 506.03 | 8.51 | 6.60 | 861.04 – | 866.03 | 14.99 | 6.60 |
| 399.38 – | 399.92 | 6.64 | 6.59 | 506.04 – | 511.03 | 8.60 | 6.60 | 866.04 – | 871.03 | 15.08 | 6.60 |
| 399.93 – | 400.48 | 6.65 | 6.60 | 511.04 – | 516.03 | 8.69 | 6.60 | 871.04 – | 876.03 | 15.17 | 6.60 |
| 400.49 – | 401.03 | 6.66 | 6.60 | 516.04 – | 521.03 | 8.78 | 6.60 | 876.04 – | 881.03 | 15.26 | 6.60 |
| 401.04 – | 401.59 | 6.67 | 6.60 | 521.04 – | 526.03 | 8.87 | 6.60 | 881.04 – | 886.03 | 15.35 | 6.60 |
| 401.60 – | 402.14 | 6.68 | 6.60 | 526.04 – | 531.03 | 8.96 | 6.60 | 886.04 – | 891.03 | 15.44 | 6.60 |
| 402.15 – | 402.70 | 6.69 | 6.60 | 531.04 – | 536.03 | 9.05 | 6.60 | 891.04 – | 896.03 | 15.53 | 6.60 |
| 402.71 – | 403.25 | 6.70 | 6.60 | 536.04 – | 541.03 | 9.14 | 6.60 | 896.04 – | 901.03 | 15.62 | 6.60 |
| 403.26 – | 403.81 | 6.71 | 6.60 | 541.04 – | 546.03 | 9.23 | 6.60 | 901.04 – | 906.03 | 15.71 | 6.60 |
| 403.82 – | 404.37 | 6.72 | 6.60 | 546.04 – | 551.03 | 9.32 | 6.60 | 906.04 – | 911.03 | 15.80 | 6.60 |
| 404.38 – | 404.92 | 6.73 | 6.60 | 551.04 – | 556.03 | 9.41 | 6.60 | 911.04 – | 916.03 | 15.89 | 6.60 |
| 404.93 – | 405.48 | 6.74 | 6.60 | 556.04 – | 561.03 | 9.50 | 6.60 | 916.04 – | 921.03 | 15.98 | 6.60 |
| 405.49 – | 406.03 | 6.75 | 6.60 | 561.04 – | 566.03 | 9.59 | 6.60 | 921.04 – | 926.03 | 16.07 | 6.60 |
| 406.04 – | 406.59 | 6.76 | 6.60 | 566.04 – | 571.03 | 9.68 | 6.60 | 926.04 – | 931.03 | 16.16 | 6.60 |
| 406.60 – | 407.14 | 6.77 | 6.60 | 571.04 – | 576.03 | 9.77 | 6.60 | 931.04 – | 936.03 | 16.25 | 6.60 |
| 407.15 – | 407.70 | 6.78 | 6.60 | 576.04 – | 581.03 | 9.86 | 6.60 | 936.04 – | 941.03 | 16.34 | 6.60 |
| 407.71 – | 408.25 | 6.79 | 6.60 | 581.04 – | 586.03 | 9.95 | 6.60 | 941.04 – | 946.03 | 16.43 | 6.60 |
| 408.26 – | 408.81 | 6.80 | 6.60 | 586.04 – | 591.03 | 10.04 | 6.60 | 946.04 – | 951.03 | 16.52 | 6.60 |
| 408.82 – | 409.37 | 6.81 | 6.60 | 591.04 – | 596.03 | 10.13 | 6.60 | 951.04 – | 956.03 | 16.61 | 6.60 |
| 409.38 – | 409.92 | 6.82 | 6.60 | 596.04 – | 601.03 | 10.22 | 6.60 | 956.04 – | 961.03 | 16.70 | 6.60 |
| 409.93 – | 410.48 | 6.83 | 6.60 | 601.04 – | 606.03 | 10.31 | 6.60 | 961.04 – | 966.03 | 16.79 | 6.60 |
| 410.49 – | 411.03 | 6.84 | 6.60 | 606.04 – | 611.03 | 10.40 | 6.60 | 966.04 – | 971.03 | 16.88 | 6.60 |
| 411.04 – | 411.59 | 6.85 | 6.60 | 611.04 – | 616.03 | 10.49 | 6.60 | 971.04 – | 976.03 | 16.97 | 6.60 |
| 411.60 – | 412.14 | 6.86 | 6.60 | 616.04 – | 621.03 | 10.58 | 6.60 | 976.04 – | 981.03 | 17.06 | 6.60 |
| 412.15 – | 412.70 | 6.87 | 6.60 | 621.04 – | 626.03 | 10.67 | 6.60 | 981.04 – | 986.03 | 17.15 | 6.60 |
| 412.71 – | 413.25 | 6.88 | 6.60 | 626.04 – | 631.03 | 10.76 | 6.60 | 986.04 – | 991.03 | 17.24 | 6.60 |
| 413.26 – | 413.81 | 6.89 | 6.60 | 631.04 – | 636.03 | 10.85 | 6.60 | 991.04 – | 996.03 | 17.33 | 6.60 |
| 413.82 – | 414.37 | 6.90 | 6.60 | 636.04 – | 641.03 | 10.94 | 6.60 | 996.04 – | 1001.03 | 17.42 | 6.60 |
| 414.38 – | 414.92 | 6.91 | 6.60 | 641.04 – | 646.03 | 11.03 | 6.60 | 1001.04 – | 1006.03 | 17.51 | 6.60 |
| 414.93 – | 415.48 | 6.92 | 6.60 | 646.04 – | 651.03 | 11.12 | 6.60 | 1006.04 – | 1011.03 | 17.60 | 6.60 |
| 415.49 – | 416.03 | 6.93 | 6.60 | 651.04 – | 656.03 | 11.21 | 6.60 | 1011.04 – | 1016.03 | 17.69 | 6.60 |
| 416.04 – | 416.59 | 6.94 | 6.60 | 656.04 – | 661.03 | 11.30 | 6.60 | 1016.04 – | 1021.03 | 17.78 | 6.60 |
| 416.60 – | 417.14 | 6.95 | 6.60 | 661.04 – | 666.03 | 11.39 | 6.60 | 1021.04 – | 1026.03 | 17.87 | 6.60 |
| 417.15 – | 417.70 | 6.96 | 6.60 | 666.04 – | 671.03 | 11.48 | 6.60 | 1026.04 – | 1031.03 | 17.96 | 6.60 |
| 417.71 – | 418.25 | 6.97 | 6.60 | 671.04 – | 676.03 | 11.57 | 6.60 | 1031.04 – | 1036.03 | 18.05 | 6.60 |
| 418.26 – | 418.81 | 6.98 | 6.60 | 676.04 – | 681.03 | 11.66 | 6.60 | 1036.04 – | 1041.03 | 18.14 | 6.60 |
| 418.82 – | 419.37 | 6.99 | 6.60 | 681.04 – | 686.03 | 11.75 | 6.60 | 1041.04 – | 1046.03 | 18.23 | 6.60 |
| 419.38 – | 419.92 | 7.00 | 6.60 | 686.04 – | 691.03 | 11.84 | 6.60 | 1046.04 – | 1051.03 | 18.32 | 6.60 |
| 419.93 – | 420.48 | 7.01 | 6.60 | 691.04 – | 696.03 | 11.93 | 6.60 | 1051.04 – | 1056.03 | 18.41 | 6.60 |
| 420.49 – | 421.03 | 7.02 | 6.60 | 696.04 – | 701.03 | 12.02 | 6.60 | 1056.04 – | 1061.03 | 18.50 | 6.60 |
| 421.04 – | 421.59 | 7.03 | 6.60 | 701.04 – | 706.03 | 12.11 | 6.60 | 1061.04 – | 1066.03 | 18.59 | 6.60 |
| 421.60 – | 422.14 | 7.04 | 6.60 | 706.04 – | 711.03 | 12.20 | 6.60 | 1066.04 – | 1071.03 | 18.68 | 6.60 |
| 422.15 – | 422.70 | 7.05 | 6.60 | 711.04 – | 716.03 | 12.29 | 6.60 | 1071.04 – | 1076.03 | 18.77 | 6.60 |
| 422.71 – | 423.25 | 7.06 | 6.60 | 716.04 – | 721.03 | 12.38 | 6.60 | 1076.04 – | 1081.03 | 18.86 | 6.60 |
| 423.26 – | 423.81 | 7.07 | 6.60 | 721.04 – | 726.03 | 12.47 | 6.60 | 1081.04 – | 1086.03 | 18.95 | 6.60 |
| 423.82 – | 424.37 | 7.08 | 6.60 | 726.04 – | 731.03 | 12.56 | 6.60 | 1086.04 – | 1091.03 | 19.04 | 6.60 |
| 424.38 – | 424.92 | 7.09 | 6.60 | 731.04 – | 736.03 | 12.65 | 6.60 | | | | |
| 424.93 – | 425.48 | 7.10 | 6.60 | 736.04 – | 741.03 | 12.74 | 6.60 | | | | |
| 425.49 – | 426.03 | 7.11 | 6.60 | 741.04 – | 746.03 | 12.83 | 6.60 | | | | |
| 426.04 – | 426.59 | 7.12 | 6.60 | 746.04 – | 751.03 | 12.92 | 6.60 | | | | |
| 426.60 – | 427.14 | 7.13 | 6.60 | 751.04 – | 756.03 | 13.01 | 6.60 | | | | |
| 427.15 – | 427.70 | 7.14 | 6.60 | 756.04 – | 761.03 | 13.10 | 6.60 | | | | |
| 427.71 – | 428.25 | 7.15 | 6.60 | 761.04 – | 766.03 | 13.19 | 6.60 | | | | |
| 428.26 – | 428.81 | 7.16 | 6.60 | 766.04 – | 771.03 | 13.28 | 6.60 | | | | |
| 428.82 – | 429.37 | 7.17 | 6.60 | 771.04 – | 776.03 | 13.37 | 6.60 | | | | |
| 429.38 – | 429.92 | 7.18 | 6.60 | 776.04 – | 781.03 | 13.46 | 6.60 | | | | |
| 429.93 – | 430.48 | 7.19 | 6.60 | 781.04 – | 786.03 | 13.55 | 6.60 | | | | |

"For remuneration in excess of $1,091.03:
(a) refer to page 10 under "Employee's Contribution—Calculation Method";
(b) the Unemployment Insurance premium is $6.60."

"*Si la rémunération dépasse $1,091.03:*
*a) se reporter à la rubrique «Cotisation de l'employé—Méthode par le calcul», à la page 10;*
*b) la prime d'assurance-chômage est $6.60.*"

---

PAYROLL JOURNAL     For the __2 Weeks__ ended __May 24__ 19 —

| Employee | Net Claim Code | Earnings | | | Deductions | | | | | | | | | Total Ded'ns | Net Pay |
|---|---|---|---|---|---|---|---|---|---|---|---|---|---|---|---|
| | | Regular | Extra | Gross | C.P.P. | U.I. Premium | R.R.P. | Income Tax Taxable Income | Ded'n | Health Ins. | Union Dues | Group Life | | | |
| Harold Evans | | 645 00 | — | 645 00 | 11 03 | | | | | | | | | | |
| | | | | | | | | | | | | | | | |
| | | | | | | | | | | | | | | | |
| | | | | | | | | | | | | | | | |
| | | | | | | | | | | | | | | | |
| | | | | | | | | | | | | | | | |
| | | | | | | | | | | | | | | | |
| | | | | | | | | | | | | | | | |
| | | | | | | | | | | | | | | | |

$132.36.

b. $135.00 less $132.36 contributed after 12 pay periods leaves $2.64 to be deducted in the 13th pay period.

It is the responsibility of the employer to keep track of the accumulated contributions for each employee. Once the maximum of $135.00 is reached, no further deduction for C.P.P. or Q.P.P. is to be made in that calendar year.

## Unemployment Insurance

Whenever a person who is both willing and able to work cannot find suitable employment, it is treated under Canadian law as a condition against which insurance is provided. While a worker is employed, he pays a portion of his earnings into an **unemployment insurance fund**. These payments are in the form of deductions made by his employer from his pay. If the worker becomes unemployed while willing and able to accept employment, he receives payments out of the fund to maintain himself and his dependants while he is out of work.

## Minimum and maximum earnings

Each province has minimum and maximum earnings in determining how much premium an employee will have to contribute by way of a deduction on his pay cheque. A schedule of minimum and maximum insurable earnings appears below. It shows that if an employee is paid weekly, he must earn at least $40.00 before U.I. premiums are deducted. It also indicates that the maximum weekly earnings which are subject to U.I. premium deduction are $200.00.

## Employees' premiums

The rate that is used as a basis to calculate the amount of premium that an employee must pay on his earnings is 1.65 per cent. This means that for every $100 of insurable earnings a person pays $1.65 to U.I., subject to the schedule of minimum and maximum earnings shown below.

## Employer's premium

The employer is required to contribute an amount equal to *1.4 times the amount of the employee's premium*. If the employee contributes $1.65, then the employer will contribute an additional $1.65 \times 1.4 = $2.31. You will be shown how to account for this later in the chapter.

### SCHEDULE OF MINIMUM AND MAXIMUM INSURABLE EARNINGS FOR VARIOUS PAY PERIODS
*TABLEAU DU MINIMUM ET DU MAXIMUM DE LA RÉMUNÉRATION ASSURABLE POUR DIVERSES PÉRIODES DE PAYE*

| Pay Period<br>*Période de paie* | Minimum<br>All Provinces, Territories and Outside Canada<br>*Toutes les provinces, tous les territoires et hors du Canada* | Maximum<br>All Provinces, Territories and Outside Canada<br>*Toutes les provinces, tous les territoires et hors du Canada* |
|---|---|---|
| Weekly—*Hebdomadaire* | $ 40.00 | $ 200.00 |
| Bi Weekly—*Quinzaine* | 80.00 | 400.00 |
| Semi-Monthly—*Bi-mensuelle* | 86.67 | 433.33 |
| Monthly—*Mensuelle* | 173.34 | 866.66 |
| 10 Pay Periods Per Year—*10 périodes de paie par année* | 208.00 | 1040.00 |
| 13 Pay Periods Per Year—*13 périodes de paie par année* | 160.00 | 800.00 |
| 22 Pay Periods Per Year—*22 périodes de paie par année* | 94.55 | 472.72 |

# How much to deduct?

The amount of premium to be deducted from an employee's pay for U.I. is determined from the U.I. Premium Tables which are included in the same booklet as the Canada Pension Plan Premium Tables. If an employee is paid on a weekly basis, all that is required to determine the amount of the premium is to refer to the weekly tables using the gross pay as the insurable earnings. The insurable earnings is that amount of pay that is subject to U.I. premium at the rate of 1.65 per cent.

However, if an employee is paid for a pay period that is other than a weekly pay period, then special rules apply. Those special rules that apply to a biweekly pay period are discussed in the following section.

SPECIAL RULES FOR BIWEEKLY PAY PERIODS
The amount of insurable earnings for a biweekly pay period is based on the following two conditions:

1. The employee must receive pay in each of the two pay weeks.
2. The gross pay for the two weeks must be equal to or greater than the minimum of $80.00 for two weeks.

The schedule below shows what happens in a number of situations.

*Example (a).* In this example the employee earns $60.00 in the first week and $60.00 in the second week for a gross pay of $120.00. This is greater than the biweekly minimum of $80.00. The insurable earnings are therefore the same as the gross pay ($120.00). The employee is credited with two insurable weeks. To determine the amount of the premium, simply refer to the tables for the biweekly pay period using $120.00 as the remuneration figure.

*Example (b).* In this example the gross pay is greater than the minimum of $80.00. The insurable earnings are $85.00 and the employee is credited with two weeks of insured earnings. The biweekly tables are used with a remuneration figure of $85.00.

*Example (c).* During the first week the employee earns $20.00 and during the second $50.00, for a combined gross pay of $70.00 for the two-week period. This is less than the minimum figure of $80.00. When this occurs, each week must be looked at separately. During the first week the pay was $20.00, which is less than the

| | Pay period ending | Week | Weekly Pay | Gross Pay | Insurable Earnings | Insured Weeks | Deduction per U.I. Tables |
|---|---|---|---|---|---|---|---|
| (a) | 12 May | 1 | $60.00 | | | | |
| | | 2 | 60.00 | $120.00 | $120.00 | 2 | $1.98 |
| (b) | 26 May | 1 | $25.00 | | | | |
| | | 2 | 60.00 | $85.00 | $85.00 | 2 | $1.41 |
| (c) | 9 June | 1 | $20.00 | | | | |
| | | 2 | 50.00 | $70.00 | $50.00 | 1 | $ .82 |
| (d) | 23 June | 1 | Nil | | | | |
| | | 2 | $40.00 | $40.00 | $40.00 | 1 | $ .66 |
| (e) | 7 July | 1 | $210.00 | | | | |
| | | 2 | 220.00 | $430.00 | $400.00 (maximum) | 2 | $6.60 |

*weekly* minimum figure of $40.00. As a result the $20.00 is *not* subject to U.I. premium deductions. In the second week the earnings are $50.00 which do exceed the minimum figure of $40.00. The insurable earnings are therefore $50.00. The employee is credited with only one week of insurable earnings and the *weekly* tables are used to determine the premium on $50.00 of insurable earnings.

*Example (d).* This example is similar to example (c). Only one week of earnings is insurable; therefore the weekly tables are used.

*Example (e).* In this example the employee's earnings of $430.00 exceed the maximum earnings figure of $400.00 (from the schedule of minimums and maximums). The employee therefore pays the maximum premium required. From the deduction tables it can be seen that the maximum premium of $6.60 for a biweekly pay period begins at the point where the remuneration reaches $400. The employee is credited with two weeks of insurable earnings.

## U.I. Premium Deduction for Harold Evans

At this point we return to Harold Evans. You will recall that he is paid on a biweekly basis and his gross pay is $645. Since his gross pay exceeds the maximum, he must pay the maximum premium. His premium of $6.60 is found in the column headed "U.I. Premium" in the biweekly tables.

**Note:** At this point it should be noted that since both the Canada Pension and the Unemployment Insurance premium tables are in the same booklet and since the same remuneration figure is used to determine each premium, both deductions can be obtained and then recorded in the journal with only one referral to the booklet.

Now that we have determined that Harold Evans must contribute $6.60 towards Unemployment Insurance, this amount is entered in the payroll journal as illustrated below.

## Registered Retirement Plans

It is very common for employees to be enrolled in a private pension plan through their place of employment. Registered retirement plans (R.R.P.) are negotiated by employees with their employer. Usually both the employees and the employer contribute a percentage of the employees' gross pay. Contributions made by the employee are tax deductible up to a maximum of $2 500 per year.

The employees of Nor-Can Groceries Ltd. have an R.R.P., the terms of which require the employees to contribute 5 per cent of their gross pay. Deductions are made each pay period. The entry to record the R.R.P. deduction for Harold Evans is shown on page 287. The company con-

| PAYROLL JOURNAL | | | | | | | | | | | For the _2 Weeks_ ended _May 24_ 19 _ | | | | | | | |
|---|---|---|---|---|---|---|---|---|---|---|---|---|---|---|---|---|---|---|
| | Net Claim Code | Earnings | | | | | | | Deductions | | | | | | | | Total Ded'ns | Net Pay |
| Employee | | Regular | Extra | Gross | C.P.P. | U.I. Premium | R.R.P. | Income Tax | | Health Ins. | Union Dues | Group Life | | | | | | |
| | | | | | | | | Taxable Income | Ded'n | | | | | | | | | |
| Harold Evans | | 645 00 | — | 645 00 | 11 03 | 6 60 | | | | | | | | | | | | |
| | | | | | | | | | | | | | | | | | | |
| | | | | | | | | | | | | | | | | | | |
| | | | | | | | | | | | | | | | | | | |

| Employee | Net Claim Code | Earnings | | | Deductions | | | | | | | | | | | Total Ded'ns | Net Pay |
| | | Regular | Extra | Gross | C.P.P. | U.I. Premium | R.R.P. | Income Tax | | Health Ins. | Union Dues | Group Life | | | | | |
| | | | | | | | | Taxable Income | Ded'n | | | | | | | | |
| Harold Evans | | 645 00 | — | 645 00 | 11 03 | 6 60 | 32 25 | | | | | | | | | | |
| | | | | | | | | | | | | | | | | | |
| | | | | | | | | | | | | | | | | | |
| | | | | | | | | | | | | | | | | | |

For the _2 Weeks_ ended _May 24_ 19 —

tributes an equal amount. The accounting for the company share will be discussed later.

## Income Tax

According to Canadian income tax laws, employers are required to make a deduction from the earnings of each of the employees for personal income taxes. The amount to be deducted depends on two factors:
1. The amount of taxable income.
2. The employee's total personal exemption.

## Taxable earnings

Taxable earnings are determined by subtracting from the gross pay the following items:
1. The employee's contribution to the Canada Pension Plan.
2. The employee's premium for Unemployment Insurance.
3. The employee's contribution to registered retirement plans.

Harold Evans contributed to all three of the above items. His contributions were as follows:

| | |
|---|---|
| Canada Pension Plan premium – | $11.03 |
| Unemployment Insurance premium – | $ 6.60 |
| Registered Retirement Plan – | $32.25 |
| | $49.88 |

Since gross pay − (C.P.P. + U.I. + R.R.P. deductions) = taxable earnings, then Harold Evans's taxable earnings are $645.00 − $49.88 = $595.12. This figure is recorded in the payroll journal, as shown at the top of page 290.

The general procedure for determining payroll deductions is standard across the country. The amount of individual deductions will vary according to differences in the terms of the plans for different provinces or organizations (for example, The Quebec Pension Plan).

The tables shown on page 289 are examples of tables currently in use. These are updated regularly by the federal government in consultation with the provincial governments.

## Personal Exemption

Every employee is required to fill out a Form TD-1, illustrated on page 288. It is used to calculate the employee's total personal exemption which is the amount of annual earnings that he may earn without being taxed. The amount varies with the employee's marital status, the number and ages of dependent children and other dependants. This form is completed whenever an employee starts a new job, whenever there is a change in the number or status of his dependants, and also at the beginning of each year. The illustration shows Form TD-1 completed for Harold Evans, who is married and has two children.

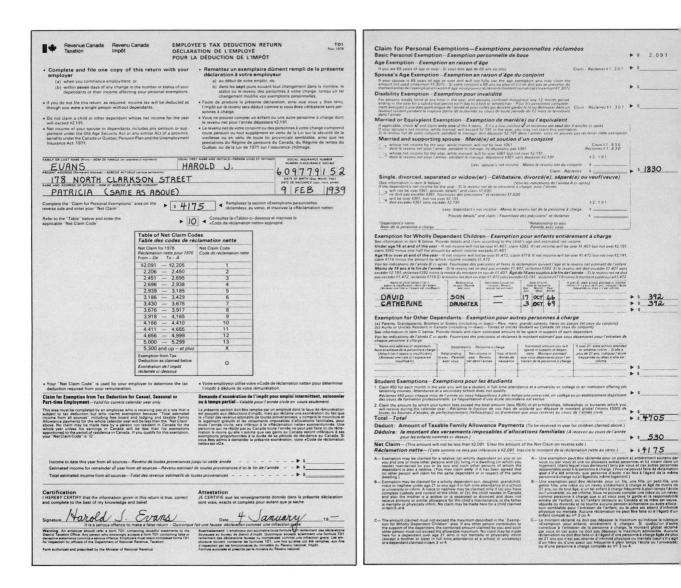

He has a total personal exemption of $4 175 and a '**net claim code**' of *10*. The net claim code is used when referring to the income tax deduction tables. A point to be noted is that the family allowance cheques that Mrs. Evans receives are deducted in calculating the total personal exemption for Mr. Evans. The rule is that the annual amount received in family allowance benefits is deducted from the parent who is declaring the children as dependants on the TD-1 Form.

## Calculating Income Tax Deductions

As with Canada pension plan and unemployment insurance, the Department of National Revenue publishes a booklet of tables for personal income taxes. The tables for the biweekly pay period are reproduced on page 289. The shaded column along the left-hand side shows biweekly pay brackets. At the top of the thirteen deduction columns are the net claim codes. To find the correct deduction, it is necessary to lo-

## TABLE 245

**BIWEEKLY TAX DEDUCTIONS**
**Basis—26 Pay Periods per Year**

**DÉDUCTIONS D'IMPÔT DE DEUX SEMAINES**
**Base—26 périodes de paie par année**

| BI-WEEKLY PAY Use appropriate bracket — PAIE DE DEUX SEMAINES Utilisez le palier approprié | IF THE EMPLOYEE'S "NET CLAIM CODE" ON FORM TD1 IS — SI LE «CODE DE RÉCLAMATION NETTE» DE L'EMPLOYÉ SELON LA FORMULE TD1 EST DE | | | | | | | | | | | | | See note on page 22. Voir remarque p. 22. |
|---|---|---|---|---|---|---|---|---|---|---|---|---|---|---|
| | 1 | 2 | 3 | 4 | 5 | 6 | 7 | 8 | 9 | 10 | 11 | 12 | 13 | |
| | DEDUCT FROM EACH PAY—DÉDUISEZ SUR CHAQUE PAIE | | | | | | | | | | | | | Column A Colonne A |
| $ 308.00 - 311.99 | 44.70 | 42.25 | 39.70 | 37.10 | 34.50 | 31.95 | 29.35 | 26.75 | 24.20 | 21.75 | 19.30 | 16.10 | 13.10 | 3.00 |
| 312.00 - 315.99 | 45.80 | 43.35 | 40.75 | 38.20 | 35.60 | 33.05 | 30.45 | 27.85 | 25.25 | 22.80 | 20.30 | 17.15 | 14.15 | 3.00 |
| 316.00 - 319.99 | 46.90 | 44.45 | 41.85 | 39.30 | 36.70 | 34.10 | 31.55 | 28.95 | 26.35 | 23.85 | 21.35 | 18.20 | 15.15 | 3.05 |
| 320.00 - 323.99 | 48.00 | 45.55 | 42.95 | 40.40 | 37.80 | 35.20 | 32.65 | 30.05 | 27.45 | 24.85 | 22.40 | 19.25 | 16.20 | 3.05 |
| 324.00 - 327.99 | 49.10 | 46.65 | 44.05 | 41.50 | 38.90 | 36.30 | 33.75 | 31.15 | 28.55 | 26.00 | 23.45 | 20.25 | 17.25 | 3.05 |
| 328.00 - 331.99 | 50.20 | 47.75 | 45.15 | 42.60 | 40.00 | 37.40 | 34.85 | 32.25 | 29.65 | 27.10 | 24.50 | 21.30 | 18.30 | 3.05 |
| 332.00 - 335.99 | 51.30 | 48.85 | 46.25 | 43.65 | 41.10 | 38.50 | 35.90 | 33.35 | 30.75 | 28.20 | 25.55 | 22.35 | 19.35 | 3.05 |
| 336.00 - 339.99 | 52.40 | 49.95 | 47.35 | 44.75 | 42.20 | 39.60 | 37.00 | 34.45 | 31.85 | 29.25 | 26.70 | 23.40 | 20.40 | 3.05 |
| 340.00 - 343.99 | 53.45 | 51.05 | 48.45 | 45.85 | 43.30 | 40.70 | 38.10 | 35.55 | 32.95 | 30.35 | 27.80 | 24.45 | 21.45 | 3.05 |
| 344.00 - 347.99 | 54.65 | 52.15 | 49.55 | 46.95 | 44.40 | 41.80 | 39.20 | 36.65 | 34.05 | 31.45 | 28.90 | 25.50 | 22.50 | 3.05 |
| 348.00 - 351.99 | 55.85 | 53.20 | 50.65 | 48.05 | 45.45 | 42.90 | 40.30 | 37.75 | 35.15 | 32.55 | 30.00 | 26.65 | 23.55 | 3.10 |
| 352.00 - 355.99 | 57.05 | 54.40 | 51.75 | 49.15 | 46.55 | 44.00 | 41.40 | 38.80 | 36.25 | 33.65 | 31.10 | 27.75 | 24.55 | 3.20 |
| 356.00 - 359.99 | 58.25 | 55.60 | 52.85 | 50.25 | 47.65 | 45.10 | 42.50 | 39.90 | 37.35 | 34.75 | 32.15 | 28.85 | 25.60 | 3.25 |
| 360.00 - 363.99 | 59.45 | 56.80 | 53.95 | 51.35 | 48.75 | 46.20 | 43.60 | 41.00 | 38.40 | 35.85 | 33.25 | 29.95 | 26.75 | 3.25 |
| 364.00 - 367.99 | 60.65 | 58.00 | 55.15 | 52.45 | 49.85 | 47.30 | 44.70 | 42.10 | 39.50 | 36.95 | 34.35 | 31.00 | 27.85 | 3.25 |
| 368.00 - 371.99 | 61.85 | 59.20 | 56.35 | 53.55 | 50.95 | 48.35 | 45.80 | 43.20 | 40.60 | 38.05 | 35.45 | 32.10 | 28.95 | 3.25 |
| 372.00 - 375.99 | 63.10 | 60.40 | 57.55 | 54.75 | 52.05 | 49.45 | 46.90 | 44.30 | 41.70 | 39.15 | 36.55 | 33.20 | 30.05 | 3.25 |
| 376.00 - 379.99 | 64.30 | 61.60 | 58.75 | 55.95 | 53.15 | 50.55 | 48.00 | 45.40 | 42.80 | 40.25 | 37.65 | 34.30 | 31.15 | 3.25 |
| 380.00 - 383.99 | 65.50 | 62.80 | 59.95 | 57.15 | 54.30 | 51.65 | 49.10 | 46.50 | 43.90 | 41.35 | 38.75 | 35.40 | 32.25 | 3.25 |
| 384.00 - 387.99 | 66.70 | 64.00 | 61.15 | 58.35 | 55.50 | 52.75 | 50.20 | 47.60 | 45.00 | 42.45 | 39.85 | 36.50 | 33.35 | 3.25 |
| 388.00 - 391.99 | 67.90 | 65.20 | 62.35 | 59.55 | 56.70 | 53.90 | 51.25 | 48.70 | 46.10 | 43.50 | 40.95 | 37.60 | 34.45 | 3.25 |
| 392.00 - 395.99 | 69.10 | 66.40 | 63.55 | 60.75 | 57.90 | 55.10 | 52.35 | 49.80 | 47.20 | 44.60 | 42.05 | 38.70 | 35.55 | 3.25 |
| 396.00 - 399.99 | 70.30 | 67.60 | 64.75 | 61.95 | 59.10 | 56.30 | 53.45 | 50.90 | 48.30 | 45.70 | 43.15 | 39.80 | 36.65 | 3.25 |
| 400.00 - 403.99 | 71.50 | 68.80 | 65.95 | 63.15 | 60.30 | 57.50 | 54.65 | 52.00 | 49.40 | 46.80 | 44.25 | 40.90 | 37.75 | 3.25 |
| 404.00 - 407.99 | 72.70 | 70.00 | 67.15 | 64.35 | 61.50 | 58.70 | 55.85 | 53.05 | 50.50 | 47.90 | 45.35 | 42.00 | 38.80 | 3.25 |
| 408.00 - 417.99 | 74.80 | 72.10 | 69.25 | 66.45 | 63.60 | 60.80 | 57.95 | 55.15 | 52.40 | 49.85 | 47.25 | 43.90 | 40.75 | 3.25 |
| 418.00 - 427.99 | 77.80 | 75.10 | 72.30 | 69.45 | 66.60 | 63.80 | 60.95 | 58.15 | 55.30 | 52.55 | 50.00 | 46.65 | 43.50 | 3.25 |
| 428.00 - 437.99 | 80.80 | 78.10 | 75.30 | 72.45 | 69.60 | 66.80 | 63.95 | 61.15 | 58.30 | 55.50 | 52.75 | 49.40 | 46.20 | 3.25 |
| 438.00 - 447.99 | 83.80 | 81.10 | 78.30 | 75.45 | 72.60 | 69.80 | 66.95 | 64.15 | 61.30 | 58.50 | 55.65 | 52.15 | 48.95 | 3.25 |
| 448.00 - 457.99 | 87.05 | 84.15 | 81.30 | 78.45 | 75.60 | 72.80 | 69.95 | 67.15 | 64.30 | 61.50 | 58.65 | 55.00 | 51.70 | 3.30 |
| 458.00 - 467.99 | 90.35 | 87.40 | 84.35 | 81.45 | 78.65 | 75.80 | 72.95 | 70.15 | 67.30 | 64.50 | 61.65 | 58.00 | 54.55 | 3.45 |
| 468.00 - 477.99 | 93.60 | 90.70 | 87.60 | 84.55 | 81.65 | 78.80 | 75.95 | 73.15 | 70.30 | 67.50 | 64.65 | 61.00 | 57.55 | 3.45 |
| 478.00 - 487.99 | 96.85 | 93.95 | 90.85 | 87.80 | 84.70 | 81.80 | 78.95 | 76.15 | 73.30 | 70.50 | 67.65 | 64.00 | 60.55 | 3.45 |
| 488.00 - 497.99 | 100.10 | 97.20 | 94.15 | 91.05 | 88.00 | 84.90 | 81.95 | 79.15 | 76.30 | 73.50 | 70.65 | 67.00 | 63.55 | 3.45 |
| 498.00 - 507.99 | 103.40 | 100.45 | 97.40 | 94.30 | 91.25 | 88.15 | 85.10 | 82.15 | 79.30 | 76.50 | 73.65 | 70.00 | 66.55 | 3.45 |
| 508.00 - 517.99 | 106.65 | 103.75 | 100.65 | 97.60 | 94.50 | 91.45 | 88.35 | 85.30 | 82.30 | 79.50 | 76.65 | 73.00 | 69.55 | 3.45 |
| 518.00 - 527.99 | 109.90 | 107.00 | 103.90 | 100.85 | 97.75 | 94.70 | 91.60 | 88.55 | 85.45 | 82.50 | 79.65 | 76.00 | 72.55 | 3.45 |
| 528.00 - 537.99 | 113.15 | 110.25 | 107.20 | 104.10 | 101.05 | 97.95 | 94.90 | 91.80 | 88.75 | 85.65 | 82.65 | 79.00 | 75.55 | 3.45 |
| 538.00 - 547.99 | 116.40 | 113.50 | 110.45 | 107.35 | 104.30 | 101.20 | 98.15 | 95.10 | 92.00 | 88.95 | 85.85 | 82.00 | 78.55 | 3.45 |
| 548.00 - 557.99 | 119.80 | 116.80 | 113.70 | 110.65 | 107.55 | 104.50 | 101.40 | 98.35 | 95.25 | 92.20 | 89.10 | 85.15 | 81.55 | 3.60 |

## TABLE 245

**BIWEEKLY TAX DEDUCTIONS**
**Basis—26 Pay Periods per Year**

**DÉDUCTIONS D'IMPÔT DE DEUX SEMAINES**
**Base—26 périodes de paie par année**

| BI-WEEKLY PAY Use appropriate bracket — PAIE DE DEUX SEMAINES Utilisez le palier approprié | IF THE EMPLOYEE'S "NET CLAIM CODE" ON FORM TD1 IS — SI LE «CODE DE RÉCLAMATION NETTE» DE L'EMPLOYÉ SELON LA FORMULE TD1 EST DE | | | | | | | | | | | | | See note on page 22. Voir remarque p. 22. |
|---|---|---|---|---|---|---|---|---|---|---|---|---|---|---|
| | 1 | 2 | 3 | 4 | 5 | 6 | 7 | 8 | 9 | 10 | 11 | 12 | 13 | |
| | DEDUCT FROM EACH PAY—DÉDUISEZ SUR CHAQUE PAIE | | | | | | | | | | | | | Column A Colonne A |
| $ 558.00 - 567.99 | 123.10 | 120.15 | 117.00 | 113.90 | 110.80 | 107.75 | 104.65 | 101.60 | 98.50 | 95.45 | 92.40 | 88.40 | 84.65 | 3.75 |
| 568.00 - 577.99 | 126.40 | 123.45 | 120.35 | 117.20 | 114.10 | 111.00 | 107.95 | 104.85 | 101.80 | 98.70 | 95.65 | 91.65 | 87.90 | 3.75 |
| 578.00 - 587.99 | 129.70 | 126.75 | 123.65 | 120.55 | 117.40 | 114.25 | 111.20 | 108.15 | 105.05 | 102.00 | 98.90 | 94.95 | 91.15 | 3.80 |
| 588.00 - 597.99 | 133.05 | 130.10 | 126.95 | 123.85 | 120.75 | 117.60 | 114.45 | 111.40 | 108.30 | 105.25 | 102.15 | 98.20 | 94.40 | 3.90 |
| 598.00 - 607.99 | 136.35 | 133.40 | 130.25 | 127.15 | 124.05 | 120.90 | 117.80 | 114.65 | 111.55 | 108.50 | 105.45 | 101.45 | 97.70 | 3.80 |
| 608.00 - 617.99 | 139.65 | 136.70 | 133.55 | 130.45 | 127.35 | 124.20 | 121.10 | 118.00 | 114.85 | 111.75 | 108.70 | 104.70 | 100.95 | 3.80 |
| 618.00 - 627.99 | 142.95 | 140.00 | 136.90 | 133.75 | 130.65 | 127.55 | 124.40 | 121.30 | 118.15 | 115.05 | 111.95 | 108.00 | 104.20 | 3.80 |
| 628.00 - 637.99 | 146.25 | 143.30 | 140.20 | 137.05 | 133.95 | 130.85 | 127.70 | 124.60 | 121.50 | 118.35 | 115.20 | 111.25 | 107.45 | 3.80 |
| 638.00 - 647.99 | 149.55 | 146.60 | 143.50 | 140.40 | 137.25 | 134.15 | 131.05 | 127.90 | 124.80 | 121.70 | 118.55 | 114.50 | 110.75 | 3.80 |
| 648.00 - 657.99 | 153.35 | 149.95 | 146.80 | 143.70 | 140.55 | 137.45 | 134.35 | 131.20 | 128.10 | 125.00 | 121.85 | 117.85 | 114.00 | 3.85 |
| 658.00 - 667.99 | 157.15 | 153.75 | 150.20 | 147.00 | 143.90 | 140.75 | 137.65 | 134.55 | 131.40 | 128.30 | 125.20 | 121.15 | 117.30 | 3.85 |
| 668.00 - 677.99 | 160.95 | 157.55 | 154.00 | 150.40 | 147.20 | 144.05 | 140.95 | 137.85 | 134.70 | 131.60 | 128.50 | 124.45 | 120.65 | 3.85 |
| 678.00 - 687.99 | 164.75 | 161.35 | 157.80 | 154.20 | 150.60 | 147.40 | 144.25 | 141.15 | 138.00 | 134.90 | 131.80 | 127.75 | 123.95 | 3.85 |
| 688.00 - 697.99 | 168.55 | 165.15 | 161.60 | 158.00 | 154.40 | 150.85 | 147.55 | 144.45 | 141.30 | 138.20 | 135.10 | 131.05 | 127.25 | 3.85 |
| 698.00 - 707.99 | 172.35 | 168.95 | 165.40 | 161.80 | 158.20 | 154.65 | 151.05 | 147.75 | 144.65 | 141.50 | 138.40 | 134.40 | 130.55 | 3.95 |
| 708.00 - 717.99 | 176.15 | 172.75 | 169.15 | 165.60 | 162.00 | 158.45 | 154.85 | 151.30 | 147.95 | 144.85 | 141.70 | 137.70 | 133.85 | 3.85 |
| 718.00 - 727.99 | 179.95 | 176.55 | 172.95 | 169.40 | 165.80 | 162.25 | 158.65 | 155.10 | 151.50 | 148.15 | 145.00 | 141.00 | 137.15 | 3.85 |
| 728.00 - 737.99 | 183.75 | 180.35 | 176.75 | 173.20 | 169.60 | 166.05 | 162.45 | 158.90 | 155.30 | 151.70 | 148.35 | 144.30 | 140.50 | 3.95 |
| 738.00 - 747.99 | 187.55 | 184.15 | 180.55 | 177.00 | 173.40 | 169.85 | 166.25 | 162.65 | 159.10 | 155.50 | 151.95 | 147.60 | 143.80 | 3.85 |
| 748.00 - 757.99 | 191.35 | 187.95 | 184.35 | 180.80 | 177.20 | 173.65 | 170.05 | 166.45 | 162.90 | 159.30 | 155.75 | 151.10 | 147.10 | 4.00 |
| 758.00 - 767.99 | 195.15 | 191.75 | 188.15 | 184.60 | 181.00 | 177.45 | 173.85 | 170.25 | 166.70 | 163.10 | 159.55 | 154.90 | 150.50 | 4.40 |
| 768.00 - 777.99 | 198.95 | 195.55 | 191.95 | 188.40 | 184.80 | 181.20 | 177.65 | 174.05 | 170.45 | 166.90 | 163.35 | 158.70 | 154.30 | 4.40 |
| 778.00 - 787.99 | 202.70 | 199.35 | 195.75 | 192.20 | 188.60 | 185.00 | 181.45 | 177.85 | 174.25 | 170.70 | 167.15 | 162.50 | 158.10 | 4.40 |
| 788.00 - 797.99 | 206.50 | 203.15 | 199.55 | 196.00 | 192.40 | 188.80 | 185.25 | 181.65 | 178.05 | 174.50 | 170.95 | 166.30 | 161.90 | 4.40 |
| 798.00 - 807.99 | 210.80 | 207.00 | 203.35 | 199.75 | 196.20 | 192.60 | 189.05 | 185.45 | 181.85 | 178.30 | 174.70 | 170.10 | 165.70 | 4.40 |
| 808.00 - 817.99 | 215.10 | 211.25 | 207.20 | 203.55 | 200.00 | 196.40 | 192.85 | 189.25 | 185.65 | 182.10 | 178.50 | 173.90 | 169.50 | 4.40 |
| 818.00 - 827.99 | 219.40 | 215.55 | 211.50 | 207.45 | 203.80 | 200.20 | 196.65 | 193.05 | 189.45 | 185.90 | 182.30 | 177.70 | 173.30 | 4.40 |
| 828.00 - 837.99 | 223.65 | 219.85 | 215.80 | 211.75 | 207.70 | 204.00 | 200.45 | 196.85 | 193.25 | 189.70 | 186.10 | 181.50 | 177.10 | 4.40 |
| 838.00 - 847.99 | 227.95 | 224.15 | 220.10 | 216.05 | 212.00 | 207.95 | 204.25 | 200.65 | 197.05 | 193.50 | 189.90 | 185.30 | 180.90 | 4.40 |
| 848.00 - 857.99 | 232.25 | 228.40 | 224.35 | 220.35 | 216.30 | 212.25 | 208.20 | 204.45 | 200.85 | 197.30 | 193.70 | 189.10 | 184.70 | 4.40 |
| 858.00 - 867.99 | 236.55 | 232.70 | 228.65 | 224.60 | 220.60 | 216.55 | 212.50 | 208.45 | 204.65 | 201.10 | 197.50 | 192.90 | 188.50 | 4.40 |
| 868.00 - 877.99 | 240.80 | 237.00 | 232.95 | 228.90 | 224.85 | 220.85 | 216.80 | 212.75 | 208.70 | 204.90 | 201.30 | 196.70 | 192.30 | 4.40 |
| 878.00 - 887.99 | 245.10 | 241.30 | 237.25 | 233.20 | 229.15 | 225.10 | 221.10 | 217.05 | 213.00 | 208.95 | 205.10 | 200.45 | 196.10 | 4.40 |
| 888.00 - 897.99 | 249.40 | 245.55 | 241.50 | 237.50 | 233.45 | 229.40 | 225.35 | 221.30 | 217.25 | 213.25 | 209.20 | 204.25 | 199.90 | 4.40 |
| 898.00 - 907.99 | 253.70 | 249.85 | 245.80 | 241.75 | 237.75 | 233.70 | 229.65 | 225.60 | 221.55 | 217.55 | 213.50 | 208.25 | 203.70 | 4.55 |
| 908.00 - 927.99 | 260.10 | 256.30 | 252.25 | 248.20 | 244.15 | 240.10 | 236.10 | 232.05 | 228.00 | 223.95 | 219.90 | 214.70 | 209.75 | 4.95 |
| 928.00 - 947.99 | 268.70 | 264.85 | 260.80 | 256.80 | 252.75 | 248.70 | 244.65 | 240.60 | 236.55 | 232.55 | 228.50 | 223.25 | 218.30 | 4.95 |
| 948.00 - 967.99 | 277.25 | 273.45 | 269.40 | 265.35 | 261.30 | 257.25 | 253.25 | 249.20 | 245.15 | 241.10 | 237.05 | 231.85 | 226.90 | 4.95 |
| 968.00 - 987.99 | 285.85 | 282.00 | 277.95 | 273.95 | 269.90 | 265.85 | 261.80 | 257.75 | 253.70 | 249.70 | 245.65 | 240.40 | 235.45 | 4.95 |
| 988.00 - 1007.99 | 294.40 | 290.60 | 286.55 | 282.50 | 278.45 | 274.40 | 270.40 | 266.35 | 262.30 | 258.25 | 254.20 | 249.00 | 244.05 | 4.95 |

| Employee | Net Claim Code | Earnings | | | Deductions | | | | | | | | | | Total Ded'ns | Net Pay |
|---|---|---|---|---|---|---|---|---|---|---|---|---|---|---|---|---|
| | | Regular | Extra | Gross | C.P.P. | U.I. Premium | R.R.P. | Income Tax Taxable Income | Ded'n | Health Ins. | Union Dues | Group Life | | | | |
| Harold Evans | 10 | 645 00 | — | 645 00 | 11 03 | 6 60 | 32 25 | 595 12 | 105 25 | | | | | | | |

cate the appropriate biweekly pay bracket in the shaded area and to follow it to the right until you arrive at the correct net claim code column. We have calculated that Harold Evans has a taxable earnings figure of $595.12 and a net claim code of 10. The correct income tax deduction for him is $105.25. It is recorded in the journal as illustrated above.

## Health Insurance

Most provinces have in operation a universal health insurance program. In most cases it is a single basic plan which pays for both doctors' fees as well as hospital expenses. Employers are authorized to deduct from the employee's pay the amount of the premium as set out by the provincial government. The premium for a single person is less than that for a person who is married and has dependent children. The rates to be used for the exercises in this text are shown below.

HEALTH INSURANCE BIWEEKLY RATES

1. Single person      Public ward    $11.00
                        Semiprivate    $12.00

2. Family (head and all    Public ward    $22.00
   dependants)           Semiprivate    $24.00

Recent years have shown an increase in health insurance plans which provide additional benefits not included in the basic health plans operated by the province. Such programs as Extended Health Care and Dental Health Care are becoming quite common. In addition to an increase in the variety of health care programs, it is quite common for employers to pay a large portion or the entire premium for the health care programs.

Harold Evans has no additional health coverage other than the basic program for which rates are shown above. His employer pays 75 per cent of the premium. Mr. Evans has semiprivate coverage.

Calculation:
Mr. Evans's portion:
25% of $24.00 = $6.00

The journal below shows the premium for Harold Evans recorded in the payroll journal.

| Employee | Net Claim Code | Earnings | | | Deductions | | | | | | | | | | Total Ded'ns | Net Pay |
|---|---|---|---|---|---|---|---|---|---|---|---|---|---|---|---|---|
| | | Regular | Extra | Gross | C.P.P. | U.I. Premium | R.R.P. | Income Tax Taxable Income | Ded'n | Health Ins. | Union Dues | Group Life | | | | |
| Harold Evans | 10 | 645 00 | — | 645 00 | 11 03 | 6 60 | 32 25 | 595 12 | 105 25 | 6 00 | | | | | | |

For the _2 Weeks_ ended _May 24_ 19 —

| Employee | Net Claim Code | Earnings | | | Deductions | | | | | | | | | | | Total Ded'ns | Net Pay |
| | | Regular | Extra | Gross | C.P.P. | U.I. Premium | R.R.P. | Income Tax Taxable Income | Ded'n | Health Ins. | Union Dues | Group Life | | | | | |
|---|---|---|---|---|---|---|---|---|---|---|---|---|---|---|---|---|---|
| Harold Evans | 10 | 645 00 | — | 645 00 | 11 03 | 6 60 | 32 25 | 595 12 | 105 25 | 6 00 | 7 00 | | | | | | |
| | | | | | | | | | | | | | | | | | |
| | | | | | | | | | | | | | | | | | |
| | | | | | | | | | | | | | | | | | |

## Union Dues 'Check-off'

Very often the employees of a medium-sized or larger business are organized into a labor union. Dues to the union are often deductions made by the employer who remits the monies periodically to the union. This obligation of the employer is usually part of the contract negotiated between the employer and the employees.

**2.01** The Company will deduct each month from the wages of each employee in the bargaining unit an amount equivalent to the normal monthly Union dues and will remit such sums deducted to the appropriate official of the Union.

This clause is taken from a contract obtained by the Brotherhood of Railway and Steamship Clerks, Freight Handlers, Express and Station Employees, Lodge No. 650. The amount that is deducted from the employee's pay depends on the union. In the case of Harold Evans, his union requires a deduction of $7.00 each pay period. The above journal shows the deduction entered.

## Group Life Insurance

Some firms make it possible for their employees to enrol in some form of group life insurance plan. Premiums are therefore handled as a payroll deduction. Premiums are paid at a specified amount per $1 000 of insurance protection. The amount of insurance that an employee may obtain depends on his gross earnings.

Harold Evans has group life insurance and pays a premium of 15 cents per week per $1 000 worth of insurance. He has a total amount of $12 000 of insurance. This means that his premium is $12 \times 15¢$, which is $1.80 per week, or $3.60 each pay period. The payroll journal below shows the premium properly entered.

## Other Deductions

There may be other deductions made from an employee's earnings if authority is granted by the employee. They are handled in a manner similar to those deductions that we have already discussed. Some of these other deductions are charitable donations, credit union contributions and purchases of bonds or shares of stock.

For the _2 Weeks_ ended _May 24_ 19 —

| Employee | Net Claim Code | Earnings | | | Deductions | | | | | | | | | | | Total Ded'ns | Net Pay |
| | | Regular | Extra | Gross | C.P.P. | U.I. Premium | R.R.P. | Income Tax Taxable Income | Ded'n | Health Ins. | Union Dues | Group Life | | | | | |
|---|---|---|---|---|---|---|---|---|---|---|---|---|---|---|---|---|---|
| Harold Evans | 10 | 645 00 | — | 645 00 | 11 03 | 6 60 | 32 25 | 595 12 | 105 25 | 6 00 | 7 00 | 3 60 | | | | | |
| | | | | | | | | | | | | | | | | | |
| | | | | | | | | | | | | | | | | | |
| | | | | | | | | | | | | | | | | | |

| Employee | Net Claim Code | Earnings | | | Deductions | | | | | | | | | | Total Ded'ns | Net Pay |
|---|---|---|---|---|---|---|---|---|---|---|---|---|---|---|---|---|
| | | Regular | Extra | Gross | C.P.P. | U.I. Premium | R.R.P. | Income Tax Taxable Income | Ded'n | Health Ins. | Union Dues | Group Life | | | | |
| Harold Evans | 10 | 645 00 | — | 645 00 | 11 03 | 6 60 | 32 25 | 595 12 | 105 25 | 6 00 | 7 00 | 3 60 | | | 171 73 | 473 27 |
| | | | | | | | | | | | | | | | | |
| | | | | | | | | | | | | | | | | |
| | | | | | | | | | | | | | | | | |
| | | | | | | | | | | | | | | | | |
| | | | | | | | | | | | | | | | | |

## Calculating Net Pay

At this point, the last deduction to be made from Harold Evans's pay has been entered. There are two steps remaining. First, add all the deductions and enter this amount in the Total Deductions column. This total is then subtracted from the gross pay of $645, giving a net pay of $473.27. This amount is entered in the Net Pay column of the journal. The illustration above shows the completed calculations for Harold Evans.

## Completing the Payroll Journal

The procedure that has been discussed and illustrated for Harold Evans is repeated for each of

the employees in the company. One line of the payroll journal is used for each employee. When all of the details for all of the employees are entered in the journal, the amount columns are totaled as shown below.

### Proving the Accuracy of the Journal

The next step is to prove the column totals of the journal. There are three steps to be performed to ensure the accuracy of the journal. You should ensure that:

1. The Regular Earnings column + the Extra Earnings column = the Gross Earnings column.
2. The sum of all the deduction columns = the Total Deductions column.
3. The Gross Earnings column − the Total Deductions column = the Net Pay column.

PAYROLL JOURNAL     For the _2 Weeks_ ended _May 24_ 19 —

| Employee | Net Claim Code | Earnings | | | Deductions | | | | | | | | | | Total Ded'ns | Net Pay |
|---|---|---|---|---|---|---|---|---|---|---|---|---|---|---|---|---|
| | | Regular | Extra | Gross | C.P.P. | U.I. Premium | R.R.P. | Income Tax Taxable Income | Ded'n | Health Ins. | Union Dues | Group Life | | | | |
| Harold Evans | 10 | 645 00 | — | 645 00 | 11 03 | 6 60 | 32 25 | 595 12 | 105 25 | 6 00 | 7 00 | 3 60 | | | 171 73 | 473 27 |
| Ronald Baker | 7 | 610 00 | — | 610 00 | 10 40 | 6 60 | 30 50 | 562 50 | 104 65 | 6 00 | 7 00 | 3 30 | | | 168 45 | 441 55 |
| Bob Funston | 8 | 590 00 | — | 590 00 | 10 04 | 6 60 | 29 50 | 543 86 | 95 10 | 6 00 | 7 00 | 3 30 | | | 157 54 | 432 46 |
| Leo Williams | 1 | 550 00 | 35 00 | 585 00 | 9 95 | 6 60 | 29 25 | 539 20 | 129 70 | 3 00 | 7 00 | 3 00 | | | 188 50 | 396 50 |
| Dennis Murray | 8 | 630 00 | — | 630 00 | 10 76 | 6 60 | 31 50 | 581 14 | 124 60 | 6 00 | 7 00 | 3 60 | | | 190 06 | 439 94 |
| | | 3025 00 | 35 00 | 3060 00 | 52 18 | 33 00 | 153 00 | 2821 82 | 559 30 | 27 00 | 35 00 | 16 80 | | | 876 28 | 2183 72 |
| | | | | | | | | | | | | | | | | |
| | | | | | | | | | | | | | | | | |
| | | | | | | | | | | | | | | | | |
| | | | | | | | | | | | | | | | | |
| | | | | | | | | | | | | | | | | |

# Recording the Payroll

When the column totals have been verified, it is necessary to record the payroll accounting entries in the general journal. There are five entries to be made in the case of Nor-Can Grocers Ltd.

1. Recording the payroll summary figures from the payroll journal.
2. Recording the employer's liability for Canada pension plan.
3. Recording the employer's liability for unemployment insurance.
4. Recording the employer's liability for the registered retirement plan.
5. Recording the employer's liability for health insurance.

## The Accounting Entries

*Entry 1.* Recording the payroll summary figures from the payroll journal.

The information for the first entry is obtained from the column totals of the payroll journal. In preparing this entry the accountant must be aware of the following:

a. The total Gross Earnings figure represents the Wages (or Salaries) expense to the business and is recorded as a debit to an expense account.

b. Each of the deductions has been made from the employees' earnings on behalf of the government or some private agency and, until remitted, represents a liability of the employer. Each deduction total, therefore, is recorded as a credit to an individual liability account.

c. The Net Pay figure represents a liability to the employees and is credited to a liability account called Payroll Payable.

The illustration below shows the first entry recorded.

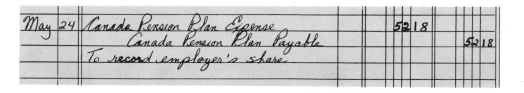

| Date 19— | | Particulars | P.R. | Debit | Credit |
|---|---|---|---|---|---|
| May | 24 | Salaries Expense | | 3060 — | |
| | | Canada Pension Plan Payable | | | 52 18 |
| | | Unemployment Insurance Payable | | | 33 00 |
| | | Registered Retirement Plan Payable | | | 153 00 |
| | | Employees' Income Taxes Payable | | | 559 30 |
| | | Health Insurance Payable | | | 27 00 |
| | | Union Dues Payable | | | 35 00 |
| | | Group Life Insurance Payable | | | 16 80 |
| | | Payroll Payable | | | 2183 72 |
| | | To record the payroll of May 24, 19 — | | | |

*Entry 2.* Recording the employer's liability for Canada pension plan.

In the discussion of the Canada Pension Plan, it was noted that the employer is required to contribute an amount equal to that made by the employee. The employer's portion is an operating expense of the business. The entry to record this obligation is shown below.

| May | 24 | Canada Pension Plan Expense | | 52 18 | |
|---|---|---|---|---|---|
| | | Canada Pension Plan Payable | | | 52 18 |
| | | To record employer's share | | | |

*Entry 3.* Recording the employer's liability for unemployment insurance.

The employer must contribute 1.4 times the employees' contributions. This amounts to

$$\$33.00 \times 1.4 = \$46.20$$

The entry to record this obligation is shown below.

| May | 24 | Unemployment Insurance Expense | | 46 20 | | |
| | | Unemployment Insurance Payable | | | 46 20 | |
| | | To record employer's share | | | | |

*Entry 4.* Recording the employer's liability for the registered retirement plan.

Both the employees and the employer contribute an amount equal to 5 per cent of the employees' gross pay towards the registered retirement plan. The amount to be contributed by each is $153.00. The entry to show the employer's liability is shown below.

| May | 24 | Registered Retirement Plan Expense | | 153 00 | | |
| | | Registered Retirement Plan Payable | | | 153 00 | |
| | | To record employer's share | | | | |

*Entry 5.* To record the employer's liability for the health insurance program.

The agreement (for Nor-Can Grocers) regarding health insurance is that the employer pays 75 per cent and the employees pay 25 per cent of the cost of the insurance. Thus the company pays three times as much as the employees. For this particular pay period the company must pay 3 × $27, or $81. The entry to record the obligation is shown below.

| May | 24 | Health Insurance Expense | | 81 00 | | |
| | | Health Insurance Payable | | | 81 00 | |
| | | To record employer's share | | | | |

## The Effect in the Accounts

Each of the five entries is then posted to the appropriate general ledger accounts. The accounts which follow show the effect of these five entries.

ACCOUNT  Canada Pension Plan Payable

| DATE | | PARTICULARS | P.R. | DEBIT | CREDIT | DR. CR. | BALANCE |
|---|---|---|---|---|---|---|---|
| May | 24 | Payroll | | | 52 18 | CR | 52 18 |
| | 24 | Employer's share | | | 52 18 | CR | 1 04 36 |

**ACCOUNT** Unemployment Insurance Payable

| DATE | | PARTICULARS | P.R. | DEBIT | CREDIT | DR. CR. | BALANCE |
|---|---|---|---|---|---|---|---|
| May | 24 | Payroll | | | 33 00 | CR | 33 00 |
| | 24 | Employer's share | | | 46 20 | CR | 79 20 |

**ACCOUNT** Registered Retirement Plan Payable

| DATE | | PARTICULARS | P.R. | DEBIT | CREDIT | DR. CR. | BALANCE |
|---|---|---|---|---|---|---|---|
| May | 24 | Payroll | | | 1 53 – | CR | 1 53 – |
| | 24 | Employer's share | | | 1 53 – | CR | 3 06 – |

**ACCOUNT** Employees' Income Taxes Payable

| DATE | | PARTICULARS | P.R. | DEBIT | CREDIT | DR. CR. | BALANCE |
|---|---|---|---|---|---|---|---|
| May | 24 | Payroll | | | 5 59 30 | CR | 5 59 30 |

**ACCOUNT** Health Insurance Payable

| DATE | | PARTICULARS | P.R. | DEBIT | CREDIT | DR. CR. | BALANCE |
|---|---|---|---|---|---|---|---|
| May | 24 | Payroll | | | 27 00 | CR | 27 00 |
| | 24 | Employer's share | | | 81 00 | CR | 1 08 00 |

**ACCOUNT** Union Dues Payable

| DATE | | PARTICULARS | P.R. | DEBIT | CREDIT | DR. CR. | BALANCE |
|---|---|---|---|---|---|---|---|
| May | 24 | Payroll | | | 35 – | CR | 35 – |

**ACCOUNT** Group Life Insurance Payable

| DATE | | PARTICULARS | P.R. | DEBIT | CREDIT | DR. CR. | BALANCE |
|---|---|---|---|---|---|---|---|
| May | 24 | Payroll | | | 1 6 80 | CR | 1 6 80 |

**ACCOUNT** Payroll Payable

| DATE | | PARTICULARS | P.R. | DEBIT | CREDIT | DR. CR. | BALANCE |
|---|---|---|---|---|---|---|---|
| May | 24 | Payroll | | | 2 1 83 72 | CR | 2 1 83 72 |

**ACCOUNT** Salaries Expense

| DATE | | PARTICULARS | P.R. | DEBIT | CREDIT | DR. CR. | BALANCE |
|---|---|---|---|---|---|---|---|
| May | 24 | Payroll | | 3 0 60 – | | DR | 3 0 60 – |

| ACCOUNT | Canada Pension Plan Expense | | | | | | | | |
|---------|------------|-----|-------|--------|--------|---------|
| DATE | PARTICULARS | P.R. | DEBIT | CREDIT | DR CR | BALANCE |
| May 24 | Payroll | | 52 18 | | DR | 52 18 |

| ACCOUNT | Unemployment Insurance Expense | | | | | |
|---------|------------|-----|-------|--------|--------|---------|
| DATE | PARTICULARS | P.R. | DEBIT | CREDIT | DR CR | BALANCE |
| May 24 | Payroll | | 46 20 | | DR | 46 20 |

| ACCOUNT | Registered Retirement Plan Expense | | | | | |
|---------|------------|-----|-------|--------|--------|---------|
| DATE | PARTICULARS | P.R. | DEBIT | CREDIT | DR CR | BALANCE |
| May 24 | Payroll | | 153 - | | DR | 153 - |

| ACCOUNT | Health Insurance Expense | | | | | |
|---------|------------|-----|-------|--------|--------|---------|
| DATE | PARTICULARS | P.R. | DEBIT | CREDIT | DR CR | BALANCE |
| May 24 | Payroll | | 81 00 | | DR | 81 00 |

## Payment to Employees

### Method 1. Paying by Cash

When employees receive their pay in cash, it is necessary to prepare each pay envelope with the correct amount of cash. In order to have the right number of bills and coins for all of the employees' envelopes, it is first necessary to prepare a 'currency requisition' form, shown below.

This form is taken to the bank together with a cheque drawn on the regular bank account for the total amount shown on the form. The cheque is cashed, and the required number of each of the bills and coins as shown on the form is received from the bank. The accounting entry for this cheque is:

Dr. Payroll Payable $2 183.72
   Cr. Bank           $2 183.72

The employees' pay envelopes are filled with currency and coins as shown by the currency requisition form. Included with each pay envelope is a statement showing the employee's earnings, deductions, and net pay. This statement may be a separate statement or may be printed on the outside of the envelope. The employee's signature is obtained at the time of paying as proof of payment.

| PAYROLL CURRENCY REQUISITION | | | | | | | | | | PAY PERIOD ENDED May 24, 19— |
|---------|--------|--------|--------|-----|-----|------|------|-----|------|
| EMPLOYEE | NET PAY | $20 | $10 | $5 | $1 | 25¢ | 10¢ | 5¢ | 1¢ |
| Harold Evans | 473 27 | 23 | 1 | | 3 | 1 | | | 2 |
| Ronald Baker | 441 55 | 22 | | | 1 | 2 | | 1 | |
| Bob Funston | 432 46 | 21 | 1 | | 2 | 1 | 2 | | 1 |
| Leo Williams | 396 50 | 19 | 1 | 1 | 1 | 2 | | | |
| Dennis Murray | 439 94 | 21 | 1 | 1 | 4 | 3 | 1 | 1 | 4 |
| | | | | | | | | | |
| Number of Coins or Bills | | 106 | 4 | 2 | 11 | 9 | 3 | 2 | 7 |
| Dollar Value | 2 183 72 | 2120.00 | 40.00 | 10.00 | 11.00 | 2.25 | .30 | .10 | .07 |

## Method 2. Paying by Cheque

Many businesses, and in particular firms having a large number of employees, prefer to pay by cheque rather than by cash. It eliminates the problem of having large sums of money around the office. Too, the canceled cheques serve as evidence that the employees did receive their pay. The cheques that the employees receive may be drawn on the company's regular bank account or on a special bank account established to meet the payroll only.

### Regular Bank Account

A separate cheque, drawn on the regular bank account, is issued to each employee for his pay. For each cheque the accounting entry, recorded in the cash payments journal, is:

| | | |
|---|---|---|
| Dr. Payroll Payable | $xxx.xx | |
| Cr. Bank | | $xxx.xx |

The sum of all the individual cheques issued in this way will be equal to the total of the Net Pay column of the payroll journal. Since each of the cheques results in a debit to the Payroll Payable account, they will have the effect of eliminating the balance in this liability account.

### Special Payroll Bank Account

To allow the Payroll Department to operate independently and to issue its own payroll cheques, many businesses set up a separate payroll bank account.

Using this method, one cheque only is drawn on the regular bank account for the amount of the total net pay. In the cash payments journal the accounting entry to record this cheque is:

| | | |
|---|---|---|
| Dr. Payroll Payable | $xxx.xx | |
| Cr. Bank | | $xxx.xx |

This cheque is cashed and the funds deposited in the special payroll bank account, thereby providing funds for the Payroll Department to meet the payroll obligation. The Payroll Department then issues separate payroll cheques to the employees as necessary. No accounting entries are required for these cheques. When all of the cheques are cashed the balance in the payroll bank account will be reduced to zero.

## Payment to Federal Government

On or before the fifteenth day of each month the employer is required to remit to the Receiver General of Canada the combined amount deducted from employees for income taxes, Canada pension, and unemployment insurance, as well as his own share of Canada pension and unemployment insurance. The amount to be paid represents deductions made in the entire previous month. For example, deductions made in August are due by September 15, deductions made in September are due by October 15, and so on. A special two-part form, PD7A (Tax Deduction-Canada Pension Plan-Unemployment Insurance Remittance Return), is used in making the payment. The upper portion is submitted with the payment while the lower portion is retained by the employer for his own records. A PD7A form for Nor-Can Grocers is illustrated on page 298.

On August 31, assume that the balances of the accounts to be paid are as follows:

| | |
|---|---|
| Employees' Income Taxes Payable | $1 455.76 Cr. |
| Canada Pension Plan Payable | 210.32 Cr. |
| Unemployment Insurance Payable | 124.32 Cr. |

One cheque is drawn for the combined amount of $1 790.40. The accounting entry to record the payment is shown below.

| | |
|---|---|
| Employees' Income Taxes Payable | 1 455.76 |
| Canada Pension Plan Payable | 210.32 |
| Unemployment Insurance Payable | 124.32 |
| Bank | 1 790.40 |

When this entry is posted, these liabilities of the previous month are satisfied.

As other liabilities resulting from payroll deductions become due, they are handled in much the same way. A cheque is issued payable to the agency involved for the appropriate amount.

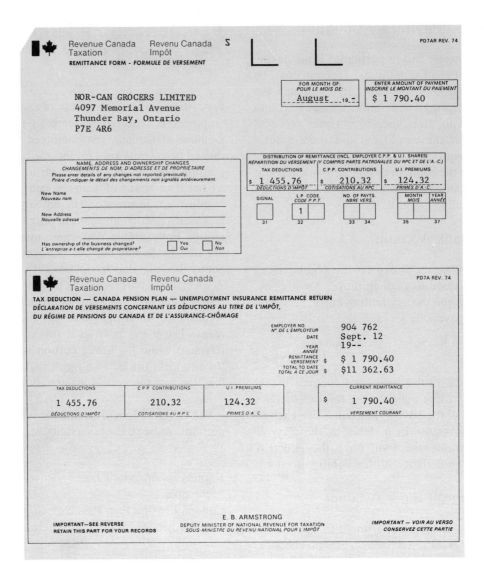

## Using the Payroll Journal as a Book of Original Entry

It should be noted at this point that it is possible to use the payroll journal in another way. We have been considering the payroll journal as a summary sheet and not as a book of original entry. As a result it was necessary to journalize the totals of the payroll into the general journal.

Many business firms, regardless of the journal system used, treat the payroll journal as a book of original entry. As a result, the first payroll entry need not be recorded in the general journal but may be posted directly from the payroll journal to the general ledger. It will still be necessary to record entries 2, 3, 4, and 5 as illus-

trated on pages 293 and 294 in the usual manner. This is necessary because the payroll journal shows only the employees' share of Canada pension, unemployment insurance, registered retirement plan, and health insurance. The employer's share of each must be recorded also.

## Basic Payroll Records

You are aware by now of the importance of written documents in the accounting process. There are three important records that are required for payroll: (1) the payroll journal, (2) the payroll cheque or payroll cash statement, and (3) the individual employee's earnings record.

| | Regular Earnings | Extra Earnings | GROSS PAY | C.P.P. | U.I. | R.R.P. | TAX | HEALTH INSCE | UNION DUES | GROUP LIFE | | TOTAL DEDUC. | NET PAY |
|---|---|---|---|---|---|---|---|---|---|---|---|---|---|
| Harold Evans — NAME | 645.00 | 645.00 | 11.03 | 6.60 | 32.25 | 105.25 | 6.00 | 7.00 | 3.60 | | 171.73 | 473.27 |

DETACH AND RETAIN THIS STATEMENT OF YOUR EARNINGS AND DEDUCTIONS
FOLD BEFORE DETACHING

NOR-CAN GROCERS LIMITED - Thunder Bay, Ontario

**Miscellaneous Deductions**

A.

B.

C.

**NOR-CAN GROCERS LIMITED**
4097 Memorial Avenue
THUNDER BAY, ONTARIO

PAYROLL 1371

DATE ___ May 24 ___ 19—

PAY TO THE ORDER OF ___ Harold J. Evans ___ $ 473.27

THE SUM OF ___ Four hundred and seventy-three ___ 27/100 DOLLARS

NATIONAL BANK OF CANADA
1867 Confederation Avenue
THUNDER BAY, ONTARIO

NOR-CAN GROCERS LIMITED

VOID

⑆94200⑆004⑈ 800 4⑈21369⑉

## 1. Payroll Journal

The payroll journal was discussed and illustrated during the discussion of the various payroll deductions. It is prepared for each pay period and is used to accumulate and calculate all of the necessary information about wages and salaries.

## 2. Payroll Cheques or Payroll Cash Statements

In most businesses, the employees are paid by cheque. Attached to each pay cheque is a voucher that shows the employee's gross pay, deductions, and the net pay. A payroll cheque is shown above.

Businesses that prefer to pay their employees by cash rather than by cheque use a payroll cash statement. It serves the same purpose as the voucher portion of the payroll cheque. It indicates the earnings, the various deductions, and the net pay.

## 3. Employee's Earnings Record

For each employee, the employer must keep an **employee's earnings record** form on which are accumulated the details of every pay. This form is shown below.

At the end of the calendar year, the columns of the employee's earnings record are totaled to obtain the information necessary for the preparation by the employer of the annual Statement of Remuneration Paid form (T-4 slip). This form is required for income tax purposes. Copies of the T-4 slips are sent to the District Taxation Office and two copies are sent to the employee. When the employee makes out his annual income tax return, he attaches one copy to the return. The illustration at the top of page 300 shows a typical T-4 slip.

NAME Evans, Harold J.   S.I.N. 609-779-152   EXEMPTION CODE 10   BIRTHDATE Feb. 9, 1939
ADDRESS 178 N. Clarkson Ave.   MARITAL STATUS Married   DEPENDENTS 2 children (with)   DEPARTMENT Warehouse   DATE STARTED May 10, 19-
Thunder Bay
PHONE 767-5781

| DATE | STANDARD EARNINGS | | | STANDARD DEDUCTIONS | | | | | | | | | DATE LEFT |
|---|---|---|---|---|---|---|---|---|---|---|---|---|---|
| May 10 | 645 00 | | 645 00 | 11.03 | 6.60 | 32.25 | 595.12 | 105.25 | 6.00 | 7.00 | 3.60 | | |
| | 1 | 2 | 3 | 4 | 5 | 6 | 7 | 8 | 9 | 10 | 11 | 12 | 13 |

| | | | NET CLAIM CODE | EARNINGS | | | DEDUCTIONS | | | | | | | | Total Deduc's | Net PAY | Cheque NO. | C.P.P. to Date | Insured Earnings to Date |
|---|---|---|---|---|---|---|---|---|---|---|---|---|---|---|---|---|---|---|---|
| DATE | EMPLOYEE | | | Regular | Extra | Gross | C.P.P. | U.I. | R.R.P. | Taxable Income | Tax | Health Insce. | Union Dues | Group Life | | | | | |
| | | | | | | | | | | | | | | | 14 | 15 | 16 | 17 | 18 |
| May 24 | Harold Evans | | 10 | 645 00 | — | 645 00 | 11.03 | 6.60 | 32.25 | 595.12 | 105.25 | 6.00 | 7.00 | 3.60 | 171.73 | 473.27 | 1371 | 11.03 | 400.00 |
| Jun 7 | Harold Evans | | 10 | 645 00 | — | 645 00 | 11.03 | 6.60 | 32.25 | 595.12 | 105.25 | 6.00 | 7.00 | 3.60 | 171.73 | 473.27 | 1492 | 22.06 | 800.00 |
| Jun 21 | Harold Evans | | 10 | 645 00 | — | 645 00 | 11.03 | 6.60 | 32.25 | 595.12 | 105.25 | 6.00 | 7.00 | 3.60 | 171.73 | 473.27 | 1603 | 33.09 | 1200.00 |

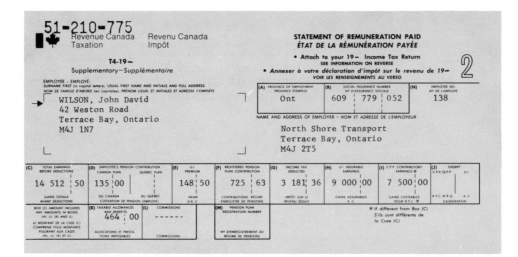

| 51-210-775 |
|---|

Revenue Canada
Taxation

Revenu Canada
Impôt

**STATEMENT OF REMUNERATION PAID**
*ÉTAT DE LA RÉMUNÉRATION PAYÉE*

T4-19—
Supplementary—*Supplémentaire*

• Attach to your 19— Income Tax Return
SEE INFORMATION ON REVERSE
• *Annexer à votre déclaration d'impôt sur le revenu de 19—*
*VOIR LES RENSEIGNEMENTS AU VERSO*

2

EMPLOYEE - *EMPLOYÉ*:
SURNAME FIRST (in capital letters), USUAL FIRST NAME AND INITIALS AND FULL ADDRESS
*NOM DE FAMILLE D'ABORD (en capitales), PRÉNOM USUEL ET INITIALES ET ADRESSE COMPLÈTE*

WILSON, John David
42 Weston Road
Terrace Bay, Ontario
M4J 1N7

| (A) PROVINCE OF EMPLOYMENT *PROVINCE D'EMPLOI* | (B) SOCIAL INSURANCE NUMBER *Nº D'ASSURANCE SOCIALE* | (N) EMPLOYEE NO. *Nº DE L'EMPLOYÉ* |
|---|---|---|
| Ont | 609 779 052 | 138 |

NAME AND ADDRESS OF EMPLOYER – *NOM ET ADRESSE DE L'EMPLOYEUR*

North Shore Transport
Terrace Bay, Ontario
M4J 2T5

| (C) TOTAL EARNINGS BEFORE DEDUCTIONS | (D) EMPLOYEE'S PENSION CONTRIBUTION CANADA PLAN / QUEBEC PLAN | (E) U.I. PREMIUM | (F) REGISTERED PENSION PLAN CONTRIBUTION | (G) INCOME TAX DEDUCTED | (H) U.I. INSURABLE EARNINGS | (I) C.P.P. CONTRIBUTORY EARNINGS ✱ | (J) EXEMPT C.P.P./Q.P.P. / U.I. |
|---|---|---|---|---|---|---|---|
| 14 512 50 | 135 00 | 148 50 | 725 63 | 3 181 36 | 9 000 00 | 7 500 00 | |
| *GAINS TOTAUX AVANT DÉDUCTIONS* | *DU CANADA / DU QUÉBEC COTISATION DE PENSION (EMPLOYÉ)* | *PRIME D'A.-C.* | *CONTRIBUTIONS, RÉGIME ENREGISTRÉ DE PENSIONS* | *IMPÔT SUR LE REVENU DÉDUIT* | *GAINS ASSURABLES A.-C.* | *GAINS COTISABLES POUR ✱ R.P.C. ✱* | *R.P.C./R.R.Q. / A.-C. EXONÉRATION* |

| BOX (C) AMOUNT (INCLUDES ANY AMOUNTS IN BOXES (H), (I), (K) AND (L)) | (K) TAXABLE ALLOWANCES AND BENEFITS | (L) COMMISSIONS | (M) PENSION PLAN REGISTRATION NUMBER |
|---|---|---|---|
| | 464 00 | ------ | |
| *LE MONTANT DE LA CASE (C) COMPREND TOUS MONTANTS FIGURANT AUX CASES (H), (I), (K) ET (L)* | *ALLOCATIONS ET PRESTATIONS IMPOSABLES* | *COMMISSIONS* | *Nº D'ENREGISTREMENT DU RÉGIME DE PENSIONS* |

✱ If different from Box (C)
*S'ils sont différents de la Case (C)*

# Devices to Assist in the Preparation of the Payroll

The manner in which the payroll is prepared depends on the number of employees and the type of office or accounting equipment that is available. An inexpensive technique designed to save time is the 'one-write' system which makes use of the pegboard or accounting board. It is a flat metal board with a row of pegs on it. Forms are placed in position on the pegs so that by using carbon paper all three basic records are produced with a single writing, as shown in the illustration below.

Another method is the accounting machine (see page 133) which is programmed to enter amounts in appropriate columns and to total these columns. This type of machine has a carriage movement to make the recording process easier. This method also makes use of carbon paper to prepare all three basic records simultaneously.

The most advanced method of preparing the payroll is by means of a computer. However, this method is expensive and usually is used only by large companies that can afford to take advantage of the computer's tremendous speed and capability.

*Accounting pegboard – payroll procedure (courtesy of The McBee Company).*

# Bookkeeping and Accounting Terms

**Payroll** The total process of calculating and preparing the employees' earnings.

**Gross Pay** Earnings before deductions.

**Net Pay** Earnings after deductions.

**Canada Pension Plan** A national pension plan sponsored by the Government of Canada.

**Unemployment Insurance** A national insurance plan against unemployment; sponsored by the Government of Canada.

**Wages** An amount paid periodically to an employee based on the number of hours he has worked or the quantity of goods he has produced. Wages are usually paid on a weekly basis to manual and mechanical workers.

**Salary** A fixed amount paid periodically to an employee for his services, regardless of the number of hours he works. Salary is usually set at a certain amount per week, per month, or per year, and is paid weekly, half-monthly, or monthly.

**Commission** An amount paid periodically to a salesman or an agent calculated as a percentage of the amount of goods or services sold.

**Personal Exemption** The amount of annual income that a person may earn that is exempt from tax; that is, tax free. The amount varies with the person's marital status and number of dependants.

**Employee's Earnings Record** A form used to provide an accumulated record of all the payroll data during a calendar year for a particular employee. One is prepared for each employee.

## Review Questions

1. Give three main reasons for keeping accurate payroll records.
2. What are the three main methods of calculating the pay for an employee?
3. What information is necessary if employees are paid a wage, and how is it obtained?
4. What is the purpose of the TD-1 form? When is it completed?
5. Why were the Canada Pension Plan and the Quebec Pension Plan introduced?
6. How are contributions to the Canada Pension Plan and the Quebec Pension Plan determined? Who is responsible for contributing?
7. Explain how you would determine the amount of income tax to be deducted from an employee's pay.
8. What is the purpose of unemployment insurance?
9. Explain who contributes to unemployment insurance and how the amount of the contribution is determined.
10. What do the rates for medical and/or hospital insurance depend on?
11. Why does the employer deduct union dues from employees on behalf of the union?
12. What is the formula or equation for calculating the net pay for an employee?
13. Describe the special form used to calculate the net pay for an employee.
14. Describe the steps that are performed to ensure the accuracy of the payroll journal.
15. Compare the advantages and disadvantages of the cash method and the cheque method of paying employees.
16. Describe the three basic records required in payroll accounting.

## Exercises

1. In each of the following cases calculate the regular earnings, overtime earnings, and the gross pay. Assume a regular work week of 40 hours.

|  | Total Hours | Regular Rate | Overtime Rate |  |  |  |  |
|---|---|---|---|---|---|---|---|
|  |  |  |  | (c) | 44½ | $5.75 | straight time |
| (a) | 46 | $5.35 | time and one half | (d) | 54 | $6.05 | time and one half |
| (b) | 43 | $6.30 | double time | (e) | 47¼ | $5.84 | time and one half |

**2. The timecards for two employees are given below.**

| Time Card | | | | |
|---|---|---|---|---|
| Week Ended | | July 23 | | 19-- |
| Soc. Ins. No. | | 642 393 438 | | |
| Name | | Frank Windsor | | |

| Day | Morning In Out | Afternoon In Out | Extra In Out | Total Hours |
|---|---|---|---|---|
| M | 7:58 12:01 | 12:58 5:01 | | |
| T | 8:07 12:00 | 12:57 5:02 | | |
| W | 7:56 12:03 | 12:59 5:00 | | |
| T | 7:59 12:02 | 1:01 5:03 | | |
| F | 7:57 12:02 | 12:59 5:01 | | |
| S | | | | |
| S | | | | |

| | Hours | Rate | Earnings |
|---|---|---|---|
| Regular Time | | 4.85 | |
| Overtime | | | |
| Gross Pay | | | |

| Time Card | | | | |
|---|---|---|---|---|
| Week Ended | | July 23 | | 19-- |
| Soc. Ins. No. | | 643 461 217 | | |
| Name | | Ray Peterson | | |

| Day | Morning In Out | Afternoon In Out | Extra In Out | Total Hours |
|---|---|---|---|---|
| M | 7:58 12:01 | 1:00 5:02 | | |
| T | 7:59 12:00 | 12:58 5:01 | 5:59 8:55 | |
| W | 7:57 12:01 | 12:59 5:02 | | |
| T | 7:56 12:01 | 12:58 5:03 | | |
| F | 7:59 12:01 | 12:59 5:01 | | |
| S | 7:58 12:01 | | | |
| S | | | | |

| | Hours | Rate | Earnings |
|---|---|---|---|
| Regular Time | | 4.65 | |
| Overtime | | | |
| Gross Pay | | | |

Determine the total number of hours worked each day and the total number of hours worked during the week. (Move the 'In' times ahead to the nearest quarter hour and the 'Out' times back to the nearest quarter hour.)
Calculate the regular and overtime earnings for each. (All hours in excess of 40 hours per week are overtime hours paid at the rate of time and one half the regular rate.)
Determine the gross pay for each.

**3. The Greenfield Real Estate Company pays its salesmen a basic salary of $325 per month plus a 2 per cent commission on the sales they make. For each of the salesmen listed below, calculate the commission and the gross earnings.**

|  | Salesmen | Net Sales |  |  |  |
|---|---|---|---|---|---|
| (a) | Bob Rennie | $90 000.00 | (d) | Allan Milroy | 39 800.00 |
| (b) | Earl Hunt | 45 500.00 | (e) | Leonard Downes | 61 750.00 |
| (c) | Gerry Anderson | 51 300.00 | (f) | Peter Johnson | 42 100.00 |

**4. What is the total personal exemption and the net claim code that would be calculated on a TD-1 for each of the following cases?**

(a) An unmarried man.

(b) A married man with a seven-year-old son. His wife does not work.

(c) A married man with a nineteen-year-old daughter attending university, and a sixteen-year-old son in school. His wife does not work. The children's earnings are each less than $1 000.

(d) A married man with a seventeen-year-old son, a fifteen-year-old daughter and a twelve-year-old daughter. His wife earns $800 a year. His children do not work.

(e) A married man whose wife earns $8 700 per year. There are no dependants.

(f) A widower with four children aged 19, 15, 13, and 9. The children's earnings have no effect on the calculations.

---

5. Using the information provided in each of the cases described below, calculate the amount of the registered retirement plan premium paid by the employee.

|  | Gross Pay | R.R.P. Rate |  |  |  |
|---|---|---|---|---|---|
| (a) | $ 685.00 | 3% | (c) | 785.00 | 5% |
| (b) | 1 250.00 | 7% | (d) | 350.00 | 2% |
|  |  |  | (e) | 925.00 | 6% |

---

6. The gross earnings listed below are for a biweekly pay period. Using the tables provided in the text, determine the amount of premium for Canada pension, unemployment insurance and for the registered retirement plan (assume that the R.R.P. rate is 6 per cent of gross pay in all cases). What is the amount of taxable earnings in each case?

|  |  |  |  |
|---|---|---|---|
| (a) | $406.19 | (d) | 642.90 |
| (b) | 920.00 | (e) | 386.50 |
| (c) | 786.59 |  |  |

---

7. In each of the following cases calculate what deduction would be made for Canada pension, unemployment insurance, registered retirement, and income tax.

(a) A person whose salary is $425.00 every two weeks, whose net claim code is 9, and whose R.R.P. deduction is at the rate of 6 per cent.

(b) A single man whose annual salary is $10 010, who is paid biweekly, whose net claim code is 1, and whose R.R.P. deduction is at the rate of 5 per cent of gross pay

(c) A married man who is paid $485 every two weeks, whose net claim code is 4, and whose R.R.P. deduction is at the rate of 7 per cent.

---

8. Suppose that in Exercise 7 each of the three men is given a raise in pay of an additional $85.00 per week.

(a) How much income tax would each pay now?

(b) Assuming that the only deductions affected by the raise in pay are C.P.P., U.I., R.R.P., and income tax, how much of the $85.00 raise would each take home?

9. (a) Prepare a payroll journal with the following headings:

Employee
Net Claim Code
Earnings (Regular, Extra, Gross)
Deductions (C.P.P., U.I. Premium, R.R.P.,
    Income Tax [Taxable Income, Ded'n])
Total Deductions
Net Pay

(b) The data below cover the two weeks ending August 12, 19—.

| Employee | Hours Worked | | Net Claim Code | Rate per Hour |
|---|---|---|---|---|
| | Week 1 | Week 2 | | |
| Alex Wilson | 40 | 48 | 9 | $6.75 |
| Peter Jones | 40 | 40 | 1 | 6.20 |
| Harold Hogan | 40 | 40 | 3 | 6.68 |
| Phil Harris | 46 | 46 | 8 | 6.60 |
| Bob Denver | 40 | 40 | 7 | 6.80 |

**Note:** Any hours over 40 hours per week are considered overtime hours and are paid for at the rate of one and one half times the regular rate.

(c) Each employee is enrolled in the registered retirement plan with contributions set at 4 per cent of his gross pay.

(d) Assuming that there are no other deductions to be made, calculate the net pay for each employee by completing the payroll journal. Use the deduction tables provided in the text.

(e) Total the columns of the journal and perform the steps to ensure the accuracy of the journal.

10. (a) Prepare a payroll journal with the following column headings:

Employee
Net Claim Code
Earnings (Regular, Extra, Gross)
Deductions – C.P.P.,
            U.I. Premium,
            R.R.P.,
            Income Tax (Taxable Income, Ded'n),
            Health Insurance
Total Deductions
Net Pay

(b) Each of the employees listed below receives a biweekly salary of $375 plus a commission of 1 per cent of the net sales that he makes for the two weeks. Record the appropriate data in the journal.

| Employee | Net Claim Code | Net Sales | Medical coverage |
|---|---|---|---|
| Eddie Albert | 1 | $12 000 | Single, Public ward |
| Bob Cummings | 9 | 9 800 | Family, Semiprivate |
| Al Fraser | 10 | 16 500 | Family, Semiprivate |
| Alex Davidson | 10 | 12 380 | Family, Semiprivate |
| Bob Pettit | 1 | 9 950 | Family, Public ward |

(c) Each employee is enrolled in the registered retirement plan and contributes 7 per cent of his gross pay.

(d) Using the deduction tables and rates given in the text, complete the payroll journal and verify.

---

11. (a) Prepare the general journal entries arising out of the payroll in Exercise 9. Assume that the employer is to match the employees' contribution to the R.R.P.

(b) Prepare the general journal entries arising out of the payroll in Exercise 10. Assume that the employer is to match the employees' contribution to the R.R.P.

---

12. The illustration below shows the column totals from the payroll of Hudson Fisheries Limited. The employer matches the employees' contributions to the R.R.P. and pays 75 per cent of the health insurance. Prepare the general journal entries to record the payroll.

| PAYROLL JOURNAL | | | | | | | | | | | | | | | | For the 2 weeks ended October 16 19— |
|---|---|---|---|---|---|---|---|---|---|---|---|---|---|---|---|---|
| | Net Claim Code | Earnings | | | | | | Deductions | | | | | | | Total Ded'ns | Net Pay |
| Employee | | Regular | Extra | Gross | C.P.P. | U.I. Premium | R.R.P. | Income Tax Taxable Income | Ded'n | Health Ins. | Union Dues | Group Life | | | | |
| | | | | | | | | | | | | | | | | |
| TOTALS | | 4982 50 | 1612 95 | 6595 45 | 116 35 | 67 34 | 329 77 | 6081 99 | 1277 22 | 40 50 | 84 — | 158 50 | | | 2073 68 | 4521 77 |

---

13. Assume that the employees in Exercise 10 are paid on a cash basis. Prepare the payroll currency requisition. Cheque number A39426 is prepared to obtain the necessary funds. Give the accounting entry for the cheque.

---

14. From the following information prepare the payroll for the period ended March 15.

(a) **The payroll journal has the following headings:**

Employee
Net Claim Code
Earnings (Regular, Extra, Gross)
Deductions – C.P.P.,
               U.I. Premium,
               R.R.P.,
               Income Tax – Taxable Income
                           – Ded'n,
               Health Insurance,
               Union Dues,
               Group Life Insurance

(b) **Each of the employees listed below is employed by E-Z Auto Sales Limited. They are paid every two weeks. The mechanics are paid on an hourly wage basis as indicated below. Any hours over 40 hours per week are paid at the time and one half rate. They belong to the I.A.M. union local and pay $6.25 in union dues each pay period. The salesmen are paid a basic salary of $180 per week plus a 2 per cent commission on all completed sales.**

| Employee | Net Claim Code | Hours Worked | Hourly Rate | Net Sales | Health Coverage | Group Life Insurance |
|---|---|---|---|---|---|---|
| Dave Durand | 1 | 80 | $5.75 | | Single, public ward | $20 000 |
| Joe Kuchma | 12 | 80 | 5.45 | | Family, semiprivate | $25 000 |
| Glen Nyman | 9 | 86 | 5.60 | | Family, public ward | $20 000 |
| Dave Bower | 7 | 86 | 5.35 | | Family, public ward | $25 000 |
| Jim Hansen | 1 | | | $16 000 | Single, semiprivate | — |
| Terry Sutherland | 13 | | | 9 600 | Family, semiprivate | $25 000 |
| Ed Milani | 11 | | | 12 400 | Family, semiprivate | $10 000 |

(c) **The rate of contribution for the R.R.P. is 5 per cent of the gross pay. The employer matches the employees' contributions.**

(d) **The employer has agreed to pay 66 per cent of the health insurance premiums.**

(e) **Group life insurance is paid entirely by the employees at the rate of 35¢ per $1 000 of insurance each pay.**

Complete the payroll journal. Where necessary, use the tables and rates provided in this chapter.

Prepare all of the accounting entries arising out of the completed payroll. The company uses separate expense accounts for Wages and for Salaries.

E-Z Auto Sales Limited pays its employees in cash. Prepare a payroll currency requisition.

# Cases

### Case 1

Lorne Morrell, a recent secondary school graduate, goes to work for Canadian Services Ltd. When he receives his first month's pay, he is amazed to see that such a large percentage of his salary has been deducted by the company. He decides it would be wise for him to discuss whether or not a mistake has been made in the calculation of his pay. He has asked for an interview with you, the office manager.

What will you tell him about the calculation of his net pay?

### Case 2

You are asked to research the following project as an aid to good employer-employee relationships. Basing yourself on the theory that happy workers are productive workers, you have planned to use some of your surplus cash to your employees' benefit. You must decide how you will invest $200 000 to its best advantage. Group insurance, mutual funds, bonds, preferred stock could be some of the areas of investment considered. In making your selection you must consider what plan would best contribute to good employer-employee relations and also whether the employees should be involved in making the decisions.

### Case 3

B. Truman has the following items deducted from his employees' payroll slips: income tax, unemployment insurance, Canada pension, group insurance, union dues and private pension plans. The employee regards these payroll deductions as an investment in the future. State what the employer does with each of the above deductions, and in each case explain why you do or do not believe that it protects the employee's future.

### Case 4

S. Jarvis Co. employs twenty workers and elects to pay its employees by cash. State the problems that are present in a cash payroll and what controls may be necessary.

### Case 5

Stirling Company, your employer, pays 75 per cent of your group insurance premiums. This amounts to approximately $220 a year. Would this amount be included in your total income for tax purposes for the year? Explain. How would the employer handle $220 in his records?

### Case 6

Matt Cook's T-4 slip indicates that his employer has withheld $3 260 in federal income tax from his salary for the year. When Cook prepares his income tax return he discovers that the total tax he is liable for amounts to $2 820. How can this happen? Explain.

### Case 7

Deductions from employees' wages for income tax are not expenses of operating the employer's business. Explain why this statement is true.

## Case 8

Western Electric uses a separate payroll bank account to handle salary and wage payments to employees. Is this a desirable practice? Explain. How would you explain a balance in the bank statement for the payroll account sent to you at the end of the month? Is it possible to have an overdraft in your payroll account? Explain.

## Case 9

As a payroll clerk for Triangle Electric, you have discovered that most employers do not attempt to reconcile total income tax withheld as shown on their T-4 slip with the amounts withheld during the year. Accordingly, the payroll clerk could understate the amount of tax deduction posted to various employees' earnings records, and overstate the tax posted on his own earnings sheet. Following the end of the year, he could then claim a refund for the excess tax shown on his own T-4 slip. Can this be prevented? Explain.

## Case 10

Submit a report on the disbursing of payroll funds in a business organization in your community. Your report should bring out the following points:
1. What type of payroll system is used: manual, one-write, accounting machine, computers? Briefly describe the system.
2. Who is responsible for control of payroll funds? Describe the employees' duties.
3. What business machines may be used in payroll computation?
4. How is pay calculated for an employee? (List all the steps involved.)
5. If salaries or wages are paid by cash, what precautions are taken to safeguard funds prior to payment?
6. List all deductions from the pay cheque.
7. Give the approximate date of issue of T-4 slips for income tax purposes.
8. Does the employer deduct union dues on behalf of the union?

## Case 11

You are the proprietor of Brite Cleaners. The following is extracted from the income statement for the fiscal year ended January 30.

| Revenue | | Expense | |
|---|---|---|---|
| Cleaning Revenue | $40 920.00 | Rent Expense | 4 800.00 |
| Storage Revenue | 954.00 | Delivery Expense | 2 930.00 |
| Laundry Revenue | 19 500.00 | Wages | 24 300.00 |
| Total Revenue | $61 374.00 | Supplies Expense | 5 250.00 |
| | | General Expense | 1 975.00 |
| | | Depreciation on Equipment | 7 560.00 |
| | | Total Expenses | 46 815.00 |
| | | Net Income | $14 559.00 |

The employees have asked for a 20 per cent raise in wages. Assuming that no other account is affected, could you grant their request and still make a profit?

You expect to earn $12 000 a year from the profit for managing the business. What percentage might you offer?

How might you cut expenses?

What might you do to increase revenue?

# 14 Adjustments for Financial Statements

One of the chief purposes of accounting is to accumulate the information necessary for the preparation of the financial statements. You have already studied this aspect of accounting in Chapter 6. Before continuing with this chapter, you should review Chapter 6.

It has been suggested throughout the text that it is expedient to let certain of the records become temporarily incorrect during the accounting period and to correct them all at one time at the end of the period. This process of correcting the records at the end of the accounting period is known as 'making the adjustments'; the corrections themselves are known as the **adjustments** or the **adjusting entries**.

The first step in preparing the financial statements is to take off a general ledger trial balance at the end of the accounting period. This is to be done on eight-column work sheet paper. You previously worked with six-column paper; the two additional columns introduced at this time are to be used for the adjustments.

The trial balance figures on the work sheet are taken directly from the general ledger at the end of the accounting period. As a result, they contain the account balances that are not up to date and which require the making of the adjustments. Although only a few adjustments are discussed at this time, they are important ones and will introduce you to the theoretical concepts involved in making adjustments of all kinds.

Before beginning the study of adjustments, a word of explanation is necessary. The topic 'adjustments' is not completely covered in this chapter but carries over into Chapter 15. Therefore, do not expect to be thoroughly informed about adjustments until you have studied both Chapter 14 and Chapter 15.

An accountant may select from two different techniques for making individual adjustments. These are: (1) the formal or traditional technique; (2) the shortcut technique. For most adjustments, either technique is equally effective. However, for certain particular adjustments one or the other of the two techniques is definitely superior. You will be informed of these particular adjustments as you proceed through the chapter.

## Adjusting Entries—Formal Technique

Let us begin the study of the formal technique of making the adjusting entries by preparing the work sheet for Cassidy Cartage, a service business. The general ledger trial balance of Cassidy Cartage as of June 30, 19–4, the end of an annual accounting period, is shown in the first two columns of the work sheet shown on page 310.

### Adjusting for Accounts Payable

One should not expect to complete the preparation of the financial statements until two to three weeks after the end of the accounting period. This period of waiting is necessary to allow time for the late arrival of purchase invoices from suppliers.

It is not an uncommon occurrence for goods and services to arrive towards the end of an accounting period, and for the purchase invoices

| Accounts | Acc. # | Trial Balance Dr. | Cr. | Adjustments Dr. | Cr. | Income Statement Dr. | Cr. | Balance Sheet Dr. | Cr. |
|---|---|---|---|---|---|---|---|---|---|
| Cassidy Cartage — Work Sheet — Year Ended June 30, 19-4 — 141 | | | | | | | | | |
| Petty Cash | 1 | 50 - | | | | | | | |
| Bank | 2 | 725 41 | | | | | | | |
| Accounts Receivable | 3 | 4 027 56 | | | | | | | |
| Allowance for Doubtful Accounts | 4 | | 26 40 | | | | | | |
| Supplies | 5 | 516 52 | | | | | | | |
| Prepaid Insurance | 6 | 216 - | | | | | | | |
| Prepaid Licences | 7 | 255 - | | | | | | | |
| Land | 8 | 8 000 - | | | | | | | |
| Buildings (Frame) | 9 | 7 280 - | | | | | | | |
| Accumulated Depreciation Bldgs. | 10 | | 2 005 40 | | | | | | |
| Furniture and Equipment | 11 | 2 950 - | | | | | | | |
| Accumulated Depreciation F+E | 12 | | 1 597 40 | | | | | | |
| Automotive Equipment | 13 | 15 600 - | | | | | | | |
| Accumulated Depreciation Autos | 14 | | 7 956 - | | | | | | |
| Accounts Payable | 21 | | 3 047 25 | | | | | | |
| Sales Tax Payable | 22 | | 238 73 | | | | | | |
| P. Marshall, Capital | 31 | | 18 387 21 | | | | | | |
| P. Marshall, Drawings | 32 | 6 000 - | | | | | | | |
| Sales | 41 | | 28 757 49 | | | | | | |
| Discounts Earned | 42 | | 56 75 | | | | | | |
| Bank Charges | 51 | 114 92 | | | | | | | |
| Building Maintenance | 52 | 474 37 | | | | | | | |
| Light, Heat, and Water | 53 | 472 19 | | | | | | | |
| Miscellaneous Expenses | 54 | 115 70 | | | | | | | |
| Telephone Expense | 55 | 151 30 | | | | | | | |
| Truck Expense | 56 | 5 704 16 | | | | | | | |
| Wages | 57 | 9 419 50 | | | | | | | |
| | | 62 072 63 | 62 072 63 | | | | | | |

for these goods and services to arrive after the accounting period is over; that is, in the next accounting period.

The accounting entries for any goods or services purchased should be recorded in the same period as that in which the goods or services are received. Therefore, for the two or three weeks following the end of the accounting period, each purchase invoice must be examined to ascertain if it pertains to goods or services received prior to the year-end. Those falling into this category must be gathered together and summarized for an adjusting entry.

Assume that the purchase invoices for Cassidy Cartage shown below are those for which an adjusting entry is required.

| Supplier | Invoice Date | Explanation | Amount |
|---|---|---|---|
| Local Telephone Co. | July 5 | Telephone bill for June | $ 15.70 |
| Arrow Garage | July 6 | Truck repairs in June | 35.50 |
| Frank's Supply | July 6 | Supplies received in June | 45.21 |
| Star Oil Co. | July 10 | Gas and oil for trucks in June | 138.50 |
| Black Lumber Company | July 10 | Repairs to building in June | 125.00 |
| Public Utilities | July 12 | Electricity for June | 15.00 |
| Public Utilities | July 14 | Water for June | 7.81 |
| Jerry's Hardware | July 14 | Miscellaneous items in June | 20.00 |

These purchase invoices are summarized into an accounting entry as shown at the top of the next column. Then they are allowed to be absorbed into the normal accounting routine in the new accounting period.

| Accounts | Acc # | Trial Balance Dr. | Trial Balance Cr. | Adjustments Dr. | Adjustments Cr. |
|---|---|---|---|---|---|
| Cassidy Cartage | | Work Sheet | | | |
| Petty Cash | 1 | 50 - | | | |
| Bank | 2 | 725 41 | | | |
| Accounts Receivable | 3 | 4 027 56 | | | |
| Allowance for Doubtful Accounts | 4 | | 26 40 | | |
| Supplies | 5 | 516 52 | | ① 45 21 | |
| Prepaid Insurance | 6 | 216 - | | | |
| Prepaid Licenses | 7 | 255 - | | | |
| Land | 8 | 8 000 - | | | |
| Buildings (Frame) | 9 | 7 280 - | | | |
| Accumulated Depreciation Bldgs. | 10 | | 2 005 40 | | |
| Furniture and Equipment | 11 | 2 950 - | | | |
| Accumulated Depreciation F & E | 12 | | 1 597 40 | | |
| Automotive equipment | 13 | 15 600 - | | | |
| Accumulated Depreciation autos. | 14 | | 7 956 - | | |
| Accounts Payable | 21 | | 3 047 25 | | ① 402 72 |
| Sales Tax Payable | 22 | | 238 73 | | |
| P. Marshall, Capital | 31 | | 18 387 21 | | |
| P. Marshall, Drawings | 32 | 6 000 - | | | |
| Sales | 41 | | 28 757 49 | | |
| Discounts Earned | 42 | | 56 75 | | |
| Bank Charges | 51 | 114 92 | | | |
| Building Maintenance | 52 | 474 37 | | ① 125 - | |
| Light, Heat, and Water | 53 | 472 19 | | ① 22 81 | |
| Miscellaneous Expense | 54 | 115 70 | | ① 20 - | |
| Telephone Expense | 55 | 151 30 | | ① 15 70 | |
| Truck Expense | 56 | 5 704 16 | | ① 174 - | |
| Wages | 57 | 9 419 50 | | | |
| | | 62 072 63 | 62 072 63 | | |

| | |
|---|---|
| Telephone Expense | $ 15.70 |
| Truck Expense | 174.00 |
| Supplies | 45.21 |
| Building Maintenance | 125.00 |
| Light, Heat, and Water | 22.81 |
| Miscellaneous Expense | 20.00 |
| Accounts Payable | $402.72 |

This accounting entry is not journalized in the books at this time. It is, however, recorded in the Adjustments column of the work sheet as shown above.

Observe that each of the amounts entered is coded with a circled numeral '1' to indicate that it forms a part of the first adjusting entry.

## Adjusting for Supplies

The Supplies account is allowed to become incorrect during the accounting period because it is too inconvenient to record the usage of supplies as it occurs. As a result, the account balance is incorrect by the cost of all the supplies used up during the period.

To adjust for supplies, it is first necessary to take a physical inventory of the supplies actually on hand on the last day of the accounting period. This involves the preparation of a listing similar to the one shown at the top of page 312. Each different item must be counted or estimated and the quantity multiplied by the most recent cost price in order to obtain a reasonable value of the supplies on hand.

The supplies adjustment debits Supplies Expense and credits Supplies with the amount that will cause the Supplies account to have a balance equal to the Supplies inventory figure. A look at the work sheet for Cassidy Cartage shows that the Supplies account has a balance of $516.52 and that there is an accounts payable debit adjustment of $45.21. This gives the account an effective balance of $561.73. To reduce this to the inventory figure of $395.25 requires an adjustment in the amount of $166.48. Accordingly, the adjusting entry for Supplies for Cassidy Cartage is:

| | | |
|---|---|---|
| Supplies Expense | $166.48 | |
| Supplies | | $166.48 |

This adjustment is recorded on the work sheet in the Adjustments column as shown on page 312. As with all such adjustments, it is not journalized in the books at this time.

## Supplies Inventory
### June 30, 19-4

| Description | Quantity | | Unit Cost | Value |
|---|---|---|---|---|
| Envelopes, #10, White | 4¾ | boxes | $5.50 | $23.38 |
| Envelopes, #8, White | 4 | boxes | 4.95 | 19.80 |
| Envelopes, Manila | 1½ | boxes | 7.50 | 11.25 |
| Envelopes, C4, Manila | 2 | boxes | 8.75 | 17.50 |
| Ball Pens, Blue | ½ | gross | 72.00 | 36.00 |
| Pencils, Black, HB | 6 | dozen | 1.50 | 9.00 |
| Pencils, Black, F2½ | 8 | dozen | 1.50 | 12.00 |
| Pencils, Red | 2 | dozen | 1.75 | 3.50 |
| Cellulose Tape, 1 cm | 3/4 | box | 24.00 | 18.00 |
| Cellulose Tape, 2 cm | 1½ | box | 30.00 | 45.00 |
| Paper Clips, Regular | 15 | boxes | 1.25 | 18.75 |
| Paper Clips, Small | 10 | boxes | 1.10 | 11.00 |
| Gummed Labels, Assorted Colors | 1¼ | gross | 75.00 | 93.75 |
| Elastic Bands, Mixed | 5 | boxes | 1.05 | 5.25 |
| | | | | $395.25 |

Cassidy Cartage — Work Sheet — Year Ended June 30, 19-4

| Accounts | Acc # | Trial Balance Dr. | Trial Balance Cr. | Adjustments Dr. | Adjustments Cr. | Income Statement Dr. | Income Statement Cr. | Balance Sheet Dr. | Balance Sheet Cr. |
|---|---|---|---|---|---|---|---|---|---|
| Petty Cash | 1 | 50 – | | | | | | | |
| Bank | 2 | 725 41 | | | | | | | |
| Accounts Receivable | 3 | 4 027 56 | | | | | | | |
| Allowance for Doubtful Accounts | 4 | | 26 40 | | | | | | |
| Supplies | 5 | 516 52 | | ① 45 21 | ② 166 48 | | | 395 25 | |
| Prepaid Insurance | 6 | 216 – | | | | | | | |
| Prepaid Licences | 7 | 255 – | | | | | | | |
| Land | 8 | 8 000 – | | | | | | | |
| Buildings (Frame) | 9 | 7 280 – | | | | | | | |
| Accumulated Depreciation Bldgs. | 10 | | 2 005 40 | | | | | | |
| Furniture and Equipment | 11 | 2 950 – | | | | | | | |
| Accumulated Depreciation F. & E. | 12 | | 1 597 40 | | | | | | |
| Automotive Equipment | 13 | 15 600 – | | | | | | | |
| Accumulated Depreciation Autos | 14 | | 7 956 – | | | | | | |
| Accounts Payable | 21 | | 3 047 25 | | ① 402 72 | | | | |
| Sales Tax Payable | 22 | | 238 73 | | | | | | |
| P Marshall, Capital | 31 | | 18 387 21 | | | | | | |
| P Marshall, Drawings | 32 | 6 000 – | | | | | | | |
| Sales | 41 | | 28 757 49 | | | | | | |
| Discounts Earned | 42 | | 56 75 | | | | | | |
| Bank Charges | 51 | 114 92 | | | | | | | |
| Building Maintenance | 52 | 474 37 | | ① 125 – | | | | | |
| Light, Heat and Water | 53 | 472 19 | | ① 22 81 | | | | | |
| Miscellaneous Expense | 54 | 115 70 | | ① 20 – | | | | | |
| Telephone Expense | 55 | 151 30 | | ① 15 70 | | | | | |
| Truck Expense | 56 | 5 704 16 | | ① 174 – | | | | | |
| Wages | 57 | 9 419 50 | | | | | | | |
| | | 62 072 63 | 62 072 63 | | | | | | |
| Supplies Expense | | | | ② 166 48 | | 166 48 | | | |

Observe that this adjustment is coded with a numeral '2' because it happens to be the second adjusting entry on this work sheet.

Notice too that a line for Supplies Expense has been started beneath the trial balance section. This was necessary because the trial balance did not include a Supplies Expense account. Whenever an adjustment affects an account that is not included in the trial balance section, the account must be written below the trial balance.

### EXTENDING THE WORK SHEET

When the accountant is certain that no other adjustment will affect a particular item on the work sheet, he may extend the item. Both the Supplies line and the Supplies Expense line of the work sheet may be extended at this time. To extend any line of the work sheet you must first find the value of the first four columns; that is, the value of the Trial Balance and the Adjustments columns. Then, transfer this value to the appropriate column of the remaining four.

For Supplies, the value of the first four columns is found to be $395.25 debit, and since Supplies is a Balance Sheet item (asset), the $395.25 is transferred to the Balance Sheet Debit column.

For Supplies Expense, the value of the first four columns is found to be $166.48 debit, and since Supplies Expense is an Income Statement item, the $166.48 is transferred to the Income Statement Debit column.

## Adjusting for Prepaid Expenses

It is a common business practice to pay in advance for certain expenses that cover a period of time and to set them up in **prepaid expense** accounts. For example, automobile licences are purchased in advance, usually for a period of one year, and are debited to an account called Prepaid Licences. Similarly, insurance coverage is purchased in advance for periods of one or three years, and is debited to an account called Prepaid Insurance.

With the passing of time, prepaid expenses gradually expire and diminish in value. For example, a truck licence costing $60 on January 1, to be in force for a period of one year, is worth $60 on January 1, but gradually diminishes in value with the passing of time. On June 30, the licence is half expired and has a value of $30. On September 30, the licence is three quarters expired and has a value of $15. Theoretically, the licence (or any prepaid expense of this type) has a value relative to the proportion of time remaining in its term.

During the course of an accounting period, however, no attempt is made to keep the prepaid expense accounts accurate. Only at the end of the accounting period, for purposes of financial statements, is accuracy of this kind important. And then, accuracy is acquired by means of an adjusting entry on the work sheet.

## Prepaid insurance adjustment for Cassidy Cartage

In this case it is first necessary to calculate the value of the unexpired insurance as of the end of the accounting period. This is done by analysing the insurance policies and preparing an insurance schedule such as the following:

*Prepaid Insurance Schedule*
*June 30, 19–4*

| Company | Policy Date | Term | Premium | Unexpired Proportion | Prepaid Insurance June 30, 19–4 |
|---|---|---|---|---|---|
| Admiral | Mar. 31, 19–4 | 1 year | $44.00 | 3/4 | $33.00 |
| International | Feb. 1, 19–2 | 3 years | $54.00 | 7/36 | $10.50 |
| Satellite | Jan. 1, 19–3 | 3 years | $90.00 | 1/2 | $45.00 |
| | | | | Total | $88.50 |

The adjustment for insurance is one that brings the Prepaid Insurance account into agreement with the prepaid insurance calculation. The accounting entry debits Insurance Expense and credits Prepaid Insurance.

The work sheet for Cassidy Cartage shows a balance of $216 for Prepaid Insurance. To bring this into agreement with the insurance schedule figure of $88.50 requires an adjustment of $127.50 as follows:

Insurance Expense      $127.50
  Prepaid Insurance          $127.50

The adjusting entry and the items extended on the work sheet are shown in the illustration at the top of the next page.

| Accounts | Acc # | Trial Balance Dr. | Trial Balance Cr. | Adjustments Dr. | Adjustments Cr. | Income Statement Dr. | Income Statement Cr. | Balance Sheet Dr. | Balance Sheet Cr. |
|---|---|---|---|---|---|---|---|---|---|
| *Cassidy Cartage* | | | | | | | | | |
| Petty Cash | 1 | 50 — | | | | | | | |
| Bank | 2 | 725 41 | | | | | | | |
| Accounts Receivable | 3 | 4 027 56 | | | | | | | |
| Allowance for Doubtful Accounts | 4 | | 26 40 | | | | | | |
| Supplies | 5 | 516 52 | | ① 45 21 | ② 166 48 | | | 395 25 | |
| Prepaid Insurance | 6 | 216 — | | | ③ 127 50 | | | 88 50 | |
| Prepaid Licences | 7 | 255 — | | | | | | | |
| Land | 8 | 8 000 — | | | | | | | |
| Buildings (Frame) | 9 | 7 280 — | | | | | | | |
| Accumulated Depreciation Bldg. | 10 | | 2 005 40 | | | | | | |
| Furniture and Equipment | 11 | 2 950 — | | | | | | | |
| Accumulated Depreciation F.&E. | 12 | | 1 597 40 | | | | | | |
| Automotive Equipment | 13 | 15 600 — | | | | | | | |
| Accumulated Depreciation Autos | 14 | | 7 956 — | | | | | | |
| Accounts Payable | 21 | | 3 047 25 | | ① 402 72 | | | | |
| Sales Tax Payable | 22 | | 238 73 | | | | | | |
| P Marshall, Capital | 31 | | 18 387 21 | | | | | | |
| P Marshall, Drawings | 32 | 6 000 — | | | | | | | |
| Sales | 41 | | 28 757 49 | | | | | | |
| Discounts Earned | 42 | | 56 75 | | | | | | |
| Bank Charges | 51 | 114 92 | | | | | | | |
| Building Maintenance | 52 | 474 37 | | ① 125 — | | | | | |
| Light, Heat, and Water | 53 | 472 19 | | ① 22 81 | | | | | |
| Miscellaneous Expense | 54 | 115 70 | | ① 20 — | | | | | |
| Telephone Expense | 55 | 151 30 | | ① 15 70 | | | | | |
| Truck Expense | 56 | 5 704 16 | | ① 174 — | | | | | |
| Wages | 57 | 9 419 50 | | | | | | | |
| | | 62 072 63 | 62 072 63 | | | | | | |
| Supplies Expense | | | | ② 166 48 | | 166 48 | | | |
| Insurance Expense | | | | ③ 127 50 | | 127 50 | | | |

Observe that this adjustment is coded with a numeral '3' and that it requires the opening of an Insurance Expense line.

## Prepaid licences adjustment for Cassidy Cartage

This adjustment is similar to that for prepaid insurance. First, it is necessary to calculate the value of the unexpired licences by means of a schedule such as the one shown below.

The adjustment for licences is one that brings the Prepaid Licences account into agreement with the Prepaid Licences Schedule. The accounting entry debits Licences Expense and credits Prepaid Licences.

The work sheet for Cassidy Cartage shows a balance of $255 for Prepaid Licences. To bring this into agreement with the schedule figure of $85.00 requires an adjustment in the amount of $170 as follows:

| Licences Expense | $170.00 | |
|---|---|---|
| Prepaid Licences | | $170.00 |

On the work sheet the adjustment (coded '4') and the items extended are as shown at the top of the next page.

---

*Prepaid Licences Schedule*
*June 30, 19–4*

| Vehicle | Cost of Licence | Term of Licence | Unexpired Proportion | Prepaid Licences June 30, 19–4 |
|---|---|---|---|---|
| 3-ton van | $80.00 | Jan. 1 to Dec. 31 | ½ | $40.00 |
| ½-ton truck | $60.00 | Jan. 1 to Dec. 31 | ½ | $30.00 |
| Station wagon | $30.00 | Jan. 1 to Dec. 31 | ½ | $15.00 |
| | | | Total | $85.00 |

---

| Cassidy Cartage | ACC # | Work Sheet | | | Year Ended June 30, 19-4 | | | | | |
|---|---|---|---|---|---|---|---|---|---|---|
| Accounts | | Trial Balance Dr. | Cr. | Adjustments Dr. | Cr. | Income Statement Dr. | Cr. | Balance Sheet Dr. | Cr. |
| Petty Cash | 1 | 50 — | | | | | | | |
| Bank | 2 | 725 41 | | | | | | | |
| Accounts Receivable | 3 | 4 027 56 | | | | | | | |
| Allowance for Doubtful Accounts | 4 | | 26 40 | | | | | | |
| Supplies | 5 | 516 52 | | ① 45 21 | ② 166 48 | | | 395 25 | |
| Prepaid Insurance | 6 | 216 — | | | ③ 127 50 | | | 88 50 | |
| Prepaid Licences | 7 | 255 — | | | ④ 170 — | | | 85 — | |
| Land | 8 | 8 000 — | | | | | | | |
| Buildings (Frame) | 9 | 7 280 — | | | | | | | |
| Accumulated Depreciation Bldgs | 10 | | 2 005 40 | | | | | | |
| Furniture and Equipment | 11 | 2 950 — | | | | | | | |
| Accumulated Depreciation F+E | 12 | | 1 597 40 | | | | | | |
| Automotive Equipment | 13 | 15 600 — | | | | | | | |
| Accumulated Depreciation Autos | 14 | | 7 956 — | | | | | | |
| Accounts Payable | 21 | | 3 047 25 | | ① 402 72 | | | | |
| Sales Tax Payable | 22 | | 238 73 | | | | | | |
| P. Marshall, Capital | 31 | | 18 387 21 | | | | | | |
| P. Marshall, Drawings | 32 | 6 000 — | | | | | | | |
| Sales | 41 | | 28 757 49 | | | | | | |
| Discounts Earned | 42 | | 56 75 | | | | | | |
| Bank Charges | 51 | 114 92 | | | | | | | |
| Building Maintenance | 52 | 474 37 | | ① 125 — | | | | | |
| Light, Heat, and Water | 53 | 472 19 | | ① 22 81 | | | | | |
| Miscellaneous Expense | 54 | 115 70 | | ① 20 — | | | | | |
| Telephone Expense | 55 | 151 30 | | ① 15 70 | | | | | |
| Truck Expense | 56 | 5 704 16 | | ① 174 — | | | | | |
| Wages | 57 | 9 419 50 | | | | | | | |
| | | 62 072 63 | 62 072 63 | | | | | | |
| Supplies Expense | | | | ② 166 48 | | 166 48 | | | |
| Insurance Expense | | | | ③ 127 50 | | 127 50 | | | |
| Licences Expense | | | | ④ 170 — | | 170 — | | | |

## Adjusting for Doubtful Accounts of Customers

An element of risk is involved in selling on credit. Although he may carefully check the credit rating of every credit customer, a businessman cannot be certain of collecting all of his accounts receivable. For a variety of reasons, such as business reversals, death, and bankruptcy, some of his customers may find it impossible to pay off their debts. Consequently, it is necessary to consider the correctness of the value of accounts receivable at the time financial statements are prepared.

| Cassidy Cartage | Accounts Receivable Aging Schedule | | | | June 30, 19-4 | | |
|---|---|---|---|---|---|---|---|
| Customer | Account Balance | 1-30 Days | 31-60 Days | 61-90 Days | 91 Days and Older | Remarks | Allowance for Doubtful Debts |
| Advance Associates | 156 50 | 52 00 | 29 40 | 75 10 | | Will be O.K. | |
| Barley Brothers | 251 20 | 55 00 | 94 12 | 102 08 | | Will be O.K. ✓ | |
| J. Bowman | 35 50 | 35 50 | | | | | |
| M. Carey | 165 25 | 102 10 | | | 63 15 | 63.15 is 7 month old disputed item Correspondence with customer is proving fruitless | 63 15 |
| Concord Company | 346 56 | 151 00 | 94 00 | 73 25 | 28 31 | Slow but sure. Has been a good customer for over 10 years. | |
| Devon Bros. | 95 62 | | | | 95 62 | Item is 10 months old and customer is in bankruptcy | 95 62 |
| Durnan + Son | 114 56 | 24 00 | 90 56 | | | ✓ | |
| Empire Traders | 26 50 | 26 50 | | | | | |
| Young + Young | 16 00 | 16 00 | | | | | |
| | 4 027 56 | 2 461 15 | 841 90 | 400 07 | 324 44 | | 260 45 |

## Allowance for doubtful accounts

At the end of each accounting period, it is necessary to analyse all of the individual customers' accounts for the purpose of determining the total of **doubtful accounts**; that is, those accounts that may not be collected. This analysis is done by preparing an Accounts Receivable Aging Schedule such as the one shown at the bottom of page 315. When preparing this schedule it will be necessary to discuss the various accounts with the credit manager.

At the end of each accounting period, the ascertained value of doubtful accounts is set up as a credit balance in an account called 'Allowance for Doubtful Accounts'. The estimated true value of accounts receivable is shown by the Accounts Receivable account and the Allowance for Doubtful Accounts account taken together. For Cassidy Cartage the estimated true value of accounts receivable is shown below in T accounts.

| Accounts Receivable | Allowance for Doubtful Accounts |
|---|---|
| 4 027.56 | 260.45 |

Estimated true value of Accounts Receivable = $3 767.11

The Allowance for Doubtful Accounts account is a 'valuation' account which must be considered in relationship to the Accounts Receivable account. There are other valuation accounts. Each one is related to an asset account and the two accounts must be looked at in conjunction with each other.

## Adjustment for doubtful accounts for Cassidy Cartage

Having determined the allowance for doubtful accounts figure, an adjusting entry is made to bring the account, Allowances for Doubtful Accounts, into agreement with the aging schedule. The accounting entry debits Bad Debts Expense and credits Allowance for Doubtful Accounts.

The work sheet shows a credit balance of $26.40 for Allowance for Doubtful Accounts. To bring this into agreement with the schedule figure of $260.45 requires an adjustment in the amount of $234.05 as follows:

Bad Debts Expense          $234.05
    Allowance for Doubtful Accounts  $234.05

On the work sheet, the adjusting entry (coded '5') and the items extended appear as shown below. Observe that since the Allowance for Bad Debts is a minus asset, it is extended to the Balance Sheet Credit column.

| Accounts | Acc # | Trial Balance Dr. | Trial Balance Cr. | Adjustments Dr. | Adjustments Cr. | Income Statement Dr. | Income Statement Cr. | Balance Sheet Dr. | Balance Sheet Cr. |
|---|---|---|---|---|---|---|---|---|---|
| Petty Cash | 1 | 50 – | | | | | | | |
| Bank | 2 | 725 41 | | | | | | | |
| Accounts Receivable | 3 | 4 027 56 | | | | | | | |
| Allowance for Doubtful Accounts | 4 | | 26 40 | | ⑤ 234 05 | | | | 260 45 |
| Supplies | 5 | 516 52 | | ① 45 21 | ② 166 48 | | | 395 25 | |
| Prepaid Insurance | 6 | 216 – | | | ③ 127 50 | | | 88 50 | |
| Prepaid Licences | 7 | 255 – | | | ④ 170 – | | | 85 – | |
| Land | 8 | 8 000 – | | | | | | | |
| Buildings (Frame) | 9 | 7 280 – | | | | | | | |
| Accumulated Depreciation Bldgs. | 10 | | 2 005 40 | | | | | | |
| Furniture and Equipment | 11 | 2 950 – | | | | | | | |
| Accumulated Depreciation F.+E. | 12 | | 1 597 40 | | | | | | |
| Automotive Equipment | 13 | 15 600 – | | | | | | | |
| Accumulated Depreciation Autos | 14 | | 7 956 – | | | | | | |
| Accounts Payable | 21 | | 3 047 25 | | ① 402 72 | | | | |
| Sales Tax Payable | 22 | | 238 73 | | | | | | |
| P. Marshall, Capital | 31 | | 18 387 21 | | | | | | |
| P. Marshall, Drawings | 32 | 6 000 – | | | | | | | |
| Sales | 41 | | 28 757 49 | | | | | | |
| Discounts Earned | 42 | | 56 75 | | | | | | |
| Bank Charges | 51 | 114 92 | | | | | | | |
| Building Maintenance | 52 | 474 37 | | ① 125 – | | | | | |
| Light, Heat, and Water | 53 | 472 19 | | ① 22 81 | | | | | |
| Miscellaneous Expense | 54 | 115 70 | | ① 20 – | | | | | |
| Telephone Expense | 55 | 151 30 | | ① 15 70 | | | | | |
| Truck Expense | 56 | 5 704 16 | | ① 174 – | | | | | |
| Wages | 57 | 9 419 50 | | | | | | | |
| | | 62 072 63 | 62 072 63 | | | | | | |
| Supplies Expense | | | | ② 166 48 | | 166 48 | | | |
| Insurance Expense | | | | ③ 127 50 | | 127 50 | | | |
| Licences Expense | | | | ④ 170 – | | 170 – | | | |
| Bad Debts Expense | | | | ⑤ 234 05 | | 234 05 | | | |

## Accounts receivable on the balance sheet

The estimated true value of accounts receivable is shown on the balance sheet in the manner shown below:

| CURRENT ASSETS | | | |
|---|---|---|---|
| Petty Cash | | $ 50.00 | |
| Bank | | 725.41 | |
| Accounts Receivable | $4 027.56 | | |
| Less Allowance for Doubtful Accts | 260.45 | 3 767.11 | $4 542.52 |

## Writing off a bad debt

When it becomes known for certain that a customer's account (or part of his account) will not be collected, the account balance (or part thereof) should be written off; that is, taken out of the books by means of an accounting entry. In the general journal, an accounting entry such as the following is made:

Allowance for Doubtful Accounts  $63.15

    Accounts Receivable (M. Carey)    $63.15

To write off the account of
M. Carey, bankrupt.

Remember that the posting to Accounts Receivable must be made twice – once to the general ledger and once to the subsidiary ledger.

## Adjusting for Depreciation

With the exception of land, every fixed asset (also known as capital equipment) is used up in the course of time and activity and therefore decreases in value. This decrease in value is known as **depreciation**.

To understand the concept of depreciation, consider the case of a businessman who purchases a new truck at a cost of $8 000 in order to begin a delivery business. After operating for five years he decides to terminate the business and in the course of its closing, the now used truck is sold for $500. Clearly, over the five-year period it cost the businessman $7 500 to own the truck and just as clearly it was essential that he have the truck in order to conduct his business.

To obtain an accurate picture of the profit and loss of his business, this man cannot ignore the $7 500 cost of the truck. Theoretically, it must be allocated as an expense of the business at the rate of $1 500 for each of the five years. The question remaining is this: since it is impossible to make a precise calculation of depreciation until the end of the life of an asset (that is, until the asset is disposed of), by what method is the depreciation calculated during the life of the asset? The most common method is to use an estimated rate for calculating depreciation based on rates laid down by government regulation.

## Net book value

Valuation accounts are used in conjunction with the fixed asset accounts. They are used to show the total amount of depreciation that accumulates during the life of an asset. At the end of every fiscal period, each fixed asset (with the exception of land) is decreased by the amount of the estimated depreciation. However, the reduction in the value of the fixed asset is not credited directly to the asset account but rather to a valuation account called Accumulated Depreciation.

A fixed asset account together with its Accumulated Depreciation account reflects the estimated true value of the asset. A typical example is the following:

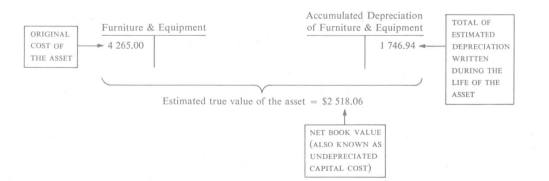

The cost of the asset less the accumulated depreciation gives the estimated true value of the asset. This is commonly known as the **net book value** or the **undepreciated capital cost**. Two accounts in respect to a fixed asset are more informative than one account because they enable the reader to see what proportion of the asset is used up. Without the valuation account this cannot be seen.

## Government rates of depreciation

Government regulations include rates of estimated depreciation (also known as **capital cost allowance**) for any possible type of capital equipment. The most commonly used of these rates are:

Brick buildings – 5% per year of net book value

Frame buildings – 10% per year of net book value

Furniture and general equipment – 20% per year of net book value

Automotive equipment – 30% per year of net book value

It is important to note that these government rates are based on the net book value (undepreciated capital cost) of the particular assets.

## Calculating the depreciation for Cassidy Cartage

The first step in calculating depreciation is to find out the net book values of the individual fixed assets. These are worked out as follows:

| | | | | |
|---|---|---|---|---|
| (i) (Frame) Buildings | Less | Accumulated Depreciation Buildings | Equals | Net Book Value Buildings |
| $7 280.00 | — | $2 005.40 | = | $5 274.60 |
| (ii) Furniture and Equipment | Less | Accumulated Depreciation Furniture and Equipment | Equals | Net Book Value Furniture and Equipment |
| $2 950.00 | — | $1 597.40 | = | $1 352.60 |
| (iii) Automotive Equipment | Less | Accumulated Depreciation Automotive Equipment | Equals | Net Book Value Automotive Equipment |
| $15 600.00 | — | $7 956.00 | = | $7 644.00 |

The second step is to multiply each of the net book value figures by the appropriate rate of depreciation in order to arrive at the respective depreciation expenses for the fiscal period (in this case one year).

| ASSET | N.B.V. | | ANNUAL RATE | | DEPRECIATION FOR YEAR |
|---|---|---|---|---|---|
| (i) Buildings (Frame) | $5 274.60 | × | 10/100 | = | $ 527.46 |
| (ii) Furniture and Equipment | $1 352.60 | × | 20/100 | = | $ 270.52 |
| (iii) Automotive Equipment | $7 644.00 | × | 30/100 | = | $2 293.20 |

**Note:** For fiscal periods of less than one year the depreciation must be calculated as follows:
1. Calculate the annual depreciation as shown above.
2. Calculate the number of days in the fiscal period.
3. Compute the depreciation for the fiscal period by applying the following formula:

$$\text{Depreciation for the period} = \text{Annual depreciation} \times \frac{\text{No. days in fiscal period}}{365}$$

## Depreciation adjustment for Cassidy Cartage

When calculated, the depreciation expense figures are set up on the work sheet as expenses and also as additions to their respective accu-

mulated depreciation totals. This is accomplished by means of an adjusting entry (or entries) which debits Depreciation Expense and credits Accumulated Depreciation. For Cassidy Cartage the adjusting entries for depreciation are:

| | | |
|---|---|---|
| Depreciation of Buildings | $527.46 | |
| Accumulated Depreciation of Buildings | | $527.46 |
| Depreciation of Furniture and Equipment | $270.52 | |
| Accumulated Depreciation of Furniture and Equipment | | $270.52 |
| Depreciation of Automotive Equipment | $2 293.20 | |
| Accumulated Depreciation of Automotive Equipment | | $2 293.20 |

On the work sheet, these adjusting entries (coded '6', '7', and '8') and the items extended appear as shown below. Because the accumu-

lated depreciation accounts are minus asset accounts, they are extended to the Balance Sheet Credit column.

Cassidy Cartage — Work Sheet — Year Ended June 30, 19–4

| Accounts | Acc # | Trial Balance Dr | Trial Balance Cr | Adjustments Dr | Adjustments Cr | Income Statement Dr | Income Statement Cr | Balance Sheet Dr | Balance Sheet Cr |
|---|---|---|---|---|---|---|---|---|---|
| Petty Cash | 1 | 50 — | | | | | | | |
| Bank | 2 | 725 41 | | | | | | | |
| Accounts Receivable | 3 | 4 027 56 | | | | | | | |
| Allowance for Doubtful Accounts | 4 | | 26 40 | | ⑤ 234 05 | | | | 260 45 |
| Supplies | 5 | 516 52 | | ① 45 21 | ② 166 48 | | | 395 25 | |
| Prepaid Insurance | 6 | 216 — | | | ③ 127 50 | | | 88 50 | |
| Prepaid Licences | 7 | 255 — | | | ④ 170 — | | | 85 — | |
| Land | 8 | 8 000 — | | | | | | | |
| Buildings (Frame) | 9 | 7 280 — | | | | | | | |
| Accumulated Depreciation Bldgs | 10 | | 2 005 40 | | ⑥ 527 46 | | | | 2 532 86 |
| Furniture + Equipment | 11 | 2 950 — | | | | | | | |
| Accumulated Depreciation F+E | 12 | | 1 597 40 | | ⑦ 270 52 | | | | 1 867 92 |
| Automotive Equipment | 13 | 15 600 — | | | | | | | |
| Accumulated Depreciation Autos | 14 | | 7 956 — | | ⑧ 2 293 20 | | | | 10 249 20 |
| Accounts Payable | 21 | | 3 047 25 | | ① 402 72 | | | | |
| Sales Tax Payable | 22 | | 238 73 | | | | | | |
| P. Marshall, Capital | 31 | | 18 387 21 | | | | | | |
| P. Marshall, Drawings | 32 | 6 000 — | | | | | | | |
| Sales | 41 | | 28 757 49 | | | | | | |
| Discounts Earned | 42 | | 56 75 | | | | | | |
| Bank Charges | 51 | 114 92 | | | | | | | |
| Building Maintenance | 52 | 474 37 | | ① 125 — | | | | | |
| Light, Heat and Water | 53 | 472 19 | | ① 22 81 | | | | | |
| Miscellaneous Expense | 54 | 115 70 | | ① 20 — | | | | | |
| Telephone Expense | 55 | 151 30 | | ① 15 70 | | | | | |
| Truck Expense | 56 | 5 704 16 | | ① 174 — | | | | | |
| Wages | 57 | 9 419 50 | | | | | | | |
| | | 62 072 63 | 62 072 63 | | | | | | |
| Supplies Expense | | | | ② 166 48 | | 166 48 | | | |
| Insurance Expense | | | | ③ 127 50 | | 127 50 | | | |
| Licences Expense | | | | ④ 170 — | | 170 — | | | |
| Bad Debts Expense | | | | ⑤ 234 05 | | 234 05 | | | |
| Depreciation of Buildings | | | | ⑥ 527 46 | | 527 46 | | | |
| Deprec. Furniture + Equipment | | | | ⑦ 270 52 | | 270 52 | | | |
| Deprec. Automotive Equipment | | | | ⑧ 2 293 20 | | 2 293 20 | | | |

## Balance sheet presentation

The estimated true value of the fixed assets is shown on the balance sheet in the following manner:

| Fixed Assets | | | |
|---|---|---|---|
| Land | | $8 000.00 | |
| Buildings | $ 7 280.00 | | |
| Less Accumulated Depreciation | 2 532.86 | 4 747.14 | |
| Furniture and Equipment | $2 950.00 | | |
| Less Accumulated Depreciation | 1 867.92 | 1 082.08 | |
| Automotive Equipment | $15 600.00 | | |
| Less Accumulated Depreciation | 10 249.20 | 5 350.80 | $19 180.02 |

## Adjusting for Accrued Wages

Certain expenses of a regular nature (such as wages and interest) are normally accounted for only on the days that payment is made. From one payment date to the next the liability for such an expense gradually builds up but is not recorded in the books of account. Not until the payment is actually due and paid is the transaction accounted for by means of an accounting entry such as:

    Wages Expense        $xxx
      Bank                        $xxx

Generally, the date of payment for such expenses as wages and interest does not coincide with the date of the end of the fiscal period. For example, consider the following illustration:

| PAY | PAY | PAY | PAY |
|---|---|---|---|
| DAY | DAY | DAY | DAY |

| Two-week pay period | Two-week pay period | Two-week pay period |
|---|---|---|

End of Fiscal Period

- - - - - - -JUNE - - - - ▶ ◀ - - - - -JULY - - - - - -

The illustration shows one of the two-week pay periods straddling the date of the end of the fiscal period. Or, expressed in other words, the date of the end of the fiscal period falls between two paydays.

This type of situation poses a problem when preparing financial statements. At the end of the accounting period there exists an unrecorded liability – for a portion of two weeks' wages in this case – which must be taken into consideration when accumulating the information for the statements. Items of this nature are known as **accrued expenses** or as **accrued liabilities.**

## Calculating the accrued wages for Cassidy Cartage

Calculating the accrued wages is most easily done after completion of the pay period straddling June 30, 19–4, and then computing the portion of the total that pertained to June.

Assuming that the total wages for the two weeks amounted to $262.15, and further assuming that of the ten working days involved, six fell in June and four in July, the accrued wages would be computed as follows:

$$\frac{\text{In last pay period, number of working days in June}}{\text{In last pay period total number of working days}} \times \text{Total wages for the last pay period}$$

$$\text{i.e.} \quad \frac{6}{10} \quad \times \quad \$262.15$$

$$= \quad \$157.29$$

## Accrued wages adjustment for Cassidy Cartage

Having calculated the accrued wages, it is then necessary to make an adjusting entry on the work sheet. The effect of the adjustment is to increase the wages expense and to set up the accrued liability for wages. The accounting entry debits Wages Expense and credits Accrued Wages Payable.

For Cassidy Cartage the adjusting entry is:

| | | |
|---|---|---|
| Wages Expense | $157.29 | |
| Accrued Wages Payable | | $157.29 |

On the work sheet, the adjusting entry (coded '9') and the items extended are shown in the illustration below. Observe that, since there was already a Wages Expense account in the trial balance section, it is not necessary to open a new line below for Wages Expense. However, it is necessary to open a new line for Accrued Wages

Payable because it is a new item. Accrued Wages Payable is a liability and is therefore extended to the Balance Sheet Credit column, as shown in the illustration below.

## Adjusting for Cost of Goods Sold

Because it is a service business, Cassidy Cartage does not require an adjustment for **cost of goods sold**. However, when preparing a work sheet for a trading business, it is necessary to know how to make this adjustment.

The cost of goods sold adjustment is not easily done by using the formal technique which we have been using. For this particular adjustment, accountants rely on the shortcut technique which handles it very effectively. (It is quite permissible to mix the two methods of making adjustments.)

The shortcut technique for making the adjustment for cost of goods sold is explained fully beginning on page 328, where it is described for the Midway Trading Company.

Cassidy Cartage — Work Sheet — Year Ended June 30, 19-4

| Accounts | Acc # | Trial Balance Dr. | Trial Balance Cr. | Adjustments Dr. | Adjustments Cr. | Income Statement Dr. | Income Statement Cr. | Balance Sheet Dr. | Balance Sheet Cr. |
|---|---|---|---|---|---|---|---|---|---|
| Petty Cash | 1 | 50 — | | | | | | | |
| Bank | 2 | 725 41 | | | | | | | |
| Accounts Receivable | 3 | 4 027 56 | | | | | | | |
| Allowance for Doubtful Accounts | 4 | | 26 40 | | ⑤ 234 05 | | | | 260 45 |
| Supplies | 5 | 516 52 | | ① 45 21 | ② 166 48 | | | 395 25 | |
| Prepaid Insurance | 6 | 216 — | | | ③ 127 50 | | | 88 50 | |
| Prepaid Licences | 7 | 255 — | | | ④ 170 — | | | 85 — | |
| Land | 8 | 8 000 — | | | | | | | |
| Buildings (Frame) | 9 | 7 280 — | | | | | | | |
| Accumulated Depreciation Bldgs. | 10 | | 2 005 40 | | ⑥ 527 46 | | | | 2 532 86 |
| Furniture and Equipment | 11 | 2 950 — | | | | | | | |
| Accumulated Depreciation F+E. | 12 | | 1 597 40 | | ⑦ 270 52 | | | | 1 867 92 |
| Automotive Equipment | 13 | 15 600 — | | | | | | | |
| Accumulated Depreciation Autos | 14 | | 7 956 — | | ⑧ 2 293 20 | | | | 10 249 20 |
| Accounts Payable | 21 | | 3 047 25 | | ① 402 72 | | | | |
| Sales Tax Payable | 22 | | 238 73 | | | | | | |
| P. Marshall, Capital | 31 | | 18 387 21 | | | | | | |
| P. Marshall, Drawings | 32 | 6 000 — | | | | | | | |
| Sales | 41 | | 28 757 49 | | | | | | |
| Discounts Earned | 42 | | 56 75 | | | | | | |
| Bank Charges | 51 | 114 92 | | | | | | | |
| Building Maintenance | 52 | 474 37 | | ① 125 — | | | | | |
| Light, Heat and Water | 53 | 472 19 | | ① 22 81 | | | | | |
| Miscellaneous Expense | 54 | 115 70 | | ① 20 — | | | | | |
| Telephone Expense | 55 | 151 30 | | ① 15 70 | | | | | |
| Truck Expense | 56 | 5 704 16 | | ① 174 — | | | | | |
| Wages | 57 | 9 419 50 | | ⑨ 157 29 | | 9 576 79 | | | |
| | | 62 072 63 | 62 072 63 | | | | | | |
| Supplies Expense | | | | ② 166 48 | | 166 48 | | | |
| Insurance Expense | | | | ③ 127 50 | | 127 50 | | | |
| Licences Expense | | | | ④ 170 — | | 170 — | | | |
| Bad Debts Expense | | | | ⑤ 234 05 | | 234 05 | | | |
| Depreciation of Buildings | | | | ⑥ 527 46 | | 527 46 | | | |
| Deprec. Furniture + Equipment | | | | ⑦ 270 52 | | 270 52 | | | |
| Deprec. Automotive Equipment | | | | ⑧ 2 293 20 | | 2 293 20 | | | |
| Accrued Wages Payable | | | | | ⑨ 157 29 | | | | 157 29 |

## Completing the Work Sheet

After recording the required adjusting entries, it is necessary to complete the work sheet in the following manner:

1. Extend each line that is not already extended. This means that for each such line the value of the Trial Balance columns and the Adjustments columns must be extended to one of the Income Statement columns or to one of the Balance Sheet columns. This must be done carefully and logically. Income and expense items are to be extended to the Income Statement section: other items are to be extended to the Balance Sheet section.

2. Total, rule, and balance the two Adjustments columns.

3. Total, rule, and balance the last four columns of the work sheet. The technique for doing this is described on pages 76 and 77.

The completed work sheet for Cassidy Cartage is shown below.

| Cassidy Cartage — Work Sheet — Year Ended June 30, 19-4 | Acc # | Trial Balance Dr. | Trial Balance Cr. | Adjustments Dr. | Adjustments Cr. | Income Statement Dr. | Income Statement Cr. | Balance Sheet Dr. | Balance Sheet Cr. |
|---|---|---|---|---|---|---|---|---|---|
| Petty Cash | 1 | 50 - | | | | | | 50 - | |
| Bank | 2 | 725 41 | | | | | | 725 41 | |
| Accounts Receivable | 3 | 4 027 56 | | | | | | 4 027 56 | |
| Allowance for Doubtful Accounts | 4 | | 26 40 | | (5) 234 05 | | | | 260 45 |
| Supplies | 5 | 516 52 | | (1) 45 21 | (2) 166 48 | | | 395 25 | |
| Prepaid Insurance | 6 | 216 - | | | (3) 127 50 | | | 88 50 | |
| Prepaid Licences | 7 | 255 - | | | (4) 170 - | | | 85 - | |
| Land | 8 | 8 000 - | | | | | | 8 000 - | |
| Buildings (Frame) | 9 | 7 280 - | | | | | | 7 280 - | |
| Accumulated Depreciation Bldgs | 10 | | 2 005 40 | | (6) 527 46 | | | | 2 532 86 |
| Furniture and Equipment | 11 | 2 950 - | | | | | | 2 950 - | |
| Accumulated Depreciation F.+E | 12 | | 1 597 40 | | (7) 270 52 | | | | 1 867 92 |
| Automotive Equipment | 13 | 15 600 - | | | | | | 15 600 - | |
| Accumulated Depreciation Autos | 14 | | 7 956 - | | (8) 2 293 20 | | | | 10 249 20 |
| Accounts Payable | 21 | | 3 047 25 | | (9) 402 72 | | | | 3 449 97 |
| Sales Tax Payable | 22 | | 238 73 | | | | | | 238 73 |
| P. Marshall, Capital | 31 | | 18 387 21 | | | | | | 18 387 21 |
| P. Marshall, Drawings | 32 | 6 000 - | | | | | | 6 000 - | |
| Sales | 41 | | 28 757 49 | | | | 28 757 49 | | |
| Discounts Earned | 42 | | 56 75 | | | | 56 75 | | |
| Bank Charges | 51 | 114 92 | | | | 114 92 | | | |
| Building Maintenance | 52 | 474 37 | | (1) 125 - | | 599 37 | | | |
| Light, Heat and Water | 53 | 472 19 | | (1) 22 81 | | 495 - | | | |
| Miscellaneous Expense | 54 | 115 70 | | (1) 20 - | | 135 70 | | | |
| Telephone Expense | 55 | 151 30 | | (1) 15 70 | | 167 - | | | |
| Truck Expense | 56 | 5 704 16 | | (1) 174 - | | 5 878 16 | | | |
| Wages | 57 | 9 419 50 | | (1) 157 29 | | 9 576 79 | | | |
| | | 62 072 63 | 62 072 63 | | | | | | |
| Supplies Expense | | | | (2) 166 48 | | 166 48 | | | |
| Insurance Expense | | | | (3) 127 50 | | 127 50 | | | |
| Licences Expense | | | | (4) 170 - | | 170 - | | | |
| Bad Debts Expense | | | | (5) 234 05 | | 234 05 | | | |
| Depreciation of Buildings | | | | (6) 527 46 | | 527 46 | | | |
| Deprec. Furniture + Equipment | | | | (7) 270 52 | | 270 52 | | | |
| Deprec. Automotive Equipment | | | | (8) 2 293 20 | | 2 293 20 | | | |
| Accrued Wages Payable | | | | | (9) 157 29 | | | | 157 29 |
| | | | | 4 349 22 | 4 349 22 | 20 756 15 | 28 814 24 | 45 201 72 | 37 143 63 |
| Net Income | | | | | | 8 058 09 | | | 8 058 09 |
| | | | | | | 28 814 24 | 28 814 24 | 45 201 72 | 45 201 72 |

## Adjusting Entries—Short-cut Technique

Many experienced accountants utilize two techniques for making the adjusting entries. These two methods are: (a) the formal technique that you have just studied, and (b) a shortcut technique that you are about to study in this section.

Both techniques are used because not all adjustments can be made using the shortcut technique. In fact, only adjustments that affect one item (e.g., Supplies or Insurance) are suited to the application of this technique.

Let us begin the study of the shortcut technique of making adjustments by examining the work sheet for Midway Trading Company after a fiscal period of one year. The Trial Balance section of this work sheet is shown at the top of the next page.

### Adjusting for Accounts Payable

Any adjustment involving more than one item is best carried out by the formal method de-

| Accounts | Acc. # | Trial Balance Dr. | Cr. | Adjustments Dr. | Cr. | Income Statement Dr. | Cr. | Balance Sheet Dr. | Cr. |
|---|---|---|---|---|---|---|---|---|---|
| Petty Cash | | 100 — | | | | | | | |
| Bank | 1 | 702 12 | | | | | | | |
| Accounts Receivable | 6 | 751 12 | | | | | | | |
| Allowance for Doubtful Accounts | | | 2 50 | | | | | | |
| Merchandise Inventory | | 12 074 — | | | | | | | |
| Supplies | | 370 — | | | | | | | |
| Prepaid Insurance | | 194 — | | | | | | | |
| Land | | 15 000 — | | | | | | | |
| Buildings (Brick) | | 12 000 — | | | | | | | |
| Accumulated Deprec. Blgs. | | | 1 711 50 | | | | | | |
| Furniture + Equipment | | 3 437 20 | | | | | | | |
| Accum. Deprec. Furn. & Equ. | | | 1 237 40 | | | | | | |
| Automobiles | | 7 800 — | | | | | | | |
| Accum. Deprec. Automobiles | | | 3 978 — | | | | | | |
| Accounts Payable | | | 9 461 21 | | | | | | |
| Bank Loan | | | 9 750 — | | | | | | |
| Sales Tax Payable | | | 251 10 | | | | | | |
| M. Philip, Capital | | | 26 214 87 | | | | | | |
| M. Philip, Drawings | | 8 751 — | | | | | | | |
| Sales | | | 59 168 10 | | | | | | |
| Sales Returns + Allowances | | 1 204 30 | | | | | | | |
| Discounts Earned | | | 516 19 | | | | | | |
| Bank Charges | | 1 140 26 | | | | | | | |
| Building Maintenance | | 375 — | | | | | | | |
| Car Expenses | | 1 846 50 | | | | | | | |
| Discounts Allowed | | 749 21 | | | | | | | |
| Duty | | 315 70 | | | | | | | |
| Freight In | | 949 14 | | | | | | | |
| Light, Heat & Water | | 417 25 | | | | | | | |
| Miscellaneous Expense | | 116 44 | | | | | | | |
| Purchases | | 30 616 90 | | | | | | | |
| Purchases Returns + Allow's | | | 1 520 — | | | | | | |
| Telephone Expense | | 484 17 | | | | | | | |
| Wages | | 7 416 56 | | | | | | | |
| | | 113 810 87 | 113 810 87 | | | | | | |

scribed in the previous section. Because the accounts payable adjustment usually involves several accounts, it is performed by means of the formal method.

Assume that the purchase invoices requiring an adjustment are as summarized here in the form of an accounting entry:

| | | |
|---|---|---|
| Car Expenses | $  147.50 | |
| Freight-in | 42.10 | |
| Miscellaneous Expense | 12.51 | |
| Purchases | 1 047.24 | |
| Accounts Payable | | $1 249.35 |

This accounting entry is recorded in the Adjustments column of the work sheet in the formal manner as shown at the top of page 324.

## Adjusting for Supplies

Any single item requiring an adjustment, supplies for example, can be adjusted by a shortcut technique. However, before the adjustment is made it is still necessary to take an inventory of supplies in the manner described on page 311. Having done this, the supplies adjustment by the shortcut method is performed as follows:

Step 1. On the Supplies line of the work sheet, write in the up-to-date supplies figure (assume $192) from the supplies inventory listing. Because Supplies is an asset, this figure is recorded in the Balance Sheet Debit column as shown below.

| ACCOUNT | TRIAL BALANCE DR. | CR. | ADJUSTMENTS DR. | CR. | INCOME STATEMENT DR. | CR. | BALANCE SHEET DR. | CR. |
|---|---|---|---|---|---|---|---|---|
| | | | | | | | | |
| Supplies | 370 — | | | | | | 192 — | |
| | | | | | | | | |

| Accounts | Acc # | Trial Balance Dr. | Cr. | Adjustments Dr. | Cr. | Income Statement Dr. | Cr. | Balance Sheet Dr. | Cr. |
|---|---|---|---|---|---|---|---|---|---|
| Midway Trading Company | | Work Sheet | | | Year Ended December 31, 19-4 | | | P. 20 | |
| Petty Cash | | 100 — | | | | | | | |
| Bank | 1 | 1 702 12 | | | | | | | |
| Accounts Receivable | 6 | 751 12 | | | | | | | |
| Allowance for Doubtful Accounts | | | 2 50 | | | | | | |
| Merchandise Inventory | | 12 074 — | | | | | | | |
| Supplies | | 370 — | | | | | | | |
| Prepaid Insurance | | 194 — | | | | | | | |
| Land | | 15 000 — | | | | | | | |
| Buildings (Brick) | | 12 000 — | | | | | | | |
| Accum. Deprec. Bldgs. | | | 1 711 50 | | | | | | |
| Furniture + Equipment | | 3 437 20 | | | | | | | |
| Accum. Deprec. Furn. + Equ. | | | 1 237 40 | | | | | | |
| Automobiles | | 7 800 — | | | | | | | |
| Accum. Deprec. Automobiles | | | 3 978 — | | | | | | |
| Accounts Payable | | | 9 461 21 | | ① 1 249 35 | | | | |
| Bank Loan | | | 9 750 — | | | | | | |
| Sales Tax Payable | | | 251 10 | | | | | | |
| M. Philip, Capital | | | 26 214 87 | | | | | | |
| M. Philip, Drawings | | 8 751 — | | | | | | | |
| Sales | | | 59 168 10 | | | | | | |
| Sales Returns + Allowances | | 1 204 30 | | | | | | | |
| Discounts Earned | | | 516 19 | | | | | | |
| Bank Charges | | 1 140 26 | | | | | | | |
| Building Maintenance | | 375 — | | | | | | | |
| Car Expenses | | 1 846 50 | | ① 147 50 | | | | | |
| Discounts Allowed | | 749 21 | | | | | | | |
| Duty | | 315 70 | | | | | | | |
| Freight In | | 949 14 | | ① 42 10 | | | | | |
| Light, Heat + Water | | 417 25 | | | | | | | |
| Miscellaneous Expense | | 116 44 | | ① 12 51 | | | | | |
| Purchases | | 30 616 90 | | ① 1 047 24 | | | | | |
| Purchases Returns + Allow's | | | 1 520 — | | | | | | |
| Telephone Expense | | 484 17 | | | | | | | |
| Wages | | 7 416 56 | | | | | | | |
| | | 113 810 87 | 113 810 87 | | | | | | |

**Step 2.** On the same line of the work sheet but in the Income Statement section, record the Supplies Expense figure. This is found by subtracting the Balance Sheet figure of $192 from the Trial Balance figure of $370. Because it represents an expense, the resultant figure of $178 is recorded in the Income Statement Debit column as shown below.

| ACCOUNT | TRIAL BALANCE DR. | CR. | ADJUSTMENTS DR. | CR. | INCOME STATEMENT DR. | CR. | BALANCE SHEET DR. | CR. |
|---|---|---|---|---|---|---|---|---|
| | | | | | | | | |
| Supplies | 370 — | | | | 178 — | | 192 — | |

When preparing financial statements from the work sheet, keep in mind that the $178 in the Income Statement section represents Supplies Expense even though it is on a line that reads Supplies.

## Checking mechanical accuracy

Many adjustments may be done by means of the shortcut technique. To assist you to perform these adjustments accurately, keep in mind the rule shown below.

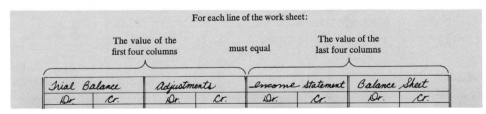

For each line of the work sheet:

The value of the first four columns   must equal   The value of the last four columns

| Trial Balance Dr. | Cr. | Adjustments Dr. | Cr. | Income Statement Dr. | Cr. | Balance Sheet Dr. | Cr. |
|---|---|---|---|---|---|---|---|

## Adjusting for Prepaid Insurance

The prepaid insurance adjustment may be performed by using the shortcut technique. However, before making the adjustment, it is necessary to calculate the value of the prepaid insurance in the manner described on page 313. Once the prepaid insurance figure is obtained, the adjustment by the shortcut method is performed as follows:

Step 1. On the Prepaid Insurance line of the work sheet, write in the unexpired insurance figure from the insurance schedule (assume $112). Because Prepaid Insurance is an asset, this figure is recorded in the Balance Sheet Debit column as shown below.

| ACCOUNT | TRIAL BALANCE | | ADJUSTMENTS | | INCOME STATEMENT | | BALANCE SHEET | |
|---|---|---|---|---|---|---|---|---|
| | DR. | CR. | DR. | CR. | DR. | CR. | DR. | CR. |
| | | | | | | | | |
| Prepaid Insce. | 194 | – | | | | | 112 | – |
| | | | | | | | | |

Step 2. On the same line of the work sheet but in the Income Statement section, record the insurance expense figure. This is found by subtracting the Balance Sheet figure of $112 from the Trial Balance figure of $194. Because it represents an expense, the resultant figure of $82 is recorded in the Income Statement Debit column as shown below.

When preparing financial statements from the work sheet, keep in mind that the $82 in the Income Statement section represents Insurance Expense even though it is on a line that reads Prepaid Insurance.

Also, with every one-line adjustment, be sure that it balances in accordance with the rule established on page 324.

| ACCOUNT | TRIAL BALANCE | | ADJUSTMENTS | | INCOME STATEMENT | | BALANCE SHEET | |
|---|---|---|---|---|---|---|---|---|
| | DR. | CR. | DR. | CR. | DR. | CR. | DR. | CR. |
| | | | | | | | | |
| Prepaid Insce. | 194 | – | | | 82 | – | 112 | – |
| | | | | | | | | |

## Adjusting for Prepaid Licences

For Midway Trading Company no adjustment for prepaid licences is required. The reason for this is that the end of the fiscal year, December 31, corresponds to the end of the licence year at which time the value of the licences is zero. If, however, an adjustment has been necessary it could have been done using the shortcut method.

## Adjusting for Doubtful Accounts

The adjustment for doubtful accounts may be performed by using the shortcut method. Naturally, before making the adjustment, it is necessary to estimate the total of the doubtful accounts in the manner described on page 316. Once this figure is established, the adjustment by the shortcut method is performed as follows:

Step 1. On the Allowance for Doubtful Accounts line of the work sheet, record the total of the doubtful accounts from the aging schedule (assume $143.20). Because Allowance for Doubtful Accounts is a minus asset, this figure is recorded in the Balance Sheet Credit column as shown below.

| ACCOUNT | TRIAL BALANCE | | ADJUSTMENTS | | INCOME STATEMENT | | BALANCE SHEET | |
|---|---|---|---|---|---|---|---|---|
| | DR. | CR. | DR. | CR. | DR. | CR. | DR. | CR. |
| | | | | | | | | |
| Allow. Doubt. Acc. | | 2 50 | | | | | | 143 20 |

Step 2. On the same line of the work sheet but in the Income Statement section, record the bad debts expense figure. This figure is calculated somewhat differently from the previous one-line adjustments. The best approach is to *balance* the Allowances line through the Income Statement Debit column. Only one figure will do it – in this case $140.70. You must be specially careful when balancing this line because the trial balance figure can sometimes be a debit figure. The balanced line for Midway Trading Company appears below.

| ACCOUNT | TRIAL BALANCE | | ADJUSTMENTS | | INCOME STATEMENT | | BALANCE SHEET | |
|---|---|---|---|---|---|---|---|---|
| | DR. | CR. | DR. | CR. | DR. | CR. | DR. | CR. |
| | | | | | | | | |
| *Allow. Doubt. Acc.* | | 2 50 | | | 140 70 | | | 143 20 |

Keep in mind when preparing the financial statements that the $140.70 figure in the Income Statement Debit column represents Bad Debts Expense even though it is on a line that reads Allowance for Doubtful Accounts.

## Adjusting for Depreciation

Each of the depreciation adjustments can be performed by the shortcut technique. Before making the adjustments, however, it is necessary to calculate the depreciation figures in the manner described on page 318. For Midway Trading Company these calculations are as follows:

CALCULATING THE NET BOOK VALUES

| | ASSET VALUE | | ACCUMULATED DEPRECIATION VALUE | | NET BOOK VALUE |
|---|---|---|---|---|---|
| Building | $12 000.00 | minus | $1 711.50 | equals | $10 288.50 |
| Furniture & Equipment | $ 3 437.20 | minus | $1 237.40 | equals | $ 2 199.80 |
| Automobiles | $ 7 800.00 | minus | $3 978.00 | equals | $ 3 822.00 |

CALCULATING THE ANNUAL DEPRECIATION FIGURES

| | NET BOOK VALUE | | RATE OF DEPRECIATION | | DEPRECIATION FOR YEAR |
|---|---|---|---|---|---|
| Building | $10 288.50 | times | 5 per cent | equals | $ 514.43 |
| Furniture & Equipment | $ 2 199.80 | times | 20 per cent | equals | $ 439.96 |
| Automobiles | $ 3 822.00 | times | 30 per cent | equals | $ 1 146.60 |

Once the depreciation expense figures are calculated, the adjustments by the shortcut method are as follows:

Step 1. On each of the Accumulated Depreciation lines of the work sheet, write in the appropriate depreciation expense figure from the calculation schedule. Because they are *expense* figures, they are recorded in the Income Statement Debit column as shown at the top of the next page.

| ACCOUNT | TRIAL BALANCE | | ADJUSTMENTS | | INCOME STATEMENT | | BALANCE SHEET | |
|---|---|---|---|---|---|---|---|---|
| | DR. | CR. | DR. | CR. | DR. | CR. | DR. | CR. |
| | | | | | | | | |
| Acc. Dep. Bldgs. | | 1711 50 | | | 514 43 | | | |
| Acc. Dep. F+E. | | 1237 40 | | | 439 96 | | | |
| Acc. Dep. Autos | | 3978 – | | | 1146 60 | | | |

Step 2. On the same lines of the work sheet but in the Balance Sheet section, record the new accumulated depreciation figures. These figures are obtained by adding the expense figures respectively to each of the trial balance figures. They are recorded in the Balance Sheet Credit column because they represent minus assets. The completed lines are shown below.

Again, keep in mind that the three figures in the Income Statement Debit column represent Depreciation Expense even though they are on lines that read Allowance for Depreciation.

| ACCOUNT | TRIAL BALANCE | | ADJUSTMENTS | | INCOME STATEMENT | | BALANCE SHEET | |
|---|---|---|---|---|---|---|---|---|
| | DR. | CR. | DR. | CR. | DR. | CR. | DR. | CR. |
| | | | | | | | | |
| Acc. Dep. Bldgs. | | 1711 50 | | | 514 43 | | | 2225 93 |
| Acc. Dep. F+E. | | 1237 40 | | | 439 96 | | | 1677 36 |
| Acc. Dep. Autos | | 3978 – | | | 1146 60 | | | 5124 60 |

## Adjusting for Accrued Wages

The accrued wages adjustment is one that may be performed by means of the shortcut method. After calculating the accrued wages figure, the adjustment is performed as follows:

Step 1. On the Wages (Expense) line of the work sheet, enter the accrued wages figure (assume $146.54). Because accrued wages represents a liability, this figure is entered in the Balance Sheet Credit column as shown below.

| ACCOUNT | TRIAL BALANCE | | ADJUSTMENTS | | INCOME STATEMENT | | BALANCE SHEET | |
|---|---|---|---|---|---|---|---|---|
| | DR. | CR. | DR. | CR. | DR. | CR. | DR. | CR. |
| | | | | | | | | |
| Wages | 7416 56 | | | | | | | 146 54 |

Step 2. On the same line of the work sheet but in the Income Statement section, record the adjusted figure for wages expense. It is merely necessary to add the trial balance figure to the accrued wages figure and record it in the Income Statement Debit column. Or, looking at it in another way, just balance the line through the Income Statement Debit column; follow the rule on page 324. The completed line showing an expense figure of $7 563.10 is shown on the next page.

| ACCOUNT | TRIAL BALANCE | | ADJUSTMENTS | | INCOME STATEMENT | | BALANCE SHEET | |
| | DR. | CR. | DR. | CR. | DR. | CR. | DR. | CR. |
|---|---|---|---|---|---|---|---|---|
| Wages | 7416 56 | | | | 7563 10 | | | 146 54 |

In this particular situation, you must keep in mind that the $146.54 in the Balance Sheet Credit column represents a liability even though it is on a line that reads Wages or Wages Expense.

## Adjusting for Cost of Goods Sold (Periodic Inventory Method)

Trading businesses, which buy and sell merchandise, require an adjustment to determine the cost of the goods that have been sold. This figure is an important one when preparing the income statement. Service businesses, on the other hand, do not buy and sell merchandise and therefore do not require a cost of goods sold adjustment. Cassidy Cartage, the business used as an example in the early part of this chapter, was a service business and as such did not require a cost of goods sold adjustment. But Midway Trading Company, the business being studied at this point, is a trading business and does require a cost of goods sold adjustment.

### Importance of cost of goods

The biggest expenditure of a trading business is the cost of its merchandise. For every sale that it makes, the merchant must buy and pay for the goods. An item that he sells for $100 may cost in the neighborhood of $75*, making it apparent that the cost of the goods is a very significant expenditure.

Since studying Chapter 8, you have been making the standard accounting entries to record the sale of merchandise. You have debited Cash or Accounts Receivable and have credited Sales and Sales Tax Payable on the basis of the selling price of the goods. The merchant and his staff

* If the cost price of an item is $75 and the selling price is $100, there will be a gross profit or markup of $25. Also, the rate of markup is $25/75 \times 100$ (Profit/Cost Price $\times$ 100) which is 33⅓ per cent.

find it no problem in coping with this accounting entry. Since the selling prices of the various goods are prominently displayed on the merchandise itself or in a convenient catalogue, it is an easy matter for the clerk to record the selling price and the sales tax by means of a cash register slip or a sales slip. For an item costing $75 and being sold for $100 the effect is:

Cash (or Accounts Receivable)  105.00
   Sales                           100.00
   Sales Tax Payable         5.00

## Basic calculation for cost of goods sold

But this accounting entry alone is insufficient. It implies that a profit of $100 is made on the sale because it does nothing to record the cost of the goods that were sold. This is not correct; the real profit is obviously only $25.

For a number of reasons, however, it is not feasible to account for the cost of goods sold during the accounting period. It is much more convenient to tidy this matter up at the end of the accounting period. It is not a complex matter at the end of an accounting period to calculate the cost of goods sold.

First, the value of the merchandise on hand at the beginning of the accounting period is known to us. This is the balance of the Merchandise Inventory account as listed in the Trial Balance columns of the work sheet.

Second, the value of the merchandise purchased during the accounting period is known to us. This is the value of the Purchases account as indicated by the first four columns of the work sheet. Or, for businesses that have a Returns and Allowances account, it is the Purchase account figure less the Purchases Returns and Allowances figure.

The merchandise on hand at the beginning of the period plus the net merchandise purchased during the period gives the total merchandise that was available for sale. Consider the following summary for Midway Trading Company.

| Merchandise Inventory at beginning of period | | $12 074.00 |
|---|---|---|
| Purchases of Merchandise during the period | $31 664.14 | |
| Less Purchases Returns and Allowances | 1 520.00 | 30 144.14 |
| Total Merchandise available for sale during the period | | $42 218.14 |

The $42 218.14 figure thus arrived at represents the total of merchandise that was available for sale during the period. But much of this merchandise will have been sold during the period. And, if it was not sold, then it will still be on hand. This statement provides us with the clue to the means of calculating the cost of goods sold. If we take an inventory of goods at the end of the period, and then subtract this closing inventory from the $42 218.14, we will have determined the cost of the goods that were sold during the period.

Assuming that the closing inventory of Midway Trading Company is $13 562, the complete basic calculation of the cost of goods sold is as shown immediately following:

| Merchandise Inventory at beginning of period | | $12 074.00 |
|---|---|---|
| Purchases of Merchandise during the period | $31 664.14 | |
| Less Purchases Returns and Allowances | 1 520.00 | 30 144.14 |
| Total Merchandise available for sale during the period | | $42 218.14 |
| Deduct: Merchandise Inventory at end of period | | 13 562.00 |
| Cost of Goods Sold during the period | | $28 656.14 |

## Cost of Goods Sold Adjustment

Before the cost of goods sold adjustment can be made, it is necessary to take an inventory of the merchandise in stock on the last day of the fiscal period. This is usually a job that requires considerable time and effort and a great deal of systematic organization. In most cases it is necessary to close down the store or plant until the operation is completed. To take the inventory, it is necessary to count and list every item in stock; to multiply the quantity of each item on hand by its cost price; and finally to total the whole listing.

Once the inventory figure is available, the cost of goods sold adjustment may be made using the shortcut method as follows:

Step 1. On the Merchandise Inventory line, write the opening inventory figure (pick up from the Trial Balance Debit column) in the Income Statement Debit column as shown below.

| ACCOUNT | TRIAL BALANCE | | ADJUSTMENTS | | INCOME STATEMENT | | BALANCE SHEET | |
|---|---|---|---|---|---|---|---|---|
| | DR. | CR. | DR. | CR. | DR. | CR. | DR. | CR. |
| | | | | | | | | |
| Mdse. Inventory | 12074 — | | | | 12074 — | | | |

Step 2. On the same line of the work sheet, record the closing inventory figure (in this case $13 562) in two places:

(a) Income Statement **Credit** column;
(b) Balance Sheet **Debit** column, as shown at the top of the next page.

| ACCOUNT | TRIAL BALANCE DR. | CR. | ADJUSTMENTS DR. | CR. | INCOME STATEMENT DR. | CR. | BALANCE SHEET DR. | CR. |
|---|---|---|---|---|---|---|---|---|
| Mdse. Inventory | 12074 — | | | | 12074 — | 13562 — | 13562 — | |

Observe that the Merchandise Inventory line is in balance at this point.

Step 3. Extend the Purchases line and the Pur- chases Returns and Allowances line to the Income Statement section of the work sheet as shown below.

| ACCOUNT | TRIAL BALANCE DR. | CR. | ADJUSTMENTS DR. | CR. | INCOME STATEMENT DR. | CR. | BALANCE SHEET DR. | CR. |
|---|---|---|---|---|---|---|---|---|
| Mdse. Inventory | 12074 — | | | | 12074 — | 13562 — | 13562 — | |
| Purchases | 30616 90 | | ① 1047 24 | | 31664 14 | | | |
| Purch. Rets + Alls | | 1520 — | | | | 1520 — | | |

At this point, the cost of goods sold adjustment is completed. Let us examine it closely to see what it has accomplished.

1. In the Balance Sheet columns, it has provided the correct closing inventory figure for inclusion on the balance sheet.
2. In the Income Statement columns, it has provided the basic ingredients for the cost of goods sold calculation of a trading business. It should be apparent to you that these figures correspond to those summarized in the middle of page 329. You will see how they are included in the income statement in Chapter 15.

It is interesting to note that almost without exception the cost of goods sold adjustment is done by the shortcut method. Some accountants will use the formal method for making all other adjustments but when it comes to adjusting for the cost of goods sold, they invariably rely on the shortcut technique.

## Completing the Work Sheet for Midway Trading Company

The remaining items on the work sheet are extended and the work sheet completed in the manner already described on page 322.

The completed work sheet for Midway Trading Company is as shown on page 331.

## Accountant's working papers

At the time financial statements are prepared it is necessary to make numerous inventories, schedules, calculations, etc. pertaining to the work sheet adjustments and other matters (e.g., bank reconciliation). It is customary to collect all papers and calculations related to the preparation of the financial statements in one file. These papers are known as the accountant's working papers.

# Bookkeeping and Accounting Terms

**Adjusting Entry** An entry made before closing the books for the period, to apportion amounts of revenue or expense to accounting periods or to operating divisions, e.g., apportionment of wages between accounting periods when the cur- rent period ends between two paydays.

**Taking Inventory** The process of counting, itemizing, and valuing the goods or stock of a business. The word [inventory] is usually restricted to designate items of tangible personal property

**Midway Trading Company**  **Work Sheet**  **Year Ended December 31, 19-4**

| Accounts | Acc # | Trial Balance Dr. | Cr. | Adjustments Dr. | Cr. | Income Statement Dr. | Cr. | Balance Sheet Dr. | Cr. |
|---|---|---|---|---|---|---|---|---|---|
| Petty Cash | | 100 — | | | | | | 100 — | |
| Bank | 1 | 1 702 12 | | | | | | 1 702 12 | |
| Accounts Receivable | 6 | 6 751 12 | | | | | | 6 751 12 | |
| Allowance for Doubtful Accounts | | | | | 2 50 | 140 70 | | | 143 20 |
| Merchandise Inventory | | 12 074 — | | | | 12 074 — | 13 562 — | 13 562 — | |
| Supplies | | 370 — | | | | 178 — | | 192 — | |
| Prepaid Insurance | | 194 — | | | | 82 — | | 112 — | |
| Land | | 15 000 — | | | | | | 15 000 — | |
| Buildings (Brick) | | 12 000 — | | | | | | 12 000 — | |
| Accum. Deprec. Bldgs. | | | 1 711 50 | | | 514 43 | | | 2 225 93 |
| Furniture + Equipment | | 3 437 20 | | | | | | 3 437 20 | |
| Accum. Deprec. Furn. + Equ. | | | 1 237 40 | | | 439 96 | | | 1 677 36 |
| Automobiles | | 7 800 — | | | | | | 7 800 — | |
| Accum. Deprec. Automobiles | | | 3 978 — | | | 1 146 60 | | | 5 124 60 |
| Accounts Payable | | | 9 461 21 | | ① 1 249 35 | | | | 10 710 56 |
| Bank Loan | | | 9 750 — | | | | | | 9 750 — |
| Sales Tax Payable | | | 251 10 | | | | | | 251 10 |
| M. Philip, Capital | | | 26 214 87 | | | | | | 26 214 87 |
| M. Philip, Drawings | | 8 751 — | | | | | | 8 751 — | |
| Sales | | | 59 168 10 | | | | 59 168 10 | | |
| Sales Returns + Allowances | | 1 204 30 | | | | 1 204 30 | | | |
| Discounts Earned | | | 516 19 | | | | 516 19 | | |
| Bank Charges | | 1 140 26 | | | | 1 140 26 | | | |
| Building Maintenance | | 375 — | | | | 375 — | | | |
| Car Expenses | | 1 846 50 | | ① 147 50 | | 1 994 — | | | |
| Discounts Allowed | | 749 21 | | | | 749 21 | | | |
| Duty | | 315 70 | | | | 315 70 | | | |
| Freight In | | 949 14 | | ① 42 10 | | 991 24 | | | |
| Light, Heat + Water | | 417 25 | | | | 417 25 | | | |
| Miscellaneous Expense | | 116 44 | | ① 12 51 | | 128 95 | | | |
| Purchases | | 30 616 90 | | ① 1 047 24 | | 31 664 14 | | | |
| Purchases Returns + Allow's | | | 1 520 — | | | | 1 520 — | | |
| Telephone Expense | | 484 17 | | | | 484 17 | | | |
| Wages | | 7 416 56 | | | | 7 563 10 | | | 146 54 |
| | | 113 810 87 | 113 810 87 | 1 249 35 | 1 249 35 | 61 603 01 | 74 766 29 | 69 407 44 | 56 244 16 |
| Net Income | | | | | | 13 163 28 | | | 13 163 28 |
| | | | | | | 74 766 29 | 74 766 29 | 69 407 44 | 69 407 44 |

which are held for sale in the ordinary course of business, or are in the process of production for such sale, or are to be currently consumed in the production of goods or services to be available for sale.

**Prepaid Expense** A short term expense prepayment; an expenditure, other than an outlay for inventory or a capital expenditure, which is expected to yield its benefits in the near future and meanwhile is carried forward to be charged to expense in the near future.

**Doubtful Account** An account or note receivable, the ultimate collectibility of which is uncertain. Also known as a **doubtful debt.**

**Bad Debt** An account or note receivable that is uncollectible.

**Write Off** To transfer to income all or a portion of the balance in an asset or liability account.

**Aging** A process of analysis of receivables by classifying the amounts according to the length of time for which they have been outstanding or for which they have been due.

**Depreciation** 1. The gradual exhaustion of the service capacity of fixed assets which is not restored by maintenance practices. It is the consequence of such factors as use, obsolescence, inadequacy, and decay. 2. The expense in an accounting period arising from the application of depreciation accounting.

**Depreciation Accounting** An accounting procedure in which the cost or other recorded value of a fixed asset less estimated residual value (if any) is distributed over its estimated useful life in a systematic and rational manner. It is a process of allocation, not valuation.

**Capital Cost Allowance** A deduction in lieu of depreciation, under *The Income Tax Act (Canada) and Regulations*, with respect to the cost of certain assets. It may differ from the amount charged for depreciation during the period.

**Book Value** The amount at which an item appears in the books of account and financial statements.

**Accrued Expense** An expense which has been incurred in an accounting period but for which no enforceable claim will be made in that accounting period by the person who rendered the service. It arises from the purchase of services (including the use of money) which at the time of accounting have been only partly performed, are not yet billable, and have not been paid for.

**Accrued Liability** A developing but not yet enforceable claim by another person, which is accumulating with the passage of time or the receipt of the service. It arises from the purchase of services (including the use of money) which at the time of accounting have been only partly performed, are not yet billable, and have not been paid for.

**Accrued Revenue** Revenue which has been earned in an accounting period but for which no enforceable claim can be made in that accounting period against the person for whom the service was rendered. It arises from the sale of services (including the use of money) which at the time of accounting have been only partly performed, are not yet billable, and have not been paid for.

**Cost of Goods Sold** The total cost of goods sold during an accounting period. Also known as **cost of sales**.

**Accumulated Depreciation** The total credit representing the expired cost of fixed assets since the assets were placed in use by a business.

## Review Questions

1. Name the two different techniques for making adjusting entries.
2. Explain why an adjustment is necessary for accounts payable.
3. Where is an adjusting entry first recorded?
4. Why are adjusting entries coded?
5. Why is an adjusting entry necessary for supplies?
6. How does one 'take inventory'?
7. What does it mean to 'extend the work sheet'?
8. What is prepaid insurance? prepaid licences?
9. What is the first step in making the adjustment for prepaid insurance? for prepaid licences?
10. Why is an adjustment necessary for doubtful accounts?
11. How is the estimated true value of doubtful accounts shown in the books of account?
12. Explain the purpose of the accounts receivable aging schedule.
13. When is a customer's account written off?
14. In your own words, explain the meaning of depreciation.
15. What is meant by the net book value of a fixed asset?
16. Briefly explain the income tax method of calculating depreciation.
17. Why is an adjustment necessary for accrued wages?
18. Which method (formal or shortcut) is used for making the accounts payable adjustment?
19. Which method is used for making the cost of goods sold adjustment?
20. What is the rule for balancing a line of the work sheet?
21. Using the shortcut method, what line of the work sheet is used to make the adjustment for depreciation of buildings? for insurance expense?
22. Explain the importance of cost of goods sold.
23. How is the closing inventory figure ascertained?

## Exercises

1. This exercise is to be done in your workbook, or as directed by your teacher.

2. Calculate the depreciation expense in each of the following cases:

| Type of Asset | Asset Account Balance | Accumulated Depreciation Account Balance | Annual Rate of Depreciation | Accounting Period |
|---|---|---|---|---|
| Building (Brick) | $29 572.50 | $13 514.21 | 5% | Jan. 1 to Dec. 31 |
| Building (Frame) | 11 263.00 | 2 946.50 | 10% | Jan. 1 to Dec. 31 |
| General Equipment | 15 072.13 | 5 516.20 | 20% | Jan. 1 to Dec. 31 |
| Automotive Equipment | 19 475.43 | 7 419.21 | 30% | Jan. 1 to Dec. 31 |
| Building (Frame) | 7 500.00 | 2 946.34 | 10% | Apr. 1 to Sep. 30 |
| Automobiles | 6 500.00 | 3 050.00 | 30% | Oct. 1 to Dec. 31 |
| Trucks | 15 073.54 | 8 455.52 | 30% | Jan. 1 to Mar. 31 |
| Building (Brick) | 125 900.00 | 53 542.10 | 5% | Jan. 1 to Jun. 30 |
| Furniture | 4 406.75 | 2 120.57 | 20% | July 1 to Dec. 31 |

3. A businessman's fiscal year-end is September 30. One of his business expenditures is for truck licences. If he spends $240 on truck licences for the calendar year, calculate the value of prepaid licences at the end of his fiscal year.

4. The details of a business's insurance policies are as follows:

| Company | Policy Date | Term | Premium |
|---|---|---|---|
| Atlantic | March 15, 19–3 | 3 years | $ 72.00 |
| Pacific | June 30, 19–4 | 2 years | 120.00 |
| Indian | June 1, 19–4 | 1 year | 84.00 |
| Arctic | September 15, 19–3 | 3 years | 156.00 |

Calculate the value of prepaid insurance as of December 31, 19–4.

5. From the following information calculate the accrued wages as of March 31, 19–8, the end of a fiscal period:

a. Total wages for the two-week period ended Friday, April 4, 19–8, are $755.40. The company works a five-day week and the employees are paid every other Friday.

b. Total wages for the two-week period ended Friday, April 10, 19–8, are $804.25. The company works a five-day week and the employees are paid every other Friday.

6. A supplies inventory count sheet is shown below.

| INVENTORY ITEM | QUANTITY |
|---|---|
| Rubber Bands | 3 boxes |
| Envelopes #8 | 10 boxes |
| Envelopes #10 | 4½ boxes |
| Envelopes, Manila | 2 boxes |
| Typewriting paper | 4M sheets |
| Letterhead | 10M sheets |
| Copy paper | 4M sheets |
| Carbon paper | 2 boxes |
| Paper clips | 12 boxes |
| Staples | 15 boxes |
| Pencils, regular | 4 doz. |
| Pencils, red | 2 doz. |

From the preceding count sheet and the cost price list below, prepare a supplies inventory sheet showing the individual items, the quantities, the cost prices, the extensions, and the final total.

Cost Prices

| Rubber bands | .75 per box |
| Envelopes, #8 | $16.90 per box |

| | | | |
|---|---|---|---|
| Envelopes, #10 | $17.50 per box | Carbon paper | $2.75 per box |
| Manila envelopes, C4 | $12.40 per box | Paper clips | .50 per box |
| Typewriting paper | $9.70 per M | Staples | $1.85 per box |
| Letterhead | $10.50 per M | Pencils, regular | $2.10 per doz. |
| Copy paper | $3.50 per M | Pencils, red | $2.40 per doz. |

**Note:** The solutions for the remaining exercises are to be kept for use again in Chapter 15.

7.  From the following trial balance and additional information, prepare the work sheet for J. P. Gorman, Consultant, for the annual fiscal period ended June 30, 19–0.

J. P. GORMAN, CONSULTANT
TRIAL BALANCE
JUNE 30, 19–0

| | | |
|---|---|---|
| Petty Cash | $ 25.00 | |
| Bank | 1 047.50 | |
| Accounts Receivable | 7 421.00 | |
| Allowance for Doubtful Accounts | | $ 7.25 |
| Supplies | 300.00 | |
| Prepaid Insurance | 280.00 | |
| Furniture and Equipment | 2 596.00 | |
| Accumulated Depreciation Furn. & Equip. | | 1 266.85 |
| Automobile | 4 800.00 | |
| Accumulated Depreciation Automobile | | 1 440.00 |
| Accounts Payable | | 521.92 |
| Sales Tax Payable | | 159.10 |
| J. P. Gorman, Capital | | 8 159.60 |
| J. P. Gorman, Drawings | 9 500.00 | |
| Revenue | | 18 072.50 |
| Bank Charges | 32.10 | |
| Car Expenses | 547.52 | |
| Miscellaneous Expense | 61.50 | |
| Rent | 1 600.00 | |
| Telephone | 112.00 | |
| Wages | 1 304.60 | |
| | $29 627.22 | $29 627.22 |

## Additional Information

a.  Purchase invoices received in July 19–0 but which pertained to goods received in June 19–0 were summarized as follows:
Supplies     $35.00
Car Expense    72.50
Misc. Expense    7.40

b.  The accounts receivable aging analysis showed the doubtful accounts at June 30, 19–0, to be $294.65.

c.  The supplies inventory taken at June 30, 19–0, amounted to $80.

d.  The prepaid insurance schedule as of June

30, 19–0, showed a total of $200 for unexpired insurance.

e. Depreciation of fixed assets is at government rates.

f. The accrued wage figure at June 30, 19–0, amounted to $175.

---

8. From the following trial balance and additional information, prepare the work sheet for Dennisson Delivery Service for the half-yearly fiscal period ended June 30, 19–5.

DENNISSON DELIVERY SERVICE
TRIAL BALANCE
JUNE 30, 19–5

| | | |
|---|---|---|
| Petty Cash | $ 100.00 | |
| Bank | 570.00 | |
| Accounts Receivable | 2 419.51 | |
| Allowance for Doubtful Accounts | 10.00 | |
| Supplies | 174.00 | |
| Prepaid Insurance | 400.00 | |
| Prepaid Licences | 1 146.00 | |
| Land | 7 000.00 | |
| Buildings (Frame) | 21 570.00 | |
| Accumulated Depreciation Buildings | | $ 7 046.90 |
| Furniture and Equipment | 8 970.00 | |
| Accum. Deprec. Furn. and Equip. | | 2 946.72 |
| Trucks | 18 472.00 | |
| Accumulated Depreciation Trucks | | 10 407.51 |
| Accounts Payable | | 3 417.40 |
| Sales Tax Payable | | 350.00 |
| Joseph Budd, Capital | | 29 797.06 |
| Joseph Budd, Drawings | 8 900.00 | |
| Revenue | | 40 721.19 |
| Bank Charges | 115.25 | |
| Miscellaneous Expense | 219.51 | |
| Telephone | 316.25 | |
| Truck Expenses | 6 901.32 | |
| Wages | 17 402.94 | |
| | $94 686.78 | $94 686.78 |

## Additional Information

a. Purchase invoices received in July 19–5 but which pertained to June 19–5 were summarized as follows:

| | |
|---|---|
| Supplies | $ 42.00 |
| Misc. Expense | 33.00 |
| Truck Expenses | 213.54 |

b. The accounts receivable aging analysis showed the doubtful accounts at June 30, 19–5, to be $77.12.

c. The supplies inventory taken at June 30, 19–5, amounted to $125.

d. The prepaid licences schedule showed that the value of unexpired licences at June 30, 19–5, amounted to $412.

e. The prepaid insurance schedule as at June 30, 19–5, showed a total of $215 for unexpired insurance.

f. Depreciation of fixed assets is at government

rates. (Remember that this work sheet is for a fiscal period of one half year.)

g. The accrued wages figure as at June 30, 19–5, amounted to $316.

---

9. From the following trial balance and additional information, prepare the work sheet of Select Trading Company for the year ended December 31, 19–6.

SELECT TRADING COMPANY
TRIAL BALANCE
DECEMBER 31, 19–6

| | | |
|---|---|---|
| Petty Cash | $ 25.00 | |
| Bank | 5 021.90 | |
| Accounts Receivable | 13 295.05 | |
| Allowance for Doubtful Debts | | $ 20.10 |
| Merchandise Inventory | 10 957.00 | |
| Supplies | 100.00 | |
| Prepaid Insurance | 180.00 | |
| Furniture and Equipment | 5 721.25 | |
| Accumulated Depreciation Furn. & Equip. | | 1 941.72 |
| Accounts Payable | | 11 517.20 |
| Sales Tax Payable | | 245.00 |
| O. Franklin, Capital | | 14 732.62 |
| O. Franklin, Drawings | 12 515.00 | |
| Sales | | 65 326.27 |
| Building Maintenance | 650.00 | |
| Delivery Expense | 1 057.15 | |
| Light, Heat, and Water | 1 315.19 | |
| Miscellaneous Expense | 170.00 | |
| Purchases | 30 704.16 | |
| Rent | 2 400.00 | |
| Telephone | 195.00 | |
| Wages | 9 476.21 | |
| | $93 782.91 | $93 782.91 |

## Additional Information

a. The accounts receivable aging analysis showed the doubtful debts at December 31, 19–6, to be $190.42.

b. Inventories taken at December 31, 19–6, were:
Merchandise     $9 567.34
Supplies             22.50

c. The prepaid insurance schedule showed that at December 31, 19–6, the value of the prepaid insurance was $136.40.

d. Depreciation of fixed assets is at government rates.

e. Purchase invoices received in 19–7 for goods and services pertaining to 19–6 were summarized as follows:
Merchandise     $756.30
Building Mntnce.     21.00
Miscellaneous Ex.     15.00

f. The accrued wages at December 31, 19–6, were calculated to be $812.

---

10. From the following trial balance and additional information, prepare the work sheet of Stirling Sales Company for the year ended June 30, 19–2.

STIRLING SALES COMPANY
TRIAL BALANCE
JUNE 30, 19–2

| | | |
|---|---:|---:|
| Petty Cash | $ 50.00 | |
| Bank | 1 292.64 | |
| Accounts Receivable | 33 412.94 | |
| Allowance for Doubtful Accounts | 5.05 | |
| Merchandise Inventory | 35 963.15 | |
| Supplies | 506.19 | |
| Prepaid Insurance | 396.00 | |
| Land | 5 000.00 | |
| Buildings (Frame) | 20 000.00 | |
| Accumulated Depreciation Buildings | | $ 6 878.00 |
| Furniture and Equipment | 4 740.26 | |
| Accumulated Depreciation Furn. & Equip. | | 2 313.04 |
| Bank Loan | | 25 000.00 |
| Accounts Payable | | 17 502.12 |
| Sales Tax Payable | | 607.50 |
| O. J. Little, Capital | | 30 333.01 |
| O. J. Little, Drawings | 14 904.15 | |
| Sales | | 156 810.51 |
| Sales Returns and Allowances | 1 926.50 | |
| Advertising | 4 465.17 | |
| Bank Charges | 1 474.10 | |
| Building Maintenance | 1 572.12 | |
| Delivery Expense | 3 416.90 | |
| Cash Short and Over | 26.70 | |
| Discounts Allowed | 2 674.15 | |
| Discounts Earned | | 742.15 |
| Freight-in | 1 946.20 | |
| Light, Heat, and Water | 1 375.46 | |
| Miscellaneous Expense | 74.12 | |
| Postage | 392.04 | |
| Purchases | 90 406.56 | |
| Purchases Returns and Allowances | | 2 472.19 |
| Telephone | 675.00 | |
| Wages | 15 963.12 | |
| | $242 658.52 | $242 658.52 |

## Additional Information

a. The accounts receivable aging analysis showed the doubtful debts at June 30, 19–2, to be $1 402.24.

b. Inventories at June 30, 19–2, were:
Merchandise    $33 592.00
Supplies          155.00

c. The prepaid insurance schedule showed that at June 30, 19–2, the value of prepaid insurance was $246.

d. Depreciation of fixed assets is at government rates.

e. Purchase invoices received in July 19–2 with respect to goods and services received on or before June 30, 19–2, were summarized as follows:
Supplies              $ 65.20
Merchandise          1 045.57
Building Maintenance     50.00
Delivery Expense        104.32
Miscellaneous Expense    24.05

f. The accrued wages at June 30, 19–2, were $316.40.

**11.** From the general ledger trial balance of Monarch Marine (after a fiscal period of six months) and the additional information necessary for the adjustments, prepare a work sheet.

MONARCH MARINE
TRIAL BALANCE
SEPTEMBER 30, 19–7

| | | |
|---|---:|---:|
| Petty Cash | $      50.00 | |
| Bank | 1 046.57 | |
| Accounts Receivable | 10 409.50 | |
| Allowance for Doubtful Accounts | | $      26.17 |
| Merchandise Inventory | 39 416.50 | |
| Supplies | 497.17 | |
| Prepaid Insurance | 395.33 | |
| Land | 24 000.00 | |
| Buildings (Brick) | 47 000.00 | |
| Accumulated Depreciation Buildings | | 7 998.37 |
| Equipment | 23 469.75 | |
| Accumulated Depreciation Equipment | | 11 693.24 |
| Delivery Truck | 4 200.00 | |
| Accumulated Depreciation Delivery Truck | | 2 759.40 |
| Accounts Payable | | 15 609.75 |
| Sales Tax Payable | | 625.00 |
| Mortgage Payable | | 3 609.00 |
| B. West, Capital | | 100 811.73 |
| B. West, Drawings | 17 200.00 | |
| Sales Revenue | | 88 764.20 |
| Bank Charges | 62.50 | |
| Building Repairs | 752.87 | |
| Delivery Expense | 1 459.61 | |
| Discounts Earned | | 315.12 |
| Freight-in | 1 796.14 | |
| Light, Heat, and Water | 1 146.19 | |
| Miscellaneous Expense | 194.17 | |
| Purchases | 42 906.70 | |
| Purchases Returns and Allowances | | 1 056.92 |
| Telephone | 215.90 | |
| Wages | 17 050.00 | |
| | $233 268.90 | $233 268.90 |

# Additional Information

a. Purchase invoices received subsequent to the year-end but pertaining to the fiscal period just ended were as follows:

| Supplier | Explanation | Amount |
|---|---|---|
| Jack's Hardware | Paint and materials for repairing buildings | $ 19.25 |
| King Oil Company | Gasoline and oil for delivery truck | 65.20 |
| Dominion Boats | Boat for resale | 565.00 |
| Best Marine Supply | Merchandise for resale | 175.00 |
| Dandy Cable | Merchandise for resale | 230.45 |

b. Depreciation is calculated at government rates (half-yearly fiscal period).
c. The accounts receivable aging analysis showed a total for doubtful accounts of $376.45.
d. Inventories taken at September 30, 19–7, were as follows:

| | |
|---|---|
| Merchandise | $41 759.40 |
| Supplies | 255.00 |

e. The following insurance policies were in force:

| Company | Policy Number | Date | Term | Premium |
|---|---|---|---|---|
| Circle | 34598 | March 31, 19–5 | 3 years | $72.00 |
| Guarantee | 234756 | June 30, 19–5 | 3 years | $40.00 |
| Prairie | 190645 | September 30, 19–6 | 3 years | $66.00 |
| Select | 23114 | September 30, 19–6 | 3 years | $270.00 |

f. Wages for the two-week period ended Friday, October 5, 19–7, were $1 214.04. The employees work a five-day week.

---

**Note: Exercise 12 is for students who have studied Chapter 13 on payroll.**

---

**12. From the following trial balance and additional information for the year ended December 31, 19–5, prepare the work sheet.**

GENERAL LIGHTING AND ELECTRIC

TRIAL BALANCE

DECEMBER 31, 19–5

| | | |
|---|---:|---:|
| Petty Cash | $      100.00 | |
| Bank | 1 469.25 | |
| Accounts Receivable | 119 007.40 | |
| Allowance for Doubtful Accounts | 24.50 | |
| Merchandise Inventory | 65 759.10 | |
| Supplies | 1 059.26 | |
| Prepaid Insurance | 470.50 | |
| Furniture and Equipment | 4 942.04 | |
| Accumulated Depreciation Furn. & Equip. | | 2 574.12 |
| Automotive Equipment | 6 574.00 | |
| Accumulated Depreciation Autom. Equip. | | 2 107.15 |
| Bank Loan | | 25 000.00 |
| Accounts Payable | | 41 964.75 |
| Sales Tax Payable | | 940.60 |
| Employees' Income Tax Payable | | 219.40 |
| R. Brooks, Capital | | 93 814.11 |
| R. Brooks, Drawings | 9 600.00 | |
| Sales Revenue | | 257 906.40 |
| Sales Returns and Allowances | 2 065.70 | |
| Advertising and Sales Promotion | 1 075.00 | |
| Bank Charges | 34.09 | |
| Bank Interest | 1 500.00 | |
| Canada Pension Plan Expense | 315.90 | |
| Car Expenses | 3 951.40 | |
| Cash Short and Over | 29.42 | |
| Discounts Earned | | 1 095.62 |
| Duty | 2 964.15 | |
| Freight-in | 1 047.24 | |
| Light, Heat, and Water | 312.95 | |
| Miscellaneous Expense | 125.94 | |
| Postage | 56.05 | |
| Purchases | 162 786.97 | |
| Purchases Returns and Allowances | | 3 746.15 |
| Rent | 12 000.00 | |
| Telephone | 941.14 | |
| Unemployment Insurance Expense | 400.15 | |
| Wages | 30 756.15 | |
| | $429 368.30 | $429 368.30 |

# Additional Information

a. The summary of purchase invoices received in 19–6 but which pertain to goods and services received in 19–5 is shown below.

| | |
|---|---:|
| Supplies | $ 49.50 |
| Furniture and Equipment | 250.00 |
| Car Expenses | 56.55 |
| Freight-in | 30.00 |
| Miscellaneous Expense | 20.10 |
| Purchases | 1 072.16 |
| | $1 478.31 |

b. Four accounts were considered to be doubtful. These four accounts are:

| Customer | Account Balance |
|---|---:|
| Morgan & Morgan | $342.19 |
| Perfect Company | 255.67 |
| J. A. Swift | 12.50 |
| W. A. Wallace | 150.00 |

c. Inventories at December 31, 19–5, were:

| | |
|---|---:|
| Merchandise | $62 056.66 |
| Supplies | 742.00 |

d. Details of insurance policies are:

| Company | Policy Number | Date | Term | Premium |
|---|---:|---|---|---:|
| Northern | 90214 | Jan. 1, 19–5 | 3 years | $ 39.00 |
| Alliance | 602294 | Mar. 31, 19–5 | 1 year | 168.00 |
| Amalgamated | 310678 | Sept. 30, 19–4 | 3 years | 120.00 |
| Anchor | 22230 | June 1, 19–4 | 3 years | 90.00 |
| Provincial | 123140 | Dec. 1, 19–3 | 3 years | 72.00 |

e. Depreciation is calculated at government rates.

f. Wages for the two weeks ended Friday, January 8, amounted to $1 105.12. The employees work a five-day week and are paid for New Year's Day, a holiday.

# Cases

## Case 1

Kilpatrick Supplies Ltd. was established January 1, 19—, by P. Kilpatrick, and since that time has made a reasonable profit each year. It has been pointed out to Mr. Kilpatrick that the business has never been able to collect all accounts owing by its customers. It shows no allowance for doubtful accounts on its balance sheet, and no bad debt expense on its income statement to reflect these uncollectible amounts. The value of the accounts receivable is at present $50 000 and 8 per cent is estimated to be uncollectible.

1. How will the practice of not recording uncollectible accounts affect (a) the income statement, and (b) the balance sheet?
2. The uncollectibles for Kilpatrick Supplies Ltd. have been 8 per cent over the past five years. This figure is regarded as too high for the industry. What changes would you suggest to bring bad debts down to a reasonable figure?

## Case 2

J. D. Fuller Company, which operates on a calendar year basis, received a $2 000 order on December 31. The merchandise, in its warehouse to fill the order, had been purchased in November for $1 300; however, it had not yet been paid for. Since the order was routine and the goods would be shipped as soon as the order was processed, the accountant treated the $2 000 as a sale on December 31 and excluded the ordered goods from the December 31 inventory. Would you approve of the procedure? Explain.

## Case 3

Through an error in counting the merchandise at the December 31 year-end, the Sutton Music Company overstated the amount of goods on hand by $10 000. Assuming the error was not discovered, what is the effect upon:

1. The net income for the year?
2. The owner's equity at December 31?

Assuming that inventory is counted and valued correctly at the subsequent fiscal year-end, what is the effect upon:

1. The net income for the subsequent year?
2. The owner's equity at December 31 of the subsequent year?

## Case 4

Mr. S. White begins a retail jewellery business on January 1. He has no stock on hand to begin with. During January he purchases $10 000 worth of jewellery and his sales amount to $3 500. On January 31, he has $7 785 worth of jewellery on hand. His expenses for January amount to $500.

1. How much has he lost or gained from the month's business? (Show your calculations.)
2. During the month of January he bought showcases and an office desk. Are these purchases operating expenses or assets? State the reason for your answer.

## Case 5

When you prepare the financial statements of the Hunter Hardware Store for the year ended June 30, 19–4, specify the instructions you would give to the accounting clerk in each of the following instances (use journal entries to illustrate your instructions):

1. On May 1, 19–4, an invoice for $400 from Sutton Office Supply for a calculator was entered in the purchases journal, but by mistake it was included in the column for Purchases.
2. On January 31, 19–4, Hunter purchased the store premises from his landlord for $62 000, of which $10 000 was for the land and $52 000 was for the building. On that date, Hunter gave the former landlord a cheque for $20 000 drawn on his personal bank account, and arranged with him to assume a mortgage for the balance. The mortgage deed states that the principal amount is to be repaid in full by Hunter Hardware Store at the end of 10 years. The interest at 9 per cent per annum is to be paid by the business on January 31 each year, commencing January 1, 19–5. The building has an estimated useful life of 20 years. (No entries have been made in the books concerning any of the above.)

## Case 6

Suppose you are the chief accountant for a small trading establishment. You wish to instruct a junior accountant in the proper procedure to follow in preparing an eight-column work sheet. Set up in point form the steps that should be followed, and also make a list of the possible trouble spots where errors are likely to occur.

## Case 7

At the end of the fiscal year, the accountant for Canadian Auto Supply Company closed the accounts and prepared the balance sheet and the income statement which showed a net income of $22 372.65. He then submitted the two statements to each of the officers of the company.

When the treasurer received the statements, he compared them with the statements of the preceding year and was surprised to find that the net income had decreased by approximately $4 000. He suspected that something was wrong. Upon making an independent check of the books, he found the following items: during the first month of the year, $1 800 was paid out for insurance, to cover a period of three years, and this entire premium had been charged to Insurance Expense for the year. He also found that $2 500 was charged to Office Supplies for the year, but that $2 200 of this was still on hand at the end of the year.

1. What errors would the treasurer point out to the accountant?
2. What should have been the correct net income for the year, presuming no other errors have been found?

## Case 8

On June 24, 19—, the collection agency in whose hands you have placed G. Plant's account for collection reports that he has collected $300 of the $500 owed you. He states the balance is uncollectible. The collection fee is 10 per cent of the amount collected.

1. Make the entry to close Plant's account and record the payment of the collection fee.
2. On November 15 of the following year, Plant pays the amount you recorded as uncollectible. Make the necessary entry or entries.

## Case 9

Mr. Davidson is in your store looking at a $625 color television set which he is interested in purchasing. Since he wants to buy on credit, you must consider certain information concerning his financial capacity.

Mr. Davidson is married and has two children. His take-home pay is $600 per month. He makes a mortgage payment of $210 per month on his house, and he recently purchased an automobile for which he is paying $110 per month.

In your opinion does Mr. Davidson have the capacity to pay for a television set at $80 per month? As credit manager will you extend credit to him?

## Case 10

Edmonds Discount Store hired four additional sales clerks on Monday, June 25, to help during its two-week Anniversary Sale. The clerks were paid a total of $1 200 on Saturday, July 7. The store's fiscal year ended on June 30, and the accountant failed to make an adjustment for accrued wages.
1. Since no entry was made until July 7, state in detail the effects on the income statement and the balance sheet for the year just ended.
2. What adjusting entry should the accountant have made?

## Case 11

Bad debts occur because accounts receivable are not always collected in full. Smith Stationery handles uncollectible receivables in the following manner: when a customer's account is found to be uncollectible, it is removed from the ledger by an entry debiting Bad Debt Expense and crediting Accounts Receivable. Explain why it would be preferable for a business to set up an allowance for doubtful accounts.

## Case 12

The M. Morrison Company, which has accounts receivable of $150 000, and an allowance for doubtful accounts of $5 200, decides to write off as worthless a past-due account receivable for $900 from D. Bader. What effect will the write-off have upon total current assets? Upon net income for the period? Explain.

## Case 13

The accountant for Burns Co. follows the practice of charging supplies to a prepaid expense account when purchased. At the end of the year an inventory of supplies is taken and the adjustment made to the prepaid expense account. This adjustment has already been made for the accounting period ended December 31. On checking over the accountant's work you discover that during the year a $50 purchase of advertising supplies was incorrectly charged to "Office Supplies on Hand". What adjusting entry would you make to correct this error?

# 15 Completing the Accounting Cycle

In order to prepare financial statements, one must be familiar with their appearance and organization. There is no single correct form of financial statements, but rather there exist certain acceptable variations, each of which is suited to a particular business or situation.

On pages 346 and 347 are shown the balance sheet and the income statement of Fraser and Associates. The statements shown are typical statements for a well-established and profitable trading business. By examining these statements you will see that they are more than just a list of debit and credit items as would appear on a trial balance. On the financial statements, the items are grouped and arranged to provide meaningful information in easily readable form. Financial statements of this type are known as classified financial statements.

## The Classified Balance Sheet

The most common classifications on the balance sheet are:

## Current Assets

Assets that are already in the form of cash or which will be converted into cash in the ordinary course of business within a period of one year. For example, accounts receivable are ordinarily collected within a period of one year and are therefore classified as current assets. Current assets are generally listed in the order of their 'liquidity'; that is, in the order of their ability to be converted into cash.

## Prepaid Expenses

Expenses paid for in advance. Such expenses are usually used up or expire within a period of one or two years.

## Fixed Assets

Assets such as buildings, machinery and equipment which are intended to be used in the operations of the business for a number of years.

## Current Liabilities

Liabilities of the business which are due within a period of one year. Current liabilities are generally listed in the order in which they must be paid.

## Long-Term Liabilities

Liabilities of the business which are not due for payment within a period of one year. Certain long-term liabilities, mortgages for example, may not be due for several years.

## Owner's Equity

The owner's share of the business at book value. In other words, the proportion of assets that belong to the owner after providing for payment of all liabilities.

FRASER AND ASSOCIATES
BALANCE SHEET
DECEMBER 31, 19–9

## ASSETS

*Current Assets*

| | | | |
|---|---|---|---|
| Petty Cash | | $      100.00 | |
| Bank | | 1 742.12 | |
| Accounts Receivable | $13 419.05 | | |
| Less Allowance for Doubtful Accounts | 374.19 | 13 044.86 | |
| Merchandise Inventory – at cost | | 15 907.00 | |
| Government Bonds – 6½ % | | 10 000.00 | $  40 793.98 |

*Prepaid Expenses*

| | | | |
|---|---|---|---|
| Insurance | | $      416.25 | |
| Supplies | | 1 530.00 | 1 946.25 |

*Fixed Assets*

| | | | |
|---|---|---|---|
| Land | | $20 000.00 | |
| Buildings – at cost | $75 742.57 | | |
| Less Accumulated Depreciation | 12 614.30 | 63 128.27 | |
| Equipment – at cost | $37 407.56 | | |
| Less Accumulated Depreciation | 18 316.41 | 19 091.15 | |
| Automobiles – at cost | $10 407.35 | | |
| Less Accumulated Depreciation | 5 307.75 | 5 099.60 | 107 319.02 |
| | | | $150 059.25 |

## LIABILITIES

*Current Liabilities*

| | | |
|---|---|---|
| Accounts Payable and Accrued Charges | $12 409.37 | |
| Bank Loan | 5 000.00 | |
| Sales Tax Payable | 440.72 | |
| Canada Pension Plan Payable | 216.40 | |
| Employees' Income Tax Payable | 517.42 | $  18 583.91 |

*Long-Term Liability*

| | |
|---|---|
| Mortgage on Property – 6% | 42 705.16 |

## PROPRIETORSHIP

*Owner's Equity*

| | | | |
|---|---|---|---|
| D. Fraser, Capital, January 1 | | $72 017.21 | |
| Add:  Net Income for year | $31 742.16 | | |
| Less Drawings | 14 989.19 | 16 752.97 | |
| D. Fraser, Capital, December 31 | | | 88 770.18 |
| | | | $150 059.25 |

## FRASER AND ASSOCIATES
## INCOME STATEMENT
### YEAR ENDED DECEMBER 31, 19–9

*Revenue*

| | | | |
|---|---|---|---|
| Sales | | $170 984.76 | |
| Less: Sales Returns and Allowances | $ 3 026.04 | | |
| Discount off Sales | 1 027.19 | 4 053.23 | |
| Net Sales | | | $166 931.53 |

*Cost of Merchandise Sold*

| | | | |
|---|---|---|---|
| Merchandise Inventory, January 1 | | $ 18 414.90 | |
| Purchases | $87 314.42 | | |
| Less: Purchase Returns & Allow's $2 016.40 | | | |
| Discount off Purchases 1 307.51 | 3 323.91 | 83 990.51 | |
| Freight-in | | 2 964.72 | |
| Duty | | 1 072.12 | |
| Total Cost of Goods Available for Sale | | $106 442.25 | |
| Deduct Merchandise Inventory, December 31 | | 15 907.00 | |
| Cost of Merchandise Sold | | | 90 535.25 |
| Gross Trading Income | | | $ 76 396.28 |

*Selling Expenses*

| | | | |
|---|---|---|---|
| Advertising and Sales Promotion | $ 2 504.00 | | |
| Delivery Expense | 1 594.23 | | |
| Salesmen's Commissions | 10 234.60 | | |
| Salesmen's Car Expenses | 5 654.30 | | |
| Depreciation of Automobiles | 2 185.56 | $ 22 172.69 | |

*Administrative Expenses*

| | | | |
|---|---|---|---|
| Bad Debts Expense | $ 304.74 | | |
| Bank Charges and Interest | 502.10 | | |
| Depreciation of Building | 7 014.25 | | |
| Depreciation of Equipment | 4 772.79 | | |
| Legal Expense | 215.00 | | |
| Audit Fee | 500.00 | | |
| General Expense | 95.00 | | |
| Insurance Expense | 128.00 | | |
| Supplies Expense | 746.12 | | |
| Office Expense | 216.40 | | |
| Postage Expense | 155.03 | | |
| Rent Expense | 84.00 | | |
| Telephone Expense | 319.54 | | |
| Canada Pension Plan Expense | 410.34 | | |
| Unemployment Insurance Expense | 380.42 | | |
| Office Salaries | 11 442.83 | 27 286.56 | 49 459.25 |
| Operating Income | | | $ 26 937.03 |

*Other Income*

| | | | |
|---|---|---|---|
| Interest on Investments | | | 4 805.13 |
| Net Income | | | $ 31 742.16 |

## Classified Income Statement

The most common classifications on the income statement are:

## Revenue

The gross earnings derived from the regular operations of the business.

## Cost of Merchandise Sold

All of the elements of cost directly connected with the acquisition of the goods which the business deals in. Included is the actual cost of the merchandise as well as any costs involved in the process of transporting the goods from their place of origin to the premises of the business.

## Selling Expenses

All expenses of the business that are directly related to the selling and delivery of the goods.

## Administrative Expenses

All expenses of a general nature that are related to the operation of the business. Expenses in this category pertain to such things as the management of the business, the maintenance of the buildings and equipment, and the running of the office.

## Other Income

Earnings that are not derived from the regular operations of the business.

## Other Expenses

Expenses that are not related to the regular operations of the business.

## Preparing the Financial Statements

Once you are familiar with the form of the financial statements, it is a relatively simple matter to prepare financial statements from the information that appears on the work sheet. It is most important that you know the source of the information for the financial statements. This source of information is the work sheet.

To prepare a balance sheet, all of the information is derived from the Balance Sheet columns of the work sheet. It is unnecessary to look elsewhere.

Similarly, to prepare an income statement, all of the information is derived from the Income Statement columns of the work sheet. It is unnecessary to look elsewhere.

So that you may see the relationship between the information on the work sheet and the information on the financial statements, the statements of Cassidy Cartage and of Midway Trading Company are shown on the following pages. The work sheets for these two businesses were completed in Chapter 14 on pages 322 and 331 respectively. You should trace the figures from the work sheets to the financial statements to help you become familiar with financial statement preparation.

The statements of Cassidy Cartage and Midway Trading Company follow the form and style shown for Fraser and Associates on pages 346 and 347. However, there are some slight differences requiring an explanation: (1) On the balance sheets for Cassidy Cartage and Midway Trading Company, no long-term liabilities appear. The reason for this is that neither of these two businesses has any long-term liabilities; (2) The income statement of Cassidy Cartage is a less classified and much simpler statement. The chief reason for this is that Cassidy Cartage is a service business and consequently has no Cost of Goods Sold section. Also no attempt has been made to separate selling expenses; (3) The income statement of Midway Trading Company is less classified in that no attempt has been made to separate the Selling Expenses. Also, Discounts Earned and Discounts Allowed are treated as Other Income and Expenses rather than as elements of Revenue and of Operating Expenses.

CASSIDY CARTAGE
INCOME STATEMENT
YEAR ENDED JUNE 30, 19–4

| | | |
|---|---:|---:|
| *Revenue* | | |
| Sales | | $28 757.49 |
| *Operating Expenses* | | |
| Bad Debts Expense | $ 234.05 | |
| Supplies Expense | 166.48 | |
| Licences Expense | 170.00 | |
| Insurance Expense | 127.50 | |
| Depreciation of Buildings | 527.46 | |
| Depreciation of Furniture and Equipment | 270.52 | |
| Depreciation of Automotive Equipment | 2 293.20 | |
| Bank Charges | 114.92 | |
| Building Maintenance | 599.37 | |
| Light, Heat, and Water | 495.00 | |
| Miscellaneous Expense | 135.70 | |
| Telephone Expense | 167.00 | |
| Truck Expense | 5 878.16 | |
| Wages | 9 576.79 | 20 756.15 |
| Operating Income | | $ 8 001.34 |
| *Other Income* | | |
| Discounts Earned | | 56.75 |
| Net Income | | $ 8 058.09 |

CASSIDY CARTAGE
BALANCE SHEET
JUNE 30, 19–4

## ASSETS

*Current Assets*
| | | | |
|---|---|---|---|
| Petty Cash | | $ 50.00 | |
| Bank | | 725.41 | |
| Accounts Receivable | $ 4 027.56 | | |
| Less Allowance for Doubtful Accounts | 260.45 | 3 767.11 | $ 4 542.52 |

*Prepaid Expenses*
| | | |
|---|---|---|
| Supplies | $ 395.25 | |
| Insurance | 88.50 | |
| Licences | 85.00 | 568.75 |

*Fixed Assets*
| | | | |
|---|---|---|---|
| Land – at cost | | $ 8 000.00 | |
| Buildings –at cost | $ 7 280.00 | | |
| Less Accumulated Depreciation | 2 532.86 | 4 747.14 | |
| Furniture and Equipment – at cost | $ 2 950.00 | | |
| Less Accumulated Depreciation | 1 867.92 | 1 082.08 | |
| Automotive Equipment – at cost | $15 600.00 | | |
| Less Accumulated Depreciation | 10 249.20 | 5 350.80 | 19 180.02 |
| | | | $24 291.29 |

## LIABILITIES AND OWNER'S EQUITY

*Current Liabilities*
| | | |
|---|---|---|
| Accounts Payable | $ 3 449.97 | |
| Sales Tax Payable | 238.73 | |
| Accrued Wages | 157.29 | $ 3 845.99 |

*P. Marshall, Equity*
| | | | |
|---|---|---|---|
| Balance July 1, 19–3 | | $18 387.21 | |
| Add: Net Income | $ 8 058.09 | | |
| Less Drawings | 6 000.00 | 2 058.09 | |
| Balance June 30, 19–4 | | | 20 445.30 |
| | | | $24 291.29 |

MIDWAY TRADING COMPANY
BALANCE SHEET
DECEMBER 31, 19–4

## ASSETS

*Current Assets*

| | | | |
|---|---|---|---|
| Petty Cash | | $ 100.00 | |
| Bank | | 1 702.12 | |
| Accounts Receivable | $ 6 751.12 | | |
| Less Allowance for Doubtful Accounts | 143.20 | 6 607.92 | |
| Merchandise Inventory – at cost | | 13 562.00 | $21 972.04 |

*Prepaid Expenses*

| | | | |
|---|---|---|---|
| Supplies | | $ 192.00 | |
| Insurance | | 112.00 | 304.00 |

*Fixed Assets*

| | | | |
|---|---|---|---|
| Land – at cost | | $15 000.00 | |
| Buildings – at cost | $12 000.00 | | |
| Less Accumulated Depreciation | 2 225.93 | 9 774.07 | |
| Furniture and Equipment – at cost | $ 3 437.20 | | |
| Less Accumulated Depreciation | 1 677.36 | 1 759.84 | |
| Automobiles – at cost | $ 7 800.00 | | |
| Less Accumulated Depreciation | 5 124.60 | 2 675.40 | 29 209.31 |
| | | | $51 485.35 |

## LIABILITIES AND OWNER'S EQUITY

*Current Liabilities*

| | | | |
|---|---|---|---|
| Accounts Payable | | $10 710.56 | |
| Bank Loan | | 9 750.00 | |
| Sales Tax Payable | | 251.10 | |
| Accrued Wages Payable | | 146.54 | $20 858.20 |

*Owner's Equity*

| | | | |
|---|---|---|---|
| M. Philip, Capital, January 1 | | $26 214.87 | |
| Add: Net Income | $13 163.28 | | |
| Less Drawings | 8 751.00 | 4 412.28 | |
| M. Philip, Capital, December 31 | | | 30 627.15 |
| | | | $51 485.35 |

MIDWAY TRADING COMPANY
INCOME STATEMENT
YEAR ENDED DECEMBER 31, 19–4

**Revenue**

| | | |
|---|---|---|
| Sales | $59 168.10 | |
| Less Sales Returns and Allowances | 1 204.30 | $57 963.80 |

**Cost of Goods Sold**

| | | | |
|---|---|---|---|
| Merchandise Inventory, January 1 | | $12 074.00 | |
| Purchases | $31 664.14 | | |
| Less Purchases Returns and Allowances | 1 520.00 | 30 144.14 | |
| Freight-in | | 991.24 | |
| Duty | | 315.70 | |
| | | $43 525.08 | |
| Deduct: Merchandise Inventory, December 31 | | 13 562.00 | 29 963.08 |
| Gross Trading Income | | | $28 000.72 |

**Operating Expenses**

| | | |
|---|---|---|
| Bad Debts Expense | $ 140.70 | |
| Supplies Expense | 178.00 | |
| Insurance Expense | 82.00 | |
| Depreciation of Buildings | 514.43 | |
| Depreciation of Furniture and Equipment | 439.96 | |
| Depreciation of Automobiles | 1 146.60 | |
| Bank Charges | 1 140.26 | |
| Building Maintenance | 375.00 | |
| Car Expenses | 1 994.00 | |
| Light, Heat, and Water | 417.25 | |
| Miscellaneous Expense | 128.95 | |
| Telephone Expense | 484.17 | |
| Wages | 7 563.10 | 14 604.42 |
| Operating Income | | $13 396.30 |

**Other Income and Expenses**

| | | |
|---|---|---|
| Discounts Allowed | $ 749.21 | |
| Less Discounts Earned | 516.19 | 233.02 |
| Net Income | | $13 163.28 |

## Analysing the Financial Statements

Primarily, financial statements are prepared for the use of managers and owners, to inform them accurately of the financial condition of the business and of the results of operation for the fiscal period. Good businessmen usually have a fair understanding of accounting matters and keep reasonably well informed of the financial affairs of the business. For these men, the end of the accounting period is a time of summing up, a time of taking stock, and a time of documenting results.

A few businessmen are ignorant in respect to accounting matters and operate their businesses relatively in the dark. For these men, it is not until after the accounting period is over and the financial statements are prepared by outside accountants that they are made aware of the condition of their businesses. Men in this category, who are not in close touch with the financial affairs of their businesses, run a greater risk of being disappointed by poor results and lack of progress.

All wise businessmen scrutinize and analyse the financial statements thoroughly. In particular, they are on the lookout for unfavorable trends, or areas of weakness that require correction. In businesses that are operating successfully, these are usually few. But in businesses that have a poor profit picture, or even a loss, the areas of weakness are usually painfully apparent. Corrective measures are then imperative.

There are numerous ways in which businessmen use financial statements to obtain meaningful information. A few of these are discussed below.

1. *Current Ratio*

   This is the ratio formed by comparing the total of the current assets to the total of the current liabilities. This ratio shows the ability of a business to pay its debts. It is important because a business that fails to pay its debts when due may be put into bankruptcy by a creditor.

   A current ratio of 2:1 is considered to reflect a safe financial condition; a current ratio of 1:1 is considered to reflect an unsafe financial condition.

   For example, consider the following two cases:

   a. Current ratio of Fraser and Associates as derived from the balance sheet on page 346.

   Total Current Assets : Total Current Liabilities
   i.e.,       $40 793.98 : $18 583.91
   Or, by dividing both numbers by $18 583.91 –
                         2.2 : 1
   This ratio of 2.2:1 is considered to reflect a safe financial condition.

   b. Current ratio of Midway Trading Company as derived from the balance sheet on page 351.

   Total Current Assets : Total Current Liabilities
   i.e.,       $21 972.04 : $20 858.20
   Or, by dividing both numbers by $20 858.20 –
                         1.1 : 1
   This ratio of 1.1:1 is considered to reflect an unsafe financial condition.

2. *Gross Income Test*

   This test yields a percentage formed by comparing the gross trading income figure with the net sales figure. For example, the gross income percentage of Midway Trading Company is calculated from the income statement on page 352 as shown below.

   $$\frac{\text{Gross Trading Income}}{\text{Net Sales}} \times 100$$

   $$= \frac{\$28\,000.72}{\$57\,963.80} \times 100 = 48\%$$

This ratio is an important one because it furnishes the owner with a quick assessment of the performance of the business. He should have some idea of what figure is sufficient to cover the remaining expenses and leave a satisfactory net income. A comparison of the percentage figure with statements of prior years or in some cases with statements of other companies in the same line of business is useful. If it is found that the gross income percentage is not satisfactory, it indicates the need either to cut costs, to improve sales, or to increase selling prices.

3. *Comparing Operating Expenses*
   A percentage comparison of expenses from year to year is a source of valuable information. Such a comparison indicates if any expenses are getting out of line, if there are any unfavorable trends, and where economies can be made in order to improve the profit picture.

In addition to their usefulness to management, financial statements must be made available for other reasons, primarily to satisfy legal requirements. For example, every businessman or incorporated company must submit detailed financial information along with the required annual income tax return. Also, every incorporated company is required to send a copy of its financial statements to each shareholder. Too, chartered banks require annual financial statements from each business to which a bank loan has been made.

# Adjusting and Closing the Books of a Proprietorship

As you are aware, for the sake of convenience during the accounting period, certain general ledger accounts are allowed to become temporarily out of date. As a result, the information contained in the general ledger cannot be used directly to prepare financial statements. It is from the work sheet that the information for the preparation of the financial statements is obtained.

Once the financial statements have been prepared, the accountant has additional work to do. He must bring the general ledger up to date and prepare the accounts for the next accounting period. This process, known as 'adjusting and closing the books', is usually done before any transactions of the next accounting period are posted.

## Objectives of Adjusting and Closing the Books

The process of adjusting and closing the books has three objectives:

1. To adjust those accounts that are not up to date.
2. To close out all Revenue, Expense, and Drawings accounts. This means to make the accounts have a nil balance. All of the accounts in the Equity section of the general ledger except the Capital account are affected. They must be closed out in order to make them ready for the next accounting period. Since these accounts are the ones used to accumulate the revenues, expenses and drawings during successive accounting periods, it is necessary that they begin each accounting period with a nil balance.
3. To bring the equity together again in one account – the Capital account. During the accounting period the owner's total equity is not contained in a single account but rather in several accounts in the Equity section of the ledger. At the end of each accounting period the value of the Equity section of the ledger is pulled together into one account – the owner's Capital account. Therefore, the balance in the Capital account usually represents the owner's correct equity only at the very end of an accounting period, or, which is the same thing, at the very beginning of the subsequent accounting period. Any changes in equity during the period are recorded in the Revenues, Expenses, and Drawings accounts.

## Adjusting and Closing Entries

To adjust and close the books of a business it is necessary to journalize and post certain accounting entries known as the 'adjusting and closing entries'. All of the information for these entries is obtained from the work sheet.

A simplified technique for obtaining the adjusting and closing entries is described below. The technique shown is appropriate for any business or any system. Too, it is appropriate whether the adjustments on the work sheet are performed by the formal method, the shortcut method, or by any combination of the two.

To adjust and close the books, only three steps are necessary:

Step 1. The first step is to journalize all and only those adjusting entries that appear in the Adjustments columns of the work sheet. This step is illustrated below and on the next page for both Cassidy Cartage (work sheet page 322) and Midway Trading Company (work sheet page 331).

### General Journal

| Date | Particulars | P.R. | Debit | Credit |
|---|---|---|---|---|
| June 30 | Supplies | | 45 21 | |
| | Building Maintenance | | 125 — | |
| | Light, Heat & Water | | 22 81 | |
| | Miscellaneous Expense | | 20 — | |
| | Telephone Expense | | 15 70 | |
| | Truck Expense | | 174 — | |
| |     Accounts Payable | | | 402 72 |
| | Adjusting for Accounts Payable | | | |
| 30 | Supplies Expense | | 166 48 | |
| |     Supplies | | | 166 48 |
| | Adjusting for Supplies Expense | | | |
| 30 | Insurance Expense | | 127 50 | |
| |     Prepaid Insurance | | | 127 50 |
| | Adjusting for Insurance Expense | | | |
| 30 | Licences Expense | | 170 — | |
| |     Prepaid Licences | | | 170 — |
| | Adjusting for Licences Expense | | | |
| 30 | Bad Debts Expense | | 234 05 | |
| |     Allowance for Doubtful Accounts | | | 234 05 |
| | Adjusting for Bad Debts Expense | | | |
| 30 | Depreciation of Buildings | | 527 46 | |
| |     Accumulated Depreciation of Bldgs | | | 527 46 |
| | Adjusting for Depreciation of Buildings | | | |
| 30 | Depreciation of Furniture & Equipment | | 270 52 | |
| |     Accum. Deprec. Furn. & Equ | | | 270 52 |
| | Adjusting for Deprec. of Furn. & Equ. | | | |
| 30 | Depreciation of Automotive Equipment | | 2 293 20 | |
| |     Accum. Depreciation Auto Equip. | | | 2 293 20 |
| | Adjusting for Deprec. of Auto. Equip. | | | |
| 30 | Wages | | 157 29 | |
| |     Accrued Wages Payable | | | 157 29 |
| | Adjusting for Accrued Wages | | | |

*Step 1 for Cassidy Cartage (which uses the formal method).*

## General Journal

| Date | Particulars | P.R. | Debit | Credit |
|------|-------------|------|-------|--------|
| Dec 31 | Car Expenses | | 147 50 | |
| | Freight - In | | 42 10 | |
| | Miscellaneous Expense | | 12 51 | |
| | Purchases | | 1 047 24 | |
| |     Accounts Payable | | | 1 249 35 |
| | Adjusting for Accounts Payable | | | |

*Step 1 for Midway Trading Company (which uses the shortcut method).*

Step 2. The second of the adjusting and closing entries is obtained from the Income Statement section of the work sheet and is one that adjusts some accounts and closes out others. This particular entry is almost the complete reverse of the two Income Statement columns of the work sheet.

In detail, this second of the adjusting and closing entries is formulated as follows:

a. Debit each of the individual items appearing in the Credit column of the Income Statement section of the work sheet to the account named at the left.

b. Credit each of the individual items appearing in the Debit column of the Income Statement section of the work sheet to the account named at the left.

c. Credit the net income figure (or debit the net loss figure) to the owner's Capital account.

When forming this entry, be sure to include all figures appearing in the two Income Statement columns of the work sheet, except for the subtotals and the totals. Also, be sure not to include any additional items. If the figures are picked up correctly from the work sheet, the accounting entry will balance.

Step 2 is illustrated below for Cassidy Cartage and at the top of the next page for Midway Trading Company.

| | | | | | | | | | | | | | | |
|---|---|---|---|---|---|---|---|---|---|---|---|---|---|---|
| June 30 | Sales | | | | | | 28 757 49 | | | | | | |
| | Discounts Earned | | | | | | 56 75 | | | | | | |
| |    Bank Charges | | | | | | | | | 114 92 | | | |
| |    Building Maintenance | | | | | | | | | 599 37 | | | |
| |    Light, Heat, and Water | | | | | | | | | 495 — | | | |
| |    Miscellaneous Expense | | | | | | | | | 135 70 | | | |
| |    Telephone Expense | | | | | | | | | 167 — | | | |
| |    Truck Expense | | | | | | | | | 5 873 16 | | | |
| |    Wages | | | | | | | | | 9 576 79 | | | |
| |    Supplies Expense | | | | | | | | | 166 48 | | | |
| |    Insurance Expense | | | | | | | | | 127 50 | | | |
| |    Licences Expense | | | | | | | | | 170 — | | | |
| |    Bad Debts Expense | | | | | | | | | 234 05 | | | |
| |    Depreciation of Buildings | | | | | | | | | 527 46 | | | |
| |    Depreciation of Furn & equip. | | | | | | | | | 270 52 | | | |
| |    Depreciation Automotive equip. | | | | | | | | | 2 293 20 | | | |
| |    P. Marshall, Capital | | | | | | | | | 8 058 09 | | | |
| | To close out the income & expense | | | | | | | | | | | | |
| | accounts to Capital account | | | | | | | | | | | | |

*Step 2 for Cassidy Cartage (which uses the formal method).*

| Dec | 31 | Merchandise Inventory | | 13 | 562 | — | | | |
|---|---|---|---|---|---|---|---|---|---|
| | | Sales | | 59 | 168 | 10 | | | |
| | | Discounts Earned | | | 516 | 19 | | | |
| | | Purchases Returns & Allowances | | 1 | 520 | — | | | |
| | | Allowance for Doubtful Accounts | | | | | | 140 | 70 |
| | | Merchandise Inventory | | | | | 12 | 074 | — |
| | | Supplies | | | | | | 178 | — |
| | | Prepaid Insurance | | | | | | 82 | — |
| | | Accum. Deprec. Buildings | | | | | | 514 | 43 |
| | | Accum. Deprec. Furn. & Equip. | | | | | | 439 | 96 |
| | | Accum. Deprec. Automobiles | | | | | 1 | 146 | 60 |
| | | Sales Returns & Allowances | | | | | 1 | 204 | 30 |
| | | Bank Charges | | | | | 1 | 140 | 26 |
| | | Building Maintenance | | | | | | 375 | — |
| | | Car Expenses | | | | | 1 | 994 | — |
| | | Discounts Allowed | | | | | | 749 | 21 |
| | | Duty | | | | | | 315 | 70 |
| | | Freight In | | | | | | 991 | 24 |
| | | Light, Heat, and Water | | | | | | 417 | 25 |
| | | Miscellaneous Expense | | | | | | 128 | 95 |
| | | Purchases | | | | | 31 | 664 | 14 |
| | | Telephone Expense | | | | | | 484 | 17 |
| | | Wages | | | | | 7 | 563 | 10 |
| | | M. Philip, Capital | | | | | 13 | 163 | 28 |
| | | To record adjustments & to close out | | | | | | | |
| | | the income & expense accounts to Capital | | | | | | | |
| | | account. | | | | | | | |

*Step 2 for Midway Trading Company (which uses the shortcut method).*

**Step 3.** The purpose of the third entry is merely to close out the owner's Drawings account to the owner's Capital account. Capital account is debited and Drawings account is credited with the balance of the Drawings account which is picked up from the work sheet – Balance Sheet Debit column: Drawings line.

The third and last of the adjusting and closing entries is shown below for both Cassidy Cartage and Midway Trading Company.

| June | 30 | P. Marshall, Capital | | 6 | 000 | — | | | |
|---|---|---|---|---|---|---|---|---|---|
| | | P. Marshall, Drawings | | | | | 6 | 000 | — |
| | | To close out Drawings to Capital | | | | | | | |

*Step 3 for Cassidy Cartage (which uses the formal method).*

| Dec | 31 | M. Philip, Capital | | 8 | 751 | — | | | |
|---|---|---|---|---|---|---|---|---|---|
| | | M. Philip, Drawings | | | | | 8 | 751 | — |
| | | To close out Drawings to Capital | | | | | | | |

*Step 3 for Midway Trading Company (which uses the shortcut method).*

## Posting the Adjusting and Closing Entries

After the adjusting and closing entries are journalized in the general journal, they are posted to the general ledger.

*Ledger of Cassidy Cartage (final position).*

The general ledgers of Cassidy Cartage and Midway Trading Company, immediately after the adjusting and closing entries have been posted, are as shown on these facing pages.

**Petty Cash #1**

| Date | | | Balance |
|---|---|---|---|
| Dec 31 | | | DR 100.00 |

**Bank #2**

| Date | | | Balance |
|---|---|---|---|
| Dec 31 | | | DR 1 702.12 |

**Accounts Receivable #3**

| Date | | | Balance |
|---|---|---|---|
| Dec 31 | | | DR 6 751.12 |

**Allow. Doubtful Accounts #4**

| Date | | | Balance |
|---|---|---|---|
| Dec 31 | | | CR 2.50 |
| 31 | | 140.70 | CR 143.20 |

**Merchandise Inventory #5**

| Date | | | Balance |
|---|---|---|---|
| Dec 31 | | | DR 12 074.00 |
| 31 | 13 562.00 | | |
| 31 | | 12 074.00 | DR. 13 562.00 |

**Supplies #6**

| Date | | | Balance |
|---|---|---|---|
| Dec 31 | | | DR 370.00 |
| 31 | | 178.00 | DR 192.00 |

**Prepaid Insurance #7**

| Date | | | Balance |
|---|---|---|---|
| Dec 31 | | | DR 194.00 |
| 31 | | 82.00 | DR 112.00 |

**Land #8**

| Date | | | Balance |
|---|---|---|---|
| Dec 31 | | | DR 15 000.00 |

**Buildings #9**

| Date | | | Balance |
|---|---|---|---|
| Dec 31 | | | DR 12 000.00 |

**Accum. Deprec. Bldgs #10**

| Date | | | Balance |
|---|---|---|---|
| Dec 31 | | | CR 1 711.50 |
| 31 | | 514.43 | CR 2 225.93 |

**Furniture + Equipment #11**

| Date | | | Balance |
|---|---|---|---|
| Dec 31 | | | DR 3 437.20 |

**Accum Deprec. Furn + Equ. #12**

| Date | | | Balance |
|---|---|---|---|
| Dec 31 | | | CR 1 237.40 |
| 31 | | 439.96 | CR 1 677.36 |

**Automobiles #13**

| Date | | | Balance |
|---|---|---|---|
| Dec 31 | | | DR 7 800.00 |

**Accum. Deprec. Autos. #14**

| Date | | | Balance |
|---|---|---|---|
| Dec 31 | | | CR 3 978.00 |
| 31 | | 1 146.60 | CR 5 124.60 |

**Accounts Payable #21**

| Date | | | Balance |
|---|---|---|---|
| Dec 31 | | | CR 9 461.21 |
| 31 | | 1 249.35 | CR 10 710.56 |

**Bank Loan #22**

| Date | | | Balance |
|---|---|---|---|
| Dec 31 | | | CR 9 750.00 |

**Sales Tax Payable #23**

| Date | | | Balance |
|---|---|---|---|
| Dec 31 | | | CR 251.10 |

**M. Philip Capital #31**

| Date | | | Balance |
|---|---|---|---|
| Dec 31 | | | CR 26 214.87 |
| 31 | | 13 163.28 | |
| 31 | 8 751.00 | | CR 30 627.15 |

**M. Philip Drawings #32**

| Date | | | Balance |
|---|---|---|---|
| Dec 31 | | | DR 8 751.00 |
| 31 | | 8 751.00 | -0- |

**Sales #41**

| Date | | | Balance |
|---|---|---|---|
| Dec 31 | | | CR 59 168.10 |
| 31 | 59 168.10 | | -0- |

**Sales Rets + Allow's #42**

| Date | | | Balance |
|---|---|---|---|
| Dec 31 | | | DR 1 204.30 |
| 31 | | 1 204.30 | -0- |

**Discounts Earned #43**

| Date | | | Balance |
|---|---|---|---|
| Dec 31 | | | CR 516.19 |
| 31 | 516.19 | | -0- |

**Bank Charges #51**

| Date | | | Balance |
|---|---|---|---|
| Dec 31 | | | DR 1 140.26 |
| 31 | | 1 140.26 | -0- |

**Building Maintenance #52**

| Date | | | Balance |
|---|---|---|---|
| Dec 31 | | | DR 375.00 |
| 31 | | 375.00 | |

**Car Expenses #53**

| Date | | | Balance |
|---|---|---|---|
| Dec 31 | | | DR 1 846.50 |
| 31 | 147.50 | | |
| 31 | | 1 994.00 | -0- |

**Discounts Allowed #54**

| Date | | | Balance |
|---|---|---|---|
| Dec 31 | | | DR 749.21 |
| 31 | | 749.21 | -0- |

**Duty #55**

| Date | | | Balance |
|---|---|---|---|
| Dec 31 | | | DR 315.70 |
| 31 | | 315.70 | -0- |

**Freight In #56**

| Date | | | Balance |
|---|---|---|---|
| Dec 31 | | | DR 949.14 |
| 31 | 42.10 | | |
| 31 | | 991.24 | -0- |

**Light, Heat + Water #57**

| Date | | | Balance |
|---|---|---|---|
| Dec 31 | | | DR 417.25 |
| 31 | | 417.25 | -0- |

**Miscellaneous Expense #58**

| Date | | | Balance |
|---|---|---|---|
| Dec 31 | | | DR 116.44 |
| 31 | 12.51 | | |
| 31 | | 128.95 | -0- |

**Purchases #59**

| Date | | | Balance |
|---|---|---|---|
| Dec 31 | | | DR 30 616.90 |
| 31 | 1 047.24 | | |
| 31 | | 31 664.14 | -0- |

**Purchases Rets + Allow's #60**

| Date | | | Balance |
|---|---|---|---|
| Dec 31 | | | CR 1 520.00 |
| 31 | 1 520.00 | | -0- |

**Telephone Expense #61**

| Date | | | Balance |
|---|---|---|---|
| Dec 31 | | | DR 484.17 |
| 31 | | 484.17 | -0- |

**Wages #62**

| Date | | | Balance |
|---|---|---|---|
| Dec 31 | | | DR 7 416.56 |
| 31 | | 7 563.10 | CR 146.54 |

*Ledger of Midway Trading Company (final position).*

## Effect of the Adjusting and Closing Entries

The objectives of the adjusting and closing entries were set out on page 354. After the adjusting and closing entries have been completed, these objectives will have been met; that is —
1. All accounts requiring an adjustment will be adjusted.
2. The Capital account will be updated.
3. All other equity accounts will be closed out.
   **Note:** The wages account of Midway Trading Company is not closed out. This exception is explained on pages 363-4.

## Post-Closing Trial Balance

The closing procedure involves the making of numerous postings and calculations of account balances. In all of this, there are many possibilities for making mechanical errors. Consequently, in order to be certain that the general ledger is in a balanced condition to begin the new accounting period, after posting the closing entries it is advisable to take off a general ledger trial balance, called the 'post-closing trial balance'. This is usually done with an adding machine and

*Midway Trading Company Post-Closing Trial Balance June 30, 19-4*

```
              0 0 T -
        1 0 0.0 0
      1 7 0 2.1 2
      6 7 5 1.1 2
        1 4 3.2 0  -
   1 3 5 6 2.0 0
        1 9 2.0 0
        1 1 2.0 0
   1 5 0 0 0.0 0
   1 2 0 0 0.0 0
      2 2 2 5.9 3  -
      3 4 3 7.2 0
      1 6 7 7.3 6
      7 8 0 0.0 0
      5 1 2 4.6 0  -
   1 0 7 1 0.5 6  -
      9 7 5 0.0 0  -
        2 5 1.1 0  -
   3 0 6 2 7.1 5  -
        1 4 6.5 4  -
              0 0 T
```

paper tape, as illustrated on this page. The paper tape is headed and stored for possible future reference.

*Cassidy Cartage Post-Closing Trial Balance June 30, 19-4*

```
              0 0 T
        5 0.0 0
      7 2 5.4 1
    4 0 2 7.5 6
      2 6 0.4 5  -
      3 9 5.2 5
        8 8.5 0
        8 5.0 0
    8 0 0 0.0 0
    7 2 8 0.0 0
    2 5 3 2.8 6  -
    2 9 5 0.0 0
    1 8 6 7.9 2  -
  1 5 6 0 0.0 0
  1 0 2 4 9.2 0  -
    3 4 4 9.9 7  -
      2 3 8.7 3  -
      1 5 7.2 9  -
  2 0 4 4 5.3 0  -
              0 0 T
```

# Reversing Entries

## Reversing Entry for Accounts Payable

When financial statements are prepared, an adjusting entry is necessary in respect to certain purchase invoices that pertain to one accounting period but which do not arrive until the next. This adjusting entry, done by the formal method, gives effect to these purchase invoices in the proper accounting period.

Once the adjusting entry for accounts payable is made, the purchase invoices are inserted into the accounting system to be processed by the ordinary accounting routine in the new period. It is necessary to do this because they must be matched with the purchase orders and receiving reports, posted to the subsidiary ledgers, and so on. The accounting routine must be adhered to strictly, as it is designed for purposes of internal control, accuracy, and efficiency. However, by processing these purchase invoices through the regular accounting system, they are entered in the books of the business a second time, this time in the new accounting period. Consequently, these particular purchase invoices are recorded in both accounting periods as shown by the following chart.

END OF
ACCOUNTING
PERIOD

| Accounting Period Just Ended | | Accounting Period Just Begun |
|---|---|---|
| + Effect of certain purchase invoices is recorded in the books of the business by means of an adjusting entry. | | + Effect of the same purchase invoices is recorded in the books of the business by means of the accounting system. |

From the above chart, you can see that the effect of the purchase invoices is felt in both accounting periods. But your common sense should tell you that this situation is not right and cannot be allowed to remain.

The situation is rectified by means of another accounting entry, called a 'reversing entry', which is made *early in the new accounting period*. This reversing entry is exactly the opposite of the adjusting entry made previously and completely cancels out the doubling effect.

For both Cassidy Cartage and Midway Trading Company the reversing entries for accounts payable are shown below. These reversing entries are exactly the opposite of the adjusting entries shown on pages 311 and 323 respectively.

| July | 1 | Accounts Payable | | 402 | 72 | | |
|---|---|---|---|---|---|---|---|
| | | Telephone Expense | | | | 15 | 70 |
| | | Truck Expense | | | | 174 | — |
| | | Supplies | | | | 45 | 21 |
| | | Building Maintenance | | | | 125 | — |
| | | Light, Heat, and Water | | | | 22 | 81 |
| | | Miscellaneous Expense | | | | 20 | — |
| | | Reversing entry for accounts payable | | | | | |
| | | adjusting entry of June 30 | | | | | |

*Reversing entry for Cassidy Cartage.*

| Jan | 1 | Accounts Payable | | 1 249 | 35 | | |
|---|---|---|---|---|---|---|---|
| | | Car Expenses | | | | 147 | 50 |
| | | Freight-In | | | | 42 | 10 |
| | | Miscellaneous Expense | | | | 12 | 51 |
| | | Purchases | | | | 1 047 | 24 |
| | | Reversing entry for accounts payable | | | | | |
| | | adjusting entry of Dec. 31 | | | | | |

*Reversing entry for Midway Trading Company.*

The total effect of the reversing entry for accounts payable is shown by the following chart.

The chart shows that the doubling effect is eliminated in the new accounting period by means of the reversing accounting entry.

| Accounting Period Just Ended | Accounting Period Just Begun |
|---|---|
| + Effect of certain purchase invoices is recorded in the books of the business by means of an adjusting entry (subsidiary ledger excluded). | + The effect of the same purchase invoices is recorded in the books of the business by means of the accounting system (subsidiary ledger included). |
| | − The opposite effect of the adjusting entry is recorded in the books of the business by means of a reversing entry (subsidiary ledger excluded). |

## Reversing Entry for Accrued Payroll

Reversing entries are also necessary for any accounting situation where the following conditions exist:

1. An adjusting entry – *by the formal method* – is made to record an item or items in the accounting period just completed.
2. The same item or items are processed in the new accounting period by means of the regular accounting routines.

Cassidy Cartage used the formal method of adjusting for accrued wages which resulted in six days' wages in the amount of $157.29 being recorded in the accounting period ended June 30. At the same time, the Payroll Department of Cassidy Cartage proceeded in its usual manner to calculate the payroll for the ten-day period ended in July and which resulted in wages of $262.15 being recorded in the new accounting period. Of special importance is the fact that the ten-day wages figure of $262.15 includes the six-day wages figure of $157.29.

The effect of the above is shown by the following chart.

| Accounting Period Just Ended | Accounting Period Just Begun |
|---|---|
| $157.29 of wages (for 6 days) recorded by adjusting entry. | $262.15 of wages (for 10 days) recorded through regular accounting routine. This amount includes the $157.29 shown at left. |

Because the $262.15 figure includes the $157.29 figure, it is apparent that the $157.29 figure is recorded in both accounting periods. This duplication is corrected by means of a reversing entry which cancels out $157.29 in the new accounting period. The reversing entry is shown below and is exactly the opposite of the adjusting entry made previously, page 321.

| July | 1 | Accrued Payroll | | 157 29 | |
| | | Wages Expense | | | 157 29 |
| | | Reversing entry for accrued wages | | | |
| | | adjusting entry of June 30 | | | |

The total accounting effect is shown by the chart below.

END OF
ACCOUNTING
PERIOD

| Accounting Period Just Ended | Accounting Period Just Begun |
| --- | --- |
| $157.29 of wages (for 6 days) recorded by adjusting entry. | $262.15 of wages (for 10 days) recorded through regular accounting routine. This amount includes the $157.29 shown at left. |
| | $157.29 of wages (for 6 days) cancelled out by reversing entry. |
| Net effect: 6 days wages at $157.29 | Net effect: 4 days wages at $104.86 |

## Shortcut Technique and Reversing Entries

No reversing entries are necessary for any adjustments performed by the shortcut technique. As you will see below, the shortcut technique has the advantage of handling reversing entry situations automatically. The accountant is thus relieved of some of his many responsibilities at this busy time.

To illustrate the way in which this works, consider the accrued wages adjustment of Midway Trading Company. This adjustment is performed by the shortcut technique (pages 327-8).

After the adjusting and closing entries have been completed, the Wages account of Midway Trading Company ends up in a credit balance position of $146.54, as shown below (from page 359).

This account has been converted temporarily into a liability account which reflects the accrued liability for wages as of the end of the accounting period, December 31.

When the first payroll is completed in the following period, say on January 9, the wages figure for this payroll will be debited to the Wages account through the normal processes of the accounting system. Assuming the gross wages figure to be $488.47, the Wages account will be debited with that amount. After posting, the account will appear as shown at right.

This payroll entry, through the normal accounting routine, has produced a debit balance in the account of $341.93. Thus, the account has not only been converted back to its normal status of expense account, but has been made to reflect automatically the proper expense figure for the new accounting period.

| Wages | | | | | #62 |
|---|---|---|---|---|---|
| Date | Particulars | P.R. | Debit | Credit | Balance |
| 19 - 4 | | | | | |
| Dec. 31 | | | | | 7 416 56 DR |
| 31 | | J. 78 | | 7 563 10 | 146 54 CR |
| 19 - 5 | | | | | |
| Jan. 9 | | J. 79 | 488 47 | | 341 93 DR |

# Full Accounting Cycle

You have now seen the full accounting cycle, that series of progressive accounting steps that must be performed during each accounting period. Specifically these steps are:

Journalizing of transactions
Posting to the general ledger and to the subsidiary ledgers
Balancing the general ledger and the subsidiary ledgers
} Performed by junior accounting clerks

Preparing the work sheet
Preparing the financial statements
Recording the adjusting, closing, and reversing entries
} Performed by the accountant or assistant accountant

# Bookkeeping and Accounting Terms

**Current Asset** Unrestricted cash or other asset that, in the normal course of operations, is expected to be converted into cash or consumed in the production of income within one year.

**Fixed Asset** A tangible long-term asset, such as land, building, equipment, etc., held for use rather than for sale.

**Current Liability** A liability whose regular and ordinary liquidation is expected to occur within one year.

**Long-term Liability** A liability which, in the ordinary course of business, will not be liquidated within one year.

**Revenue** The gross proceeds from the sale of goods and services (generally after deducting returns, allowances and discounts).

**Selling Expenses** Expenses of an organization relating to the selling or marketing of its goods or services, as contrasted with expenses incurred for other specialized functions such as administration, financial, and manufacturing.

**Administrative Expenses** Expenses of an organization relating to the overall direction of its affairs, as contrasted with expenses incurred for other specialized functions, such as manufacturing, selling or financing.

**Current Ratio** The ratio of current assets to current liabilities.

**Gross Profit** The excess of net sales over the cost of goods sold. Also known as **gross income.**

**Working Capital** The excess of current assets over current liabilities.

**Closing Entry** An entry made at the end of an accounting period for the purpose of transferring the balances in nominal accounts (revenue, income, expense or loss) to the capital (or retained earnings*).

**Reversing Entry** An entry made at the beginning of an accounting period to bring into the accounts for the period any accrued amounts set up at the end of the preceding period.

* Discussed in Chapter 17.

# Review Questions

1. Explain what is meant by classified financial statements.
2. Name the classifications shown on the balance sheet of Fraser and Associates, on page 346.
3. Name the classifications shown on the income statement of Fraser and Associates, page 347.
4. Do all classified financial statements follow exactly the same format? Explain.
5. What is the source of information for the financial statements? Explain in detail for both the balance sheet and the income statement.
6. Briefly explain the uses to which financial statements may be put.
7. How is the current ratio calculated?
8. How is the gross income percentage calculated?
9. What are the three objectives of adjusting and closing the books?
10. What does it mean to close an account?
11. Revenue, expense, and drawings accounts must be closed out at the end of the accounting period. Explain.
12. Where does one obtain all of the information for the adjusting and closing entries?
13. How many steps are required to adjust and close the books? Explain briefly.
14. What is the purpose of the post-closing trial balance?
15. Under what conditions is a reversing entry necessary?
16. Can reversing entries be avoided? Explain.
17. List all of the steps in the full accounting cycle.
18. What is working capital?
19. Define 'current asset'.
20. Define 'fixed asset'.

# Exercises

1.  Armstrong Company has current assets of $210 000 and current liabilities of $98 000. Calculate the current ratio of Armstrong Company and express your opinion as to its adequacy.

2.  J. Frankland's business has current assets of $375 000 and current liabilities of $410 000. Calculate the current ratio and express your opinion as to its adequacy.

3.  Given the following:

|  | Co. A | Co. B | Co. C |
|---|---|---|---|
| Net Sales | $475 000 | $310 000 | $257 600 |
| Gross Trading Income | 285 000 | 127 100 | 28 336 |

... for each company calculate the gross income percentage.

4.  The following are the operating figures for the James Company:

| | |
|---|---|
| *Revenue* | |
| Sales | $48 075 |
| | |
| *Operating Expenses* | |
| Bad Debts | $    315 |
| Supplies Expense | 157 |
| Licences | 250 |
| Insurance | 975 |
| Depreciation of Building | 1 020 |
| Depreciation of Furniture and Fixtures | 1 675 |
| Depreciation of Automobiles | 3 072 |
| Bank Charges | 215 |
| Building Maintenance | 1 574 |
| Light, Heat, and Water | 2 746 |
| Miscellaneous Expense | 105 |
| Telephone Expense | 747 |
| Truck Expense | 2 769 |
| Wages | 10 437 |
| | $26 057 |
| Operating Income | $22 018 |
| *Other Income* | |
| Discounts Earned | $    746 |
| Net Income | $22 764 |

Convert each amount into a percentage of the sales figure. Make the calculations to one decimal place. Record these percentages in a column immediately to the right of the money figures. Adjust the percentage figures if necessary so that the percentage column totals properly.

---

5. The following classification is used in preparing the financial statements of ABC Company.

Current Assets
Prepaid Expenses
Fixed Assets
Current Liabilities
Long-term Liabilities
Owner's Equity

Revenue
Cost of Goods Sold
Selling Expenses
Administrative Expenses
Other Income
Other Expenses

Classify each of the following items into one of the above categories. With a few items a choice is possible.

Accounts Receivable
Accounts Payable
Accumulated Depreciation of Buildings
Advertising
Allowance for Bad Debts
Audit Fee
Bad Debts Expense
Bank
Bank Charges
Bank Loan
Buildings
Canada Pension Plan Expense
Delivery Expense
Depreciation on Automobiles
Depreciation on Building
Discounts Allowed
Discounts Earned
Duty
Employees' Income Tax Payable
F. Franks, Capital
F. Franks, Drawings
Freight-in
General Expense

Insurance Expense
Interest Income
Investment in Bonds
Legal Expense
Merchandise Inventory
Mortgage Payable
Office Expense
Office Salaries
Prepaid Insurance
Postage Expense
Purchases
Rent Expense
Sales
Sales Returns and Allowances
Sales Tax Payable
Salesmen's Commissions
Salesmen's Car Expenses
Supplies
Supplies Expense
Telephone Expense
Unemployment Insurance Expense
Wages

---

6. This exercise is to be done in your workbook, or as directed by your teacher.

7. The results of operations for C. Simpson for the years 19–1 and 19–2 are shown below:

| | 19–1 | 19–2 |
|---|---|---|
| *Revenue* | | |
| Sales | $361 800 | $315 844 |
| | | |
| *Cost of Merchandise Sold* | | |
| Opening Inventory | $ 25 072 | $ 31 719 |
| Purchases | 137 916 | 146 209 |
| Freight-in | 3 812 | 4 702 |
| | $166 800 | $182 630 |
| Deduct: Closing Inventory | 31 719 | 65 080 |
| Cost of Goods Sold | $135 081 | $117 550 |
| | | |
| *Gross Trading Income* | $226 719 | $198 294 |
| | | |
| *Selling Expenses* | | |
| Advertising | $ 1 076 | $ 1 102 |
| Delivery Expense | 5 192 | 4 865 |
| Salesmen's Salaries | 26 437 | 25 096 |
| Car Expenses | 9 711 | 9 542 |
| Depreciation of Automobiles | 7 215 | 5 767 |
| Total Selling Expenses | $ 49 631 | $ 46 372 |
| | | |
| *Administrative Expenses* | | |
| Bad Debts | $ 574 | $ 2 472 |
| Depreciation of Building | 2 075 | 1 904 |
| Depreciation of Equipment | 1 974 | 1 812 |
| Legal and Audit | 500 | 550 |
| Insurance | 400 | 416 |
| Office Expenses | 372 | 450 |
| Rent | 10 000 | 12 000 |
| Telephone | 317 | 450 |
| Canada Pension Plan Expense | 356 | 375 |
| Unemployment Insurance Expense | 412 | 475 |
| Wages | 12 902 | 13 074 |
| Total Administrative Expenses | $ 29 882 | $ 33 978 |
| | | |
| *Total Expenses* | $ 79 513 | $ 80 350 |
| *Net Income* | $147 206 | $117 944 |

To this comparative statement add a third column to show the changes from year 19–1 to 19–2. Show decreases in brackets or preceded by a minus sign.

Indicate the most significant change and offer an explanation for it.

**8. From the work sheet for J. P. Gorman (Chapter 14, Exercise 7) –**

Prepare the income statement and the balance sheet.

Journalize the adjusting, closing, and reversing entries in a two-column general journal.

---

**9. From the work sheet for Dennisson Delivery Service (Chapter 14, Exercise 8) –**

Prepare the income statement and the balance sheet.

Journalize the adjusting, closing, and reversing entries in a two-column general journal.

---

**10. From the work sheet for Select Trading Company (Chapter 14, Exercise 9) –**

Prepare the income statement and the balance sheet.

Journalize the adjusting, closing, and reversing entries in a two-column general journal.

---

**11. From the work sheet for Stirling Sales Company (Chapter 14, Exercise 10) –**

Prepare the income statement and the balance sheet.

Journalize the adjusting, closing, and reversing entries in a two-column general journal.

---

**12. From the work sheet for Monarch Marine (Chapter 14, Exercise 11) –**

Set up the general ledger accounts in T account form from the trial balance figures.
Prepare the income statement and the balance sheet.
Journalize the adjusting and closing entries in a two-column general journal.

Post the adjusting and closing entries to the general ledger T accounts and calculate the account balances.
Take off a post-closing trial balance of the general ledger.

---

**13. From the work sheet for General Lighting and Electric (Chapter 14, Exercise 12) –**

Set up the general ledger accounts in T account form from the trial balance figures.
Prepare the income statement and the balance sheet.
Journalize the adjusting and closing entries in a two-column general journal.
Post the adjusting and closing entries to the

general ledger T accounts and calculate the account balances.
Take off a post-closing trial balance of the general ledger.
Calculate the current ratio and the gross income percentage.

**14.** The general ledger trial balance of King Chemical Company, after a fiscal period of one year, is as follows:

KING CHEMICAL COMPANY
GENERAL LEDGER TRIAL BALANCE
DECEMBER 31, 19–3

| No. | | Account | Debit | Credit |
|---|---|---|---|---|
| 1 | Petty Cash | $ 50.00 | |
| 2 | Bank | 593.74 | |
| 3 | Accounts Receivable | 12 519.50 | |
| 4 | Allowance for Doubtful Accounts | 4.70 | |
| 5 | Merchandise Inventory | 20 416.50 | |
| 6 | Supplies | 575.75 | |
| 7 | Prepaid Insurance | 312.00 | |
| 8 | Furniture and Equipment | 4 010.00 | |
| 9 | Accum. Deprec. Furn. & Equip. | | $ 2 716.50 |
| 10 | Automobiles | 7 800.00 | |
| 11 | Accum. Deprec. Automobiles | | 5 124.60 |
| 21 | Bank Loan | | 15 000.00 |
| 22 | Accounts Payable | | 15 741.62 |
| 23 | Sales Tax Payable | | 672.14 |
| 24 | Employees' Income Tax Payable | | 602.51 |
| 31 | F. C. Wallace, Capital | | 27 441.20 |
| 32 | F. C. Wallace, Drawings | 15 946.15 | |
| 41 | Sales | | 140 567.07 |
| 51 | Bank Charges | 141.05 | |
| 52 | Canada Pension Plan Expense | 405.00 | |
| 53 | Car Expenses | 3 509.10 | |
| 54 | Duty | 1 075.92 | |
| 55 | Freight-in | 4 074.75 | |
| 56 | Light, Heat, and Water | 147.16 | |
| 57 | Miscellaneous Expense | 79.52 | |
| 58 | Postage | 112.40 | |
| 59 | Purchases | 73 416.95 | |
| 60 | Rent | 11 760.00 | |
| 61 | Telephone | 565.70 | |
| 62 | Unemployment Insurance | 286.00 | |
| 63 | Wages | 50 063.75 | |
| | | | $207 865.64 | $207 865.64 |

Set up the above information in general ledger accounts.

Prepare a work sheet for the company for the year ended December 31, 19–3.
Use the following additional information:

(i) The total of the estimated doubtful accounts as shown by the December 31, 19–3, aging analysis is $516.90.

(ii) Purchase invoices received in January 19–4 pertaining to goods and services received in 19–3 are summarized as follows:

| | |
|---|---|
| Supplies | $ 75.00 |
| Purchases | 967.25 |
| Car Expenses | 135.75 |
| Misc. Expense | 74.01 |
| | $1 252.01 |

(iii) Inventories taken at December 31, 19–3, are:

| | |
|---|---|
| Merchandise | $18 450.00 |
| Supplies | $ 250.00 |

(iv) The prepaid insurance schedule as of December 31, 19–3, showed the value of prepaid insurance to be $116.25.

(v) Capital cost allowances are calculated at government rates.

(vi) The gross wages for the first payroll in January amounted to $1 140. Half of this amount pertained to the 19–3 fiscal year and half to the 19–4 fiscal year.

Prepare a balance sheet and an income statement.
Journalize the adjusting and closing entries.
Post the adjusting and closing entries and calculate the account balances.
Take off a post-closing trial balance.
Journalize the reversing entry (or entries).
Post the payroll journal figures for the pay period ended January 6, 19–4, from the following payroll summary figures:

| | |
|---|---|
| Gross Wages | $1 140.00 |
| Canada Pension Plan Deductions | 16.70 |
| Income Tax Deductions | 78.50 |
| Unemployment Insurance Deductions | 13.90 |
| United Appeal Deductions | 12.00 |
| Net Wages | 1 018.90 |

Calculate the new balance in the Wages expense account to see if the account reflects correctly the wages expense for the first working week of 19–4.
Calculate the current ratio and the gross income percentage.

**15.** On December 31, 19–4, the end of a fiscal year, the general ledger trial balance of Dominion Furniture is as follows:

DOMINION FURNITURE

TRIAL BALANCE

DECEMBER 31, 19–4

| No. | | | | |
|---|---|---|---|---|
| 1 | Petty Cash | $ 50.00 | | |
| 2 | Bank | 1 047.21 | | |
| 3 | Accounts Receivable | 10 467.04 | | |
| 4 | Allowance for Doubtful Accounts | | $ | 25.94 |
| 5 | Merchandise Inventory | 12 375.16 | | |
| 6 | Supplies | 362.04 | | |
| 7 | Prepaid Insurance | 243.00 | | |
| 8 | Land | 9 500.00 | | |
| 9 | Buildings – Frame | 7 500.00 | | |
| 10 | Accum. Deprec. Buildings | | | 2 579.25 |
| 11 | Furniture and Equipment | 2 150.00 | | |
| 12 | Accum. Deprec. Furn. & Equip. | | | 1 172.00 |
| 13 | Automobiles | 4 875.00 | | |
| 14 | Accum. Deprec. Automobiles | | | 1 462.50 |
| 21 | Accounts Payable | | | 3 076.21 |
| 22 | Sales Tax Payable | | | 315.20 |
| 23 | Employees' Income Tax Payable | | | 84.50 |
| 24 | Canada Pension Plan Payable | | | 31.10 |
| 25 | Loan Payable – Due March 31, 19–9 | | | 20 000.00 |
| 31 | J. K. Smit, Capital | | | 8 706.59 |
| 32 | J. K. Smit, Drawings | 12 500.00 | | |
| 41 | Sales | | | 85 904.15 |
| 42 | Sales Returns and Allowances | 2 074.10 | | |
| 51 | Advertising | 200.00 | | |
| 52 | Bank Charges | 35.00 | | |
| 53 | Building Repairs and Maintenance | 746.09 | | |
| 54 | Canada Pension Plan Expense | 234.00 | | |
| 55 | Car Expenses | 946.80 | | |
| 56 | Cash Short and Over | 13.50 | | |
| 57 | Discounts Allowed | 1 516.15 | | |
| 58 | Discounts Earned | | | 1 075.21 |
| 59 | Duty | 357.00 | | |
| 60 | Freight-in | 907.40 | | |
| 61 | Interest on Loan | 900.00 | | |
| 62 | Light, Heat, and Water | 112.00 | | |
| 63 | Miscellaneous Expense | 56.50 | | |
| 64 | Postage | 94.60 | | |
| 65 | Property Taxes | 804.90 | | |
| 66 | Purchases | 40 915.78 | | |
| 67 | Purchases Returns and Allow. | | | 1 010.44 |
| 68 | Telephone | 212.50 | | |
| 69 | Unemployment Ins. Expense | 151.20 | | |
| 70 | Wages and Salaries | 14 096.12 | | |
| | | $125 443.09 | | $125 443.09 |

Set up the general ledger of Dominion Furniture as of December 31, 19–4.
Prepare a work sheet for Dominion Furniture for the year ended December 31,
19–4. Use the shortcut technique for adjustments wherever possible. Use the
following additional information:

(i) The total estimated value of doubtful
accounts per the aging analysis is $152.

(ii) Purchase invoices received in January
19–5 which pertain to goods and services
received in 19–4 are summarized below:

| | |
|---|---|
| Purchases | $1 200.50 |
| Building Repairs and Maintenance | 105.00 |
| Car Expenses | 41.02 |
| Freight-in | 25.00 |
| | $1 371.52 |

(iii) Inventories taken at December 31, 19–4,
are:

| | |
|---|---|
| Merchandise | $14 650.00 |
| Supplies | $    150.00 |

(iv) The details of insurance policies as at
December 31, 19–4, are:

| Company | Policy Date | Term | Premium |
|---|---|---|---|
| Acme | July 1, 19–2 | 3 years | $  72.00 |
| Inland | April 1, 19–4 | 3 years | 96.00 |
| Empire | Dec. 31, 19–1 | 3 years | 120.00 |
| Imperial | Sept. 30, 19–4 | 1 year | 36.00 |

(v) Capital cost allowances calculated at
government rates.

(vi) The gross wages and salaries for the first
pay in January 19–5 totaled $305 for 10
working days. Three working days are in
19–4 and seven are in 19–5.

(vii) The loan payable of $20 000 bears interest
at a rate of 6 per cent per annum. Interest
payments are made half-yearly on
March 31 and September 30. Interest has
been paid to September 30 only. (An
adjustment is necessary in respect to
accrued interest payable.)

Prepare a balance sheet and an income statement.
Journalize the adjusting and the closing entries.
Post the adjusting and the closing entries and calculate the account balances.
Take off a post-closing trial balance.
Journalize the reversing entry (or entries).
Post the debit to Wages and Salaries account for the first pay in 19–5. Calculate
the account balance to see if it properly reflects the expense for the new pay
period.
Post the debit to Interest on Loan account for the first interest payment on
March 31, 19–5. Calculate the account balance to see if it properly reflects the
interest expense for the new period.
Calculate the current ratio and the gross income percentage.

# Cases

### Case 1
Condensed financial statements of Company A and Company B appear below.

AS OF DECEMBER 31, 19—

|  | Company A | Company B |
|---|---|---|
| *Current Assets* | | |
| Cash | $ 6 000 | $ 7 000 |
| Accounts Receivable | 21 000 | 22 000 |
| Inventories | 23 000 | 91 000 |
| Total Current Assets | $ 50 000 | $120 000 |
| *Fixed Assets* | | |
| Fixed Assets, at cost less Accumulated Depreciation | 525 000 | 210 000 |
| Total Assets | $575 000 | $330 000 |
| *Current Liabilities* | | |
| Accounts Payable | $ 20 000 | $ 25 000 |
| Bank Loan | 5 000 | 5 000 |
| Total Current Liabilities | $ 25 000 | $ 30 000 |
| *Long-Term Liabilities* | | |
| 5% Bonds Payable | 100 000 | 100 000 |
| Capital | 450 000 | 200 000 |
| Total Liabilities and Capital | $575 000 | $330 000 |

INCOME STATEMENT
FOR THE YEAR ENDED DECEMBER 31, 19—

|  | Company A | Company B |
|---|---|---|
| Sales | $500 000 | $800 000 |
| Cost of Goods Sold | 375 000 | 576 000 |
| Gross Income | $125 000 | $224 000 |
| Operating Expenses | 85 000 | 199 000 |
| Operating Income | $ 40 000 | $ 25 000 |
| Bond Interest | 5 000 | 5 000 |
| Net Income | $ 35 000 | $ 20 000 |

Prepare a detailed analysis of the financial data for the two companies and interpret the results from the point of view of a prospective investor. Include in your analysis the following calculations:

a. amount of working capital
b. current ratio
c. gross income ratio to sales
d. operating income ratio to sales
e. net income ratio to sales

Explain in your report the significance of each ratio you calculate.

## Case 2
If the following errors are not corrected, state whether the net income would be more or less, and give the amount of the difference.

1. The $4 200 cost of installing a new machine in a factory was charged to Repair Expense.
2. A $35.50 credit to Discounts Earned was erroneously credited to Discounts Allowed.
3. A journal entry in the amount of $1 500 was posted as a $150 debit to Furniture & Fixtures and as a $150 credit to Accounts Payable.

## Case 3

On September 1, 19–1, the Whiting Company purchased a three-year fire insurance policy and charged the entire premium of $900 to Insurance Expense. There were no other insurance premiums paid during the term of this policy. No adjustment for the unexpired portion was made when the books were closed at December 31, 19–1. At December 31, 19–2, Mr. Whiting decided to set up an unexpired Insurance account and to adjust the results for both 19–1 and 19–2. What journal entry or entries should be made?

## Case 4

Because of the cost and inconveniences of taking inventory, the Sutton Hardware Store, owned by C. Wallace, takes inventory only at the end of the calendar year. The gross profit of the business is stable and averages 40 per cent.

The accounts of January 31 had balances as follows:

| | |
|---|---|
| Inventory January 1 (obtained by actual count of merchandise) | $ 51 920 |
| Sales | 103 850 |
| Operating Expenses | 29 875 |
| Purchases | 45 920 |

From these facts estimate the inventory at January 31, and prepare an estimated income statement for January.

## Case 5

The comparative statement of income for James O'Halloran shows that his sales have increased 40 per cent over the sales of the previous year, but his net income has decreased 15 per cent. Give two possible causes.

## Case 6

At the end of the accounting period you prepare a trial balance and the financial statements. You do not, however, prepare any adjusting and closing entries. What effect will this omission of adjusting and closing entries have on your records at the end of the next accounting period?

## Case 7

If the cost of a new calculator ($700) purchased for office use was recorded as a debit to Purchases, what would be the effect of the error on the balance sheet and income statement in the period in which the error was made?

## Case 8

The ending merchandise inventory of the O'Hara Co. as of December 31, 19—, is $98 100. What entry is made to show this item in the accounts of the company? Is this a closing entry or an adjusting entry? Explain.

## Case 9

During the taking of physical inventory at December 31, 19—, certain merchandise which cost $2 500 was counted twice; the inventory was therefore overstated by $2 500. What is the effect of this error on the cost of goods sold? on net income for the year? on total assets?

## Case 10

After studying your balance sheet you decide you do not need all of your $25 900 in capital to operate the business. You decide to withdraw some of your capital and invest it in 'blue chip' stocks of Canadian corporations. What are some of the decisions you will have to make in order to determine how much you can safely withdraw?

## Case 11

E. C. Percy, owner of Percy Plumbing and Heating, asks you to analyse the operating results of the business for the last two years with a view to advising him as to the reasons for a decrease in net income.

Your partially completed analysis is shown below. Finish the analysis by completing the Per Cent columns. (Do not write your answers in the textbook.) Follow this up by preparing a list of questions and comments that you would make to Mr. Percy. Restrict your comments to significant items only.

### Percy Plumbing and Heating
### Income Statement
### Year Ended March 31, 19 – 5
(with comparative figures for 19 – 4)

| | 19 – 4 Amount | 19 – 4 Per Cent | 19 – 5 Amount | 19 – 5 Per Cent |
|---|---|---|---|---|
| **Revenue** | | | | |
| Sales | 58 254 | 100.0 | 43 534 | 100.0 |
| **Direct Expenses** | | | | |
| Materials Used | 29 802 | | 23 978 | |
| Wages | 6 380 | | 6 752 | |
| Truck Repairs | 776 | | 654 | |
| Truck Licence | 80 | | 80 | |
| Gasoline and Oil | 650 | | 1 158 | |
| Depreciation of Truck | 1 650 | | 1 156 | |
| Insurance | 736 | | 918 | |
| Business Licence | 370 | | 362 | |
| Depreciation of Equipment | 134 | | 108 | |
| Workmen's Compensation | 318 | | 384 | |
| Unemployment Insurance | 68 | | 90 | |
| Business Tax | 14 | | 14 | |
| | 40 978 | | 35 654 | |
| **Indirect Expenses** | | | | |
| Telephone | 870 | | 1 090 | |
| Office Supplies | 48 | | 168 | |
| Accounting Fee | 160 | | 150 | |
| Postage | 60 | | 20 | |
| Interest and Bank Charges | 770 | | 526 | |
| Sales Promotion | 312 | | 394 | |
| Legal Expenses | 362 | | | |
| Miscellaneous Expenses | | | 122 | |
| | 2 582 | | 2 470 | |
| **Total Expenses** | 43 560 | | 38 124 | |
| **Net Income** | 14 694 | | 5 410 | |

# Supplement to Chapter 15

## Universal Lumber Company Exercise

**Read the introductory information and make notes of the business transactions that you will be required to make on your own initiative.**

### Introductory Information

You have taken a position as accountant for the Universal Lumber Company. You are to commence duties on December 15, 19–4, the arrangement being that you are to work with the present accountant until his departure at the end of the month. It is expected that during that time you will become sufficiently acquainted with the company's books, records, and office procedures to enable you to take over full responsibility for their preparation.

During the introductory period you learn the following facts and information:

1. The business is three years old.
2. The owner is James Wiseman.
3. The company's fiscal year coincides with the calendar year.
4. The owner demands interim financial statements at the end of each month, to show in columnar form the results of operation for the month just completed, as well as the results of operation for the year to date.
5. In the office there is an adding machine and a calculator which are rented by the company from Office Rentals Co. The monthly rentals of $10 and $15 are due on the fifteenth of each month.

6. The company offers a 2 per cent discount on all sales if payment is received from the customer within 10 days of the date of the sales invoice.
7. Sales tax at the rate of 10 per cent applies on all sales.
8. The company has a National Pacific Railway siding. Most of the material purchased is transported to the company premises by rail.
9. On the fifteenth and on the last day of each month the proprietor draws $725 out of the business.
10. The detailed information in respect to payroll is as follows:
    a. Payday is every other Friday. The first payday in the new year is Friday, January 10.
    b. All employees are paid on a salary basis.
    c. The method of payment is by cash. The cash to meet the payroll is obtained by issuing and cashing one cheque for the total amount required.
    d. The payroll for January 10 is to be made up from the following minimum information:

| Employee | Weekly Salary | Net Claim Code | Weekly United Appeal Donation | Account to be Charged |
|----------|--------------|----------------|-------------------------------|----------------------|
| C. Barney | $200.00 | 6 | $1.00 | Wages |
| A. Scott | 200.00 | 3 | 1.50 | Wages |
| E. Kollar | 180.00 | 7 | 1.00 | Wages |
| B. Brody | 180.00 | 12 | .50 | Wages |
| F. Duncan | 170.00 | 13 | 1.25 | Wages |
| D. Ellis | 240.00 | 13 | .50 | Office Salaries |
| Accountant (you) | 260.00 | 1 | —— | Office Salaries |

(Assume for convenience that all employees are at least 18 years of age and under 70 years of age)

e. Each employee is enrolled in the company registered retirement plan. Contributions are made at the rate of 5 per cent of the gross pay on each pay period. The employer matches the employees' contributions.

f. R.R.P. contributions made by the employees and the employer are accumulated by the company and remitted to the Insurance Company of Canada at the end of each month in which the deductions were made.

g. Employees' income taxes, employees' and employer's contributions to the Canada Pension Plan, and the employees' and employer's contributions to the Unemployment Insurance Fund are remitted to the Receiver General on the fifteenth day of each month following that in which the deductions are made (one cheque).

h. The United Appeal Fund contributions of the employees are accumulated by the company and remitted to the local organization at the end of the quarter.

11. Sales tax is remitted on the fifteenth of each month for the deductions of the previous month, payable to the Provincial Treasurer.

12. The complete chart of accounts for the business is as follows:

| Account Number | Account Name |
|---|---|
| 1. | Bank |
| 2. | Petty Cash |
| 3. | Accounts Receivable |
| 4. | Allowance for Bad Debts |
| 5. | Merchandise Inventory |
| 6. | Office Supplies |
| 7. | Prepaid Insurance |
| 8. | Land |
| 9. | Building |
| 10. | Accumulated Depreciation Building |
| 11. | Office Equipment |
| 12. | Accumulated Depreciation Office Equipment |
| 13. | Trucks |
| 14. | Accumulated Depreciation Trucks |
| 21. | Bank Loan |
| 22. | Accounts Payable |
| 23. | Canada Pension Plan Payable |
| 24. | Unemployment Insurance Payable |
| 25. | Registered Retirement Plan Payable |
| 26. | Employees' Tax Deductions Payable |
| 27. | United Appeal Payable |
| 28. | Sales Tax Payable |
| 31. | James Wiseman, Capital |
| 32. | James Wiseman, Drawings |
| 41. | Sales |
| 42. | Discount Allowed |
| 45. | Purchases |
| 47. | Freight-in |
| 51. | Bad Debts |
| 52. | Building Maintenance |
| 53. | Depreciation of Building |
| 54. | Depreciation of Office Equipment |
| 55. | Depreciation of Trucks |
| 56. | Insurance Expense |
| 57. | Interest and Bank Charges |
| 58. | Legal Expense |
| 59. | Miscellaneous Expense |
| 60. | Office Expense |
| 61. | Office Supplies Used |
| 62. | Office Salaries |
| 63. | Pension Fund Expense |
| 64. | Power Expense |
| 65. | Property Taxes |
| 66. | Telephone |
| 67. | Truck Expense |
| 68. | Unemployment Insurance Expense |
| 69. | Wages |

13. The general ledger trial balance at December 31 was as follows:

|  | Debit | Credit |
|---|---|---|
| Bank | $ 5 173.13 | |
| Petty Cash | 100.00 | |
| Accounts Receivable | 8 642.81 | |
| Allowance for Bad Debts | | 93.62 |
| Merchandise Inventory | 24 812.55 | |
| Office Supplies | 650.00 | |
| Prepaid Insurance | 352.20 | |
| Land | 12 000.00 | |
| Building | 17 000.00 | |
| Accumulated Depreciation Building | | 2 424.63 |
| Office Equipment | 1 339.00 | |
| Accumulated Depreciation Office Equipment | | 653.42 |
| Trucks | 11 400.00 | |
| Accumulated Depreciation Trucks | | 7 489.80 |
| Bank Loan | | 5 000.00 |
| Accounts Payable | | 11 416.70 |
| Canada Pension Plan Payable | | 192.16 |
| Unemployment Insurance Payable | | 135.12 |
| Employees Tax Deductions Payable | | 1 226.60 |
| Sales Tax Payable | | 1 502.17 |
| James Wiseman, Capital | | 51 335.47 |
| | $81 469.69 | $81 469.69 |

14. The subsidiary ledger trial balances at December 31 were as follows:

*Accounts Receivable*

| | |
|---|---|
| Bayvue Village Estates (Nov. 30) | $2 365.53 |
| Carlton Home Builders (Nov. 30) | 1 672.16 |
| Evergreen Gardens (Dec. 27) | 1 848.88 |
| Keele Estates (Aug. 23) | 120.43 |
| J. Martin (Mar. 16) | 10.42 |
| B. Starr (Apr. 1) | 83.20 |
| Superior Construction Co. (Dec. 28) | 2 542.19 |
| | $8 642.81 |

*Accounts Payable*

| | | |
|---|---|---|
| Lumber Wholesalers | Terms, N60 | $5 627.42 |
| Plywood Suppliers | Terms, N60 | 4 320.60 |
| Wood Moulding Co. | Terms, N60 | 1 468.68 |
| | | $11 416.70 |

15. The following information is to be used by the accountant to prepare simple financial statements.

a. *Bad Debts:* The Allowance for Bad Debts is calculated on a specific account basis. The balance in this account at December 31 of $93.62 was to cover J. Martin's account of $10.42 and B. Starr's account of $83.20, both of which were over one year old.

b. *Prepaid Insurance:* The annual insurance premium is $2 113.20 payable in advance on each February 28. The Prepaid Insurance account balance of $352.20 at December 31 represents the unused portion (the 2 months of January and February) of the insurance premium calculated as follows: 2/12 × $2 113.20 = $352.20.

c. *Fixed Assets:* Fixed assets are depreciated in accordance with the rules and regulations of the federal government. Detailed information in respect to the fixed assets is as follows:

*Brick Buildings*
Cost Price                           $17 000.00
Rate of Depreciation – 5 per cent, reducing balance.
Accumulated Depreciation
    after 3 years is                  $2 424.63

*Office Equipment*

| Cost Price: | | |
|---|---|---|
| Steel Desk | $ | 325.00 |
| Steel Desk | | 325.00 |
| Filing Cabinet | | 120.00 |
| Swivel Chair | | 72.00 |
| Swivel Chair | | 72.00 |
| Typewriter | | 425.00 |
| | | $1 339.00 |

Rate of Depreciation – 20 per cent, reducing balance.
Accumulated Depreciation
    after 3 years is                  $653.42

*Trucks*

| Dodge Van | $ 4 600.00 |
|---|---|
| Ford ½ Ton | 2 900.00 |
| G.M.C. Stake | 3 900.00 |
| | $11 400.00 |

Rate of Depreciation – 30 per cent, reducing balance.
Accumulated Depreciation
    after 3 years is                  $7 489.80

16. The business uses a synoptic journal and a two-column general journal in its accounting system. The next page number for the synoptic journal is 62, and for the general journal, 31. (**Note:** This exercise may be done using any system of journals preferred. If some other system is used, the student is to select his own page numbers.)

17. The bank reconciliation statement as at December 31, 19–4, is as follows:

*Universal Lumber*
*Bank Reconciliation Statement*
*December 31, 19–4*

| | | | |
|---|---|---|---|
| Balance per bank statement | | | $4 228.91 |
| Add outstanding deposit | | | 121.50 |
| | | | $4 350.41 |
| Deduct outstanding cheques | | | |
| | 635 | $ 47.50 | |
| | 639 | 156.20 | |
| | 640 | 300.00 | 503.70 |
| Balance per general ledger | | | $3 846.71 |

**Set up the three ledgers.**
**Set up the two journals.**
**Record the accounting entries for the transactions in the journals. You are told directly about most of the transactions but some you must remember to originate yourself, from the notes made according to the introductory information. Post daily to the subsidiary ledgers.**

*Transactions*
January
2 *Sales Invoice*
    –No. 1462, to Ontario Carpentry Co., $625 plus sales tax.

3 *Sales Invoice*
    –No. 1463, to Evergreen Gardens, $575 plus sales tax.

6 *Cash Receipt*
   –From J. Martin, $10.42, on account.
   *Purchase Invoice*
   –From Industrial Oil Co. Ltd., $54, for gas
   and oil used in the trucks; N,30.

7 *Purchase Invoice*
   –From Lumber Wholesalers, $1 214.62,
   for lumber; N,60.

8 *Cheque Copies*
   –No. 641, to Lumber Wholesalers, $2 000,
   on account.
   –No. 642, to Plywood Suppliers, $1 500,
   on account.

9 *Cash Receipt*
   –From Bayvue Village Estates, $2 365.53,
   on account.

10 *Cash Receipt*
   –From Ontario Carpentry Co., $673.75,
   on account.

14 *Purchase Invoice*
   –From National Pacific Railway, $37.14,
   freight on lumber; N,30.

15 *Cash Receipt*
   –From cash sales; $3 412.53; for the amount
   of sales plus the sales tax.

17 *Cheque Copy*
   –No. 648, to petty cash; $?; to replenish the
   petty cash fund for the following petty cash
   vouchers: Office Expense, $14.12; Truck
   Expense, $62.40; Building Maintenance,
   $19.25.

20 *Sales Invoice*
   –No. 1464, to Bayvue Village Estates,
   $1 250 plus sales tax.

22 *Cash Receipt*
   –From Carlton Home Builders, $1 672.16,
   on account.

23 *Cheque Copy*
   –No. 649, to Wood Moulding Co.,
   $1 468.68, on account.

24 *Cheque Copy*
   –No. 650, to Local Telephone Co., $37.50,
   telephone bill for the month.

27 *Cash Receipt*
   –From Evergreen Gardens, $2 481.38,
   on account.

28 *Sales Invoice*
   –No. 1465, to Carlton Home Builders,
   $982.49 plus sales tax.
   *Cash Receipt*
   –From Superior Construction Co.,
   $2 542.19, on account.

29 *Cheque Copy*
   –No. 652, to Yorktown Hydro, $47.89,
   hydro bill for the month.

30 *Sales Invoices*
   –No. 1466, to Ontario Carpentry Co.,
   $3 687.98 plus sales tax.
   –No. 1467, to Evergreen Gardens,
   $4 846.73 plus sales tax.

31 *Sales Invoice*
   –No. 1468, to Parker Bros., $400.75 plus
   sales tax.
   *Purchase Invoice*
   –From Lumber Wholesalers, $6 234.65,
   for lumber received; freight prepaid; N,60.
   *Cash Receipt*
   –From cash sales, $3 245.44, for the amount
   of sales plus sales tax.
   *Cheque Copies*
   –No. 653, to Lumber Wholesalers, $4 000,
   on account.
   –No. 654, to Municipality of Yorktown,
   $23.50, for monthly instalment of property
   taxes.

**Balance the journals and post to the general ledger.**
**Balance the general ledger and the subsidiary ledgers as at January 31, 19–5.**
**Prepare the bank reconciliation statement as at January 31, 19–5. The bank**
**statement for January is shown on page 382.**

## CANADIAN CENTURY BANK

In account with:

### UNIVERSAL LUMBER COMPANY

| Debits | Credits | Date | Balance |
|---|---|---|---|
| | Balance Forward | Dec. 31 | 5 555.33 |
| | 121.50 | Jan.  2 | 5 676.83 |
| 47.50  (635) | | 3 | 5 629.33 |
| | 10.42 | 6 | 5 639.75 |
| 156.20  (639) | | 8 | 5 483.55 |
| | 2 365.53 | 9 | 7 849.08 |
| 300.00  (640) | | | |
| 2 296.54  (643) | 673.75 | 10 | 5 926.29 |
| | 3 412.53 | 15 | 9 338.82 |
| 1 500.00  (642) | | | |
| 725.00  (644) | | | |
| 2 000.00  (641) | | 16 | 5 113.82 |
| 95.77  (648) | | 17 | 5 018.05 |
| 1 553.88  (646) | | 20 | 3 464.17 |
| 25.00  (645) | | 21 | 3 439.17 |
| 1 502.17  (647) | 1  672.16 | 22 | 3 609.16 |
| 2 296.54  (651) | | 24 | 1 312.62 |
| 1 468.68  (649) | 2 481.38 | 27 | 2 325.32 |
| | 2 542.19 | 28 | 4 867.51 |
| 37.50  (650) | | 29 | 4 830.01 |
| 25.40  (D.M. for Bank Interest) | | 31 | 4 804.61 |

Using the following information, prepare the work sheet and financial statements, and record the adjusting, closing, and reversing entries as required at the end of the accounting period.

a. The Allowance for Bad Debts at January 31 is to allow for B. Starr's account of $83.20 and Keele Estates' account of $120.43.

b. The lumber inventory at January 31 is valued at $23 773.31.

c. The office supplies on hand at January 31 are valued at $622.91.

d. The accrued payroll is to be estimated on the basis of the gross salaries for the period ending February 7 being the same as for the period ending January 24.

e. There are no unprocessed accounts payable vouchers pertaining to January.

Prepare a post-closing trial balance.

Journalize the following transactions for February. Post daily to the subsidiary ledgers.

## Transactions

February

4 *Non-routine Entry*

–The G.M.C. truck was in a serious collision and damaged beyond repair. The insurance company, Insurance Underwriters, agreed that Universal Lumber Company could keep the wreck (from which spare parts could be obtained) and that a cheque for $1 205 in full settlement would be forthcoming in the near future.

5 *Cash Receipt*

–From Keele Estates, $120.43, on account.

*Cheque Copies*

–No. 657, to National Pacific Railway Co., $37.14, on account.

–No. 658, to Industrial Oil Co. Ltd., $54, on account.

6 *Cheque Copies*

–No. 659, to Lincoln Motors Limited, $165, repairs to Mr. Wiseman's personal car.

–No. 660, to Large and Small Ltd., $28.91, C.O.D. order of carbon paper.

*Cash Receipt*

–From Evergreen Gardens, $5 224.77, on account.

7 **Note:** Mr. Barney terminated his employment with the company effective at 5 p.m. A Mr. J. Lee was hired to replace him; work to commence on Monday morning February 10. Mr. Lee's salary was set at $180 per week and his TD-1 form showed a net claim code of 1. Mr. Lee made no other commitments.

*Cash Receipt*

–From Mr. Charles Carlton, owner of Carlton Home Builders, $1 100.29; for balance of account plus $38.18 cash sale of lumber plus sales tax, less cash discounts.

10 *Cheque Copies*

–No. 662, to John Carmichael, $43.20, painting of buildings.

–No. 663, to Lumber Wholesalers, $5 000, on account.

11 *Sales Invoices*

–No. 1469, to Evergreen Gardens, $1 272.68, plus sales tax.

–No. 1470, to Carlton Home Builders, $3 542.01, plus sales tax.

–No. 1471, to Bayvue Village Estates, $1 672.97, plus sales tax.

12 *Bank Debit Memorandum*

–$120.43, cheque from Keele Estates, deposited on February 5, was returned – "Not Sufficient Funds".

*Purchase Invoice*

–From Wood Moulding Co., $3 742.62, for lumber; N,30.

13 *Purchase Invoice*

–From National Pacific Railway Co., $36.24, for freight charges on lumber; N,30.

*Cash Receipt*

–From Bayvue Village Estates, $1 375, on account.

14 *Cash Receipt*

–From cash sales, $4 731.98, for the amount of sales plus the sales tax.

17 *Cheque Copies*

–No. 668, to Peter Douglas and Son, $150, cash payment for legal services.

–No. 669, to Plywood Suppliers, $2 820.60, on account.

*Cash Receipt*
–From James Wiseman, the owner, $3 000, to increase his equity in the business.

18 *Cheque Copy*
–No. 670, to Tom's Local Garage, $65.42, cash payment of invoice for truck repairs.

19 *Sales Invoice*
–No. 1472, to Ontario Carpentry Co., $2 288.60 plus sales tax.

21 *Cash Receipt*
–From Ontario Carpentry Co., $2 000, on account.
–From cash sales, $2 591.82, for the amount of sales plus the sales tax.

24 *Cheque Copy*
–No. 672, to petty cash fund, $?; to reimburse the petty cash fund for the following petty cash vouchers: Office Expense, $2.10; Truck Expense, $30.72; Office Supplies, $42.60; Miscellaneous Expense, $21.06.

25 *Purchase Invoice*
–From Plywood Suppliers, $2 381.11, for lumber; N,60.

26 *Purchase Invoice*
–From Industrial Oil Co. Ltd., $58.70, for gas and oil used in the trucks; N,30.

*Purchase Invoice*
–From National Pacific Railway Co., $27.01, for freight on lumber; N,30.

27 *Cheque Copies*
–No. 673, to Yorktown Hydro, $59.10, cash payment of monthly hydro bill.
–No. 674, to Municipality of Yorktown, $23.50, for monthly instalment on property tax.
–No. 675, to Local Telephone Co., $37.50, telephone bill for the month.

28 *Cheque Copy*
–No. 676, to Insurance Underwriters, $2 113.20, annual insurance premium.

28 *Cash Receipt*
–From cash sales, $5 440.82, for the amount of sales plus the sales tax.

*Sales Invoices*
–No. 1473, to Ontario Carpentry, $2 565.53, plus sales tax.
–No. 1474, to Parker Bros., $1 320, plus sales tax.
–No. 1475, to Bayvue Village Estates, $680.70, plus sales tax.

*Cash Receipt*
–From Parker Bros., $440.83, on account.

Balance the journals and post to the general ledger.
Balance the general ledger and the subsidiary ledgers as of February 28, 19–5.

Prepare the bank reconciliation statement as at February 28, 19–5. The bank statement for February is shown on the next page.

## CANADIAN CENTURY BANK

In account with:

## UNIVERSAL LUMBER COMPANY

| Debits | Credits | Date | Balance |
|---|---|---|---|
| | Balance Forward | Jan. 31 | 4 804.61 |
| 47.89 (652) | 3 245.44 | | |
| 23.50 (654) | | Feb. 3 | 7 978.66 |
| 4 000.00 (653) | | | |
| 725.00 (655) | | 4 | 3 253.66 |
| 572.00 (656) | 120.43 | | |
| 37.14 (657) | 5 224.77 | 6 | 7 989.72 |
| 2 296.54 (661) | 1 100.29 | 7 | 6 793.47 |
| 54.00 (658) | | 10 | 6 739.47 |
| 120.43 (D.M. for N.S.F. cheque) | | 11 | 6 619.04 |
| 43.20 (662) | | | |
| 28.91 (660) | | 12 | 6 546.93 |
| | 1 375.00 | 13 | 7 921.93 |
| 165.00 (659) | 4 731.98 | 14 | 12 488.91 |
| 5 000.00 (663) | | 15 | 7 488.91 |
| 25.00 (664) | 3 000.00 | 17 | 10 463.91 |
| 725.00 (665) | | 18 | 9 738.91 |
| 1 842.07 (666) | | | |
| 1 035.96 (667) | | 20 | 6 860.88 |
| 2 261.47 (671) | 4 591.82 | 21 | 9 191.23 |
| 96.48 (672) | | 24 | 9 094.75 |
| 2 820.60 (669) | | | |
| 65.42 (670) | | 25 | 6 208.73 |
| 150.00 (668) | | 27 | 6 058.73 |
| 23.40 (D.M. for Bank Interest) | | 28 | 6 035.33 |

Using the information shown below, prepare the work sheet and financial statements, and record the adjusting, closing, and reversing entries as required at the end of the accounting period.

a. An analysis of the accounts receivable ledger indicated that B. Starr's account and Keele Estates' account are doubtful.
b. The lumber inventory at February 28 is valued at $20 667.93.
c. The office supplies on hand at February 28 were valued at $658.09.
d. For accrued payroll, estimate on the basis of the gross payroll for the period ending March 7 being the same as for the period ending February 21.
e. The following purchase invoice received in March pertained to goods received in February:

Plywood Suppliers' invoice of March 5, $170.50, for lumber.

**Prepare a post-closing trial balance.**

# 16 Partnerships

Your study so far has dealt with only one type of business organization, the single proprietorship. The text has emphasized basic accounting concepts and skills in as simple a setting as possible. The single proprietorship, however, is not the only type of business organization. Partnerships and corporations are other types of business organizations which are very common in the business world. In respect to volume of business, corporations are the most significant by far.

## Partnership

A **partnership** exists where two or more persons (called partners) join together in a business and share in its profits or losses. A company's name (also known as the 'firm' name) indicates if it is a partnership; for example: H. Gregg & Sons; Peters and Associates; Black and Morris.

Each province in Canada has its own Partnership Act to govern the operations of partnerships within its provincial boundaries. There is little difference in the partnership acts of the various provinces.

## Partnership Accounts

The main difference in accounting for a partnership, as compared to that for a single proprietorship, is in respect to the Capital and Drawings accounts. As you know, a single proprietorship is owned by one person for whom there is a single Capital account and a single Drawings account. A partnership, which is owned by two or more persons, requires a Capital account and a Drawings account for each of the partners. Partnerships having a number of partners will require a number of Capital and Drawings accounts.

A simple, graphic comparison of the books of a single proprietorship and those of a partnership (with three partners) is shown below. Observe that the principal difference between the two forms of business organization is reflected in the Capital and Drawings accounts.

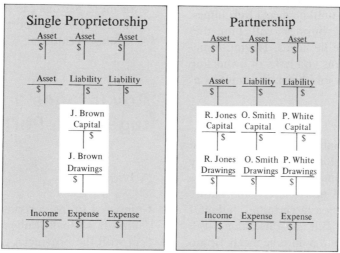

*Comparison of the accounts for a single proprietorship and for a partnership.*

387

In the day-to-day accounting for a partnership there is little that is new. Most transactions are handled in the usual manner.

The most distinguishing aspect of partnership accounting is in regard to the capital accounts. This is where new accounting theory is encountered. These accounts represent each partner's individual stake in the business and must be maintained accurately, and in accordance with the wishes of the partners as stated in a partnership contract agreed to by all of the partners. This aspect of partnership accounting is an end-of-accounting-period activity, at which time the partnership net income or net loss is calculated and then distributed to the partners.

# Reason for Partnerships

Partnership is a common form of business organization. The main reason for choosing the partnership, as opposed to some other form of business organization, is usually convenience. Particular circumstances vary, however. To help you understand the circumstances under which partnerships come into being, consider the simple case histories described below.

## Case 1.
For some time Jack Brian has wanted his own business but has lacked the courage to go on his own. He has been afraid of the financial risk and of the heavy responsibility that he would have to bear alone. It is not until he meets Bob James, who agrees to go into business with him, that Jack finds the courage he needs. Having someone to share the burdens and risks of ownership has allowed Jack to view things in a more optimistic light.

## Case 2.
For several years Bill Salino has been the general manager of a large building firm. Bill knows the business thoroughly and is anxious to go into business for himself. Unfortunately, the nature of the business requires a large initial outlay of funds – far more than Bill can raise alone. Bill is frustrated in his ambition until he meets Bruno

Moro who has the necessary funds and who is looking for a business opportunity in which to invest. The two men agree to enter business as partners. By combining their individual resources the two men are able to achieve a goal that neither could reach independently.

## Case 3.
J. R. Hall has been in business for a number of years and has built up a profitable and expanding business. Mr. Hall sees a good future in the business for his son whom he persuades to join him in the partnership of J. R. Hall and Son. For both father and son the partnership is a convenient way of sharing ownership and keeping the business in the family.

Generally, the formation of a partnership is not as simple a matter as suggested by the above case histories. The case histories serve their purpose, however, by demonstrating that:
a. partnership provides the means whereby two or more persons can pool their financial resources in order to put together funds that could not be raised by any of them separately;
b. partnership provides the means whereby two or more persons may bring different resources, e.g. money, expertise, personal connections, talent or experience, together in a business venture;
c. partnership provides a simple, convenient way for members of a family to co-operate in the operation and continuance of a family business;
d. partnership provides the means whereby two or more persons can provide each other with the emotional support needed to undertake a business venture.

# Advantages and Disadvantages of a Partnership

## Advantages

Compared to the corporation it is simple to organize. It is usually only necessary to register the firm with the provincial government and to pay a nominal fee in accordance with regulations.

It allows for the bringing together of greater financial resources and more varied resources than does the single proprietorship.

It is not subject to double taxation as is the corporate form of business enterprise. A corporation is itself subject to annual income tax. In addition, the shareholders of the corporation are required to pay personal income tax on any dividends that they receive from the corporation.

## Disadvantages

It has limited life. The death, insolvency, or incapacity of any of the partners usually ends the partnership automatically by law. The remaining partners must arrange to pay out the departed partner's equity and to register a new partnership in order to carry on the business.

There is unlimited liability. Every partner is jointly liable for any or all of the debts of the partnership. This means that an unsatisfied creditor may sue any one partner for total payment of a partnership's debt. If the creditor wins his law suit, it is the sued partner who must pay the creditor, even to the extent that he has to sell his personal property and suffer personal hardship. The sued partner in turn has the lawful right to recover from the other partners, but it is usually a time-consuming, costly and inconvenient process. In extreme circumstances the other partners may not be able to pay, in which case the sued partner is the victim of what is essentially unfair treatment.

There is mutual agency. This means that all of the partners are bound by the acts of any one of them, provided that the acts are within the normal scope of the firm's activities. If one of the partners happens to make a poor business decision, the others cannot disclaim responsibility except in special circumstances.

# Partnership Agreement

The formation of a partnership is not a simple matter. As you have seen, partnerships are formed for various reasons, resulting in a variety of ownership situations.

It would be unwise for anyone to enter into a partnership without first obtaining legal advice. A lawyer will attend to the registration of the firm, provide professional opinion to safeguard the interests of the individual partners, and prepare the **partnership agreement**. The partnership agreement is a legal contract which sets forth the specific terms and conditions of the partnership. By having such an agreement, dissatisfaction and inharmonious relationships are avoided from the very beginning, and the partnership has a better chance for success and survival.

Included in a partnership agreement are the following details:
— the firm name and address
— the partners' names and addresses
— the date of formation of the partnership
— the nature of the partnership business
— the duties of the individual partners and the amount of time that they are expected to devote to the business
— the amount of capital to be contributed by each of the partners
— the salaries (if any) to be paid to each of the partners
— the rate of interest (if any) to be paid on each of the partners' capital balances
— the ratio of sharing income and loss
— the procedure to be followed in the case of unforeseen termination of the partnership, by the death or bankruptcy of a partner, etc.

# Partnership Acts

The Partnership Acts of the various provinces serve as general protective measures for persons entered into partnerships. The terms of these acts, however, are not equitable in all circumstances. In particular, the condition that 'in the absence of a partnership agreement, profits and losses are to be divided equally' may be unfair in many instances. The possibility of being bound by the terms of a provincial partnership act is strong reason for ensuring that there is an effective partnership agreement.

# Accounting for Simple Partnership Formations

There is no simple set of rules to be followed in establishing the accounts of a partnership. Circumstances vary greatly and each case must be considered separately. This is one of the reasons why professional opinion should be obtained.

To introduce you to accounting for partnerships, and to add to your understanding of partnerships in general, some additional partnership situations are described below. Bear in mind that these are simplified case studies and are not to be thought of as typical. Their purpose is to show the accounting treatment separate from the legal complexities.

## Case 1. Purchase of a part interest from the owner of an existing business

Henry Harris is the owner of a well-established and profitable business. He has an equity in the business of $30 000. Recent expansion has placed a heavy burden on Mr. Harris; he feels the need of assistance at a senior level of responsibility. Jack Ray, a bright young engineer, has agreed to go into business with Mr. Harris and to provide the much needed assistance. The two men form a partnership with the following terms and conditions:
1. Jack Ray is to pay $15 000 to Henry Harris personally for a one-half interest in the business.
2. Net income or net loss of the partnership is to be shared equally.
3. Jack Ray is to gradually assume an equal share of the management responsibility.

After the partnership arrangements are formally attended to and the $15 000 is paid to Mr. Harris, an accounting entry is made in the books of the existing business to establish the partnership. The entry is:

Henry Harris, Capital   15 000
    Jack Ray, Capital           15 000

With the posting of this entry, the two partners have equal balances in their Capital accounts, indicating that they have an equal share in the net assets of the business.

This is an example of a case in which:
  (i)  there is already an existing business;
 (ii)  no new capital is introduced into the business;
(iii)  any money which changes hands between the partners does so privately, outside of the business.

## Case 2. Formation of a new business by investment of cash

Frank Henderson and Charles Wright have been long-time senior employees of Paper Products Company. The two men are dismissed from their positions when the company is taken over by a large corporation. Both men have worked in the paper products business since leaving high school and have no other skills or experience except in this particular line of work.

For several reasons the two men decide that it is their best course of action to establish a paper products business of their own. They agree to form a partnership in which both are equal partners. To establish the business, $50 000 capital is needed to obtain the necessary furniture and equipment. By mortgaging their homes and selling some investments the two men each raise $25 000 in cash. After obtaining the necessary legal and accounting advice, and depositing the $50 000 cash in a business bank account, the partnership of Henderson, Wright Paper Products is established. The first accounting entry in the new set of company books is the following:

Bank                     50 000
   Frank Henderson, Capital      25 000
   Charles Wright, Capital       25 000

This is an example of a situation in which:
  (i)  there is no existing business;
 (ii)  an entirely new business is formed;
(iii)  new capital in the form of cash is introduced into the business;
(iv)  no money changes hands privately.

## Case 3. Introduction into a business of a partner who invests cash and other assets

T. Wolfe has a small prosperous business which is growing rapidly. His equity is $75 000. The business has progressed to the stage where additional facilities and equipment are necessary, but Mr. Wolfe does not have the capital with which to finance the expansion. R. Hulf has agreed to enter into partnership with Mr. Wolfe on the condition that he (Hulf) contribute $10 000 cash and a building valued at $40 000 into the business. It is part of the agreement that the partners' Capital accounts be kept in a 60:40 ratio and that Wolfe and Hulf share net income or net loss in the ratio of 60:40, respectively. The accounting entry to record the incoming partner's investment is recorded in the existing set of books as follows:

| Bank | 10 000 | |
| Building | 40 000 | |
| R. Hulf, Capital | | 50 000 |

The business now has the funds required for expansion. The two partners now have Capital accounts in accordance with the agreement.

This is an example of a situation in which:
- (i) there is already an existing business;
- (ii) new capital in the form of cash and a building is introduced into the business;
- (iii) no money changes hands privately.

## Case 4. Two existing businesses join together

F. Marston and J. Lawson each own a small drugstore. Their stores are located within a few blocks of each other. Their small business operations are threatened by the coming of a large shopping center which will include a large drugstore as one of its units. It is expected that the new center will seriously affect the small nearby stores.

Rather than risk financial failure the two men decide to join together to lease and operate the new drugstore in the shopping center. In preparation for the move the two men arrange to have their business assets evaluated by an independent appraiser.

The move to the new store is to take place on July 1, 19—. On that day the new business is to assume the following assets and accounts payable of the former businesses at the appraised values:

| | Marston | Lawson |
|---|---|---|
| Accounts Receivable | $ 5 000 | $ 6 000 |
| Merchandise Inventory | 25 000 | 19 000 |
| Supplies | 500 | 350 |
| Store and Office Equipment | 7 500 | 8 200 |
| Delivery Equipment | 4 000 | 4 800 |
| Total Assets | $42 000 | $38 350 |
| Accounts Payable | $12 500 | $10 000 |
| Owner's Equity | $29 500 | $28 350 |

It is further agreed between the partners that: 1) each of them is free to sell or dispose of any other business property as he sees fit; 2) Lawson must bring his equity up to the value of Marston's by contributing cash to the partnership; this amounts to $1 150.

The accounting entries to set up the partnership in a new set of books are as follows:

| July 1 | Accounts Receivable | 5 000 | |
| | Merchandise Inventory | 25 000 | |
| | Supplies | 500 | |
| | Store and Office Equipment | 7 500 | |
| | Delivery Equipment | 4 000 | |
| | Accounts Payable | | 12 500 |
| | F. Marston, Capital | | 29 500 |
| | To record the appraised assets and accounts payable of F. Marston. | | |

| July 1 | Bank | 1 150 | |
| | Accounts Receivable | 6 000 | |
| | Merchandise Inventory | 19 000 | |
| | Supplies | 350 | |
| | Store and Office Equipment | 8 200 | |
| | Delivery Equipment | 4 800 | |
| | Accounts Payable | | 10 000 |
| | J. Lawson, Capital | | 29 500 |
| | To record the appraised assets and | | |
| | accounts payable and cash | | |
| | contribution of J. Lawson. | | |

The new firm is now ready to operate. The two partners have equal investments as agreed upon.

This is an example of a situation in which:

(i) there are two existing businesses which join together;

(ii) a new business is formed which takes over most of the assets and the accounts payable of the individual proprietorships;

(iii) no money changes hands privately between the partners.

The previous case studies describe simple partnership formations. From studying only these simple cases you may falsely conclude that all partnership formations are simple. This is not the case. The reality is that there are usually some complexities in all partnership formations, and that professional advice is almost always necessary. The following case study illustrates a more complex but common situation.

## Case 5.

John Brown has built a thriving taxi business in a small suburban location. He is the sole owner of the only commercial licence to operate a taxi business in his area. His total investment in the business is $40 000. This includes four cars, radio and office equipment, and a small building. The profitability of the business is indicated by the net income figures of the latest three years – $45 000, $48 000, and $50 000 respectively. Profits are expected to continue at this level or to improve.

Because Mr. Brown is approaching retirement age, he is endeavoring to sell a one-half interest in the business in order to obtain cash for his personal use and to reduce his direct involvement in the business.

G. Smith has discussed the possibility of purchasing an interest in the business, but the two men have not come close to arriving at a price.

Smith argues that since the book value is $40 000, a fair price for a one-half interest would be half of that, or $20 000. Brown counterargues that since the business is expected to earn approximately $50 000 annually and that as an equal partner Smith's share would be $25 000 annually, Smith should expect to pay much more than the proposed $20 000. He argues further that the price of a business depends on its earning power and not on its book value, and that in the case of his business a fair market value would be in the range of $200 000.

No solution is given for the above case. The accounting required will depend on the agreement reached between the parties. Negotiating a fair price takes much hard bargaining, and in many instances outside professional advice as well.

The above case indicates that there are times when a business *is* worth more than its book value. This happens when a business enjoys above average profitability. Factors contributing to this may be exceptional management, a superior location, or something else, but whatever the reason, it results in above average profits.

The sale of a business or the introduction of new partners may occur in a number of different ways, and can involve **bonus** payments, or payments for **goodwill** (the value of a business in excess of its book value). No attempt is made here to elaborate on these numerous variations because it is an objective of the text not to go beyond basic accounting concepts. The topic is mentioned only to indicate that complexities do arise in accounting for partnerships.

# Apportioning Net Income or Net Loss to the Partners

In a one-owner business the handling of net income, net loss, and drawings in the accounts is a straightforward matter. In a partnership it is not. An important new consideration exists – that of *correctly recording the changes in equity in the individual partners' Equity accounts.* This is a matter of considerable importance because:

1. it may be agreed that interest be paid to the partners based on the balance in their Capital accounts;
2. in the event of a partnership termination, the net assets of the partnership are distributed to the partners in the ratio of their Capital account balances.*

During the fiscal period there is usually no problem in properly recording changes in the partners' Capital and Drawings accounts. It is at the end of the fiscal period of a partnership that new accounting theory is employed – to apportion the net income or the net loss to the partners in accordance with the conditions laid down in the partnership agreement.

## Factors Affecting Apportionment of Net Income or Net Loss

Three factors affect the calculation for apportioning the net income or net loss to the partners. These are **salaries**, **interest**, and **income- or loss-sharing ratio**.

The procedure for handling remuneration to partners is strongly influenced by legality. The

*The one exception to this rule is an advanced topic and is not discussed in this text.

law considers that a partner participates in a partnership for a share in the earnings of the business – not for a salary or for interest on his investment. Therefore, when salaries or interest are part of the scheme for apportioning net income, they are mathematical factors only. They are used to make the calculation of the apportionment at the end of the fiscal period, but no recognition of them is required in the accounts.

Any payments by way of remuneration to partners are properly charged to partners' Drawings accounts. (The size of the amounts drawn may be reckoned by anticipating what the respective shares of net income will be.)

The three factors that affect the *calculation* of the apportionment of net income or net loss to the partners can now be discussed.

## 1. Salaries (if any) allowed to partners

A partner's share of net income (or net loss) often includes an amount to compensate him for active participation in the management of the business. For example, if one partner participates full time in the operation of the business and another participates not at all, then it is only right that the one partner's share of net income includes something for his time and effort, whereas the other's does not. This is generally regarded as being salary.

Salaries allowed to partners are an apportionment out of net income before it is divided in the income-sharing ratio.

## 2. Interest (if any) allowed on invested capital

A partner's share of net income (or net loss) may include an amount to compensate him for the size of his investment in the business. For example, if one partner's investment in the business is $100 000 and another's is $20 000, an agreement to pay interest at 8 per cent would reward the partners with $8 000 and $1 600, respectively, for the use of their capital.

Like salaries, interest is an allocation out of net income before applying the income-sharing ratio.

### 3. Income- (or Loss-) sharing ratio

Salaries and interest are prior charges against the net income or net loss when calculating the apportionment. After providing for these, the balance of net income or net loss is divided in the income-sharing ratio.

The establishment of the income-sharing ratio is something to be approached carefully before any partnership agreement is finalized. Many factors need to be considered, such as:

a. The special skills and abilities that the partners bring to the firm;
b. The special abilities of the partners to bring new business to the firm through their personal contacts and reputation in the community;
c. If there is no provision for salaries, the time spent in the business by the partners;
d. If there is no provision for interest, the amount of capital invested by the partners. In a business that requires mostly capital, income is often divided in the ratio of the Capital account balances.

It should be kept in mind that in the absence of a partnership agreement, income and loss are divided equally in accordance with government regulation. Such an equal division does not take into consideration any special contributions of individual partners and may not be equitable in all circumstances.

# Statement of Distribution of Net Income

Once the net income or net loss of the business is determined in the customary manner, the distribution of net income calculation may be made. The following examples show the way in which the calculations are made:

### Case 1.

Morris and Graves are partners. Their Capital accounts are $50 000 and $20 000 respectively. Their partnership agreement stipulates that:
  (i) Graves is allowed a salary of $11 000, Morris none;
  (ii) interest is allowed on the balance in the Capital accounts at the rate of 10 per cent;
  (iii) after allowing for salaries and interest, the balance of net income is divided equally.
At December 31, 19—, the end of their fiscal year, the partnership net income was $65 312.08.

The **statement of distribution of net income** may be prepared as shown below. You should study the calculations thoroughly.

### Case 2.

On June 30, 19—, the partnership of Watts, Tate, and Barlow completes a fiscal year with a

---

**MORRIS AND GRAVES**
**STATEMENT OF DISTRIBUTION OF NET INCOME**
**YEAR ENDED DECEMBER 31, 19—**

| | Morris's Share | Graves's Share | Total |
|---|---|---|---|
| Net Income available for distribution | | | $65 312.08 |
| Salary allowed to Graves | | $11 000.00 | $11 000.00 |
| Interest at 10 per cent allowed on Capital account balances | $ 5 000.00 | 2 000.00 | 7 000.00 |
|    Morris: 10% of $50 000 = $5 000 | | | |
|    Graves: 10% of $20 000 = $2 000 | | | |
| Balance of net income divided equally | 23 656.04 | 23 656.04 | 47 312.08 |
| Totals | $28 656.04 | $36 656.04 | $65 312.08 |

net income figure of $20 000. The partnership agreement specifies that net income or net loss is to be allocated to the partners according to the following terms:

1. Salaries allowed:  Watts,  $9 000
   Tate,  $4 500
   Barlow,  nil
2. Interest allowed on Capital account balances at 8 per cent. (The partners' Capital account balances were: Watts, $40 000; Tate, $50 000; Barlow, $100 000.)
3. The remaining net income or net loss to be divided as follows: Watts, 25%; Tate, 25%; Barlow, 50%.

For the partnership of Watts, Tate, and Barlow the statement of distribution of net income may appear as shown below. Note that in this particular case the total of the salaries and interest is greater than the net income figure and that this requires special handling on the statement.

### WATTS, TATE, AND BARLOW
### STATEMENT OF DISTRIBUTION OF NET INCOME
### YEAR ENDED JUNE 30, 19—

| | Watts's Share | Tate's Share | Barlow's Share | Total |
|---|---|---|---|---|
| Net Income available for distribution | | | | $20 000 |
| Salaries allowed to partners | $ 9 000 | $4 500 | — | $13 500 |
| Interest allowed on Capital accounts at 8 per cent | 3 200 | 4 000 | 8 000 | 15 200 |
| Watts:   8% of $ 40 000 = $3 200 | | | | |
| Tate:    8% of $ 50 000 = $4 000 | | | | |
| Barlow: 8% of $100 000 = $8 000 | | | | |
| Allocation of balance of net income in income- and loss-sharing ratio of 1:1:2 | –2 175 | –2 175 | –4 350 | –8 700 |
| Totals | $10 025 | $6 325 | $3 650 | $20 000 |

# Financial Statements of a Partnership

Financial statements for a partnership include more than the balance sheet and the income statement. In addition, a partnership requires a statement of distribution of net income, which you have just studied, as well as a **statement of partners' capital**, which will be explained shortly.

The financial statements of a partnership are usually constituted as follows:

Statement No. 1   The Balance Sheet
Statement No. 2   The Income Statement
Statement No. 3   Statement of Partners' Capital
Statement No. 4   Statement of Distribution of Net Income

In preparing financial statements for a partnership be mindful of the fact that information found on statement 4 is needed in order to complete statement 3, and that information found on statement 3 is needed in order to complete statement 1. Therefore, it is necessary to complete statement 4 before statement 3 and to complete statement 3 before statement 1. Statement 2 may be prepared at any time because the other statements have no bearing on it.

The study of the preparation of the four statements begins below. It is based on the simplified work sheet for Jones, Ross, and Warner.

| ACCOUNTS | TRIAL BALANCE DR. | TRIAL BALANCE CR. | ADJUSTMENTS DR. | ADJUSTMENTS CR. | INCOME STATEMENT DR. | INCOME STATEMENT CR. | BALANCE SHEET DR. | BALANCE SHEET CR. |
|---|---|---|---|---|---|---|---|---|
| Petty Cash | 100 — | | | | | | 100 — | |
| Bank | 3700 — | | | | | | 3700 — | |
| Accounts Receivable | 37461 — | | | | | | 37461 — | |
| Allowance for Doubtful Accounts | | 1956 — | | | 102 — | | | 2058 — |
| Supplies | 1500 — | | | | 625 — | | 875 — | |
| Prepaid Insurance | 900 — | | | | 484 — | | 416 — | |
| Investment in Property | 20000 — | | | | | | 20000 — | |
| Furniture and Equipment | 7000 — | | | | | | 7000 — | |
| Accum. Deprec. Furn. & Equip. | | 3490 — | | | 702 — | | | 4192 — |
| Automobiles | 12000 — | | | | | | 12000 — | |
| Accum. Deprec. Automobiles | | 4875 — | | | 2137 50 | | | 7012 50 |
| Accounts Payable | | 5962 — | | ① 175 — | | | | 6137 — |
| M. Jones, Capital | | 19452 12 | | | | | | 19452 12 |
| M. Jones, Drawings | 18500 — | | | | | | 18500 — | |
| G. Ross, Capital | | 15137 09 | | | | | | 15137 09 |
| G. Ross, Drawings | 14000 — | | | | | | 14000 — | |
| A. Warner, Capital | | 25410 79 | | | | | | 25410 79 |
| A. Warner, Drawings | 22396 — | | | | | | 22396 — | |
| Sales | | 82940 — | | | | 82940 — | | |
| Advertising | 3000 — | | | | 3000 — | | | |
| Automotive Expense | 4600 — | | | | 4600 — | | | |
| General Expense | 350 — | | ① 175 — | | 525 — | | | |
| Light, Heat & Water | 600 — | | | | 600 — | | | |
| Rent | 2400 — | | | | 2400 — | | | |
| Telephone | 1290 — | | | | 1290 — | | | |
| Wages | 9426 — | | | | 9536 — | | | 110 — |
| | 159223 — | 159223 — | 175 — | 175 — | 26001 50 | 82940 — | 136448 — | 79509 50 |
| Net Income | | | | | 56938 50 | | | 56938 50 |
| | | | | | 82940 — | 82940 — | 136448 — | 136448 — |

Work sheet of Jones, Ross, and Warner (which uses the shortcut method of adjustments).

Statement 4

JONES, ROSS, AND WARNER
STATEMENT OF DISTRIBUTION OF NET INCOME
YEAR ENDED DECEMBER 31, 19—

Net Income available for distribution      $56 938.50

| | M. Jones | G. Ross | A. Warner | Total |
|---|---|---|---|---|
| Salaries allowed to partners | | $ 5 000.00 | $ 5 000.00 | $10 000.00 |
| Interest on Capital Accounts | $ 1 945.21 | 1 513.71 | 2 541.08 | 6 000.00 |
|     M. Jones    $19 452.12 at 10% | | | | |
|     G. Ross     $15 137.09 at 10% | | | | |
|     A. Warner   $25 410.79 at 10% | | | | |
| Balance of net income divided in | | | | |
|     ratio of 2:1:2 | 16 375.40 | 8 187.70 | 16 375.40 | 40 938.50 |
| Total distribution to partners | $18 320.61 | $14 701.41 | $23 916.48 | $56 938.50 |

## Statement of Distribution of Net Income (Statement 4)

The net income figure of $56 938.50 to be apportioned to the partners is picked up from the work sheet. Additional information necessary to make the apportionment is found in the partnership agreement as follows:

1. G. Ross and A. Warner are to receive annual salaries of $5 000 each;
2. Interest is allowed on partners' capital at the rate of 10 per cent;
3. After allowing for salaries and interest, the balance of net income or net loss is apportioned in the ratio of 2:1:2 to Jones, Ross, and Warner, respectively.

This information is used to prepare the statement of distribution of net income.

## Statement of Partners' Capital (Statement 3)

The statement of partners' capital shows the continuity of the partners' Capital accounts for the fiscal period. Except for lack of space, this information would be included in the Equity section of the balance sheet. However, with possibly several partners to account for, it is customary to show the information on a separate statement. The statement begins with the Capital account balances as shown on the previous year's statement, continues by summarizing the increases and decreases for the current fiscal period, and arrives at the current end-of-period balances.

The information for this statement is usually picked up from two sources: the work sheet and the statement of distribution of net income. The only exception to this is where a partner has increased his capital investment during the fiscal period so that the balance in his Capital account does not coincide with the figure shown on the prior statement. In this event it is necessary to analyze the partner's Capital account in order to ascertain the amount of the increase to be shown on the current statement.

For Jones, Ross, and Warner, the statement of partners' capital is shown below.

---

Statement 3

JONES, ROSS, AND WARNER
STATEMENT OF PARTNERS' CAPITAL
YEAR ENDED DECEMBER 31, 19—

|  | M. Jones | G. Ross | A. Warner | Total |
|---|---|---|---|---|
| Capital Balances January 1 | $19 452.12 | $15 137.09 | $25 410.79 | $60 000.00 |
| Add: Share of Net Income for Year (Statement 4) | 18 320.61 | 14 701.41 | 23 916.48 | 56 938.50 |
|  | $37 772.73 | $29 838.50 | $49 327.27 | $116 938.50 |
| Deduct: Drawings for Year | 18 500.00 | 14 000.00 | 22 396.00 | 54 896.00 |
| Capital Balances December 31 | $19 272.73 | $15 838.50 | $26 931.27 | $62 042.50 |

## Balance Sheet (Statement 1)

The balance sheet of a partnership differs only in respect to the Equity section. The final capital figures are taken from Statement 3. The balance sheet for Jones, Ross, and Warner appears below.

Statement 1

JONES, ROSS, AND WARNER
BALANCE SHEET
DECEMBER 31, 19—

### ASSETS

| | | | |
|---|---|---|---|
| *Current Assets* | | | |
| Petty Cash | | $ 100.00 | |
| Bank | | 3 700.00 | |
| Accounts Receivable | $37 461.00 | | |
| Less Allowance for Doubtful Accounts | 2 058.00 | 35 403.00 | $39.203.00 |
| *Prepaid Expenses* | | | |
| Supplies | | $ 875.00 | |
| Insurance | | 416.00 | 1 291.00 |
| *Investment* | | | |
| Property – at cost | | | 20 000.00 |
| *Fixed Assets* | | | |
| Furniture and Equipment | $ 7 000.00 | | |
| Less Accumulated Depreciation | 4 192.00 | $ 2 808.00 | |
| Automobiles | $12 000.00 | | |
| Less Accumulated Depreciation | 7 012.50 | 4 987.50 | 7 795.50 |
| | | | $68 289.50 |

### LIABILITIES

| | | |
|---|---|---|
| *Current Liabilities* | | |
| Accounts Payable | $ 6 137.00 | |
| Accrued Wages | 110.00 | $ 6 247.00 |

### PARTNERS' EQUITY

| | | |
|---|---|---|
| *Partners' Capital* (Statement 3) | | |
| M. Jones | $19 272.73 | |
| G. Ross | 15 838.50 | |
| A. Warner | 26 931.27 | 62 042.50 |
| | | $68 289.50 |

## Income Statement (Statement 2)

The income statement is prepared in the customary manner. For Jones, Ross, and Warner it appears below.

|  |  | Statement 2 |
|---|---|---|
| JONES, ROSS, AND WARNER | | |
| INCOME STATEMENT | | |
| YEAR ENDED DECEMBER 31, 19— | | |
| *Income* | | |
| Sales | | $82 940.00 |
| *Operating Expenses* | | |
| Advertising | $3 000.00 | |
| Bad Debts | 102.00 | |
| Automotive Expense | 4 600.00 | |
| Depreciation of Automobiles | 2 137.50 | |
| Depreciation of Furniture and Equipment | 702.00 | |
| General Expense | 525.00 | |
| Insurance | 484.00 | |
| Light, Heat, and Water | 600.00 | |
| Rent | 2 400.00 | |
| Supplies | 625.00 | |
| Telephone | 1 290.00 | |
| Wages | 9 536.00 | 26 001.50 |
| Net Income | | $56 938.50 |

## Closing Entries for a Partnership

The theory of closing entries has been discussed fully on pages 354 and 355. A slight modification in procedure is required when closing the books of a partnership. A new factor to consider is the existence of more than one Capital account and more than one Drawings account.

Step 1. The first step in the closing entry process is the same for a partnership as for a proprietorship. It is to journalize all and only those adjusting entries that appear in the Adjustments columns of the work sheet. For Jones, Ross, and Warner there is a single adjustment, as shown below.

Dec. 31  General Expense      $175.00
                 Accounts Payable                $175.00
             Adjustment for accounts payable

Step 2. The second step of the closing entry process for a partnership is essentially the same as previously explained. It affects some adjustments and closes out the revenue and expense accounts. This entry is the same as for a proprietorship except that where previously the net income figure was credited (or the net loss figure debited) directly to the owner's Capital account, in a partnership it is placed in a temporary or 'holding' account called Income Summary. (Subsequently, the net income (or net loss) figure is transferred out of the Income Summary account to the partners' Capital accounts according to the figures determined on the distribution of net income statement.) As before, the figures for this second closing entry come from the Income Statement section of the work sheet. For Jones, Ross, and Warner the second of the closing entries is:

| | | |
|---|---|---|
| Dec. 31 Sales | | 82 940.00 |
| Allowance for Doubtful Debts | | 102.00 |
| Supplies | | 625.00 |
| Prepaid Insurance | | 484.00 |
| Accum. Deprec. of Furniture and Equipment | | 702.00 |
| Accumulated Depreciation of Automobiles | | 2 137.50 |
| Advertising | | 3 000.00 |
| Automotive Expense | | 4 600.00 |
| General Expense | | 525.00 |
| Light, Heat, and Water | | 600.00 |
| Rent | | 2 400.00 |
| Telephone | | 1 290.00 |
| Wages | | 9 536.00 |
| Income Summary | | 56 938.50 |
| To close revenue and expense accounts | | |
| to Income Summary account | | |

The Income Summary account at this stage appears as shown below.

Income Summary

| Dec 31 | | | 56 938.50 | Cr 56 938.50 |
|---|---|---|---|---|

Step 3. The final line of the statement of distribution of net income (page 396) provides the figures needed to close out the Income Summary account to the partners' Capital accounts. For Jones, Ross, and Warner this entry is as follows:

| | | |
|---|---|---|
| Income Summary | 56 938.50 | |
| M. Jones, Capital | | 18 320.16 |
| G. Ross, Capital | | 14 701.41 |
| A. Warner, Capital | | 23 916.48 |
| To apportion net | | |
| income to partners | | |

The Income Summary account is now closed out and each partner's Capital account has been increased by his respective share of net income, as shown below:

Income Summary

| Dec 31 | | | 56 938.50 | Cr 56 938.50 |
|---|---|---|---|---|
| Dec 31 | 56 938.50 | | | Nil |

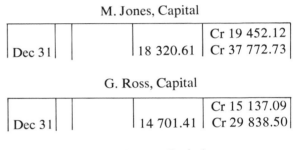

M. Jones, Capital

| | | | | Cr 19 452.12 |
|---|---|---|---|---|
| Dec 31 | | | 18 320.61 | Cr 37 772.73 |

G. Ross, Capital

| | | | | Cr 15 137.09 |
|---|---|---|---|---|
| Dec 31 | | | 14 701.41 | Cr 29 838.50 |

A. Warner, Capital

| | | | | Cr 25 410.79 |
|---|---|---|---|---|
| Dec 31 | | | 23 916.48 | Cr 49 327.27 |

Step 4. The final closing entry closes out each partner's Drawings account to his Capital account. The amounts for this entry are picked up from the work sheet. For Jones, Ross, and Warner these entries are as follows:

| | | |
|---|---|---|
| M. Jones, Capital | 18 500.00 | |
| G. Ross, Capital | 14 000.00 | |
| A. Warner, Capital | 22 396.00 | |
| M. Jones, Drawings | | 18 500.00 |
| G. Ross, Drawings | | 14 000.00 |
| A. Warner, Drawings | | 22 396.00 |
| To close out Drawings accounts | | |
| to Capital | | |

After completion of this four-step closing procedure for a partnership, the ledger accounts will be adjusted and closed out as necessary, and the partners' Capital accounts will reflect the proper balances as at the fiscal year-end. For the partnership of Jones, Ross, and Warner, the Capital accounts at this stage are as shown below.

M. Jones, Capital

| | | | Cr 19 452.12 |
|---|---|---|---|
| Dec 31 | | 18 320.61 | Cr 37 772.73 |
| Dec 31 | 18 500.00 | | Cr 19 272.73 |

G. Ross, Capital

| | | | Cr 15 137.09 |
|---|---|---|---|
| Dec 31 | | 14 701.41 | Cr 29 838.50 |
| Dec 31 | 14 000.00 | | Cr 15 838.50 |

A. Warner, Capital

| | | | Cr 25 410.79 |
|---|---|---|---|
| Dec 31 | | 23 916.48 | Cr 49 327.27 |
| Dec 31 | 22 396.00 | | Cr 26 931.27 |

It can be seen clearly that the partners' Capital accounts at this point agree with the statement of partners' capital, and with the Equity section of the balance sheet.

# Termination of Partnerships

A partnership may be terminated for a number of reasons. Depending on the circumstances, it may be sold as a going concern, or it may be liquidated, in which case the business ceases to operate. A liquidation involves the disposal of the partnership assets for cash, the payment of the partnership debts, the apportionment to the partners of the gain or loss on disposal of the assets, and the payment of the bank balance to the partners.

Upon the death of a partner, a partnership is legally terminated. The family or estate of the deceased partner is entitled to receive his share in the worth of the business. Where the remaining partners wish to continue to operate the business under a new partnership arrangement, provision can usually be made in advance, usually through life insurance, to have sufficient funds available to pay out the deceased's share. Otherwise it may be necessary for the remaining partners to borrow heavily, or even to liquidate the partnership against their wishes.

Accounting for partnership termination usually involves enough complexities that partners find it advisable to obtain the professional services of lawyers and public accountants. The topic is discussed here to give you a general idea of the process through a very simplified case.

The partnership of King and Queen Sales has two partners, A. King and B. Queen, who have mutually agreed to liquidate the business. At December 31, 19—, after the closing entries are posted, the trial balance of King and Queen Sales is as shown on page 402.

## Step 1. Conversion of Assets into Cash

It is necessary to convert the assets into cash. Gains or losses on disposal and any expenses of liquidation are charged to an account called Gain or Loss on Realization.

a. The net accounts receivable are sold to a collection agency at a discount of 25 per cent. A cheque for $1 518.75 is received from the collection agency.
   The entry to record this transaction is:

| | | |
|---|---|---|
| Bank | 1 518.75 | |
| Allowance for Doubtful Accts | 275.00 | |
| Gain or Loss on Realization | 506.25 | |
| Accounts Receivable | | 2 300.00 |

   Sale of Accounts Receivable
   to Ace Collection Agency
   at a discount of 25 per cent

b. The inventory and the equipment are sold at public auction for $2 100.00 and $5 300.00, respectively. The entries to record these transactions are:

```
                        KING AND QUEEN SALES
                      POST-CLOSING TRIAL BALANCE
                         DECEMBER 31, 19—

    Bank                                    $  5 700.00
    Accounts Receivable                        2 300.00
    Allowance for Doubtful Accounts                          $    275.00
    Inventory                                  3 700.00
    Land                                      12 000.00
    Buildings                                 33 000.00
    Accumulated Depreciation Buildings                          2 925.00
    Equipment                                 12 575.00
    Accumulated Depreciation Equipment                          4 075.00
    Bank Loan                                                  14 000.00
    Accounts Payable                                           8 000.00
    Mortgage Payable                                          10 000.00
    A. King, Capital                                          20 000.00
    B. Queen, Capital                                         10 000.00

                                            $69 275.00      $69 275.00
```

| Bank | 2 100.00 | |
| Gain or Loss on Realization | 1 600.00 | |
| Inventory | | 3 700.00 |

Sale of inventory at public
auction.

| Bank | 5 300.00 | |
| Accum. Deprec. Equipment | 4 075.00 | |
| Gain or Loss on Realization | 3 200.00 | |
| Equipment | | 12 575.00 |

Sale of equipment
at public auction

c. The land and buildings with the existing mortgage are sold for $65 000.00 less a 5 per cent real estate commission. A cheque for $51 750.00 is received. The entry to record this transaction is:

| Bank | 51 750.00 | |
| Mortgage Payable | 10 000.00 | |
| Accum. Deprec. Buildings | 2 925.00 | |
| Land | | 12 000.00 |
| Buildings | | 33 000.00 |
| Gain or Loss on Realization | | 19 675.00 |

Sale of property for $65 000,
less 5 per cent real estate commission

After the above entries are posted, the remaining accounts are:

| Bank | $66 368.75 | |
| Bank Loan | | $14 000.00 |
| Accounts Payable | | 8 000.00 |
| A. King, Capital | | 20 000.00 |
| B. Queen, Capital | | 10 000.00 |
| Gain or Loss on Realization | | 14 368.75 |

## Step 2. Payment of Partnership Debts

The partnership debts are normally settled before any allocations to the partners are considered.

a. The bank is directed to deduct from the company bank account an amount that will pay off the bank loan and any accrued interest. A bank debit memo is received debiting the account for $14 097.05 – $14 000.00 principal and $97.05 interest. The accounting transaction is:

Bank Loan                              $14 000.00
Gain or Loss on Realization                97.05
    Bank                               $14 097.05
Settlement of bank loan
and accrued interest

b. Cheques are issued in settlement of all accounts payable. The entry to give effect to
these cheques is:

Accounts Payable                       $8 000.00
    Bank                                $8 000.00
Settlement of all outstanding
accounts payable

After these two entries are posted, the partnership accounts are:

Bank                                   $44 271.70
A. King, Capital                            $20 000.00
B. Queen, Capital                            10 000.00
Gain or Loss on Realization                  14 271.70

## Step 3.  Apportionment of Gain or Loss on Realization to Partners

The balance in the Gain or Loss on Realization
account is apportioned to the partners in the
income- and loss-sharing ratio. King and Queen
share income and losses in the ratio of 3:2, respectively. Therefore, King receives 3/5 and
Queen 2/5 of the balance of $14 271.70; that is,
$8 563.02 and $5 708.68, respectively. The accounting entry to record the apportionment is:

Gain or Loss on Realization   $14 271.70
    A. King, Capital                  $8 563.02
    B. Queen, Capital                  5 708.68
Apportionment of gain on
realization to partners in
the ratio of 3:2 for King
and Queen, respectively

After this step the accounts of the partnership
are:
Bank                          $44 271.70
A. King, Capital                   $28 563.02
B. Queen, Capital                   15 708.68

## Step 4.  Payment of Cash to Partners

Where all of the partners have credit balances in
their Capital accounts,* the distribution of cash
to the partners is made in proportion to their
Capital account balances. In this case the accounting entry to record the payment to the partners is:

A. King, Capital               $28 563.02
B. Queen, Capital               15 708.68
    Bank                               $44 271.70
Cheques to partners closing
out the partnership

*Note: Where one or more partners has a debit balance
in his Capital account, a special set of rules applies.
These rules are not discussed here because they are
considered to represent a topic of an advanced nature.

# Bookkeeping and Accounting Terms

**Partnership** The relation which exists between
persons carrying on a business in common with a
view to profit. This term does not apply to the
relation which exists between members of a corporation.

**Corporation** See page 433.

**Insolvency** The inability of an individual or corporation to pay its debts as they become due.

**Goodwill** An intangible asset of a business when
the business has value in excess of the sum of its
net assets.

**Liquidation** The winding up of the affairs of an
organization; the accounts of its debtors and
creditors are settled, and any remaining assets
are distributed to its owners.

# Review Questions

1. What is meant by 'partnership'?
2. From an accounting point of view where does the main difference between a proprietorship and a partnership lie?
3. Partnerships are formed for a variety of reasons. Describe two situations in which a partnership might be formed.
4. Briefly, and in your own words, note the advantages and disadvantages of the partnership form of business organization.
5. Explain the purpose of the partnership agreement.
6. In your opinion what are the three most important items contained in a partnership agreement?
7. Explain the reason for a provincial Partnership Act.
8. When forming a partnership it is advisable for the persons involved to obtain professional assistance. Briefly explain why.
9. In your own words explain why cash is not always introduced into a new partnership.
10. New accounting theory for partnerships pertains to year-end activity. Why is this so?
11. State the factors that affect the apportionment of net income or net loss.
12. For what reason does a partner get interest? salary?
13. A partnership usually requires two additional financial statements. Name them.
14. In what order would you prepare the four financial statements for a partnership? Explain.
15. The closing entries for a partnership are not exactly the same as for a proprietorship. Explain why this is so.
16. Name the four steps in the termination of a partnership.

# Exercises

## Partnership Formation Exercises

1. Powell and James form a partnership in which Powell contributes $20 000 and James contributes $10 000. The two men agree that their capital interest in the business will be in the ratio of their respective capital contributions.

   Give the accounting entry to establish the partnership.

---

2. Foster, Harris, and Russell join together to begin a new business. Foster contributes a building valued at $35 000; Harris contributes equipment valued at $25 000; and Russell contributes $20 000 cash. It is agreed among the men that their capital accounts will reflect their individual contributions.

   Give the accounting entry to record the partners' contributions.

---

3. Fleming is the sole owner of a cleaning business in which he has an equity of $27 000. In order to finance a modernization of the plant, Fleming has agreed to take Monroe into partnership. Monroe has agreed to contribute $27 000 cash into the business for a one-half interest.

   Give the accounting entry to record the introduction of Monroe into the business.

**4.** Baxter is the sole owner of a men's clothing store. His equity in the business is $22 000. He makes a deal with Gregory to sell him a one-half interest in the business for $15 000 cash. The money is to be paid directly to Baxter. No new funds are introduced into the business.

Give the accounting entry to record Gregory's interest in the business.

**5.** McLean, Tracey, and Reynolds reach a decision to go into a new business of building recreational trailers. McLean is regarded as a wizard at this type of thing and it is agreed that his know-how is to be his contribution to the partnership. The other men have little to offer in the way of specific skills. Their contribution to the partnership is to be in the form of cash – $15 000 each. All three men will work full time in the business. Although Tracey and Reynolds put up the total cash between them, the three men agree that all the capital accounts will be equal.

Give the accounting entry to establish the partnership.

**6.** I. James, W. Walsh and P. Norris are sole proprietors working independently as public accountants. They decide to join together in partnership in order to be able to specialize in different aspects of accounting and to facilitate the purchase of a new office building.

The partnership is to come into existence on June 1, 19—, at which time the appraised assets and liabilities of the individual firms are to be transferred to a new set of books for the partnership. It is agreed that capital balances are to be brought up to the level of the partner with the largest equity by the direct contribution of cash to the partnership.

The appraised values of the assets and liabilities on June 1 are as shown below:

|  | I. James | W. Walsh | P. Norris |
|---|---|---|---|
| *Assets* | | | |
| Bank | $ 1 500 | $ 1 200 | $    800 |
| Accounts Receivable | 4 700 | 3 800 | 4 200 |
| Supplies | 740 | 630 | 315 |
| Office Equipment | 1 100 | 3 000 | 1 500 |
| Automobiles | 5 000 | 4 200 | 5 500 |
| Total Assets | $13 040 | $12 830 | $12 315 |
| *Liabilities* | | | |
| Accounts Payable | $ 1 350 | $ 1 700 | $    950 |
| *Owner's Equity* | $11 690 | $11 130 | $11 365 |

Give the accounting entries to set up the new partnership.

## Distribution of Net Income Exercises

**7.** C. Lemaire, R. Kennedy, B. Henning, and S. Dudley are lawyers in partnership. They have just completed their December 31, 19—, fiscal year with a net income figure of $126 040.28. In their partnership agreement it is stipulated that Lemaire and Kennedy, the senior partners, are to receive salaries of $12 500 before distributing the remainder of net income equally. Calculate the net income of each of the partners. Show your calculations.

8. Black and Associates is a loan company with four partners: R. Allen, M. Hamilton, R. Cooper, and T. Cavanaugh. Their respective Capital account balances are: $12 000, $24 000, $18 000, and $30 000. If their partnership agreement states that net income or net loss is to be divided in the ratio of their Capital account balances, calculate how they would divide a net income of $110 040. Show your calculations.

9. Barnes, Doby, and Barnes are in a partnership in which the partners, A. Barnes, W. Doby, and S. Barnes, share income and loss in the ratio of 4:4:3. Their partnership agreement further stipulates that (1) S. Barnes receives a salary of $10 000, the others none; (2) interest is to be allowed at 9 per cent on the Capital account balances held throughout the year. These were $20 000, $35 000, and $5 500 for A. Barnes, W. Doby, and S. Barnes, respectively.

Prepare a statement of distribution of net income for the year ended April 30, 19—. The net income was $87 199.21.

10. Chambers Brothers has just completed its December 31, 19—, fiscal year with a net income figure of $26 070. Using the information shown below, prepare the statement of distribution of net income for Chambers Brothers.

Additional information:
1. A. Chambers receives a salary of $8 000;

R. Chambers receives a salary of $12 000.
2. The balance of net income is divided equally.

11. For the year ended June 30, 19—, Expert Investors had a net income of $19 640.40. Using the additional information shown below, prepare the statement of distribution of net income for Expert Investors.

Additional information:
1. The partners are J. Hunter and C. Lamont.
2. The balances in the partners' Capital accounts are: Hunter, $12 000; Lamont, $30 000.
3. Hunter is to receive a salary of $15 000;

Lamont, $7 500.
4. Interest is to be allowed on Capital account balances at the rate of 8 per cent.
5. The balance of net income or net loss is divided equally.

## Financial Statement Problems

12. From the work sheet opposite and the additional information shown below, prepare (1) the statement of distribution of net income, (2) the statement of partners' capital, and (3) the Equity section of the balance sheet for Frame Brothers.

Additional information:
1. A. Frame receives a salary of $10 000;
   G. Frame receives a salary of $8 000.

2. A. Frame and G. Frame divide the remainder of net income in the ratio of 2:1, respectively.

13. From the work sheet opposite and additional information shown below, prepare (1) the statement of distribution of net income, (2) the statement of partners' capital, and (3) the Equity section of the balance sheet.

Additional information:
1. Each partner receives a salary of $12 000.
2. Interest is allowed on Capital account balances at the rate of 8 per cent.

3. K. Oakes, R. Oakes, and B. Reid divide the remainder of net income in the ratio of 3:2:2. respectively.

| ACCOUNTS | TRIAL BALANCE DR. | CR. | ADJUSTMENTS DR. | CR. | INCOME STATEMENT DR. | CR. | BALANCE SHEET DR. | CR. |
|---|---|---|---|---|---|---|---|---|
| Petty Cash | 50- | | | | | | 50- | |
| Bank | 31270 | | | | | | 31270 | |
| Accounts Receivable | 940716 | | | | | | 940716 | |
| Allowance for Doubtful Accounts | | 315- | | | 65- | | | 380- |
| Merchandise Inventory | 27055- | | | | 27055- | 28575- | 28575- | |
| Supplies | 740- | | | | 415- | | 325- | |
| Prepaid Insurance | 316- | | | | 204- | | 112- | |
| Furniture and Equipment | 19073- | | | | | | 19073- | |
| Accum. Deprec. Furn. & Equip. | | 490720 | | | 283316 | | | 774036 |
| Automobiles | 2664290 | | | | | | 2664290 | |
| Accum. Deprec. Automobiles | | 1137312 | | | 458093 | | | 1595405 |
| Bank Loan | | 5000- | | | | | | 5000- |
| Accounts Payable | | 572115 | | ①89927 | | | | 662042 |
| Sales Tax Payable | | 79160 | | | | | | 79160 |
| Employees' Income Tax Payable | | 40210 | | | | | | 40210 |
| A. Frame, Capital | | 20000- | | | | | | 20000- |
| A. Frame, Drawings | 1058306 | | | | | | 1058306 | |
| G. Frame, Capital | | 20000- | | | | | | 20000- |
| G. Frame, Drawings | 1056670 | | | | | | 1056670 | |
| Sales | | 13570270 | | | | 13570270 | | |
| Bank Charges | 450- | | | | 450- | | | |
| Canada Pension Plan Expense | 375- | | | | 375- | | | |
| Light, Heat, and Water | 97020 | | | | 97020 | | | |
| Miscellaneous Expense | 19220 | | | | 19220 | | | |
| Purchases | 4731220 | | ①84160 | | 4815380 | | | |
| Rent | 12000- | | | | 12000- | | | |
| Telephone | 600- | | ①5767 | | 65767 | | | |
| Unemployment Insurance Expense | 14675 | | | | 14675 | | | |
| Wages | 37420- | | | | 37420- | | | |
| | 20421287 | 20421287 | 89927 | 89927 | 13551871 | 16427770 | 10564752 | 7688853 |
| Net Income | | | | | 2875899 | | | 2875899 |
| | | | | | 16427770 | 16427770 | 10564752 | 10564752 |

| ACCOUNTS | TRIAL BALANCE DR. | CR. | ADJUSTMENTS DR. | CR. | INCOME STATEMENT DR. | CR. | BALANCE SHEET DR. | CR. |
|---|---|---|---|---|---|---|---|---|
| Petty Cash | 100- | | | | | | 100- | |
| Bank | 149874 | | | | | | 149874 | |
| Accounts Receivable | 1328588 | | | | | | 1328588 | |
| Allowance for Doubtful Accounts | | 2450 | | | 58821 | | | 61271 |
| Supplies | 41270 | | | | 9695 | | 31575 | |
| Prepaid Insurance | 80410 | | | | 34310 | | 461- | |
| Investment in Property | 70000- | | | | | | 70000- | |
| Furniture and Equipment | 5856- | | | | | | 5856- | |
| Accum. Deprec. Furn. & Equip. | | 194690 | | | 78182 | | | 272872 |
| Automobiles | 1607284 | | | | | | 1607284 | |
| Accumulated Deprec. Automobiles | | 706021 | | | 270379 | | | 9764- |
| Accounts Payable | | 156497 | | ①145- | | | | 170997 |
| Employees' Income Tax Payable | | 85- | | | | | | 85- |
| Canada Pension Plan Payable | | 3075 | | | | | | 3075 |
| K. Oakes, Capital | | 35000- | | | | | | 35000- |
| K. Oakes, Drawings | 1520031 | | | | | | 1520031 | |
| R. Oakes, Capital | | 35000- | | | | | | 35000- |
| R. Oakes, Drawings | 1509535 | | | | | | 1509535 | |
| B. Reid, Capital | | 20000- | | | | | | 20000- |
| B. Reid, Drawings | 1000930 | | | | | | 1000930 | |
| Fees Earned | | 7277026 | | | | 7277026 | | |
| Canada Pension Plan Expense | 22916 | | | | 22916 | | | |
| Car Expenses | 340907 | | ①90- | | 349907 | | | |
| Light, Heat, and Water | 101715 | | | | 101715 | | | |
| Miscellaneous Expense | 32763 | | ①55- | | 38263 | | | |
| Postage | 96446 | | | | 96446 | | | |
| Rent | 4800- | | | | 4800- | | | |
| Telephone | 63329 | | | | 63329 | | | |
| Unemployment Insce. Expense | 14721 | | | | 14721 | | | |
| Salaries | 1361940 | | | | 1411940 | | | 500- |
| | 17348259 | 17348259 | 145- | 145- | 3030624 | 7277026 | 14789517 | 10543115 |
| Net Income | | | | | 4246402 | | | 4246402 |
| | | | | | 7277026 | 7277026 | 14789517 | 14789517 |

## Adjusting and Closing Entry Exercises

**14.** In a two-column general journal record the adjusting and closing entries for Frame Brothers introduced in Exercise 12. Before undertaking this exercise, make sure that your solution to Exercise 12 has been corrected.

**15.** From the work sheet in Exercise 13, prepare the adjusting and closing entries for Oakes, Oakes, and Reid in a two-column general journal. Be sure that your solution to Exercise 13 has been corrected before beginning this exercise.

## Partnership Liquidation Exercises

**16.** Jackson, Johnson, and Wilson have decided to liquidate their partnership. The post-closing trial balance of the partnership on March 31, 19—, is as follows:

| | | |
|---|---:|---:|
| Bank | $ 3 199 | |
| Accounts Receivable | 7 061 | |
| Allowance for Doubtful Debts | | $ 350 |
| Merchandise Inventory | 12 950 | |
| Supplies | 1 720 | |
| Prepaid Insurance | 400 | |
| Equipment | 15 795 | |
| Accumulated Depreciation of Equipment | | 4 500 |
| Automobiles | 12 500 | |
| Accumulated Depreciation of Automobiles | | 7 350 |
| Accounts Payable | | 6 425 |
| E. Jackson, Capital | | 10 000 |
| C. Johnson, Capital | | 10 000 |
| F. Wilson, Capital | | 15 000 |
| | $53 625 | $53 625 |

From the information shown below, prepare the accounting entries to liquidate the partnership.

1. The partners share income and losses as follows:
   Jackson – 30 per cent
   Johnson – 30 per cent
   Wilson  – 40 per cent
2. The accounts receivable are sold to a collection agency for $4 000 cash.
3. The merchandise inventory is sold to another company for $8 000 cash.
4. Insurance is cancelled and a refund cheque for $300 is received from the insurance company.
5. The supplies, equipment, and automobiles are sold at public auction and realize the following amounts: supplies, $500; equipment, $6 500; and automobiles, $6 200.
6. All of the accounts payable are paid in full.

**17.** The partnership of Gare and Martin is being liquidated due to the illness of one of the partners. The company books were closed on January 31, 19—. The post-closing trial balance is as shown below:

| | | |
|---|---|---|
| Bank | $ 22.00 | |
| Accounts Receivable | 2 950.00 | |
| Allowance for Doubtful Accounts | | $ 275.00 |
| Merchandise Inventory | 8 942.00 | |
| Supplies | 416.00 | |
| Prepaid Insurance | 212.00 | |
| Land | 20 000.00 | |
| Buildings | 17 000.00 | |
| Accumulated Depreciation Buildings | | 3 680.60 |
| Equipment | 6 800.00 | |
| Accumulated Depreciation Equipment | | 4 609.20 |
| Automobiles | 12 710.00 | |
| Accumulated Depreciation Automobiles | | 8 746.20 |
| Accounts Payable | | 3 200.00 |
| Bank Loan | | 2 800.00 |
| Mortgage Payable | | 25 741.00 |
| C. Gare, Capital | | 10 000.00 |
| H. Martin, Capital | | 10 000.00 |
| | $69 052.00 | $69 052.00 |

**Using the additional information shown below, prepare the accounting entries to liquidate the partnership.**

1. The partners share income and loss equally.
2. $275 of accounts receivable is written off. The balance of accounts receivable is collected quickly by offering a 10 per cent cash discount for immediate payment.
3. The merchandise inventory, supplies, and equipment are sold at public auction. The following amounts are realized in cash: inventory, $7 500; supplies, $100; equipment, $2 500.
4. The insurance is cancelled and a refund cheque in the amount of $162 is received from the insurance company.
5. The land and buildings are sold through a real estate agent for $48 000. The agreement calls for the purchaser to take over the existing mortgage on the property and for the seller to pay a real estate commission of 5 per cent on the selling price.
6. The owners decide to purchase the two company automobiles at the current market values as determined by an independent car appraiser. C. Gare takes a car with a market value of $2 200; H. Martin takes a car with a market value of $2 100. The market value of the cars is charged to the partners' respective Capital accounts.
7. The bank loan is settled.
8. All of the accounts payable are paid in full.

# Cases

### Case 1
Tony Calderone, Jim Kidd, Frank Morris, and Mario Capiletti are experienced construction men who have become acquainted through their work. The men are presently employed by different companies in the house building industry. Tony is a carpenter, Jim is an accountant, Frank is a heavy equipment operator and maintenance man, and Mario is a concrete and masonry man.

At a meeting one day the men talk seriously about joining forces – to work for themselves. Although they do not have all the necessary skills themselves, they have a great deal of collective experience and know a great many people in the trades.

They discuss their plan with the head of a financial institution who assures them of the availability of a substantial line of credit as well as mortgage money for the homes to be built; the one condition is that the four men themselves invest $50 000 in the business.

Together, the men can raise this amount of capital and are eager to proceed with the plan. Tony and Frank are of the opinion that they should take on work immediately and work out the details of the business organization later. Jim and Mario are more cautious and insist that the details be worked out in advance.

What course of action should the men follow? Give reasons for your choice.

## Case 2

Fred Norris is the sole owner of Hilltop Ski Area, which he has developed over the last ten years. The ski area has excellent hills and very reliable snow conditions. Since its beginning it has been increasingly profitable. In the most recent fiscal year its net income figure was $62 000.

Over the years it has been Fred Norris's policy to use the profits of the business to pay off the large debts that he incurred for the original property and equipment. Consequently the position of the business is regarded as being good, with property presently valued at $1 000 000, and with no large debts. The only adverse aspect of the business is that the equipment is either completely worn out or obsolete.

In order for the ski area to retain its popularity it is essential that modern chair lifts and hill-grooming equipment be obtained. The cost of the new equipment is $600 000. Neither Fred nor the business has that amount of money available. Bank financing is available but at an interest rate of 10½ per cent, which would cost the business $63 000 a year for the interest alone. Fred is of the opinion that the new equipment would attract additional skiers to the area and that an increase in gross revenues of approximately $50 000 could be expected.

An offer is made to Fred by Harry Watson, a man with great confidence in the future of skiing. Harry offers to put up the $600 000 for the new equipment on the condition that he have a one-half interest in all aspects of the business.

What advice would you give to Fred Norris? What is your opinion of Harry's offer? Give reasons for your answer.

## Case 3

Hutton and Inman hastily formed a partnership which was expected to last for only two or three years. The nature of the business was to buy and sell metric supplies in order to take advantage of the changeover to the metric system of measurement.

Hutton is an expert on metrication, having lived and worked for a number of years in a country that uses the metric system. Inman knows nothing of the metric system, but expects to study it and be expert in a very short time.

In the process of establishing the business, Inman can raise only $8 000 of the $15 000 that he had promised. Hutton has to come up with his own share of $10 000 plus the $7 000 balance of Inman's share, for a total of $17 000.

Prior to officially registering the partnership the two men had discussed a tentative income-sharing plan which would compensate each partner according to his contribution of capital, time, and talent. But because Hutton became very busy in a hurry the two men had never gotten together to make an agreement official and the business carried on without one.

The business did well financially thanks to the efforts of Hutton, who had to do most of the work. Inman never could master the metric system of measurement and was of little help except to unpack goods that arrived and to package and mail them for shipment. Inman also took a lot of time off for golf in the summer and for curling in the winter.

At the end of the first year of operation the business had a net income of $38 000. When it came time to discuss the profit split, Inman told Hutton that the Partnership Act stated specifically that the profits had to be divided equally and that there was nothing that either of them could do about it.

Express your views on this situation.

## Case 4
Andrews, Brown, and Collins are all graduate engineers who form a partnership in which each man is to work full time in the business. To get the business started the men contribute cash as follows: Andrews, $25,000; Brown, $20 000; and Collins, $5 000.

The men ask your opinion about their income- or loss-sharing arrangement. State your views in this regard.

## Case 5
Davidson is a young and talented man in the photography and graphics field. He is anxious to form a business of his own because of his confidence that many of the people for whom he has done work would come to him if he were on his own. Unfortunately, the equipment and special facilities for this line of work are expensive. The cost would be approximately $40 000, a sum which he does not have.

Edwards is a friend who is willing to put up the required capital for an interest in the business.

If Davidson and Edwards were to form a partnership in which Edwards put up the capital and Davidson did all the work, what profit sharing arrangement would you suggest for them?

## Case 6
Fraser and Gregg are two men who form a partnership in the wholesale auto parts business. Fraser has put up $40 000 and Gregg $50 000 of the required capital. The agreement reached by the two men is to the effect that Gregg is to work full time in the business and Fraser is to work 25 per cent of his time. Neither man brings any particular skills or experience to the business.

These two men have not as yet made a decision regarding the profit-sharing ratio. What suggestions would you make to them?

## Case 7
D. R. Johnson is a lawyer with a well-established and profitable legal practice which he has built up on his own over a period of twenty years. In the past few years the demands of his business have been exceptionally heavy, forcing him to work many more hours than normal. He has not been able to spend nearly as much time with his family as he would like, and last year he was forced to give up his summer vacation because of an important case.

To help relieve the workload, Mr. Johnson employed Lorne Fox, a law student, to work with him on a part-time basis. Lorne began working during the summer months when his classes were not in session and in the evenings during the school term. The arrangement worked out well for both parties. Lorne proved to be an able and energetic student who soon demonstrated his value. At the same time, he was acquiring the experience that he wanted. Mr. Johnson's workload was reduced considerably.

With Lorne's graduation approaching, Mr. Johnson finds himself facing the unpleasant prospect of losing him. Lorne will be a lawyer fully qualified to move into his own office or to take a position with another lawyer. Mr. Johnson has been very happy with Lorne, does not want to see him leave, and above all does not want to return to the long, arduous working days.

What advice would you give to Mr. Johnson? Give reasons for your choice.

## Case 8

G. Barton, an office employee, has just inherited a service station and garage from a deceased uncle. Because he has not been happy with his present job he is excited about the possibility of going into business as a service station operator. Unfortunately he has no knowledge of automobile mechanics or car servicing.

The service station has not been operated since his uncle's death six months earlier, but its modern equipment and facilities are in good condition. Mr. Barton feels that it is too good an opportunity for him to pass up and he is confident of his own business instincts and ability for hard work.

What advice would you give Mr. Barton? Be prepared to support your position with good reasons.

## Case 9

R. Price and G. Good have been together in partnership operating a wholesale business for about five years. Although the business is very profitable, the two partners have had to draw heavily upon their personal resources in order to get the business started and to see it through an almost immediate period of expansion.

On January 31, 19—, the balance sheet of the partnership is as shown below.

PRICE AND GOOD
BALANCE SHEET
JANUARY 31, 19—

| | | | |
|---|---|---|---|
| *Current Assets* | | | |
| Cash | | $ 438.00 | |
| Accounts Receivable | $ 15 072.00 | | |
| Less Allowance for Doubtful Accounts | 2 000.00 | 13 072.00 | |
| Merchandise Inventory | | 125 000.00 | $138 510.00 |
| *Prepaid Expenses* | | | |
| Insurance | | $ 415.00 | |
| Supplies | | 1 432.00 | 1 847.00 |
| *Fixed Assets* | | | |
| Land | | $ 35 000.00 | |
| Buildings | $145 000.00 | | |
| Less Accumulated Depreciation | 32 075.00 | 112 925.00 | |
| Furniture and Equipment | $ 72 000.00 | | |
| Less Accumulated Depreciation | 48 456.00 | 23 544.00 | |
| Automobiles | $ 12 473.00 | | |
| Less Accumulated Depreciation | 5 903.00 | 6 570.00 | 178 039.00 |
| | | | $318 396.00 |

*Current Liabilities*

| | | |
|---|---|---|
| Accounts Payable | $112 500.00 | |
| Bank Loan | 50 000.00 | $162 500.00 |
| *Mortgage Payable* | | 65 400.00 |
| *Owners' Equity* | | |
| R. Price, Capital | $ 45 248.00 | |
| G. Good, Capital | 45 248.00 | 90 496.00 |
| | | $318 396.00 |

On February 1, G. Good is killed in an automobile accident. Lawyers for the deceased quickly point out to Price that Good's death legally terminates the partnership, and that Good's family is urgently in need of Good's portion of the value of the partnership.

Price is fully aware that he will have to comply with the request of Good's lawyers. He has his own future to think about, however, and hopes to be able to continue to operate the business because it has proven to be a successful and profitable one.

Discuss this case, giving consideration to the following questions:

1. What problem is Price faced with?
2. What courses of action are open to him?
3. What precautionary measures could he take to avoid a similar situation with a future partnership?

# 17 Corporations

A **corporation**, also known as a limited company, is an organization which by law is given a legal identity independent of the persons who own it.

Corporations range in size from small to very large. In Canada they are identified by the word 'Limited' or 'Ltd.' as part of the company name. Examples of corporation names are: Pace Contracting Limited and Northwestern Broadcasting Ltd. Almost all large business enterprises operate under the corporate form of business organization.

Accounting for corporations may not be a simple matter, particularly when you are dealing with large companies. It is not an objective of this text to explore advanced or specialized accounting theory. Its purpose is to examine corporation accounting from a fundamental point of view, explaining basic concepts that apply to corporations in general. Thus you will gain an understanding of this form of business organization which is so prominent in our society.

## Major Purpose of Corporations

The original purpose of the corporate form of business organization was to facilitate the accumulation of large amounts of capital, and to spread the financial risk involved in costly business ventures. To raise a large amount of capital for a business venture from a small number of people usually proved to be no easy task.

The corporation concept allows for the raising of capital from a large number of persons, each one individually undertaking a relatively small financial risk for a share in the anticipated profits. For example, if you assume that a capital investment of $2 000 000 is required to put a new mine into operation, it is a remote possibility that the capital for the venture could be raised from a few persons, say four, each contributing one-half million dollars. There is much more likelihood of the capital being raised from a large number of persons, say about 200 000, each one contributing $10 or more. Each contributor would receive a share certificate (also known as a stock certificate) indicating that he owns a share in the venture. He would thus become a **shareholder** or **stockholder** in the company and would receive a portion of the profits (if any) in proportion to the number of shares that he owns.

He would have no legal obligation beyond the full contribution for his shares.

## Characteristics of Corporations

1. The owners of a corporation are its common shareholders. For a small private corporation there may be a single shareholder, but for a large public corporation there are usually many shareholders. Each common* share in a corporation carries one vote at any shareholders' meeting. A shareholder who owns 50 common shares of a corporation is entitled to 50 votes, whereas one who owns 10 common shares is entitled to 10 votes.

*A corporation may have different kinds of shares, as will be explained later. It is the common shares that carry the privilege of ownership.

2. An incorporated company is a separate legal entity in the eye of the law. It is regarded as an artificial legal 'being', separate from those who own it. Its existence continues regardless of anything that may happen to any of its shareholders. In a number of respects it has the rights and obligations of a real person. It can buy and sell property in its own name; it can sue or be sued in its own name; it can enter into legal contracts in its own name; and it must pay its own income tax and other taxes.

3. The shareholders have no liability for any actions of the corporation except to the extent of their capital contribution. They have what is known as limited liability. In this respect the corporate form of business ownership is quite different from the single proprietorship or the partnership.

4. For the protection of shareholders and prospective shareholders, corporations are subject to government control. The laws of the federal government in regard to corporations are found in the Canada Business Corporations Act. Each of the provinces has a similar act. These acts lay down the numerous rules and regulations which people must strictly follow in forming and operating limited companies. If the scope of a company's operations is national, it will usually choose to operate under the Canada Act. If the scope of a company's operations is confined to a particular province, it will likely choose to operate under the Companies Act for that province. One unfortunate aspect of company law is its complexity; parts of it are difficult to read and understand.

   To incorporate a company, a formal request is made to the government by one or more petitioners. Permission, if granted, is given in the form of a document called a **charter** or **letters patent** which contains the following information:
   - the name of the company
   - the purpose of the company
   - the address of the head office of the company
   - the amount of capital authorized

   **Note:** Authorized capital is the maximum amount of capital that the charter allows the company to raise. If, at a subsequent time, the company wishes to increase the authorized capital, it must apply for permission which may be given in the form of 'Supplementary Letters Patent'.
   - the number of shares authorized
   - the names, addresses, and occupations of the petitioners for the formation of the company and the number of shares to be taken by each
   - the number of directors.

5. Company policy is not decided by the shareholders but by a committee of the shareholders called a **board of directors**. Directors are elected by the shareholders from among themselves at the annual shareholders meeting. Control of the company is usually in the hands of a few shareholders who have large holdings of company shares. Directors do not run the day-to-day operations of the company, but they regulate the affairs of the company by passing bylaws and making policy decisions.

6. The daily operations of the company are in the hands of hired company officers or executives. They are the president, vice-president(s), secretary, treasurer, general manager, and so on. The executive positions of a company are established in the bylaws passed by the board of directors.

7. To control a corporation, one must theoretically own fifty per cent of the shares plus one. In actual fact, because of the extensive distribution of shares and the lack of participation by a great many shareholders, a corporation can be effectively controlled with a much smaller percentage holding of shares.

## Advantages and Disadvantages of Corporations

### Advantages
The liability of the shareholders is limited to the amount of their investment in shares of the company.

The power of the directors is kept under strict control by government regulations.

Large investments of capital can be assembled more easily.

The existence of the company continues despite the death, insolvency, or incapacity of any of its shareholders.

New capital can be brought into the business by selling additional shares.

Except for the contribution for his shares, a shareholder is not affected if a company fails or if it is involved in legal entanglements.

Shares of a public company may be easily acquired or disposed of through a stockbroker.

A person can enjoy ownership in a company without having the responsibility of management.

### Disadvantages

Most individual shareholders have no say in the running of the company. A shareholder can run for the board of directors and he can vote (one vote per share) at the election of directors.

A corporation pays income tax at a high rate. In addition, when the profits of the company are distributed to the shareholders, the shareholders are also required to pay income tax on these dividends. In effect, this is double taxation.

Government controls are quite strict. Corporation law is often difficult to read and to understand.

There are fees and legal expenses involved in incorporating a company.

Minority shareholders have little influence in the conduct of the business.

## Accounts of a Corporation

As compared to proprietorship and partnership, the accounts of a corporation differ basically in respect to the owners' equity. Whereas the accounts of a proprietorship or partnership have Capital and Drawings accounts for each of the owners, the accounts of a corporation have neither. In the simplest of corporations the equities of all the shareholders are recorded collectively in two accounts: (1) the **Capital Stock** account, and (2) the **Retained Earnings** account. In simplified form the accounts of a corporation appear as shown below:

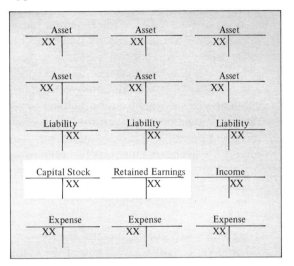

It is a characteristic unique to corporation accounting that the owners' equity is separated into two parts: (1) capital invested by the shareholders, which is represented by the Capital Stock account, and (2) capital earned by the business, which is represented by the Retained Earnings account.

## Capital Stock

When company shares are sold initially, the proceeds of the sale are credited to a Capital Stock account. The simplest accounting entry to record the sale of shares is:

| | | |
|---|---|---|
| Bank | $xxx | |
| Capital Stock | | $xxx |
| To record the issue | | |
| of capital stock for cash | | |

The Capital Stock account has a credit balance which represents the accumulation of the proceeds from all sales of shares made directly from the company to its shareholders.

# Retained Earnings

The nature of this account is described almost perfectly by its name – Retained Earnings. In simple corporations the account is affected by two types of accounting activity.

1. *Net Income or Net Loss*

   As you will see later, at the end of each fiscal period the net income or the net loss of a company is transferred to the Retained Earnings account. Net income represents a credit to the account and net loss a debit.

   Normally the Retained Earnings account has a credit balance representing the net accumulation of income from profitable operations. It is possible, however, for the account to have a debit balance – a state of negative retained earnings. This usually follows a severe loss or a series of losses. When the Retained Earnings account has a debit balance, it is known as a **deficit**.

2. *Dividends*

   The shareholders of a company are its owners who expect to receive some of the company profits – called **dividends**. Whether or not any dividends are paid is at the discretion of the board of directors. It is the directors who have the power to declare a dividend; that is, to vote a payment to shareholders out of the accumulated net profits in the Retained Earnings account. A dividend payment has the effect of reducing the credit balance in the Retained Earnings account.

   See page 424 for a detailed discussion of dividends.

## Retained Earnings – Summary

The following diagram shows how income, loss, and dividends affect the Retained Earnings account.

Retained Earnings

| Debits: Net Loss<br>Dividends | Credit: Net Income |
|---|---|

Under normal circumstances the dollar value of credit entries exceeds the dollar value of debit entries, giving the account a credit balance. Payment of a dividend is not allowed if it will create a debit balance in the Retained Earnings account.

The balance in the Retained Earnings account reflects the amount of accumulated free earnings retained within the company.

The Retained Earnings account is not closed out to the Common Stock account.

# Organization Costs

Substantial costs can be incurred in incorporating a company. These initial costs include the fee to obtain the charter from the government, legal fees paid to company lawyers, and costs for miscellaneous items such as the company seal. Where large issues of shares are sold through the services of an investment dealer, the commission paid to the investment dealer is an organization cost.

Initial costs of incorporation are charged to an account called **Organization Costs**. Accounting theory regarding organization costs varies. The most common treatment is to write the amount off as an expense over a period of years as allowed by government regulation. On the balance sheet the item appears as an intangible asset.

# Simple Balance Sheet of a Corporation

A simple balance sheet for a corporation is shown at the top of the next page. The illustration shows the manner in which the two components of Shareholders' Equity – Capital Stock and Retained Earnings – are presented.

```
                    CROWN INDUSTRIES LIMITED
                         BALANCE SHEET
                         JUNE 30, 19 –

            ASSETS                          LIABILITIES

Current Assets                      Current Liabilities
Bank                   $10 500      Accounts Payable            $17 800
Accounts Receivable     25 350
Merchandise Inventory   20 742          SHAREHOLDERS' EQUITY
                       $56 592      Capital Stock
                                    Authorized and Issued
Fixed Assets                        10 000 Common Shares        $100 000
Land                   $35 000      Retained Earnings           $ 51 292
Plant and Equipment     75 000                                  $151 292
                      $110 000

Organization Costs      $2 500
Total                 $169 092      Total                       $169 092
```

## Statement of Retained Earnings

This is a simple statement prepared for each set of financial statements. The details are obtained by analysing the Retained Earnings account. A sample statement is shown below.

```
              Statement of Retained Earnings
            For the year ended December 31, 19-3

                                                     19-3
Balance at Beginning of Year                    $   301 000
Add Net income for the year                         993 000
                                                $1 294 000

Deduct Dividends paid                           $   561 000


Balance at End of Year                          $   733 000
```

# Share Records

The Capital Stock account shows the total proceeds from the sale of shares by the company to shareholders. Except for extremely small or private companies it does not provide any other information about the shareholders. Additional information about the shareholders is required, however, particularly their names and addresses and the number of shares held. This information is kept by the company in a separate book called the stock certificate book.

## The Stock Certificate Book

For all but large public corporations, those whose shares are traded on a 'stock exchange', the detailed information relative to shareholders is kept in a **stock certificate book**. The stock certificate book is similar to a cheque book of the type that has both cheques and stubs. Instead of cheques the stock certificate book contains preprinted blank stock certificates and stubs as shown below.

Each time that the company makes a sale of a share or shares, details of the transaction are recorded. The name of the buyer (shareholder), the number of shares bought, and the date of issue of the share certificate are recorded by the company secretary on the front and back of a blank share certificate and on the attached stub, as illustrated on the next page. The share certificate is then detached and exchanged with the purchaser for the price of the shares. The stub remains in the stock certificate book – the company's permanent record of its shareholders.

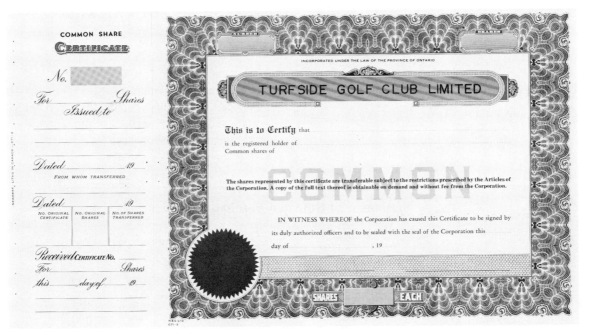

*Blank stock certificate and stub.*

*Stock certificate and stub with entries (front).*

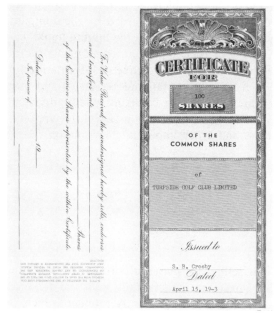

*Stock certificate and stub with entries (back).*

## Transferring Shares

An important feature of corporations is the transferability of shares. That is, one person can sell or give his shares to another person. When such an exchange takes place, an important procedure must be followed in order both to effect the transfer of stock certificates, and keep the stock certificate book up to date.

Step 1. The selling shareholder endorses the certificate; that is, he completes the reverse side of the share certificate, indicating the number of shares to be transferred, the name(s) and address(es) of the new shareholder(s), the date, and his signature. (See illustration on the next page.)

Step 2. The endorsed certificate is sent to the secretary of the company.

Step 3. The company secretary, upon receiving the endorsed share certificate, does the following:

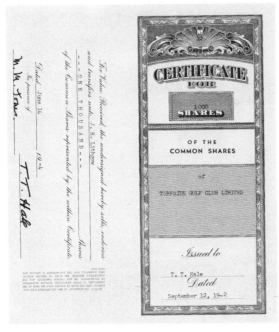

*Endorsed stock certificate.*

a. He cancels the share certificate and its stub by writing or stamping the word 'cancelled' on each.

b. He staples the cancelled certificate to its stub in the stock certificate book.

c. He prepares new certificates, and stubs, as indicated by the endorsement. The new certificate or certificates will be for the same number of shares as the cancelled certificate.

More than one new certificate may be necessary because:

(i) the seller of the shares may have sold them to more than one person, in which case each buyer receives a new share certificate on which is stated the number of shares allocated to him;

(ii) the seller may have sold only a portion of the stated share value of the old certificate, in which case he and the buyer each receive a new share certificate on which is stated the number of shares allocated to him.

Step 4. The company secretary issues the new share certificate(s) to the respective owner(s).

In respect to transfer of shares (as compared to sale of new shares), any money that changes hands is done privately, outside of the organiza-tion. No money is paid by or received by the company, nor is the number of company shares increased or decreased. Therefore, no accounting entries are required in the company accounts.

The stock certificate book is kept as up to date as possible. A corporation requires up-to-the-minute information about its shareholders, so that it can send out notices of meetings, dividend cheques, and financial statements and company reports to the proper persons.

A requirement of public corporations, those whose shares are traded through a stock exchange, is that their share records be maintained by a registrar, and that changes in ownership of shares be effected by a transfer agent. A number of firms are in the business of providing both of these services for corporations.

## The Minute Book

The law requires that the actions and decisions of every shareholders' meeting and of every directors' meeting be recorded by the company secretary in a book called the **minute book**. The minute book is an important record of a corporation and an important source of information for its own accounting staff and its outside auditors. In it are recorded the company bylaws, dividend declarations, policy decisions, executive appointments, and other important information.

# Accounting for the Issue of Shares

When selling its shares a corporation must be very careful to comply fully with the requirements of the Companies Act under which it operates.

## Par Value Shares

In planning for an issue of shares it may be decided to set a predetermined value on the shares. This value, known as the **par value**, is printed on the share certificate. Round amounts, such as $1, $10, $25, and $100 are usually chosen as par values, the values chosen being the amounts that the directors believe will be attractive to the buyers. In actual fact the shares may be sold for either the par value or, if the issue is popular and the demand great, for more than the par value; that is, at a premium. In most jurisdictions, the law does not permit the sale of par value shares for less than par value, that is, at a discount, except in the case of mining companies.

Some accounting situations that can arise in respect to the issuing of par value shares are explained below.

1. *Sale of par value shares for cash*
   Example: 5 000 shares having a par value of $10 each are sold at par for cash.
   Accounting entry:

   | | | |
   |---|---|---|
   | Bank | 50 000 | |
   | Capital Stock | | 50 000 |

   To record the sale for cash of 5 000 common shares, $10 par value, at par

2. *Sale of par value shares for assets other than cash*
   Example: 5 000 shares having a par value of $10 each are sold at par in return for a building valued at $50 000.
   Accounting entry:

   | | | |
   |---|---|---|
   | Buildings | 50 000 | |
   | Capital Stock | | 50 000 |

   To record the sale of 5 000 common shares at $10 par for a building located at 751 Cross Place, evaluation of Stone & Associates

3. *Sale of par value shares at a premium*
   Example: 1 000 shares with a par value of $100 are sold for cash at a 10 per cent premium.
   Accounting entry:

   | | | |
   |---|---|---|
   | Bank | 110 000 | |
   | Capital Stock | | 100 000 |
   | Premium on Capital Stock | | 10 000 |

   To record the sale for cash of 1 000 common shares, par value $100, at a premium of 10 per cent

4. *Sale of par value shares at a discount*
   (**Note:** In most jurisdictions corporations are not permitted to sell par value shares at a discount, except for mining companies.)
   Example: 2 000 shares having a par value of $25 are sold for $22 each.
   Accounting entry:

   | | | |
   |---|---|---|
   | Bank | 44 000 | |
   | Discount on Capital Stock | 6 000 | |
   | Capital Stock | | 50 000 |

   To record the sale for cash of 2 000 common shares, par value $25, for $22 each

## No Par Value Shares

Because it frequently happens that shares having a par value cannot be sold for the par value figure, another type of share is commonly used. This is the **no par value share**. The advantage of no par value shares is that they can be sold at any price established from time to time by the board of directors. Shares of equal rank, put up for sale at different times, may be sold at different prices according to demand and general market conditions.

The accounting for the issue of no par value shares is simple because no discount or premium situations exist. Consider the following series of share transactions in respect to one company's no par value shares:

1. 1 000 no par value common shares are issued for cash at $9 on February 2.
   The accounting entry is:

   | | | | |
   |---|---|---|---|
   | Feb 2 | Bank | 9 000 | |
   | | Capital Stock | | 9 000 |

   Sale of 1 000 no par value shares at $9 for cash

2. 5 000 no par value common shares are issued for cash at $8.50 on June 15.
   The accounting entry is:

   | | | | |
   |---|---|---|---|
   | June 15 | Bank | 42 500 | |
   | | Capital Stock | | 42 500 |

   Sale of 5 000 no par value shares at $8.50 for cash

3. 500 no par value shares are issued for equipment valued at $5 000 on August 20.
   The accounting entry is:

   | Aug 20 | Equipment | 5 000 | |
   |---|---|---|---|
   | | Capital Stock | | 5 000 |
   | | Sale of 500 no par value shares for equipment valued at $5 000 | | |

# Dividends

## Dividend Policy

Dividends are payments out of retained earnings to the shareholders of a company on a pro rata basis. Each share receives an equal dividend. Retained earnings represents a company's net accumulation of earnings that are free for distribution to shareholders in the form of dividends.

Whether a dividend is distributed or not depends on the directors. It is they who have the ultimate responsibility for deciding on the disposition of retained earnings, whether to use them for company expansion, for example, or whether to distribute them to shareholders as dividends. The ordinary shareholder has no direct say in this matter. Normally, dividends are not declared unless a company is earning satisfactory profits on a regular basis.

When dividends are declared, they are declared to shareholders of record on a certain date, to be paid at a subsequent time. The date of record, therefore, is an important one, and is one reason why stock records must be kept current and accurate.

Dividends are usually stated at so much a share; for example, 10¢ a share or $1 a share. Once they have been voted by the board of directors, the payment of dividends becomes a legal obligation of a company. If the company fails to make payment, the shareholders can sue in the courts.

The various companies acts protect the interests of shareholders. Regarding dividends, the acts state that dividends may not be declared if the following two requirements cannot be met: (1) sufficient cash is available to make the payment, and (2) a credit balance exists in the Retained Earnings account sufficiently large that the dividend entry will not put the account into a debit position.

## Accounting for Dividends

Accounting for dividends is usually done in two steps as follows:

1. To set up the liability when the dividend is declared:

   | Retained Earnings | xxxx | |
   |---|---|---|
   | Dividends Payable | | xxxx |

2. To record the payment of the dividend:

   | Dividends Payable | xxxx | |
   |---|---|---|
   | Bank | | xxxx |

# Different Classes of Shares

## Common Shares (Common Stock)

A corporation's basic class of stock is known as **common stock**. Holders of common stock have certain rights including the following:
1. The right to vote at shareholders' meetings – one vote per share.
2. The right to receive any common dividends that are declared – in proportion to the number of shares held.
3. The right to share in the remaining assets (after creditors have been paid) if the corporation is liquidated.

## Preferred Shares (Preferred Stock)

A corporation may issue more than one class of stock. If this is the case, there are both common stock, with the rights described above, and **preferred stock**. There are several types of preferences that can be given to preferred stock. This text deals only with the two simplest types.

## Ordinary Preferred Stock

The simplest type of preference stock is one preferred as to dividends but having no voting rights. A preferred stock of this type might be described as:

6% preferred non-voting stock, par value $100

This means simply that a holder of a share of this stock has a prior right each year to dividends at the stated rate. The preferred shareholders must be paid their preferred dividend, at the stated rate per annum on par value ($6 for the share described above), before any dividend may be paid to the common shareholders. Unless specifically stated, preference shares do not carry with them the right to vote as do common shares.

The fact that preferred shares exist in a company does not guarantee that an annual preferred dividend will be paid. A corporation that is not profitable, for example, will not normally declare a dividend. If a dividend is not declared, a preferred shareholder can only hope for better luck in the following year. If a dividend is declared, however, the preferred dividend must be looked after first, before anything is considered for the common shareholders.

On the other hand, if a company is profitable and paying dividends regularly, the common shareholders may receive more dividends than the preferred shareholders. The preference dividend is restricted to the amount stipulated whereas the amount of a common dividend is limited only by the earning capacity of the company.

## Example

Saunders Company Limited is incorporated with capital stock as follows:

5% Preferred  –  50 000 shares – $10 par value
    Common  – 100 000 shares –  no par value

a. In 19–2 the net income of the company is $30 000. Early in the following year it is decided to declare the preferred dividend as well as a common dividend of 5 cents a share. The following dividends are paid:

| | |
|---|---|
| Preferred stock  –  5% | $25 000 |
| Common stock  –  5¢ a share | 5 000 |
| Total dividends paid | $30 000 |

b. In 19–3 the company experiences a very poor year with a net income of only $10 000. It is decided to declare no dividends for the year.

c. In 19–4 the company enjoys an exceptionally good year in which the net income is $90 000. Early in the following year it is decided to declare the preferred dividend as well as a common dividend of 75 cents a share. The following dividends are paid:

| | |
|---|---|
| Preferred stock  –  5% | $25 000 |
| Common stock  –  75¢ a share | 75 000 |
| Total dividends paid | $100 000 |

## Cumulative Preferred Stock

In any year, if no dividend is declared, a preferred stockholder loses his right to receive the dividend *unless the preferred shares are cumulative*. Any 'arrears' of dividends, that is, any unpaid preferred dividends of prior years, must be paid in full to the holders of cumulative preferred shares before any dividend may be paid to the common shareholders.

## Example

Glen Company Limited is incorporated with the following capital stock:

6% Preferred– 25 000 shares  – $10 par value
    Common – 10 000 shares  –  no par value

a. In 19–2, because of a poor working capital position, no dividends are declared. In prior years the dividends on the preferred shares were paid in full.

b. In 19–3 the working capital situation is corrected and dividends are declared as follows:

(i) On Preferred stock

| | | |
|---|---|---|
| – 19–2 arrears 6% | $15 000 |
| – 19–3      6% | 15 000 |
| Total dividend on preferred stock | $30 000 |

(ii) On Common stock

| | |
|---|---|
| – $4 a share | 40 000 |
| Total dividend for 19–3 | $70.000 |

### Reason for Issuing Preferred Stock

Usually, preferred stock is issued (instead of more common stock) so that the present shareholders can acquire additional capital without relinquishing any control of the company. Preferred stock is preferred as to dividends but normally carries no voting rights. Also, the issuing of preferred shares allows for potentially higher dividends to the common shareholders. In a very profitable year a company may be able to pay a much larger dividend to the common stockholders than it is required to pay to the preferred stockholders.

### Accounting for Preferred Shares

The accounting entries for preferred stock are identical in principle to those for common stock. It is only necessary to remember that there is a separate ledger account for each class of stock. In a company that has two classes of shares there will be two Capital Stock accounts as shown below.

Preferred Stock    Common Stock

xxxx              xxxx

## Appropriations

Instead of voting for a dividend to shareholders, the directors may decide that it is in the best interests of the company to use accumulated earnings for some other purpose. The most common 'other' purpose is company expansion. Retained earnings are used in order to save the interest expense on borrowed funds, or to retain company control that might be jeopardized if new shares were issued. The feeling of the directors might be that the company can realize greater profits as a result of the expansion, and that although the shareholders will be disappointed at receiving little or no dividends in the near term, they will more than make up for this by receiving increased dividends in the future.

A credit balance in the Retained Earnings account suggests to shareholders that there is an accumulation of earnings that can be made available to them in the form of dividends, particularly if there is ample cash on hand. The directors of the company, however, may have some other purpose in mind for such retained earnings; a new building, for example.

To make their intentions clear to shareholders, it is normal for the directors, by resolution, to segregate a portion of the balance in the Retained Earnings account into a special purpose account called an Appropriation account. For example: the directors of Dartco Limited intend to use accumulated company profits to pay for a new building to cost $250 000. To make their intention clear to the shareholders, the board, on June 5, 19—, votes to appropriate $250 000 to pay for the new building.

The appropriation is entered in the accounts in the following way:

June 5  Retained Earnings          250 000
            Appropriation for New Bldg    250 000
            To record resolution
            of board of directors
            on June 3, 19—

The effect in the accounts is:

Retained Earnings

| Mar 31 | | | Cr 265 000 |
| Jun  5 | | 250 000 | Cr  15 000 |

Appropriation for New Building

| Jun  5 | | | 250 000 | Cr 250 000 |

It can be seen from the above that the appropriation serves to (1) reduce the expectation of receiving dividends by reducing the balance in the Retained Earnings account, and (2) show the purpose for which a particular portion of retained earnings is intended.

Because it does not represent cash funds, the Appropriation account is not used to pay for the new plant. Once the objective of the appropriation is achieved – in our example, cash funds generated from company profits are used to pay for the new building – the Appropriation account is no longer required and the balance is returned to the Retained Earnings account. This increased balance in the Retained Earnings account is free for dividends as soon as the company builds up sufficient cash, and whenever the directors choose to spend it in that way.

## Contributed Surplus

In published reports of public companies an equity item called **contributed surplus** occurs so frequently that it deserves an explanation. Contributed surplus arises primarily from:

1. Premium or discount on stock transactions;
2. Gifts of plant or property from outsiders;
3. Donations of stock or assets from shareholders.

In the accounting for such transactions, the entries are put into one or more accounts in the Equity section. On financial statements they are usually combined and shown on the balance sheet as one item called Contributed Surplus.

## Equity Section—Presentation on the Balance Sheet

Shown below and on the next page are four samples of the Equity sections of balance sheets as taken from published reports of Canadian companies.* The basic components of shareholders' equity, as well as the variation in presentation, are well illustrated by these examples. Observe the common practice, when dealing with large dollar figures of rounding them off – to the nearest dollar or thousand dollars.

*The names of the companies have not been disclosed because of minor changes or deletions made by the author.

### SHAREHOLDERS' EQUITY

**Capital Stock**
Authorized – 5 000 000 shares without nominal or par value
Issued        – 4 201 600 shares                                10 300 000

**Retained Earnings**                                          25 572 000

**Appropriation for Land Acquisition**                          1 470 000

                                                                37 342 000

                                                               $62 014 000

### Shareholders' Equity

Share capital
Authorized, 3 000 000 common shares without
                nominal or par value
Issued and outstanding, 1 572 016 shares          $  4 867 440
Contributed surplus                                    402 980
Retained earnings                                    5 916 481

                                                    $11 186 901

                                                    $53 840 308

*Two samples of the Equity sections of corporate balance sheets.*

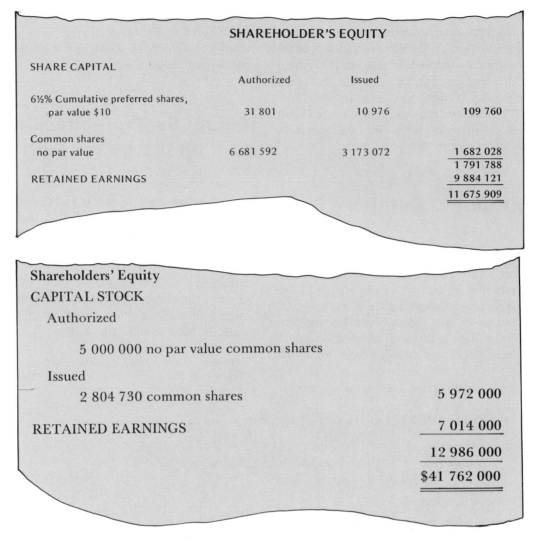

**SHAREHOLDER'S EQUITY**

| SHARE CAPITAL | Authorized | Issued | |
|---|---|---|---|
| 6½% Cumulative preferred shares, par value $10 | 31 801 | 10 976 | 109 760 |
| Common shares no par value | 6 681 592 | 3 173 072 | 1 682 028 |
| | | | 1 791 788 |
| RETAINED EARNINGS | | | 9 884 121 |
| | | | 11 675 909 |

Shareholders' Equity

CAPITAL STOCK

Authorized

    5 000 000 no par value common shares

Issued

    2 804 730 common shares    5 972 000

RETAINED EARNINGS    7 014 000

12 986 000

$41 762 000

*Two samples of the Equity sections of corporate balance sheets.*

# Market Value of Company Shares

Shares of a corporation may be bought or sold on the open market. All that is necessary is that a buyer and a seller agree on a price, and effect the transaction. The share certificate is transferred to the new owner in the manner described in a previous section.

In respect to public companies, those complying with the requirements of a **stock exchange**, shares are bought and sold ('traded') through the facilities of stockbrokers who are members of a stock exchange. In Canada there are four stock exchanges, the Canadian Stock Exchange, the Montreal Stock Exchange, the Toronto Stock Exchange, and the Vancouver Stock Exchange. There are many stockbrokers with offices throughout the country. Their services are available for a commission. On the basis of instructions from their clients they put through share transactions at the stock exchange building. This is known as trading on the floor of the stock exchange.

The sales data of all transactions on each of the stock exchanges are listed daily in the financial pages of the larger newspapers.

# Toronto

QUOTATIONS FOR NOVEMBER 5, 19— PREPARED BY THE TORONTO STOCK EXCHANGE

*Part of financial page of newspaper, showing transactions of the Toronto Stock Exchange.*

For any particular stock, the price of the last trade is generally regarded as being its current 'market price'. The market price of a stock is not a fixed figure, therefore, but one that may change whenever a new transaction takes place. Prices fluctuate according to buying and selling forces. If investors find a stock attractive they tend to bid the price up. A bad report on a stock will almost certainly cause its market price to drop.

There is no direct relationship between the **issue price** of a stock, as reflected in the accounts, and the **market price** for that stock. The issue price is a one-time price, fixed at the time of issue. The market price fluctuates according to market forces. Generally, if a company is profitable, the market price of its stock will be steady or rising. If it is not profitable, the market price of its stock will fall.

## Adjusting and Closing Entries for a Corporation

The closing procedures for a corporation involve only two steps as described below:

1. Journalize the adjustments as they appear on the work sheet.
2. Close out the Income and Expense accounts to the Retained Earnings account. Except for the utilization of the Retained Earnings account, the method is exactly as described on page 354 regarding the single proprietorship.

There are no Drawings to be closed out in corporation accounts.

## Income Tax Cycle for Corporations

Corporations, by law, must pay income tax on their earnings at a fairly high rate. Therefore, income tax is an important expense item for a corporation.

The federal law requires that (1) a corporation pay its income tax on an estimated basis throughout its corporate fiscal year (the procedure for estimating the income tax for any year is prescribed by government regulation), and (2) settle its account for that year within the subsequent three months. More specifically, before the last day of each month of each fiscal year a corporation must remit to the Receiver General an amount equal to one twelfth of its estimated income tax for that year. Then, within three months of the corporation's year-end, the company must remit the balance of any unpaid tax; that is, the excess, if any, of the actual tax calculated for the year over the sum of the instalments paid for the year.

To illustrate, assume that Superior Products Limited is incorporated on November 1. Its first fiscal year ends on the following October 31. Assume further that the determination of its estimated income tax for the year is $15 000. The required monthly instalment, one twelfth of this amount, is $1 250.

On October 31, the fiscal year-end of the company, twelve instalment payments will have been made. The Income Tax account will have a debit balance of $15 000 as shown below:

## INCOME TAX EXPENSE

| DATE | PARTICULARS | DEBIT | CREDIT | BALANCE | |
|---|---|---|---|---|---|
| Nov 30 | | 1 250 | | 1 250 | Dr |
| Dec 31 | | 1 250 | | 2 500 | Dr |
| Jan 31 | | 1 250 | | 3 750 | Dr |
| Feb 28 | | 1 250 | | 5 000 | Dr |
| Mar 31 | | 1 250 | | 6 250 | Dr |
| Apr 30 | | 1 250 | | 7 500 | Dr |
| May 31 | | 1 250 | | 8 750 | Dr |
| Jun 30 | | 1 250 | | 10 000 | Dr |
| Jul 31 | | 1 250 | | 11 250 | Dr |
| Aug 31 | | 1 250 | | 12 500 | Dr |
| Sep 30 | | 1 250 | | 13 750 | Dr |
| Oct 31 | | 1 250 | | 15 000 | Dr |

## Income Tax on the Work Sheet

First, remember that a corporation must itself pay income tax. When preparing the company's work sheet the Income Tax Expense account is one of the items in the Trial Balance section as shown below:

## WORK SHEET

| ACCOUNTS | TRIAL BALANCE | | ADJUSTMENTS | | INCOME STATEMENT | | BALANCE SHEET | |
|---|---|---|---|---|---|---|---|---|
| | DR | CR | DR | CR | DR | CR | DR | CR |
| Income Tax Exp | 15 000 | | | | | | | |

Remember that the $15 000 figure represents an estimate of the company's tax and not the actual tax figure. The actual tax figure still remains to be calculated, based on the company's net income before tax.

## Net Income Before Income Tax

Before the company's actual income tax for the year can be calculated, it is necessary to ascertain its **net income before income tax**. It is this figure that the income tax calculation is based on. To ascertain the company's net income before income tax:

1. *Except for the Income Tax line*, complete the work sheet making adjustments as necessary, up to the point of being ready to take column totals.
2. Either (a) from the figures in the Income Statement section of the work sheet prepare an income statement to the point of the net income before income tax figure. A sample of a corporation's income statement is shown on the next page;

## ROBIN HOOD MINES LIMITED

### Statement of Income
For the year ended December 31, 19-3

|  | 19-3 | 19-2 |
|---|---|---|
| **Revenue** | | |
| Bullion production | $3 271 000 | $1 988 000 |
| Interest | 55 000 | 15 000 |
| | 3 326 000 | 2 003 000 |
| **Expense** | | |
| Development | 285 000 | 187 000 |
| Mining | 367 000 | 296 000 |
| Milling | 198 000 | 138 000 |
| Fees and charges for the use of underground facilities of parent company | 348 000 | 290 000 |
| Mine management, office and general | 161 000 | 122 000 |
| Head office administration and general | 71 000 | 36 000 |
| Marketing | 15 000 | 9 000 |
| Provision for tax under the Mining Tax Act, Ontario | 198 000 | 131 000 |
| | 1 643 000 | 1 209 000 |
| **Operating Income** | 1 683 000 | 794 000 |
| **Other Expense** | | |
| Amortization of deferred development and administrative expenditures | 163 000 | 136 000 |
| Provision for depreciation of buildings, machinery and equipment | 21 000 | 6 000 |
| | 184 000 | 142 000 |
| **Income Before Income Taxes** | 1 499 000 | 652 000 |
| Income taxes | 506 000 | 222 000 |
| **Net Income for the Year** | $ 993 000 | $ 430 000 |
| **Earnings per Share** | $.33 | $.14 |

It is customary for public companies to prepare the income statement in comparative form, showing the results for the current year and for the preceding year.

or (b) using an adding machine, take off totals of each of the two columns in the Income Statement section and find the difference between them. The figure represents the net income before income tax. (These are not the column totals to be recorded on the work sheet.)

## Completing the Work Sheet

Based on the net income before tax figure determined above, and in accordance with government rules and regulations, the actual income tax for the year is calculated. For purposes of continuing our example, assume for General Products Limited a tax figure of $17 010.

The Income Tax line of the work sheet can now be extended. Enter the actual tax figure of $17 010 in the Income Statement section, Debit column. Then balance the line through the Balance Sheet section; a credit figure of $2 010 will be produced. This line of the work sheet now appears as follows:

| | WORK SHEET | | | | | | | |
|---|---|---|---|---|---|---|---|---|
| ACCOUNTS | TRIAL BALANCE | | ADJUSTMENTS | | INCOME STATEMENT | | BALANCE SHEET | |
| | DR | CR | DR | CR | DR | CR | DR | CR |
| IncomeTaxExp | 15 000 | | | | 17 010 | | | 2 010 |

The $17 010 figure represents the income tax expense for the year. The $2 010 figure represents the liability for income tax at the company's fiscal year-end.

The work sheet may now be totaled and completed in the usual manner, and the financial statements prepared. The $2 010 liability is included on the balance sheet among the current liabilities. Income tax expense on the income statement is shown in the example on page 431.

## Closing Entry

Closing the books in the usual manner will produce a credit balance of $2 010 in the Income Tax account as shown below. At this point of time the account correctly reflects the tax liability of $2 010.

| INCOME TAX EXPENSE | | | | |
|---|---|---|---|---|
| DATE | PARTICULARS | DEBIT | CREDIT | BALANCE |
| Oct 31 | | | | 15 000 DR |
| 31 | | | 17 010 | 2 010 CR |

# Bookkeeping and Accounting Terms

**Corporation** A legal entity as determined by statute, separate and distinct from its owners, with a capital divided into shares which, when issued, are held by shareholders whose liability is limited to the amount of the capital for which they have subscribed. Also called a **limited company**.

**Shareholder** The legal owner of shares of a limited company. Also called **stockholder**.

**Charter** The document by which a corporation is created under the provisions of the Canada Business Corporations Act, or the corresponding act of a province. Also known as **letters patent**.

**Board of Directors** The committee of persons elected by the shareholders of a limited company to be responsible for supervising its affairs.

**Retained Earnings** The accumulated balance of income less losses of a corporation, after dividends and other appropriate charges or credits have been taken into account.

**Dividend** An amount of earnings declared by the board of directors for distribution to the shareholders of a corporation in proportion to their holdings, having regard for the respective rights of various classes of stock.

**Cumulative Dividends** Dividends paid at a fixed annual rate on preferred stock, which, if not paid in one year, are carried forward as an additional priority of preferred shareholders in future income distributions.

**Par Value** The nominal or face value of a share.

**No Par Value Stock** Shares of capital stock which have no nominal or par value.

**Common Stock** The class of capital stock representing the residual equity in the company's assets and earnings.

**Share** One of the equal parts into which each class of the capital stock of a limited company is divided.

**Preferred Share** A class of share capital with special rights or restrictions as compared with other classes of stock of the same company. The preference will generally attach to the distribution of dividends at a stipulated rate. Such shares normally have no voting rights to elect the company's directors. Also known as **preferred stock**.

**Shareholders' Equity** The interest of the shareholders in the net assets of a limited company.

**Appropriation** A setting aside of accumulated earnings to an account so as to restrict the use of such accumulated earnings for a specific purpose.

# Review Questions

1. Give the name of a limited company in your community.
2. What is the most significant feature of the corporate form of business ownership?
3. What is a shareholder?
4. In your own words explain what is meant by a corporation being an artificial legal being.
5. Explain what is meant by limited liability.
6. Why are corporations subject to greater government control than partnerships or proprietorships?
7. Name the official document that gives approval to the formation of a limited company.
8. How does a person become a director of a

company? What does a director do?

9. Name the usual executive officers of a corporation. What functions do they perform?
10. Name the two accounts in which the shareholders' equity of a simple corporation is recorded. Describe how these two accounts separate the equity into two distinct parts.
11. What is the name given to negative retained earnings? Explain how negative retained earnings come about.
12. Is a shareholder assured of receiving dividends? Explain.
13. Explain the purpose of the stock certificate book.
14. Explain the meaning of 'endorsement' as it applies to stock certificates.
15. Explain the difference between a par value common share and a no par value common share.
16. How is the issue price associated with a no par value share determined?
17. Why might a company choose to issue preferred shares instead of issuing more common shares?
18. What is the purpose of making an appropriation?
19. Explain the difference between the book value and the market value of company shares.
20. With shares of public companies changing hands daily, how does the company know who is to receive dividends?

# Exercises

## Exercises on Formation of Corporations

**1. J. Franklin Limited is incorporated with an authorized capital of 1 000 shares of common stock having a par value of $10 a share. The petitioners, J. Franklin, R. Franklin, and S. Franklin, each subscribe for 200 shares.**
**Journalize the following transactions:**

## Transactions

May 1 Each of the petitioners pays $2 000 cash for his shares.
5 Legal fees for incorporation in the amount of $1 500 are paid.
20 400 shares are sold to T. Wilson for $4 000 cash.

---

**2. E. G. Winters Limited is a company just incorporated with an authorized capital of 100 000 common shares having a par value of $10.**
**Journalize the following selected transactions of E. G. Winters Limited:**

## Transactions

Feb. 6 The petitioners pay cash, amounting to $135 000, for their shares.
8 Incorporation expenses of $3 000 are paid by cheque.
15 10 000 shares are sold through an investment dealer to the general public at par. A cheque for the full issue price is received from the dealer.
27 5 000 shares are sold through the investment dealer to the general public at a premium of 2 per cent. A cheque for the full price is received from the dealer.
28 A cheque is sent to the investment dealer in the amount of $4 530 representing his commission of 3 per cent of the selling price of shares sold.

3. **Plastic Products Limited** is a new company which has just received its charter authorizing the issue of 1 000 common shares having no par value. The five petitioners each agree to take 100 shares at an agreed price of $100.

Journalize the following selected transactions:

## Transactions

Mar 3 The petitioners each make payment to the company by cheque for the full price of their shares.

7 Legal and incorporation expenses of $2 000 are paid by cheque.

10 Property valued at $35 000 is acquired in return for 200 shares.

14 300 shares are sold to various new shareholders, realizing $51 000 cash.

---

4. **Colorful Decor Limited** is incorporated with an authorized capital stock of 10 000 shares of no par value.

Journalize the following transactions of the company:

## Transactions

Sept 1 2 500 shares are issued in return for cash to each of the petitioners at a price of $10 a share.

3 Legal fees of incorporation are paid; $2 500.

5 2 500 shares are issued in return for a building at an agreed value of $30 000.

**Prepare a balance sheet as of September 5, 19–2.**

---

5. **R. Peters, M. Mowbray, and G. Glen** are in the process of changing their partnership over to a limited company. Immediately prior to the changeover, the net assets of the company amounted to $120 000. The partners' Capital account balances were $60 000, $30 000, and $30 000, respectively.

If the authorized capital of the limited company is 10 000 shares with a par value of $10:

1. Calculate the number of shares that each of the partners will receive.
2. Show the detail that will be entered on each new share certificate.

3. Give the accounting entry to convert the partnership into a limited company. With this entry the books of the partnership will become the books of the corporation.

---

6. **W. Murray, M. Walters, and F. Stevens** operate a partnership in which they share income and loss and maintain their Capital accounts in the ratio of 3:3:2, respectively. The three men have applied for and received letters patent to incorporate their business under the name of Master Products Limited, effective June 30, 19——. The letters patent authorize capital stock of 16 000 no par value common shares.

After closing the books at June 30, the trial balance of the partnership is as follows:

MURRAY, WALTERS, AND STEVENS
POST-CLOSING TRIAL BALANCE
JUNE 30, 19—

| | | |
|---|---:|---:|
| Bank | $ 4 250 | |
| Accounts Receivable | 18 450 | |
| Allowance for Doubtful Debts | | $ 1 350 |
| Supplies | 516 | |
| Prepaid Insurance | 1 008 | |
| Land | 20 000 | |
| Buildings | 35 000 | |
| Accumulated Depreciation of Buildings | | 4 992 |
| Furniture and Equipment | 7 250 | |
| Accumulated Depreciation of Furn. and Equip. | | 3 538 |
| Automobiles | 7 845 | |
| Accumulated Depreciation of Automobiles | | 4 001 |
| Bank Loan | | 3 000 |
| Accounts Payable | | 13 438 |
| W. Murray, Capital | | 24 000 |
| M. Walters, Capital | | 24 000 |
| F. Stevens, Capital | | 16 000 |
| | $94 319 | $94 319 |

The partners have agreed to revalue the land and the buildings and to adjust these accounts to the appraised values immediately prior to incorporation. Any gain or loss on appraisal, and any expenses of appraisal or incorporation, are to be recorded in the partnership accounts as a direct charge or credit to the partners' Capital accounts. It is also agreed that the books of the partnership will continue and become the books of the corporation.

**On June 30, journalize the effect of the revaluation of the land and buildings. Land is appraised at $36 000 and buildings at $75 000 (the accumulated depreciation on buildings remaining unchanged).**
**Journalize the payment on June 30 of the following remittances made by cheque:**

a. Appraiser's fee, $1 200;
b. Incorporation and legal fees, $2 640.

**Convert the partnership books into those of the new limited company by closing out the partners' adjusted Capital accounts to a Common Stock account.**

**All of the authorized shares are to be distributed to the partners. The distribution is to be made in the ratio of their final Capital account balances as partners.**
a. Calculate the number of shares that each partner will receive;
b. Calculate the value per share to be recorded in the company's minute book.

7. **Mountain Mining Company of Canada Limited has three classes of shares authorized:**

1. No par value common shares;
2. 8 per cent non-cumulative preferred shares having a par value of $10 (known as Class 1 Preferred Stock);
3. 9 per cent cumulative preferred shares having a par value of $10 (known as Class 2 Preferred Stock).

**Journalize the following share transactions of the company:**

Transactions

April  2  Sold for cash: 50 common shares for $5 000.
6  Sold for cash: 100 Class 1 preferred shares at par.
9  Sold: 1 200 common shares in exchange for land and buildings valued as follows: Land   $40 000
Buildings $80 000.
15  Sold for cash: 50 Class 1 preferred shares at a premium of 10 per cent.
29  Sold for cash: 100 Class 2 preferred shares at a discount of 5 per cent.

8. **This exercise is to be done in your workbook, or as directed by your teacher.**

## Dividends Exercises

9. **The issued capital stock of Marwell Limited is:**

No par value common shares, 76 700 shares;
6 per cent preferred shares, par value $10,   27 500 shares.

**Calculate the total dividend on the preferred stock.**
**Calculate the total dividend on the common stock if the rate is to be 26 cents per share.**
**Show the journal entries necessary to record the declaration of both of the above dividends. Date of declaration is April 12.**
**Show the journal entries necessary to record the payment of the above dividends. Date of payment is April 30.**

10. **The capital stock of EFG Co. Ltd. has remained as shown below for several years.**

Common Stock – no par value; 10 000 shares
Preferred Stock – par value $25; 6 per cent cumulative; 40 000 shares

For the last few years the net income of the company has been too small to fully pay the preferred dividends. Dividend payments on the preferred shares have been as follows:

19–2 $50 000
19–3 $25 000
19–4 $16 000

19–5 has been a profitable year, with the company earning a net income of $154 000. It has been proposed that the entire year's profit be paid out in dividends.

**If this is done, how much per share will the common shareholders receive? Show your calculations.**

---

**11.   At December 31, 19–7, the end of a fiscal year, Vintage Products Limited has fully paid capital stock as shown below.**

Common Stock – 500 000 shares of no par value
Preferred Stock – 5 per cent cumulative;
100 000 shares; par value of
$25 per share

Dividends on preferred shares are fully paid up to December 31, 19–5. No preferred dividends have been paid since that time.

**Calculate the total amount of dividends on preferred shares that must be paid before any dividends can be paid on the common shares.**

**On December 31, 19–7, if the balance in the Retained Earnings account is $900 000 Cr. and the balance in the Bank account is $700 000 Dr., calculate the greatest dividend per share that can be paid on the common shares.**

**If the dividends calculated in both cases above are declared by the directors on January 3, 19–8, give the accounting entries to record them.**

**If the dividends above are paid on January 15, 19–8, give the accounting entries to record the payment.**

---

**12.   The following is an analysis of the share certificate book of Haskin Associates Limited:**

| Certi-ficate Number | Name of Shareholder | Number of Shares | Date of Issue of Certificate | Date of Cancellation of Certificate | Comments |
|---|---|---|---|---|---|
| 1 | E. J. Boynton | 50 | Mar. 1, 19–1 | Apr. 12, 19–5 | Replaced by #15 |
| 2 | A. P. Scully | 100 | Mar. 1, 19–1 | Sep. 9, 19–3 | Replaced by #10 |
| 3 | J. Felton | 150 | Apr. 30, 19–1 | | |
| 4 | D. T. Tyrone | 200 | Sep. 6, 19–1 | Apr. 6, 19–3 | Replaced by #7 and #8 |
| 5 | A. Browser | 150 | Feb. 19, 19–2 | | |
| 6 | F. Minelli | 50 | Sep. 20, 19–2 | | |
| 7 | B. Carson | 100 | Apr. 6, 19–3 | Aug. 3, 19–4 | Replaced by #12 |
| 8 | E. J. Boynton | 100 | Apr. 6, 19–3 | | |
| 9 | A. Browser | 1 000 | July 4, 19–3 | | |
| 10 | J. Felton | 100 | Sep. 9, 19–3 | | |
| 11 | F. Minelli | 500 | May 15, 19–4 | | |
| 12 | W. Childs | 100 | Aug. 3, 19–4 | | |
| 13 | C. Fraser | 200 | Jan. 19, 19–5 | | |
| 14 | P. Yonge | 100 | Mar. 16, 19–5 | | |
| 15 | A. Browser | 50 | Apr. 12, 19–5 | | |

A dividend of $10 a share is declared on October 15, 19–4, to be paid to shareholders of record on December 31, 19–4.

For purposes of preparing the accounting entry and the dividend cheques, ascertain who the shareholders of record are on December 31, 19–4, and the total holdings of each.

Show the journal entry to record the declaration of the dividend.

Show the journal entry to record the payment of the dividend.

## Retained Earnings Exercises

**13.** Show the effect (if any) of the following items in the Retained Earnings account of Meg Limited.

1. Dec. 31, 19–5  Net Income, $76 000.
2. Mar. 15, 19–6  Appropriation for New Building, $50 000.
3. Dec. 31, 19–6  Net Income, $86 000.
4. Mar. 15, 19–7  Appropriation for New Building, $50 000.
5. Dec. 31, 19–7  Net Income, $92 000.
6. Jan. 20, 19–8  Declaration of Dividend, $75 000.
7. Mar. 15, 19–8  Appropriation for New Building, $50 000.
8. Apr. 20, 19–8  Dividend paid, $75 000.
9. Aug. 31, 19–8  New building completed and paid for, $150 000.
10. Dec. 31, 19–8  Net Income, $103 000.

Show the accounting entries required for items 2, 6, 8.

Once the building project is completed, what should be done with the Appropriation account? In your opinion what was the purpose of the account?

**14.** Shown below is the Retained Earnings account for Morris Switzer Limited. The accountant's comments in analyzing the account are written in the Particulars column. Prepare the statement of retained earnings for the year ended December 31, 19–4.

### RETAINED EARNINGS

| DATE | PARTICULARS | DEBIT | CREDIT | BALANCE |
|---|---|---|---|---|
| 19-3 | | | | |
| Nov 30 | Balance Forwarded | | | CR 102 746 21 |
| Dec 31 | Closing of net income | | 156 212 02 | CR 258 958 23 |
| 19-4 | | | | |
| Jan 15 | Dividend declaration | 150 000 00 | | CR 108 958 23 |
| Jun 30 | Appropriation business expansion | 100 000 00 | | CR    8 958 23 |
| Dec 31 | Closing of net income | | 142 012 72 | CR 150 970 95 |

## Exercises on Equity Section of Balance Sheet

**15.** **The shareholders' equity of P.R.O. Limited is made up of the following items:**

*Common Stock*
Authorized, 50 000 shares; par value $10; issued and fully paid, 20 000 shares.

*Retained Earnings*
$7 542.00

**Prepare the Shareholders' Equity section of the balance sheet.**

**16.** **The shareholders' equity of Alpine Products Limited is comprised of the following:**

*Common Stock*
Authorized, 10 000 shares; no par value; issued and fully paid, 10 000 shares; book value of issued shares, $94 216.

*Retained Earnings*
$26 412.
*Appropriation*
For land acquisition, $50 000.

**Prepare the Equity section of the balance sheet.**

**17.** **The shareholders' equity of Kingston Investments Limited consists of:**

*Common Stock*
Authorized, 5 000 shares; no par value; issued and fully paid, 5 000 shares; book value of issued shares, $54 260.

*Preferred Stock*
6 per cent cumulative preferred; par value $25; authorized, issued, and fully paid, 20 000 shares.
*Contributed Surplus*
Premium on preferred stock, $40 000.

**Prepare the Shareholders' Equity section of the balance sheet.**

## Exercises on Work Sheet, Income Tax, and Financial Statements

**18.** **This exercise is to be done in your workbook, or as directed by your teacher.**

**19.** **This exercise is to be done in your workbook, or as directed by your teacher.**

# Cases

## Case 1

Jerry Walker, with his wife and brother, is the owner of a small limited company. Of a total of 1 000 common shares, Jerry owns 990, his wife and brother each own five.

By patiently plowing the company earnings back into the business and by taking out the minimum in the way of dividends, Jerry has brought the business along successfully. Earnings have been steadily improving but have never been large.

The business has reached a critical point at which, with a larger plant at a cost of $400 000, it could capitalize on a booming market and be assured of net income (over and above the costs of financing the expansion) in the range of $150 000 annually.

Jerry has no additional capital of his own. The current interest rates are 10 per cent or more. What alternative ways are there for Jerry to finance the expansion? Which method would you recommend? Give reasons for your choice.

## Case 2

In regard to the purchase of its shares, J. P. Johnson Limited does not require full and immediate payment. The company has a plan that allows people to *subscribe* for its shares by making a down payment on the purchase price and contracting to pay the balance of the purchase price on an instalment basis.

Devise what you think is a fair way to handle a situation such as this in the accounts. Consider (1) the extent of the shareholders' liability, (2) the voting privileges of the shareholders, (3) the presentation on the balance sheet of any new accounts that you may think are necessary. Explain fully.

## Case 3

An acquaintance of yours, Mr. Farmer, comes to you with a proposition regarding the purchase of some shares that he owns in a medium-sized company. He acquired these shares some time ago as an investment and claims that he would like to sell them at this time because he needs cash in order to take advantage of another investment opportunity.

Mr. Farmer shows you the following breakdown of the shareholdings of the company:

| | | |
|---|---|---|
| Mrs. Adams | 30 shares | A widow who inherited her shares upon the death of her husband. She has shown no interest whatever in the company affairs, and is quite satisfied that it must be an excellent company because she receives a dividend cheque from them regularly. |
| R. Baker | 40 shares | He acquired his shares from a third person in settlement of a debt. He attends the company meetings regularly and is highly critical of the management. Whenever he suggests a change, however, he is always voted down. |

| S. Clarke | 65 shares | He is the secretary-treasurer of the company, a position that he has held for 15 years. He is also one of the three company directors. |
|---|---|---|
| M. Dunn | 100 shares | He is the general manager, president, and a director of the company which he started 15 years ago. |
| C. Everett | 10 shares | He had his shares given to him. He does not know anything about the company and is not interested. He would be willing to sell his shares for a fair price. |
| Mr. Farmer | 150 shares | |
| Mrs. Greig | 35 shares | Mrs. Greig is a wealthy lady who travels a great deal. She has had no known direct involvement in any affairs of the company. It is not known how she acquired her shares. |
| H. Harris | 70 shares | He has been the vice-president for the last ten years, is the brother-in-law of the president and is also a director. |

It is Mr. Farmer's opinion that the company could earn substantially higher profits with new management and that by acquiring his shares you would become the shareholder with the largest individual holdings. You would stand a good chance of gaining control of the company by getting the support or acquiring the shares of the four small shareholders. He points out that the three men who run the company own only 235 shares out of a total of 500.

Mr. Farmer is asking $50 000 for his shares. This is a fair price. You have the management skills, the technical expertise, and the experience to handle the company.

Decide on a course of action and give reasons for your decision.

## Case 4

The Jones family owns 24 per cent of the common stock of a large corporation. It is common knowledge that this family has control of the company. How is it possible that the Jones family can control the company without having the theoretical 50 per cent of the shares plus one?

## Case 5

The following analysis of XYZ Limited has been made by an investment company.

| Year | Number of Common Shares | Amount of Dividends Paid on Common Shares | Amount of Net Income | Market Value Per Share |
|---|---|---|---|---|
| 19–1 | 50 000 | $62 500 | $215 000 | $48 |
| 19–2 | 57 000 | 62 700 | 275 000 | 55 |
| 19–3 | 67 000 | 63 650 | 375 000 | 57 |

Calculate the rate of dividend for each year.

Calculate the rate of earnings per share for each year.

In your opinion why is the market value of the stock increasing at a time when the rate of dividends is decreasing?

## Case 6

An investment analyst has compiled the following information in respect to three public companies:

|  | ABC LTD. | PQ LTD. | XYZ LTD. |
|---|---|---|---|
| Number of common shares | 50 000 | 400 000 | 120 000 |
| Number of preferred shares | nil | nil | nil |
| Total shareholders' equity | $650 000 | $4 600 000 | $1 800 000 |
| Net income for last five years |  |  |  |
| 19–6 | 250 000 | 1 400 000 | 480 000 |
| 19–5 | 200 000 | 1 500 000 | 475 000 |
| 19–4 | 175 000 | 1 800 000 | 510 000 |
| 19–3 | 125 000 | 2 400 000 | 435 000 |
| 19–2 | 75 000 | 2 500 000 | 450 000 |

In the columns provided in your workbook calculate:

a. the net book values per share;
b. the earnings per share for the 19–6 year;
c. the average earnings per share for the last five years.

The current market values of the stocks are:

|  | ABC LTD. | PQ LTD. | XYZ LTD. |
|---|---|---|---|
|  | $90 | $35 | $60 |

Assuming that in all three companies the total earnings are regularly paid out in dividends, answer the following questions:

What factors influence the market price of the companies' shares?

Explain the difference in the market price of the shares of the three companies.

If you were required to select one of the three companies to invest in, which company would you select? Explain your choice.

## Case 7

Jake Takem, a young and aggressive entrepreneur, saw an opportunity of making some quick and easy money, provided that he could come up with $50 000. Unfortunately Jake was broke, but he had heard about the way in which corporations raise money by selling shares to the public. He decided to explore this possibility. He surmised that if he were to set up a company with 100 000 shares, he could keep control by putting 50 001 shares in his own name, and he could sell the remaining 49 999 to the general public at $10 each. Without putting up a cent of his own he then would have close to the $50 000 he needed. Jake was quite pleased with the whole scheme.

To put his plan into action Jake first paid a visit to a lawyer and explained his plan. The lawyer informed Jake of the following:

1. He would have to comply in all respects to the numerous requirements of the Companies Act.
2. He would have to seek permission of the government to set up his company by applying for Letters Patent and paying a fee.
3. Most important, he would have to prepare a *prospectus* for which there was page upon page of legislative requirements.

Hearing all of this annoyed Jake. He left the lawyer's office in an angry mood exclaiming about the unfairness of government regulations and about oppression of the little man.

Is Jake right? Does government regulation work for or against the little man? Explain.

## Case 8

The board of directors of Grover Contracting Company Limited is meeting on January 10, 19–4, to decide on the payment of dividends to shareholders. The following data have been collected for the meeting to help the directors in their discussion:

Net income, year ended December 31, 19–3 – $150 000
Cash on hand, January 10, 19–4 – $ 95 000
Retained earnings, January 10, 19–4 – $156 750
Total current assets, January 10, 19–4 – $ 99 000
Total current liabilities, January 10, 19–4 – $104 000

Capital Stock:
Common: 50 000 shares, no par value,
issued and fully paid
(Last common dividend, $2 a share for the
19–2 year)
Preferred, 6 per cent cumulative: 150 000 shares,
issued and fully paid, par value $1 500 000.
(Preferred dividends are fully paid up to and
including the 19–2 year. There were no
preferred dividends in 19–3 or 19–4.)

1. Based on the information given above, what decision should the directors make? Give your opinion and show your calculations.
2. If in 1 above you were of the opinion that a dividend should be paid, give the accounting entries to record the declaration of the dividend, and the payment of the dividend.

# Index